"*Stiles himself a Prize fighter*"

New-York Runaways, 1706-1768

Compiled by
Joseph Lee Boyle

CLEARFIELD

Copyright © 2020 by
Joseph Lee Boyle

All Rights Reserved.

Printed for Clearfield Company by
Genealogical Publishing Company
Baltimore, Maryland
2020

ISBN 9780806359038

INTRODUCTION

The majority of the individuals in this compilation are runaway servants and slaves, but quite a number of runaway apprentices, both men and women, military deserters, with horse thieves, rapists, burglars, jail breakers, an occasional murderer, and other lowlifes are represented.

Tracking an individual by name may often lead to a dead end as multiple names were common, and middle names were not often used at this time. Joshua Frost used the alias Kettenger, James Bill, used the alias Bradford, and Thomas Partridge, the alias Wilson. Jacob Nice advertised for "Thomas Higgins, otherwise John Higgins, otherwise John Ornals." Some of the runaway Negroes also used aliases such as Jack, alias Salem.

Some runaway ladies used multiple names such as Mary Hulburt, alias Mary Lyons, alias Mary Kearney. Eleanor Debutcher, alias Catherine Cotton, may have been married to a man named John Sims. William McCew advertised a reward for William/Robert Erwin who "has stolen from me the subscriber, my servant maid, a girl of about 26 years of age; being a fat jolly girl."

Some of the multiple names that appear are likely due to spelling or pronunciation errors such as Elizabeth Carpenter/Cardender/Carpder and John Nicolls/Nichols/Nickles. Names not common in English such as Johannes/Johannis Finckensor/Frokinger, may have been quite creatively spelled by the advertisers. There are also nicknames such as "old Brass" for William Stewart, "Silver Heels" for Mary Allen, and "French Milliner" for Charles Gerome.

Multiple spellings of names sometimes appear in the same ad. When ads are published in different newspapers or even in the same paper, discrepancies in the ads sometimes appear. If the variations are substantial, the separate ads are included. The reader should be prepared for phonetic spellings of people they are interested in such as Margaret Henery/Hendry, Thomas Hamersley/Hamersly, and of course Jonson/Johnston/Johnson is always subject to challenge. In a few cases letters were indistinct and thus appear in brackets.

Some of the runaways were well skilled. Butchers, coopers, carpenters, blacksmiths, shoemakers and taylors (tailors) are represented. Runaway slave York was "the most ingenious with his Tongue and Hands, of any of his Colour; can make Bridles and Saddles, and understands the taning Business, and farming, very well." Skills of others might be questionable such as "an Irish servant man, named Florence Crawley, pretends to be a surgeon," and Mordecai Hart "pretends to be a Scholar." Some skills such as that of a ditcher, fuller, and wool comber no longer exist, and have you lately heard of a tinker or "battoeman." In many ads privateers and privateering are mentioned indicating skills at sailing.

It is impossible to know how many runaways there really were. The first New York newspaper did not begin publishing until 1726, and no newspapers were published in New Jersey or Delaware for the entire period covered.

Also printed handbills were often circulated, and some masters may have only advertised with them. Given that so many of the servants appear to be scapegraces, one wonders why their masters spent money to advertise for them, let alone pay a reward for their return. Those who were useful workers with lots of time remaining were likely to be the most sought after. Masters were likely to ignore those who left for a few days of dissipation, particularly planters during the agricultural slow season. Several ads seem to have been intended to let the runaway know how little the master thought of them as very low rewards were posted.

Some masters may have not wanted to pay the cost of the ads. Those masters whose servants absconded from more remote parts of the colony may not have bothered to advertise them. Subscribers who waited lengthy periods to advertise must have greatly reduced the chance of capturing the rogue. Cornelius Van Ranst waited "upwards of two Year" to advertise for a Mulatto Man slave named John. Cato ran away from Benjamin Westervelt in October 1764, but was not advertised until May 1765.

Some of the escapees were rather agile despite physical problems and restraints. J. Sebastian Stephany recorded his "Negro Fellow" Pompey ran away, though his "left Legg is a wooden one." Rose, or Grace, ran away from James Carroll though "lame in one of her Legs, with a broken Shin." A Negro man named Scipio ran away though he "had his arms pinioned behind him." Irish Servant Man John Read though only twenty years old "walks limping, owing to Rheumatick Pains in the great Toe of his Right Foot."

Many of the runaways were very fond of alcohol such as George Hames who was "much given to swearing and drinking" as was James Bishop "apt get drunk, and when so, is a very talkative, searing, rude, quarrelsome Fellow." Blacksmith John Bell, "hard-favoured, talks much and loud, and is a hard drinker." Some of the ladies imbibed such as Mary Godfrey, from Liverpool, "very liquorish, and has something lewd in her Behaviour, is much addicted to lying, and generally betrays herself by her Talkativeness." William Walters and his wife "are much given to drink."

Advertisements by men whose spouses "eloped" from them are usually not included as there is rarely much detail included. Men never appeared in advertisements for having left from their ladies.

Some enchanting ladies are included such as a fifteen-year-old "Indian Servant Wench" named Kate. She had run away before as she had an iron collar about her neck, and her master believed "in all Probability will equip herself in Men's Cloths, and inlist for a Soldier, as she did once before, but was detected." Another charmer was the thieving Moll Rogers. "This wretch has been a great plunderer and disturber of the repose of the honest people of this province, particularly the country, for a long course of time, and has actually been in the hands of the authority time after time, and yet is as daring as ever in her villainy."

Sad stories are found such as seven-year old Betsy Williams who "stray'd and lost herself in this City." Eve Hukel a runaway German servant girl was only twelve years old. Family quarrels are also represented with fifteen-year old Frederick Haber running away after his father "moderately corrected" him for frequenting a Public House and skipping Divine Service in 1732.

Stories that might have been scandalous for the day such as the runaway Negro Robin who was "supposed he is gone off with a likely young White Girl, by whom it is reported she is with Child; and Tis thought she will protect him under the Character of being her Servant." A runaway Spanish Negro Man named Domingo "is supposed to harbour in or about the Swamp, having been seen with one Mary Carney, a white Woman, that frequently used to harbour him at her Lodgings…."

Some interesting physical traits appear in the ads. One of the few men over six feet tall was Welch born Francis Jones, who was six feet three inch "by Trade a Tanner, and Stiles himself a Prize fighter." Others such as burglar Edward Lee escaped from prison in New York by sawing off his irons rendered "one large Iron Bar in the Chimney broke in sunder, and another much bent, by which Means, 'tis thought he got down to the Dungeon below his Prison, from whence he could get out without any Difficulty." Sheriff Roberts offered a hefty reward of twenty pounds for escaped prisoners who attacked their jailers and "rose upon them, knocked them down, and forced the keys from them, opened the doors and made their escape."

This work includes individuals with New York connections who did not run away in that colony, such as Ebenezer Mirrit who ran away from

Pennsylvania, but "says he was born away above New York, and his Friends live there, so that he will make that Way." Alexander McCormack, a Ditcher, was advertised in New Jersey but "has a Wife in New-York, named Mary, with a Son about 18 Months old."

Several of the men were well travelled. In 1765, John Duncan advertised a Negro man named Charles who was captured at Braddock's defeat in 1755, taken to Montreal in Canada, and when the British captured Montreal on 1760, wound up the property of Walter Rutherford of New York. Jacob claimed to have served in "Roger's Rangers three Years, and was at the Battle of Ticonderoga," and had the scar of a bullet on his wrist, but "he has been found in many Lies." Others had served on privateers and may have had extensive experience at sea. Before he broke prison in 1730, James Chambers went around "carrying a great Monkey for a Shew." One wonders how he obtained the animal and what happened to it.

The upheavals of the War of the Austrian Succession, and French and Indian War, which became part of the Seven Years War, certainly reduced the number of white servants available, As most came from or through the British Isles there would have been danger at sea, reducing the number of people sent from Europe, as well as an increased demand for cannon fodder to fill the ranks of armies there and in the Americas. During these wars the military activities in North America are likely to have encouraged some masters to send their servants as legitimate substitutes or simply to assuage their consciences.

This compilation lists all individuals mentioned. If an individual is listed with more than one name, all the names appear in the index. While many of the Negroes and some Indians are listed as slaves, many are not, so they may have been paid servants, though it is likely that most were slaves. People described as mixed Indian and Negroe blood such as the "Negro man named Stephen...is part Indian" are indexed in both ways, as Nanny/Nanney/Fanny described as "between the Indian and Negro Breed." Those designated as "Mustees" are also listed separately as they were of unspecified mixed races.

I have retained the original spelling, punctuation, and capitalization of the ads. Illegible words or letters are in brackets. Sometimes the ads in different papers are very similar and only the ad which occurs first in time is included, with references to the later ones. Minor differences in the advertisements are considered to be capitalization, spellings such as trousers/trowsers and 7/seven. If the ads are substantially different, each appears at the time it is first run. The majority are advertised in only one paper, many in two. Advertisements that are largely illegible are not included.

Newspapers Consulted:

It should be noted that none of these newspapers had a complete run for the period. Some, such as *Weyman's New-York Gazette*, were published less than one year. Also, there were no newspapers published in Delaware or New Jersey for the entire period, colonies where ads for New-York runaways might have appeared. Newspapers from south of Maryland were not consulted.

The American Weekly Mercury
The Boston Chronicle
The Boston Evening-Post
The Boston Gazette
The Boston News-Letter
The Boston Post-Boy
The Connecticut Courant
The Connecticut Journal
The Independent Reflector
The Maryland Gazette
The New-England Courant
The New-England Weekly Journal
The New-Hampshire Gazette
The New-London Gazette
The New-London Summary
The Newport Mercury
The New-York Chronicle
The New-York Evening Post
The New-York Gazette
The New-York Gazette, or Weekly Post-Boy
The New-York Journal; or, The General Advertiser
The New-York Mercury
The New-York Weekly Journal
The Newport Mercury
The Pennsylvania Chronicle
The Pennsylvania Gazette
The Pennsylvania Journal, or Weekly Advertiser
The Providence Gazette
The Rhode-Island Gazette
Weyman's New-York Gazette

1706

RAn-away from her Master Nicholas Jamain of New-York Merchant, the beginning of September last, A short thick Indian Girl, named Grace, aged about 17 years, her face is full of Pock holes, very few hairs on her Eyebrows, a very flat Nose, and a broad mouth; she speaks English, Dutch and French, the last best. Whoever shall apprehend and take up the said Servant, and deliver her unto Mr. Andrew Fanueil Merchant in Boston: If taken up in the Provinces of Massachusetes-Bay and New Hampshire; if in Connecticut-Colony, to Mr. John Clark at Saybrook; If at Rhode-Island Colony, to Mr. William Barbutt; In Pensilvania to Mr. Benj. Godfrey; In Carolina to Messieurs Guerard and Pacqueran; If in the Province of New-York at Albany to Col. Peter Schuyler; and other part of said Province to her Master Jamain, 3 pounds, shall forthwith be paid to any one that shall deliver the said Indian Woman to any of the persons above mentioned, besides reasonable Charges.

The Boston Post-Boy, From January 13, to January, 20, 1706; From February 10, to February 17, 1706; From February 24, to March 3, 1706; From March 10, to March 17, 1706.

1714

DEserted from Her Majesty's Service the 18th of August last at New-York, *John Smith* a Serjeant in his Excellency Brigadier *Hunter's* Company, a Tall slender Man, aged about 26 years, of a fair Complexion, wears his own Hair, of a sandy colour and curles, he was born in the North of Ireland, he speaks Scotch best, had on a Red Coat lin'd with yellow, the Sleeves fac'd with black, and a gray Wastcoat. Whoever shall apprehend the said Deserter and him safely convey to his Excellency the Governor of New-York, or give any true Intelligence of him so as he may be found again, shall be sufficiently rewarded besides all necessary Charges paid.

The Boston News-Letter, From August 30, to September 6, 1714.

RAn away from his Master, *Gilbert Ash* of the City of New-York Merchant; A Lusty Indian Man, named *Joseph Emery*, aged about 26 Years, he has bushy Hair, a Squinting Look, with a Cinamon coloured Coat lin'd with Red, a white Cotton Wastcoat, and speckled Shirt. Whoever shall apprehend the said Run-away, and him safely convey to his said Master at New-York, or give any Intelligence of him, so as his Master may have him again, shall have Twenty Shillings reward, besides all reasonable Charges paid.

The Boston News-Letter, From October 18, to October 25, 1714.

1720

THESE are to give Notice That there is lately arrived here at Boston from beyond Sea, a certain Person that wants to speak with one Daniel Pougher an English Man, born at Leicestershire in Old England, a Butcher by Trade, a Quaker by Profession, was marryed at New-York, liv'd some time in Rhode-Island, said to live somewhere in New-England; who is hereby desired to come to John Campbell in Cornhill, Boston, or write him word where he may be spoke with, or if any Person or Persons knows where he lives, they'l do well to inform, that thereby the said Pougher may reap the benefit and advantage intended for him.

The Boston News-Letter, From Monday December 12, to Monday December 19, 1720.

1721

W*Hereas John Mattuse Uresher, a Dutch Man aged about 28 Years, a middle sized Man, One Cheek bigger than the to'ther, wears a bob Wigg, a fad colour'd Stuff Coat trim'd with Silver, a flower'd Silk Wastecoat and Breeches, or a Pea Jacket, speaks very thick and but little English, late Privateer belonging to Capt. Jennings, has lately barbarously murdered one William Bostick of New-York Butcher, and is fled from Justice. All Persons are desired to apprehend the said John Mattuse Uresher, and give Notice to some Magistrate of New-York, that he may be sent for and proceeded against according to Law.*

The Boston Gazette, From May 1, to May 8, 1721.

1726

WIlliam Fletcher, *a bought Servant is Run away from his Master the 19 of last Month, and carried with him some Paper Money belonging to his said Master. Whoever can apprehend said Servant, or discover by Letter where he is, so that he may be apprehended, shall have* Five Pounds *paid by the Collector of his Majesty's Customs in* New-York. *Or if he will give security for his good Behaviour, he shall be forgiven. He had on, when he went away, a dark colour'd Kersey Coat with Brass Buttons, and lined with Duroy, has Leather Breetches, short dark Hair, by Trade a Brush-maker, pretends to be a Turner, he makes Mops, makes and mends Bellows.*

The New-York Gazette, From April 11, to April 18, 1726.

1727

RUn away from Mr. Walter Dongan, of Staten-Island, a servant Man named William Dulany, an Irishman, speaks pretty good English, but has a little brogue on it; he's a short, thick, well set young Fellow, about 20 Years old, has dark brown thick hair, he wears a black Duroy Suite of Cloths, he has also two leather pair of Breetches, one new, the other old, has 3 Shirts and a good Hat: Whoever secures him and brings him to the said Mr. Dongan, or to Mr. Thomas Scurlock, in New-York, shall have Forty Shillings, Reward, and all reasonable Charges.
The New-York Gazette, From June 26, to July 3, 1727.

RUN away from Capt. Mathew Norris, a Lusty Young Negro Man, named John Henricus, he speaks very good English & Welch, and had on when he went away, a Pea-Jacket, Striped Waistcoat and Breetches, Gray Worsted Stockings and Round Toes Shoes. Whoever will secure the said Negro, and bring him to the Post-Office in New-York, shall have Forty Shillings Reward.
The New-York Gazette, From August 28, to September 4, 1727; From September 4, to September 11, 1727, From September 11, to September 18, 1727.

Province of New-York, September 22.
On the 17th of August, Run away from Daniel Denton of Goshen in Orange-County, named Owen Doadel, an Irish-man; he is of middle Stature, has strait black Hair, a fresh Countenance, a crooked Toe upon each Foot, has a dark brown Coat, black Button-holes, no Buttons, (unless put on since he Ranaway) two pair of coarse Linnen Breeches. Whoever shall take up said Servant-man, and Secure him, so that his Master may have him again, or bring him home, or to John Everit at Jamaica on Long-Island, shall have Three Pounds as a Reward, and all Reasonable Charges.
The New-York Gazette, From September 23, to October 2, 1727.

1728

RUn away the 4th of August, from John Moor of the City of New-York, Merchant, a Negro Man named Caesar; he is of Tall stature; has taken with him several suits of Cloaths, viz. To Camblet Coats one brown the other whitish; also, an old homespun Coat; Two suites of Ozenbrig Jackets and Bretches; one Pair of Leather Bretches good Stockings and Shoes and some

Shirts. He reads and writes English and its believed he has got himself a sham Pass Whoever apprehends and secures the said Negro and gives Notice, so that his Master can have him again, shall have a Reward and all reasonable Charges.
N. B. He was taken up some time past, but slip away at Kings-Bridge.
The New-York Gazette, From August 12, to August 19, 1728; From August 19, to August 26, 1728.

1729

RUN away from the Brigantine *Frances, John Young* Master, the 15th of this Instant *February*, a Servant Man named *Joseph Hammond*, aged about 20 Years, a short well-set Fellow, black Hair, had on a red Duffils Watch coat over his other Cloaths. Whoever apprehends the said Servant, and brings him to Capt. *John Young* or to his Master *John Moore* of *New-York*, Merchant, shall have a Reward of Three Pounds, and all reasonable Charges.
The New-York Gazette, March 16, 1729, to March 23, 1729.

RUN away about the ninth of this Instant *June*, from *James Alexander* of *New-York*, a Negroe Man named *Yaff*, about 35 Years old; he formerly belonged to Mr. *Trent* and before him to Coll. *Ingoldey*; he was seen at *Elizabeth-Town* after he run away with a great Coat trimmed with Red, and an old Fustian Coat: He was born in this County, and reads and writes. He is a sensible cunning Fellow, and probably has got a pass forged. Whoever takes up the said Negroe, and secures him so that his said Master may have him again, shall have Four Pounds Reward, and all reasonable Charges.
The New-York Gazette, June 23, to June 30, 1729; June 30, to July 7, 1729; July 7, to July 14, 1729; July 14, to July 21, 1729.

1730

RUN away from the *John Galley*, of *Dublin*, Capt. *Richard Murphy*, a Servant Man named *William Gilliam*, a black-Smith by Trade, he is short and well-set, he was but indifferently Cloathed when he went away, having but part of a Shirt to his Back, and yellow coloured Jacket with Pewter Buttons, his Hair very short, wearing an old Wig over it. He is supposed to be gone towards *Philadelphia*. Whoever takes up said Servant, and secures him, so that the said Murphy may have him again, or give Notice to *Richard Ashfield* in *New-York*, or to *Andrew Bradford* in *PhilGelphis*, [sic] shall have Forty Shillings Reward, besides all reasonable Charges,

paid by   Richard Ashfield.
The American Weekly Mercury, From Tuesday December 30, to Tuesday, January 6, 1729 [sic]; *The American Weekly Mercury,* From Tuesday, January 6, to Wednesday, January 14, 1730. See *The New-York Gazette,* From December 30, to January 6, 1730.

RUN away from the Janny Galley, of *Dublin,* Captain *Richard Murphy* a Servant-Man named *William Gilliam,* a Black-smith by Trade. He is short and well-set, he was but indifferently Cloathed when he went away, having but Part of a Shirt to his Back, and a yellow coloured Jacket with Pewter Buttons, his Hair very short, wearing an old Wig over it. He is supposed to be gone towards *Philadelphia.* Whoever takes up said Servant, and secures him, so that the said *Murphy* may have him again, or gives Notice to *Richard Ashfield* of *New-York,* shall have *Forty Shillings* Reward, besides all reasonable Charges,
paid by   Richard Ashfield.
The New-York Gazette, From December 30, to January 6, 1730. See *The American Weekly Mercury,* From Tuesday December 30, to Tuesday, January 6, 1729.[sic]

WHereas three Prisoners for Debt broke out of the common Goal for *Westchester*-County, on Sunday Night, being the Twenty ninth of *March* last past; one of them named *David Orvis.* is a tall lusty Man thin faced have very short dark Hair; and at the time of breaking Goal little or no Cloaths on his back, and is about 36 years of Age; one other named *James Chambers,* is a short thick set Man, about 30 years old. having then on old Duroy Cloaths, and went formerly about the Country with one *Waring* carrying a great Monkey for a Shew: The other named *A[l]set Garrison.* is a lusty young Fellow. of a ruddy Complexion, had then on him an old blue Coat of Camblet. Whoever takes up the said Prisoners or either of them and brings them to *Gilbert Willet.* High-Sheriff or to *Jeremiah Fowler,* Under-Sheriff of said County of *Westchester* shall have *Forty Shillings* Reward for each Prisoner, and all reasonable Charges
paid by me   *G. Willet,* Sheriff
The New-York Gazette, From April 21, to April 28, 1730.

RUn away from *Cornelius De Peyster* of the City of *New-York,* a Negro Man named *Quash,* he is about 24 years of Age; a likely young Fellow, he has thick Lips and has lost some of his upper Fore-Teeth. Whoever can take up said Negro, and bring him to his Master, or secure him and give Notice, so that his Master can get him again, shall have *Forty Shillings* Reward and all reasonable Charges.

The New-York Gazette, From May 11, to May 18, 1730.

RUn away from *Nicholas Matthison*, of the City of *New-York*, Brewer, One Servant Man named *Henry Fincher*, about 26 years of age: He is by Trade a House-Carpenter, a Mason and a Pump Maker; some time past he lived with Mr. *Hold* in the City, Brewer. He had on, when he went away, a sute of Broad cloth Cloathes of a Choakalet Colour, and wears a speckled Cap; he is a West County Man, speaks pretty good *English*, and went away about the 28th of *April* last. He is of middle stature. Whoever can take up said Servant Man and bring him to his Master, or secure him and give Notice, so that his Master can have him again, shall have *Five Pounds* Reward, and all Reasonable Charges,
    paid by *Nicholas Matthison.*

The New-York Gazette, From May 11, to May 18, 1730.

RAN away from *David McCamly* of *Orange County*, in the Province of *New-York*, a Servant Man named *John Andrew*, (late a Servant to Alderman *Stuyvesant* of *New-York*) aged 18 or 19 years, tall of Stature, small Visage; had on at his Departure, an old Brown Worsted Drugget Coat, Oznabrigs Wastcoat and Breeches, grey Stockings, pretty good Shoes, a very old Hat, and a brown worsted Cap, and can speak very good *English* and *Dutch*. Whoever can secure the said Servant, and send Word to his Master, or to Mr. *James Wallace*, Merchant in *New-York*, shall be sufficiently Rewarded for their Pains.

The New-York Gazette, From July 3, to July 10, 1730.

RAN away on Sunday the 12th Instant *July*, from *Philip Livingston*, two *Irish* Servants, the one named *Michael Highland*, who is a tall lusty thick well set Fellow, brown Complection, short brown Hair, blue Eyes, a large Scar on one of his Legs. The other named *John Whilen*, is of middle Stature, fair Complection, sandy short curl'd Hair, blue Eyes, and is a Shoemaker by Trade; they have taken with them brown Frize close-body'd Coats, the Back lin'd with brown Flannel, narrow Sleeves, & Bath-mettle Buttons made after the French Fashion, two ditto Wastcoats, four pair of Leather Breeches, four pair Ozenbrigs ditto, five Guinea-Stuff Shirts, and four strong Holland Linen ditto, five pair Stockings, two Felt Hats, two Silk-romal Handkerchiefs, two Cotton ditto, one Worsted Cap, a Bayonet, and sundry other Things. Whoever shall apprehend and secure the said

Servants, so that they may be delivered to their said Master, shall receive for each Servant, the Sum of *Three Pounds*.
Philip Livingston.
The New-York Gazette, From July 13, 1730, to July 20, 1730; From July 20, to July 27, 1730; From July 27, to August 3, 1730.

RUN away last Tuesday Night two Negro Men, both branded *R N* upon their Shoulders: one remarkably Scarrified o'er the Fore-head, cloth'd with a Pair of Trousers only; the other with a Coat and Pair of Trousers. Whoever brings the said Negroes to *Jason Vaughan* in *New-York,* shall have *Thirty Shillings* Reward and all reasonable Charges paid.
The New-York Gazette, From August 24, to August 31, 1730; From August 31, to August 7, 1730.

R*UN away from* Richard Bishop, *a Servant Man named* John Farrant, *about nineteen years of Age of a fresh Complexion about five Feet and a half High, he had on when he went away, a brown livery Coat and Breeches the Coat lined and cuffed with blue, a blue Shoulder Knot a black natural Wig, and a Pair of red Stockings. Whoever takes up the said Servant and brings him to Mr.* Charles Robinson *at Capt.* Courter's *on the Dock shall have*
Five Pounds *Reward.*
The New-York Gazette, From August 10, to August 17, 1730; From August 17, to August 24, 1730.

RUn away from *John Bell,* of the City of *New-York,* a Servant Man named *John Sinclair,* about 24 or 25 years of Age, is of low stature, fresh Complexion, Round Faced, has short curled Hair of a light Colour, and is marked or stained with Powder or Ink on his Right Wrist with *I S* and three Spots: He wears a light Coloured Duroys Coat & Wastecoat with small Buttons, and dark coloured Duroys Breeches with silk Puffs of a Purple Colour; he has a new Hat; and has taken with two Ozenbrigs Wastecoats and one pair of Breeches of the same, a pair of blue striped Breeches and two pair of Trowsers.
Whoever can take up and secure said Servant, so that his Master can have him again, shall have *Forty Shillings* Reward, and all reasonable Charges, paid by   *J. Bell.*
The New-York Gazette, From November 2, to November 9, 1730; From November 9, to November 16, 1730.

1732

RUn away from *John Haskell* of the City of New-York, a Servant Man who went by the Name of *John Smith*, aged about 25 years, of short stature, a fresh Ruddy Complexion and short brown Hair; He walks Limping, speaks light a North Britain; he has been used to the Sea, and when he went away he had on a Pee Jacket. Whoever apprehends said Servant and brings him to John Haskell in *New-York*, or secures and gives Notice so that his Master may have him again, shall have *Twenty Shillings*
          and all Reasonable Charges.
    The New-York Gazette, From April 28, to May 5, 1732; From May 5, to May 11, 1732.

RUN away on Thursday last from Robert Bevan, a Servant Maid named Margery Brown, of a thick short Stature, had on when she went away, a speckled Jacket, plain quilt Petticoat. Whoever brings her to her said Master shall be reasonable rewarded, by Robert Bevan.
    It is supposed she may be about this City at this present.
    The New-York Gazette, From June 12, to June 19, 1732.

Whereas Frederick Haber, aged near sixteen Years, who for some time frequented a certain Publick House, and absented himself from Divine Service, being moderately corrected by his Father *Christian Haber*, of *Queens-bury*, in the Camp, in the County of *Albany*, for the above Facts, Ran away on the 17th of July last: He is a slender Youth of middle Stature, brown Eyes, brown short Hair, brown Complexion, flattish Nose, had lately the Small-Pox, he had on when he went away, a homespun Vest and Breeches, with Pewter Buttons, blue Stockings, a good Felt Hat, and took with him 3 white Shirts, a Leather Breeches, a strip'd Holland ticken Vest. Whoever can take up and secure the said Frederick so that his Father may have him again, shall have a reasonable Reward, and all Charges,
          paid by   *Christian Haber.*
    The New-York Gazette, From July 31, 1732, to August 7, 1732.

RAN away from *James Wallace* of *New-York* Mercht a Servant Man named John Ivey, of a middle stature, pretty slender, very small Legs, and something inclining to a stoop in his walk, pie Fac'd long dark colour'd Hair curl'd when dress'd, commonly wears it under a Cap aged about 30 Years born in *Barnstaple* in the West of *England*, by Trade a Cooper. He had on when he went away a grey Coat trim'd with Black and Leather

Breeches. Whoever secures said Servant and brings him to his said Master shall have Four Pounds as a Reward and all reasonable Charges paid.

The New-York Gazette, From October 23, to October 30, 1732; From November 13, to November 20, 1732; From November 20, to November 27, 1732.

RAN away from *Joseph Reade* of the City of *New-York*, Mercht. the 14th of *November* 1732, a likely Mullatto Servant Woman, named *Sarah*, she is about 24 Years of Age, and taken with her a Callico Suit of Cloaths, a striped Satten Silk Wast-coat, Two Homespun Wast-coats and Petty-coats; she is a handy Wench, can do all sorts of House-work, speaks good English and some Dutch. Whoever takes up the said Servant, and will bring her to her late Master, shall have *Five Pounds* as a Reward and all reasonable Charges paid.

The New-York Gazette, From November 11, to November 20, 1732; From November 20, to November 27, 1732.

1733

RUN away on Tuesday last, from Nathaniel Hazard of *New-York*, a lusty Lad about 18 or 19 Years of Age, named *Robert Hill*, a West County Man, tall and well set, with short brown Hair; had on when he went away a Cinnamon colour'd plain course Kersey Coat, with large flat metal Buttons, a pair of Tow Trowsers, thick Shoes, an old Felt Hat, a Brick-maker by Trade, and understands something of the Farmers Work.

Whoever takes up the said Servant, and brings him to his Master, or secures him that he may be had again, shall have Forty Shillings as a Reward, and all reasonable Charges, paid by *Nathaniel Hazard.*

The New-York Weekly Journal, January 7, 1733; December 31, 1733. No explanation for the date range.

RUN away on Thursday Night last about Ten a Clock from *John Cannon*, of the City of *New-York*, three Negro Men, with a Sloop belonging to said *Cannon*, Burthen about Thirty five Tons. Whoever takes up said Sloop and Negroes and secures them so that the Owner may have them again, shall have Twenty Pounds Reward, and all necessary Charges
            paid by   *John Cannon.*

The New-York Gazette, From January 30, to February 6, 1733; From February 6, to February 13, 1733; From February 13, to February 20, 1733.

RAN away on the 17th of this Instant *May*, from the Printer hereof. an Apprentice Lad, named *James Parker*, by Trade a Printer, aged about 19 Years, he is of a fresh Complection, with short yellowish Hair; having on a yellowish Bengall Coat, Jacket and Breeches, lined with the same, and has taken with him a brown colour'd coarse Coat, with flat Mettal Buttons, Two Frocks, Two Shirts, One Pair of strip'd Ticken Jacket and Breeches. Whoever takes up and secures the said Apprentice, so that his said Master may have him again, shall have *Twenty Shillings* as a Reward, and all reasonable Charges,
    Paid by *William Bradford.*
 The New-York Gazette, From May 14, to May 21, 1733. See *The New-York Gazette,* From May 21, to May 28, 1733.

RAN away on the 17th of this Instant *May*, from *William Bradford* an Apprentice Lad, named *James Parker*, by Trade a Printer, aged about 19 Years, he is of a fresh Complection, with short yellowish Hair; having on a yellowish Bengall Coat, Jacket and Breeches, lined with the same, and has taken with him a brown colour'd coarse Coat, with flat Mettal Buttons, Two Frocks, Two Shirts, One strip'd Ticken Jacket and Breeches. He has likewise —— or taken away several other Goods, as Linnen of several sorts, Silk and Worsted Stockings, Silk Handkerchiefs, Books, Knives, two Composing Sticks and other Tools belonging to the Printing Trade. Whoever takes up and secures the said Apprentice, so that his Master may have him again, shall have *Forty Shillings* as a Reward, and all reasonable Charges, paid by *William Bradford.*
 The New-York Gazette, From May 21, to May 28, 1733. See *The New-York Gazette*, From May 14, to May 21, 1733;

RUN away from *Thomas Rodman* of *Flushing*, the 3d of this Instant, an Irish Servant Woman, about 24 Years of age, of a middle Stature, pretty much Pock freckled, has a scar on one of her Cheeks, speaks pretty good English, but has something of the Irish-Brogue, she took with her an Orange coloured Gown and Petticoat home spun Made, a speckled Calico Gown lined with White and a blew quilted Petticoat. Whoever shall take her up and convey her to her Master or secure her and give notice so that he can have her again, shall have Twenty-Shillings Reward and reasonable Charges.
 The New-York Gazette, From June 18, to June 25, 1733.

RUN away from *Thomas Hall*, of the City of *New-York*, Cordwainer, two Servant Men, the one named *Thomas Holland*, of a middle Stature black Complexion and a blach [sic] Beard, aged about 35 Years, had on when he went away a dark brown broad Cloath Coat, a pair of Leather Breeches, a dark Whig. He is an Irish Man, very well shap'd and has small Feet.

The other named *John Sulivan*, a short well sett Fellow, of a fair Complexion and fresh Colour, has on when he went away an Iron gray broad Cloath Coat, Wastcoat and Breeches, light blew Worsted Stockings, round toe'd Shoes almost new, he wears his own Hair which is light colour'd and curl'd, he wears a checker'd Shirt white and red. He is an Irish Man, about 18 Years of Age, and has very thick Legs.

Whoever takes up the said Servants or either of them and brings them or him to their Master in *New-York*, or secures them so that they may be had again, shall have three Pounds for each or either of them as a Reward and all reasonable Charges
                paid by   *Thomas Hall.*
New-York, June 25*th*, 1733.
    The New-York Gazette, From July 16, to July 23, 1733.

A Young Indian Fellow named *Teer*, about 18 or 19 Years of Age, is Run away from his Master *James Jackson* of *Flushing*; he is a strait slim fellow speaks English and nothing else: He run away the latter end of May last, and had on when he went away a good Beaver Hat, a homespun Coat of a yallowish colour with brass Buttons, a home-spun Shirt Leather Breeches and large Buckles in his Shoes: He had long black Hair, but it may be supposed he has cut his Hair, and perhaps sold his hat. Whoever takes up the said Indian fellow and bring him to his said Master in *Flushing*, or secures him so that he may be had again, shall have three Pounds as a Reward and all reasonable Charges
                paid by   *James Jackson.*
    The New-York Gazette, From July 16, to July 23, 1733; From July 30, to August 6, 1733; From August 13, to August 20, 1733.

R*AN away the* 18*th of* August 1733, *from* Jacobus van Cortlandt *of the City of* New-York, *a Negro Man Slave, named* Andrew Saxton, *a very black tall Fellow, walks lamish with his left Leg: the Thumb of his left Hand is somewhat stiff by a Wound he had in his Hand formerly; the Shirts he had with him and on his Back are mark'd with a Cross on the left Breast; He professeth himself to be a* Roman Catholick, *speaks very good* English, *is a Carpenter and Cooper by Trade, and has Tools for both Trades with Him; he had on a Pair of Trowsers, but 'tis uncertain what other Cloaths he has with him. Whoever takes up and secures the said Negro Man, and gives*

Notice thereof to his said Master, so as he may be had again, shall have Forty Shillings if takes within Ten Miles of the City of New-York, *and Three Pounds in farther, as a Reward, and all reasonable Charges, paid by* Jacobus Van Courtlandt.

The New-York Gazette, From August 27, to September 3, 1733; From September 10, to September 17, 1733; From September 17, to September 24, 1733; From October 1, to October 8, 1733; From October 8, to October 15, 1733.

RAN away on the 28th of *August* last, from *Robert Todd*, of the City of *New-York*, a Servant Man, named *Martin Morrow*, of a short Stature and swarthy Complexion, aged about 40 Years; he is a *French-man*, and has something of the *Irish* Brogue; when he went away he had a speckled Shirt and an old Wastcoat. Whoever takes up said Servant and secures him so that his said Master may have him again, shall have 30 *Shillings* Reward, and all reasonable Charges.

The New-York Gazette, From October 8, to October 15, 1733; From October 15, to October 22, 1733; From October 22, to October 29, 1733.

1734

RUN away on Tuesday last, from *William Legget* of *West-chester*, two *Nantucket Indians*, who are Brothers; the Elder is about 23 Years old, is named *Job*, and the Younger about 20 Years old, is named *Hezekiah*, they are strong lusty Fellows, and had on home-spun Cloaths, they runaway with my Peteauger, which is pretty large, has a Round-house, was lately Stove, and is new fitted, they had with her two Ceder Masts, and Sails, one small Oar and Paddle, but no Rudder, they were seen to go past *Frog's-Point* on Wednesday morning about sun rising, and therefore are gone Eastward.

If any Person can procure me my Peteauger, Sails, &c. again; or take the said Indians and bring them to me, or secure them and give Notice, so that I can have them, shall have *Thirty Shillings* Reward for the Peteauger, and the same Sum for each of the said Indian Men, besides all reasonable Charges, paid by   *William Legget.*

The New-York Gazette, From March 3, to March 11, 1734.

Run away from *Johanna Kelsall* of the City of *New-York*, a Negroe Man known by the Name of Johnsey here in Town, but writes his Name *Jonathan Stow*, about 25 Years of Age, of short Stature, bandy Legs, blubber Lips, yellow Complexion, his Hair is neither right Negro nor

Indian, but between both, and pretty long, he had on when he went away a homespun Jacket, a Pair of Trowsers, and a speckled Shirt.

    Whoever takes up the said Negro and secures him, or brings him to his Mistress, shall have 40 Shillings Reward and all Reasonable Charges
            paid by me   *Johanna Kelsall.*
The New-York Weekly Journal, August 24, 1734.

    Run away from *Thomas Rigby*, of the City of *New-York*, Joyner, an indented Servant Man named *John Howey*, about 21 Years of Age, he is an Irish Man, and a Joyner by Trade, of a middle Stature, very round Back'd, thin Beard, he wears a Wigg, had on when he went away, a blew Duffels Coat, Ozenbrigs West-Coat, and a Pair of Buck-Skin Britches, a speckl'd Shirt, a new Felt Hat, and a Pair of Yarn Stockings.

    Whoever takes up the said Servant, and brings, him to his Master, shall have 5 Pounds as a Reward, and all reasonable Charges
            paid by   *Thomas Rigby.*
The New-York Weekly Journal, October 14, 1734; October 21, 1734.

AN Indented Servant Man, named *Ralph Maulkin*, on Friday last, Run away from the Ship called *Mainwaring*, having on a dark brown Coloured Sailors Jacket and dark Coloured Breeches, an Old Hat slouching over his Ears, and an Old pair Shoes. He is very much Pock-fretten. Whoever shall take up said Servant, secure him and give Notice, or bring him to Mr. *Williams* at *Boston Richardsons* in *New-York*, or to the Printer hereof, shall have *Three Pounds*, as a Reward, besides all reasonable Charges.
The New-York Gazette, From October 21, to October 28, 1734.

    Run away from *Hugh Waddell*, of the City of *New-York*, Merchant, a Servant Man named *Adam Gray*, about 19 Years of Age, had on when he went away a blew Coat, edged with Red, and yellow Metal Buttons, a red Wast-coat with yellow Metal Buttons, Leather Breeches very greasy, gray Stockings, a Pair of small Steel Buckles in his Shoes, and wears a black Wigg. He allso took with him a Steel Gray Cloath Coat trim'd and lin'd with Black, and a Snuff coloured Wast-Coat.

    Whoever takes up the said Servant and brings him to his Master, or secures him so that he may be had again, shall have 30 *s*. as a Reward and all reasonable Charges
            paid by   *Hugh Waddell.*
The New-York Weekly Journal, October 14, 1734; October 21, 1734; October 28, 1734; November 4, 1734; November 11, 1734.

1735

RUN away from *John Dunlap* of the City of *New-York*, Coardwainer, one indented Servant Man, named *John Morsby*, is an *Irish-man*, a Shoe-maker by Trade, about Thirty years of age, is of middle stature, he has black Hair and a thick blach Beard; had on, when he went away, a sad coloured Broadcloth Coat, a Linsey-woolsey striped Wastcoat, brown Yarn Stockins newly footed, blew Breeches trimed with black; and Two speckled Shirts, one is Cotton, the other is Linnen. Whoever shall take up said Servant and convey him to his Master, or secure him and give Notice, so that he may be had again, shall have *Three Pounds* Reward, and all reasonable Charge.

The New-York Gazette, From December 30, 1734, to January 7, 1735.

RUN away, the 4th of this Instant *Feb.* from *Francis Richardson* of *Philadelphia*, Gold-smith, an Apprentice Lad named *Isaac Marceloe*, born in *London* but of French Extraction which may be discovered by his speech, of short Stature and thin Visage, limps in his gate as if he had been Lame. He was formerly Apprentice to *William Heurtin*, Gold-smith, in *New-York*. Had on when he went away, a grey Cloath Coat which had been his Masters and was turn'd for him, a brown Cloath Jacket with most of the Buttons off, a pair of Plush Breeches with Horn Buttons turn'd round and tip'd with Silver, a thick pair of mil'd grey Stockings and a pair of old Shoes worn thro', he has a light Wigg and a Cap with him. Whoever takes up and secures the said Lad so that his Master may have him again, shall have *Thirty Shillings* as a Reward and reasonable Charges,
    paid by me *Francis Richardson.*
N. B. 'Tis suppose the above Runaways are in Company.

The American Weekly Mercury, From Tuesday February 11, to Tuesday February 18, 1735.

RUN away about the beginning of May, a Servant Man named Samuel Hunter, about fifty years of Age, and talks broad Scotch, was born in Dumfrieze in Scotland; by Trade a Taylor, he wears his own Hair, and had on when he went away, a blue Camblet Coat. Whoever secures the said Samuel Hunter, and gives notice to the Printer hereof shall have two Pistoles Reward and all reasonable Charges.

The New-York Gazette, From May 26, to June 2, 1735; From June 2, to June 9, 1735; From June 9, to June 16, 1735; From June 16, to June 23, 1735; From June 23, to June 30, 1735; From July 21, to July 28, 1735.

RUN away the 5th Instant from John Bell of the City of New-York, Carpenter, an Apprentice Boy named James Harding, aged about 19 Years, being a tall well-set Lad of a fresh Complection, he wears a Wig, he spley-footed, [sic] and Shuffles with his feet as he walks, has a Copper colour'd Kersey Coat with large flat white Mettle Buttons, a grey Duroy Coat lined with Silk, it is pretty much faded by wearing, abroad blue striped Wast-Coat and Breeches and a pair of blue striped Tickin Breeches, in warn whether [sic] he often bleeds at the Nose. Whoever takes up said Apprentice within the City of New-York, or ten Miles off, and brings him to his Master, or secures him and give Notice, so that he can be had again, shall have Forty Shillings, and if further off the Sum of Four Founds, and reasonable Charges,
          paid by   John Bell.
The New-York Gazette, From June 2, to June 9, 1735.

RUN away from the Ship James and Joseph, John Butler Commander on the 29th Instant, a Servant Man named Joseph Woodward, about 19 or 20 Years of Age, fresh Complection, and a round Face, about 5 Foot 5 Inches high and wellset, having on a dark colour'd Wig, and a light colour'd thick Cloth Coat, little fac'd, and a green Wastcoat, and a white pair of Breeches.

    Whoever will secure the said Servant, or bring him to Cadwalider Williams, Merchant in New-York, or to John Butler Commander, of the abovesaid ship, shall have Thirty Shillings Reward, and all reasonable Charges.

The New-York Gazette, From June 23, to June 30, 1735; From July 21, to July 28, 1735; From July 28, to August 4, 1735.

RAnaway from *John Lester* of *Hempstead* in *Queens-County* on *Nassau Island*, a Servant Man, named *William Macoy* (an Irish Man) about twenty-five years of Age, he is pretty much Pock-freeten: He had on when he went away, a Red Duffils Coat, a brown Broad cloth Wastcoat, a light coloured Durois Coat, and a black Caliminco Wastcoat and Breeches.

    Whever can take up said Servant and convey him to his Master, or to *William Bradford* in *New-York*, or secure and give Notice, so that his Master can have him again, shall have *Twenty Shillings* Reward, and all Reasonable Charges,
          paid by   *John Lester.*
The New-York Gazette, From December 8, to December 15, 1735; From December 15, to December 23, 1735.

1736

RUN away from Edmund Peers, *of* New-York, *a Servant Maid, named* Grissel Miller, *a Scotch Girl aged about* 20 *Years; had on when she went away, a black Crape Gown, and a quilted Petticoat, a Pair of blew Stockings white clocks, a new Pair of Shoes, she speaks broad Scotch, middle size, full breasted.* Whosoever takes her up and brings her to Henry Hartley, *at the* Compass *and* Horse-Shoe, *in* Strawberry-Alley, Philadelphia, *shall have* Forty Shillings *Reward and reasonable Charges paid by* Henry Hartley.
   The Pennsylvania Gazette, From May 20, to May 27, 1736; From May 27, to June 3, 1736.

☞ Run away from *William Finn* of *Goshen*, in the County of *Orange* and Province of *New York*. A Servant Man named *James Rodman*, an Irishman, of about Twenty Years of Age, of a middle Stature and well Built, he is very much Pockbroken, and has one of his little Fingers cut off, in the middle Joynt, he had on when he went away, a Linnen Fly Coat and a Demity Vest and Breeches, and a light colour'd pair of Worsted Stocking, he wares a Cap, and had a new felt Hat when he went away. Whoever takes up the said Servant, and secures him so that his said Master may have him, shall have Twenty Shillings reward, and all reasonable Charges,
   paid by said,   *William Finn.*
   The New-York Weekly Journal, June 7, 1736.

RAN away from *John Wallace* of the City of New-York, a Servant Man, named *Joseph Brook*, but perhaps has changed his Name to *Thomas Ward*, or some other Name, He is mark'd on one of his hands with I. B. has a home-spun grey Coat, brown Ozenbrigs, or whitish Cloth Breeches, blackish Woolen Stockins, and brass Buckles, has a white Shirt, a Woolen Cap, a Silk Muzlain Handkerchief, and an old Felt Hat: he is a well-set Man, Pock-fretten, of pale Complection, is pretty Deaf, and his Head stands a-wry. There is another Man along with him, not so tall as he is, who had on a Redish Coat, has Redish Eyes and squints, and is of brownish Complexion. Whoever shall take up said *Joseph Brook*, and bring him to his Master, or secure him & give Notice, so that his Master can have him again, shall have *Forty Shillings*, if taken within 20 Miles of the City of the City [sic] of *New-York*, if further off, *Three Pounds* and reasonable Charges.
   The New-York Gazette, From September 20, to October 4, 1736.

RAN away from the Printer hereof an Apprentice Boy named *Sam Daily*; he is lurking about in this City. All Persons are hereby fore-warned not to entertain or conceal, nor to convey away said Apprentice, as they will answer it at their Peril.
The New-York Gazette, From November 8, to November 15, 1736; From November 15, to November 22, 1736.

RAn away from on board the Neptune Snow the 17th past, a Servant Boy named *Edward Rowley*, born in *Worstershire* in *England*, speaks broad West Country he is round face'd, short Nose, some-what Pock-fretten; had on when he went away, a grey Kersey Pee-Jacket, a striped Home-spun Jacket under it a Speckled Shirt, a Worsted Cap, narrow cropt Hat and painted, a pair of Trowsers, and old Shoes.

Whosoever takes up said Boy and brings him to the Vessel, or to the Printer hereof, shall be very well Rewarded.
The New-York Gazette, From November 15, to November 22, 1736; From November 22, to November 29, 1736.

RUN away about the 6th of November past from Mathew Clarkson, a Servant Man named Johannes Poluck, born in Switzerland, about Twenty Years of age, of a middle Stature, hath two Thumbs on the right Hand, and keeps it bound over with a Rag, came over from Holland, in the Brigt. Prince Frederick, Joseph Willson, Master, to New York, about the middle of September last: Had on, a new Felt Hat, a double worsted striped Cap, a double breasted Pea Jacket with flat brass buttons, two ozenbrigs Shirts, new leather breeches, two pair woollen Stockings, new Shoes & two cotton romal Handkerchiefs. Whoever apprehends the said Servant & delivers him in the Goal of Philadelphia, any Goal in New Jersey or at New York, giving Notice to Mr. Arent Hassert of Philadelphia, Gerardus De Peyster at New Brunswick, or Mathew Clarkson in New York shall receive Three Pounds reward and reasonable Charges.
The Pennsylvania Gazette, December 16, 1736.

1737

RUN away from *Arent Bradt* of *Schinectady*, in the County of *Albany*, on Sunday the 10th of *April* last, a Negroe Man named *William Smith*, he is an Indented Servant; he is a pretty lusty well set Fellow, full fac'd, and in colour like the *Madagascar* Negroes, Speaks *English*, *High* and *Low* Dutch, understands all Sorts of Husbandry work, and something of the Trade of a Blacksmith, since he run away he has been seen at *Katskills*, and is supposed now to be in the *Jerseys* were he lived some time ago. Any Person that take up said Negroe Man servant, and secure him so that his Master may have him again, shall have *Three Pounds* reward, and all reasonable Charges.

The New-York Weekly Journal, May 2, 1737; May 9, 1737; May 16, 1737; May 23, 1737.

R*AN away from Mr.* James Jones *of Whitestone on* Long-Island, *upon Wednesday last, in the Night, an Irish Servant Boy, about* 16 *years Old, he is mark'd with the Small-Pox, and of Sanguine Complexion, short Chubbed Size, has black Hair, and had on, when he went away, a black Cloth Waistcoat and Breeches and a Frock. He has carried away a Home-spun Jacket and Breeches, and an Old Bever Hat, and two White Shirts; his Name is* James Mac Langhlin. *Whoever shall take up said Servant Boy and convey him to his Master, or secure him and give Notice, so that his Master can have him again, shall be very well Rewarded, and all Charges*
    paid by   JAMES JONES.
The New-York Gazette, From May 9, to May 16, 1737.

RUN away from *Cornelius Quackenbusch*, Baker of the City of *New York*, an Apprentice Boy, named *John Lane*, aged about 14 years, has dark brown Hair, a large Scar under the right Jaw, had on when he went away a homespun Linnen Jacket Ozanbrigs Breeches and a Course Felt hat. Whoever takes him up and secures him so that his Master may have him again shall have 20 *s.* and all reasonable Charges.

The New-York Weekly Journal, July 11, 1737.

R*AN away from* John Wooly *in the Township of* Hempstead *in* Queens-County, *on Nassau-Island, in the Province of* New-York, *a Negro Man, about the Age of Twenty Three years; had on when he went away, a course Felt Hat, a grey Home-spun Drugget Coat, about half worn, a Vest of the same, short Toe-Oznabrig Trowzers, grey Yarn Stockins, He is a Middle-sized Negro, he lisps a little upon the Dutch. His Master has been inform'd that has got a Pass along with him.*

  Whoever takes up said Negro and conveys him to his Master, or to John Byvank *in the City of* New-York, *or secures him and gives Notice, shall have Forty Shillings as a Reward, and all Reasonable Charges.*

The New-York Gazette, From July 11, to July 18, 1737.

RUN away from Samuel Hopson *of* New-York Ferry, *Butcher, a Servant Man Named* Anthony Roberts, *a short chuffy* [sic] *Fellow, a ruddy Complection, dark colour'd strait Hair, Aged about* 21; *Had on when he went away an Oznabrigs Jacket, Shirt and Breeches with Buckles, a short Brim'd greasy Hat, is a West Country Man, and retains something of the accent.*

Twenty Shillings *as a Reward, and all reasonable Charges for taking and securing the said Servant so that his Master May have him again.*

The New-York Weekly Journal, July 25, 1737; August 1, 1737.

RUN away from the Brigantine Joanna, Samuel Payton *Master, an Irish Servant Man named* Charles Mc'Cammel *aged about* 25 *Years a tall lusty Man, wearing his own black Hair, having on a dark Frize Coat and a brownish Wastcoat and Breeches. Whoever takes up the said Servant and brings him to* Mr. Cornelius Van Horne *or said* Payton *shall be rewarded and all Charges.*

N. B. *The Servant having been offer'd* 8 *Shillings for his Hair, it's suppos'd he may have cut it off, he speaks very good* English.
New-York, August 21, 1737.

The New-York Weekly Journal, August 29, 1737.

RAN away the 15th of *November* Instant from *Jeremiah Gardner,* a Man who goes by the Name of *William Story,* (but suppose his true Name is *John Bond)* he is a thick short well-set Man, and had Bushy sandy Hair, and wears an old blue Vest laced with Canvas, and has a blew Shirt, appearing like a Sailor. Whoever takes up and brings the said Servant Man to Messieurs *Latouch* and *Hay* in *New-York,* or secures him and gives Notice, so that he may be had again, shall have *Forty Shillings* and all reasonable Charges.

The New-York Gazette, From November 14, to November 21, 1737.

1738

RUN away from Capt. Langden of the City of New-York a Servant Maid named *Catherine Weissenburg,* about 17 Years of Age, Middle stature, Slender, black ey'd, brown Complexion, speaks good English, altho a Palantine born; had on when she went away, a homespun striped wastcoat and Peticoat, blew-stockings and new Shoes, with her a Calico Wraper, and a striped Calamanco Wraper, besides other Cloaths:

Whoever takes her up and brings her home, or secures, her so that she may be had again, shall have *Twenty Shillings* Reward, and all resonable Charges; and all Person are forewarned not to entertain the said Servant at their Peril.
The New-York Weekly Journal, January 22, 1738.

THese are to give Notice. That last *Saturday* Night (19th of *July*) then broke out of Goal in *Jamaica* on *Long-Island* in the Province of *N. York*, one *William Higgins* a middle-sized Man, near Fifty years of Age, a long Visage, brown and Sanguine Complection, has short grey Hair, and a Mole on his Right Cheek; he is very Talkative, and stammers in his Speech. Was cloathed when he went away, with an Old Home-spun Coat and Jacket, a pair of Old Sheep-skin Breeches, and a broad-brim'd Bever Hat, Old Shoes and Stockins,

And one *Amos Langdon*, a tall slender Man, about Thirty years of Age, of a dark Complection, dark brown Hair, a Roman Nose, slow of Speech, is a Weaver by Trade; He had on when he went away, and Old grey Worsted Coat, a Double breasted Camblet Jacket of a Snuff Colour, a pair of Old Leather Breeches, grey Home-spun Stockins, Dog-skin Shoes, and a Narrow-brim'd Bever-Hat half worn.

Whoever takes up these two Men, or either of them, and bring them, or him, to the said Goal in *Jamaica*, or can secure them, and give Notice, so that the Goal-keeper can get them again, shall receive for *William Wiggins* the Sum of *Ten Pounds*, and for *Amos Langdon* Three Pounds, and reasonable Charges,
              paid by   GEORGE REYNOLDS, *Under-Sheriff.*
The New-York Gazette, From July 24, to July 31, 1738; From July 31, to August 7, 1738; From August 7, to August 14, 1738; From August 14, to August 21, 1738; From August 21, to August 28, 1738; From August 28, to September 4, 1738; From September 4, to September 11, 1738; From September 25, to October 2, 1738.

RAN away from *Jonas Foster* of the Township of *Hempstead* on *Long-Island*, a Servant Boy, named *William Butterfield*, about 19 years of Age, he is a thick squat youth, and very Remarkable by having a bald Head, which came by a scald. He had on, when he went away, a striped Flannel Jacket, and a blue one over it; a New pair of Shoes, but no Stockins, and a pair of brown Trouzers, besides a bundles of Cloathes he took along with him, unknown to his Master. This Lad is of a brown Complection.

Whoever shall take up said Run-away servant, and convey him to his Master, or to *Joi[s] Siv[ec]k* in *New-York*, or secure him, and give Notice,

so that his Master can have him again, shall have *Twenty Shillings* Reward, and all reasonable Charges
     paid by   JONAS FOSTER.
The New-York Gazette, From August 7, to August 14, 1738; From August 28, to September 4, 1738; From September 4, to September 11, 1738.

RUN away from *Stephen Wood, of* Staten Island, *an Apprentice Lad named* Isaac Lakerman, *a short slender fresh coloured Lad*, about 19 *Years of Age, a Shoemaker by Trade, he wore a Cap, had on when he went away, a good Castor Hat an all Woollen Coat and Vest, of an olive Green color, a pair of specled Trowsers, and sundry sorts of Shoemakers Tools, which he took from his said Master. Whoever takes up the said Run away and secures him so that his said Master may have him again shall have* Forty Shillings Reward and all reasonable Charges
     paid by,   STEPHEN WOOD.
N. B. He is very apt to blirk [sic] *with his Eyes if steadily look'd upon.*
The New-York Weekly Journal, August 21, 1738; August 28, 1738.

RUN away from *Frederick Zepperly* of *Reinbeck*, in *Dutchess, County* Black Smith, a Copper, Coloured Negro Fellow, named Jack, aged about 30 Years, speaks nothing but English, and has been much used to the Sea, short of Stature. thin Face, strong bearded and hair longer than Negroes commonly have, and reads English, he had on when he went away an Orange Coloured Drugget Fly Coat some what faced, with brass Bottons, a Homespun Linnen Coat two striped Linsey Woolsey Wastcoats and two pair of Breeches of the same, also one pair of Leather Breeches a pair of Worsted Stockings, and a pair of New Blew Stockings, New square toed Shoes. with Brass Buckles, two homespun Shirts, and a very good hat.
 Whoever takes up the said Run away and secures him so that his Master may have him again or give him notice of him to *Henery Beekman, Esq*; or to *John Peter Zenger*, shall have *Forty Shillings* Reward and all reasonable Charges.
The New-York Weekly Journal, October 2, 1738; October 9, 1738.

RAN-away, on the 16th of *September*, from *Charles Decker*, of *Richmond* County upon *Staten-Island*, a Malatto Slave named *Harry*, about 24 Years of Age, of middle Stature, blew Eyes, blackish Hair, and a fair Skin for a Malatto, he speaks good Dutch but his English something broken: He had on when he went away a lightish Duroy Coat, a blue grey Kersey Jacket, and a pair of tow Cloth Trowsers, a white Shirt, a narrow brimm'd Beaver Hat, gray woollen Stockings, new round toe'd Shoes, and Silver Buckels.

Whoever takes up said Slave and secures him so that his Master may have him again, shall have *Forty Shillings* Reward and reasonable Charges.

The New-York Gazette, From October 2, to October 9, 1738.

1739

RUN away from *Gabriel Crooke*, a Negro Man named *Jupiter* of a middle Stature, about 25 Years of Age; had on when he went away, a Carsey Coat and Jacket, a Pair of Yellow Leather Britches, good Shoes and Stockings. Whoever will take up and Secure the said Negro Man so that his Master may have him again shall have 30 Shillings as a Reward and all reasonable Charges.

The New-York Weekly Journal, January 14, 1739; January 21, 1739; January 28, 1739.

RUN away from *James Willey*, Cooper of the City of *New-York*, an indented Servant Man named *John Scott*, of a middle Stature, black Hair, and sometimes wears a Cap, has on a Brown dark Coloured Kersey Coat, a Pair of good Buckskin Britches, a striped Linsey Woolsey Jacket, and spickled Shirt; he has a very large Scar on the right Side of his under Jaw.—Whosoever takes up the said Servant, and brings him back to his said Master or Secures him so that he may be had again, shall have Five Pounds as a Reward and all reasonable Charges

                Paid by   *James Willey.*

The New-York Weekly Journal, January 28, 1739.

RAN-away from *John Markham*, living in the *Highlands* near Goshen, an Indented Servant Man named *John Hickey*, an Irish Man, about 18 Years of age, he is five Foot three Inches High, has short red Hair, of a thin Visage and full of Freckles, and has something of the Irish Accent in his Speech; he had on a brown Coat, Vest and Breeches.

Whoever takes up the said Servant and conveys him to his Master or to *John Dyer* in *New-York*, or secures him and gives Notice so that he may be had again, shall have *Forty Shillings* Reward and reasonable Charges.

The New-York Gazette, From February 20, 1739.

R*An away about two Months ago, from* Moses Gombauld *of the City of* New York, Merchant, *an Indian Boy named* Pero, *about* 18 *Years of Age,* *that speaks* French, English *and* Spanish *but all bad. He had on went he went away, a lap'd double breasted blue Jacket and Breeches, and has thick bushy Hair.*

Whoever shall take up the said Indian Boy, and bring him to his abovesaid Master to New York, *or to Mr.* Stephen Bourineau, *Merchant in* Boston, *shall have Three Pounds Reward, and all reasonable Charges paid.*
The Boston Evening Post, March 19, 1739; March 26, 1739; April 2, 1739; April 9, 1739. See *The Boston Gazette*, From May 14, to May 21, 1739.

RAN-away about two Months ago, from his Master, *Moses Gombauld* of the City of *New-York*, Merchant, an Indian Boy named *Pero*, about Eighteen Years of Age, speaks *French, English* and *Spanish* but all bad. He had on went he went away, a lap'd double Breasted blue Jacket and Breeches, and has thick bushy Hair. Whoever shall take up the said Indian Boy, and bring him to his abovesaid Master to *New-York*, or to Mr. *Stephen Bourineau*, Merchant in *Boston*, shall have *Three Pounds* Reward *New-York* Money, or *Nine Pounds* our Money.
The Boston Gazette, From May 14, to May 21, 1739. See *The Boston Evening Post*, March 19, 1739.

RAn away the 30th of last Month, from *Anthony Engelbert*, of this City, Stone-Cutter, a High-*Dutch* Servant Man, nam'd *George Henry Keriger*, about 21 Years of Age, of middle Stature, thick set, brown Complexion, and short black Hair. He has been some time in the County, speaks good English, and is something Foolish in his way of Discourse. He had on an Old round Hat, a yellow-brown-Linsey-woolsey Jacket, a coarse check Shirt, Old Leather Breeches, or Old Trowsers, and New Shoes tied with Strings.
Whoever brings home, or secures the said Servant, and give Notice to his Master, or to *William Bradford* in *New-York*, so that he may have him again, shall have *Forty Shillings* as a Reward, and all reasonable Charges paid By   *Anthony Engelbert.*
The New-York Gazette, From June 4, to June 11, 1739.

RAN away the 4th of this instant *August* from *Joshua Delaplaine* of *New-York*, Joyner, an Apprentice Lad about 18 years of Age, his Name is *James Howard*, is a well-set Lad, of a sandy Complexion, has short Hair, and had on a full Trim'd Drugget Coat and Breeches, a New Turned Fustion

Waistcoat, a good Hat, Shoes and Trowzers. He can work pretty well at the Joyners Trade.

Whoever shall take up said Apprentice and bring him to his Master, or secure and give Notice to his Master, or to *Benjamin Bagnel*, Watch-maker in *Boston*, or to *Samuel Holmes* in *Newport, Rhode-Island*, or to *Henry Slideborn* in *Philadelphia*, shall have Thirty Shillings as a Reward, and all reasonable Charges,

             paid by   JOSHUA DELAPLAINE.

The New-York Gazette, From July 30, to August 6, 1739.

RAN away from the Sloop Venus, whereof *Robert Bollard* is Master, a Servant Man, his Name is *Daniel Mackeffee*, he is a thick short well-set Fellow about 20 years of Age, he wears a Cap, but the rest of his Cloaths are uncertain. Whoever shall take up said Servant & bring him to Capt. *Bollard* on board the Sloop Venus, or to Mr. *Merrils* at the sign of the Ship on the New Dock, shall be very well Rewarded for doing the same. All Masters of Vessels, Boats, &c. are desired and fore-warned not to entertain nor carry off said *Daniel Mackeffee*, as they will answer the contrary at their Peril.

The New-York Gazette, From August 27, to September 2, 1739.

RAN away from the Hon. *George Clarke*, Esq; Lieutenant Governor of *New-York*, a Servant Man, Named *John Makist*, Taylor. Aged about two or three and Twenty; he is a short thick set Man, has black Hair, Speaks broad Scotch, and very bad English, he had on when he went away, a Cloath colour'd figur'd Fustian Coat, turned up and lined in Part or wholly with Yellow, for a Hat a blue Bonnet, good Leather Breeches, good Stockins and Shoes; he had likewise a blue Dufields Great Coat, and carried a Blanket with him. He was brought into the Province about thirteen or fourteen Months ago, by Mr. *Campble*; he understands Country Work, having been altogether in a Stable.

Whoever takes up and secures the said Servant, so that his Master may have him again, shall have a Reward of *Three Pounds*, and all reasonable Charges paid him.

The New-York Gazette, From October 22, to October 29, 1739; From October 29, to November 5, 1739; From November 5, to November 12, 1739; From November 12, to November 19, 1739.

RAN away from *John Obrian*, of *Eastchester* in the County of *Westchester*, a Servant Man, named *Daniel Taylor*, he is about 17 or 18 Years Old, has long black Hair, the Hair on the Crown of his Head has been lately cut off, when he was sick. He came lately from the *Highlands* in *Scotland*, he is a tall slim Youth, has a pale sickly Countenance, having been lately sick, He had on an Old Watch-Coat, of an Olive Color, and an Old Linsey Woolsey Waistcoat of a Redish Colour, with Brass Buttons. A pair of Trouzers, and Leather Breeches under them, a pair of Brogues on his Feet.

Whoever takes up said Servant and convey him to his Master or secures him, and give Notice, so that his Master may have him again, shall have *Thirty Shillings*, and all reasonable Charges
              paid by   *John Obrian.*

The New-York Gazette, From October 22, to October 29, 1739; From October 29, to November 5, 1739; From November 12, to November 19, 1739.

RAN from William Sims of the City of New-York one Indian Man, named James Mahane, about 25 years old, he was born in Long-Island, and formerly lived with Obadiah Smith in Smiths Town: He is a tall slim Fellow, he had on an old brown Coat and a Home-spun greyish Waistcoat. Whoever shall take up and secure this Indian Fellow, and convey him to his Master, or give Notice, so that he can have him again, shall have Twenty Shillings and all Reasonable Charges.

The New-York Gazette, From October 29, to November 5, 1739; From November 5, to November 12, 1739; From November 12, to November 19, 1739.

RAN away from the Hon. *George Clarke*, Esq; Lieutenant Governour of *New-York*, a Servant Man, Named John *M'c Intaylor*, Aged about two or and Twenty; he is a short thick set Man, has black Hair, speaks broad *Scotch*, and very bad *English*; he had on when he went away, a Cloath colour'd figur'd Fustian Coat, turned up and lined in Part or wholly with Yellow, a Hat and blue Bonnet, good Leather Breeches, good Stockins and Shoes; he had likewise a blue Duffills Great Coat, and carried a Blanket with him. He was brought into the Province about thirteen or fourteen months ago, by Mr. *Campble*; he understands Country Work, having been altogether in.

Whoever takes up and secures the said Servant; so that his Master may have him again, shall have a Reward of *Three Pounds*, and all reasonable Charges paid him.

The New-York Gazette, From October 29, to November 5, 1739; From November 5, to November 12, 1739; From November 12, to November 19, 1739.

1740

New-York, February 4. 1739. [*sic*]
RAN away some Time in August last from Thomas Betts, Esq; of Flat-Bush, in Kings County, a Negro Named Coffey. He understands Playing on the Violin, also all sorts of Husbandry Work, he is a black Fellow, and some what Pock-broken, he hath Thick Lips, and has a Scarr on one of his Leggs. He had on when he went away a Home-spun Coat lin'd with the same.
  Whoever can take up said Negro Man, or secure him and give Notice to his *M*aster shall have Three Pounds Reward; & all Reasonable Charges
     paid by   THOMAS BETTS.
The New-York Gazette, From February 5, to February 12, 1740; From February 19, to February 26, 1740; From February 26, to March 4, 1740.

RAN away from Charles Arding of the City of New-York, Taylor, one Servant Man, named James Keys, a Taylor by Trade, is about 14 years of age; he is a slender Youth of middle Stature, and is pock-broken, He is an Irish-man, and has the Brogue on his Tongue, He had on when he went away, an old silk Camblet Coat lined with red Salunet and breeches of the same; a Pair of Ribbed Stockins of a bluish Colour.
  Whoever shall take up said Servant, and convey him to his said Master, or secure him and give Notice, so that his Master, can have him again, shall have Forty Shillings as a Reward, beside all reasonable Charges,
  The New-York Gazette, From March 25, to March 31, 1740; From April 7, to April 14, 1740.

RUN away from *Thomas White*, of *Shrewsbury* a certain lusty Negro Fellow called *James*, he has had his Right Shoulder out, and is still so, which by lifting up his Arm may be soon discover'd; he had on when he went away a Homespun Coat, thread Stockings, and a new pair of Pumps. Whosoever takes up the said Negro, and Secures him so that his Master may have him again shall have *Twenty Shillings* as a Reward, and all reasonable Charges
     paid by   *Thomas White.*
The New-York Weekly Journal, June 23, 1740; June 30, 1740.

RUN away about a Month ago one John Higgins alias Eagon a Servant Man about 17 Years of Age, of a middle Stature thin faced; had on a Gray Jacket with trowsers thin black Hair; an Irish Man who Served part of his time

with one Wright in *Long Island*, is apt to get in Liguor and then delights much in Singing, he was seen here at New York, this Week with a black Eye Whoever Secures the said *Higgins* alias *Eagon* and delivers him to me at New York, shall have a Pistole reward and all reasonable Charges
                    paid by   *William Cosby Sheriff.*
                                          New York, July 5 1740.
    The New-York Weekly Journal, July 7, 1740.

RUN away the first of *October* 1740, from *John Breese*, of the City of *New-York*, Leather-Dresser, a Mulatto *Indian Slave* Named *Galloway*, Aged 21 Years, about five foot four, Inches high, a thin Body and Face, markt with the Small-Pox, he was Born, in the Fort at *Albany*, can speak Duth [*sic*] and lived many Years with *Paul Richards*, Esq: some Years Majer [*sic*] of this City; had on when he went away a dark gray homespun Jacket lin'd with the same, a pair of Linnen Breeches, and new Shoes; on the 3 Instant he was seen and challenged by Coll. *Philipse's* Mill, and escaped by asserting he was sent in pursuit, of a *Cuba* Man Run away, and took the Road towards *New-England*, he loves Rum and other strong Liquors, and when Tipsey, is a brave fellow, and very abusive. Whoever Secures the said Slave so that his Master or his Attorney may dispose of him shall have *Forty Shillings*, Reward and Reasonable Charges
                    paid by.   *John Breese.*
    The New-York Weekly Journal, November 3, 1740; November 11, 1740.

1741

WIlliam Durrem *is run away from his Master* Sam. Bavard, *of the City of* N. York, *he is an* Irish *Servant about 30 Years of Age, had on when he went away a dark Drab Cloath Coat, red Shaloon Lining, and large Brass Buttons; he endeavoured to enlist for Cuba, but being disappointed, he said he would ship himself with any other Vessel. Therefore public Notice is hereby given to all Persons not to entertain the said Servant in order to convey him away, and all Masters of Vessels are forewarned not to transport the said Servant, for they will be sued upon the Bond for their Clearance.*
    The New-York Weekly Journal, January 4, 1741; January 11, 1741; January 18, 1741; January 24, 1741; February 1, 1741.

RUN away from *John Sayre*, of the City of *New-York*, Taylor, a Servant Man, named *John M' Call*, an Irishman of a middle Stature, Fat and well set, light gray Eyes, and short black Hair, but wares a Wig or Cap, he is pretty much pitted with the Small-Pox, he has a Scar on the upper part of his forehead, but a Wig or Cap will cover it, he is a Taylor by Trade, and can make either Men or Women's Cloths; he had on when he went away a brown duroys Coat lined with double fold Stuff, the Body in lined with Linen, he had a light coloured Camblet wastecoat trim'd with black, and a pair of Olive couloured Cloth Breeches, and a pair of gray Yarn Stockings and a black velvet Stock. Whoever will take up this Servant Man and bring him to his said Master, or secure him so that he may have him again shall have *Five Pounds* Reward, and all reasonable Charges
        paid by me.   *John Sayre.*
   The New-York Weekly Journal, April 13, 1741; April 29, 1741; May 11, 1741.

RUN away from on Board the Snow *Elizabeth*, Capt. *Patrick Hepburn*, belonging to *Aberdeen,* an Apprintice, belonging to the said Capt. named *Francis Ray*, about 18 Years of Age, a Scotch Man small Stature, brown Complexion, wears a Cap, had on when he Run away, a Blew Wast Coat, Trowsers, two pair of wollen Stockings, he speaks broad Scotch. Whoever apprehends said Apprentice, and brings him to his Master, or secures him so that his Master may have him again, shall have a Pistole Reward and Reasonable Charges of   *Patrick Hepburn.*
   The New-York Weekly Journal, June 29, 1741; July 6, 1741; July 20, 1741.

RUN away the 11th of this instant from *Robert Hogg*, of the City of *New-York*, a Servant Man, named *Francis Jones* a Welchman born, he is a Tall thin Man of a sickly Couler, about six feet three Inches high or there about, by Trade a Tanner, and Stiles himself a Prize fighter, and if he has not changed his Dress, he had on when he went away a felt Hat, a new worsted Cap, a Surtute frize Coat, a new Check'd Shirt, a pair of Silk Camblet Breeches, a pair of new Homespun thread Stockings, a new pair of Shoes, and sundry Old Cloaths. Whoever takes up said Servant, and Secures him, or brings him, to his said Master, shall have *Twenty Shillings* Reward, and all Reasonable Charges
        paid by me.   *Robert Hogg.*
   The New-York Weekly Journal, July 13, 1741; July 20, 1741; July 27, 1741; August 24, 1741.

1742

RUN away from *Cornelius Van Rans*, of the City of *New York Sale Maker*, a Negro Fellow, about 20 Years of Age, of a very black Complexion, named *Prince*, very much Noted by his Coarse Speech, had on when he went away, a short brown Jacket, and a pair of Tarry Trowsers. Whoever takes up the said Negro Fellow, and secures him so that his Master may have him again, shall have 20s, as a Reward and all reasonable Charges
    by *Cornelius Van Rans.*
The New-York Weekly Journal, January 24, 1742; January 31, 1742.

RUN away about two Months ago, from Patrick Steward, Taylor, in New York, a Scotch Servant Man, named William Landram, about 28 years of Age, well set, fresh complexion'd; had on when he went away, a light grey homespun Suit of Cloaths, a fair Wig, a pair of large plain white metal Buckles. He may have other Cloaths on, for he took with him more than one Suit. Whoever secures said Servant, so that his Master, or Edward Graham, in New York, or Archibald Campbell, in Philadelphia, Joyner, may have him again, shall have Thirty Shillings Reward. N. B. If said Servant returns of his own Accord; Edward Graham assures him, he shall be pardon'd for all that has past, and shall not be compell'd to serve any more Time than if he had not eloped.
The Pennsylvania Gazette, April 15, 1742.

RUN away on the 18th of this Instant, from Samuel Boyer, of New York, Butcher, an Irish Servant Man, named John McMahon, a Butcher by Trade, about 25 Years of Age, a short thick Man, very much pockfretten, sour Countenance; had on when he went away, an olive colour'd cloth Coat and Breeches, white linnen Jacket, white Shirt, a pair of light colour'd Stockings, double channel'd Pumps, mended: Also took with him a white flannel Jacket, and a blue and white striped homespun Jacket, one white linnen Coat and Jacket. Whoever takes up said Servant, and brings him to John Saunders, Huntsman, in Philadelphia, or to said Boyer, in New York, shall have Three Pounds Reward, and reasonable Charges, paid by John Saunders aforesaid, or Samuel Boyer.
The Pennsylvania Gazette, April 29, 1742.

RUN away from *Johannes Bratt*, of the County of *Albany*, a Servant Man, the 8th of May last, named *Dennis Brian*, aged about 21 Years, of a lusty Stature, short Black Curl'd Hair, he has a mark in his forehead seemenly cut, and another on his Throat as if had been a swelling. He had on when he

went away an old dark colour'd Coat, with Pewter Buttons, Leather Breeches, and a white Shirt, something Pockfretten. Whosoever takes him up and secures him so that his Master may have him again and gives Notice to Capt. *Peter Winn* of *Albany*, or *John Peter Zenger* of New York Printer, or to his Master shall have *Forty Shillings* Reward and all reasonable Charges paid him.   *Albany June* 17th 1742.
The New-York Weekly Journal, June 28, 1742; July 12, 1742.

RUN away on Wednesday the 10th Inst. from Richard Chew, near Timber Creek, in West-Jersey, a Servant Man named Ephraim Colam, about 35 Years of Age, tall and slim, no Hair, stoops a little, and is troubled with a Phthisick; Had on, a worsted Cap, blue grey Great-Coat, striped linsey woolsey Jacket, oznabrigs Shirt, leather Breeches, with a new Seat to them, oznabrigs Trowsers, good Shoes, ty'd with Strings, and grey yarn Stockings. Whoever takes up and secures the said Servant so that his Master may have him again, shall have Forty Shillings Reward, and reasonable Charges,   paid by   Richard Chew.
Note, he was born on Long Island.
   The Pennsylvania Gazette, December 2, 1742; December 7, 1742; December 14, 1742; December 21, 1742.

1743

RAN away on Sunday the 10*th of April, from* Peter Low, *of the City of* New-York, *Bolter, a Servant Man named* John Piercy, *about* 30 *Years of Age, he is a well set lusty Fellow, smooth Skin, dark colour'd Eyes, he speaks pretty thick, and much like a West Country Man: He had on when he went away, a white Wigg or Cap, a blue double breasted Surtout Coat, a grey drab coloured Kersey Coat and Breeches, with white Metal Buttons, a white tow cloth Vest, and which Stockings, one white and check Shirt.*
   Whoever takes up and secures said Servant so that his Master may have him again, or gives Notice to Townsend White in Philadelphia, shall have Twenty *five Shillings Reward and reasonable Charges.*
   The Pennsylvania Journal, or, Weekly Advertiser, May 5, 1743; May 12, 1743; May 19, 1743; May 26, 1743; May 26, 1743; June 2, 1743; June 9, 1743; June 16, 1743; June 23, 1743.

RUN away from *Rice Williams* of the City of *New-York*, a Servant Man named *Thomas Davis*, about 20 Years of Age, has a down Look, a pale Complexion and limps when he walks, it is occasioned by the Loss of his grate Toe: Had on when he went away a dark colour'd Coat, a Linnen

Complexion and limps when he walks, it is occasioned by the Loss of his grate Toe: Had on when he went away a dark colour'd Coat, a Linnen Jacket, a Worsted Cap, two Ozenbrigs Shirts, a Pair of blue Cloath Breeches, a Pair of new Shoes with Brass Buckles, Yarn Stockings, he is a Welsh Man and has the Brogue very much. Whoever takes up said Servant, and brings him to his Master, or secures him so that he may be had again shall have Forty Shillings as a Reward and all reasonable Charges
          paid by   RICE WILLIAMS.

The New-York Gazette, From August 13, to August 20, 1744; September 24, 1744; October 1, 1744; October 15, 1744; October 29, 1744.

RUN away from Joseph Lawrence of Flushing, a Negro Man, named Peter is a middle Sized Fellow and speaks good English; had on when he wemt away a [ ] Duffils Jacket, [ ] Breeches, a Tow Shirt, and old Felt Hat, a striped Worsted Cap. Whoever takes up the said Negro, and secures him, so that his said Master may have him again shall be well rewarded for their trouble, and all reasonable Charges
          paid by me.   Joseph Lawrenc.

The New-York Gazette, From August 13, to August 20, 1744.

RAN away from John Thorn at White-Stone-Ferry in Flushing, a new Negro Fellow named Prince, he can't scarce speak a Word of English; he is a short Fellow, about 20 Years of Age, had on when he went away nothing but an Ozenbrigs Shirt, and a Pair of Tow Trowsers, and a striped worsted Cap; he also has taken with him a short Gun well mounted with Brass. Whosoever takes up the said Negro Fellow and Gun, and brings him to his said Master, shall have three Pounds Reward and all reasonable Charges,
          paid by me,   JOHN THORN.

The New-York Evening Post, December 31, 1744; January 7, 1745; January 21, 1745.

1745

RUN away from George Elsworth, of Dutches County, an indented Servant Malatto named *Isaac Cromwell*, he is a tall well set Fellow, mauger Jaw'd, [sic] speeks good English and Dutch, he has taken with his 3 fine Mares, the oldest is 7 or 8 Year, of a Strawberry Rown, one is a cole Black of 3 Years old and Paces very well, two are Branded **G. E.** the third is a Coult of a Year old this Spring, of a sorral colour. Whosoever takes up said Servant and brings him to his Master, or secures him so that he may be had again, shall have Ten-Pounds Reward and all reasonable Charges,

paid by George Elsworth.
The New-York Evening Post, March 4, 1745; March 11, 1745.

RUN away from *George Kelly* Black Smith of *Philadelphia*, a Servant Man, named *Thomas Cavenaugh*, an *Irishman* aged about 22 Years, wears a Cap and a Brownish Westcoat, he has been in the Work House at *New-York* and was taken out, but made his escape in the Evening. Whoever secures the said Servant, so that his said Master may have him again, shall have *Forty Shillings* Reward, and all reasonable Charges
paid by the said, *George Kelly*,
The New-York Weekly Journal, April 1, 1745; April 8, 1745.

RUN away from the Clinton Privateer, Captain Seymour, of New York, an Irish Servant Man, born in Dublin, named Arthur Byrn, a lively, well set Fellow, about 38 Years of Age, is very much given to Drinking, writes a good Hand, and reads well. Had on a Homespun Coat, blue Jacket and Breeches; and 'tis supposed he has a brown Broad Cloth Jacket and Breeches, and other good Clothes, fit for a Sailor, Whoever takes up and secures said Servant, or brings him to the Subscribers, near Prince Town, East Jersey, shall have Four Pounds Reward, and reasonable Charges, paid by John Muirhead and Hugh McCan. N. B. He was seen in Philadelphia in March last, and may have gone on board some Vessel from that Port.
The Pennsylvania Gazette, May 2, 1745.

THIS is to give Notice, to all Person or Persons Whatsoever; especialy Capts. of Privateers or Merchantmen, not to take on board their respective Vessels, a Servant Man named *Richard Renold*, belonging to me the under named *James Wiley*.
This is farther to forwarn and Persons, especially Ale-Houses, Taverns or Play-Houses, not to Trust or entertain said Servant upon any Account whatsoever. If in case he be found playing along Streets of a Week-Day, they are desired to bring to his Master, and be satisfied for their Trouble
by me, *James Wiley.*
The New-York Evening Post, September 30, 1745; October 7, 1745.

1746

Run away last Friday Night, from *Jonathan Brown* of *Rye*, in the County of *West-Chester*, a *Mulatto Negro* Man called *Hector*, (but supposed to have altered his Name to *James Weldon*) aged about 30 Years, he is a Tall Lusty

Fellow, and has a remarkable Blemish in each Eye, had on, a darkish Colour'd Woolen Coat, Country Make, a brown Jacket, old Buck-Skin Breeches, and an old Beaver-Hat. Whosoever secures the said *Negro* and gives Notice to his Master, or the Printer hereof, shall have forty Shillings Reward, *New-York* Money, and all reasonable Charges paid by me.
Rye, December 16*th,* 1745.
The New-York Evening Post, January 6, 1746; January 20, 1746; February 10, 1746; February 15, 1746.

RUN away from *Wessel Tenbrook,* living near *Rockey-Hill,* a Negro Man Slave named *Pompee,* a tall well-set Fellow, about 6 Foot long, and very black; about 25 Years of Age, speaks good English, and tolerable good Dutch; he is brought up in *West-Chester,* and lately came from Esopus, had on when he went away a pair of blew Stockings an old Buck-skin Breeches, a linsey woolsey Jacket, and an old white Kersey Coat. Whoever takes up said Negro and brings him to his Master at *Rockey-Hill,* or secures him so that he may be had again, shall have 30 Shillings as a Reward, and all charges   paid by   *Wessel Tenbrook.*
The New-York Evening Post, May 5, 1746.

Philadelphia, May 8, 1746.
RUN away on the 3d inst. from the subscriber, an apprentice lad, named James Jacobs, about 18 or 19 years of age, tall and slender, of a pale complexion, long visage, long nose, long dark hair, if not cut off, by trade a carpenter, and was born at New-York. Had on when he went away, a brown kersey Coat, with large brass buttons, a brown linnen vest, both leather and linnen breeches, grey worsted stockings, and cotton ditto, new shoes, large silver buckles, with brass anchors, a pair of wrought brass buckles, and a good castor hat. Whoever takes up said apprentice, and brings him to the subscriber, or secures him in any goal in Pennsylvania government, shall have Three Pounds reward, and reasonable charges; or if taken in any other government, Ten Pounds, and reasonable charges,
              paid by   ISAAC TAYLOR.
N. B. 'Tis probable he may change his clothes.
The Pennsylvania Gazette, May 8, 1746; May 15, 1746; May 29, 1746.

Philadelphia, July 24. 1746.
WHEREAS several Persons inlisted in my Company, have absented themselves without Leave. I therefore require every Man to appear at the Sign of the George, in Philadelphia, or at the Bear, in Frankford, on Monday at 10 o'Clock; otherwise they'll be looked upon as Deserters. And I

forwarn all persons against entertaining them, as they may depend upon being prosecuted according to Law. Deserted from the said Company, RICHARD WILLIAMS, and SAMUEL SWANSON. Richard Williams, a Butcher, about 4 Foot 8 Inches high, dark Complexion; has been a Privateering in the Marlborough; has a Mother lives in New York, and has been seen sometime since there. Samuel Swanson, a Taylor, sandy Complexion, about 5 Foot 7 Inches high; lived in Second street, in Philadelphia, and was lately seen in Darby, and supposed to be concealed there by some of his Friends. Any Person who takes up either of the said Deserters, and brings them to the Sign of the George, in Philadelphia, shall have TWO PISTOLES Reward for each. If either of them is taken up in New York, it's desired they may be put in some of the Companies there, the Captain paying the Reward. Swanson was enlisted before the Carthagena Expedition, and deserted.
      CHRISTOPHER CLYMER.
The Pennsylvania Gazette, July 24, 1746.

                Philadelphia, July 31. 1746.
Deserted from Capt. Trent's Company, RICHARD WILLIAMS, and SAMUEL SWANSON. Richard Williams, a Butcher, about 5 Foot 8 Inches high, dark Complexion; has been a Privateering in the Marlborough; has a Mother lives in New York, and has been seen sometime since there. Samuel Swanson, a Taylor, sandy Complexion, about five Foot 7 Inches high; lived in Second street, in Philadelphia, and was lately seen in Darby, and supposed to be concealed there by some of his Friends. Any Person who takes up either of the said Deserters, and brings them to the Sign of the George, in Philadelphia, shall have TWO PISTOLES Reward for each. If either of them is taken up in New York, 'tis desired they may be put in some of the Companies there, the Captain paying the Reward. Swanson was enlisted before upon the Carthagena Expedition, and deserted.
      WILLIAM TRENT.
The Pennsylvania Gazette, July 31, 1746.

LATELY deserted from His Majesty's Service, out of a company of Foot under the command of Capt. *Charles Mackintosh*, designed on the Expedition against *Canada*, the following Persons, viz.
 Isaac Holms, an Irishman born, about five Foot ten Inches high, slender bodies, aged about 36 Years, roman Nose, thin Face wears a homespun Coat and Trousers.

Peter M''Donald, an Irishman, of about five Foot ten Inches high, well-set, aged about 30 Years, sandy complexion, a talkative Person, and has for some time past sail'd out of *Philadelphia*.

John Scott, also an Irishman, about five Foot eight Inches high, brown complexion, well-set, and well dressed.

William Taylor, this country born, about five Foot nine Inches high, middling set, aged about 24 Years, thin Face, and lives at *North-Castle*, in *West-Chester* County.

William Stewart, (*alias*) old Brass, born in the West of *England*, about five Foot nine Inches high, a talkative, drunken Person; a Tinker by trade aged about 57 Years.

Amaziah Bush, New-England born, about six Foot High, a likely well-set Man, aged about 30 Years, wears a blew cloath Coat, red plush Breeches, and short black curl'd Hair.

Thomas Wiswal, also a *New-England* Man, about five Foot ten Inches high slender Body'd, has lately had the small Pox, and much pitted with it, aged about 25 Years.

Whosoever takes up said Deserters, or either of them, and delivers them to *Stephen Bayard*, Esq: at *New-York*, or to their said *Company* at *Albany*, shall have 4 Pounds Reward and all reaseable Charges
      paid by *Charles Mackintosh.*

The New-York Evening Post, September 1, 1746; September 15, 1746; September 29, 1746; October 6, 1746; October 13, 1746; October 27, 1746; November 10, 1746; November 17, 1746; November 24, 1746; December 1, 1746; December 8, 1746; December 15, 1746; December 29, 1746. Ads from November 24 on do not list Wiswal.

DEserted from Captain *Richard Langdon's* Company at *Albany*, the following two Persons, *Marthinus Johnson* of *Statten-Island* and *Henry M'' Peck*, who not long since lived at chief Justice *De Lancey*, Whoever takes up any of said Deserters, or secures them so that they may be had again shall have 40 Shillings as a Reward.

The New-York Evening Post, September 8, 1746; October 13, 1746; October 20, 1746; October 27, 1746; November 10, 1746; November 17, 1746; November 24, 1746; December 1, 1746; December 8, 1746; December 29, 1746; January 5, 1747; January 19, 1747; January 26, 1747.

DEserted from Capt. Nathaniel Richard's *Company of Foot design'd on the Expedition against* Canada, *the following Persons, viz.*

Samuel Donum, New-England born aged 25 Years well set about 5 Feet 9 Inches high a Sailor.

John Christopher a short spare Man with bushy Hair, 28 Years of Age.

Samuel Hickenbottom, a short well set Man With sore Lips and has a By-word, (in a Minuet) about 40 Years of Age, and drinks hard, a Sailor.

John Cox, living at Basken-Ridge, a tall Fellow with Bushy Hair, aged about 40 Years.

Timothy Stouten about 5 Feet 10 inches high living at Basken-Ridge of a fair Complexion.

Morgan Smith, an Irishman born, aged 50 Years well set about 5 Feet 8 Inches high a Weaver by Trade.

Whoever apprehends the said Deserters or either of them, and secures them so that they may be had again shall receive Four Pounds Reward for each, and all reasonable Charges

paid by me, Nathanial Richards.

The New-York Evening Post, September 8, 1746; September 15, 1746; September 29, 1746; October 6, 1746; October 13, 1746; October 20, 1746; October 27, 1746; November 10, 1746; November 17, 1746. The ads from October 20 on do not list Morgan Smith.

LAtely Deserted from Capt. Albartus Teebout in a Company of Foot in the present Expidition, the following Persons, *Johannis Rose, Robert Hunter, David Goald, John Hiddiels, Joshua Mous, Richard M" Farrel, Abner Brush, Daniel Norris, John Grasset, Robert Coomes.* This is therefore to give Notice, if and Person [sic] Person or Persons whatsoecr will apprehend any of the above Deserters, shall have three Pounds for each or either of them as a Reward and all reasonable charges

paid by   *Cornelia Teebout.*

The New-York Evening Post, September 15, 1746.

LAtely deserted from his Majesty's Service, out of a Company of Foot, under the command of Capt. Natheniel Richards, designed on the Expedition against Canada, John Dunkin, about five feet six Inches high, between 40 and 50 Years of Age; had on when he went away a white Waistcoat, a darke colour'd Watch-coat, a Pair of new Buck-skin Breeckes, new Stockings, new Pumps, and wairs black Hair, is a Shoe-maker by Trade. Whoever takes up said Deserter, and secures him so that he may be had again, shall have 40s. Reward and all reasonable Charges

paid by   *Nathaniel Richards.*

The New-York Evening Post, October 6, 1746; October 13, 1746; October 20, 1746; October 27, 1746; November 10, 1746; November 17, 1746.

RUN away from *Barent Van Deventer*, of *Flat-Bush*, on *Long-Island*, in *Kings County*, a Negro Man named *Handrick*, alias *Hank*, of middle stature, had on When he went away a Linning striped, Jacket, a Pair of Humespun Breeches, a Blewish Pair of Stockings, and an old Pair of Shoes, a good Felt Hat: He speaks good English and Dutch, and tells People he is a free Negro. Whoever takes up said Negro, and brings him to his said Master, or secures him so that he may be had again, shall have 30 Shillings Reward, and all Reasonable charges
     paid by me. *Barnet Van Deventer,*
The New-York Evening Post, September 29, 1746; October 6, 1746; October 13, 1746; October 20, 1746; October 27, 1746; November 10, 1746; November 17, 1746; December 1, 1746.

LAtely Deserted from Capt. *Albartus Teebout* in a Company of Foot in this present Expidition, the following Persons, *Johaunis Ross, Robert Hunter, David Goald, John Hiddiels, Joshua Mous, Richard M"Farrel, Abner Brush, Daniel Norris, John Grasset, Robert Coomes*, This is therefore to give Notice, if any Person or Persons whatsoever will apprehend any of the above Deserters, shall have three Pounds for each or either of them as a Reward and all reasonable charges
     paid by Cornelia Teebout.
The New-York Evening Post, September 29, 1746; October 6, 1746; October 13, 1746; October 20, 1746; October 27, 1746; November 24, 1746.

RUN away from Anthoney Byvanck, a Molatto spanish Slave, named WILL, aged 22 Years, he is a well set Fellow, and general wares a Wigg, and says he is a free Man. Had on when he went away, a blew Jacket and a striped one, a Pair of Ozenbrigs Trousers, has taken several Linnen Cloathing with him. Whoever takes up the said Molatto Slave, and brings him to his Master or secures him so that he may be had again shall have 30 Shillings Reward, and all reasonable Charges.
The New-York Evening Post, October 13, 1746; October 20, 1746; October 27, 1746; November 10, 1746; November 17, 1746; November 24, 1746; December 1, 1746.

            Albany *Nov.* 14th, 1746.
DESerted from Capt. Nathaniel Richard's *Company of Foot, at Albany, the following Person, viz.*

Michill van Dervoort, *born on* Long-Island; *by Trade a Shoe-maker, about 5 Foot 10 Inches, wears his own Hair.*
David Harper, *a sailor about 5 Foot 8 Inches wares a Cap.*
Philip Duley, *an Irishman, about 5 Foot 8 Inches, wares his own Hair.*
Frederick Ennis, *an Irishman, about 5 Foot 8 Inches.*
Martin Salm, *a Jersey-man, by Trade a shoemaker about 5 Foot 3 Inches, wares a Cap.*
John Ederenton, *an Englishman, about 5 Foot 6 Inches well-sett, smooth faced, generally wears a gray Wigg.*
Thomas Croker, *about 5 Foot 7 Inches, an Irishman, has a cast in one of his Eyes, wares his own Hare.*
William M" Koy, *a scotchman about 5 Foot 8 Inches.*
John Darby, *an Irishman, about 6 Foot, has his own Hair.*
Hendrick Sickles, *a Jersey-man, kept Tavern fromerly in Freehold, about 5 Foot 9 Inches.*
Laurence Van Cleef, *Born upon Statten-Island by Trade a Wheelwright, about 6 Foot and an Inch, he lately had the small-pox, wares his own Hair.*
William Strong, *an Irishman, about 5 Foot 8 Inches, well set.*
John Stilwill, *about 6 Foot and an Inch, a well set likely Fellow, when he Talks lisps pritty much, kept the Ferrey formerly at the Narrows. Had on when he went off a silver laced Hat, a snuff colour'd Coat.*
Whoever apprehends the Said Deserters or either of them, and secures them so that they may be had again shall receive 40 *shillings Reward for each, and all reasonable Charges paid by* Warner Richard *near the City-Hall, or* John Richard, *living on the Broad-way.*
Nathanial Richard.
The New-York Evening Post, November 24, 1746; December 1, 1746; December 8, 1746; December 15, 1746; December 29, 1746; January 5, 1747; January 19, 1747; January 26, 1747.

Philadelphia, December 2. 1746.
DESERTED the 18th Instant, from Capt. BEVERLY ROBINSON'S company, of foot, now lying in fort George in New York, the four following soldiers, viz. James Shaw, an Irishman, about 5 foot 4 inches HIGH, of a dark complexion, full faced, pock fretten, and well set, aged 23 years. Philip Radman, an Irishman, about 5 feet 5 inches high, a labourer, has brown eyebrows, ruddy face, a scar on the upper lip, a cast in the right eye, and is well set, aged about 20 years. William Harris, born in Maryland, about 5 foot 8 inches high, of a light complexion, stoops in the shoulders, speaks slow, and is a carpenter by trade, aged about 20 years. Hugh Tully, an Irishman, about 5 foot 8 inches high, a sawyer by trade, of a light brown

complexion, smooth faced; wears his hair, and affects an odd kind of speech at times: He has been drummer in the dragoons in Ireland, and is about 30 years of age. Whoever apprehends the said deserters, or either of them, so that they may be brought to their quarters, shall have Three Pistoles reward for each, and all reasonable charges,
     paid by BEVERLY ROBINSON.
The Pennsylvania Gazette, December 2, 1746.

1747

RUN away from Capt. Benjamin Bethell, *Master of the Sloop Increase, an Irish Servant Man named* Alexander Mc'Collister, *about* 5 *Foot* 10 *Inches high, a thin spare Fellow: Had on when he went away a dark Kersey Jacket, a pair of Oznabrigs Trowsers and Yarn Stockings. Whosoever apprehends the said Fellow, and delivers him to* Thomas Burch *at Mr.* William Bradford's, *shall receive* Thirty Shillings *Reward, and all reasonable Charges,*
     paid by the said Thomas Burch.
The New-York Gazette, Revived in the Weekly Post-Boy, January 19, 1747; February 2, 1747.

RUN away on Sunday the 15*th of February, from Capt.* Abraham Kip, *of the City of* New-York, *an Indian Fellow named* Tierce, *about* 19 *Years of Age, Long-Island born, and can speak nothing by English; of a middlng Stature, short Hair, and a fair Complexion for an Indian: Had on when he went away, a light colour'd Cloth Coat with slash Sleeves, and indifferent good Hat, and a pair of Trousers. Whoever takes up the said Fellow, and brings him to his Master, or secures him, so that he may be had again, shall have* Twenty Shillings *Reward, and all reasonable Charges*
     paid by Abraham Kip.
The New-York Gazette, Revived in the Weekly Post-Boy, February 23, 1747; March 2, 1747. See *The New-York Gazette, Revived in the Weekly Post-Boy,* May 4, 1747.

Deserted the 24*th* February, *from the* Virginia *Company quarter'd in the Fort at* New-York, *the three following Soldiers, viz.*
  George Malcolm, *an Irishman, about* 6 *Feet high, aged* 36 *Years. short black Hair, very much mark'd with the Small Pox and freckled, a stoop in his Shoulders, knock-keed, has a drolling Speech; a Labourer.*

Archibald Hanna, *an Irishman, about 5 Feet 6 Inches high, aged about 22 Years, brown Complexion, a Scar over the left Eye, an upright Walk; a Sawyer by Trade.*

James Row, *an Irishman, about 5 Feet 5 Inches high, aged 25 Years, a Weaver by Trade, of a brown Complexion, smooth-faced, a small Stoop in his Shoulders; they carried off their Regimentals.*

Whoever apprehends the said Deserters, or either of them, that be or they be brought to their Quarters, shall receive Two Pistoles *Reward for each,   paid by   Beverly Robinson.*

The New-York Gazette, Revived in the Weekly Post-Boy, March 2, 1747; March 9, 1747; March 16, 1747; March 23, 1747.

*R*UN *away the 20th of* March, *from* Benjamin Burling, *of* Flushing, *a Servant Maid named* Mary Bouls, *Old England born, but last from Ireland, of a very red Complection, red Hair, and middle Size; carried with her a new striped Cambleteen Gown, with the rest of her Apparel. Whoever apprehends the said Servant, and secures her so that she may be had again, shall have* Forty Shillings *Reward, and all reasonable Charges,*
         paid by   Benjamin Burling.

The New-York Gazette, Revived in the Weekly Post-Boy, March 30, 1747; April 6, 1747.

Deserted from on board a Vessel bound for Louisbourgh, on Thursday the 9th Instant, and cross'd over to Long Island, *James Howath*, of General Fuller's Regiment and Capt. Scott's Company; about 22 Years of Age, thin fac'd, somewhat inn knee'd 5 Feet 9 Inches high without Shoes, short dark brown Hair, has a thick undistinct Way of speaking; wore when he went off a light colour'd Frock and red Waistcoat. He robb'd his Captain and deserted from the Flagg of Truce which put into Boston about 5 Months ago: Whoever shall apprehend the said Howath, and give Information to Stephen Bayard, Esq; Mayor of New-York, shall receive Five Pounds Reward, and whoever harbours or conceals the said Deserter shall be prosecuted according to Law.
         Hugh Scott.

The New-York Gazette, Revived in the Weekly Post-Boy, April 13, 1747; April 20, 1747; April 27, 1747.

*D*eserted the 22d *of* March, *from the Subscriber's Company near* Albany, *the four following Men, viz.*

Anthony Furnance, *born in Madera, about 25 Years of Age, 5 Foot 6 Inches high, swarthy Complexion, black curl'd Hair, black Eyes; he talks broken English, and very quick.*

Samuel Burnham, *an Englishman, about 5 Feet 6 Inches high, about 40 Years of Age, swarthy Complection, dark Eyes, and squints a little, short black Hair a little curled; he generally laughs when he speaks, and is a remarkably ill-looking Fellow.*

Mathias Franks, *a fresh colour'd young Fellow, about 5 Feet 10 Inches high, short black Hair, and has a very remarkable Limp when he Walks; he was born in London.*

Thomas Insull, *an Englishman, about 25 Years of Age, and about 5 Feet 10 Inches high, flax colour'd Hair, fair Complexion and grey Eyes.*

They have all on, narrow brimm'd Felt Hats, coarse dark grey Coats, Breeches of the same, and blue Jackets, all such as the Maryland Forces are cloathed with; they went off in a Batto and carried a Blanket with them to made a Sail of. Whoever apprehends them or either of them, and brings them to their Quarters, shall be paid Three Pounds for each, and all reasonable Charges,
              By   Dudley Crofts.

The New-York Gazette, Revived in the Weekly Post-Boy, April 13, 1747; April 20, 1747; April 27, 1747.

*R*UN *away from* Theunis De Klerk, *of* Tappan, *in* Orange *County, a Negro Man named Sippeo, about 30 Years of Age, of a middle Size, is well set, speaks good and proper English, and has a hoarse Voice: Had on when he went away, a brown short Watch-Coat, a light colour'd red Jacket, a white Jacket bound round the Edge with some other Colour, and a Felt Hat cock'd up and fastned on the Crown. Whoever takes up said Negro, and brings him to his Master, or unto* William Vredenburgh *in* New-York, *shall have* Forty Shillings *Reward, and all reasonable Charges,*
              paid By   Theunis De Klerk.

The New-York Gazette, Revived in the Weekly Post-Boy, April 20, 1747; April 27, 1747; May 18, 1747; May 25, 1747.

DESERTED *from Capt.* John Honeyman*'s Company near* Albany, *the six following Men, viz.* John Lounsberry, William Williams, Jores Banker, Ruben Buxton, Daniel Simkin, *and* John Burtow. *If they will return directly he will pardon them; but if they do not, he will punish them as Deserters, according to the Governor's Proclamation.*

The New-York Gazette, Revived in the Weekly Post-Boy, April 20, 1747; May 4, 1747; May 11. 1747; May 18, 1747.

*D*ESERTED at sundry Times, from Capt. *James Parker's* Company, at *Albany,* the following Men, viz. Daniel Lacy, David Wells, William Murfey, Gersham Store, *an Indian,* James M"Carty, Alexander, M"Carty, Francis Buckelew, Daniel Rice, John Afey, Thomas Nelson, Andrew M"Cullom, and Barnet Sutphen. *Whoever takes up and Secures either of the said Men, and give Information thereof to* John Deare, *Esq; Sheriff of* Amboy *or to the Subscriber in the same Place shall have THREE POUNDS Reward and all reasonable Charges*
      paid by THOMAS ROBINSON,
             Lieut. of the Company.
N. B. *If all or either of the said Men, return by the first of May next, and deliver themselves up to the Sheriff of* Amboy *or to the Lieutenant of the Company, they shall receive Pardon, otherwise not.*
 The New-York Gazette, Revived in the Weekly Post-Boy, April 27, 1747; May 4, 1747; May 11, 1747; May 18, 1747; May 25, 1747.

*R*UN away on April *the 25th, from Capt.* Abraham Kip, *in* New-York, *an Indian Man, about Eighteen Years old, and speaks good English: Had on when he went away, a grey Cloth Jacket, an old Pair of Trowsers, and an Iron Ring about his Neck and one about his Legs, with a Chain from one to the other. Whoever takes up and secures the said Indian, so that he may be had again, shall have TWENTY SHILLINGS Reward, and all reasonable Charges paid by* ABRAHAM KIP.
 The New-York Gazette, Revived in the Weekly Post-Boy, May 4, 1747; May 11, 1747; May 18, 1747; May 25, 1747. See *The New-York Gazette, Revived in the Weekly Post-Boy,* February 23, 1747.

*D*ESERTED from on board Capt. *Philemon Saunders,* off the East End of *Long-Island,* in a Boat belonging to the Vessel, who therewith landed at *Montoge,* the following Recruits enlisted for Sir WILLIAM PEPPERRELL'S Regiment, viz *Luke Collens,* Serj. *Thomas Dunahoe, James McCaniel, Daniel O'Dowley, John Davis, Hezekiah Shaw, Robert Eiles, William Thompson, James Alexander, Charles Wiggins, John Wherton, William Dowhanty, James Mackadee, Cornelius Grimes, John Steward,* and *Edward Nutlees;* as also *James McBriage,* deserted from *Louisbourg.* Whoever takes up any of the said Deserters, and secures them in any of his Majesty's Goals, or will bring them to Messrs. *Colman* and *Sparhawk,* or Lieut. *Edmund Dwight* in *Boston,* or to any Officer belonging to the said Regiment, shall have a *Guinea* Reward for each and reasonable Charges paid. *Edmund Dwight.*
          Boston, May 19, 1747.

N. B. If any of the above Deserters will deliver themselves up to any Officer in said Regiment, so as to proceed to their Duty at *Louisbourg,* they shall be kindly received, and their past Offence forgiven.
The Boston Weekly News-Letter, May 21, 1747; June 11, 1747; *The Boston Weekly Post-Boy,* June 1, 1747; June 15, 1747.

New-York, May 25. 1747.

MADE his Escape form on board the Privateer Brig. Pollux, *on the 20th Instant, a Mulatto Man, named* Storde, *aged about 23 Years, of a middle Stature, and Pock-broken, by Trade a Carpenter; his Cloaths unknown. Whoever takes up said Mulatto, and delivers him to Mr.* Daniel Stiles, *at Capt.* John Waldron's *in this City, shall have five Pounds Reward, and all reasonable Charges*
           paid by said   Stiles.
The New-York Gazette, Revived in the Weekly Post-Boy, May 25, 1747; June 1, 1747; June 8, 1747.

Run away from Samuel Tingley, *a Negro Man named* Andrew; *had on when he went away, a blue Cloth Waistcoat, and green Breeches. Whoever takes up the said Negro, and brings him home, shall have* Thirty Shillings *Reward, and reasonable Charges,*
           paid by   Samuel Tingley.
The New-York Gazette, Revived in the Weekly Post-Boy, June 22, 1747; June 29, 1747; July 13, 1747.

New York, June 13. 1746.

RUN away from the subscriber, an Irish servant man, named William Patterson, about 22 years of age, he is a well set young fellow, about 5 foot 7 inches high, of a sandy complexion, his hair cut off, sometimes wears a wig, but mostly a cap: he took with him a new castor hat, fine broad cloth vest, of a light colour, a fine new linnen jacket, speckled shirt, striped trowsers, oznabrigs drawers, pewter buckles in his shoes. Whoever takes and secures said servant, so that his master may have him again, shall have Three pounds reward,
           paid by   NICHOLAS BAYARD.
N. B. His father is a miller at Christine mills, and it is supposed he is gone that way, in Company with one James Williams and his wife, who are also run away from hence. He has changed his name to John O'Connor.
The Pennsylvania Gazette, June 25, 1747. See *The New-York Evening Post,* June 29, 1747.

New-York, June 13th.

RUN away from the Subscriber, an *Irish* Servan [*sic*] Man, named *William Patterson*, about 22 Years of Age, he is a well set young Fellow, about 5 foot 7 Inches high, of a sandy Complection, his Hair cut off, sometimes wears a Wigg, but mostly a Cap, he took with him a New Castor Hat, without a lining, a good fine Broad-Cloath Vest of a light Colour, a fine new linnen Jacket, a Speckled Shirt a broad striped linnen Trowsers, a wide Ozenbrigs Drawers over it, and a broad pair of pewter Buckles in his Shoes. Whoever takes up said Servant, and brings him to his Master, or secures him so that he may be had again shall have Three Pounds Reward,
   paid by *Nicholas Bayard.*
 N. B. His Father is a Miller at *Christeen* Mills, and it is supposed he is gone that way, in company with one *James Williams* and his Wife, who are also Run away from hence.
 (He has changed his Name to John O'Konnor)
 The *New-York Evening Post*, June 29, 1747; July 13, 1747; July 27, 1747; August 3, 1747; August 17, 1747; August 24, 1747; September 7, 1747; September 21, 1747; September 28, 1747; October 5, 1747; October 19, 1747; October 26, 1747. See *The Pennsylvania Gazette*, June 25, 1747.

New-York, June 8. 1747.

RUN away from his Master *Leonard Hoff*, on the 30*th* of last month, a Negro man named *York*, about 23 Years of Age. a portly tall Fellow, very Black; had on when he went away, a Linsey Woolsey Grey Coat & Jacket, and the sleeves of his Jacket are made of blue Druget, Shirt and short narrow Trowsers made of homespun Linnen, and a pair of shoes with double soals, grey coarse yarn Stockings, an old coarse Hat, cut in the shape of a Sailors leather Cap. Whoever takes up the said Negro man and secures him either in this City Goal, or brings him to his master living at *Middletown*, in *Monmouth* County, shall have *Forty Shillings* as a Reward, and all reasonable Charges
   paid by the said LEONARD HOFF.
The New-York Weekly Journal, July 6, 1747.

Rye, July, 20th.

RUN away from the Subscriber, an Apprentice Boy, about 19 Years of Age, named *Moses Billing*, of a middle Stature and has a Blemish in his right Eye. Had on when he went away, a brown Homespun Coat, a brown Linnen Vest, a good Bever Hat, a pair of new Shoes. Whoever takes up said Apprentice, and brings him to his Master, or secures him so that he may have him again shall have Thirty Shillings as a Reward, and all reasonable Charges paid by, *James Horton.*

The New-York Evening Post, July 20, 1747; July 27, 1747; August 17, 1747; August 24, 1747; August 31, 1747; September 7, 1747; September 14, 1747; September 21, 1747.

New-York, July 20th.
RUN away from the Subscriber, a Negro Man named *Cato*, formerly belonging to *Gilbert Wessels*, and did usually follow Chimney Sweeping: He is a short well set Fellow about 26 Years of Age. Had on when he went away, speckled Trowsers, a white Shirt, blew Jacket, linnen Handkerchief, a Bever-Hat, Whoever takes up the said Negro, if taken in Town shall have Twenty Shillings, if taken up in the Country, shall have Forty Shillings Reward,
    paid by *Matthew Senthus.*
The New-York Evening Post, July 20, 1747; July 27, 1747; August 17, 1747; August 24, 1747.

Run away of Friday Morning last, from the Sloop Trial, William Rose Master, *lying at the Mayor's Wharfe, a Servant Boy named* Richard King, *about 15 Years of Age, but small, with a pale and sickly but sharp Look; had on a blue Sailor's Jacket napt; a pair of good Shoes, and new grey Stockings, narrow ozenbrigs Trousers and ozenbrigs Shirt very dirt, a strip'd worsted Cap, and a good Felt Hat. Whoever returns him on board the said Sloop, shall have a Pistole Reward.*
    New-York, Sept. 21. 1747.
The New-York Gazette, Revived in the Weekly Post-Boy, September 21, 1747.

ALBANY, October 10.
RUN away on the 1st Instant from *Folkert Hendrick Dow*, a Mallato Man Slave, named *SAM*, aged about 40 Years, well set, an much Pock-broken, Talks English and Dutch, he pretends to be free: Had on when he went away a flowered Fustian Jacket, a pair of Leather Britches, and Trowsers, and is supposed he is gone with some of the New Levies, either to *New-Jersey* or *Pensylvania*. Whoever takes up said slave, and brings him to his Master, or the Printer hereof shall have four Pounds as a Reward and all reasonable Charges
    paid by *Folkert Hendrick Dow.*
The New-York Evening Post, October 19, 1747; October 26, 1747; November 9, 1747.

RUN away from Robert Sherer, *of the* Fish-Kills, *in* Dutchess *County, and Colony of* New-York, *A Negro Slave named* Harry, *aged upwards of* 40 *Years; had on when he went away, a woollen Hat, a worsted Cap, homespun Shirt half worn, homespun Coat, Flannel Waistcoat, homespun Breeches, blue Stockings, pretty good Shoes: he has been gone upwards of* 3 *Months, and it is supposed he is conveyed or carried off by some ill minded and malicious Persons. Whoever can find out, or take up and secure said Slave, and give Notice thereof, so that his Master may have him again, shall have* Three Pounds *Reward,*
    paid by JOHN SHERER.
 N. B. He was taken up and put in New-York *Goal, last May was a two Years.*
 The New-York Gazette, Revived in the Weekly Post-Boy, November 2, 1747; November 9, 1747; November 16, 1747; November 23, 1747; November 30, 1747; December 6, 1747; December 21, 1747.

RUN away on the first of October last, from the Widow of Alderman *Van Gelder, A Negro Man named* Frank, *of a tauny Complexion, speaks good* English *and* Dutch; *had on when he went away, a striped Flannel Jacket, Ozenbrigs Trousers, old Shoes but no Stockings; he has since changed his Cloaths, and has been seen since his Elopement, to wear a red Duffels great Coat. Whoever takes up said Negro, and brings his to his Mistress, or to* Victore Hyer, *living near the* English *Church, shall have* Forty Shillings *Reward, and all reasonable Charges.*
          New-York, *Nov,* 16, 1747.
 The New-York Gazette, Revived in the Weekly Post-Boy, November 16, 1747; November 23, 1747; November 30, 1747; December 6, 1747; December 21, 1747.

Run away the 18*th* November *Instant, from* Thomas Saunders, *in* New-York, *an Irish Servant Man, named* Nathaniel Robeson; *of a middle Stature, long Visage, pretty good Complexion, and no Hair; had on when he went away, a white Coat, a Pair of Leather Breeches, and Trousers, thread Stockings, a linnen Wastcoat, check Shirt, coarse Hat and Cap, and old Shoes:*
 Whoever takes up said Servant and secures him, so that his Master may have him again shall have Forty Shillings *Reward.*
 The New-York Gazette, Revived in the Weekly Post-Boy, November 30, 1747; December 6, 1747; December 14, 1747; January 4, 1748.

1748

RUN away last Saturday Morning, an Apprentice Lad named Joseph Loughton, *thin faced, black Complection, and is Lame in one Leg, which occasions him to limp, is about* 18 *Years of Age: Had on when he went away, a light colour'd Cloth Pea-Jacket, red Vest and Breeches, new Shoes, yarn Stockings, a Cap, and an old Hat painted: He has also a blue Coat with red Cuffs, and a red Over-Coat. Likewise run away, a hired Boy, about* 17 *or* 18 *Years old, but small; named Joseph Dart, of a dark Complexion, and very talkative: Had on a dark colour'd Cloth Pea-Jacket, a new great red Coat, a new blue Vest, a Leather Cap, and sometimes a Hat, and is suppos'd to have intic'd the other away. They are both English.*

Whoever secures either of them, so that they may be brought to Justice, or to their Master Ralph Hylton, *shall have Forty Shillings Reward for each, and all reasonable Charges,*
    paid by said Hylton, *or Mr.* John Cruger.
The New-York Gazette, Revived in the Weekly Post-Boy, January 11, 1748; January 18, 1748; February 8, 1748.

RUN away from Doctor Standard, *at* East-Chester, *a Negro Man named* Hamstead, *of a short Stature, pretty full Face marked with the small Pox: Had on when he went away, a Beaver Hat, a Surtout of West Country Kersey of a light Colour, since has been seen have upon that a Riding Coat of blue Cloth, Leather Breeches, Yarn Stockings, sharp toed Shoes; supposed not to be far from House. Whoever takes up the said Negro and secures him, so that his Master may have him again, shall have* Forty Shillings *Reward, and all reasonable Charges borne,*
    by THOMAS STANDARD.
The New-York Gazette, Revived in the Weekly Post-Boy, March 14, 1748; March 28, 1748.

STOLEN about a Fortnight ago, out of the House of Capt. Thomas Hutchinson, *near the Fly-Market, the following Goods, viz. A large square silver Snuff Box, with wrought Flourishes on Top and Bottom, and gilt inside; a Set of rais'd China; a Pair of Silver handle Scissars; two laced Cambrick Caps; some Handkerchiefs and Aprons; a Copper Pot of a Pint & half; and several Household Goods: Some other Things lost at the same Time, have been found in the Possession of* Ellinor Sinnet, *now in Goal. If any Person will give Intelligence of the said Snuff-Box, so that the Owner may have it again, shall have* Thirty Shillings *Reward; and a reasonable*

Reward for any of the other Goods. If pawn'd or sold; the Money return'd with Thanks.
   The New-York Gazette, Revived in the Weekly Post-Boy, April 9, 1748; May 2, 1748.

***R**UN away the Eighth of this Instant* May, *from Capt.* Francis Brett, *of the* Fish Kills, *in* Ulster *County, a Mulatto Slave, named* Peter, *aged about* 20 *Years,* 6 *Foot high, pretty fair for a Mulatto, but Negro Hair, a Scar over both his Eyes: Had on a yellowish Fly Coat of Broad Cloth, Leather Breeches, grey homespun Stockings, a Beaver Hat, a grey homespun Jacket, a Linnen Shirt, and a Tow Club Shirt. Whoever takes up said Negro, and gives Notice to his said Master, or to the Printer hereof, so that he may be had again, shall have* Forty Shillings *Reward, and all reasonable Charges, paid by* FRANCIS BRETT.
   The New-York Gazette, Revived in the Weekly Post-Boy, May 16, 1748; May 23, 1748.

***R**UN away on the* 30th *Instant, From* William Rogers, *of* Oyster-Bay, *an* Irish *Servant Lad named* Henry Mc.Queede, *about* 11 *Years of Age, and very much freckel'd: Had on when he went away, a blue Jacket, Check Shirt, and Leather Breeches. Whoever secures said Servant, and gives Notice thereof to his said Master, or to* William Peters *in* New-York, *shall have* Twenty Shillings *Reward.*
   The New-York Gazette Revived in the Weekly Post-Boy, June 6, 1748; June 13, 1748; June 27, 1748.

***R**UN-AWAY on Friday Morning last, from* Resolved Waldron *of this City, Baker, a Negro Man named* Wan, *by Trade a Baker, a yellow Fellow about* 25 *Years old, much pock mark'd, and goes a little limping: Had on when he went away, a white Cloth Pea Jacket lin'd with blue, an Ozenbrigs Shirt, Sailors Trowsers, a pritty old Hat and old Shoes.*
   Whoever takes up and secures the said Negro Man, so that his Master may have him again, shall have Forty Shillings *Reward, and all reasonable Charges, paid by* RESOLVED WALDRON.
   The New-York Gazette, Revived in the Weekly Post-Boy, June 13, 1748; June 27, 1748. See *The New-York Gazette, Revived in the Weekly Post-Boy,* August 29, 1748.

***R**UN away from the Executors of Capt.* Beezley, *a* Spanish *Negro Man named* Domingo, *about* 40 *Years of Age, pitted with the Small Pox, has a*

Scar under his Left Eye Brow, speaks bad English: Had on when he went away, a brown Cloth Jacket, a Check Shirt, an old Hat flapt, a striped blue and white Trowsers, is supposed to harbour in or about the Swamp, having been seen with one Mary Carney, *a white Woman, that frequently used to harbour him at her Lodgings near the Stockadoes. Whoever takes up said Negro, and secures him, so that he may be had again, shall receive* Twenty Shillings *Reward,*
    by   JAMES MILLS.
The New-York Gazette, Revived in the Weekly Post-Boy, June 27, 1748; July 4, 1748; July 11, 1748; July 18, 1748.

*R*UN *away the 5th of* June *last, from* Samuel Wickham, *of* Goshen, *in the County of* Orange, *a Negro Man named* Jack, *about* 22 *Years of Age,* 5 *Foot high, very black, this Country born, and speaks good* English: *Had with him when he went away, an old Felt Hat, two new Two Shirts* [sic] *and a fine one, one pair of old Trousers, a pair of Thread Stockings, one old gray Kersey Coat, a new homspun Duroy Coat, a Linnen Jacket, and Holland Cap. Whoever takes up or secures said Fellow, so that his Master may have him again, shall have* Forty Shillings *Reward, and all reasonable Charges,*
    paid by me   SAMUEL WICKHAM.
N. B. *It is thought he took with him a bay Mare.*
The New-York Gazette, Revived in the Weekly Post-Boy, July 11, 1748.

*R*UN *away on the* 30*th of* July *last, from* Samuel Hodge *of this City, an* Irish *Servant Girl named* Margaret Kelly, *but is supposed will change it to that of* Henery, *about* 18 *Years of Age, tall and slender, and of a pale Complexion: Had on when she went away, a blue and white short Gown, also a brown strip'd yellow check'd One, a red quilted Petticoat,* 2 *white Linnen Aprons, and a check'd One. Whoever secures said Servant, so that her Master may have her again, shall have* Forty Shillings *Reward, and all reasonable Charges,*
    paid by   Samuel Hodge.
The New-York Gazette Revived in the Weekly Post-Boy, August 1, 1748. See *The Pennsylvania Gazette*, August 11, 1748, and *The New-York Gazette Revived in the Weekly Post-Boy*, August 29, 1748.

        Philadelphia, *August* 11. 1748.
Run away, on the 31st of July last, from Samuel Hodge, of the City of New-York, peruke maker, an Irish servant girl, named Margaret Kelly, (but may alter it to that of Hendry) about eighteen years of age, tall and slender, pale

complexion, dark brown hair, sharp nose, and has a dimple in her chin: Had on a cherryderry [sic] gown, checked yellow and green, and a short gown, with one side blue printed linnen, and the other small red and white striped holland; a red quilted petticoat, and a blue ditto, two white aprons, and a check one. She came into this city on the third instant, and it is supposed (if she is gone from hence) that she is gone towards Brandywine. Whoever takes up said servant, and brings her to John Stoop's, taylor, in Second street, Philadelphia, or to her master, at New-York, shall have Three Pounds reward, and reasonable charges,

    paid by SAMUEL HODGE.

 N. B. All masters of Vessels, and others, are warned not to harbour or conceal her at their Peril.

 The Pennsylvania Gazette, August 11, 1748; August 18, 1748; August 25, 1748. See *The New-York Gazette, Revived in the Weekly Post-Boy,* August 1, 1748, and *The New-York Gazette, Revived in the Weekly Post-Boy,* August 29, 1748.

RUN away on Friday the 12th Instant, from James Swan, of New-York, an Irish Servant Man named *Cornelius Malley,* about 18 Years of Age, slender bodied, and pretty fresh colour'd, about 5 Foot 6 Inches, speaks with the Brogue: Had on when he went away, a Felt Hat lin'd with Leather, a Bird's Eye Handkerchief, a green Flannel Jacket, Check Shirt Ozenbrig Trowsers, a pair of dark blue ribb'd Stockings and a pair of old Pumps. Whoever secures said Servant, so that his Master may have him again, shall have Twenty Shillings Reward, and all reasonable Charges,

    paid by JAMES SWAN.

 The New-York Gazette, Revived in the Weekly Post-Boy, August 15, 1748; August 21, 1748; August 29, 1748; September 5, 1748; September 12, 1748.

RUN-AWAY from Samuel Hodge *of the* City of *New-York,* an Irish Servant Girl, named *Margaret Kelly,* aged about eighteen Years, middling tall and slender, long visag'd, of a pale Complexion, dark brown hair, a long sharp Nose, with a Dimple in her Chin: Had on when she went away, a check dark brown and yellow Cherredery Gown, a blue quilted Peticoat, a check Apron, and a yellow Silk Handkerchief. She run away the 31st day of July last, and was taken up hard by *Ringwood,* where she left her Cloaths, and said was encouraged to go there again; She was brought home the 15th of this Instant, and ranway [sic] the Day following. All Persons are forewarned to harbour her at their Peril, and whoever will take her up, so that her

Master may have her again, shall have Forty Shillings Reward, and reasonable Charges
           paid by   SAMUEL HODGE.
The New-York Gazette, Revived in the Weekly Post-Boy, August 29, 1748; September 5, 1748; October 10, 1748. See *The New-York Gazette, Revived in the Weekly Post-Boy*, August 1, 1748, and *The Pennsylvania Gazette*, August 11, 1748.

R*UN-AWAY on Friday the 26th of this* Instant, from RESOLVED WALDRON, Baker, a Negro Man named *Wan*, by Trade a Baker, a yellow Fellow about 25 Years old, much pock mark'd, and goes a little limping: Had on when he went away, an Oznabrigs Shirt, Sailors Trowsers, an old Hat, with old Shoes but no Stockings. Whoever takes up and secures the said Negro Man, so that his Master may have him again shall have Forty Shillings Reward, and all reasonable Charges
           paid by   RESOLVED WALDRON.
The New-York Gazette, Revived in the Weekly Post-Boy, August 29, 1748. See *The New-York Gazette, Revived in the Weekly Post-Boy*, June 13, 1748.

Run-away from Adam Van Allen *of* Kinderhook *the 21st of* August *last, an* Negro Man named Hannibal, *aged about twenty five Years, is a square well set fellow, about 5 Foot and a half high, pretty black and much pock mark'd, especially about the Nose, has a Scar above his Right Eye: It is uncertain what Cloaths he has on. Whoever takes up said Negro, and secures him so that his Master may have him again, shall have Three pounds reward, and reasonable Charges*
           paid by said   Adam Van Allen.
The New-York Gazette, Revived in the Weekly Post-Boy, September 5, 1748; September 12, 1748; September 19, 1748; September 26, 1748.

           New-York, September 19th. 1748.
RUN away from *John Roe*, of *Oyster-Bay* on *Long-Island*, an Apprentice Boy, named *Comfort Baily*, about 19 Years of Age, thick sett, five Feet five Inches high, had on when he went a way an old blue Jacket with a new patch on one shoulder, white homspun shirt, Tow Trowsers, Felt Hatt, white Linnen Cap, is a Shoe-maker by Trade. Whosoever takes up the said Apprentice, secures him so that his Master may have him again, shall have twenty shillings Reward and all reasonable charges
           paid by   *John Roe of* Oyster-Bay,

or Benjamin Roe in New-York.
The New-York Evening Post, September 19, 1748.

RUN away about a Fortnight ago, from the Subscriber hereof, a Negro Man named Jack, *about 5 Foot 8 Inches high, speaks hoarse and was Drummer on board the Ship* Brave-Hawk*: Had on when he went away, a light colour'd blue Jacket double Breasted; a speckled Shirt, striped Holland Trowsers, new Worsted Cap, an old Felt Hat, and Shoes and Stockings. Whoever takes up and secures said Negroe, so that his Master may have him again, shall have* Forty Shillings *Reward, and all reasonable Charges   paid by*   JOSEPH HAYNES.
The New-York Gazette, Revived in the Weekly Post-Boy, October 17, 1748; October 24, 1748; October 31, 1748.

Philadelphia, October 20. 1748.
RUn away from the Morning star privateer, of New York, an Irish servant man, named Hugh Kelly, belonging to Samuel Hodge, of New York, Perriwig maker; he is of low stature, has a long sharp nose, black beard, is long visage, and much addicted to drinking. He left the Privateer at Bermuda, and came in a vessel to this place, but is supposed to be gone towards Virginia, or lurking about Christine. Whoever takes up and secures said servant, so as he may be had again, shall have Three Pounds reward,
         paid by   William   Cannon,   taylor,   in   Front   street, Philadelphia, or said Samuel Hodge, in New York.
The Pennsylvania Gazette, October 20, 1748.

RUN away from John Pell, *of the Mannor of* Pelham, *a Negro Wench named* Bell, *a Boy named* Janneau, *a Girl named* Tamer, *another named* Dinah, *and another named* Issabel; *also a Negro Man named* Lewis. *Whoever will take up said Negroes, and bring them to* John Pell *aforesaid, shall have* Five Pounds *Reward, and all reasonable Charges,*
         paid by   JOHN PELL.
The New-York Gazette, Revived in the Weekly Post-Boy, November 14, 1748.

RUN-AWAY from Luykas Joh. Wyngaard, *of the City of* Albany, *Merchant, a certain Negro Man named* Simon, *of a middle Size, a slender spry Fellow, has a handsome smooth Face, and thick Legs; speaks very good* English: *Had on when he went away, a blue Cloth Great Coat. Whoever takes up the said Negro, and brings him to his Master, or to Mr.* John Livingston, *at*

New-York, *shall receive* Three Pounds, New-York *Money, Reward, and all reasonable Costs and Charges,*
        paid by   JOHN LIVINGSTON.
The New-York Gazette, Revived in the Weekly Post-Boy, November 21, 1748; November 28, 1748; December 5, 1748; December 12, 1748.

BROKE out of the Goal of Richmond *County, in the Night of the* 14th *of* November *Inst.* one Benjamin Reed, *a Man about* 40 *Years of Age, and* 5 *Foot* 10 *inches high; has a Scar almost round his left Wrist, by the Cut of a Broad-Ax, which makes him something stiff: Had on when he broke out, a light coloured Coat, and red Plush Breeches. Whoever takes up and secures the said* Benjamin Reed, *so that the Sheriff may get him again, shall have* Five Pounds *Reward, and all reasonable Charges,*
        paid by   NICHOLAS LARZELERE, Sheriff.
The New-York Gazette, Revived in the Weekly Post-Boy, November 28, 1748; December 5, 1748; December 12, 1748; December 19, 1748.

Run-away on the first of *November* last, from *John Tuthill* of the *Oyster-Ponds* on the East End of *Long-Island,* a Mulatto Man Slave, named *Toney,* aged about 19 Years: Had on when he went away, a Felt Hat, a brown Camblet Coat, a red Jacket, and speckled Trowsers. Also run away in Company with him, an Indian Man named *Jack,* belonging to *John Petty* of the same Place, aged about 18 Years, and has his Hair cut off: Had on when he went away, an old Beaver Hat, lightish colour'd close bodied Coat, a red Jacket, Leather Breeches, and speckled Trowsers, with short Hair. Whoever takes up the said *Tony* and sends him to his Master, or to *Obadiah Wells* in *New-York,* shall have Forty Shillings as a Reward, and Twenty Shillings for doing the same with the said *Jack,* and all reasonable Charges paid by *John Tuthill* and *John Petty,* or if delivered to said *Wells,* shall be paid by him.
        JOHN TUTHILL,   JOHN PETTY,   OBADIAH WELLS.
The New-York Gazette, Revived in the Weekly Post-Boy, December 5, 1748. See *The New-York Evening Post,* December 12, 1748.

RUN away on the first of *November* last, from *John Tuthill* of the *Oyster-Ponds* on the *East* End of *Long-Island,* a Melatto Man Slave, named *Toney,* aged about 19 Years, had on when he went away, a Felt Hatt, brown Camblet Coat, red Jacket and Speckled Trowsers: Also runaway in Company with him, an Indian Man named *Jack,* belonging to *John Petty* of the same Place, about 18 Years of Age, had on when he went away, an old Beaver Hatt, lightish colour'd close bodied Coat, red Jacket, a Pair of

Leather Breeches, and speckled Trowsers, with short Hair. Whosoever takes up the said *Toney* and sends him to his Master, or to *Obadiah Wells* in *New-York*, shall have forty Shilings Reward, and twenty Shillings for taking the said *Jack*, if in company with him, and all reasonable Charges paid by John Tuthill and John Petty, or if delivered to said *Wells*, shall be
     paid by him. John Tuthill,
         John Petty, Obadiah Wells.
The New-York Evening Post, December 12, 1748; December 19, 1748; March 20, 1749; March 27, 1749. See *The New-York Gazette, Revived in the Weekly Post-Boy*, December 5, 1748.

1749

             Philadelphia, March 28. 1749.
RUn away from his master, Joseph Gray, at the sign of the Conestogoe waggon, a servant man, named John Bell, was born at Albany, of Dutch and Swedish parents, is of small size, about 33 years of age, has very little hair, and is bald on the crown of his head: Had on when he went away, an old beaver hat, white shirt, old lead colour'd broadcloth coat, turn'd, old olive colour'd fustian jacket, old coarse blue plush breeches, grey worsted stockings, and old shoes. He says his mother lives at New-York. Whoever brings said servant to Joseph Gray, or secures him, so as his master may have him again, shall have Three Pounds reward, and reasonable charges,
    paid by JOSEPH GRAY.
The Pennsylvania Gazette, March 28, 1749; April 5, 1749; April 13, 1749. Third ad does not have the location and date at the top.

RUN away from *Nicholas Bayard*, an Indian Man Slave, named *James*, about 40 Years of Age, well sett, about 5 Foot 10 Inches high, wears his own Hair, and formerly liv'd with *Gabriel Legett* at *West-Chester*: Whoever takes him up, and secures, him so that his Master can have him again, shall have Twenty Shillings Reward, and all reasonable Charges
    paid by *Nicholas Bayard.*
The New-York Evening Post, May 15, 1749; May 22, 1749.

RUN away from Francis Bloodgood, *a* Madagascar *Negro Man, named* Tom, *of a middle Size, well-set, and near* 30 *Years old; he speaks pretty good English, and can read: We hear he has got a sort of an Indenture, whereby he pretends to be free: Had on when he went away, a lightish colour'd Great Coat, a plain brown streight-bodied Coat, red Waistcoat without Sleeves, Buckskin Breeches without a Seam between the Legs, and a*

coarse grey *Cap. Whoever takes up and secures the said Negro, so that his Master may have him again, shall have Three Pounds Reward, and all reasonable Charges paid;*
     by me FRANCIS BLOODGOOD.
 N. B. As he is a cunning Fellow, the Person who takes him up is desired to be cautious, lest he deceive them.
 The *New-York Gazette Revived in the Weekly Post-Boy*, May 15, 1749; May 22, 1749.

RUN away on the 30th Day of May last, from Obadiah Huntt, *of the City of* New-York, *an* Irish *Servant Boy named* Thomas Price, *about 16 Years of Age: Had on when he went away, a yellow striped homespun Jacket, with a pair of Leather Breeches and Trowsers, a Felt Hat, and dark brown hair: he has a Brother named* George Price, *that sails out of* Philadelphia *in Mr.* Allen's *Employ, and 'tis thought he is gone that Way. Whoever takes up and secures said Servant, so that his Master may have him again, shall have* Thirty Shillings *Reward, and all reasonable Charges paid, by* OBADIAH HUNTT.
 The *New-York Gazette, Revived in the Weekly Post-Boy*, June 12, 1749; June 19, 1749; June 26, 1749.

RUN away from Capt. Thomas Hutchinson, *the 13th Inst. a bought Servant Maid for four Years, named* Mary Allen, *but by many called* Silver Heels, *of a brown Complexion, black Hair, a little Pock broken, a very awkward Gaite in her Walking, and pretty tall: Had on when she absconded from her said Master, a brown Camblettee Gown, homespun Shift, two striped homespun Petticoats. Whoever brings the said* Mary Allen *to her Master at City-Hall, shall have* Thirty Shillings *Reward; and if any Person or Persons harbours, or gives Entertainment to the said* Mary Allen, *shall be prosecuted as the Law directs.*
     THO. HUTCHINSON.
 The *New-York Gazette, Revived in the Weekly Post-Boy*, June 26, 1749; July 3, 1749; July 10, 1749.

Run away the 21st Instant from William *and* Benjamin Hawxhurst, *of* Oyster-Bay, *on* Long Island, *a Negro Man named* Tom, *a middle size yellow Fellow, and is pretty well cloath'd: Took with him a black Horse, with a white Snip or Spot on his Nose. Whoever takes up and secures the said Negro and Horse, shall have a reasonable Reward paid by* WILLIAM *and*

BENJAMIN HAWXHURST.
The New-York Gazette, Revived in the Weekly Post-Boy, June 26, 1749; July 3, 1749; July 10, 1749.

THIS is to give Notice, to any Person or Persons Whatsoever, to apprehend one *Jacob Oger*, born in *Germany*, a likely Man about thirty Years of Age, for robing *Elenor Erwin* on the Highway on Sunday last, of the following Goods, viz. six Yards and a Half of Cambrick, three Yards of scollop'd Lace, two Yards and Half a Quarter of Holland, half a Yard of Chinch, four Ounces of fine white Thread, two Fans, three Quarters of an Ounce of black and red sewing Silk, a Card of red Stone sleave Buttons, a Gold Ring with a Stone in it: Whoever takes up said *Jacob Oger* and brings him to *Jacob Hollet* at the *Race-Horse*, in the *Bowery Lane*, or the Serjeant *John Ferrel* near the *Bowling Green*, that he may be delivered up to Justice, shall have Forty Shillings Reward, and all reasonable Charges paid: If any of the above mentioned Goods be offered for Sale, those they are offer'd too are desired to stop them. It is supposed he is gone towards Pennsylvania.
New-York, July 5*th*, 1749.

The New-York Evening Post, July 10, 1749; July 24, 1749; July 31, 1749; August 7, 1749.

Run-away about two Months ago, from James Mills, *of this City, a Negro Man named* Bolton, *a short ill looking Fellow, about* 30 *Years of Age, flat Nose, and Teeth black with Tobacco, he is a Chimney-sweeper, and had but very ordinary Cloaths of when he went away: Whoever takes up the said Negro Man, and brings him to his Master, shall have Three Pounds Reward, and all reasonable Charges*
        paid by   JAMES MILLS.
The New-York Gazette, Revived in the Weekly Post-Boy, September 4, 1749; September 11, 1749.

NEW YORK, August 28.
Thursday and Friday last the famous infamous vagrant TOM BELL made his appearance in this city, but being discovered a little sooner than he could wish, he left the place before Friday noon, otherwise would have been secured:—'Tis somewhat surprizing that this fellow should so many years continue rambling here in America, playing dishonest pranks; for as he is now pretty well known throughout the country, his impositions pass only upon innocent and unwary people; tho' several honest persons have suffered at times, because they have been suspected to be like him: He must certainly now be a pain to himself, as well as an injury to society; and as he

seems almost incurable in that sort of life, it is not unlikely but his craft may one day fail him, and he have the just reward of his demerits on a triple tree.
The Pennsylvania Gazette, August 31, 1749

Run-away on the 17th Inst. from John Betts, *of* Jamaica, *on* Long-Island, *a Mulatto Fellow, named* Isaac, *aged about 24 Years, of a middle Size; Had on when he went away, a very good Head of Hair, a good Felt Hat, a brown Coat, Linnen Vest and Breeches, a Pair of blue Yarn Stockings, and good Shoes. Whoever takes up the said Fellow, and brings him to the Owner, or secures him shall have* Three Pounds *Reward, and all reasonable Charges paid them, by* JOHN BETTS.
The New-York Gazette Revived in the Weekly Post-Boy, September 25, 1749; October 2, 1749; October 9, 1749; October 16, 1749.

RUN away the second of October *Instant, from* John Groesbeek *of* New-York, *a Negro Man named* Harry, *a lusty Fellow, about 28 Years of age, yellow Complexion, upwards of 6 Foot high, is born at* Albany *talks good* Dutch *and* English, *understands to play on the Fiddle; he had on when he went away, an Ozenbrigs Shirt, a striped red and brown Homspun Jacket, and a Bear-skin one over it, a striped Worsted Cap, small Hatt, Cloth Breeches, and a Pair of Ozenbrigs Trowsers over it, a Pair of fine blue Worsted Stockings, new Shoes, Steel Buckles, one of his Ancles bend, inwards from a Cut thereon; it is supposed he is gone to the* West-Jerseys: *Whoever takes up the said Negro, and secures him so that his Master may have him again, shall have* Forty Shillings *Reward, and reasonable Charges paid, by* John Groesbeek.
The New-York Evening Post, October 16, 1749; October 30, 1749.

Run-away from Peter De Lancey, *Saturday the 7th of* October, *Inst. a Negro Man named* Sam, *of about 27 Years of Age: He is a tall Fellow, with thick Lips, has a flat Nose, is bow Legged, and speaks English: Had on when he went away, a homespun Coat, and a short pair of Trowsers. Whoever takes up the said Fellow, or secures him so that his Master gets him again, shall have* Thirty Shillings *Reward; if taken out of the Government,* Three Pounds, *and all reasonable Charges, paid by* PETER DE LANCEY.
The New-York Gazette Revived in the Weekly Post-Boy, October 16, 1749.

Run away from the sloop Speedwell, in New York, on Saturday night last, Nathan Solly master, two seamen; one named Thomas Nicholls, a small statur'd man, long thin visage, very swarthy, long nose, pock mark'd, and wears a light colour'd wig; the other named George, a middle sized man, full fac'd, red pimples, occasioned by drinking; and if they have not changed their clothes, are dress'd in blue jackets, check shirts, white tarry trowsers, old shoes and stockings, old hats, and are very dirty. The night they went away, the above master's chest was broke open, and 12 or 14 £. in money take out of it; also a light brown ratteen coat, with white metal buttons, racoon hat, pretty much worn, with a small hole in the crown, a pair black breeches, 3 pair worsted stockings, one pair dark blue, the others a light colour, two check, and two white shirts, a gingham waistcoat, two or three caps, and some paper; and it is thought the above seamen have committed the robbery. Whoever apprehends and secures said semen, so as they may be had again, shall have Three Pounds reward fore each, and reasonable charges,
          paid by   NATHAN SOLLY.
The Pennsylvania Gazette, October 19, 1749.

Run-away from Adrian Ryersz, *on* Staten-Island, *the* 12th *of* October *Inst. a Negro Man named* Hector, *speaks good English, is about five Foot six Inches high, well set, with a Scar on his left Hand, and has a down Look: Had on when he went away a good Beaver Hat, a blue Coat lin'd with light colour'd Shalloon, a white Jacket and Shirt, a good Pair Calf Skin Shoes, and a blue Pair of Stockings. Whoever takes up and secures the said Negro, so that his Master may have him again, shall have* Forty Shillings *Reward, and all reasonable Charges*
          paid by   ADRIAN RYERSZ.
The New-York Gazette Revived in the Weekly Post-Boy, October 23, 1749; October 30, 1749; November 6, 1749. See *New-York Gazette Revived in the Weekly Post-Boy*, July 27, 1752

Run-away Friday last from the Subscriber, from the Sign of the Horse and Cart *in this City, a Servant Man named James Fitch, born in New-England, aged about* 28 *Years, a pretty tall slim Fellow, long Visag'd, dark Eyes and Wore a Cap; Had on when he went away, an old pale blue Coat, a light colour'd Jacket and Breeches, white Stockings, and a large Beaver Hats; He lately had the Fever and Ague, and looks poorly.*

    Whoever takes up and secures the said Servant in any of his Majesty's Goals, and gives Notice thereof to Mr. John Lake, *Merchant in* New-York, *or to the Subscriber living in* Canterbury, *in the County of* Windham, *and*

Colony of Connecticut, *shall have Forty Shillings Reward, and all reasonable Charges*
        paid by   DAVID NEVINS.
The New-York Gazette Revived in the Weekly Post-Boy, November 13, 1749; November 27, 1749.

1750

R UN-away from John Innes, *on* Long-Island, *the Fifth of* October *last, a Negro Woman named* Bett, *formerly the Property of the Widow Mary Cornell, of* Cow-Neck, *and last seen at her House since run away: Had on, a new Duffils Pettycoat and Jacket, speaks good English, a slender Wench, with a large Scar on her Breast right under her Chin. Whoever takes up and secures the said Negro, so that her Master may have her again, shall have* Forty Shillings *Reward, and all reasonable Charges,*
        paid by   JOHN INNES.
The New-York Gazette, Revived in the Weekly Post-Boy, January 8, 1750; January 15, 1750; January 22, 1750; January 29, 1750.

RUN-away, from Cornelius Vanhorne *of the City of* New-York, *Merchant, on or about the* 22d *of December last, a Servant Man, named James Wisely, of about 26 Years of Age, of a short Stature, a squat brown Man, brown Hair when grown, but now wears a brown Wig: Had on when he went away, a coarse blue Ratteen or Peniston Pea Jacket, lined with green, a blue and a red Cloth Jacket faced with Velvet, a dress'd Sheep-Skin Breeches, a pair of homespun Stockings, a Leather Jockey Cap, is a pretty talkative Fellow, pretends to be a Coachman, and brought up to attend a Table. Whoever takes up and secures said Servant, so that he may be had again, shall have a Pistole Reward, and all reasonable Charges,*
        paid by   CORNELIUS VANHORNE.
The New-York Gazette, Revived in the Weekly Post-Boy, January 8, 1750; January 15, 1750; January 22, 1750.

RUN away on the Fourth of February *last, from* Robert James Livingston, *a tall likely Negro Wench, named* Nell, *about 36 Years of Age: Had on when she went away, a blue Peniston Petticoat, a short blue and white homespun Gown, with a short blue Duffils Cloak and Straw Bonnet; she is mark'd with nine Spots on each Temple, and nine on her Forehead. Whoever takes up said Wench, so that her master may have her again, shall have* Twenty Shillings *Reward, and all reasonable Charges,*
        paid by   ROBERT JA. LIVINGSTON.

The New-York Gazette Revived in the Weekly Post-Boy, March 19, 1750; March 26, 1750.

Run-away *on the 25th of* March *last, from* James Banks, *of* Newark, *in the County of* Essex, *an Irish Servant Man named* Arthur Harvey, *(formerly Servant to* Solomon Comes *of* Staten-Island*) is about* 20 *Years of Age, of short Stature, has a down Look, with short dark Hair: Had on a brown great Coat, and a Snuff coloured Pea Jacket. Also ran away with him, a Negro Man about the same Age, has a long Face, strait Nose, of a middle Stature, and had on a good red great Coat, a Butter-nut coloured Coat and Jacket, and some other Cloaths besides, and has taken with him a Gun. Likewise run off, a Lad named* Nathaniel Ward, *Son to Nathaniel Ward of* Newark, *is of tall Stature, aged about* 16 *Years, and has white Hair; Had on a light blue Camblet Coat, and a deep blue Frize Jacket. Whoever takes up and secures all or either of the said Persons, so that their respective Owners may have them again, shall have for each* THREE POUNDS, *and all reasonable Charges*
                  paid by   James Banks,   Jonathan Sergeant,
                                 and Nathaniel Ward.
    The New-York Gazette Revived in the Weekly Post-Boy, April 2, 1750; April 9, 1750; April 16, 1750.

BROKE *out of* New-York *Goal, last Saturday Night, two Prisoners for Felony; one of them named* James Green, *a likely well-set Man, born, and well known in* New-England; *the other named* James Leech: *Whoever apprehends and secures said Green, shall have Five Pound Reward,*
                paid by   JOHN AYSCOUGH, Sheriff.
    The New-York Gazette Revived in the Weekly Post-Boy, May 21, 1750; May 28, 1750.

Run-away from on board the Snow *Friendship,* Henry Swetnam, Master, the 25th Inst. Four Sailors, named *Charles Clemens, John Gover, William Blackmore,* and *John Duggan,* supposed to be gone to *Philadelphia; Clemens* is a Welchman, about 5 Foot 6 Inches high, well set and Pockbroken; *Gover* is an Irishman, fair Complexion; *Blackmore* is a West-Countryman, about 6 Foot, brown Complexion and well set; *Duggan* is an Irishman, about 6 Foot, fair Complexion and well set: Any Person who shall apprehend the said Sailors, or any of them, and secures them in any of his Majesty's Goals, shall have FIVE POUNDS Reward,
               paid by me   HENRY SWETNAM.

The New-York Gazette Revived in the Weekly Post-Boy, May 28, 1750; June 4, 1750.

Stolen or stray'd from Undrell Budd*'s Door, at* Maroneck, *in* Westchester County, *the* 27*th of May, in the Evening, a likely black Mare about* 14 *Hands high, with a Hunting Saddle with a Dear-Skin Seat and Leather Housing, and Bridle; paces and has a Star in her Forehead, some white on one of his hind Feet, but has neither Brand nor Mark: She is thought to be taken away by a Man travelling along, whose Name is said to be* Samuel Rogers, *a middle sized well set Man, who had on a blue Coat with white metal Buttons, dirty Leather Breeches, and a short Wig; and 'tis said has a stump Finger. Any Person securing the said Mare and Saddle, so that the Owner may have her again, shall have* Forty Shillings *Reward, and reasonable Charges*

    paid by   NEHEMIAH PALMER.

The New-York Gazette Revived in the Weekly Post-Boy, June 4, 1750; June 11, 1750; June 18, 1750; June 25, 1750.

RUN away, from *James Mc. Hugh* a *Scotch-Irish* Servant Boy, named *Michael Daugherty*, about 16 Years old, and well Set. Had on when he went away, a Flannel Jacket, a pair of Leather Breeches, a black pair of Worsted Stockings, and a Black Wigg; Talks much upon the *Scotch Irish* Brogue. Whoever takes up and secures the said Servant so that his Master may have him again shall have *Forty Shillings* as a Reward and all Reasonable Charges

    Paid by Me   *James Mc. Hugh.*

N. B. He has a scalded Head by which he may be known, he has likewise changed his Cloaths and taken the Road towards Rh. Island.

The New-York Weekly Journal, June 11, 1750; July 2, 1750; August 6, 1750.

Run away, from the subscriber, of Falls township, Bucks county, the 10th ult. a lusty young Negroe fellow, named Frank, about 5 feet 8 inches of stature, down look, speaks very slow, and seems very shy: took with him several clothes, such as strip'd jackets and breeches, white shirts, and white stockings, a light colour'd cloth frock, lined with green, white metal buttons, blue camblet breeches, good hat, new shoes, and a large pair of carv'd buckles. The said Negroe was born in Barbados, but has liv'd in New York several years and understands the baking business, and butchering, having lived lately with Frederick Bekers of York. Any person

that secures the said fellow, so as his owner may have him again, shall have Three Pounds reward, if taken in York government, and Thirty Shillings, if taken in this government, and all reasonable charges,
    paid by ISAAC SHANO.
  N. B. All masters of vessels or others, are forbid to carry him off at their peril. He has a large swelling or lump on his forehead.
The Pennsylvania Gazette, August 2, 1750.

R UN away from David Vander Heyden, *of* Albany, *an Irish Servant Man, called* Edward Rubie, *of a middling Stature, pitted with the small Pox, and has brown Hair. Whoever takes up the said Servant, and secures him so that his Master may have him again, and gives Notice thereof to his said Master, or to* Dirk Vander Heyden, *of* New-York, *shall have Three Pounds Reward, and all reasonable Charges,*
    paid by DAVID VANDER HEYDEN.
The New-York Gazette Revived in the Weekly Post-Boy, August 13, 1750; August 27, 1750.

Run-away about four Weeks ago, from Simon Cregier, *of the City of* New-York, *a Negro Wench, named* Phaebe, *aged about 45 Years, middle sized, and formerly belonged to Mr.* Cornelius Van Wyck, *at Great Neck; she is well known at that Part of* Long-Island, *and about* Flushing; *She had a Note with her to look for a Master, but has not return'd again; Her Cloaths uncertain. Whoever takes up and secures said Negro Wench, so that her Master may have her again, shall have* Forty Shillings *Reward and all reasonable Charges,*
    paid by SIMON CREGIER.
The New-York Gazette Revived in the Weekly Post-Boy, August 27, 1750; September 10, 1750; September 15, 1750.

Whereas one Peter Walsh, *an* Irish *Servant Man, belonging to* Richard Clark Cook, *hath absented himself from his said Master: These are therefore to forewarn all Persons, not to harbour the said* Peter Walsh, *on the Penalty of being prosecuted as the Law directs. Any Person taking up the said Servant, and brings him to his said Master, shall have* Ten Shillings *Reward: He is said to be about Town: Had on when he went away, a blue Coat daubed with Paint, a brown Cloth Pee Jacket, and an Ozenbrigs Waistcoat and Breeches.*
    RICHARD CLARK COOKE.

N. B. *The said* Peter Walsh *is a Painter by Trade, blind of an Eye, and Pock broken.*
The New-York Gazette Revived in the Weekly Post-Boy, September 20, 1750; September 27, 1750.

New-York, September 26th, 1750.

RUN away from *Leonard Reed* Cooper, near the City-Hall, an indented Servant Man, named Hugh M'Vicar, aged about 20 Years, a Cooper by Trade, of a middle Stature fair Complection, is Mark'd with a Ring-Worm on one of his Arms and one of his Knees, is Pock broken round his Nose. Had on when he went away, a Kersey Jacket and Breeches, a pair of Duck Trowsers, with a Seam all round the Thigh, a pair of homespun gray Stockings, good Shoes, large metal Buckles, and a felt Hat; he took with him some Shirts and Trousers unknown. Whoever takes up said Servant, and brings him to his Master, or secures him so that he may be had again shall have Five Pounds Reward, and all reasonable Charges
paid by *Leonard Reed.*
N. B. This is to forwarn all Captains of Vessels not to carry off the said Servant on their Peril.
The New-York Evening Post, October 1, 1750. See *The New-York Gazette Revived in the Weekly Post-Boy*, October 15, 1750.

New-York, October 8*th* 1750.

YEsterday Run away from *Nicholas Bayard*, a Servant Man named *James Caselicth*, a *Bristol* Man born, he came here in *May* last, in the Ship *Griffin*, Capt. *John Goad*, from *Liverpool*; he is a well set Fellow, fresh Colour'd, aged about 25 Years, he pretends to be a *Coachman*, and at other Times a *Barber*, he had on when he went a way, an Ozenbrigs Coat, a green Ratein Vest, a new brown Cloath Breeches, and a new brown Wigg, a Beaver Hat about half worn, he has also took with him, a red Ratein Coat with Brass Buttons, in one of the Sleves of said Coat was a long Cut, as also a speckled Trowsers, he has lost one of his upper Teeth in the for Part of his Mouth; whoever takes up said Servant, and brings him to his said Master, or secures him in Goal so that his Master may have him again shall have three Pound Reward   paid by   *Nicholas Bayard.*
The New-York Evening Post, October 8, 1750; October 22, 1750; November 19, 1750; January 7, 1751. See *The New-York Gazette Revived in the Weekly Post-Boy*, October 8, 1750.

RUn away Yesterday, from *Nicholas Bayard*, of this City, a *Bristol* Servant Man, named *James Caselick;* he came here in *May* last, in the *Griffin*, Capt.

Goad, from *Liverpool*: He is a well set Fellow, fresh colour'd, aged about 25 Years; he pretends to be a Coach-man, and at other Times a Barber: Had on when he went away, an Ozenbrigs Coat, a green Ratteen Vest, new brown Cloth Breeches, new brown Wig, and a Beaver Hat about half worn; he also took with him, a red Ratteen Coat with Brass Buttons, one of the Sleeves having a long Cut in it, as also a speckled Trowsers; he has lost one of his upper Teeth in the fore Part of his Mouth. Whoever takes up said Servant, and brings him to his Master, or secures him so that his said Master may have him again, shall have *Three Pounds* Reward,
    paid him, by NICHOLAS BAYARD.
 The New-York Gazette Revived in the Weekly Post-Boy, October 8, 1750; October 22, 1750; October 29, 1750. See *The New-York Evening Post*, October 8, 1750.

*R*UN *away, from* Cornelia Rutgers, *of the City of* New-York, *a Negro Man, called* Hector, *well-set, thick and of middle Stature, thick Lips, speaks thick and fast; he formerly belonged to Mr.* Newcom, *at* Poughkeepsie, *in* Dutchess *County: It is suppos'd he had on when he went away, a light colour'd Kersey Pea-Jacket, lined with red, an Ozenbrigs Shirt and Trowsers, and Shoes and Stockings. Whoever takes up and brings, or sends the said Negro to his said Mistress, shall have* Thirty Shillings *Reward, if taken within the City and County of* New-York; *but if without the said County,* Three Pounds *Reward, and all reasonable Chares,*
    paid by the said CORNELIA RUTGERS.
 The New-York Gazette Revived in the Weekly Post-Boy, October 8, 1750; October 15, 1750.

      FIVE POUNDS, Reward.
*R*un-away *on Tuesday the 25th of* September, *from* Leonard Reed, *Cooper, near the City-Hall, in this City, an indented Servant Man, named* Hugh M"Vicar, *aged about* 20 *Years, a Cooper by Trade, of a middle Stature, fair Complexion, is mark'd with a Ring-Worm on one of his Arms, and one of his Knees, is Pock-broken round his Nose. Had on when he went away, a Kersey Jacket and Breeches, a pair of Duck Trowsers, with a Seam all round the Thigh, homespun grey Stockings, good Shoes, large metal Buckles, and a felt Hat; he took with him some Shirts and Trowsers unknown. Whoever takes up said Servant, and brings him to his Master, or secures him so that he may be had again, shall have* Five Pounds *Reward, and all reasonable Charges*
     paid by LEONARD REED.
 N. B. *This is to forewarn all Masters of Vessels and others, not to carry off the said Servant at their Peril.*

The New-York Gazette Revived in the Weekly Post-Boy, October 15, 1750; October 22, 1750. See *The New-York Evening Post,* October 1, 1750.

RUn away the 9th of last Month, from *Isaac Medway* of the City of *Albany,* in the Province of *New-York,* an Irish servant Man named *Roger Mc.''Donalson,* is a thick, short well set fellow, with Black Eyes, short black Hair, an stammers much in his speech, and pretends to be a Saylor: Had on when he went away. a half Kersey Vest with white metall Buttons, a pair of good Buckskin Breeches, Yarn Stockings, and a half-worn Beaver Hatt Whoever takes up the said servant and secures him so that his Master may have him again shall have *Three Pounds* as a Reward and all reasonable Charges
                paid by.   ISAAC MEDWAY.
The New-York Weekly Journal, October 22, 1750; October 22, 1750; November 26, 1750; December 3, 1750; December 15, 1750; December 22, 1750.

1751

*R*UN *away from his Master* Hugh Grangent, *a Mulatto Fellow named* John, *he speaks* French *very well, and is supposed to be in this Town, having a Wife at the Widow* Bownes *in* Smith*'s Fly. Whoever apprehends said Fellow, and delivers him in the Goal or Work-House, or to* John Willett, *shall have* Twenty Shillings *Reward,*
            paid by   JOHN WILLETT.
The New-York Gazette Revived in the Weekly Post-Boy, January 14, 1751; January 21, 1751; February 4, 1751.

RUN away from Capt. *John Roberts* about 10 Days ago, a Negro Boy, called *Ben*; of a yellowish Colour, about 5 Feet high, aged near 17; is a Chimney-Sweeper, and pretty well known in this City: Had on a blue Watch-Coat, and some other Cloaths: Whoever secures him, and gives Notice, so that he may be had, shall have a reasonable Reward: And all Persons are forewarned of entertaining him, at their Peril.
New-York Gazette Revived in the Weekly Post-Boy, February 11, 1751; February 18, 1751.

*R*UN *away Sunday night, the* 3*d Instant, from* Judah Hays, *a Negro Wench, named* Sarah, *aged about* 30 *Years; she is a likely Wench of a Mulatto Complexion, was brought up at* Amboy, *in Col.* Hamilton*'s family, and has*

had several Masters in the Jerseys: She dresses very well, has a good Parcel of Cloaths, and speaks good English. Whoever takes up the said Wench, and brings her to her said Master, or secures her in any County Goal, so that he may have her again, shall receive Forty Shillings *reward, and all reasonable Charges.* Whoever entertains said Wench, shall be prosecuted with the utmost Rigour of the Law. All Masters of Vessels, Boat men, &c. are forewarned of conveyed said Wench away, as they shall answer the same.
        JUDAH HAYS.
 New-York Gazette Revived in the Weekly Post-Boy, February 18, 1751; February 25, 1751; March 4, 1751; March 11, 1751; March 18, 1751. See *The Pennsylvania Gazette,* February 19, 1751.

          New York, February 7, 1750-1.
Run away last Sunday night, from Judah Hays, a Negroe wench, named Sarah, aged about 30 years; she is a likely wench, of a Mulatto complexion, was brought up at Amboy, in Col. Hamilton's family, and has had several Masters in the Jerseys: She dresses very well, has a good parcel of cloaths, and speaks good English. Whoever takes up the said wench, and brings her to her said master, or secures her in any county goal, so that he may have her again, shall receive Forty Shillings reward, and reasonable charges. Whoever entertains said wench, shall be prosecuted with the utmost rigour of the law. All masters of vessels, boat men, &c. are forewarned of conveyed said wench away, as they shall answer the same.
        JUDAH HAYS.
 N. B. Said wench has robb'd her said master, in apparel, &c. upwards of Fifty Pounds.
 The Pennsylvania Gazette, February 19, 1751. See *New-York Gazette Revived in the Weekly Post-Boy,* February 18, 1751.

***R**UN-away, the 3d Inst. from* Francis Dudley, *of this City, Carpenter, an* Irish *Maid Servant, named* Mary Sullivan, *of low stature, fair Complexion, and has the Brogue on her Tongue: Had on when she went away, a brown and yellow strip'd Stuff Gown, fac'd and rob'd* [sic] *with green Silk, and has been since seen with a blue Gown on, and a blue Petticoat. Whoever brings home the aforesaid Servant to her Master, shall receive* Twenty Shillings *Reward, and all reasonable Charges,*
     paid by me   Francis Dudley.
 N. B. *This is to fore-warn all Masters of Vessels, and others, not to harbour the above-mention'd Servant, upon Pain of being prosecuted to the utmost Rigour of the Law.*

New-York Gazette Revived in the Weekly Post-Boy, March 4, 1751; March 18, 1751; March 25, 1751; April 1, 1751.

RUN-away, from Andrew Oliver, *of* Marble-town, *in* Ulster *County, on the 23d of* April *last, a Servant Man named* Nathaniel Wilkinson, *about* 24 *Years of Age,* 5 *Feet* 10 *inches high: Had on when he went away, a Worsted Cap, and little Felt Hat, a half worn brown Drugget Coat and Waistcoat, Leather Breeches, and a Woollen check Shirt; he is of a heavy Gait, has a down-look, a large Mouth, thick Lips, pale blue Eyes, speaks good* English, *but slow, and says he was born in* Maryland. *Whoever takes up and secures said Run-away, so as his Master may have him again, shall have* FORTY SHILLINGS *Reward, and all reasonable Charges*
        paid, by me   ANDREW OLIVER.
New-York Gazette Revived in the Weekly Post-Boy, May 6, 1751; May 20, 1751; May 27, 1751.

RUN-away on the 22d *Day of last Month, from* Robert Woodhouse, *of this City, Cordwainer, an Apprentice Lad named* James Sheerer, *about* 17 *Years of Age, of a pale Complexion, dark Hair, and has a Swelling on the left Side of his Throat: Had on when he went away, a worsted Cap, strip'd Homespun Jacket and Leather Breeches. Whoever takes up and secures the said 'Prentice so that his Master may have him again, shall have* Twenty Shillings *Reward, and reasonable Charges,*
        paid by   ROBERT WOODHOUSE.
    N. B. Whoever harbours or entertains the aforesaid Apprentice shall be prosecuted according to Law.
New-York Gazette Revived in the Weekly Post-Boy, June 3, 1751; June 10, 1751; June 17, 1751; June 24, 1751.

Run-away on Sunday the 30th *of* June *last, from* Gilbert Hyatt, *of the City of* New-York, *two Apprentices; one named* Joseph Ryder, *aged about* 18 *Years, about* 5 *Feet* 4 *Inches high, a well-set Fellow, and works well at the Shoemaker's Trade: Had on when he went away, a blue Broad-cloth Coat, which has been turn'd, and is full long for him, a white Fustian double breasted Jacket, half worn brown Wig, a Pair of blue Broad cloth Breeches with a blue Patch upon one of the Knee, and a half-worn Castor-Hat. The other named* Joseph Baker, *of the same Trade, about* 17 *Years of Age, a thick short Lad: When he went away, he had on a blue Penistone Jacket faced with red, a Pair of new yellow Leather Breeches, grey Yarn Stockings, a pair of good Pumps, and a half-worn Beaver Hat. Whoever takes up and*

secures the said two Apprentices, or either of them, so that their said Master may get or obtain them, or either of them, or brings them, or either of them to their said Master, shall have Five Pounds *Reward for each of them, and all reasonable Charges
paid, by* GILBERT HYATT.
N. B. *Whoever harbours or entertains said Apprentices, shall be prosecuted to the utmost Rigour of the Law.*
New-York Gazette, Revived in the Weekly Post-Boy, July 15, 1751; July 22, 1751; July 29, 1751; August 5, 1751.

NEW YORK, July 29.
Friday last one Jonathan Woodman, a Native of Narraganset, was committed to our Goal, for uttering Counterfeit Twenty Shilling Bills of this Colony, in Imitation of the Impression dated December 10,1737: He confesses he has passed ten of them: They are done on a Copper Plate, and may be easily distinguished by those who know the Difference of Copper Plate from common Printing Letters: But that the unskill'd may not be imposed on, it is noted, that the two xxs. near the Arms, are not of an equal Size in the Counterfeit, but are in the True, and the Word N. YORK in the Flourish, has no Point between the N. and YORK, as in the true Bills; also the Word EBORAC in the Arms, is EBORAO in the Counterfeit, and the whole Bill appears more irregular than in the true Bills: He says, there are two others concerned with him, one of whom was in Town when he was taken up, but immediately made off, and went by the Name of Dr. Dunsten, whom he believes to be the Signer of the Bills, and it is probable he has passed more of them, these two being just on going home when apprehended. There was found on him a Number of New Hampshire Four Pound Bills, which are supposed to be counterfeit, and which the Man himself confesses he believes to be so. The other Person concerned, he says, he does not know, but as he heard from his Accomplice, from whom he says he had the Bills; but as he often prevaricates in his Stories, we must leave it to Time to unriddle this Mystery of Iniquity.
The Pennsylvania Gazette, August 1, 1751. See *The New-York Gazette Revived in the Weekly Post-Boy,* August 5, 1751.

NEW-YORK, August 5.
Tuesday last one *James Bill,* alias *Bradford,* a Narraganset Man, was apprehended near Second-River in *New-Jersey,* and committed to our Jail, as one of those concerned with *Jonathan Woodman,* mentioned in our last, in counterfeiting the Twenty Shilling Bills of Credit of this Province: The other called Doctor *Dunsten,* is not yet taken. 'Tis said, this *Bill* had been taken up and committed to Jail at *Hackinsack* a few Years ago, for uttering

counterfeit *Jersey* Bills, from whence he made his Escape; but tis hoped he will now meet with the Reward of his Ingenuity. Their Trials we hear, are put off till next Term.
    New-York Gazette Revived in the Weekly Post-Boy, August 5, 1751.
    See *The Pennsylvania Gazette*, August 1, 1751.

*R**UN** away the* 30*th Day of* June *last, from* Philip Smith *of the* Fish-Kills *in* Dutchess County, *in the Province of* New-York, *a Negro Fellow named* Harry, *aged about* 20 *Years, of a short Stature, well-set, and very black: He had with him when he went away, one Linnen Shirt, two Tow Shirts, and a Woollen Shirt, a Pair of Tow Breeches, and three Pair of Woollen Stockings:—Whoever takes up and secures the said Negro, so that his Master may have him again, shall have* Thirty Shillings *Reward, and all reasonable Charges: And, 'tis at their Peril who entertains him.*
PHILIP SMITH.
    New-York Gazette, Revived in the Weekly Post-Boy, August 5, 1751; August 12, 1751. See *New-York Gazette, Revived in the Weekly Post-Boy*, August 19, 1751.

*R**UN** away the* 30*th of last Month from the Sloop* Neptune, Morris Underdown *Master, now lying in the Harbour of* New-York, *a Servant Man named* John Cox, *a Gardener by Trade, aged about* 28 *Years, of a dark Complexion, black Eyes with a small Cast in them, with short black Hair: He had with him a new plain red Jacket, and another of a purple Colour, with black Flowers on it, a Pair of wide Oznabrigs Trowsers, and a Pair of narrow strip'd Trowsers, white cotton Stockings, new Pumps, plain Silver Buckles, and a good Felt Hat. All Persons are forewarned to entertain him at their Peril. And, Whoever takes up and secures the said Servant so that his Master may have him again, shall have* FIVE POUNDS *Reward, and all reasonable Charges,*
        paid by   MORRIS UNDERDOWN.
    New-York Gazette, Revived in the Weekly Post-Boy, August 5, 1751; August 12, 1751; August 19, 1751.

*R**UN** away the* 30*th of* June *last, from Philip Smith of the* Fish-Kills *in* Dutchess-Countie, *in the Province of New-York, a Negro Fellow named* Harrie, *aged about* 20 *Years, of a short Stature, well-sett, and very black: He had with him when he went away, one Linnen Shirt, two Tow Shirts, and a Woollen Shirt, a Pair of Tow Breeches, and three Pair of Woollen Stockings: Whoever takes up and secures the said Negro, so that his Master*

may have him again, shall have Thirty Shilling Reward, *and all reasonable Charges: And, 'tis at their Peril who entertains him.*
PHILIP SMITH.
New-York Gazette, Revived in the Weekly Post-Boy, August 19, 1751.
See *New-York Gazette, Revived in the Weekly Post-Boy,* August 5, 1751.

R*UN away from* Josiah Martin, *living on the Edge of* Hampstead-Plains, *a young Indian Fellow, middle siz'd and well set; had on when he went away, an Ozenbrigs Shirt, Waistcoat and Trowsers, and a brown Waistcoat overall, also, a Pair of Indian Shoes, and as he has carried away his Bed and Blankets, 'tis thought he may dress himself like an Indian; his name is* Jacob, *and last Year liv'd with the Chief-Justice. His Hair is but half grown. Whoever will secure the said Fellow, so that he may be deliverd to the said* Josiah Martin, *or to Mr.* David Algee, *at Mrs.* Breese*'s in* New-York, *shall have* Thirty Shillings *Reward, and all reasonable Charges, paid by either of the Persons before-mentioned.*
New-York Gazette, Revived in the Weekly Post-Boy, August 26, 1751; September 9, 1751.

R*UN away, on Friday the* 16*th August, from* James Thompson, *of* Ulster County and Province of New-York; *an Irish Servant Man, named* Matthew McIntire, 18 *or* 19 *Years of Age, about* 5 *Foot* 6 *Inches, much Pock-broken, stoop shoulder'd, and wore his own Hair of a blackish Colour: Had on when he went away, an old Kersey Pea Jacket, speckled Shirt, Oznabrigs Trowsers, new Shoes and white Mettal Buckles, but without Stockings, and an old Wooll Hat cut very narrow in the Brim. Whoever takes up and secures said Servant, so that his Master may have him again, shall have* Thirty Shillings *Reward, and all reasonable Charges,*
paid by JAMES THOMPSON.
New-York Gazette Revived in the Weekly Post-Boy, September 2, 1751; September 9, 1751; September 16, 1751; September 23, 1751; September 30, 1751.

R*UN away the* 3*d Instant, from* John Willett, *of* Hamstead Plains, *a Negro Man named* Holliday, *a likely Fellow, about* 23 *Years of Age, speaks good English: Had on when he went away, a whitish Linnen Coat with green Cuffs, and a small Cape to it; he is about* 5 *Feet high and thin made. Whoever takes up said Fellow, and secures him in the Goal at* Jamaica, *or*

the Work-House at New-York, *or delivers him to said* Willett, *shall receive* Twenty Shillings *Reward from*
JOHN WILLETT.

The New-York Gazette Revived in the Weekly Post-Boy, September 9, 1751; September 16, 1751; September 23, 1751.

R*UN away, on Sunday the 25th of August last, from* Matthew Hornbeck, *of* Cocksocky, *in the County of* Albany, *and Province of* New-York, *a.* Bermudian *Negro Fellow named* Dick, *about* 21 *Years old, and his Hair much like that of an Indian's: Had on when he went away, a blue Jacket, Ozenbrigs Shirt and Trowsers, Shoes and Stockings, and a Hat painted Red. Whoever takes up and secures said Negro, so that his Master may have him again, shall have* FORTY SHILLINGS *Reward, and reasonable Charges,*
paid by MATTHEW HORNBECK.
N. B. *All Masters of Vessels are forbid to carry him off at their Peril.*

The New-York Gazette Revived in the Weekly Post-Boy, September 9, 1751; September 23, 1751.

W*HEREAS* William Hana, *Apprentice to* John M'Mullin, *Cordwainer, near the Old-Slip-Market, in* New-York, *absented himself from his said Master's Service, the Twenty-first Instant, and is supposed to be gone to* New London; *if he returns to his Master, he shall be received, and all Faults forgiven: He is five Feet six or seven Inches high, of a fresh Complexion, large Cheeks taper to the Chin, small Eyes, large Eye-brows, and round Forehead; was born in New-York: Had on when he went away, a light brown Cloth Coat lined with blue, and Gold Twist Buttons, blue Cloth Breeches, a dark brown Wig, and Check Shirt. Whoever takes up and brings him to his said Master, or secures him in any Goal, so that his Master may have him again, shall receive Forty Shillings Reward, and all reasonable Charges; and whoever entertains or harbours said Apprentice, will be prosecuted with the utmost Rigour of the Law.*
N. B. *All Masters of Vessels, Boatmen, and others, are forewarned from carrying off said Apprentice at their Peril.*

The New-York Gazette Revived in the Weekly Post-Boy, October 28, 1751; November 4, 1751; November 11, 1751; November 18, 1751; December 2, 1751.

R*UN* away, from on board a sloop at *Poghkeepsie,* in *Dutchess* County, an Irish Servant man, named *Nicholas Mc.Daniel,* aged about 20 years, came lately from Ireland with Capt. *Anderson,* and is about 5 feet 10 or 11 Inches

high; carried with him a Gun, and is supposed to have gone down along the West Side of *Hudson's* river, to Pennsylvania: Had on, a brown Pea Jacket, a Cap, and a new Woollen Hat; he speaks but indifferent English, has a wild Look, says one *Henry Mulhall,* in *Amboy,* is his uncle; he has a Brother at *Poghkeepsie,* who is also a Servant to *James Isaiah Ross,* of *New-York,* Merchant, and came over in the same Vessel. Whoever takes up the said *Nicholas Mc.Daniel,* and secures him, so that the said *James Isaiah Ross,* his Master, may have him again, shall have FIVE POUNDS Reward, and all reasonable charges,
    paid by JAMES ISAIAH ROSS.

The New-York Gazette, Revived in the Weekly Post-Boy, November 18, 1751; November 25, 1751; *The Pennsylvania Gazette,* November 21, 1751; December 5, 1751. Minor differences between the papers. *The Pennsylvania Gazette* shows the servant's last name as "M'Daniel."

R*UN away from* THOMAS VAN WYCK, *of* Oysterbay *on* Long-Island, *the 8th of this Instant, a Negroe Man named* Caesar, *aged about* 23 *Years, of a pretty black bold face, with large white in his Eyes, and may pretend to be free; his right Hand has been bruised, by which Means 'tis not so big as the other: Had on when he went away, a Felt Hat, white Woollen Cap, a grey Kersey Coat, a homespun Check Shirt, a pair of wide Trousers, with Leather Breeches under them, bluish stockings, and new Shoes. Whoever takes up and secures said Negroe, so that his Master may have him again, shall have* Forty Shillings *Reward, and reasonable Charges,*
    paid by THOMAS VAN WYCK.

The New-York Gazette Revived in the Weekly Post-Boy, November 18, 1751.

            New-York, 16th December 1751.
R*UN away, from* John Willet, *of* Flushing, *a lusty yellow Wench, aged about* 26 *Years; She has lost the two first Joints of one of her little Fingers, and has been gone about* 18 *Months. If any Person will inform her Master where she is, so that he may have her again, they shall be well rewarded.*

The New-York Gazette Revived in the Weekly Post-Boy, December 23, 1751.

JUST imported by *William Donaldson,* in the Snow *St. Andrew,* from *Scotland....*

  N. B. Run-away, last Week, from said Snow, a Servant Man named *William Mc.Donald;* is a short well-set Man, wears his own Hair, which is bushy and grey; about 40 Years of Age: Had on when he went away a blue Coat, with red Facings, and a Scots Bonnet; he as seen at *Harlem* last Week.

Whoever takes him up, and returns him to the Vessel, shall have *Four Pounds* Reward; or upon sending Notice where he is secured, shall have *Twenty Shillings*,
        paid by   WILLIAM DONALDSON.
The New-York Gazette Revived in the Weekly Post-Boy, December 23, 1751; December 30, 1752.

Run *away last Night, from* Moses Clement, *in the Broad-way, an Irish Servant Maid named* Mary Lookwhite, *of a middle Stature, red Face, fair Complexion and a bold Look; had on when she went away, a light brown Camblet Gown, a brown quilted Petticoat, a pair of Stays, white Apron and a white Handkerchief: Whoever takes up said Servant, or secures her, so that her Master may have her again, shall have* Twenty Shillings *Reward, and all reasonable Charges paid. Whoever harbours or entertains said Servant, or if any Masters of Vessels should offer to carry her off, they shall be prosecuted to the utmost Rigour of the Law.*
    The New-York Gazette Revived in the Weekly Post-Boy, December 30, 1751; January 6, 1752; January 13, 1752.

1752

RUN-away from *Samuel Neilson* of Kingston, on the 11th Day of this Instant, a High Dutch or Polish Servant Lad, about 19 Years of Age, named *John Danel Ragen*, speaks but poor English, he is about five Feet and a half high, pretty well set, had on when he went away, a blew Cloth Coat, a striped Flannel Waistcoat, new Oznaburg Shirt and Trowsers, a pretty good Felt Hat, and a pair of new Shoes, with Steel Buckles, and he is thought to go towards *New-York*; whosoever takes up said Servant, and secures him, so that his Master may have him again, shall have FORTY SHILLINGS Reward, and all reasonable Charges
        paid, by said   SAMUEL NEILSON.
The New-York Gazette Revived in the Weekly Post-Boy, May 18, 1752; May 25, 1752; June 1, 1752; June 8, 1752; June 15, 1752.

RUN *away from* PETRUS VEILE, *of* Dutchess *County, on Tuesday the 12th of* May, *an* English *Servant Man, named*John Walker, *aged about i Years, about 5 Foot 6 Inches high, Red-hair'd and much freckl'd in his Face, and pretty Round-Shoulder'd: Had on when he went away, a brown Cloth Jacket and Breeches, a speckled Short, a Parir of wide Trowsers, very much mender, and a Pair of Thread Stockings; it is thought he is gone to* New-York, *or to the* Jersies. *Whoever takes up the said Servant, so that his*

Master may have him again, shall have Forty Shillings *Reward, and all reasonable Charges*
                paid, by   PETRUS VIELE.
N. B. *The said Servant has been in this Country before.*
    The New-York Gazette Revived in the Weekly Post-Boy, May 18, 1752; May 25, 1752; June 1, 1752; June 8, 1752.

RUN away together on Monday the 18th Instant, from *Elias Degrushe*, of this City, Rope-maker, at the upper end of Broadway, two Servant Men; one named *Richard Poole*, a West Countryman, and has that Accent on his Tongue; of a middle Stature, black Complexion, and has a large scar near his left Eye, had on when he went away short black Hair, a new English Castor-Hat, a half-worn light-colour'd Frize Coat, scorch'd at the Bottom of the left Skirt, a blue Serge Jacket, and a red Cloth one without Sleeves, a Check Shirt, blue Camblet Breeches, brown Yarn Stockings, and new Shoes with broad rimm'd Brass Buckles in them. He may probably pass for a Rope-maker. The other named *Thomas Jenkins*, a *Welsh-man*, about 21 Years old, of a middle Stature, smooth-fac'd, pretty round-shoulder'd, and has a small Cast in one of his Eyes; had on when he went away, a half-worn Beaver-Hat, worsted Cap, a light-colour'd Cloth Coat, a blue Serge Waistcoat and a Flannel one, Check Shirt, light colour'd Dimity Breeches, Yarn Stockings and new Shoes. Whoever takes up and secures the said Servants, or either of them, again, shall have THREE POUNDS Reward for each, and all reasonable Charges,
                paid by   ELIAS DEGRUSHE.
N. B. It is supposed they are gone towards *New-England.*
    The New-York Gazette Revived in the Weekly Post-Boy, May 25, 1752; June 8, 1752; June 22, 1752.

R*UN away last* Saturday, *a likely mulatto Fellow, named* Crook; *aged about 22, speaks* French *and* English, *pretends to be free; had on a brown Homespun Jacket, Homespun Shirt, a blue flower'd Handkerchief on his Head, no Hat, and is bare-foot.* THIRTY SHILLINGS *Reward will be given for taking him up, or securing him in Jail,*
                paid by   WILLIAM BAYARD.
    The New-York Gazette, Revived in the Weekly Post-Boy, June 8, 1752.

RUN away from *Daniel Dunscomb*, of the City of *New-York*, Cooper, an Apprentice Lad named John Stevens, about 20 Years of Age, near five Foot six Inches high, with brown Hair, very talkative, and pretty much pitted with the Small Pox: He is an English Lad a Cooper by Trade, but Professes to be a Sailor, and has been several Voyages a Privateering out of this Place. He had on when he went away, a green Frize Jacket with round Pewter Buttons, a light blue Cloth Breeches with red Puffs and Pewter Buttons, a white flower'd Jacket, two Shirts one check and the other white, an English Caster Hat, a Pair of brown Thread Stockings, a Pair of good Shoes with Metal Buckles, a Spanish Gregoe or great over Coat, and has taken an old rusty Back-Sword with him; he has since been seen in *Phillipses* Manour, and was traveling towards *Albany*. Whoever takes up said Apprentice and brings him to his Master, or secures him so that his Master may have him again, shall have *Three Pounds* Reward and all reasonable Charges

     paid, by Daniel Dunscomb.

N. B. All Persons whatsoever, are forewarned not to entertain or conceal said Apprentice, on their Peril.

The New-York Evening Post, June 29, 1752; July 6, 1752; July 13, 1752; July 20, 1752.

RUN-away on the 10th of this instant June, from the Subscriber, of this City, Baker, a Dutch (or German) Servant Man, named Valentine Arnold, about 18 or 19 Years of Age, a short Fellow, speaks pretty good English, and has short Hair: Had on when he went away, a brown Linnen Jacket, Check Shirt, white homespun Trowsers, a Linnen Cap, a new Felt Hat, a dark blue Pair of new Worsted Stockings, a Pair of Pumps, and a large Pair of Pewter Buckles; he is a Loaf Bread Baker by Trade, and inclines much to the Sea. Whoever takes up and secures said Servant, so that his Master may have him again, shall have FORTY SHILLINGS, if taken within Thirty Miles of this City, and THREE POUNDS Reward, if further, and reasonable Charges

     paid by OWEN JONES.

N. B. All Masters of Vessels are forbid to carry him off.

The New-York Gazette Revived in the Weekly Post-Boy, June 29, 1752; July 6, 1752; July 13, 1752; July 20, 1752.

NEW-YORK, July 20.

Tuesday Night last Edward Lee, who was committed to Jail about Three Weeks ago, for breaking open Mr. Perry's House, and robbing the same of a considerable Quantity of Cash, found means to escape out of the Prison: He was not miss'd until the next Day, when the Goaler went to carry him his Victuals, and then they found his Irons saw'd off, and one large Iron Bar in the Chimney broke in sunder, and another much bent, by which

Means, 'tis thought he got down to the Dungeon below his Prison, from whence he could get out without any Difficulty.

The said Edward Lee is but about 21 Years of Age, and has on a Sailor-like Habit, five Feet nine Inches high: If any Person apprehends him, that so he may be secured again, a Reward of FIVE POUNDS, and reasonable Charges, will be
                paid by   JOHN AYSCOUGH, Sheriff.

The New-York Gazette Revived in the Weekly Post-Boy, July 20, 1752; July 27, 1752, *The Pennsylvania Gazette*, July 23, 1752. Minor differences between the papers.

Run *away, from* ADRIAN RYERSZ, *of* Staten Island, *on the seventh of this Inst.* July; *a Negroe Man named* Hector, *about 5 Feet 6 Inches high, speaks good English, and has a Scar on his left Hand, near his little Finger, has taken with him, two Pair of Trousers and one Shirt: Whoever takes up the said Negro, and secures him, so that his Master may have him again, shall have* Forty Shillings *Reward, and all reasonable Charges*
                paid, by   ADRIAN RYERSZ.

The New-York Gazette Revived in the Weekly Post-Boy, July 27, 1752; August 3, 1752; August 17, 1752; August 24, 1752. See *The New-York Gazette Revived in the Weekly Post-Boy*, October 23, 1749.

RUN *away on Wednesday the 22d Instant* July, *from* GEORGE BURNS, *Tavern-keeper, near the* Long-Bridge, *in* New-York; *a Servant Man, named* Thomas Bubount James, *(but is called* Thomas James *for Shortness) born in* London; *a full-fac'd likely Man, about 22 Years of Age, very little Beard, and about 5 Feet 5 Inches high: Had on when he went away, an Ozenbrigs Jacket and Breeches, white Shirt and striped, a Pair of ribb'd grey Stockings, old Shoes pretty high heel'd, black Wigg, an old Felt Hat, walks as if lame, by losing a Joint of the great Toe of his right Foot, having been frost-bitten in coming from* Halifax, *last Winter. Whoever takes up and secures said Servant, so that his Master may have him again, shall have* Forty Shillings *Reward, and all reasonable Charges,*
                paid by me   GEORGE BURNS.

The New-York Mercury, July 27, 1752; August 3, 1752; August 10, 1752; August 17, 1752; August 31, 1752; September 18, 1752; September 25, 1752.

RUN *away the 2d Day of this Instant* August, *from* WILLIAM DARLINGTON, *of the City of* New-York, *Peruke-Maker; two Servant men, one named* John Owens, *a* Welshman, *but speaks good English; is a*

tall well-set Fellow, about 25 Years of Age, has a Mark on his right Underjaw, like as if it were an old Cut; had on when he went away, a brownish Cloth Coat, white Jacket, with small Metal Buttons, white Shirt, Leather Breeches, with Metal Buttons, a white Wig, has had an Issue in each Arm, is pretty fresh-colour'd, and has a large Nose: The other is also a Welshman, *named* Francis Nuttle, *of low Stature, white-looked, black Eyes, talks quick and something lisping, pretends to be a Sailor, much given to Laughing; had on a white Broadcloth Coat, Black Silk Jacket, Leather Breeches with Metal Buttons, a good Beaver-Hat, a black Wig resembling his own Hair, a Pair of new Pumps, white Shirt, but may have taken check'd Ones also; they are both Perriwig-makers, but may pretend to be Sailors. Whoever secures said Servants, or either of them, so as their Master may have them, or either of them again, shall have* FIVE POUNDS *Reward for each, if taken out of this Province, but if taken in this Province, Fifty Shillings for each, besides reasonable Charges,*
    paid by   WILLIAM DARLINGTON.

 N. B. *Since they have been gone, 'tis reported they have been seen at this City* Ferry-Stairs, *in old Jackets, with Wallets, and wanted to go over to the Jersies, so 'tis supposed they have got other Apparel. The short Fellow is bald in the Forehead, and it is also thought they have got false Passes.*
 New-York Gazette Revived in the Weekly Post-Boy, August 10, 1752.

R*UN away, from Mr.* RICHARD LYNEALL, *Fencing-Master, in* Beaver-Street, New-York, *on Wednesday the 12th Instant, an indented Servant, named* John Smith, *about 34 Years of Age, by Trade a Clock-Maker, and plays on the Fiddle, about 5 Foot 6 Inches high, sallow Complexion, talks much, and with the French Accent: Had on when he went off, an old Felt Hat old grey Wig, an old blue Camblet Coat with Gold-twist Buttons, a white Jacket, and checker'd white Fustain Breeches, white Stockings, and old Shoes, with Brass Buckles; the Finger next to his Little-finger on his Right-hand he can't bend, says he was born in* Shropshire *in* Old England. *Whoever secures said Servant, and gives Notice to said* Lyneall, *shall be well rewarded, and all reasonable Charges paid.*
 New-York Gazette Revived in the Weekly Post-Boy, August 17, 1752; September 25, 1752.

R*UN away from Doctor* WILLIAM RAND *of* Boston, *on the third Day of* July *last, an indented* German *Servant Man, named* (in German) Jean Jacob Ducard, *but in his Indenture is called* George Ducart; *about 22 Years old, is well set, of a Brown Complexion, and has brown Hair. He took with him a Suit of blue Cloaths, with Metal Buttons, a Pair of Leather Breeches, Ozenbrigs Frock and Trowsers, and Yarn Stockings. He also took from his*

Master, a Silver hilted Sword, a Cross-cut Saw, and a fine French Gun. He is supposed to be gone towards Philadelphia, but 'tis said, has been lately seen in New-York, in the Employ of a Butcher.

Whoever takes up said Servant, and secures him in Goal, shall have Three Pounds Reward, paid by the Printer or this Paper; or return'd to Boston to his Master, Three Pistoles Reward, and all reasonable Charges.

New-York Gazette Revived in the Weekly Post-Boy, September 25, 1752; October 2, 1752.

*R*UR-away, [sic] *from* Philip Livingston, *of* New-York, *on the* 28*th of* October *last, a Negro Man lately imported from* Africa. *His Hair or Wooll is curled in Looks,* [sic] *in a very remarkable Manner. He is a very likely lusty Fellow, and cannot speak a Word of English or Dutch, or any other Language but that of his own Country. He was seen last Monday, on* New-York *Island, and is now supposed to be in the Woods near* Harlem. *Whoever takes up the said Fellow, and delivers him to his said Master, shall receive* THREE POUNDS *as a Reward,*
From   PHILIP LIVINGSTON.

The New-York Mercury, November 6, 1752; New-York Gazette Revived in the Weekly Post-Boy, November 13, 1752; November 20, 1752. Minor differences between the papers, RUN and Locks are spelled correctly in the *Gazette*.

RUN away on Thursday the 14th Instant, from on board the Ship *St. Andrew*, JAMES COOPER, Master, Two Servants, one a *Frenchman*, named *Pierre Joseph Carre*, alias *Bellross*, a likely Fellow, about 30 Years of Age, middle Stature, with long bushy black Hair, and commonly wears a white Coat, but had other Cloaths, and is a very nimble active Man: The other a High *German* Woman, named *Christina Wilhelmen*, about 30 Years of Age, a thick short Woman, of a swarthy Complexion, has a very broad full Face. Whoever takes up the said Servants, and brings them to said Ship, or to the Printer hereof, shall have FORTY SHILLINGS Reward for each, and all reasonable Charges,
paid by   HENRY PATERSON.

New-York Gazette Revived in the Weekly Post-Boy, December 18, 1752; December 25, 1752.

1753

*R*UN-away *on the* 20*th Instant, from* Daniel Connar, *of the County of* Westchester, *an Irish Servant Man, named* Thomas Brown, 28 *Years of*

Age, and about five Feet high; well-set, of a ruddy Complexion, and has the mark of a small Bile on his left Cheek, near his Ear, not quite heal'd: Had on when he went away, a red and white Cap, a blue Jacket with Leather Buttons, and a white Flannel One under it, with Leather Buttons also, a Pair of old strip'd Holland Breeches, patch'd on the Knees, a Pair of old Trowsers, grey Yarn Stockings about half worn, and old Pumps cap'd and soal'd: His Hair is cut off. Whoever takes up and secures said Servant, so that his Master may have him again, shall have THREE POUNDS Reward, and all reasonable Charges
     paid by   DANIEL CONNAR.
The New-York Mercury, March 26, 1753; April 2, 1753.

RUN-away, on the 16th *of* April *last, from the subscriber, at* Fish-Kills, *in the province of* New-York, *an* Irish *Servant man, named* John Erwine, *about* 16 *years of Age,* 5 *feet three or four inches high, pretty slender, short black hair, his face much freckled, brown eyes, wants several of his teeth in his upper jaws; and can't look one straight in the face in conversation, and seems not to have the command of his head, by its frequent involuntary motions, proceeding from his bashfulness: Had on when he went away, a coarse plain blue frock with round carv'd brass buttons, a short green jacket wanting sleeves, a check shirt, and had one made of wool. He came to this county with Capt* Woodstock *last fall, and speaks good english. Whoever takes up and secures said servant, so that his master may have him again, shall receive* Forty Shillings *reward, and all reasonable charges paid by*   FRANCIS WILSON.
The New-York Mercury, May 7, 1753; May 28, 1753.

RUN-away on the 30th *ult. from on board the brig* Sea-Nymph, Henry Bethune, *master, an Irish servant boy, named* James Knowland, *about* 17 *years of age, speaks good english, and is a little battle ham'd: Had on when he went away, a black wig, check shirt, blue waistcoat, breeches and stockings, ozenbrigs trowsers double-channel pumps about half worn, and carried with him another suit of the same; and 'tis supposed he is gone towards* Philadelphia. *Whoever apprehends the abovesaid servant, and brings him to his master, on-board said vessel, lying opposite Mr.* Richard Haddon's *on the* New-Dock, *shall receive* Forty Shillings *reward, and all necessary charges paid,*
     by me,   HENRY BETHUNE.
  N. B. All Masters of Vessels and others, are hereby cautioned against concealing or carrying off said Servant, as they would avoid the Penalty of the Law.

The New-York Mercury, July 2, 1753.

R*UN-away on* MONDAY, *the* 16*th inst. from* Roger Magrah, *of this city, taylor, an* Irish *servant Man, named* Richard Fitz Morris, *a taylor by trade, about 23 years old, short and well-set, round visag'd, of a pale complexion, and came to this Country about* 8 *Weeks ago, with Capt.* Brown *from* Cork: *Had on when he went away, a light colour'd wig, coarse hat, a mouse colour's cloth coat, with blue lining, slash sleeves, and gold twist buttons much tarnish'd, black stockings, much worn, woollen shag breeches, made for strings, but had none; white shirt, and took a check one with him; and may perhaps wear a pair of French ozenbrigs trowsers. Whoever takes up and secures said servant, so as his master may have him again, shall have* Three Pounds *reward, and reasonable charges*
paid, by ROGER MAGRAH.
N. B. *Went away at the same time from* Capt. Goodwin, *a servant man, named* Michael Arrowsmith, *a barber by trade, and may pretend to be a sailor, a* Bristol-*man born; and 'tis suppos'd they are together, and may have chang'd cloaths. There is* 40s. *reward for taking of him up.*
The New-York Mercury, July 23, 1753; August 13, 1753. See *The Pennsylvania Gazette,* August 2, 1753, for Fitz Morris.

New York , July 17, 1753.
RUN away on Monday, the 16th inst. from Roger Magrah, of this city, taylor, An Irish servant Man, named Richard Fitz Morris, a taylor by trade, about 23 years old, short and well set, round visag, of a pale complexion, and came to this country about seven weeks ago with Capt. Brown from Cork: Had on when he went away, A light colour'd wig, coarse hat, mouse colour cloth coat, with blue lining, slash sleeves, and gold twist buttons, much tarnish, black stockings, much worn, woollen shag breeches, made for strings, but had none, white shirt, and took a check one with him, and may perhaps wear a pair of French ozenbrigs trowsers. Whoever takes up and secures said servant, so as his master may have him again, shall have Three Pounds reward, and reasonable charges,
paid by ROGER MAGRAH.
N. B. He may change his name and clothes, and is a county of Cary man.
The Pennsylvania Gazette, August 2, 1753. See *The New-York Mercury,* July 23, 1753.

Thirty Shillings Reward, besides all reasonable Charges, to be paid by the Subscriber, for taking up, returning, or securing of Abraham Terrel, an Apprentice, who departed from his Service on the 18th of May last, is about

18 Years of Age, middle Size, of a brown Complexion, his Hair grows nearer his Eyes than common, a bold awkward Fellow, apt to swear: Had on when he went away (tho' he left his out Cloaths behind) a Beaver Hat but little worn, a Vest of blue and white Colour lin'd with red; he was lately seen at White-Stone on Long-Island, and in Service of Benjamin Waters, and on Thursday the 26th of July last, was at New-York. All Masters of Vessels, and others, are hereby forewarned, either to harbour of carry him off, on pain of being prosecuted with the Rigour of the Law, by his Master,
JAMES MITCHELL, of Elizabeth-Town.
New-York Gazette: or, the Weekly Post-Boy, August 6, 1753.

RUN away on Sunday, the 5th inst. from William Nicholson, Ship chandler, in New York, A German servant man, named Christianus Fredericus Heisterberg, about 30 years of age, smooth faced, with a small scar between his eyes, has an innocent look, is about 5 feet 6 inches high, and walks stooping: Had on when he went away, A light colour'd cloth jacket and breeches, homespun striped jacket, check shirt, black stockings, old double channel pumps, and pewter buckles, with brass chapes and tongues. Whoever takes up said servant, and secures him, so as his master may have him again, shall have Five Pounds reward, and all reasonable charges, paid by WILLIAM NICHOLSON.
N. B. He speaks Latin, and but little English, and pretends to be a limner.
The Pennsylvania Gazette, August 16, 1753.

RUN-away on Sunday the 26th of August *last, from* John Griffin, *of* Mamoranack, Westchester *county, and province of* New-York, *a* French *servant man, named* Anthony Lavolet, 23 *years old, about 5 feet 4 inches high, of a fair complexion, strait black hair, pretty short, has a brisk lively look, can talk pretty good* English, *but may easily be discovered to be a* Frenchman: *Had on when he went away, a broad cloth coat, of a light brown colour, a brown linnen jacket, a pair of wash leather breeches, but may wear trowsers, as he carried a pair with him; and wears his hair cock'd Alamode.*
RUN-away at the same time and is supposed to be gone in company with the above-mentioned Anthony Lavolet, *from* Isaac Guion, *of* New-Rochel, *and province aforesaid, a* French *servant man, named* Glove De Boutemant, *6 feet high, a likely sprightly man, of a fair complexion, wears his own black hair, pretty long, and for the most part ty'd up, and can work a little at the cooper's trade: Had on when he went away, a blue homespun coat, with mix'd blue shalloon lining, and white metal buttons, a brown*

jacket, and buttons of the same colour, a felt hat a pair of wash leather breeches, with metal buttons, and a flap before; a pair of new worsted stockings, and good shoes; but may possibly have chang'd his stockings, as he carried two or three pairs with him. Whoever takes up and secures either of the above servants, so that their masters may have them again, shall receive 40s. reward for each, and all reasonable charges
    paid, by John Griffin, Isaac Guion.

The New-York Mercury, September 3, 1753; September 17, 1753; September 24, 1753; October 1, 1753; October 8, 1753.

       FIVE POUNDS, Reward.
RUN-away on the 28th ult. from the subscriber, an *English* servant man, named *John Nicholas*, aged about 24 years, of a middle stature, yellow complexion, and pitted a little with the small-pox, speaks good English, and took with him, a little black dog or bitch, which was accustomed to follow him: had on when he went away, a blue jacket, with a large patch on the back, a pair of fine grey cloth breeches, with a long pair of check trowsers, which he us'd to wear over them, a check shirt, a new strip'd silk handkerchief, an old felt hat, with the edge bound with tarr'd canvas, and a pair of good shoes, with large pewter buckles; he was imported hither by Capt. *Stephen Richard*, who sold him to one *Alexander Sterling*, (who follows coasting from *Maryland* and *Virginia* hither) from whom the subscriber bought him: It's thought that he is gone towards *Maryland* or *Virginia*, or ship'd himself in some vessel from this port, he being a tolerable seaman. Whoever apprehends the said servant, or secures him in any goal, so as his master may have him again, shall have FIVE POUNDS reward if taken out of this government, or FORTY SHILLINGS if taken within it, and all reasonable charges
    paid by *WILLIAM KELLY.*

The New-York Mercury, October 8, 1753; October 15, 1753; October 22, 1753; November 5, 1753.

RUN-away on the 11th Instant, from *Carden Proctor*, of this city, watch-maker, an *English* servant girl, named *Mary Wright*, about 23 years of age, thick and short, and of a brown complexion: Had on when she went away, a short strip'd cotton gown, a blue quilted petticoat, and took a brown and light coloured one with her, and may change them, the better to escape. Whoever takes up and secures the above run-away, so that her master may have her again, shall receive *THIRTY SHILLINGS* reward, and all reasonable charges,
    paid by CARDEN PROCTOR.

N. B. She was brought in here by Capt. *Grinnell,* from *London,* and lived some time with Mr. *Dyer,* in this city.

The *New-York Mercury,* October 15, 1753; October 22, 1753; October 29, 1753; November 5, 1753; November 12, 1753; November 19, 1753; November 26, 1753; December 3, 1753; December 10, 1753; December 17, 1753.

RUN-away on the 5th ultimo, from Captain Charles Ware, *of the city of* New-York, *a negro man, named* Joe, *or* Joseph, *short and well sett, about* 38 *or* 40 *years of age, pitted with the small-pox, speaks good* English, *lately came with his master from the* Bay, *and pretends to be free; he can play the bangeo: Had on when he went away, a red waistcoat, with metal buttons, an olive colour'd stuff coat, an old blue great coat and a darkish wig, or woollen cap. Whoever apprehends him, and brings him to his master Mr.* Charles Ware, *or to* Evert Byvanck, *shall have TWENTY SHILLINGS reward, and all reasonable charges*
        paid by   CHARLES WARE.

The *New-York Mercury,* November 5, 1753; November 12, 1753; November 19, 1753; December 3, 1753; December 10, 1753.

RUN-away about the 14th inst. from Patrick Moss *of* Hampstead *on* Long-Island, *a mulatto fellow named* Tom, *about 30 years old, five feet and half high, well set: Had on when he went away, a brown homespun coat and jacket, a pair of leather breeches, a check'd woollen shirt, and had with him, a white linnen shirt, a pair of linnen breeches, and two pair of stockings; he wears black curl'd hair, and had on an old beaver or castor hat, can play of the violin, and speaks good* English. *Whoever takes up and secures the said mulatto fellow, so as his master may have him again, shall have FORTY SHILLNGS as a reward, and all reasonable charges*
        paid, by me   PATRICK MOTT.

The *New-York Mercury,* November 19, 1753; November 26, 1753; December 3, 1753; December 10, 1753; December 17, 1753; December 24, 1753; December 31, 1753.

1754

Whereas Peter Sennet, *Taylor, who for some time past, resided in this city, is now absconded, and has taken from* Sarah Sappen, *a long scarlet cloak, a red taffety gown, and a black Horse hair hat, and is supposed to be gone towards* Philadelphia. *Whoever takes up and secures the said Peter Sennet,*

so that the said cloaths may be had again, shall have THIRTY SHILLINGS *Reward, paid by* SARAH SAPPEN.
The New-York Mercury, February 11, 1754.

New-York, December 11, 1753.
R UN away, on September 2d. 1753, *from his Master* Chauncey Graham, *of* Rumbout, *in* Dutchess *County, and Province* of New-York, *a likely lusty Negro Man, named* Cuff, *about* 30 *Years old, well sett, has had the Small Pox, is very black, speaks* English *pretty well, and very s[lipp], he is a plausible smooth Tongue Fellow, has with him a pair of greenish Plush Breeches about two thirds worn, and a pair of Russel ditto, [colo]ured green and yellow, two white Shirts, two pair of middling short tow Trowsers, one Pair of Thread Stockings knit in Squares, on Pair of fi[ne b]lue Wool ditto flower'd, one Diaper Cap, one white Cotton ditto, one blue [br]oad Cloth Jacket with red Lining, one blue homespun Coat lined with str[ipe]d Linsey Woolsey, or Woolen, &c. He is a strong smoaker, and supposed to [ha]ve a sham Pass.—Whoever shall take up and secure said Servant, so that his Master may have him again, shall have a* PISTOLE *Reward, and all reasonable Charges,*
paid by Chauncey Graham.
N. B. *All Masters of Vessels are forbid to carry off said Servant, as they would not incur the utmost Rigour of the Law in that Case made and provided.*
Boston Evening Post, February 18, 1754.

BROKE out of Somerset Goal, the 20th of May last, two Prisoners who were committed on Suspicion of Felony, one of them named Enoch Hannawell, 23 Years of Age, 5 Foot 8 Inches high, has a young-like Look: Had on when he went away, a blue-grey homespun Coat, Waistcoat and Breeches, Stockings almost the same Colour, and a Linnen Cap; he was born at Westchester in New-York Government. The other about 30 Years of Age, 5 Foot 7 Inches high, thick set, with black Hair and Beard, thick Legs, sour Look, named John Murphy: Had one when he went away, a light colour'd Kersey Jacket, no Coat, old bluish mix'd Stockings, old Shoes. Whoever secures them, so that he may have them again, shall have Forty Shillings Reward for each of them, and all reasonable Charges,
paid by ABRAHAM VANDORN, Sheriff.
The New-York Gazette: or, the Weekly Post-Boy, June 3, 1754.

R UN-away on the 17*th of* March *last, from* Daniel Brewster, *of* Brookhaven, *in the county of* Suffolk, *on* Long-Island, *a negro fellow*

named Jerry, *26 years old, about five feet seven inches high, well-made, can talk good english, is a sly cunning fellow, and can play well on the violin; was taken up at* Flushing, *the 15th of April, but made his escape the next day: Had on when he went away, a homspun coat, a dark colour'd kersey jacket, leather breeches, shoes, and clouded stockings, wears a cap, and has a large scar on the back of one of his hands. Whoever takes up and secures the said negro, so that his master may have him again, shall have FORTY SHILLINGS reward, and all reasonable charges paid, by* DANIEL BREWSTER.
The New-York Mercury, June 3, 1754; June 17, 1754; July 1, 1754.

RUN-away, on sunday the 9th Instant, from James McHugh, *of the city of* New-York, *a* German *servant man, named* Johann Ernst Frederick Zaensker, *5 foot 10 inches high, slender, smooth fac'd, well-looking, has remarkable long fingers, speaks bad* English, *but writes and speaks in the* French *language very well; writes a good hand in the* German *way, and can play well on the spinnet or harpsicord, being brought up as an organist: Had on when he went away, a brown knap coat, breeches of the same, blue ribb'd stockings shoes much worn, with large brass buckles. Whoever takes up and secures the said Run-away, so as his master may have him again, shall have FORTY SHILLINGS reward, and all reasonable charges paid by* JAMES McHUGH.
The New-York Mercury, June 24, 1754; July 1, 1754; July 8, 1754; July 15, 1754.

RUN away on Wednesday the 24th of May last, from James Wilson, *of the City of* New-York, *Stone-cutter. a Servant Boy, named* Alexander Pertt, *about 19 Years old, of a fair Complexion, with his own Hair, very fair and bushy; and about 5 Feet 8 Inches high. He had on when he went away, a dark drugget Coat, with Mohair Buttons, lin'd with Shalloon of the same Colour, a brown Linen Jacket, with Sleeves, and under it a thick Swan-Skin Jacket, without Sleeves; a pair of large Buck-Skin Breeches, with Buttons cover'd with Leather, one pair of light coloured Worsted Stockings, his Shoes much wore, and has one speckled Shirt of a large Check. Whoever takes up and secures said Servant, so that his Master may have him again, shall have* 40 SHILLINGS *Reward, and all reasonable Charges paid by* JAMES WILSON.
N. B. *He is of* Scotch *Extraction, and has took with him a half-worn Wool Hat.—He went off in Company with* Alexander Pert, James Robinson, *and* James M'Claren, *all Scotchmen.*
Boston Evening-Post, July 1, 1754.

R UN-away on wednesday the third inst. from Le Chevalier Deane, *of this city, a negro man, named* Jack, *a tall slim fellow, very black, and speaks good* English. *Had on when he went away, a Spanish waistcoat, one side red, and the other white, a check'd shirt, ozenbrigs trowsers, a pair of shoes, and am hat. Whoever takes up and secures the said negro, so as his master may have him again, shall have TWENTY SHILLINGS reward, and all reasonable charges*
           paid, by   Le CHEVALIER DEANE.
The New-York Mercury, July 8, 1754; July 22, 1754. See *The New-York Mercury*, August 19, 1754.

R UN-away on sunday the second day of June last, from Charles Ware *of the city of* New-York, *a high* Dutch *servant woman, named* Margrietta Plymun, *about 23 years old, short and well set, and formerly lived with Mr.* Edward Graham, *merchant in this city: Had on when she went away, a light coloured stuff gown, a blue baze jacket and pettycoat, a black quilted pettycoat, a good white apron and handkerchief, and two check'd aprons: Whoever takes up and secures said servant woman, so that her Master may have her again shall receive TWENTY SHILLINGS reward, and all reasonable charges*
           paid, by   CHARLES WARE, *or* EVERT BYVANCK.
The New-York Mercury, August 5, 1754; August 12, 1754; August 19, 1754.

R UN-away on the 27th ult. *from* Samuel Farmar, *of* New-York, *an* Irish *Servant Lad, named* Patrick Flanley, *about 19 years old, middle Stature, black Eyes, short black Hair thin fac'd, much pock broken, and has large Teeth before; his Tongue plainly discovers his Country; and when he is questioned, or would speak in haste, stammers and stutters, so that he can scarce bring out his Words, and is by Trade a Leather Breeches Maker and Skinner: Had on when he went away, a grey homespun Cloth Coat almost new, lin'd with blue Shalloon in the fore Part, and with brown Tow Cloth in the Back, Mohair Buttons, a Leather Fawn Skin Vest, Hair Outside, but almost worn off, lin'd with scarlet Shalloon, a new Ozenbrigs Shirt, a pair of purple Sheepskin Breeches, Yarn Stockings, and a Pair of old round-toe'd Pumps. Whoever takes up and secures said Servant, so that his Master may have him again, shall receive FORTY SHILLINGS Reward, and all reasonable Charges,*
           paid by   SAMUEL FARMAR.

The New-York Mercury, August 5, 1754; August 19, 1754; August 26; September 9, 1754; September 16, 1754.

RUN-away on Saturday the 27th of July, from Stephen Leach, *of this city, taylor, a* Lancashire *servant girl, named* Lydia Mary Anne Williams, *about 20 years of age, a brown complexion, much pock-broken, her face and nose is commonly much enflam'd, walks something stooping, and has a sly look: Had on, a stuff gown with red and white stripes, which has several spots of tar in it, and a remarkable one on one of the shoulders. Whoever takes up and secures said servant girl, so that her master may have her again, shall receive FORTY SHILLINGS reward, and all reasonable charges*
    paid, by   STEPHEN LEACH.
The New-York Mercury, August 12, 1754.

RUN-away on sunday the 11th instant, from *Le Chevalier Deane*, of this city, a negro man, (who formerly belonged to *William P. Smith*, Esq;) named *John*, about five feet nine inches high, pretty slender, very black, and has a grey beard; he is a sly, suttle, cunning fellow, speaks good *Spanish* and *English*, and pretends to have been a great traveller: Had on when he went away, a *Spanish* waistcoat, one side red, and the other white, a check'd shirt, ozenbrigs trowsers, a pair of shoes, and a hat. Whoever takes up and secures the said negro, so as his master may have him again, shall receive THIRTY SHILLINGS reward, and all reasonable charges
    paid, by   Le CHEVALIER DEANE.
The New-York Mercury, August 19, 1754; September 2, 1754; September 9, 1754; September 30, 1754. See *The New-York Mercury*, July 8, 1754.

RUN-away, on wednesday the 4th instant, from *Mary Wright*, of this city, an English servant girl, named *Mary Pyra*, about 5 feet 6 inches high, 22 years old, of a fair complexion, short hair, cut down in her neck: Had on when she went away, a striped blue and white cotton gown, a red and yellow silk handkerchief, a blue and white checked linnen apron, a crossbar'd stuff pettycoat, brown and yellow, a red quilt, and a black horse hair hat. Whoever takes up and secures said servant girl, so that her mistress may have her again, shall receive TWENTY SHILLINGS reward, and all reasonable charges,
    paid by   MARY WRIGHT.
 N. B. All masters of vessels are forewarned not to carry her from this place; and any person that shall entertain her, shall be prosecuted at the law directs.

The New-York Mercury, September 9, 1754.

Run-away, *from Daniel Campbell of Schenectady, and county of Albany, an Irish servant man named Nicholas Welch, a taylor by trade, 20 years old, speaks bad English, is about 5 feet 8 inches high, thin visag'd, and his nose somewhat longer than common: Had on when he went away, a new blue drugget coat, with brass buttons, a brown cloth waist coat with mohair buttons, two pair of breeches, one of of fine blue cloth, the other fly coloured, and pretty old, wears a brown wig, and 'tis thought took another along with him, two pair of worsted stockings, old shoes with steel buckles, had two check shirts and one white one, and a silk handkerchief about his neck. Whoever takes up said servant, and brings him to his Master in Schenectady, or to the high Sheriff in Albany, shall have THIRTY SHILLINGS reward, in taken in Albany; if out of Albany THREE POUNDS, and if out of the government, FIVE POUNDS, and all reasonable charges,*
    paid by   DANIEL CAMPBELL.
The New-York Mercury, October 7, 1754; October 14, 1754; October 21, 1754.

Run-away, *on the 4th inst. from* Daniel Tuthill, *of* Southold, *a light-coloured mulatto fellow, named* Caesar, *about 23 years old, pretty tall, and has a mole under his left eye: Had on when he went away, an old beaver hat, a dark coloured grey kersey great coat, a light-coloured jacket and breeches, the same of the coat, grey stockings, and old shoes. Whoever takes up and secures said slave, so that his master may have him again, shall receive* TWENTY SHILLINGS *reward, and all reasonable charges*
    paid by,   Daniel Tuthill, *or*
       Obadiah Wells, *in* New-York.
N. B. 'Tis supposed the fellow above-mentioned is either in *New-York,* or gone to the *Jersies;* therefore, all masters of vessels are forbid to carry him off, at their Peril.
The New-York Mercury, December 23, 1754; January 6, 1755; January 13, 1755; January 20, 1755.

1755

Run-away, on monday the 6th instant, from the subscriber, living near the *Meal-Market,* a mulatto boy, named *Charles*; he is a short follow, [*sic*] and very much pitted with the small-pox; has black curled hair, is left lip is out, and walks remarkably limping: Had on when he went away, a light coloured cloth coat and breeches, grey homespun stockings, and a pair of new shoes, with buckles. Whoever takes up the said boy, and delivers him to his

mistress, shall have TEN SHILLINGSS reward, if taken within the city of *New-York*; and TWENTY SHILLINGS, if taken elsewhere, and all reasonable charges,
        paid by   MARY FERRARI.
    N. B. All persons are hereby forbid to harbour the said boy; and all masters of vessels are forbid to carry him off at their peril.
    The New-York Mercury, January 13, 1755.

Run-away from Patrick Deaver, *of* Schoharie, *in the county of* Albany, *and province of* New-York, *an* Irish *servant man, named,* George Hames, *aged about* 24 *years,* 5 *feet* 6 *inches high, of a fresh sandy complexion, bold look, wants his two upper fore-teeth, has a large scar on his forehead, is much given to swearing and drinking, stoops in his walk, and is by trade a mason: Had on when he went away, a brown, or dark greyish coat, with a small black cape to it; and was seen in* Livingston*'s manor, on his way to* New-York. *Whoever takes up and secures said servant, so that his master may have him again, or acquaints Mr.* Robert Lottridge, *inn-holder in* Albany, *shall have* THREE POUNDS *reward, and all reasonable charges*
        paid, by   PATRICK DEAVERS.
    N. B. All masters of vessels are forewarn'd not to carry off the said servant, or they shall be sued on the bond of their clearance.
    The New-York Mercury, April 21, 1755; April 28, 1755; May 12, 1755; May 19, 1755.

Run-away, *on tuesday the first of* April *last, from* John Van Zandt, *a* German *servant man, named* Barnet Shilling, *a short well-set fellow,* 21 *years of age, of a fresh colour, and speaks little or no english: Had on when he went away, a blue coat, brown jacket, and a blue under one, with brown sleeves, brown yarn stockings, felt hat, with a gold button, brown hair, just trimmed. Whoever takes up and secures said servant, so that his master may have him again, shall receive* FORTY SHILLINGS *reward, and all reasonable charges*
        paid, by   JOHN VAN ZANDT.
    N. B. He run-away in company with another German *servant man belonging to* David Provoost, *of* New-York, *merchant: He is a lusty fellow, and had on a white coat, when he went away.*
    The New-York Mercury, May 12, 1755.

Run-away, *the* 19*th ult. from* Nicholas Bayard, *of the city of* New-York, *a* german *servant lad, named* Philip Barnet Kremer, *about* 5 *feet* 6 *inches*

high, 18 years of age, fat and well-set, and of a fair complexion: Had on when he went away, a snuff coloured cloth coat, with gold twist buttons, a linnen vest, leather breeches, a brown cut wig; and took with him a pair of indian shoes, and new ozenbrigs shirt. Whoever takes up and secures said servant, so that his master may have him again, shall have THREE POUNDS reward, and all charges
paid, by NICHOLAS BAYARD.
The New-York Mercury, June 2, 1755; June 16, 1755; July 7, 1755.

THIRTY POUNDS Reward.
On the 29th of April last, *Thomas Douglas*, aged about 25 years, pale complexion, freckle faced, with short red hair, enlisted with Lieutenant Richard Bayly, of Sir Peter Halkett's regiment; had been several years in this country, and, amongst others, has serv'd Col. Foreman, and Capt. M'Guire, both living on the south branch in Hampshire, and has been employed as an under trader amongst the Indians: Upon the 17th of May the above Thomas Douglas deserted from Lieutenant Bayly, and robb'd him of a considerable sum; a fusee, the maker's name mark'd on it, Timothy Hughes; and a side highland pistol, the maker's name on it, John Campbell; and also a soldier of his knapsack, and what belong'd to him. Whoever apprehends the aforesaid Thomas Douglas, and delivers him to Sir Peter Halkett, or the officer commanding his regiment, shall receive THIRTY POUNDS currency reward, and reasonable charges.
PETER HALKETT.
N. B. The above person, if taken, must be carried to the camp at Wills's-Creek, or where ever the regiment shall be, and all reasonable charges will be paid.

The New-York Mercury, June 2, 1755; June 9, 1755; June 16, 1755; June 23, 1755.

East-Chester, April 18th 1755.
R*An away the* 16*th of this Instant April, from* John Hunt *and* Israel Honeywell, *jun. Executors of* William Pinkney, *sen. late of* East-Chester, *deceased, a very likely Negro Man of a yellow Complexion, aged about* 30 *Years, is a tall slender long leg'd Fellow, born at* East-Chester *named* Methias, *a streight limb'd Fellow: Had on a good pair of leather Breeches, and very well cloathed; he carried away with him a small Bay Horse well set, about* 14 *Hands high, went a small pace, which he stole, likewise a good hunting Saddle, with a blue plush Housing, bound with russet Leather: It is suppos'd some evil minded Person has given him a pass to Travel, as a free Man. He is a very handsome Fellow, speaks good* English. *Whoever shall take up the said Negro and Horse, and bring them either to*

said Hunt *or* Honeywell, *living in* West-Chester, *or secure him in any of his Majesty's Goals, shall have* Five Pounds *New York Money Reward, and all reasonable Charges paid by us,* John Hunt.
Israel Honeywell, jun.
Boston Evening Post, June 23, 1755; June 30, 1755; July 7, 1755.

Run-away, *on friday the* 20*th ult. from* John Haydock, *of the city of* New-York, *a* German *servant girl, named,* Maria Derota, 18 *years of age, well-set, of a brown complexion, walks very fast, has a felion [sic] on her right thumb, and a bile on the same arm; and is pretty much pitted with the small-pox: Had on when she went away, a short striped purple and white gown, took a calicoe one with her, and two homespun pettycoats. Whoever takes up and secures said servant girl, so that her master may have her again, shall have* FORTY SHILLINGS *if in the province, and* THREE POUNDS, *if out of the same, as a reward, and all reasonable charges paid, by* JOHN HAYDOCK.
The New-York Mercury, June 23, 1755; June 30, 1755; July 7, 1755; July 21, 1755.

Run-away *on saturday the* 10*th of June last, from* Henry Hardcastle, *of the city of* New-York, *carver, an apprentice lad named* John Mooney, *round faced, about 5 feet 5 inches high, and pretty slender: Had on when he went away, a white flannel jacket, a cut wig, and black breeches. Whoever takes up and secures the said apprentice, so that his master may have him again, shall receive* FORTY SHILLINGS *reward, and all reasonable charges, paid by* HENRY HARDCASTLE.
N. B. *All masters of vessels and others, are forbid to carry him off, or harbour him at their peril.*
The New-York Mercury, July 7, 1755.

***R**UN-away, on sunday the* 17*th instant, from* Benjamin Blage, *of this city, distiller, a german servant girl, named* Margreta Myer; *has a large roman nose, and short curled hair: Had on when she went away, an ozenbrigs josey, a blue cloth pettycoat, and a blue quilted one, leather shoes, with white mettal buckles, and white thread stockings. Whoever takes up and secures said servant girl, so that her master may have her again, shall have* FORTY SHILLINGS *reward, and all reasonable charges paid, by* BENJAMIN BLAGE.
The New-York Mercury, August 25, 1755; September 1, 1755; September 22, 1755; September 29, 1755.

Run-away, on sunday the 24th instant, from *Thomas Dobson*, of the city of *New-York*, a servant man, named, *John Baptist Freidure*, about 5 feet 6 inches high, aged 28 years, is pitted with the small pox, has dark hair, is pretty slender, and of a pale complexion: He came from *Brabant*, in *Germany*, about twelve months ago, and speaks mostly *French*. He had on when he went away, a beaver hat cock'd in the *French* mode, a brown forrest cloth coat, an olive-coloured cloth vest, ozenbrigs shirt, tow cloth trowsers, black leather breeches, and stockings of a mixed blue colour; he understands dressing of leather: Whoever takes up said servant, and brings him to the subscriber, shall receive *three pounds* reward,
    from THOMAS DOBSON.
 The New-York Mercury, September 1, 1755; September 22, 1755; September 29, 1755; October 13, 1755.

Run-away on sunday the 21st instant, from *Edward Laight*, of the city of *New-York*, currier, an Irish servant lad, named *James Moore*, about five feet six inches high, pretty slim, of a dark brown complexion, grey eyes, and dark eye-brows: Had on when he went away, a beaver hat, and brown wig, both old; a brown cloth coat, and fustian jacket, a white shirt, a pair of half worn bukskin breeches, white thread stockings, good shoes, large square steel buckles, and speaks with something of the brogue.
 Whoever takes up said servant, and secures him, so that his master may have him again, shall have *Twenty Shillings* reward if taken in town; if out of town, *Forty Shillings*, and all reasonable charges
    paid by EDWARD LAIGHT.
 N. B. All masters of vessels, and others, are forbid to carry him off, or harbour him at their peril.
 The New-York Mercury, September 29, 1755; October 6, 1755; October 13, 1755; October 27, 1755; November 10, 1755. Last two ads show he ran away the 21st. "ultimo."

*R*UN-away, the latter end of October last, from Paul Demere, of Albany, a Welch *servant man, about 5 feet 7 inches high, well made, has thick legs, and streight black hair: He had on when he went away, a grey coat with a cape to it, and a pair of red breeches. Whoever takes up and secures said servant man, so that his master may have him again, shall receive* FORTY SHILLINGS *reward, and all reasonable charges paid in New York,*
    by JOHN LAWRENCE.
 The New-York Mercury, November 10, 1755; November 17, 1755; December 1, 1755; December 12, 1755.

Run away, about three weeks ago, from Hendrick Schinkle, *of* Claverack, *and province of* New-York, a German *servant girl, named* Elizabeth Kout, *thick, and well-set, has been in the country about three years, and can speak* French, High *and* Low-Dutch. *Had on when she went away, a mix'd russel gown, strip'd homespun pettycoat, and has been seen in this city about a week ago. Whoever takes up and secures said servant girl, so that her master may have her again, or will bring her to* John Will, *pewterer, in the* Fly, *in* New-York, *shall receive* Forty Shillings *reward, and all reasonable charges paid,*
    by   HENDRICK SCHINKLE.
 The New-York Mercury, November 17, 1755; November 24, 1755.

1756

Broke out of the city-hall of Albany, *the* 21st *of* January, 1756, Philip Shoemaker, *and* Cornelius Dally. *Philip Shoemaker is by trade a weaver, born at the* East Camp, *in the manor of* Livingston, *and is a short well set fellow, about five feet one inch high, and has a mole on his cheek, talks* High-Dutch, Low-Dutch, *and* English. *Cornelius Dally, is a cooper by trade, about five feet four inches high, lean and thin visag'd, and very mean in apparel. Whoever takes up the said persons, shall have a reward of* Ten Pounds, *or* Five Pounds *for each of them,*
    paid by me   PATRICK MAGEE, *Goaler.*
 The New-York Mercury, February 9, 1756; February 23, 1756; March 1, 1756.

Run-away from the subscriber, on monday the 19th *ultimo, a mulatto fellow, named,* Whitehaven, *a carver by trade, is thick and well-set, about 5 feet 4 inches high, black curl'd hair, and can speak both English and Dutch. Whoever takes up and secures said mulatto fellow, so that he may be had again, shall have* FORTY SHILLINGS *reward, and all reasonable charges paid, by*   SAMUEL BRIDGE.
 The New-York Mercury, February 9, 1756.

BROKE out of the City-Hall at *Albany*, the 21st of *January*, 1756, *Philip Shoemaker* and *Cornelius Derry.*—*Philip Shoemaker* is a short well-set Fellow, about 5 Feet and 1 Inch high, a Mole on his Cheek; Born in the East-Camp in the Manor of *Livingstone*; and is by Trade a Weaver; talks High-Dutch, Low-Dutch and English.—*Cornelius Derry*, a Cooper by Trade, about 5 Feet 4 inches high, lean, and thin visaged; and very mean in Apparel. Whoever takes up said Men, shall receive *Ten Pounds* Reward, or *Five Pounds* for one of them,

paid by me, *Patrick M'Gee*, Jaylor.
The Boston Weekly News-Letter, February 19, 1756; February 26, 1756.

Run *away from the subscriber, a negro man named* Jack, *he is about 5 feet, 7 inches high, speaks broken* English; *had on when he went away from Mr. Henry Ludlow's (to whom he was hired as a baker) a blue duffils great coat. Whoever secures him, shall have* Forty Shillings *reward,*
         paid by   DAVID CLARKSON.
The New-York Mercury, April 5, 1756; April 12, 1756; April 19, 1756; April 26, 1756; May 3, 1756; May 10, 1756; May 17, 1756.

DESERTERS from his Majesty's 44th Regiment, commanded by the Honourable Colonel GAGE.
....
THIRTY SHILLINGS Reward for each of the following Men, viz.
....

Jacob Cole, born in New-York, about 26 years of age, 6 feet high, remarkably strong and active, has short black hair, by trade a weaver, supposed to be now at work about North Wales; he was lately charged with sheep-stealing.
....

Whoever secures any of the above deserters, and gives notice to Capt. Samuel Hobson, of said regiment, in Philadelphia, shall receive from him the rewards offered.—Or if any of said Deserters will surrender themselves to him, or any other Officers, in fourteen days from the date hereof, they will be pardoned. Given under my hand this third day of April, 1756.   SAMUEL HOBSON.

N. B. As some of these deserters have been advertised before, there will be no further time allowed for their surrendering but what is now offered.
The Pennsylvania Gazette, April 8, 1756.

RUN-AWAY *on the 22d day of* June *last, from* Henry Allen, *of* Great-Neck, *on* Nassau-Island, *a malatto slave named* Licum, *aged about 24 years, and about 5 foot 10 inches high, well-set, walks stooping, with a down look; had on when he went away, black curled hair, a half worn felt hat, a brown tow shirt, and tow trowsers, a brown jacket with pewter buttons, and blue worsted linning, one shirt of* Irish *linnen, and a pair of half worn broad cloth breeches. Whoever takes up and secures said fellow,*

in any of his majesty's goals, so that his master may have him again, shall have Five Pounds *reward, and all reasonable charges,*
   paid by   HENRY ALLEN.
 The New-York Mercury, July 5, 1756; July 12, 1756; July 19, 1756; July 26, 1756; August 2, 1756; August 9, 1756; August 16, 1756; August 23, 1756; August 30, 1756; September 6, 1756; September 13, 1756; September 27, 1756.

THIS *is to give notice, that this day, at night the following persons broke* Dutchess County *goal, viz,* Ichabod Hubbel, Daniel Galusha, Patrick Colford, *debtors;* Samuel Jones, Simeon Toms, *and* Abijah Smith, *these three last were confined at the suit of the crown;* Ichabod Hubbel, *is about* 5 *feet,* 10 *inches high, well built, of a good ruddy complexion, a talkative, brisk man, wants part of his finger on his left hand, middle aged;* Daniel Galusha, *is about six foot high, aged about* 55 *years, well set, full-faced man, farmers by trade or occupation;* Patrick Colford, *is about* 5 *foot,* 8 *inches high, middle sized, has a remarkable mole on his right cheek, by trade a carpenter and joiner;* Samuel Jones, *a slender man, about five foot, eight inches high, pale visage, branded on both cheeks, though not very visable, and both ears cropt;* Simeon Toms, *aged about* 30 *years, a slender man, sandy complexion, very apt to swear;* Abijah Smith, *is about* 5 *foot* 9 *inches high, aged* 28 *years, a well set young man, quite fresh colour'd, very red on his cheeks. Whoever shall apprehend all, or any, of the above mentioned prisoners, and shall deliver him, or them, to* CLEAR EVERIT, *high-sheriff, of said county, his under-sheriff, or goaler, so as they may be secured, in any of his majesty's goals in* America, *notifying said sheriff thereof, shall receive the following rewards, for* Ichabod Hubbel, *the sum of* Five Pounds *reward, and for each other,* Three Pounds *reward, and all reasonable charges,*   June 5, [*sic*] 1756.
   paid by   CLEAR EVERIT, *sheriff.*
 The New-York Mercury, July 5, 1756; July 12, 1756; July 19, 1756; July 26, 1756; August 2, 1756; August 9, 1756; August 16, 1756.

            New-York, 24th July, 1756.
JOHN BELL, *a blacksmith by trade, lately a prisoner in* Orange *town goal, in* Orange *county, feloniously broke and escape out of the said goal (this being the second escape) he is a well-set man, somewhat stooping, brown complexion, hard-favoured, talks much and loud, and is a hard drinker. Any person who shall retake and secure the said* John Bell, *in any of his Majesty's goals, or shall convey him to the high-sheriff of* Orange *county,*

shall be paid the sum of FOUR POUNDS *current money of* New York, *as a reward, by*
JOSEPH SACKET, *sheriff of* Orange *county.*
The New-York Mercury, July 26, 1756; August 2, 1756; August 9, 1756; August 16, 1756.

New-York, July 26, 1756.
DESERTED *from Captain* Wettersroom, *of his majesty's* Royal Regiment of North Americans, *commanded by his Excellency the Right Hon, the Earl of* LOUDON, *&.* Charles Ross, *born in* Stirling *shire, in* Scotland, *aged 34, five feet 8 inches high; is a sailor, has dark hair and blue eyes: Had on when he went off, only a check shirt and trowsers, Also* William Smith, *born in* Pennsylvania, *aged 25, five feet 10 inches high, a labourer: Had on when he went away, a blue waistcoat and check shirt, a brown wig and leather breeches. Whoever secures the above deserters in any of his majesty's goals, or delivers him to the commander of said regiment at* New-York, *or* Philadelphia, *or the above named captain, shall receive* FIVE POUNDS *currency reward for each.*
G. C. WETTERSROOM.
The New-York Mercury, July 26, 1756; August 2, 1756; August 9, 1756; August 16, 1756; August 23, 1756.

RUN *away on Saturday the* 31st *ultimo, from the ship* Betsey, *of* London, Thomas Castleton, *master, a white lad, named* ROBERT CASTLE, *between 12 and 13 years of age, of a fair complexion, and black eyes: Had on when he went off, a green waistcoat, a worsted cap, a pair of trowsers, and black breeches under them, grey stockings, and a pair of old shoes. Whoever takes up and secures said boy, or delivers him to his said master on board, or to Mrs.* De Forest's, *shall be well rewarded for their trouble.*
The New-York Mercury, August 2, 1756; August 9, 1756; August 16, 1756; August 23, 1756.

RUN-away on the 18th day of *July* last, from *Joseph Concklin*, of *Southold*, on *Long-Island*, an indian boy named *Shadrac*k, is a stout well-made fellow, and about 16 years of age: Had on when he went away, a mixed kersey coat, the under part of the sleeves of a different colour, a flannel shirt, and a pair of deer skin breeches. Whoever takes up said boy, and secures him, so that his master may have him again, shall have FIVE DOLLARS reward, and all reasonable charges
paid, by me   *JOSEPH CONCKLIN.*

The New-York Mercury, August 9, 1756; August 16, 1756; August 23, 1756; August 30, 1756; September 6, 1756; September 13, 1756.

RUN-AWAY, *on monday the 9th day of* August *instant, from* William Mott, *of* Great-Neck, *in the township of* Hempstead, *in* Queen's *county, on* Long-Island, *a negro man slave named* Joe, *of a middle size, a thick well-set likely fellow, pretty full faced, and black; as a small round scar on his left cheek, this country born, speaks pretty good* English, *and is about* 29 *or* 30 *years of age. Had on when he went away, a grey homespun coat with pewter buttons, white linnen jacket, a speckled linnen handkerchief about his neck, a felt hat, tow trowsers, a pair of old pumps with buckles: He carried with him a jacket the same of the coat. Whoever takes up and secures the said negro fellow, so that his master may have him again, shall have* THREE POUNDS *reward, and all reasonable charges paid, by* WILLIAM MOTT.
The New-York Mercury, August 16, 1756; August 23, 1756; August 30, 1756; September 6, 1756.

RUN-away on friday the 20th inst. *August,* from *Thomas Hamersley* of the city of *New-York*, goldsmith, a negro fellow named *Duke*, about 5 feet 5 inches high, has very thick lips, and of a yellow cast, and can work at the goldsmith's business: Had on when he went away, a speckled shirt and trowsers. Whoever takes up and secures said negro fellow, so that his master may have him again, shall have TWENTY SHILLINGS reward if taken in town, if off the island FORTY SHILLINGS, and all reasonable charges paid,
by THOMAS HAMERSLY.
The New-York Mercury, August 30, 1756. See *The New-York Gazette*, February 20, 1764.

RUN *away from the subscribers, on monday the* 23d *instant August, two new negro fellows, the one a lusty well-set fellow: Had on when he went away, a light coloured fustian coat, and a pair of large duck trowsers, and took with him four white and check shirts, and has large bumps on his wrists, which looks as if they were swelled, and answers to the name of* Hector. *The other a less, thin-faced fellow: Had on when he went away, a striped flannel jacket, and a pair of leather breeches, and answers to the name of* Caesar. *They can neither talk nor understand much* English. *Whoever takes up and secures said negroes, so that their masters may have them again, shall receive* TWENTY SHILLINGS *reward, and all*

reasonable charges paid for each of them,
                by JOHN SMITH,   AND WILLIAM PEARSON.
    The New-York Mercury, August 30, 1756.

DESERTED *from the honorable lieutenant general* Otway's *regiment of foot, and Captain* Bellew's *company, now quartered at* Albany, John Philips, *aged* 42 *years,* 5 *feet* 7 *inches high, born in* Effington, *in* Devonshire, *full-faced, short brown hair, and corpulent body: He went off on sunday the* 20*th of* August*: Had on a brown coat, black plush Waistcoat, and buckskin breeches.*

Deserted also, from on board the Mary *transport, the* 18*th of* August*, lying at* New-York, *three men belonging to the said regiment, viz.* Benjamin Jackson, *full-faced, of a brown complexion, has a cast in his eyes, and a down look, is about* 5 *feet* 8 *inches high, born in England, and by trade a butcher, aged about* 33 *years.* Thomas Scot, *has a smooth comly face, and of a fair complexion, aged* 25 *years,* 5 *feet* 10 *inches high, no trade, and born in* Ireland. John Patterson, *of a swarthy complexion, full faced, aged* 26 *years,* 5 *feet* 7 *inches high, black eyes, no trade, and born in* Scotland. *Whoever apprehends any of the said deserters, and secures them in any goal on this continent, shall receive* TWENTY SHILLINGS *reward for each, besides what is allowed by act of parliament for apprehending deserters. The money to be paid by the commanding officer of said regiment at* Albany, *or by*
        Mr. Hugh Wallace,   *merchant, in* New-York.
    The New-York Mercury, September 6, 1756; September 13, 1756; September 20, 1756; September 27, 1756; October 4, 1756.

THERE *is now confined in* Casco-Bay *goal, in the province of* New-Hampshire, *for assaulting a white man, a negro fellow, who calls himself* Black Peter, *and confesses that he belonged to* New-York *about* 12 *Years ago, but said he had no master. Any person claiming said negro fellow, by applying to* Hugh Ryder, *on* Canon's Dock, *in* New-York, *may be farther informed concerning him.*
    The New-York Mercury, September 13, 1756; October 4, 1756.

                        New-York, October 8. 1756.
DESERTED *from the 40th regiment of foot, now lying at* Halifax, *in* Nova-Scotia, JAMES BIRD, *or* BOYDE, *born in* Ireland, *about* 26 *years of age,* 5 *feet* 7 *inches in statue,* [sic] *black hair a little longish, of a long visage, and had on when he went away, a blue coat, with a red waistcoat, blue*

breeches, and pepper and salt stockings. Whoever apprehends the said deserter, so as to secure him in any of his majesty's goals, and give notice thereof to any of the officers of the said regiment, shall have two guineas reward. N. B. *His right eye is much bruised.*
The New-York Mercury, October 11, 1756; October 18, 1756; November 11, 1756.

RAN-*away about the first of* October, *from* James Brown, *of* Westchester *county, in the Manor of* Cortlandt, *and Province of* New-York, *a negro man named* Dick, *but sometimes calls himself* Richard, *about 22 years old, and can read and wright: Had on when he went away, an old felt hat, red duffils great coat, leather waistcoat and breeches, a check'd woollen shirt, blue stockings, and a pair of shoes without heels; is of a middling stature, and something scarefied in the forehead; he carried with him, a light-coloured serge suit of cloths. Whoever takes up and secures said negro, so that his master may have him again, shall receive* FORTY SHILLINS *reward; and all reasonable charges paid,*
    by Jonathan Brown, *of* Rye,   *or* JAMES BROWN.
The New-York Mercury, October 25, 1756; November 1, 1756.

RUN-*away, from* Anthony Sarly, *about the 20th of August last, a negro boy named* Hector, *about 13 or 14 years of age, well-set, his under lip considerably thicker than the upper, and has a small scar on his forehead: Had on a grey bearskin jacket and ozenbrig trowsers, had neither shoes nor stockings, formerly belonged to Mrs.* Houtvat, *and was remarkable for concealing himself under stoops. For bringing him home,* THREE POUNDS *reward, and all reasonable charges will be*
    paid, by   ANTHONY SARLY.
The New-York Mercury, October 25, 1756; November 1, 1756.

New York, October 11, 1756.
TWENTY-FIVE POUNDS Reward.
A Person who called himself John Pattison, having short hair, an olive coloured thick set coat, a pair of short check trowsers, yarn stockings, and has an impediment in his speech, about 32 years old, is 5 feet 6 inches high, of slender make, and has told others he has two sisters married in or about Prince-Town; told a person on Wednesday last was se'ennight to the subscriber, as a servant, who called himself Edward Brewer, and a house-carpenter by trade, born in Ireland, pock-mark'd, well-set, black eyes, about

5 feet 4 inches high, with an old striped jacket, a check shirt, and short narrow dirty ozenbrigs trousers; and as there is great reason, from the said Pattison's informing the subscriber that he lived in East-Jersey, when in fact his place of residence is on or near-Duck creek, in the lower counties on Delaware, and his being seen lurking about the vessel that the said Brewer was on board of on the Day following, and both disappearing the same day, that they are gone off together; the subscriber will pay any Person that takes up and secures the said Edward Brewer, if out of this government, Five Pounds; and also Fifteen Pounds for taking up the said Pattison, provided such person can prove that the said Pattison was in any respect aiding or assisting the said servant in making his elopment as aforesaid.
    WILLIAM KELLY.
 N. B. The said Pattison and Brewer came to this Town from the southward, by the stage last Wednesday was se'ennight.
 The above reward will be paid by Townsend White, in Philadelphia, if the persons are brought to him.
 The Pennsylvania Gazette, November 4, 1756; November 25, 1756.

RUN-away, the 25th of *October* last, a negro man named *Franck*, about 20 years old, five feet high, and looks somewhat squinting with the left eye; he speaks *English* and *Portugueze*, and pretends to be a free man: These are to forewarn all captains of privateers and others from taking him on board, or conveying him away, if apprehended and brought to *Ever Byvanck*, 20s. reward will be paid for taking him up.
    EVERT BYVANCK.
 The New-York Mercury, November 8, 1756.

RUN-AWAY from the ship *Lord Dunlute*, Capt. *Caldwell*, JOHN CHRISTELL, about 5 feet 7 inches high, of a swarthy complexion, black eyebrows, and black eyes: Had on a buckled wig, brown coat and striped tick westcoat, old shoes, and coarse sheep's grey yarn stockings, check shirt, is a very ill-looking fellow, and looks down, can speak *Irish* of the *Ulster* dialect; when he speaks *English*, 'tis with the *Scots* accent, and arrived here from Newry a few days since. Whoever secures, or gives intelligence, so that he can be found (or if listed, whoever will inform what company he is enlisted in) shall have three pounds
    paid by JAMES THOMPSON.
 The New-York Mercury, December 27, 1756; January 3, 1757.

1757

RUN-AWAY, *on tuesday the 25th ultimo, from* Edward Earle, *of the city of New-York, felt-maker; an Irish servant man, that goes by the name of* ANDREW DAMSEL, *a weaver by trade, a thin, spare man, about five feet five inches high, wore his own hair of a light pale colour, and has a scar on his under lip: Had on when he went away, a light blue homspun coat, with a small cape, and strip'd ticken breeches.—Whoever takes up and secures said servant, so that his master may have him again, shall receive* FIVE POUNDS *reward, and all reasonable charges*
     paid by EDWARD EARLE.
 The New-York Mercury, February 14, 1757; February 21, 1757; February 28, 1757.

             Annapolis, February 21, 1757.
RUN away from this city on Thursday, the 17th instant, a servant man, named John Down, born in New-York, a blockmaker by trade, aged about 30 or 35 years, about 5 feet 8 inches high, very much freckled, red hair, and has had one of his legs broke, which is bent: Had on and took with him an old beaver hat, dark brown wig, an old dark great coat, a light broadcloth coat, with gold buttons, and lined with blue silk, a cloth of tease waistcoat, a green plush waistcoat, a pair of leather breeches, one pair of white, one pair of mixed worsted hose, and a pair of thread ditto, a pair of new pumps, two ruffled shirts over the hands, and two check shirts, some stocks, and several other sorts of wearing apparel; also a sett of blockmaker's tools, and a sett of pump tools. Whoever secures or delivers him to Mr. Enoch Story in Philadelphia, or to the subscriber, shall have THREE POUNDS reward.
     ZACHARIAH HOOD.
 The Pennsylvania Gazette, March 10, 1757; March 24, 1757.

DESERTED from New-York, the following Persons belonging to the Second Batalion of His Majesty's 62d, *or,* Royal American Regiment,
DANIEL STAGNER, of Capt. Greem's Company of Grenadiers, about 5 Feet 7 Inches high, without Shoes, 26 Years of Age, born in Germany, ruddy Complexion, round Visag'd, brown Eyes and Hair, by Occupation a Labourer, went off in his Regimental Cloths the 7th December.
 Eavan Sayers, of Capt. Greem's Company of Grenadiers, about 5 Feet 11 Inches high, without Shoes, 22 Years of Age, born in South-Britain, fair Complexion, round Visag'd, grey Eyes, and wore a Wig, went off in brown Cloths, the 30th December, by Trade a Carpenter.
 Frederick Stager, of Capt. Greem's Company of Grenadiers, 5 Feet 7 Inches high, without Shoes, 22 Years of Age, born in Germany, black

Complexion, round Visag'd, brown Eyes, and black Hair, by Trade a Minor, went off in his Regimental Cloths, the 7th January.

Lawrence Mackett, of Capt. Chombrier's late Company, 5 Feet 5 Inches and a Half high without Shoes, 38 Years of Age, born in Ireland, fair Complexion, round Visag'd, grey Eyes, and fair Hair, inlisted in Pennsylvania, went off in his Regimental Cloths, the 10th of March.

Michael Huttur, of Colonel Disseaux's, Company, about 5 Feet 4 Inches high without Shoes, 20 Years if Age, brown Complexion, black Eyes and Hair, born in Germany, by Trade a Shoemaker, went off in his Regimental Cloths, the 16th of March.

Michael Long, of Col. Disseaux's Company, 5 Feet 7 Inches high, without Shoes, 20 Years of Age, fair Complexion, round Visag'd, grey Eyes and dark Hair, born in Ireland, inlisted in Pennsylvania, went off in a blue Surtout Coat, which he stole, with Shirts, Stockings, &c. by Occupation a Labourer.

William Chapman, of Capt. Rollar's late Company, 5 Feet 5 Inches high, without Shoes, 22 Years of Age, brown Complexion, round Visag'd, grey Eyes, and brown Hair, born in South Britain, inlisted at Easton, went off the 16th of March, supposed in a blue Surtout Coat, with he stole, with Shorts, Stockings, &c. by Occupation a Labourer.

Philip Keef, of Captain Rollar's late Company, about 5 Feet 7 Inches high, without Shoes, 22 Years of Age, born in Ireland, dark Complexion, round Visag'd, brown Eyes and Hair, inlisted in the Jersies, by Occupation a Labourer, went off the 16th of March, in a blue Surtout Coat, which he stole, with Shirts, Stockings, &c.

Francis Bradly, of Col. Disseaux's Company, about 5 Feet 3 Inches high without Shoes, black Complexion, long Visag'd, black Eyes and Hair, born in Dublin, in Ireland, by Occupation a Labourer, inlisted in the Jersies, went off the 17th of March, in his Regimental Cloths.

The above three Deserters, mentioned in blue Surtout Coats, took with them also, a blue Coat, with Gold Vellum Holes, and Gold Twist Edging, which was also stolen.

Whoever takes up and secures any of the above Deserters, and gives Notice to the Commanding Officer of the Batalion, at New-York, shall receive *Forty Shillings* Reward for each. All Masters of Vessels, and others, are forbid to conceal or carry off said Deserters, at their Peril.

The New-York Gazette, March 21, 1757; April 4, 1757.

DESERTED the 18th of *March*, 1757, from Lieutenant General *Charles Otway's* regiment of foot, and major *Fletcher's* company, *William Gatefield*, born at *Bursit, Gloucestershire*; 26 years of age, 5 feet 8 inches and half high, well-made, pale-faced, fair hair, short and curled; took with

him his arms and ammunition, and is supposed to have gone off in a regimental coat of the *New-York* regiment. Deserted at the same time, from said company, *Walter Walsh*, born in the town of *Cashell*, in the county of *tipperary*, in *Ireland*, 27 years of age, 5 feet 4 inches and an half high, pitted with the small-pox, thin-visaged, dark brown hair, and in-knee'd, took with him his army and ammunition, and the same coat as the above. Deserted also, *James Barton*, of Col. *Moore*'s company, 5 feet 8 inches high, well-set, pitted with the small-pox, and of a brown complexion. Deserted likewise, *William Wright*, of Capt. *Bellew*'s company, 5 feet 9 inches high, pitted with the small-pox, of a swarthy complexion, has small black eyes, wears a dark brown cut wig, born in *Birmingham*, in *England*, 30 years old, and by trade a button-maker. Whoever takes up, and secures any of the above deserters in any goal, shall have 20*s*. sterling reward,
          paid by   Mr. *Hugh Wallace*, Merchant, in *New-York*,
The New-York Mercury, March 28, 1757; April 11, 1757; April 18, 1757; April 25, 1757.

RUN-AWAY, *on tuesday the* 19*th instant, from his master,* GEORGE SCOT, *mariner, an apprentice lad, named* GEORGE GLEN, *about* 18 *years of age,* 5 *feet* 5 *inches high, of a fair ruddy complexion: Had on when he went away a blue jacket and ozenbrigs trowsers, wears his own hair, of a light pale colour: He is by trade a silver buckle cutter. Whoever takes up and secures the said apprentice, so as his master may have him again, shall have* 40 *s. reward, and all reasonable charges*
          paid by   GEORGE SCOT, *or*
          GEORGE FOLLIOT, *merchant, in* New-York.
The New-York Mercury, April 25, 1757; May 2, 1757; May 9, 1757.

RUN AWAY *on thursday the 21st. of April instant, from* Jacob Van Schaick, *jun. a negro man, named* RICK: *He is about* 23 *years old, and had on when he went away, a pair of leather breeches, and strip'd woollen trowsers, and a shirt of the same, yellow peniston jacket, old shoes, and no hat. Whoever takes up the said negro, and brings him to* Henry Dumont, *in* New-York, *shall be reasonably rewarded for their trouble. If the said negro will return to his master, he will be pardoned.*
N. B. If he returns of his own Accord, his Faults will be forgiven.
    The New-York Mercury, April 25, 1757; May 2, 1757. See *The New-York Gazette: or, The Weekly Post-Boy*, May 16, 1757.

R*UN AWAY the* 25*th of April last, from* Thomas Robinson, *of* Brookhaven, *in the County of* Suffolk, *on* Long-Island, *a Negro Man named* Ned, *about*

23 Years of Age; he stole a Barge, and was seen last the Thursday following in the Sound, opposite to Lloyd's Neck, steering to the Westward, The Barge has lost Part of her Stern, and several of her Timbers broke. He has a crooked Knee. Had on when he went away, a new grey Kersey Coat, a new Pair of Pumps. The said Negro can both read and write, and probably has wrote himself a Pass. Whoever takes up said Negro, and secures him, so that his Master may have him again, shall have Twenty Shillings Reward, and all reasonable Charges
     paid, by THOMAS ROBINSON, jun.
The New-York Gazette: or, The Weekly Post-Boy, May 10, 1757; June 6, 1757; June 20, 1757; July 4, 1757.

RUN away from Jacob Van Schaick, jun. a Negro Man, named Rieck: Had on when he went away, Leather Breeches and striped woollen Trowsers, and a Shirt of the same; and a yellowish Peniston Vest, old Shoes, and no Hat. Whoever takes up the said Negro, and brings him to Henry Dumont, of this City, shall be reasonably rewarded for the same,
     by me, Jacob Van Schaick.
N. B. If he returns of his own Accord, his Faults will be forgiven.
The New-York Gazette: or, The Weekly Post-Boy, May 16, 1757. See The New-York Mercury, April 25, 1757.

RUN-away, from Jacobus Kip, of Kipsbay, the 9th instant, a negro man named Tom, about 5 feet 3 inches high, near 40 years old, something bendy-leg'd: Had on when he went away, a felt hat, worsted cap, ozenbrigs shirt, green napt vest, grey homspun coat, red rib'd everlasting breeches, woollen stockings, pretty good shoes, with brass buckles. Whoever takes up said negro, and secures him, so that his master may have him again, shall receive a reward of Twenty Shillings, if taken on this island; and Forty Shillings, if taken elsewhere.
The New-York Mercury, May 23, 1757; May 30, 1757; June 13, 1757; June 20, 1757.

RUN away from Moses Clement at Queensbury, a negro man, named George, about 25 years of age, he is a tall lusty fellow, and has a swelling in one knee: He had on when he went away, a new blue great coat, and a handkerchief yed [sic] about his head. Whoever takes takes up the said negro, and brings him to his master living in New-York, opposite Oswego-Market, shall have Twenty Shillings reward, and all reasonable charges,
     paid by MOSES CLEMENT.

The New-York Gazette: or, The Weekly Post-Boy, May 23, 1757; May 30, 1757; June 13, 1757; June 20, 1757; July 11, 1757.

FIVE POUNDS REWARD.
RUN *away on* Thursday *the* 28*th Inst. from* Rachael Low, *of this City, a Negro Man named* Charles, *aged about* 23 *Years, about* 5 *Feet* 6 *Inches high, pretty likely, and well set, speaks pretty good English, and some Dutch, this Country born: Had on when he went away, an Oznabrigs Shirt and Trowsers, blue Jacket without Sleeves, a Castor Hat, also took with him a blue Cloth Coat, red Vest, and red Everlasting Breeches, several Shirts and other wearing Apparel. Whoever takes up said Negro, or secures him so that his Mistress may have him again, shall receive Five POUNDS reward, and all reasonable Charges paid, by applying to the said* Rachael Low, *or to* Peter Low, *in* Broad-Street, *or to* Henry Kip, *near the* Merchants-Coffee-House.
N. B. *All Commanders of Vessels are forwarn'd to conceal or harbour said Negro.*
The New-York Gazette: or, The Weekly Post-Boy, May 30, 1757.

RUN-*away, on wednesday the* 25*th of* May *inst. from the sloop* Ranger, *Captain* Bethel, *a negro fellow named* Frank, *about* 44 *years old, and* 5 *feet* 6 *inches high: Had on when he went away, a blue duffils jacket, and ozenbrigs trowsers. Whoever takes up and secures said negro fellow, so that his master may have him again, shall receive* FORTY SHILLINGS *reward, and reasonable charges paid, by the printer hereof, or*
By Benjamin Bethel.
The New-York Mercury, May 30, 1757; June 13, 1757; June 30, 1757.
See *The New-York Gazette: or, The Weekly Post-Boy*, June 6, 1757.

RUN *away, on Wednesday Morning the* 24*th of* May *last, from the sloop* Ranger, Benjamin Bethell, *Master, a Negro Man, named* Frank, *about* 5 *Feet and* 6 *Inches high: Had on when he ran away, Ozenbrigs Shirt, speckled Shirt, Shoes and Stockings, he is Bermuda born. Whoever takes him up and brings him to the Printer, or to the said Bethell, shall have* FIVE POUNDS *reward, and all reasonable Charges,*
paid by BENJAMIN BETHELL.
The New-York Gazette: or, The Weekly Post-Boy, June 6, 1757; June 13, 1757; June 20, 1757; June 27, 1757; July 4, 1757 See *The New-York Mercury*, May 30, 1757; June 13, 1757; June 30, 1757.

RUN *away together the 26th of May last, the following Negro Men, viz, From Jacob Mersereau, living in Richmond County, Staten-Island, a Negro Man, named Jack, about 5 Feet 9 Inches high, speaks good English and Dutch, and is a Weaver by Trade: Had on when he went away, a Homspun Coat, a striped blue and white Vest, about 21 or 22 Years of Age. From Jacob Van Horne, in Bergen County, a Negro Man, named Jack, about 5 Feet 9 Inches high, and is much the Colour of an Indian: Had on when he went away, Homespun Cloaths. From Jacob Van Buskirk, of Bergen County aforesaid, a Negro Man, named Cuff, about 5 Feet 3 Inches high: Had on Homspun Cloaths, and can play upon the Fiddle. Whoever takes up and secures any or all of the said Negroes, or will deliver them to Mr. Othis Vantile, or Rem Symonson at the Ferry on Staten-Island, or to their respective Masters, shall have* FIVE POUNDS *Reward, and all reasonable Charges,   paid by the said Vantile and Symonson,*
    on their Delivery, or their Owners.
    The New-York Gazette: or, The Weekly Post-Boy, June 13, 1757; June 20, 1757; June 27, 1757; July 25, 1757.

RUN-AWAY *from* Judah Hayes, *of the city of* New-York, *a* German servant woman, *named* Dorothy Cicere, *aged about 25 years, middle stature, and pretty lusty; brown complexion, one thumb being short, speaks bad* English: *Had on when she left her said master, a stript home-spun josie and blue baize petticoat; also a red and white callicoe gown, and a josie and petticoat of the same. Whoever apprehends said servant, and secures her, so as her said master may have her again, shall have* forty shillings reward, *and reasonable charges*
    paid, by JUDAH HAYES.
    The New-York Mercury, June 27, 1757; July 4, 1757; July 18, 1757; July 25, 1757.

RUN-away; on saturday the 25th instant from John Alexander, on the city of New-York, an Irish servant lad, named William Ashton, about 15 years old, of a swarthy complexion, short black hair, talks a little on the Irish accent: Had on when he went away, a white flannel jacket, check shirt, yarn stockings, red breeches; and carried with him a grey cloth coat and breeches, a red stamped linnen waistcoat, a new felt hat, and a pair of new shoes. Whoever takes up and secures said lad, so that his master may have him again, shall receive FIVE POUNDS reward, and all reasonable charges
    paid, by   JOHN ALEXANDER.
    The New-York Mercury, June 27, 1757; July 4, 1757.

R*UN away from* Cornelius Newkerk, *a lusty Negro Man named* Claus, *about* 35 *Years old, is much Pock-broken, can read and write both* English *and* Dutch, *pretends to cypher, and has a very heavy Gate. Had on a light colour'd Silk-Camblet Coat, lin'd with Shalloon, a flower'd Stuff Waistcoat lin'd with the same as the Outside, a Wash-Leather Breeches, almost white with wearing and Washing, light colour'd Worsted Stocking, one Pair of home-spun blue Woolen Stockings; took two Pair of Shoes, big Brass Buckles, Brass Knee-Buckles; one fine Garlix Linnen Shirt, one homespun Shirt, a Beaver Hat much worn; had a Quantity of small Silver with him, and its likely will forge a Pass. Whoever takes up the said Negro, and gives Notice thereof to* Andrew Breasted, sen. *or* Isaac Ryckman, *in* New-York, *and secures him, so that his Master may have him again, shall have* THREE POUNDS *Reward, and all reasonable Charges paid by* CORNELIUS NEWKERK.

The New-York Gazette: or, The Weekly Post-Boy, July 4, 1757; July 11, 1757; August 1, 1757.

R*UN-away, from* Anthony Ten Eyck, *of the city of* New-York, a negro fellow named *Don Pedro*, lately brought in here by Captain *Dixon*, about 5 feet and a half high, a very black, well-made fellow: Had on when last seen, a red jacket and trowsers. Whoever takes up and secures said negro fellow, so that his master may have him again, shall receive FORTY SHILLINGS reward, and reasonable charges,

from   Anthony Ten Eyck.

The New-York Mercury, July 4, 1757; July 11, 1757; July 18, 1757; July 25, 1757; August 8, 1757.

D*Eserted the 9th Instant,* July, *from a recruiting Party of Capt.* Crookshank*'s Independent Company, under the Command of Lieut.* M'Keane,—James Smith, *born in* Ireland, *aged 26 Years, has short black Hair, of fresh Complexion, 5 Feet 6 Inches high, well made, and formerly lived in* Eusopus; *speaks Dutch. He went off in a new blue Jacket, Trowsers, &. Captains in Privateers, and others, are to take Notice not to carry him off, as they will be proceeded against according to Law.*

Two Pistoles, *besides what the Law allows Reward for apprehending and securing the said Deserter so that he may be had again.*

The New-York Gazette: or, The Weekly Post-Boy, July 11, 1757; July 18, 1757; July 25, 1757; August 1, 1757.

Jamaica, Long-Island, July 6, 1757.

WHereas this Day about One o'Clock in the Morning, John Jones *and* John Sighmont Fisher, *two Men inlisted in his Majesty's Service, has deserted from the House of* Joseph Howard, *Tavern-Keeper at the* Half-Way House *'twixt* Jamaica *and the* Ferry. Jones *was born in* Ireland, *aged* 35 *Years, five Feet* 7 *Inches, his Hair and Complexion dark brown, and is of a thick and crooked built: Had on a dark grey Jacket, Trowsers, and dresses like a Sailor.*—Fisher *was born in the* Dutch Countries, *speaks bad English, but High and Low Dutch he speaks extremely well, is* 5 *Feet* 3 *Inches, fair Complexion, fair short Hair shaved to the back of his Head: Had on a brown Coat, and red Jacket without Sleeves. They carried away the Landlord's Great Coat, a white Cloth Coat he used to wear in the Church, his Gun and other Things no yet missed.*

Two Pistoles Reward, besides what the Law allows for apprehending and securing the said Deserters.

The New-York Gazette: or, The Weekly Post-Boy, July 11, 1757; July 18, 1757; August 8, 1757.

R*UN-AWAY, from the subscriber, on thursday the* 14*th instant, a mulatto fellow named,* Mingo Booth, *about* 28 *years old: Had on when he went away, a speckled shirt, duck trowsers, with a bound hem at the bottom, and had the nail jam'd off one of his fingers, the day before he went away. Whoever takes up and secures said fellow, so that his master may have him again, shall receive forty shillings reward, and all reasonable charges*
    paid by   JESSE HALLOCK.

The New-York Mercury, July 18, 1757; July 25, 1757; August 8, 1757; August 22, 1757.

RUN away from the subscriber, living at *Tapan,* in the county of *Orange,* and province of *New-York,* the 10th instant, a servant man named *Henry Sniffen,* of a brown complexion, thin visaged, brown hair, and stutters very much: Had on when he went away, an ozenbrigs shirt, wide trowsers, red jacket, a pair of magasoons, [*sic*] and an old hat. RUN away with him at the same time, a negro man named *Cuffey,* a lusty well made fellow, talks bad *English,* and goes stooping: Had on when he went away, an old hat, ozenbrigs shirt, old breeches, white woollen stockings. 'Tis imagined they will change or sell their cloaths as they are both much addicted to liquor. Whoever takes up and secures both the above run-aways, so that they may be had again, shall receive FOUR POUNDS reward, or *Forty Shillings* for each of them,
    paid by   ROBERT CAMPBELL.

The New-York Mercury, July 18, 1757; July 25, 1757; August 8, 1757; August 22, 1757.

RUN-away on wednesday night, the 13th of *June* inst. from on board a sloop in the harbour of *New-York*, a negro man named *Cambridge*, and it's supposed will change his Name: Had on when he went away a brown homespun coat, with yellow buttons, ozenbrigs shirt and trowsers, blue yarn stockings, shoes almost new ty'd with leather thongs, a white linnen cap, felt hat half worn, has lost two of his fore teeth, and speaks broken English. Whoever takes up and secures said negro, so that his master may have him again, shall receive FORTY SHILLINGS reward, and all reasonable charges paid by ABRAHAM FONDA.
The New-York Mercury, July 18, 1757; July 25, 1757; August 8, 1757.

RUN away from THOMAS WILDE, *of Philipsborough, on the* 24*th of July; an Indian Fellow, named* Jacob, *aged about Twenty Years, of a middle Stature, speaks good English: Had on when he went away, a Felt Hat whipt round with yellow Silk, a brown Coat and Waistcoat, light-blue Breeches and Stockings, one Tow Shirt and one fine, a Pair of single soal'd Shoes; his Hair is off:*
Whoever secures the said Servant, so that his Master may have him again, shall have Forty-shillings *Reward, and reasonable Charges paid by* THOMAS WILDE.
N. B. All Masters of Vessels, and Others, are forbid to carry off the said Fellow, at their Peril.
The New-York Gazette: or, The Weekly Post-Boy, August 1, 1757; August 8, 1757; August 22, 1757; August 29, 1757.

ANTHONY MULLAR, deserted yesterday Evening from his Majesty's Service. Had on a green camblet coat and waistcoat, narrow silver laced hat, and black leather breeches, aged 27 years, 5 feet 7 inches high, black complexion, black short hair tied behind, born in Germany, speaks bad English. SIX POUNDS reward for taking up and securing him,
paid by Lieut. MacAulay,
at mr. Edward Graham's, Mert. New-York.
The New-York Gazette: or, The Weekly Post-Boy, August 1, 1757.

RUN-AWAY, *on saturday the 23d ultimo, from* Francis Van Dyck, *of the city of* New York, *cutler, An apprentice lad, named* John Annow, *aged about* 15 *years, near five foot high, and pock-broken: Had on when he went*

away, *a blue camblet coat, a pair of ozenbrigs trowsers, and a wool hat, and has light coloured hair. Whoever takes up and secures said apprentice lad, so that his master may have him again, shall receive thirty shillings reward, and all reasonable charges*
paid, by FRANCIS VAN DYCK.
The New-York Mercury, August 1, 1757; August 8, 1757.

R*UN away from the Subscriber, living in* New-York, *a* High-Dutch *Servant Man, named* Mordecai Hart, *of about* 27 *Years of Age, about* 5 *Feet* 6 *Inches high, of a sandy Complexion, but wares an old brown Wig, his fore Teeth much rotten, pretends to be a great Scholar, can talk* French *and* Spanish, Greek *and* Hebrew, *has some Time been a Pedler in* York *Government; he had on when he went away, a light-colour'd homespun Jacket, coarse white Shirt and Trowsers, a Pair of new Shoes, with large Nails in the Heels, a Pair of coarse brown Stockings, a half-worn Felt Hat: He has been seen Yesterday, going over King's Bridge, and is supposed to be gone to* Rhode-Island. *Whoever takes up and secures said Servant, and brings him to* York, *or any other Goal, so as his Master may know, shall have* Forty-shillings *Reward, and reasonable Charges paid by the Subscribers. His Master may be found at* Barnet Borhite's, *Lime-burner, in* Montgomery's-street, New-York.
Jno. Dougherty, Barnet Borhite. N. York, Aug. 6th, 1757.
The New-York Gazette: or, The Weekly Post-Boy, August 8, 1757; August 29, 1757; September 12, 1757; September 27, 1757.

Albany, August 20, 1757.
RUN away from his Master, *John Bourk*, aged about 20. He is a short stout young Man, of 5 Feet 2 Inches high, of a fair Complexion, and particularly bald on his Head. Had on when he went off, a Pigtail'd Wig, a sharp cock'd Hat, a blue Coat and Breeches; and was formerly Servant to Capt. Willcox, in Philadelphia, who sold him to Mr. Johnson, Paymaster to His Majesty's Forces in North-America: He was afterwards sold to Mr. Farrel, Sutler to the 35th Regiment at Albany, to whom he belongs. This is to forewarn all Persons whatsoever, not to entertain him, as they will be prosecuted as the Law directs. And whoever apprehends him, or causes him to be taken, so that he may be brought to his said Master John Farrell, shall receive FIVE PISTOLES for their Trouble, and no Questions asked.
The New-York Gazette: or, The Weekly Post-Boy, August 29, 1757.

New-York, August 23, 1757.
RUN or let away this Day from *Lane's Ferry*, a Negro Man named Scipio, who had his Hands pinioned behind him, and belonged to the sloop

Margaret and Mary, John Baddeley, Master, of So. Carolina. His Name is *Scipio*, about five feet five Inches high, of a middling Bulk, a little Pockmarkt, his Mouth extends more than common, has a large Bump over one of his Eyes, his Buttocks pretty well marked with the Lash, speaks pretty good English, though somewhat thick; was born at St. Christophers, and says he understands something of the Cooper's Business. Had on when he went away, an Oznabrigs Frock and Trowsers, and a Worsted Cap. Whoever takes up the said Negro, and delivers him to Capt. John Schermerhorn, in New-York, shall receive Three Pounds reward, and all reasonable Charges. Any person that harbours or carries the said Negro off in any Boat, Barque or Vessel whatever, may depend on being prosecuted to the utmost Rigour of the Law.

The New-York Gazette: or, The Weekly Post-Boy, August 29, 1757; September 12, 1757; September 19, 1757; September 26, 1757; October 3, 1757. See *The New-York Mercury*, August 29, 1757.

RUN, *or let away, on the* 23d *inst. from* Lane's-Ferry, *a negro man named* Scipio, *who had his arms pinioned behind him, and belonged to the sloop* Margaret *and* Mary, John Baddeley, *master, of* South-Carolina; *he is about 5 feet 5 inches high, pretty well set, and a little pock mark'd: His mouth extends more than common; had a large bump over one of his eyes, his buttocks well mark'd with the lash, speaks tolerable* English, *though somewhat thick; was born at* St. Kitts, *and pretends to something of the cooper's business: Had on when he went away, an ozenbrig frock and trowsers, and a worsted cap. Whoever takes up the said negro, and delivers him to Captain* John Schermerhorn, *in* New-York, *shall receive* THREE POUNDS *reward, and all reasonable charges. And any person that harbours or carries the said negro off, in any boat, barque or vessel whatsoever, may depend on being prosecuted to the utmost rigour of the law.*

The New-York Mercury, August 29, 1757; September 5, 1757; September 12, 1757; September 19, 1757. See *The New-York Gazette: or, The Weekly Post-Boy*, August 29, 1757.

RUN away, on the 2d of September Instant, from the Subscriber, living in Salem, in Salem County, West New Jersey, an Irish Servant Man, named Edward Rubie, says he was bred in the City of Cork, and that he served his Time in Philadelphia to a Ship carpenter; pretends to know something of sawing with a Whip saw; has been a Privateering, and in the Army, and says he was discharged at Cape-Breton; has a Brother living in the Highlands of York, where he taught School some Time, from whence he

ran away, and came to Piles-Grove, in Salem County, where he also taught School for some Time, then ran away from his Bail, took a Horse with him, forged an Order on Capt. Cox in Philadelphia, got some Money, was advertised in the Pennsylvania Gazette, and put in York Goal, over Sasquehanna, from whence he was brought and put into Salem Goal, and there begin and indebted Servant for three Years from February 1757: Had on when he went away a light colour'd Bearskin Jacket, two check Shirts, and Trowsers of the same, new Shoes, with large Brass Buckles, and a half worn Beaver Hat. He is a middle aged Man, about five Feet five Inches high, has short curled Hair, much Pock-marked, and can play on the Flute; it is supposed he is gone towards New-York. Whoever takes up and secures said Servant in any Goal, so as his Master may have him again, shall have Two Pistoles Reward, and reasonable Charges,
   paid by GABRIEL COPPNER.
The Pennsylvania Gazette, September 8, 1757; September 29, 1757.

RUN-AWAY from the subscriber, Isaac Brush, on *Huntington*, on *Long-Island*, on the 20th of *August*, a negro man, named NED; had on a kersey jacket, wide trowsers, and an old felt hat; his right knee bends much in.— Whoever takes up and secures said fellow, so that his master may have him again, shall have forty shillings reward, and all reasonable charges paid,
   By me *ISAAC BRUSH.*
The New-York Mercury, September 12, 1757; September 26, 1757.

           New-York, September 19, 1757.
RUN away on the 28th Day of August last, from John Lasher, *of this City, an Apprentice Lad, named Michael Pheffer, about 17 Years old, of short stature, round visag'd, black Eyes, and stoops in his Walk. Had on when he went off, a Bearskin Coat, green Jacket, a short striped Pair of Trowsers, black stockings, wore pumps, and had a Cap, and a Castor Hat. He is a Cordwainer by Trade, and was seen to go through* Rye *on Tuesday last, enquiring his Way to Horse-Neck, and is supposed designs for* Rhode-Island.
  Whoever takes up and secures the said Apprentice, so that his Master may have him again, shall have two Pistoles Reward, and reasonable Charges, paid by JOHN LASHER.
  The New-York Gazette: or, The Weekly Post-Boy, September 19, 1757; September 26, 1757; October 3, 1757; October 10, 1757; October 17, 1757.

RUN away from Caleb Ferris, *of* East-Chester, *a Negro Man slave called* Joe, *aged about* 25 *Years. He is a lusty well set Fellow every Way, about five Feet Ten Inches high, thick shoulder'd, full round Face, speaks altogether English, his Hair is frizzled, being half Indian. He has been a Voyage privateering, and is a great Fiddler. He has a large Leg and broad Foot, and commonly wears Sailors Habit. He was born at* Westchester, *and sometimes pretends to be free.*

Whoever takes up the above described Slave, and will secure him so that his Master may have him again, shall have Six *Pounds Reward,*
         paid by   CALEB FERRIS.

N. B. *I hereby forbid and forwarn all Persons dealing with, entertaining or employing him, under any Pretence whatsoever. And I further forwarn al Masters of Vessels, Captains of Privateers, from taking him on board, or carrying him off under any Pretence whatsoever.*
September 25, 1757.   C. F.

The New-York Gazette: or, The Weekly Post-Boy, October 3, 1757; October 10, 1757; October 17, 1757; November 7, 1757; November 21, 1757; November 28, 1757.

DESERTED from the three following companies of the XXVth regiment of foot, the 12th instant, October, 1757, at *Fort-Edward.*

Major's Company. *JAMES PENNY,* 20 *years of age,* 5 *feet,* 6 *inches and* 3/4ths *high, short brown hair, fresh complexion, round fac'd, speaks very slow, born at* Grannarn *in the county of* Antrim, Ireland; *by trade a shoemaker: Had on his regimental coat and hat, a brown linen vest and breeches. Inlisted in* York-Town, *province of* Pennsylvania.

Capt. Fletcher's Company, JOHN O'BRIEN, *aged* 32 *years, well made, sandy complexion, thin fac'd, pock mark'd, with some freckles, by trade a shoemaker, born in the city of* Kilkenny, *in Ireland: Had on his regimental coat and hat, and linen breeches. Inlisted in* Carlisle Town *in the province of* Pennsylvania.

Capt. Bellew's Company. HUGH COLQUHOON, *aged* 30 *years, i feet* 11 *inches high, well made, a little stoop in his shoulders, of a fresh complexion, short dark brown hair, which curl'd at the ends, and mark'd with the small-pox; born at* Strabane, *in Ireland: Went off with his arms, regimental coat and hat, linen vest and breeches. Inlisted at* Lancaster, *in the province of* Pennsylvania, *was then a pedlar, but formerly an Indian trader.*

Ditto. RICHARD ALAGON, *aged* 36 *Years, born in* Old-England, 5 *feet* 9 *inches high, well made, of a sandy complexion, large eye brows, an impediment in his speech, by trade a pettiaugar-man: Went off with his arms*, had on his regimental coat, with a blue surtout over it, a dark grey vest and drawers.

Twenty-Shillings, sterling, reward will be given for apprehending each of said deserters,
                  by HENRY FLETCHER, Major.

The New-York Mercury, October 31, 1757; November 7, 1757; November 14, 1757.

Description of Deserters from His Majesty's 44th Regiment of Foot, whereof Major-General James Abercrombie, in Commander;

JOhn Shirley, 5 *feet* 8 *inches and* 3 *qrs. high;* 28 *years of age; born in Ireland, by calling a labourer, black complexion, black hair, strong made, mark'd with the Small-Pox*,

James Margison, 5 *feet* 9 *inches high*, 23 *years of age, born in England; by calling a labourer, fair complexion, fair hair, roun'd fac'd, a cut on his nose*.

Richard Prichard, 5 *feet* 5 *inches high*, 30 *years of age, born in Ireland, by calling a labourer, black complexion, black hair, round fac'd, well made*,

Jacob Haily, 5 *Feet* 7 *Inches high*, 27 *Years of Age, born in Germany, by calling a labourer, swarthy complexion, Black round fac'd, well made*.

Richard Livesly, 5 *feet* 7 *inches high*, 29 *years of age, born in England, by trade a weaver, fair complexion, short fair hair, thin fac'd, mark'd with the small-pox*.

Marmaduke Smith, 5 *feet* 6 *Inches high*, 21 *years of age, born in England, by trade a gun-smith, swarthy complexion, black hair, round fac'd, well made*.

Thomas Smith, 5 *feet* 7 *inches high*, 28 *years of age, born in Scotland, by calling a labourer, black complexion. black hair, thin fac'd, speaks French and Dutch*.

James Sheringham, 5 *feet* 6 *inches high*, 36 *years of age, born in England, by calling a school-master, black complexion, black hair, round fac'd, well made*.

The New-York Gazette: or, The Weekly Post-Boy, November 7, 1757; November 14, 1757.

RAN-away on the 8th of *November*, Inst. from James Carrol, of this City, a Negro Wench, aged about five or six and thirty Years old, or thereabouts, called Rose, formerly called Grace, talks but indifferent English. Had on when she went away, a striped Homespun Joseph, an old red Cloth Peticoat, white Yarn Stockings, and old Shoes, lame in one of her Legs, with a

broken Shin. Whoever secures the said Wench, shall have Twenty shillings Reward, and all reasonable Charges
    paid by JAMES CARROLL. November 21, 1757.
The New-York Gazette: or, The Weekly Post-Boy, November 21, 1757; November 28, 1757; December 5, 1757.

R*UN-away on saturday the* 19*th instant, from the sloop SWAN, lying in the harbor of* New-York; *an apprentice named* Samuel Haynes, *about seventeen years of age, fair complexion'd: Had on when he went away, a grey fear-nothing jacket, oznabrigs shirt and trowsers, yarn stockings, half worn shoes, a mill'd cap, and an indifferent hat; whoever brings the said* Samuel Haynes, *to the subscriber, shall have a PISTOLE reward,*
    From JACOB VAN WAGENEN.
N. B. *All masters of vessels are forbid to carry him off at their Peril.*
The New-York Mercury, November 28, 1757; December 5, 1757.

THOMAS FOINE, matross, in capt. Godwin's company of the royal regiment of artillery, deserted Sept. 27, 1757, from on board the Morning-star, in her passage from New-York to Albany: had on when he deserted, his regimental coat, waistcoat, hat, and blue shag breeches; is an ignorant man, and subject to fits; 5 feet 9 inches high; born at Maidstone in Kent; a labourer.—CHARLES AYRES, matross in the above company, born at Reading in Berkshire, 5 feet 9 inches high, well set, chews tobacco between his under lip and teeth, and talks very fast: Had on when he deserted an old narrow gold lac'd hat, regimental coat, blue waistcoat and blue shag breeches.—Likewise deserted from the detachment of the royal artillery, at New-York, commanded by lieut. Thomas Collins; JOHN BEAR, matross, born in Germany: Had on when he went away, a plain blue coat, red waistcoat, and buckskin breeches; speaks very slow; 5 feet 9 inches high, and pitted with the small pox; a carpenter.

  Any person who shall apprehend and secure the above deserters, and give notice thereof to the commanding officer of the royal artillery at Albany, or to lieut. Thos. Collins, of the said corps at New-York, shall receive 20 shillings sterling for each.
  The New-York Mercury, November 28, 1757; *The New-York Gazette: or Weekly Post-Boy,* December 5, 1757; December 12, 1757. Minor differences between the papers.

DESERTED from His Majesty's 22d Regiment of Foot, commanded by Col. EDWARD WHITMORE, and said Company at *Albany* Camp, September 12;

FRANCIS HAYS, 23 *years of age, 5 feet 6 inches and 3 quarters high, short black hair, round visag'd; by trade a stocking-weaver; born in Deceiworth, Leicestershire; went off in his regimental cloaths.*

ROBERT BOYLE, *of Capt.* French's *company, October 17th;* 25 *years of age, 5 feet 8 inches and a half high, brown hair, full fac'd, dark complexion, born in the north of Ireland, a good Latin scholar, and writes a good hand; went off in his regimentals.*

GEORGE MAXWELL, *of Capt.* Zobel's *company, from the hospital at* Albany, *September 4th;* 22 *years of age, 5 feet 7 inches and a half high, black hair, dark brown complexion; a Labourer; born in Glasgow, in Scotland; went off in the regimentals of the Royal-Scots.*

Whoever shall secure any of the above deserters in any goal, or guard, and give notice to the commanding-officer of the regiment, at *Schenectady*, shall, for each deserter so secured, receive TWENTY SHILLINGS sterling, reward.

The New-York Gazette: or Weekly Post-Boy, December 5, 1757; December 12, 1757; December 26, 1757.

RUN-*away about the 7th of 8th of this Instant* December, *from the Subscriber, the three following Servaent Men, viz.* Richard Welch, *by Trade a Tanner, about 45 Years old, and of a dark Complexion:* John Douglass, 23 *Years old, and a Wheel-wright by Trade: And* Patrick Machree, *a Labourer. They are Strangers in the Country. Whoever takes up and secures the above run-away, shall have* THREE POUNDS *Reward, or* TWENTY SHILLINGS *for each, and all reasonable Charges,*
    paid by ROBERT ALEXANDER.
The New-York Mercury, December 19, 1757; December 26, 1757.

New-York, Decemb, 24*th.* 1757.
RAn away last Night from the Sloop *Walter, William Price,* Master, lying in *Rotten Row*; a Negro Man, named *Ralph*; about 25 Years of Age, about 5 Feet 4 Inches high, smooth-faced, thick Lipped; speaks good *English*. Had on, when he went away, a blue Jacket, and a Drab colour'd Do. and a white Flannel Waistcoat, a grey pair of Stockings, much wore, with a pair of black worsted one's under them. Any Person taking up the said Negro, and bringing him to Mr. *Waddel Cunningham,* Merchant in *New-York,* or to Mr. *Alexander Hamilton,* Merchant in *Philadelphia,* shall receive 5 Dollars Reward, and reasonable Charges.

The New-York Gazette, December 26, 1757; January 3, 1758; January 9, 1758; January 16, 1758; *The New-York Mercury*, December 26, 1757; January 2, 1758; January 9, 1758; January 16, 1758; January 21, 1758; January 30, 1758. Minor differences between the papers. See *The New-York Gazette: or, The Weekly Post-Boy*, December 18, 1758.

1758

DEserted from his Majesty's ship *Scarborough*, at *New-York*, the undermentioned Men; THOMAS GLAND, a native of Ireland, aged upwards of 40 years; about 5 feet 5 inches and a-half high; pale fac'd, with dark brown Hair,—Had on his Regimental Cloaths; (red Cloth, with blue-and-white Worsted Large) stoops much, and formerly kept a Suttler's shop on the Ohio; and can speak an Indian Language.

JOHN M'EVEY, Aged about 28 Years, 5 Feet 5 Inches high; pale fac'd; with dark brown Hair: Had on his Regimental Cloths, and a scolop'd Gold lac'd Hat, and other Clothes of his Master's. The Marine Officers. [the above-mentioned are Marines]

JOHN BURN, a seaman, a Native of Ireland; aged about 26 Years, 5 Feet 6 Inches high, fair Complexion, a little freckled with red Hair, Had on a blue Jacket, Trowsers, and a Worsted Cap.

Whoever apprehends them, or any other Seaman or Marine, stragling, or attempting to desert from the said ship, shall, on their bringing them onboard her, receive as a Reward, Three-Pounds Ten shillings, Currency of New-York, for each Person.

The New-York Gazette: or, The Weekly Post-Boy, January 2, 1758; January 9, 1758; January 16, 1758; January 30, 1758.

RUN away from the subscriber, about 5 weeks ago, a young Negro Man called Hannibal, *alias,* Sandy, *born at* Barbados: *He is about 5 Feet high, thick liped, with big Cheeks; has a down Look, and a Scar under his Chin; and talks much: Had on when he went away, a brown short jacket with Hooks and Eyes, and a striped double-breasted do. Leather Breeches, and an old Hat and Wig. Whoever secures the said Negro, so that his Master may have him again, shall have* FORTY SHILLINGS *Reward, and all reasonable Charges*

        paid, by   Cornelius Tiebout.

The New-York Mercury, January 2, 1758; January 16, 1758; January 21, 1758; January 30, 1758. See *The New-York Gazette: or, The Weekly Post-Boy*, January 9, 1758.

R*UN away from the subscriber, about five weeks ago, a young negro man called* Hanibal, *alias* Sandy, *born at* Barbados: *He is about 5 feet long, thick lip'd, and thick cheek'd, has a down look, and a scar under his chin; a fellow that will talk much; had on when he went away, a brown short jacket with hooks and eyes, a black and white strip'd homespun double-breasted jacket, a leather pair of breeches, and an old wigg and hat. Whoever secures the said negro, so that his master may have him again, shall have forty shillings reward, and all reasonable charges*
                    paid, by   Cornelius Tiebout.
    The New-York Gazette: or, The Weekly Post-Boy, January 9, 1758; January 16, 1758; January 30, 1758; February 6, 1758. See *The New-York Mercury*, January 2, 1758.

DESERTED from *Perth-Amboy*, the 20th Instant, JOHN MAGEE, from the Company of Rangers whereof HEZEKIAH DUNN, is Captain. Said MAGEE is about 5 Feet high, 45 Years of Age, red fac'd, had on when he went away Provincial Clothing, *viz.* A grey lapell'd Waistcoat, and an under green Jacket, a Leather Cap, and Buck-skin Breeches. Whoever will secure said Deserter, and lodge him in any Goal, or bring him to said Regiment, now at *Albany*, shall have 20*S.* sterling Reward,
                  paid by   Capt. HEZEKIAH DUNN.
    The New-York Gazette: or, The Weekly Post-Boy, January 9, 1758; January 16, 1758.

RUN away on Sunday last the 29th *January*, from Philip Duley, living in Bloomandall, on York-Island, a Negro Man, called Tom, late the Property of Jacobus Kip, about four Foot, [sic] five Inches high, well set, speaks broken English; had on, when he went away, a brown Cloath Coat, Buttons of the same, Buckskin Breeches, grey Yarn Stockins, Brass Buckles in his Shoes, a good Felt Hat, with a Pewter Button on it, work'd like a Hair Button: Whoever takes up the same Negro, and secures him so that his Master may have him again, shall have twenty Shillings Reward, and all reasonable Charges
                  by   PHILIP DULEY.
    The New-York Gazette: or, The Weekly Post-Boy, February 6, 1758; February 13, 1758; February 20, 1758.

DEserted from a recruting Party of the 22d Regiment under the Command of Ensign Brereton, at Brunswick, the 19th Day of Jan. 1758.

John Wooters, Corporal in said Regiment; he is of a dark Complexion, broad, well made, 32 Years of Age, five Feet, eight Inches high, wore a silver-laced Hat, a regimental Coat, with a white Shoulder-knot, a spotted Flannel Waistcoat, and scarlet Britches: Whoever apprehends the said John Wooters, shall upon Application to the Commanding Officer of said Regiment, at Schennectidy, or Ensign Brereton, at Philadelphia, receive the Sum of twenty Shillings Reward, besides what is allowed by Act of Parliament.

The New-York Gazette: or, The Weekly Post-Boy, February 13, 1758; February 20, 1758; February 27, 1758; March 6, 1758; March 20, 1758.

DESERTED *from Ensign* Swetanham*'s Recruiting Party, belonging to his Majesty's 17th Regiment, commanded by Colonel* JOHN FORBES, David Carter, *formerly a Drummer in the* New-York Regiment. *Whoever takes up the said Deserter and gives Notice to the Colonel in* New-York, *or the commanding Officer at* Albany, *shall have* 20s. *Reward, above what is allowed by Act of Parliament. If said Deserter will surrender himself in 14 Days from the Date hereof, to Colonel* FORBES, *he will be pardoned. February* 13, 1758.

The New-York Mercury, February 13, 1758; March 6, 1758.

Albany, *January* 26, 1758.
RUN away from *Edmond Matthews*, of Livingston's-Manor, about the Beginning of this Month, a Negroe Fellow of about 20 Years of Age, has a smooth Face, and is very thick built; had on when he went away, a Bearskin Coat, white Cloth Breeches, a blue-and-white strip'd Holland shirt, and a grey Pair of stockings.—It is tho't he will try to go out in some of the Privateers.—Whoever takes up and secures the said Negro, so that his Master may have him again, or gives Notice to James Carrol, of the City of New-York, Butcher, or at the New-Printing-Office, in Beaver-street, shall have 40s. Reward, and all Charges paid.

The New-York Gazette: or, The Weekly Post-Boy, February 27, 1758; March 6, 1758; March 20, 1758; March 27, 1758.

RUN away on the 27th of February last, from Richard Kip, of this City, an Apprentice Lad, named, Stephen Palmer, about 19 years and 5 months old, is about 5 feet 6 Inches high, has a round Visage, black Eyes, and black Hair: Had on when he went off, a green Jacket, with a green under One, blue Breeches, grey stockings, large Pewter Buckles, Castor Hat, has a check shirt, is a cooper by trade, and is seen every Day in the City. Those

apprehending the said Apprentice so that his Master may have him again, shall have three Dollars Reward, and Charges
    paid by Richard Kip.
The New-York Gazette: or, The Weekly Post-Boy, March 13, 1758; March 20, 1758; March 27, 1758; April 3, 1758; April 10, 1758.

RUN-*away from the Snow* Four-Cantons, Christopher Heysham, *Master, an Apprentice Lad named* Patrick Randle: *He is a short set Fellow, about* 22 *Years of Age; and had served some Time to the Blacksmith's Trade: Had on when he went away, a Pair of new Shoes, a brown Coat, a white Flannel Jacket, with Hooks and Eyes, for Buttons.* Whoever takes up and secures said Patrick Randle, *so that his Master may have him again, shall receive* Twenty Shillings *Reward,*
    paid by CHRISTOPHER HEYSHAM.
The New-York Mercury, March 13, 1758; March 20, 1758; March 27, 1758.

DESERTED from the New-York Provincial Forces, under the Command of Francis Moore, of this City, THOMAS GAFFE, a Smith by Trade, about 25 Years old, of a fair Complexion, and 5 Foot 9 Inches high. Whoever takes up the said deserter, and brings him to Col. DeLancey shall have £. 3 Reward, clear of all Charges,
    from FRANCIS MOORE.
The New-York Mercury, March 27, 1758; April 3, 1758; April 10, 1758.

DEserted from Col. *John St. Clair's* Company, of the 4th Battalion of the *Royal-American* Regiment, at *New-York,* in their Regimentals, on Sunday the 19th of March, 1758; JACOB LINK, aged 20 Years, 5 Feet 3 Inches high, of a fresh smooth Complexion, brown Hair, blue Eyes, round-visag'd, born in the Province of *Pennsylvania,* and Parish of *Ganistoga,* and listed at *York-Town,* by Captain Bosomworth. FRANCIS REFFLY, aged 21 Years, 5 Feet 9 Inches high, fresh Complexion, brown Hair, brown Eyes, long Visage, born in the Province of *Pennsylvania,* at *Germantown*; listed by Ensign *M'Cleur,* at *Donegal,* 1757. Whoever apprehends the said Deserters, shall receive *Twenty Shillings Sterling* Reward for each of them,
    from Captain *Rutherford,* of the said Battalion.
The New-York Mercury, March 27, 1758; April 3, 1758; *The New-York Gazette: or, The Weekly Post-Boy,* April 3, 1758. Minor differences between the papers.

Flatbush, on Long-Island, March 21, 1758.
DEserted from the Third Battalion of the *Royal American* REGIMENT, and in Capt. *William Leteler's* Company, JOHN CAMPBELL, private Soldier, about 22 Years of Age, 5 Feet 6 Inches and a Half high, light brown Hair, some-what mark'd with the Small-Pox: He had on when he deserted, a drabb-colour'd Waistcoat, and a Pair of Leather Breeches. Whoever takes up the said Deserter, and delivers him to Lieutenant *Herring,* Adjutant to the Fourth Battalion of the Royal American Regiment, or secures him in any of his Majesty's Goals, shall have TWENTY SHILLINGS Reward.
The New-York Gazette: or, The Weekly Post-Boy, March 27, 1758; April 3, 1758.

Deserted in their Regimentals;
FRom Major John Rutherford's *Company, of the 4th Battalion of* Royal Americans, *on* Monday *the 20th Instant;* CHRISTENAR STEVENAR, *aged* 28 *Years,* 5 *Feet* 7 *Inches high, round Visage, blue Eyes, fair hair, born in* Hanover, *and inlisted in* Pennsylvania, *by Capt.* Schlosser.
Deserted the same Day from said Company;
PETER LANGSTON, *aged* 22 *Years,* 5 *Feet* 8 *Inches high, round Visage, blue Eyes, brown Hair, born in* Hamburgh, *and inlisted in* New-York.—Whoever apprehends said Deserters, shall receive *Twenty Shillings* Sterling for each of them,
from Capt. *Rutherford,* of said Battalion.
The New-York Gazette: or, The Weekly Post-Boy, April 3, 1758.

DESERTED from Captain Moore's Company, belonging to one of the New-York Provincial Regiments, the following Persons, viz.
John Belcher, born in New-Jersey, 22 Years of Age, of a brown Complexion, and 5 Feet 10 Inches high.
John Fitzgerald, born in Ireland, 26 Years of Age, of a brown Complexion, 5 Feet 4 Inches high.
Thomas Wiel, born in London, 24 Years of Age, of a fair Complexion, 5 Feet 6 Inches high.
William Watens, born in Liverpool, 19 Years of Age, of a brown Complexion, 5 Feet 2 Inches high.
Roger Connely, born in Ireland, 27 Years of Age, of a brown Complexion, 5 Feet 8 Inches high.
Edmund Murphey, born in Ireland, 20 Years of Age, of a fair Complexion, 5 Feet 7 Inches high.
Whoever takes up and secures any of the above Deserters, and will convey them safe to New-York, shall, besides having all reasonable

Charges paid, receive Twenty Shillings Reward for each,
    paid by GERARD G. BEEKMAN.
The New-York Mercury, May 8, 1758; May 15, 1758; May 22, 1758.
See *The New-York Gazette: or, The Weekly Post-Boy*, July 17, 1758.

                New-York, May 8, 1758.
RUN *away on* Monday *last, from* John Hastier, *of this City, Goldsmith, a lusty well-set Negro Man, named* Jasper, *about* 5 *Feet* 6 *Inches high, speaks good English, and understands the Silversmith's Trade. Had on when he went away, a brown Forest Cloth Coat with flat Pewter Buttons, blue Waistcoat, with same Sort of Buttons; a Leather Breeches, with the like Buttons, old Hat, brown Yarn Stockings, and old Shoes. Whoever takes up the said Negroe, and secures him so that his Master may have him again, shall have* FOUR POUNDS *Reward, and all reasonable Charge*
    paid by JOHN HASTIER.
The New-York Gazette: or, The Weekly Post-Boy, May 15, 1758; May 22, 1758; June 5, 1758.

DESERTED from Captain Jaquet's Company of Battoe Men, at Albany, the 2d Instant, James Stinson, and Michael M'Gill, both born in Ireland, and enlisted at New-Castle on Delaware; the former a Labourer, a slim tall Man, of a pale Complexion, and was married to a hump-backed Woman called Margery Curry: Had on when he deserted, a half-worn brown homespun Jacket, and a white one under it, and Buckskin Breeches. Michael M'Gill is of a middle Size, and black Hair: Had on when he deserted, a Lead-coloured Jacket; as they both had Blankets and Guns, some Provisions, and a Canoe, 'tis imagined they are gone by Water, and will endeavour for Pennsylvania. Whoever takes up and secures said Deserters, so that their Captain may have them again, shall have Thirty Shillings Reward, and all reasonable Charges
    paid, by JOSEPH JAQUET.
The New-York Mercury, May 15, 1758; May 29, 1758.

DESERTED from his Majesty's Sloop Hunter, Captain John Laforey, Commander, Michael Purcel, Seaman, aged 22 Years, 5 Feet ten Inches high, born at Kilkenny, in Ireland, by trade a House-Carpenter; of a brown Complexion, and wears a Wig: Had on when he went away, a Flannell Jacket, with red Flowers. Whoever apprehends him, shall be intitled to the Reward of THREE POUNDS Sterling, according to his Majesty's

Proclamation for taking up straggling Seamen;
to be paid by   Mr. White
Agent-Victualler at New-York.
The New-York Mercury, May 15, 1758; May 22, 1758; May 29, 1758.

RUN-away, from on board the Duke of Cumberland, Transport, Thomas Hurry, Master, on the Night of the 18th Instant, two Apprentice Lads; one named John Paul, 21 Years of Age, is pitted with the Small-pox, has an Impediment in his Speech, about 5 Feet 7 Inches high, and one of his Legs is much larger than the other: Had on when he went away, a grey Wig, a round Hat, and Seamen's Cloathing. The other is called Samuel Polly, aged 19 Years, short, and well-set, round visaged, wears a Wig, and had on Seamen's Cloaths. Whoever brings one, or both of them, to Thomas Hurry, Master of the Ship above mentioned, at Capt. Barns's Wharf, shall have a Reward of Four Pounds for each. If the above Apprentices are taken up, after Capt. Hurry sails, and are brought to Capt. Jefferies, in New-York, they shall have Forty Shillings Reward for each.
The New-York Mercury, May 22, 1758; May 29, 1758.

RUN-*away, from the Subscriber, living at Flushing, on Long-Island, the 16th Instant, a Negro Man Slave, called York, born in the Province of New York, speaks very fluent good English, 28 Years old, about 5 Feet 8 Inches high, well-made, and very black: It's likely he may pretend to be free, and have a Pass, as he attempted to get one some Time ago: He is a spry active, complaisant Fellow, and the most ingenious with his Tongue and Hands, of any of his Colour; can make Bridles and Saddles, and understands the taning Business, and farming, very well. 'Tis impossible to describe his Cloathing, as he never kept them at his Master's. Who ever takes up and secure the above Negro Man, so that his Master may have him again, shall receive (if take up out of the Province) Forty Shillings Reward, and all reasonable Charges paid; and if within the Province,* Twenty Shillings, *and all reasonable Charges,*
paid, by   WILLIAM KEESE.
The New-York Mercury, May 22, 1758; June 5, 1758; June 12, 1758; June 19, 1758.

RUN-away from Judah Hays, of the City of New-York, Merchant, on Tuesday the 23d inst. a German Servant Woman, named Dorothy Sifirey, a well-set, middle sized Woman, about 30 Years old, and speaks very bad English: Had on when she went away, a striped linsey Josey, and a blue

Half-thick Pettycoat: She has also taken with her, a striped Bird's-Eye Stuff Gown, one red Calico, do. a red Calico Josey and Pettycoat, and sundry other wearing Apparel. She is remarkable, by having lost one Part of her right Thumb, so that the Nail is quite grown over the Flesh. Whoever takes up said Servant, and brings her to her Master, or secures her, so that her Master may have her again, shall receive FORTY SHILLINGS Reward, and all reasonable Charges,
    paid by JUDAH HAYS.
  N. B. All Masters of Vessels, and other Persons, are forbid to carry off said Servant; and any Person harbouring her may depend they will be prosecuted to the utmost Rigour of the Law.
  The New-York Mercury, May 29, 1758; June 12, 1758; June 19, 1758; June 26, 1758; July 10, 1758; August 21, 1758; August 28, 1758; September 4, 1758; September 11, 1758; September 18, 1758; September 25, 1758; October 2, 1758. See *Pennsylvania Journal and Weekly Advertiser*, June 22, 1758, and *The New-York Mercury*, September 4, 1758.

RUN-away, on the 20th of May last, from the Subscriber, living at North-Castle, County of Westchester, and Province of New-York, an Indian Servant Wench named Kate, is about 15 Years of Age, of a middling Size, and her Hair a little curl'd: Had an Iron Collar about her Neck, when she went away, and in all Probability will equip herself in Men's Cloths, and inlist for a Soldier, as she did once before, but was detected. She had a Pass for one Week, to look for a Master. Whoever takes up and secures said Wench, so that her Master may have her again, shall receive TWENTY SHILLINGS Reward,
    paid by AARON FORMAN, Jun.
  The New-York Mercury, June 12, 1758; June 19, 1758; June 26, 1758; July 3, 1758; July 10, 1758.

WHEREAS James Roseman, late a Soldier in the 27th Regiment, and discharged for having Convulsion Fits, went away from the Service of Capt. Ormsby of the 35th Regiment, on Tuesday the 6th of June Instant, without any Sort of Provocation. This is therefore to caution all Persons whatsoever, not to entertain said Roseman, as they will be prosecuted as the Law directs. Said Roseman is about 24 Years of Age, five Feet eight Inches high, wears a plain Soldier's Coat, with Buff Lapells and Cuffs, a short green Waistcoat, and Soldier's Breeches, was born at Killishandria, in the North of Ireland, and speaks with a strong Irish Accent.
  The New-York Mercury, June 12, 1758; June 19, 1758; June 26, 1758.

New-York, May 26, 1758.

RUN-away from JUDAH HAYS, of the City of New-York, Merchant, on Tuesday Night last, a German Servant Woman, named Dorathy Sifirey, a well-set, middle sized Woman, about 30 Years old, and speaks very bad English: Had on when she went away, a striped linsey Josey, and a blue Half-thick Pettycoat: She has also taken with her, a striped Bird's-Eye Stuff Gown, one red Calico, do. a red Calico Josey and Pettycoat, and sundry other wearing Apperel. She is remarkable, by having lost one Part of her right Thumb, so that the Nail is quite grown over the Flesh. Whoever takes up said Servant, and brings her to her Master, or secures her, so that her Master may have her again, shall receive Forty Shillings Reward, and all reasonable Charges,
        paid by   JUDAH HAYS.

N. B. All Masters of Vessels, and other Persons, are forbid to carry off said Servant; and any Person harbouring her may depend they will be prosecuted to the utmost Rigour of the Law.

The Pennsylvania Journal and Weekly Advertiser, June 22, 1758; June 29, 1758; July 6, 1758. See *The New-York Mercury*, May 29, 1758, and *The New-York Mercury*, September 4, 1758.

RUN-away, on Friday the 23d Instant, from on board the Snow Prince of Wales, now in this Harbour, an indented Servant Man named John Brown, a Shoe-maker by Trade, about 19 Years of Age, of a swarthy Complexion, and has black streight Hair: Had on when he went away, two short blue Jackets, and a Pair of green Cloth Breeches. Whoever takes up and secures said Servant, and will bring him to Waddell Cunningham, Merchant, in New-York, shall have 20s. Reward, and all reasonable Charges paid.

The New-York Mercury, June 26, 1758; July 3, 1758; July 17, 1758.

RUN-*away, from the subscriber, living in New-York, next Door to Mr. Livingston's sugar-house, on friday the 23d instant, a negro woman named Cuba, about 25 years of age, born in the west-indies, and speaks broken English: Had on when she went away, a homspun josey and pettycoat, and a white apron; has a wen or swelling in the middle of her stomach. Took along with her, a child, a girl of about twenty months old, named Peggy. Twenty shillings reward for whoever takes her up and secures her, so that her master may have her again, with all reasonable charges,*
        paid by   WILLIAM ALBRESPY.

The New-York Mercury, June 26, 1758.

New-York, June 30, 1758.

RUN away last Night from *John Leversage*, of this City, Boat-builder; an Apprentice named *Thomas Hodge*, six Foot high, of a smooth thin Visage, pale Complexion, about 23 Years old: Had on a red Jacket, lined with white Flannel, a new Pair of Oznabrigs Trowsers, wore a black Wig, had a Castor Hat, blue Worsted stockings, half-worn shoes, and a Pair of Square Copper Buckles, with a Check Shirt. Whoever takes up and secures the said Apprentice, so that his Master may have him again, shall have *Thirty shillings* Reward, and reasonable Charges

   paid by JOHN LEVERSAGE.

N. B. All Masters of Vessels are forbid to carry him off, as they must answer the Contrary according to Law.

The New-York Gazette: or, the Weekly Post-Boy, July 3, 1758; July 10, 1758; July 31, 1758.

RUN away from Messrs. *Thomas* and *Benjamin Forsey*, Merchants, in *Albany*; A Negro Man that is known by the Name of *Phoenix*: Had on when he went away, a strip'd Flannel Waistcoat, Oznabrigs shirt, ditto Trowsers, 5 Feet 9 Inches high, speaks good English, a little lame, one Ancle somewhat larger than the other, a Speck on one Eye, and about Twenty-six Years of Age. Whoever takes up said Negro, and brings him to his Masters, or sends them Intelligence so that he may be had, shall receive Forty shillings Reward, and all reasonable Charges paid.

  Thomas & Benjamin Forsey. *Albany, June* 29, 1758.

The New-York Gazette: or, the Weekly Post-Boy, July 3, 1758; July 17, 1758; July 24, 1758. See *The Boston Gazette, and Country Journal*, July 10, 1758.

New-York, June 22, 1758.

R*UN away on* Monday *last, from his Master,* Stephen Leech, *of this City, an Apprentice Lad named* James Springer, *wears short black Hair, is full fac'd, is pitted with the Small-Pox, is very lusty and fat, and something Knock-knee'd: He had on when he went away, a light-colour'd Cloth Coat, Check Shirt, an Olive-colour'd Thickset Pair of Breeches, brown Worsted Stockings and no Hat. Whoever takes up and secures the said Runaway, shall have* 40s. *Reward, and Charges*

   paid, by me STEPHEN LEECH.

Note, Twenty shillings Reward if put into Goal, so that he may be had again.

The New-York Gazette: or, the Weekly Post-Boy, July 3, 1758; July 10, 1758.

Jamaica, on Long-Island, June 29, 1758.

RUN away on the 24th of this Instant June, from Jamaica, on Long-Island, James Thorn, *by Trade a Carpenter, of about 5 Feet 8 Inches high, has red Hair, and a freckled sandy Complexion, and has the Scar of a Musket-Ball on the Outside of his right Leg. Had on when he went away a blue Great Coat, a red Plush Waistcoat, without Sleeves: Has an ordinary Hat with a narrow Silver Lace on it; and a cut Wig. He carry'd away with him a well-set, lively, brisk Chesnut-colour'd Horse, six Years old, of about 13 Hands and 2 or 3 Inches high, with a small Star on his Forehead, and a Snip on his Nose, having a black Mane and Tail; with a Brand, which the Subscriber cannot recollect: He also took a Russel Hunting Sadle, having a green Worsted Girt, without Housing Whoever takes up and secures that Person above described, so that he may be bro't to Justice, and the Horse at the same Time recovered, so that the Owner may have him again, shall have* FORTY SHILLINGS *Reward for both Man and Horse, or* TWENTY SHILLINGS *for either; and reasonable Charges*
    paid by, Caleb Whealton.
  The New-York Gazette: or, the Weekly Post-Boy, July 3, 1758; July 17, 1758; July 24, 1758; July 31, 1758.

New-York, June 9, 1758.
RUN away from Mr. Thomas Scramshire, *of this City, the 5th Instant, a Mulattoe Wench, named Fanny, about 5 Feet 4 Inches high, and talks good English; has a smiling Countenance, and black curl'd Hair, full breasted; she had on when she went away, a small black silk Hat, a long cross barr'd blue and white Stuff Gown, and an old red quilted Petticoat, with a Bundle of several other Things, the Contents as yet unknown.—Whoever takes up, secures, or discovers where the said* Fanny *is harboured, so that her Master may have her again, shall receive 20s. Reward, if taken up in Town, and 40s. if cross'd any Ferry; with all other reasonable Charges which may arise thereupon: And whoever shall offer to harbour or entertain the said Wench, may depend upon being prosecuted to the utmost Rigour of the Law, by me,* Thomas Scramshair.
  The New-York Gazette: or, the Weekly Post-Boy, July 3, 1758.

RUN-away from *Thomas* and *Benjamin Forsey*, Merchants, in *Albany*, A Negro Man that did formerly belong to Dr. *Donald Cummings* of *Casco-Bay*, known by the Name of *Phenix*, five Feet nine Inches high, about 26 Years of Age, speaks good English; Had on when he went away, a stript Flannel Waistcoat, Oznabrigs shirt, ditto Trowsers, a little lame, one Ancle a little larger than the other, with a Speck in one Eye. Whoever shall take up said Negro, and bring him to his Masters, or sends them Intelligence so that he may be had, shall receive *Five Dollars*, and all reasonable Charges paid by Thomas & Benjamin Forsey.

Albany, June 29, 1758.

The Boston Gazette, and Country Journal, July 10, 1758; July 17, 1758; July 24, 1758. See *The New-York Gazette: or, the Weekly Post-Boy*, July 3, 1758.

RUN-away from Judah Hays, of the City of New-York, Merchant, on Tuesday the 23d of May, a German Servant Woman, named Dorothy Sifirey, a well-set, middle sized Woman, about 30 Years old, and speaks very bad English: Had on when she went away, a striped Linsey Josey, and a blue Half-thick Pettycoat: She has also taken with her, a striped Bird's-Eye Stuff Gown, one red Calico, ditto; a red Calico Josey and Pettycoat, and sundry other wearing Apparel. She is remarkable, by having lost one Part of her right Thumb, so that the Nail is quite grown over the Flesh. Whoever takes up said Servant, and brings her to her Master, so that her Master may have her again, shall receive SIX POUNDS Reward, and all reasonable Charges,
paid by   JUDAH HAYS.

N. B. All Masters of Vessels, and other Persons, are forbid to carry off said Servant.

The New-York Mercury, July 10, 1758; July 17, 1758; August 21, 1758; August 28, 1758; September 4, 1758; September 11, 1758; September 18, 1758; September 25, 1758; October 2, 1758. See *The New-York Mercury*, June 27, 1757, *The New-York Mercury*, May 29, 1758, and *Pennsylvania Journal and Weekly Advertiser*, June 22, 1758.

New-York, July 13, 1758.

*R*UN *away from* Stephen Leech, *on Wednesday last, a Servant Lad named* Timothy Sheels, *born at* Larne *in* Ireland, *about 5 Feet eight Inches high, of a pale Complexion, and is much pitted with the Small-pox, had on when he went away, a Snuff coloured Coat, a light grey Pair of Breeches, and wears his own Hair, somewhat short; and when he laughs is remarkable for shutting his Eyes.*

RUN-AWAY also at the same Time a Scotch Servant lad named James Morrison, *of a fair Complexion, has a down sly Look, and is about five Feet three Inches high, had on when he went away, a double Breast green Jacket lin'd with white Flannel, and a strip'd one under it, a Pair of black Everlasting Breeches, and a Pair of black worsted Stockings rib'd. Whoever takes up the above Servants and delivers them to their Master in*

New-York, *shall have ten Pounds Reward for both, and five Pounds for either.*
    N. B. *The above Lads were Taylors by Trade. All Masters of Vessels, or others are forbid to carry them off.*
    The New-York Gazette: or, the Weekly Post-Boy, July 17, 1758; July 24, 1758. See *The New-York Mercury,* July 17, 1758.

Albany, June 25, 1758.

DESERTED *out of the Guard-room in* Albany, *the* 22d *of* June, THOMAS M'KENZIE, *Soldier in the* 42d *Regiment, and in Captain* Gardon Graham's *Company, he went off in his Regimentals, about five Foot four Inches and an half high, aged* 20; *well made, round visage, darkish brown Hair, black Eyes, and a little marked with the small Pox, fluent in the English Tongue, and by Trade a Carpenter; he brought with him a Woman, whom he calls his Wife. Whosoever takes up the said Deserter, and secures him in any of his Majesty's Goals, shall have forty Shillings Reward.*
    The New-York Gazette: or, the Weekly Post-Boy, July 17, 1758; July 24, 1758; August 7, 1758.

New-York, July 11, 1758.

DESERTED *from the several undermentioned Companies belonging to the* New-York *Regiment the following Persons, viz.*
    JOHN EVANS, of M'Ever's, 5 *Feet* 6 *inches high,* 25 *Years old, brown Complexion, Carpenter by Trade, black Hair, born in* England. —— *JEFFERIES, of* Moore's, 5 *Feet* 11 *Inches,* 24 *Years old, dark Complexion, JOHN SUTTON, of ditto,* 5 *Feet* 8 *Inches,* 26 *Years old, fair, born in* Virginia. *HENRY WALTON, of ditto,* 6 *Feet high,* 35 *Years old, dark Complexion, born in* Pennsylvania. *HENRY COOLY, of ditto,* 5 *Feet* 6, 29 *Years old, an Indian, born in* New-York. *JOHN FITZGERALD, of ditto,* 5 *Feet* 9, 29 *Years old, dark Complexion, born in the* Jerseys. *JOHN BELCHER, of ditto,* 5 *Feet* 8, 30 *Years old, dark Complexion, born in the Jerseys. JOHN COLLIN, of ditto,* 5 *Feet* 7, 23 *Years old, fair Complexion, born in* Ireland. *JOHN GERBUS, of ditto,* 5 *Feet* 8, 29 *Years old, fair Complexion, born in* Germany. *JOHN CONWAY, of ditto,* 5 *Feet* 7, 28 *Years old, fair Complexion, born in* Ireland. *JOHN M'ALSTER, of ditto,* 5 *Feet* 6, 25 *Years old, born in* Ireland. *THOMAS KERNON, of ditto,* 5 *Feet* 8, *born in* Ireland.—*All the foregoing inlisted at* New-York.
    JOHN MILLER, sen. *of ditto,* 5 *Feet* 6, *brown Complexion, born in* England, *inlisted at* Philadelphia. *GABRIEL DICKER, of* Smith's *Company.* Robert Robertson, *of* Potter's; Amos Wilkot *of ditto.* Thomas Pay, *of* Steyversant's. Zepheria Cornie, *of ditto.*

Daniel Mills *of* Pauling's, *Labourer,* 5 *Feet* 10, *aged* 51, *ruddy, Connecticut born.* Henry Stevens *of* Johnston's; Joseph Decker, *of* Van Veight's; Joseph Duddon, *of ditto,* Rufford Ridden, *of ditto,* Abraham Rice, *of* Yate's.

Andrew Rice *of ditto.* Deliverance Conkling, *of* Verplank's, 5 *Feet* 1-2, 25 *Years old, ruddy, born at* Philadelphia; Benjamin Akerly, *of ditto,* 5 Feet 9, *aged* 23, *ruddy,* Long-Island *born.* John Williams *of ditto,* 5 *Feet* 10, 34 *Years old, black Hair,* Long-Island *born;* William Johnson, *of ditto,* 5 *Feet* 10, *aged* 24, *red Hair,* Long-Island *born*; William Brock, *of ditto,* 5 Feet 8, *aged* 34, *brown Hair.* —— Downs, *of* Lockwood's, *Mariner,* 5 *Feet* 4 1-2, *aged* 23, *ruddy Complexion, sandy Hair.* Abraham Mezgan, *of* Bradgsley's, 5 *Feet* 11, *Blacksmith, born in the* Jerseys; John Yates *of ditto,* 6 *Feet high, aged* 24, *a Sadler*; Robert Beslee, *of ditto,* 5 *Feet* 10, *a Farmer born in* Boston; John Eliot, *of ditto,* 5 *Feet* 7, *a Farmer born in* Connecticut. Henry Miller, *of* Seely's 5 *Feet* 4, *aged* 24, *of a red Complexion, born in* Germany, i*nlisted at* Ulster County: John Conner, *of* Hawlet's, 5 *Feet* 6, 30 *Years old, fair Complexion, born in* Ireland, *inlisted in* Queens-County: Hamilton Blackwood, *of ditto,* 5 *Feet* 9, *aged* 29, *Mariner, of a brown Complexion, born in* Ireland, *inlisted in* Queens-County. William Steel, *of ditto,* 5 *Feet* 6 *Inches high,* 25 *Years old, dark Complexion, born in* England, *and inlisted at* Queens-County.

Whoever apprehends any, or either of the aforesaid Deserters, and gives proper Notice to the Commissioners in New-York, shall have forty Shillings Reward.

The New-York Gazette: or, The Weekly Post-Boy, July 17, 1758. See *The New-York Mercury,* May 8, 1758.

New-York, July 16, 1758.
RUN away on the 10th of this inst. July, from James Swan, of this city, pilot; a negro man named York, about 5 feet 8 inches high, of a slender make, talks pretty good English, is a good cook, can play on the violin, and shave, and dress wigs;—He had on when he went away, old shoes, and carv'd silver buckles, blue and red worsted plush breeches, old trowsers, check'd shirt, a blue jacket, a small-cropt hat, with yellow worsted binding round it; and steps pretty long: He formerly belonged to Lawrence Lawrance, [*sic*] of this city, merchant.—Whoever takes up the said negro, and secures him so that his master may have him again, shall have, if within the city, 20s. if between it and King's Bridge, 30s. and 40s. in farther, and all reasonable charges,

paid by   JAMES SWAN.

All masters of vessels, and captains of privateers, are forwarned from carrying him to sea, or harbouring him on board their vessels, as they may expect to answer it at their peril.

The New-York Gazette: or, the Weekly Post-Boy, July 17, 1758; July 24, 1758; July 31, 1758; August 7, 1758; August 21, 1758.

RUN-away from Stephen Leach, on Wednesday last, a Servant Lad named, Timothy Sheels, born at Larne, in Ireland, about 5 Feet 8 Inches high, of a pale Complexion, and is much pitted with the Small-pox: Had on when he went away, a Snuff coloured Coat, a light Grey Breeches, and his own Hair; when he laughs he is remarkable for shutting his Eyes.

Run-away also at the same Time, a Scotch Servant lad named James Morrison, of a fair Complexion, has a down sly Look, and is about five Feet three Inches high: Had on when he went away, a double-breasted Jacket, with strip'd Flannel one under it; black Everlasting Breeches, and a Pair of black ribb'd worsted Stockings. Whoever takes up the above Servants and delivers them to the said Stephen Leach, of this City, Taylor, shall have Ten Pounds Reward for both, and Five Pounds for either. All Masters of Vessels, or others are forbid to carry them off.

The New-York Mercury, July 17, 1758. See *The New-York Gazette: or, the Weekly Post-Boy*, July 17, 1758.

RUN away from IDE MYER, *on the 29th of June last, a Molato Wench, named* Ohnech, *but goes by the Name of* Hannah, *and pretends to be free: She is about* 4 *Feet* 4 *Inches high, and* 28 *Years of Age, is well set, and speaks both* English *and* Dutch *very well, and had on when she went away a home spun Josey and a Petticoat, a blue short Cloak and white Cap; whoever takes up and secures said Wench, so that her Master may have her again, shall receive Twenty Shillings reward, and all reasonable Charges paid by me* IDE MYER.

N. B. *All Persons are forewarned to entertaiher, [sic] and as Masters of Vessels to carry her off, at their Peril.*

The New-York Gazette: or, the Weekly Post-Boy, July 17, 1758; July 31, 1758; August , 1758. See *The New-York Mercury*, July 24, 1758.

New-York, July 11, 1758.

DESERTED from the several undermentioned Companies, belonging to the New-York *Regiment the following Persons, viz.*

of Moore's.... *HENRY COOLY, of ditto,* 5 *Feet* 6, 29 *Years old, an Indian, born in* New-York.

Benjamin Akerly, *of ditto,* 5 *Feet* 10, 34 *Years old,* Long-Island *born.* John Williams, *of ditto,* 5 *Feet* 10, 34 *Years old, black Hair,* Long Island *born;*

William Johnson, *of ditto, 5 Feet* 10, *aged* 24, *red Hair*, Long-Island *born*....

Whoever apprehends any, or either of the aforesaid Deserters, and gives proper Notice to the Commissioners in New-York, shall have forty Shillings Reward.
The New-York Gazette: or, The Weekly Post-Boy, July 24, 1758.

RUN-away at different times from on board the Tartar Frigate, captain Hugh M'Quoid, commander, since her arrival in New-York, William Phillips, Patrick Kelly, Arthur Neill, John Hurst, Ambrose Osborne, John Chadwicke, Samuel Cooper, William Jones, Thomas Gardner, Bartholomew Kennedy, Robert Murphy, John M'Girr, John Christian, David Gilliland, John Orr, James Hutchinson, John Kennedy, Robert Bell, Arthur Gill, James Collier, James Searisbrook, Christopher Johnston, David M'Cullough and Thomas Raffele, servants to said ship: Whoever takes up and secures any of said servants, so as they may be had again, shall receive a reward of TWENTY SHILLINGS for each, from the above Hugh M'Quoid or Greg and Cunningham, Merchants, in New-York. All persons are cautioned not to entertain them, as they will be prosecuted according to law.
The New-York Mercury, July 24, 1758; August 14, 1758; August 21, 1758.

RUN-away from IDE MYER, on the 29th of June last, a Mulatto Wench named Ohnech, but goes by the Name of Hannah, and pretends to be free; she is about 4 Feet 4 Inches high, is well set, and speaks both Dutch and English very well: Had on when she went away a Home-spun Josey and Pettycoat, a blue short Cloak, and white Cap. Whoever takes up and secures said Wench, so that her Master may have her again shall receive Twenty Shillings reward, and all reasonable Charges
     paid by me IDE MYER.
The New-York Mercury, July 24, 1758; July 31, 1758; August 14, 1758; August 21, 1758. See*The New-York Gazette: or, the Weekly Post-Boy*, July 17, 1758.

RUN-*away, from Hobuck, Yesterday, a Negro Fellow named Robin, lusty, and well-made, talks good Dutch and English, smooth-skin'd, and is about 36 Years old. He took with him, two Coats, one of Ratteen, with red Lining, and the other of Bearskin. All Masters of Vessels are hereby fore-warned not to carry him off at their Peril. Whoever takes up, and secures said Run away, in New-York, so that he may be had again, shall have* Twenty

Shillings *Reward; if out of the City,* Forty Shillings *Reward, and all reasonable Charges,*
    paid by Samuel Bayard, *living opposite the Old-English Church.*
The New-York Mercury, July 31, 1758; August 7, 1758; August 14, 1758; August 21, 1758.

RUN away on Wednesday *last from* Elizabeth Carpder, *of this City, a likely young Negro fellow about* 18 *or* 20 *Years old, named* Venture, *of a middle Size. He had but light cloathing on when he went away.*

Whoever takes up and secures the said Negro fellow, so that his Mistress may have him again, shall have Twenty Shillings reward if taken up in this City; and Forty Shillings if taken out of it, with all reasonable Charges paid,
    By ELIZABETH CARPENTER.
The New-York Gazette: or, the Weekly Post-Boy, August 7, 1758; August 14, 1758; August 21, 1758. See *Weyman's New-York Gazette,* April 30, 1759, *Weyman's New-York Gazette,* July 16, 1759, and *The New-York Gazette,* September 29, 1760; *The New York Gazette,* July 13, 1761.

DESERTED from Captain Boughey Skey, *of His Majesty's* 43d. *Regiment, recruiting at* NEW-YORK, THOMAS PAGE, *born in* Deal, *in* Old-England, *is by Trade a Peruke-Maker, aged* 33 *Years, round fac'd, grey Eyes, something corpulent: Had on when he deserted, a Regimental Hat with a white Worsted Lace, an old grey Wigg, a brown Coat with Metal Buttons, a stamp'd Linen Waistcoat, and Leather Breeches; hath resided for some Time past at* Hampstead, *on* Long-Island.—*Whoever secures the above Deserter, and brings him to Capt.* Skey, *in* NEW-YORK, *or lodges him in any of His Majesty's Goals, and gives him Information thereof, so as he may get him, shall receive Two Pistoles Reward, over and above His Majesty's Bounty allowed for taking up Deserters.*
The New-York Gazette: or, the Weekly Post-Boy, August 7, 1758; August 14, 1758; August 21, 1758.

RUN-away on the 6*th Instant at Night, from on board the Tartar Frigate, Capt.* Hugh M'Quoid, John Withers, *an indented Servant to said Capt.* M'Quoid, *having upwards of* 4 *Years and half of his time to serve; the said* Withers *was born in Belfast, in the Kingdom of Ireland, bred a Shoe-maker, of a fair Complexion, wears his own Hair, and is about* 18 *Years of Age. All*

Commanders of Vessels are hereby cautioned not to take away said Withers; and all Persons whatsoever are strictly required not to entertain him, as they will be prosecuted with the utmost rigour of the **LAW**.

    The New-York Mercury, August 7, 1758; August 14, 1758; August 21, 1758.

New-York, July 22, 1758.

WHERE AS a *Mulatto Man slave named* JOHN, *a Sailmaker by Trade, belonging to the Heirs of the late Widow* Van Ranst *hath absented himself from the Service of the Subscriber upwards of two Year, and still absents himself: These are therefore to forwarn all Persons whatsoever, not to entertain, conceal, harbour or employ the said Mulatto in any Shape whatsoever, as the Subscriber is advised, and determined to prosecute all such with the utmost Rigour of the Law,*

CORNELIUS VAN RANST,

Twenty Shillings Reward will be given to any Person who will discover who entertains the beforementioned Slave.

    The *New-York Gazette: or, the Weekly Post-Boy*, August 21, 1758; September 11, 1758; September 19, 1758. Only the first ad has the date and location at the top.

FIVE POUNDS REWARD,

FOR taking up and securing one William Connel, but says his Name is William Weaver, and passed by that Name when out a Privateering in the Sloop Fox, Captain Crew, and Brig Prince of Orange, Captain Dixon; He is a well-set Man, about 45 Years of Age, of a fresh Colour, and has a Scar on his Forehead above his Eye; is about 5 Feet 6 Inches high: Took with him a large Wallet made of Oznabrigs; left his Lodgings in New-York the 11th of August Instant, and took with him the Sum of £.21 18*s*. 6*d*. New-York Money, belonging to George Remer, of the County of Somerset, and Province of East-New-Jersey. Whoever will bring the said William Connell, to Lewis Stewart, Merchant in New-York, shall have the above Reward.

    The *New-York Mercury*, August 28, 1758; September 4, 1758; September 11, 1758; September 18, 1758.

RUN away on the 13*th of* August *Instant, from* William Peartree Smith *Esq; of Elizabeth-Town in* New-Jersey; *A Negro Man called* Prince, *had on a Leather Cap, Linnen Waistcoat and Breeches, coarse blue Stockings, a thick pair of Shoes, speaks* English *and* Dutch, *has lived in* Jamaica *in the* West-Indies *with Mr.* Simon Parsco, *and in* Dutchess-County, *in* New York Colony *with Mr.* Nixon, *has been lately seen in* New-York, *and it is said*

has passed King's-Bridge, *where he shewed a Pass and pretended that he belonged to a Butcher in* New-York, *and was going into the Country to fetch Cattle for his Master: Whoever secures him in any of his Majesty's Goals, so that his Master may have him again, shall be well rewarded.*
The New-York Gazette: or, the Weekly Post-Boy, September 4, 1758.

RUN-away from Stephen Fitzpatrick, Taylor, in NEW-YORK, an Apprentice Boy, named James Stewart, about 15 Years of Age, small of Stature, fair Complexion, thin visag'd, a little mark'd with the Small-Pox: Had on when he went away a striped Flannel Jacket, double breasted, with Hooks and Eyes; a new Felt Hat, a Pair of light coloured Fine Cloth Breeches, almost Thread-bear, or Check Trowsers. Whoever takes up said Boy, and secures him so that his said Master may have him again, shall have THIRTY SHILLINGS Reward, and all reasonable Charges
          paid, by   STEPHEN FITZPATRICK.
The New-York Mercury, September 11, 1758.

R UN away from the Subscriber, living at Philipsbourg, *a Mulatto Servant Man, named* Henry, *aged* 23 *Years; about 5 Feet* 8 *Inches high; had a Scar on his Forehead; took with him a greasy Beaver Hat; wore a brown homespun Coat; took away with him a blue Jacket, and several other Things; he plays very well on the Violin.—Whoever secures the said Mulatto so that his Master may have him again, shall have 20s. Reward, and all reasonable charges*
          paid by   Samuel Devenport.
The New-York Gazette: or, The Weekly Post-Boy, September 18, 1758; September 25, 1758; October 2, 1758; October 9, 1758.

New-York, September 14, 1758.
R UN away yesterday morning from Joseph Griswold, of this City, distiller; a middle-siz'd negro man, aged about 40, speaks little or no English, as he mostly living with the French: Had on when he went away, a short blue sailor's jacket and trowsers, a check shirt, and old hat. His name in Frank, or Francois.—Whoever takes up and secures the said negro fellow, so that his master may have him again, shall have Twenty shillings reward, and all reasonable charges
          paid, by   JOSEPH GRISWOLD,   *Living in Pearl-street.*
The New-York Gazette: or, The Weekly Post-Boy, September 25, 1758; October 2, 1758; October 9, 1758; October 16, 1758.

RUN-away, on Saturday Night last, from on board the Ship Nancy, Ralph Foster, Commander, lying at Crommeline's-Wharff, an Apprentice Lad, named John Riddle, aged 23 Years, well-set, of a brown Complexion, wears his own brown curled Hair, is 5 Feet 5 Inches high, has a Scar on the Back of his Left Hand, and speaks broad Scotch: Had on when he went away, a dark-coloured, thread-bear worn Coat, a striped Waistcoat, and a Scotch Bonnet; or perhaps he may be in a Sailor's Dress, having used the Sea some Time. All Masters of Vessels are forbid to carry him off. Whoever takes up and secures said Apprentice, so that his Master may have him again, shall receive FIVE PISTOLES Reward, and all reasonable Charges.
    RALPH FOSTER.   Sept. 25, 1758.
The New-York Mercury, September 25, 1758; October 2, 1758; October 9, 1758.

*B*ROKE *out of the Goal of the City of* New-York, Friday *Night the* 22*d Instant,* Joseph Simson, *by Trade a Carpenter, born in* New-Jersey, *is about* 30 *Years of Age, of a Sandy Complexion, had a Wife at* Poughkeepsie, *and is an excellent Hand at stealing Horses. Whoever takes up and secures said* Joseph Simson, *shall have* FIVE POUNDS *Reward,*
    paid by JAMES MILLS.
The New-York Gazette: or, The Weekly Post-Boy, September 25, 1758; October 2, 1758; October 9, 1758; October 16, 1758; *The New-Mercury*, September 25, 1758.

RUN-away on Monday the second Instant, from Benjamin Williams, a Negro Man, named Bristol, about 5 Feet 7 Inches high, aged about 26 Years: Had on when he went away, a red Jacket, brown Great-Coat, brown Camblet Breeches and wide Trowsers, a pair of new Shoes, with Strings, and a new felt Hat: Whoever takes up said Negro Fellow and brings him to is said Master, at Newark, or to Daniel Nap, in New-York, shall have Forty Shillings Reward, and all reasonable Charges,
    paid by BENJAMIN WILLIAMS.
The New-York Mercury, October 9, 1758; October 16, 1758; October 23, 1758.

                 Albany, Octob. 12. 1758.
DEserted from the 47th Regiment, *Jacob Fisher* a Dutchman, speaks good *English,* about 5 Feet 5 Inches high, a squat Man of a fresh Complexion, long Nose, and light colour'd Hair; had on when he deserted a short red plain Coat, with white Cuffs. He was inlisted about three Years ago at *Lancaster,* in *Pennsylvania* Government, and has Relations living there; he

has stolen and carried away with him, 43 Johannes and 106 Dollars. Whoever secures the said Deserter, shall have Three Guineas Reward, over and about what is allowed by Act of Parliament for apprehending and securing Deserters. *N. B.* Any Person or Persons that secures him, or causes him to be secured, and Notice given to the Commanding Officer of the 47th Regiment, or brings him to the Regiment at *Brunswick* in the *Jerseys,* shall be entitled to the Reward, with all Expences paid.

Boston Evening Post, October 23, 1758; November 6, 1758. See *The New-York Gazette: or, the Weekly Post-Boy,* October 23, 1758, and *The Boston Weekly Advertiser,* November 6, 1758.

Albany. October 13, 1758.

DEserted this Day from the 47th Regiment, *Jacob Fisher,* a Dutchman, speaks good *English,* about five Feet five Inches high; a thick squat Man; of a fresh Complexion, long nos'd, a light colour'd Hair; had on when he deserted, a short red Coat, with white Cuffs: He was inlisted about three Years ago at *Lancaster,* in *Pennsylvania* Government; and has relations living there: He has stole and carried with him 43 thirty six Shilling Pieces, and 106 Dollars:—Whoever secures the said Deserter, shall have *Three Guineas* Reward over and above what is allowed by Act of Parliament for apprehending and securing Deserters.

NB. The Person or Persons, who secures him, or causes him to be secured, and Notice given to the commanding Office [*sic*] of the 47th Regiment, or to the New Printing Officer in Beaver-street, shall be intituled to the Reward, and all Costs paid.

The New-York Gazette: or, the Weekly Post-Boy, October 23, 1758. See *Boston Evening Post,* October 23, 1758, and *The Boston Weekly Advertiser,* November 6, 1758.

DEserted from the 47th Regiment, *Jacob Fisher* a Dutchman, but speaks good English; he is about Five Feet 5 Inches high, a squatt Man of a fresh Complexion, has a long Nose, and light-colour'd Hair. Had on when he Deserted, a short, plain red Coat with white Cuffs; he was Inlisted about three Years ago at *Lancaster,* in *Pennsylvania*-Government, and has Relations living there.—He has stolen and carried away with him, 43 Johannes and 106 Dollars. Any Person or Person that secures the above Deserter, or causes him to be secured, and Notice given to the Commanding Officer of the 47th Regiment, or brings him to the Regiment at *Brunswick* in the *Jerseys,* shall have THREE GUINEAS Reward over and above what is allowed by Act of Parliament for the apprehending and securing Deserters, and all Expences paid.   *Boston, October* 23, 1758.

The Boston Weekly Advertiser, November 6, 1758; November 13, 1758. See *Boston Evening Post,* October 23, 1758, and *The New-York Gazette: or, the Weekly Post-Boy,* October 23, 1758.

RUN away on Monday *the* 30*th of* October, *from Mr.* Abraham Sebring, *in the Broad-Way; a Dutch Servant Maid, named* Margaret Elbert, 22 *Years of Age, is a High Dutcher, speaks but indifferent* English*; has blue Eyes, sandy colour'd Hair; had on when she went off, a Brown cross barred Gown, and a blue weaved Quilted Petticoat, and the lower End of the same not Quilted:*—*Whoever secures the same, so that her Master may have her again, shall have* Forty Shillings *Reward, and all reasonable Charges paid by* ABRAHAM SEBRING

The New-York Gazette: or Weekly Post-Boy, November 6, 1758; November 13, 1758; November 27, 1758; December 23, 1758.

New-York, November 5, 1758.
Deserted from Captain *Skey*, of his Majesty's 43d Regiment, recruiting at *New-York*,
JOHN SILEA, *born in* Old England, *aged* 21 *Years,* 5 *Feet* 10 *Inches high, pale Complexion, short brown Hair; had on, when he went off, a white Flannel Jacket, spotted with Black, a Pair of Trowsers, an old Pair of Stockings, mended in the Heels with red Cloth.*
Also deserted from said Captain Skey.
WILLIAM HEATH, *born in* Wales, Montgomery Shire, *bred a Mariner, aged* 24 *Years,* 5 *Feet* 5 *Inches high, well fac'd, and well made: Had on, when he went off, a green Jacket, with high colour'd Breeches: Whoever secures the said Deserters, or either of them, shall have ONE PISTOLE Reward over and above his Majesty's Bounty, for taking up Deserters.*

NB. *It is supposed that they have entered on Board some Privateer. All Commanders of Privateers, and Masters of other Vessels, are desired not to ship said Deserters, as they will be prosecuted to the utmost Rigour of the Law, if found to be on board their Vessel, or harboured on any Pretence whatsoever.*

Any Persons who will discover any one that hath enticed or influenced the said Deserters to abscond his Majesty's Service, shall have FIVE GUINEAS Reward.

The New-York Gazette: or Weekly Post-Boy, November 13, 1758; November 20, 1758.

Albany, Octob. 12. 1758.
DEserted from the 47th Regiment, *Jacob Fisher* a Dutchman, speaks good *English*, about 5 Feet 5 Inches high, a squat Man of a fresh Complexion,

long Nose, and light colour'd Hair; had on when he deserted a short red plain Coat, with white Cuffs. He was inlisted about three Years ago at *Lancaster*, in *Pennsylvania* Government, and has Relations living there; he has stolen and carried away with him, 43 Johannes and 106 Dollars. Whoever secures the said Deserter, shall have Three Guineas Reward, over and about what is allowed by Act of Parliament for apprehending and securing Deserters.

N. B. Any Person or Persons that secures him, or causes him to be secured, and Notice given to the Commanding Officer of the 47th Regiment, or brings him to the Regiment at *Brunswick* in the *Jerseys*, shall be entitled to the Reward, with all Expences paid.

Boston Evening Post, November 23, 1758; December 6, 1758.

Run-away, the 30th ultimo, at night, from James Jackson, of New Windsor, boatman, an Irish servant man, named John Handlin, five feet six inches high, 24 years old, a fresh coloured well-looking young fellow: Had on when he went away, a new bearskin coat, striped holland jacket, leather breeches, tow trowsers, clouded worsted stockings, a new blue duffils great coat, without either buttons or button holes; and took with him a short blue coat with black cuffs. Whoever secures said servant, and will bring him to John Durham, shoe-maker, near the Old-Slip, in New-York, shall have Forty Shillings reward, and all reasonable charges paid, by JAMES JACKSON.

The New-York Mercury, December 1, 1758; December 8, 1758; December 15, 1758; December 22, 1758; December 29, 1758.

DEserted the 5th of this Instant December, *from the* LIGHT-INFANTRY, *of Lieut.* Backus's *Recruiting Party, one* John Williams, *born in* Old-England, *aged about* 35 *Years; has black Hair, and wants two of his Fore-Teeth; has also a Scar on his upper Lip, and is about* 5 *Feet* 7 *Inches high.*—

Captains of Privateers, &c. are forbid, on Pain of being prosecuted with the utmost Rigour of the Law, to harbour or carry off the said Deserter:—LIKEWISE, Whosoever takes up and secures the said Deserters, shall have 20 Dollars Reward.

The New-York Gazette: or, the Weekly Post-Boy, December 11, 1758; December 18, 1758. The second ad shows the lieutenant's name as Bicker.

RUN away, on the 27th Day of May, 1757, from Thomas Lee, of Cortland Manor, in West Chester County, and Province of New York , a Dutch Servant Man, named John Milcus Freits, about 5 Feet 8 Inches high, of a dark Complexion, has long brown Hair, a long Visage, well set, has very large Joints to his great Toes, is broken bellied, and speaks broken English. Whoever takes up said Servant, and secures him in any Goal, so that his Master may have him again, shall have Three Pounds Reward, and reasonable Charges,
    paid by THOMAS LEE.
The Pennsylvania Gazette, December 14, 1758

New-York, December 18, 1758.
RUN away on the 23d of *December*, 1757, from the sloop *Walter*, of *Maryland*, then lying at *Hunter's-Quay*, in *New-York*; A Negro Fellow named RALPH; *Maryland*-born; about 22 Years of Age; of a middle Stature, and about 5 Feet 6 Inches high; speaks hoarse and thick, and is a great Chewer of Tobacco; flat Nose, and very thick lip'd, and wide-mouth'd; He has been scalded on the Back of his left Hand, and up his Arm, by which Scar thereof appears; and is of a swarthy Complexion: He has a greet many Dents in the Top of his Head, which seem to be the Ward-end of a Key: He has the use of his left Hand better than his Right; and is what is commonly called left-handed: He has had the Small-Pox, but not much pitted. It's expected he is on board some of the Privateers belonging to this City. Whoever takes up and secures the above Negro, so that his Master may have him again, shall have *FIVE POUNDS* Reward, if in or near *New-York*, the Reward will be paid by *Samuel Bowne*, Merchant; if in *Philadelphia*, by *Reese Meredith*, Merchant; and if in *Maryland*,
   by *James Campbell*, (the Owner) in *Charles-County*;
    besides all reasonable Charges.
The New-York Gazette: or, The Weekly Post-Boy, December 18, 1758; December 23, 1758; January 1, 1759; January 8, 1759. See *The New-York Gazette*, December 26, 1757.

DEserted the 5th *of this Instant* December, *from the* LIGHT-INFANTRY, *of Lieut.* Bicker's *Recruiting Party, one* John Williams, *born in* Old-England, *aged about* 35 *Years; has black Hair, and wants two of his Fore-Teeth; had also a Scar on his upper Lip, and is about* 5 *Feet* 7 *Inches high.—*
  Captains of Privateers, &c. are forbid, on Pain of being prosecuted with the utmost Rigour of the Law, to harbour or carry off the said Deserter:—LIKEWISE, Whosoever takes up and secure the said Deserter, shall have 20 Dollars Reward.

The New-York Gazette: or, The Weekly Post-Boy, December 18, 1758.

DESERTED from Captain Stewart's Company of the First Battalion of the Royal American Regiment, JOHN KNITE, and ANDREW STAGNER, KNITE is a strong made Man, full faced, brown Hair, about five Foot Ten Inches high. STAGNER has fair Hair, about Five Foot Nine Inches high, and well made: Whoever secures the Deserters and puts them in any Goal, shall have Twenty Shillings Reward, besides whats allowed by Act of Parliament.
N. B. They deserted from Albany the second Instant.
The New-York Gazette: or, The Weekly Post-Boy, December 23, 1758.

1759

DESERTED *from his Majesty's* 44*th Regiment, from Hampstead, on Long-Island; John Smith, about 5 Feet 5 Inches high, and about 21 Years old; fair short Hair, pale Complexion, Had on when he went off, a short plain Coat with yellow facings and round Cuffs; has a short Nose, round Face, a little thick lipped and speaks English with the German Accent. Whoever can give intelligence of him to Captain Falconer, at Hampstead, shall receive three Dollars Reward, besides the Allowance for apprehending Deserters.*
The New-York Mercury, January 1, 1759; January 15, 1759.

RUN-away, from the Snow Mary-Anne, laying at Burling's-Slip, the 12th Instant, a Negro Man called Tom, Bermuda born, about 23 Years of Age, 5 Feet 10 Inches High: Had on when he went away, a green Jacket, check Shirt, red Woollen Trowsers, with an Ozenbrigs Pair over them; he wears a Silver Bob sometimes in his Ear. Whoever takes up the said Fellow, and delivers him on board said Snow, to Henry Tucker, at Mr. Peter Evouts, or to Mr. Peter Keteltas's, before the Departure of said Snow, for London, which will be in a few Days, shall receive 3 Pistoles Reward,
         paid by   HENRY TUCKER, Jun.
The New-York Mercury, January 15, 1759.

RUN-away, from the Subscriber, the 28th of December last, a Negro Man about 22 Years old, a tall slender Fellow, speaks good English, and formerly belonged to Colonel Martin, at the Great-Plains: Had in when he went away, a blue Duffils Watch Coat, a light brown Cloth Coat, Black Calimancoe Breeches, and a check Shirt. Whoever takes up and secures the said Negro Fellow, so that he may be had again, shall receive FORTY

SHILLINGS Reward, and all reasonable Charges,
          paid by   SUSANNA BOSKIRK.
The New-York Mercury, January 15, 1759; January 22, 1759.

RUN-away, from Richard Harris, of Staten-Island, the 4th Instant, a Negro Man, named Tom, speaks good English, about 30 Years of Age. Run-away at the same Time, a Negro Boy named Harry, 14 Years old, has an Impediment in his Speech, speaks good French, and has lost one of his Fore-Teeth: They both had light coloured Kersey Jackets, with white flowered Mettal Buttons; Harry had a Cap on such as Marines generally wear, and Tom has a Great-Coat with a Cap to it that covers his Head on Occasion. Whoever takes up and secures said Negroes, so that their Master may have them again shall receive Twenty Shillings Reward for each, and all reasonable Charges
          paid by   RICHARD HARRIS.
The New-York Mercury, January 15, 1759; February 5, 1759. See *The New-York Mercury*, April 30, 1759.

                    TEN POUNDS REWARD.
RUN-away on Wednesday Night last, from the Subscriber, a Negro Fellow named Jack, well set and not very black: Had on when he went away, a brown Pee-Jacket, and a blue under one, he took with him a pair of Buckskin Breeches. Whoever takes up and secures said Negro Fellow, so that his Master may have him again, shall receive Ten Pounds Reward, and all reasonable Charges
          paid, by   WILLIAM BROWNEJOHN.
All Masters of Vessels and others, are forbid to carry of [sic] said Fellow at their Peril.
The New-York Mercury, January 22, 1759; January 29, 1759; February 5, 1759; February 12, 1759; February 26, 1759; March 19, 1759.

RUN-away the 25th Instant, from the Privateer Ship St. George, James Devereux, Commander, the five following Persons, viz. John Young, smooth-faced: Had on a brown Pee Jacket, and an under green Jacket, and wears a brown Wig. Andrew Charles, a Taylor by Trade, tall and smooth faced: Had on a close bodied light coloured Coat, wears a Wig, and of a pale Complexion. George Horn, a German, smooth-faced, fresh coloured, wears his Hair, and had on a blue Jacket and a red Cap. Thomas Jameson, a Taylor by Trade, a short well set Man: Had on a blue Jacket, and a blue mill'd Cap. John Smith 22 Years old thin-visaged, and generally wears a

blue Surtout Coat. Whoever takes up all, or any of the Men above-mentioned, and delivers them to Capt. Devereux, on board the St. George, shall have Twenty Shillings Reward for each of them, and all reasonable Charges paid by   JAMES DEVEREUX.
The New-York Mercury, January 29, 1759; February 5, 1759; February 12, 1759.

RUN-away from the Subscriber, on Saturday the 3d Instant, a Servant Girl named Bridget Nealan, of a sandy Complexion, much freckled, of a middle size, and about twenty Years of age: Had on when she went away, a blue quilted Petticoat, a brown josey, speckled Apron and Handkerchief. Whoever takes up and secures said Servant Girl, shall have Twenty Shillings Reward, and all reasonable Charges
paid, by   ARTHUR M'NEEL.
The New-York Mercury, March 5, 1759.

RUN-away about three Months ago, from George Norton, of Huntington, Suffolk-County on Long-Island, a Mulatto Slave named Simon, about 35 Years old, of a yellow Complexion, five Feet 8 Inches high, curled bushey Hairs, and wants the under Lappit of his Right Ear. Whoever takes up and secures the said Slave, so that his Master may have him again, shall receive Forty Shillings Reward, and all reasonable Charges,
paid by   GEORGE NORTON.
The New-York Mercury, March 5, 1759; March 19, 1759; March 26, 1759.

Albany, March 5, 1759
DESERTED from his Majesty's 55th Regiment of Foot, and the Hon. Major John West's Company, John Watson, aged 21 Years, 5 Feet 6 Inches high, by Trade a Labourer, born at Dalranck, in the Shire of Inverness, North-Britain, had dark brown curley hair, grey Eyes, of a swarthy Complexion, broad shouldered, and well-limbed.

William Otterson, aged 22 Years, 5 Feet 7 and Half Inches, a Labourer, born at Newtown, in the County of Down, has short black curley Hair, round faced, of a fresh Complexion, thick Legs, stout and well-made. Whoever secures the above Deserters, in any of his Majesty's goals, and gives Notice thereof to the commanding Officer of the Regiment at Albany, shall receive two Guineas Reward for each of them.
The New-York Mercury, March 12, 1759; March 19, 1759; March 26, 1759; April 2, 1759; April 9, 1759; *Weyman's New-York Gazette*, March 12, 1759; March 19, 1759; March 26, 1759; April 9, 1759.

Minor differences between the papers. *Weyman's* shows Watson's home town as Dalraneck, and Otterson as "short and well made."

DESERTED from his Majesty's 48th Regiment of Foot, and of Colonel Burton's Company, Mark Williams, aged 30 Years, five Feet seven Inches high, by Trade a Labourer, born in Norwich, New-England, dark brown short Hair, swarthy Complexion, a small Lisp in his Speech. Had on when he went away, a Frize Coat and Waist-coat, Leather Breeches, his present Residence is in, or about, North Stratford. Whoever apprehends the said Mark Williams, shall have Twenty Shillings Reward, over and above what is allow'd by Act of Parliament.

The New-York Mercury, March 19, 1759; April 9, 1759; April 16, 1759; April 30, 1759.

Betsy Williams, a Child of 7 Years of Age, has stray'd and lost herself in this City. She was bound to Mrs. Ward, on Cow Foot Hill, and is the Daughter of a poor widow Woman, who has been at great Expences looking for her; she therefore humbly requests, if any one knows any Thing of the said Child, to acquaint Robert Richards, Cooper, at Peck's slip, who will reward them for their Trouble: Or to acquaint the Widow *Budd*, in *Maroneck*, who will likewise reward them for their Trouble.

Weyman's New-York Gazette, March 19, 1759.

RUN-away from John Leake, of New-York, the 18th of March last, a Negro Wench named Bet, aged about 20 Years; was born at Jamaica, on Long-Island, a yellow Complexion, of a middling Stature, long curl'd Hair, speaks good English a little Lisping, a round full Face and Breast; took sundry Cloaths with her, a short red Cloth Cloak, a Velvet Bonnet, a Calico Gown, a strip'd Homespun ditto, a strip'd Homespun Petticoat, and several other Things. Whoever takes up and secures said Wench, so that her Master may have her again, shall receive Forty Shillings Reward and all reasonable Charges paid, by   JOHN LEAKE.
It is supposed she is gone towards Albany.

The New-York Mercury, April 2, 1759; April 9, 1759.

DESERTED from a recruiting Party of the 46th Regiment, from on board a Sloop bound to Albany, Cornelison, Master; John Fisher, about 5 Feet 5 inches high, of a dark Complexion, aged 28 Years, born in Prussia, by Trade a Butcher; went off in brown Cloaths. Whoever will secure the said

Deserter in any of his Majesty's Goals, and give Information thereof to any officer of the said Regiment, shall receive Twenty Shillings Sterling Reward, over and above what is allowed by Act of Parliament.
The New-York Mercury, April 2, 1759; April 9, 1759; April 16, 1759; April 23, 1759; April 30, 1759.

WHEREAS several Men have lately deserted his Majesty's 80th Regiment of Foot, and particularly Samuel Cunningham, born in the Province of Pennsylvania, twenty two Years of Age, five Feet three Inches in height, dark complexioned, round visaged, grey ey'd, brown Hair. Had on when he deserted, a red Jacket and Waistcoat, Bird ey'd. John Cunningham, born in the aforesaid Province, twenty-five Years of Age, five Feet six Inches in height, dark Complexion, round visaged, brown Eyes, brown Hair: Had on when he deserted, a light coloured Jacket and blue Waistcoat. John Pardy, born in Ireland, twenty one Years of Age, dark complexioned, long visaged, dark grey Eyes, red brown hair, well made, 5 Feet 10 Inches high: Had on when he deserted, a blue Jacket and Leather Cap. Michael Dooly, born in Ireland, 25 Years of Age, five Feet two Inches in height, dark Complexion, round visaged, dark grey Eyes, black curl'd Hair: Had on when he deserted, a Sailor's blue jacket. Daniel Mac Manus, born in Ireland, 25 Years of Age, five Feet six Inches, and a half high, fair Hair, sandy Complexion, well made, had been in the Pennsylvania Service, and was inlisted at New-York: Had on when he deserted, a light blue, Sailor made Waistcoat, coarse Oznabrigs Keir, blue Cloth Legings, wore a Bonnet, and took all his Arms and Accoutrements with him. Mathew Hopkins, aged 30 Years, 5 Feet and 1 Inch high, is, or pretends to be a very good Seaman, and is very talkative when drunk, round visaged, dark Complexion, short frizled Hair, was born in the North of Ireland. Edward Norman, born in the same Place, about 5 feet nine Inches high, long Visage, fair Complexion, fair streight Hair: Had on when they deserted, Sailors short Jackets, blue Legings and Trowsers: Norman is supposed to be about twenty-three Years of Age, and served his Time to the Sea. Whoever takes up any of the above Deserters, and lodges them in any Goal, until they can be sent to the Regiment, shall have Forty Shillings Reward, paid by the commanding Officers, besides what is allowed by Act of Parliament.
The New-York Mercury, April 16, 1759; April 23, 1759; April 30, 1759; May 7, 1759; May 14, 1759.

RUN-AWAY *from Richard Harris, of Staten-Island, the 16th of April, a Negro Man, named Tom, speaks good English, and about 30 Years old: Had on a light coloured Kersey Coat and Jacket, with Metal Buttons,*

Buckskin Breeches, with a Watch Coat with a Cap to it; he plays on the Fiddle, and carried one with him. Whoever takes up and secures said Negro, so that his Master may have him again, shall receive Three Pounds Reward, and all reasonable Charges

       paid, by   Richard Harris.

 N. B. He was seen at Raway the 17th, and at Woodbridge the 18th of April. All Persons are forbid to harbour, conceal, or entertain him on their Peril, or carry him off.

 The New-York Mercury, April 30, 1759; May 7, 1759; May 14, 1759.
 See *The New-York Mercury*, January 15, 1759.

 RAN AWAY last Friday from *Elizabeth Carpender*, a negro man named *Venture*, about five foot high, walks shambling, or loose kneed; with striped upper jacket, and red under ditto, leather breeches, and red cap; supposed to be in the out parts of the town, or gone on board some of the transports. All persons are hereby forbid to harbour the said negro; and whoever brings him to his mistress, *Elizabeth Carpender*, shall have *Forty Shillings* reward.

 Weyman's New-York Gazette, April 30, 1759; May 1, 1759. See *The New-York Gazette: or, the Weekly Post-Boy*, August 7, 1758, *Weyman's New-York Gazette*, July 16, 1759, *The New-York Gazette*, September 29, 1760, and *The New-York Gazette*, July 13, 1761.

 RUN-away, a few days ago, Anthony Otlay, from the Ship Hopewell, Capt. George Masterman, an indented servant, aged 25 years, of a brown complexion, pitted with the small-pox, wears a blue or green jacket, is about six feet high: Also, Robert Stringer, aged 18 years, of a brown complexion, about five feet high, pitted with the small-pox, with short brown hair; had on a short jacket; supposed to be skulking about the town until the departure of the ship. Whoever secures one or both of the above servants, and gives notice thereof to Sidney Breese, shall be rewarded beyond expectation.

 The New-York Mercury, May 7, 1759; May 14, 1759.

 RUN-AWAY, *on saturday the 28th of April last, from John Duryee, bolter, of this city,* servant boy named John Markeshin, *but calls himself John Markessixhe, about five feet high, a very yellow complexion, and has a down look: Had on when he went away, a mouse coloured bearskin coat, a blue camblet jacket, and blue serge breeches; a pair of blue or white stockings, a pair of large silver buckles; he enlisted in the province service, and was discharged; it is imagined he is gone on board one of the transports: All masters of vessels and others, are hereby forbid to harbour*

the said servant boy. Whoever takes up said servant and brings him to his master, at Peck's-slip, shall have twenty shillings and all reasonable charges paid, by JOHN DURYEE.
The New-York Mercury, May 7, 1759; May 14, 1759; May 21, 1759.

RUN AWAY last Tuesday from *John Dudley*, baker, a young lad about 13 years of age, 3 [sic] feet high, born in this city; had on when he went away, a swanskin jacket, a pair of buckskin breeches, and had two remarkable marks, viz. a spot on the crown of his head, which had no hair, and another on the right side, without hair likewise. Whoever takes and secures said apprentice, shall have a reasonable reward, and all charges
            paid, by   JOHN DUDLEY.
    N. B. This is to forbid all master of vessels, and others, not to harbour or engage said apprentice, on penalty of suffering according to law.
Weyman's New-York Gazette, May 7, 1759; May 14, 1759; May 28, 1759.

                      Green-Bush, Albany County, May 8, 1759.
DESTERED this Day, from Major Whiting's Company, of the Rhode-Island Regiment, William Smith, about 5 Feet 6 Inches high, black strait Hair, aged 26 Years, born in England, talks very fast, and was bred a Sailor. Deserted also, Mathias Mount, and James Cross. Whoever takes up and secures the said Deserters, in any of his Majesty's Goals, so that they may be recovered, shall have Ten Dollars Reward for each, and reasonable Charges paid, by
    GERARD G. BEEKMAN, in New-York.
The New-York Mercury, May 14, 1759; May 21, 1759; May 28, 1759.

DESERTED from one of the New-York Provincial Regiments, and Captain James Holmes's Company, the following Soldiers, viz. John Blackwood, by Trade a Cooper. 5 Feet 9 Inches high, 29 Years of Age, of a dark Complexion, light Eyes, and bright Hair. Charles Williams, a Labourer, 18 Years of Age, of a dark Complexion, light Eyes, and light Hair. Benedict Arnold, by Trade a Weaver, 18 Years of Age, dark Complexion, light Eyes, and black Hair. Whoever takes up and secures the said Deserters, or either of them, in any of his Majesty's Goals, so that they may be sent to the Regiment, shall receive 40s. Reward for each, and all reasonable Charges,
            paid by   Thomas Willet, in Westchester County.
The New-York Mercury, May 21, 1759; May 28, 1759; June 11, 1759.
See *Weyman's New-York Gazette*, May 21, 1759.

DESERTED from the *New-York* Regiment, and Captain *James Holme*'s company;

John Blackwood, by trade a cooper, 5 feet 9 inches high, 29 years of age, dark complexion, light eyes, and bright hair.

Charles Williams, labourer, 18 years of age, dark complexion, light eyes, and light hair.

Benedict Arnold, by trade a weaver, 18 years of age, dark complexion, light eyes, and black hair.

Whoever takes up and secures the said deserters, or either of them, in any of his majesty's goals, so that they may be sent to the regiment, shall receive Forty Shillings reward for each, and all reasonable charges,

          paid by   THOMAS WILLET, in *West Chester* county.

Weyman's New-York Gazette, May 21, 1759; May 28, 1759; June 11, 1759. See *The New-York Mercury*, May 21, 1759.

          Scotack, Near Albany, May 20, 1759.

DESERTED from his Majesty's first Highland Battalion, commanded by the Honourable ARCHIBALD MONTGOMERY, and from the Honourable Capt. John Gordon's Company, Donald M'Neelage, aged Twenty-three Years, Five Feet Ten Inches high, fair Complexion, Flaxen Hair, long Visage, with a Roman Nose, by Trade a House-Carpenter, born in the Shire of Argyle, in Scotland; he speaks both Earse and English: Any Person who apprehends the said Donald M'Neelage, and secures him in any of his Majesty's Goals, so that he may be recovered, shall receive Five Guineas Reward, over and above what is allowed by Act of Parliament: Reasonable Charges will be allowed, and the Reward

          paid by   Hugh Wallace, Merchant, in New-York.

The New-York Mercury, June 4, 1759; June 11, 1759; June 18, 1759; June 25, 1759; July 2, 1759; *The Pennsylvania Gazette*, June 21, 1759. Minor differences between the papers, the *Gazette* shows he deserted from Scotick, and that the reward could also be paid by "Serjeant John Suter, opposite the New Market, in Philadelphia."

RUN away from Dennis Hicks, *of* Philipsborough, *on the 5th Inst.* June, *a negro man, named,* William, *aged about 20 Years; had on a homespun blu-cloth coat, lined with striped homespun flannel, a dark Ruteteen waistcoat, and sheep skin breeches, with Tow Trowsers over them; he has a black mold on the right side of his face, near his nose, and had very large Ears, speaks good English, and pretends to be free: he is supposed to be gone to* Bedford, Horseneck, *or* Hartford: *he is of middle size, and of a thin Visage, with his hair cut off. All Persons are forewarn'd to harbour him; and all*

Masters of Vessels forbid to carry him off at their peril. FORTY SHILLINGS *Reward for securing him in any Goal, so that I may have him again, and reasonable Charges*
      paid by Dennis Hicks.
The New-York Gazette, June 11, 1759; June 18, 1759; June 25, 1759; July 9, 1759; July 30, 1759. See *The New-York Gazette*, August 20, 1759, *The New-York Gazette*, July 14, 1760, and *The New-York Gazette*, December 29, 1760.

RUN away last Tuesday, from *John Rikor*, of *Horseneck*, a Mulatto Woman, named *Sarah Street*, very much pock-marked, has long curled Hair, and a Piece of her Ear cut off. Whoever takes up and secures the said Mulatto, so that the said Rickor may have her again, shall have 20s Reward, and all reasonable Charges
   paid by *John Welch*, in *Beaver-street, New-York*,
      or by the said *Rikor*, in *Horseneck*.
Weyman's New-York Gazette, June 18, 1759; June 25, 1759; July 30, 1759; *The New-York Gazette*, August 13, 1759; September 3, 1759. See *The New-York Mercury*, June 25, 1759.

     Thirty-nine Pounds Reward.
    Deserted from the *New-York* REGIMENT.
   From Capt. *Hulet's* Company raised on *Long-Island,*
JAMES HAMSEN, born in *New-York*, 19 years of age, 5 feet 7 inches high, grey eyes, dark complexion, brown hair, a labourer. BENJAMIN LEWIS, born in *Rhode-Island*, 23 Years of age, 5 feet 2 inches and an half high, brown eyes, sandy hair, and a ruddy complexion, a labourer. MATTHEW CAN, born in *Bucks County, Pennsylvania*, 21 years of age, 5 feet 4 inches high, blue eyes, ruddy complexion, light hair, a labourer. VINCENT HODGE, born in Germany, 45 years of age, a tailor by trade, 5 feet 8 inches high, brown eyes, sandy hair. ROBERT KATIENS. 28 years of age, 5 feet 5 inches high, brown complexion and hair, a fisherman.
   From Capt. Wright's Company, Long-Island:
DANIEL CHAPMAN, born in *Connecticut*, by trade a ship carpenter, 5 feet 11 inches and an half high, grey eyes, sandy complexion, and hair. THOMAS JONES, born in *New-Jersey*, by trade a weaver, 5 feet 11 inches and an half high, brown eyes and hair. SAMUEL PALMER, born in *Connecticut*, 5 feet 9 inches high, brown eyes, sandy hair, a labourer.
   From Capt. Moss's Company, Long-Island; JAMES COMBS, born in *New-Jersey*, by trade a weaver, 5 feet 11 inches and an half high, brown eyes and hair.

From Capt. Potter's, *Long-Island*; JOHN JONES, born in Ireland, 41 years of age, 5 feet 8 inches high, light complexion, well set, and wears a wig.

From Capt. Tuthill's *Comp. Long-Island*: DAVID MURPHY, 47 years of age, 5 feet 5 inches high, born in born in *Scotland*, by trade a nail-maker, dark complexion.

From the Company raised in King's *County, Long Island;*
THOMAS CHELWELL, born on *Long-Island*; by trade a labourer, 26 years of age, 5 feet 11 inches high, fair complexion. And CHARLES POWERS, inlisted in Kings County, Long-Island.

Any Persons securing any of the above DESERTERS, in the Goal of *New-York* or *Albany*, shall have THREE POUNDS Reward, paid by the commissary for each.

Weyman's New-York Gazette, May 21, 1759; May 28, 1759; June 11, 1759; June 18, 1759; June 25, 1759; July 2, 1759.

RUN *away last Tuesday Night, from Horse-Neck, a Mulatto Woman, named Sarah Street, very much Pock-marked, has long curled Hair, and a Piece of her Ear cut off: Whoever secures the said Mulatto, shall have Twenty Shillings Reward, and all reasonable Charges*
    paid by John Welch, in New-York,
      or by John Ryker, at Horse-Neck.   June 18, 1759.
The New-York Mercury, June 25, 1759. See *Weyman's New-York Gazette*, June 18, 1759.

Thirty-nine Pounds Reward.
Deserted from the *New-York* REGIMENT.
From Capt. *Hulet's* Company raised on *Long-Island*,
JAMES HAMSEN, born in *New-York*, 19 years of age, 5 feet 7 inches high, grey eyes, dark complexion, brown hair, a labourer....

From the Company raised in King's County, *Long-Island*;
THOMAS CHELWELL, born on *Long-Island*; by trade a labourer, 26 years of age, 5 feet 11 inches high, fair complexion....

Any Persons securing any of the above Deserters, in the Goal of New-York or Albany, shall have THREE POUNDS Reward, paid by the commissary for each.

Weyman's New-York Gazette, July 2, 1759.

R*UN-away on the 3d Instant from the Snow Irish Oak John Sample Master; lying in New-York Patrick Hughes, an Apprentice about* 19 *Years of Age,* 5 *Feet* 7 *Inches high, smooth Fac'd, fair Complexion, large Feet and his Legs*

much Swelled. Had on when he run away, a white Flannel Jacket, Canvas Trowsers and a Cap or Wig. Whoever secures the said Hughes, and brings him to Mr. George Bryan, Merchant in Philadelphia or Mr George Folliot, Merchant in New-York, shall have Three Pounds Reward and reasonable Charges paid by either of the same Gentlemen,
          JOHN SAMPLE   GEORGE BRYAN.
The Pennsylvania Journal, and Weekly Advertiser, July 12, 1759; July 26, 1759.

RUN away last Sunday, from *Elizabeth Carpenter*, of this city, a negro man, named *Venture*, of a middle stature: Had on when he went away, a pair of leather breeches, and striped jacket, and wore a worsted cap. Whoever takes up and secures the said negro, so that his mistress may have him again, shall have *Forty Shillings* reward, and reasonable charges,
          paid by   ELIZABETH CARPENTER.
   N. B. All masters of vessels and others, are forbid to carry him off; or harbour him at any rate, at they must answer it by law.
Weyman's New-York Gazette, July 16, 1759; July 30, 1759; August 6, 1759; *The New-York Gazette*, August 13, 1759; August 20, 1759; September 3, 1759; September 24, 1759; October 8, 1759; October 15, 1759. See *The New-York Gazette: or, the Weekly Post-Boy*, August 7, 1758, *Weyman's New-York Gazette*, April 30, 1759, and *The New-York Gazette*, July 13, 1761.

RUN away on the 12th of this instant June, from Ulster County, York Government, a labouring man, named Cornelius Smith, about 5 Feet 8 Inches high, marked pretty much with the Smallpox, short black hair: Had on, a green Coat, red plush Vest and Breeches, and felt Hat; he says he served his Time at the Forks of Delaware. He took a bay Horse with him, the Property of John Milegan, about 13 Hands and a Half high, paces and trots, branded on the near Thigh with the Letter A, about 10 years old; also Saddle and Bridle, the Saddle is plated round the Seat with Brass. He was seen at Prince Town, and it is believed he will make for some Part of Pennsylvania, as he is well acquainted there; he has a Pattern for a Suit of clothes with him unmade, the Coat of blue Broad cloth, the Vest of Scarlet, and Breeches of Manchester Velvet. Whoever secures the said Man and Horse, so as the Owner may have the Horse again, and Opportunity of prosecuting the Man, shall have Five Pounds Reward, and reasonable Charges,
          paid by   John Milegan.
The Pennsylvania Gazette, June 21, 1759.

RUN-away on Monday the 4th Instant, from West-chester, a Negro Man, called Lamdon, about 5 Feet 8 Inches high, about 30 Years of Age, has lost some of his fore Teeth, and is mark'd under one of his Eyes: Had on when he went away, a blue broad Cloth Coat, but has different Cloaths with him, wore a Wig, and talks indifferent good English. Whoever takes up said Fellow and brings him to his Master, or secures him in any of his Majesty's Goals, so that he may be had, shall receive Thirty Shillings Reward, and all reasonable Charges
              paid, by   GABRIEL LIGGET, at Westchester,
                      or GABRIEL LIGGET, [sic] in New-York.
The New-York Gazette, June 11, 1759; June 19, 1759; *The New-York Mercury*, June 11, 1759; June 18, 1759; June 25, 1759.

DESERTED His Majesty's Service, from Albany one Hezekiah Wright, of Col. Fitch's Regiment and Maj. Durkee's Company; he is a mulatto fellow about 28 years old, belong to Norwich, about 5 feet 8 inches high: Also one Jona [E]ws, a transient Person who deserted from this Town; he is about 18 years of age, said to belong to Haddam: Whoever shall apprehend said Deserters and convey them to the abovesaid Regiment, shall have Three Pounds Reward and all necessary charges paid by me
            ELIHU HIDE, Ens. in said Regt.
The New-London Summary, or, The Weekly Advertiser, July 11, 1759.

TAKEN up, and now in the Goal at Goshen, in Orange County, a Negro Man named (as he says) Jacob; has a Scar upon his Chin under his upper Lip; has the Negro Mark with a Cut on each Cheek in his own Country; has had the Small-pox, and a little pitted with it; has a Scar on his right Wrist, he says it was shot with a Ball; is five Feet seven Inches and Half high, is about 25 or 30 Years old, has a green Jacket lined with red, Buckskin Breeches, blue Indian Stockings, five white Shirts, with Chitterlings; has a Gun Iron mounted, spotted Silk Handkerchief; he says he was in Roger's Rangers three Years, and was at the Battle of Ticonderoga; that he belonged formerly to one Daniel M'Coy, in New-York, who lived near the Old-Slip, and that his Master had given him free for serving three Years in the Rangers, and that Mr. Livingston's Negro Wench Rose, had his Freedom Paper; he is a spry able Fellow, he has been found in many Lies, and has been charged with Pilfering. Whoever owns the said Negro may have him upon paying the Charges.
            EBENEZER KELLER.
The New-York Mercury, July 23, 1759; July 30, 1759; August 6, 1759.

153

RUN AWAY about a Fortnight ago, from *John Lavenue*, at *Albany* an *English* servant man, named *John Exelby*, aged 28 years, black complexion, about 4 foot 9 inches in nature, well set, very much pitted with the small-pox; his upper lip turns much up to his nose, and had a ranger's green waistcoat on, with his hat cut in the form of a jockey cap. *Forty Shillings* reward to any person who will take up and bring said servant to the Printer hereof, or secures him in any goal, so that his master may have him again; and reasonable charges
    paid by *JOHN LAVENUE.*
 N.B. It is supposed he is either sculking about *New-York*, or gone to the *Jersey's* or *Philadelphia*, from whence he first came.
 Weyman's New-York Gazette, July 30, 1759; August 6, 1759; *The New-York Gazette,* September 3, 1759.

RUN-AWAY, *on Friday the 18th Day of May, from James I. Ross, of the Nine-Partners, County of Dutchess, and Province of New-York, a Negro Man named Dick, but was sometimes called Martin; speaks good English and Dutch, about* 33 *Years of Age, pretty tall and slim: Had on when he went away, a Woollen check'd Shirt, and took a check'd Linnen one with him, a blue knapt Jacket lined with yellow Flannell, Linnen Trowsers, and took a Pair of Check Trowsers with him, a Pair of blue and white Stockings, a great Coat, and a brown Worsted Cap. Whoever takes up and secures said Negro, so that his Master may have him again, shall receive* THREE POUNDS *Reward, and all reasonable Charges,*
   paid by JAMES I. ROSS.
 The New-York Mercury, July 30, 1759; August 6, 1759; August 13, 1759; August 20, 1759.

RUN-*away, the Beginning of July last, from Johannis Roorbach, of New-York, a Negro Man named Tone, or Anthony; is about* 25 *Years old, has little or no Beard, is about five Feet* 6 *or* 7 *Inches high, of a Madagascar Breed, has a big Mouth, and a good set of large Teeth, which he don't fail to show when he laughs; was seen in several Parts of the City; but the last Time was seen to go in a Wood Boat. Whoever takes up said Fellow, and brings him to his Master, or secures him so that his Master may have him again, shall receive* 20 *s. Reward, and all reasonable Charges*
   paid, by JOHANNIS ROORBACH
 The New-York Mercury, August 6, 1759; August 13, 1759; August 20, 1759. See *The New-York Gazette,* August 13, 1759

RUN away the beginning of *July*, 1759, from *Johannes Roorbach*, in *New-York*, a negro man named *Toon*, or *Anthony*, 25 years old, has little or no beard, about 5 feet 6 or 7 inches high, of a Malagsco breed, has a big mouth, and a good set of large teeth, which he never fails to shew when he laughs, was seen in several parts of the city, but last to go in a wood boat. Whoever takes up the said fellow and brings him to his master, or secures him so that he may be had again, shall have *Twenty Shillings* reward, and reasonable charges paid.

The New-York Gazette, August 13, 1759; August 20, 1759. See *The New-York Mercury*, August 6, 1759.

RUN-away on Friday the 3d Instant, from Joshua Levy, a Negro Man, named Prince, about 30 Years of Age, has two Cuts on his Cheek, and a hole in each Ear: Had on when he went away, a brown Jacket lined with blue Flannel, and has Metal Buttons. Whoever takes up and secures said Negro, and brings him to his said Master, living in Batteau-Street, New-York, shall receive Forty Shillings Reward and all reasonable Charges
    paid, by JOSHUA LEVY.
N. B. All Masters of Vessels or others are forbid to carry off or harbour said Fellow at their Peril.

The New-York Mercury, August 13, 1759; August 20, 1759; August 27, 1759; September 3, 1759.

RUN-AWAY from the Subscriber, living in Battoe Street, New-York, the 25th of July last, a Negro Man about 30 Years old, named Primus, 5 Feet 8 Inches high, and had a Sore on his Right Shin. Whoever takes up and secures said Fellow, so that his Master may have him again, shall receive Forty Shillings Reward, and all reasonable Charges,
    paid by NICHOLAS STIKE.

The New-York Mercury, August 13, 1759; August 20, 1759; August 27, 1759; September 3, 1759; September 10, 1759.

           New-York, August 7, 1759.
Run away from *Bartholomew Coxetter*, Taylor, an Irish Servant Girl, named, Margaret M"Chelhow, about 14 Years old, pock-marked. Had on when she went away, a blue and white striped homespun Josey and Petticoat, and a Pair of old black stuff shoes. Whoever brings the said servant to her master, living in King street, between Mr. Joseph Reade, Merchant, and Mr. Smith, Attorney, and opposite to Judge Horsemanden's, shall have Twenty shillings Reward, and reasonable Charges
    paid by *Bartholomew Coxetter.*

N. B. It is supposed she is gone towards New Windsor, in the Highlands.
The New-York Gazette, August 20, 1759; August 27, 1759; September 3, 1759; September 17, 1759; September 24,1759; October 1, 1759.

RUN away from *Dennis Hicks,* of Philipsburgh, in Westchester County, and Province of New-York, a mulatto Slave, named Bill, aged about 20 Years. Had on a brown Camblet Waistcoat, without sleeves, and one camblet ditto lined with silk; a pair of new blue stockings, and a pair of new shoes; a pair of Leather Breeches, with old Trousers, and one pair of striped ditto; a coarse felt hat stitched round the Brim with white Yarn. he has a long sharp nose, with a black Mole on the right Side of his Face, near his Nose: has very large Ears, speaks very good English, and pretends to be free: He says he has a White Mother, and was born in New England. He is of a middle size, and has a thin Visage, with his Hair cut off. All Persons are forbid to harbour him, and all Masters of Vessels are forbid to carry him off, as they will answer it at their Peril. Forty shillings Reward for securing him in any Goal, or bringing him to me, so that I may have him again, and reasonable Charges
           paid by   *Dennis Hicks.*
N. B. This Fellow was advertised in the New York Papers the 5th of June, and in Newhaven the 11th of June; was afterwards taken up in Waterbury, and was put into Litchfield Goal, from thence he was brought to Bedford, and there made his Escape from his Master again. Those who apprehend him, are desired to secure him in Irons. He was taken up by Moses Foot, of North Waterbury, in New-England. It is likely he will change his Clothes, as he did before. The Mole abovementioned is something long.
The New-York Gazette, August 20, 1759; August 27, 1759; September 10, 1759; September 17, 1759; September 24, 1759. See *The New-York Gazette,* June 11, 1759, *The New-York Gazette,* July 14, 1760, and *The New-York Gazette,* December 29, 1760.

New-York, August 20, 1759.
Run away last Friday the 17th Instant, from Joshua Hetfield, of White Plains, in Westchester County, Province of New-York, a Negro Man, named, Will, is of middle stature, and pretty well set; in long visag'd, and aged about 26 years: He is Country born, and talks good English: Had on when he went away, a Homespun Jacket, without sleeves, the front and back of which are of different Colours; and a homespun tow shirt and trowsers. Whoever takes up and secures the said Negro in any goal, so that

his Master may have him again, or gives Notice thereof to either Capt. Abraham Hetfield, or Dr. Graham, both of White Plains, Westchester County, or to W. Weyman, in New York, shall have 40s Reward if taken about twelve Miles from Home, and 16s if taken under, and all reasonable Charges paid by　　Joshua Hetfield.

Captains of Privateer, and all masters of Merchantmen, and others, are forbid to carry him of, or to harbour him at any rate, as they may expect to be prosecuted for the same.

The New-York Gazette, August 20, 1759; August 27, 1759; September 3, 1759; September 17, 1759; September 24, 1759. See *The New-York Gazette*, November 26, 1759.

　　　　　　　　　　　　　　NEW-YORK, AUGUST 31, 1759.

RUN away from his Bail, John Bellamy, Mariner: He is 22 Years of Age, or thereabouts, born in London; had on when he went off, a blue napt Jacket, lin'd with white Flannel, a Check Shirt, a Pair of Breeches, the Cloth representing Diamonds, and sometimes red Everlasting, blue Stockings, a Pair of new square-toe'd Pumps, with, round white Metal Buckles, set with Stones; and had round his Neck, a blue Silk Bird-ey'd Handkerchief; is of a sandy Complexion, round visag'd, very much freckled and swarthy, sturdy and well set, waddles in his Walk, and has harsh Pronunciation.

Whoever takes up the above-mentioned Person, and secures him in any of His Majesty's Goals, shall have, if taken within Sixteen Miles of this City, Forty Shillings, and if farther, Three Pounds Reward, and all reasonable Charges
　　　　　　　paid, by　　LAWRENCE SWEENY, Penny-Post;
living in Bayard-street, New-York. N. B. There is some Reason to believe he is gone to Philadelphia or Rhode-Island.

The New-York Mercury, September 3, 1759; September 10, 1759.

DESERTED *from the 4th Battalion of the Royal American Regiment, at Oswego, the 8th of August Inst. Nicholas Morris, 5 Feet 6 Inches high, about 30 Years of Age, full visaged, light brown Hair, and was born in the County of Kilkeny, in Ireland. William Campbell, 5 Feet 4 Inches and a Half high, about 28 Years of Age, brown Complexion, thin visaged, black Hair, and was born in the County of Donegal in Ireland. Archibald Danolson, 5 Feet 6 Inches high, about 30 Years of Age, brown Complexion, round visaged, brown Hair, and was born in Ireland. John Knapshneider, 5 Feet 5 Inches and a Half high, about 28 Years of Age, brown Complexion, long visaged, black Hair, and was born in Germany, John Ryan, Drummer, 5 Feet 4 Inches high, about 20 Years of Age, thin visaged, brown Hair, and*

was born in Pennsylvania. Simon Lutz, 5 Feet 4 Inches high, about 22 Years of Age, brown Complexion, long visaged, brown Hair, and was born in Germany. Robert Reese, 5 Feet 7 Inches high, about 26 Years of Age, fair Complexion, full visaged brown Hair, and as born in Wales.
The New-York Mercury, September 3, 1759; September 10, 1759.

RUN-AWAY from the Subscriber on Tuesday last, a young Lad about 19 Years of Age, named Benjamin Weatherly: Had on a Homespun striped Jacket, an old hat, a Worsted Cap, and a pair of blue Breeches; was bound to be a Pilot, and is well-set. Whoever takes up said Lad, and confines him, so that his Master may have him again, shall receive Twenty Shillings Reward and all reasonable Charges
        paid by   THOMAS CROOKSHANKS, Pilot.
N. B. All Masters of Vessels and others, are forbid to employ or carry off said Run-away, otherwise they may expect to be treated according to Law.
The New-York Mercury, September 10, 1759; October 1, 1759.

RUN away on Sunday the 16th Instant, from Richard Dongan, of Staten-Island, a negro Man named Tom, about 30 Years of age; a thick short fellow, about five feet four inches high. Had on when he went away, a brown Kersey Jacket, lined with white flannel, a check Shirt, and Trowsers. Whoever takes up said Negro, and brings him to his said Master, shall have FORTY SHILLINGS Reward, and all reasonable Charges
        paid by   RICHARD DONGAN.
                              Staten Island, Sept. 20, 1759.
The New-York Gazette, September 24, 1759; October 8, 1759; October 15, 1759; November 26, 1759; December 3, 1759.

RUN-AWAY from the Subscriber, living at the Great-Nine-Partners, in Dutchess County, a Negro Man, named Jack Green, about 5 Feet 8 Inches high, well-made, and a strong Fellow: Had on when he went away, a blue Jacket, and Check Trowsers. Whoever takes up and secures said Negro Fellow, so that his Master may have him again, shall receive Twenty Shillings Reward, and all reasonable Charges,
        paid by   JOEL GILLET.
N. B. He took a dark Bay Horse with him.
The New-York Mercury, October 1, 1759; October 8, 1759; October 22, 1759.

RUN-away *on Monday the* 17*th Inst. from the Subscriber, living in the Township of East-Chester, a Negro Man named* Rob, *aged about* 27 *Years,* 5 *Feet* 3 *Inches high, humf-backed, and is this Country born: Had on when he went away a red Jacket. Whoever takes up and secures said Negro, so that his Master may have him again, shall receive Three Pounds Reward, and all reasonable Charges*
              paid, by   DAVID FOWLER.
    N. B. All Captains of Vessels and others, are forbid to harbour, employ, or carry off said Fellow.
    The New-York Mercury, October 8, 1759; October 15, 1759; October 22, 1759. See *The New-York Mercury*, November 24, 1760, and *The New-York Mercury*, December 29, 1760.

RAN away on Wednesday the 26th of September last, from Capt. *Thomas Davis*, of the City of *New-York*, a Mulatto Wench named *Fanny*, with her young Child about eight Months old, is pretty tall: had on when he [sic] went away, a red and white striped Cotton Gown, and a striped blue and white homespun Petticoat, with a Cap without any Border. Whoever takes up the said Wench, and brings her to the said Thomas Davis, at the Sign of the Harliquin, at the White Hall Slip, shall have Twenty *Shillings* Reward, and all reasonable Charges
              paid by   THOMAS DAVIS.
    The New-York Gazette, October 1, 1759; October 8, 1759; October 15, 1759; *The New-York Mercury*, October 8, 1759; October 22, 1759; October 29, 1759; November 5, 1759. Minor differences between the papers.

RAN away from Major Edmund Matthews, of the Camp, in the County of *Albany*, in the Province of *New-Yor*k, a Servant Man, named William Sarefield, is of a dark Complexion, has a down look, black Hare, [sic] of a short Stature; he carried away with him a blue Waistcoat of Damask, a striped Pair of Breeches, two Pair of black worsted Stockings, a Pair of old Pumps, a felt hat, an old ruffled Shirt, and several other Things; he commonly wears a black Cravat about his Neck. At the same Time runaway also, from the said Matthews, a negro Man and Woman; also a white Girl, of about 13 Years of age, talks English, and High and Low Dutch, and has short black Hair, thick size, and swarthy Complexion, and is very talkative. The Negro Man and Woman is much marked with the Small Pox. The Negro Man speaks middling good English, Dutch and French, is well made, very mannerly in his Way, and understands most all sorts of labouring Work: The Negro Woman talks Dutch and English, understands all sorts of House Work. Whoever takes up the said Runaways, and secures them so that their Master may have them again, shall have Ten Pounds, New-York Currency Reward, and all reasonable Charges paid, by   EDMOND MATTHEWS.

The New-York Gazette, October 8, 1759; October 15, 1759; October 22, 1759; November 5, 1759. See *The New-York Mercury*, October 8, 1759.

RUN-away from Major Edmond Mathews, of the County of Albany, in the Province of New-York, a Servant Man, named William Sarefeald, dark Complexion, down look, black Hair, of short Stature; he carried away with him a blue Waistcoat of Damask, a striped pair of Breeches, two pair of black Stockings, a pair of old Pumps, a felt hat, an old ruffled Shirt, and several other Things; he commonly wears a black Cravat about his Neck. The same Time run-away also, from said Mathews, a Negro Man and Woman; also a white Girl, of about thirteen Years of Age, talks English, high and low Dutch; has short black Hair, thick Size, and swarthy Complexion, and is very talkative. The Negro and Negro Woman is much marked with the Small-Pox, the Negro-man speaks middling good English, Dutch and French; well made, very mannerly in his Way, and understands most Sorts of Labouring Work: The Negro Woman talks Dutch and English, and understands all sorts of House Work. Whoever takes up said Run-aways, and secures them so that their Master may have them again, shall have Ten Pounds, New-York Currency, Reward, and all reasonable Charges paid, by   EDMOND MATHEWS.

The New-York Mercury, October 8, 1759; October 15, 1759; October 22, 1759. See *The New-York Gazette*, October 8, 1759.

RUN-away, on Sunday the 23d ultimo, from John Puglsey, John Hunt, and Arabella Hedy, all of the Town of Westchester, and Province of New-York, the following Negros, viz. a Negro Follow, [sic] Jerrey, between 30 and 40 Years of Age: Had on when he went away, a brown Cloth Coat, with a red Collar, and had no Lining; and is a well set round shouldered Fellow. Another Negro Fellow, about 35, named Bohenah, well set, with a light Woolen Coat, and a Wool hat: They took a Negro Wench with 3 Children with them, one of which is a Girl of 11 Years old; a Boy of 4, and another about 2 Years old. Whoever takes up and secures the above Negroes, so that their Owners may have them again, shall receive Forty Shillings for each of the Fellows, and Twenty for the Wench, and each of her Children, as a Reward,   paid by   JOHN PUGLSEY, JOHN HUNT,
and ARABELLA HEDY. October 8, 1759.

The New-York Mercury, October 8, 1759; October 15, 1759; October 22, 1759; November 5, 1759

RUN away from Major Edmond Matthis of Albany, in the Province of New-York, the following People, viz. A Servant Man named William Fairfield, of a dark Complexion, down look, black Hair, and of a middling Stature. Also a Negro Man and Woman, and a white Girl with them, about 14 Years of Age, who talks good English, high and low Dutch; the Negro Man is much pitted with the Small Pox, and speaks good English: tis supposed they are all together: They took with them a great many Cloaths, and its probable with often alter their Dress. Whoever takes up said Runaways, and safely conveys them to their abovesaid Master, shall have Ten Pounds (25 Dollars) New-York Currency Reward, and all necessary Charges paid.
     EDMOND MATTHIS.   Albany, Octob. 1, 1759.
 The Boston Gazette, and Country Journal, October 9, 1759; October 22, 1759; November 5, 1759.

RUN-away, on Sunday, the Fourteenth Instant, from Jacob Van Wagenan, of the City of New-York, a Negro Fellow named Tom, about 22 Years old, 5 Feet 9 Inches high, and was marked on the Cheeks: Had on when he wen away, a brown Coat and Watch Coat, with a Velvet Jocky Cap. Whoever takes up the said Negro Fellow in the City of New-York, so that his Master may have him again, shall receive 20s. and if out of the City 40s. as a Reward, with all reasonable Charges,
    paid by JACOB VAN WAGENAN.
 The New-York Mercury, October 22, 1759; October 29, 1759; November 5, 1759; November 19, 1759.

RUN away from Major Matthews, on Matthew's Island, near Albany; a short thick-set Negro about 23 Years of Age, and has one of his Ears cut off; speaks good English, and had pretty good Cloaths: Whoever apprehends and secures the same, so as his Master may have him again, shall have THREE POUNDS Reward, and all reasonable Charges,
    paid by, Major EDWARD MATTHEWS,
 The New-York Gazette, October 30, 1758; November 20, 1758.

RUN-AWAY, from the Subscriber, living at Newtown, on Long-Island, the 30th ult. a German, named John Christophel Miller, by Trade a Cooper: Had on when he went away a light brown Broad-Cloth Coat, a Jacket of light-coloured cut velvet, and a Pair of black Everlasting Breeches. He wore a Cap, and went away considerable in Debt to Jacob Reader. Whoever will inform the said Reader where Miller is gone, so that he may

apprehend him, shall receive 40s. Reward, and all reasonable Charges, paid by   JACOB READER.
The New-York Mercury, November 5, 1759; November 12, 1759; November 19, 1759.

DESERTED the 11th of November, 1759, from Albany, Abraham Hinds, Matross, in Captain Martin's Company, of the Royal Regiment of Artillery; he is a thic chubby Fellow, about 20 Years of Age, born at Bristol, of a dark Complexion, full faced, dark brown Hair, has a Scar near his Throat on the right Side: Had on at the Time of his deserting, a plain blue Coat, a Flannel Waistcoat and blue breeches. Whoever apprehends and secures the said Deserter, and gives Notice thereof to Francis Stephens, Esq; Store keeper of his Majesty's Ordnance at New-York, or to John Hawkins, Esq; Commissary to the Artillery at Albany, shall receive a Guinea Reward, over an above what is allow'd by Act of Parliament.
The New-York Mercury, November 19, 1759; November 26, 1759.

RUN AWAY the 29th Day of October, from Richard Barnes, of Harison's Purchase, in West-Chester County, and Province of New-York, a Negro Man named Peter, but may change his Name: He is about 26 Years of Age, short and well-set, has had the Small-Pox, but had it easy, and shows it but very little, turns his Feet pretty much out when he walks or runs, is a sly, bold looking Fellow: Had on when he went away, a good Felt Hat, a new Woollen Jacket, or a dark Colour, an old Jacket under it, one or two Shirts, a Pair of old Woollen Breeches, and one Pair of blue Stockings; but it is very likely he will change his Cloaths. Whoever takes up the said Negro, and will secure him, so that I may have him again, or will bring him home to me, living in Harison's Purchase aforesaid, shall receive, if taken within 20 Miles of the Purchase, Twenty Shillings, and if farther, Forty Shillings Reward, and all reasonable Charges,
paid, by me   RICHARD BARNES.
N. B. He said that he would go to some other Country, or up to our Army. All Captains of Privateers, and other Vessels, are hereby forwarned from carrying off said Negro, as they may expect to answer the same at their Peril; and all other Persons are cautioned against harbouring him.
The New-York Gazette, November 26, 1759; December 31, 1759; January 7, 1760; January 14, 1760.

RUN-away the 23d of this instant, from Joshua Hatfield of the White Plains, in the county of West-Chester, in the Province of New-York, a

Negro man named Will, about 27 years of age, of a midling stature, thin faced, inclined to the consumption; had on when he went away, a great coat and close bodied coat under it, and breeches of grey home-spun cloth, a jacket of two colours, black stockings, and a pair of pumps; wears a cap, a felt hat, and a band cut off the hat: Whoever shall take up said Negro and bring him to his master, or secure him so that he may be had again, shall have 20 s. reward, if within 15 miles, if more 40 s. and all reasonable charges paid; forbidding all persons to conceal or carry off said Negro, upon the penalty of the law,

New-York, November 26, 1759.

The New-York Gazette, November 26, 1759; December 3, 1759. See *The New-York Gazette,* August 20, 1759.

RUN-*away from William Smith, of the City of New-York Block-Maker, last Wednesday Morning, the 21st of November ultimo, an Apprentice Lad, named William Edward, Bristol Born, about* 18 *Years of Age, and has a Scar in his left Cheek: Had on when he went away a blue Jacket, and a Pair of Thickset Breeches; has short Hair, and is about five Feet five Inches high. Whoever takes up and secures the said Apprentice Lad, so that his Master may have him again, shall receive Twenty Shillings Reward, and all reasonable Charges*

paid, by   *WILLIAM SMITH.*

The New-York Mercury, November 26, 1759; December 3, 1759; December 10, 1759; December 17, 1759.

RUN-away from the Subscriber, about ten Days ago, a Negro Fellow named Harry, who formerly belonged to Mr. Hildreth, of this City, Distiller, aged about 27 Years, five Feet 10 Inches high, well-limb'd, and is a stout well made Fellow, and can talk French, Spanish, Dutch and English: Had on when he went away, a brown Jacket and Breeches, wears a Scotch Bonnet, and was seen in Town on Sunday last. Whoever takes up and secures the said Negro Fellow so that his Master may have him again shall receive Forty Shillings Reward, and all reasonable Charges

paid, by Charles Lewis,

near the Sign of the Three Tons. November 24, 1759.

The New-York Mercury, November 26, 1759.

RUN away from on board the Letter of Marque Ship Prince Ferdinand, of Liverpool, Captain Hugh McQuoid, Commander, on Saturday Night last, Robert Lauder, an indented Servant to said Ship; said Robert Lauder is about 18 or 19 Years of Age, long visaged, wears his own hair, lately cut, marked with the Small-pox, speaks the Scotch Dialect very thick, and about 5 Feet 8 Inches high; he carried off with him several Things not his own Property. Any Person securing the said Lauder, and giving information thereof to said Capt. McQuoid, or Philip Livingston, Esq; in New-York, shall receive 40s. Reward. All Commanders of Ships are desired not to entertain him on pain of being prosecuted at the Law directs.

The New-York Mercury, November 26, 1759; December 3, 1759

ON Sunday Night, the 25th of November last, Run away from their Masters, Captain Isaac Sheldon, and Captain Hayt, both of this Port, two Apprentice Boys, the one named John Price, aged about 13 years; had on when he went away, a blue pee jacket, and blue breeches; of a slim stature, a brown complexion, and wore his own hair. The other named James M'Hugh, aged about 14 years, of a small stature, and a fair complexion. There is great reason to believe these boys were inveigled away to Philadelphia, by one Samuel Gill, a Guernsey man, about 23 years of age, and talks broken English, who was a sailor with Captain Sheldon in his last voyage, to whom the said John Price is an apprentice. Whoever takes up the said Samuel Gill, and two boys, and confines them so that their masters may have them again, and the said Gill meet his desert, [*sic*] shall have Forty Shillings reward, and all reasonable charges, paid by their said masters.

The New-York Gazette, December 10, 1759; January 14, 1760; January 21, 1760; *The New-York Mercury*, December 10, 1759; December 17, 1759; December 24, 1759. Minor differences between the papers. In the *Mercury* the second captain's name is "Hait" and Gill is to meet his "Deserts."

RUN-away from Jacob Eage, of Cambel-hall, in Ulster-County, the 2d of December instant, a Servant Woman named Mary M'Clean, aged about 25 Years, of a pale Complexion, middling lusty, was born in Scotland and speaks bad English: Had on when she went away, a Homespun Josey and Petticoat, and a new check Apron. Whoever takes up and secures said Servant, so that her Master may have her again, shall receive *Three Pounds* Reward, and all reasonable Charges
        paid by me   Jacob Eage.
The New-York Mercury, December 17, 1759; December 24, 1759; December 31, 1759; January 1, 1760.

New-York, December 31, 1759.

RUN away, from Charles Lewis, of the City of New-York, Mariner, the 20th Instant, a Negro Fellow, named, HARRY, about 5 Feet nine Inches high: Had on when he went away, an old green Jacket, and a white one under it, wore a Cap, and Woollen ribb'd Stockings, and had an Iron Collar round his Neck. Whoever takes up said Negro Fellow and secures him, so that his Master may have him again, shall receive Twenty Shillings Reward, and all reasonable Charges

   paid, by CHARLES LEWIS.

N. B. He has got an Iron Collar about his Neck, under his Shirt Collar, not visible, under the Collar, or his Hanerchief be removed.

The New-York Gazette, December 31, 1759. See *The New-York Mercury*, December 24, 1759.

1760

RAN-away last Tuesday night, from Adam Gilchrist, Taylor, in New-York, an Irish Servant Girl, named Catherine Pallester, about 30 years of age, remarkably short, being only between four and five feet stature, has black hair, and black eye brows, is of fresh colour and full of chat, and withall the fore finger of her right-hand is sore. Had on when she went away, a black and white check stuff gown, a new striped homespun petticoat. Took with her a brown camblet gown, one check linnen ditto, and two homespun joseys, one of them not made; a green sattin hat lined with red, and an old scarlet cloak without a cape, and arm-holes. Whoever takes up and secures the said servant, so that her master may have her again; shall have FORTY SHILLINGS reward, and reasonable charges

   paid by Adam Gilchrist.

N. B. All Captains of vessels and others are forbid to harbour her, or carry her off; 'tis tho't she is gone with some soldier or sailor.

The New-York Gazette, January 7, 1760; January 14, 1760.

RUN AWAY from his Bail, the 4th of this instant, Charles Hambleton, by Trade a Silver-smith, and Minor, as he pretends; of a dark Complexion, wears his Hat commonly flapping, with a blue or snuff colour'd Coat, about 5 Feet 8 Inches high, wants some of his Teeth, talks fast, and much on the Irish Tone, wears commonly a Sheep's grey Great coat, very short; aged about 40 Years, and is supposed to be gone into the Jerseys.—Whosoever takes up the said Hambleton, and secures him in any Goal in America, or delivers him to his Bail, or the Sheriff of New-York, shall receive Five Pounds Reward, and all reasonable Charges paid.

   JAMES CARRALL.

The New-York Gazette, January 7, 1760; January 28, 1760.

RUN AWAY, *on Monday last the 7th Instant, from* William Puntiner, *of this city, an English servant man, named* Nicholas Goddard, *by trade a tinman, of a small thin stature, aged about* 30, *remarkable for an extraordinary large scar under his chin, of a down look, and wears his own black hair. Had on when he went away, a light colour'd forrest cloth coat, and had a half-worn beaver hat. Whoever takes up and secures the said servant, so that his Master may have him again, shall have* Forty Shillings, *if taken upon this island, or* Five Pounds, *if taken up off the island, and all reasonable charges,*
    paid by   WILLIAM PUNTINER.
The New-York Gazette, January 14, 1760; January 28, 1760; February 11, 1760; March 10, 1760; March 31, 1760; *The New-York Mercury*, February 11, 1760; February 13, 1760; February 25, 1760. Minor differences between the papers.

RUN AWAY, *on Tuesday last the 8th Instant, from Capt.* John Taylor, *of this City, a Negro Man, named* JACK, *of short stature, Mulatto colour, wears his own bushy hair, pitted with the small pox, this country born, and, besides English, can talk very good Dutch. Had on when he went away, a blue watch coat, and Sailor's blue jacket, has trowsers, and dressed sailor like; had a hat, but may throw it aside for a cap.*

 Whoever takes up and secures the said Negro, so that his master may have him again, shall have Forty Shillings *reward, and reasonable charges paid by his master.*

 N. B. He gives out to be a free man. All Masters of Vessels are forbid to carry him off, as they must answer it according to Law.
The New-York Gazette, January 14, 1760; January 28, 1760; February 13, 1760; March 3, 1760; March 10, 1760.

DESERTED *from his Majesty's* 46th *Regiment, at Schenectady, commanded by the Hon. Lieut. General Thomas Murray, the following Persons, viz.* George Long, *belonging to Captain Delancey's Company, aged* 21 *Years,* 5 *Feet* 10 *Inches high, born in Queen's County, in Ireland, is a Wooll-Comber to Trade; is of a dark brown Complexion, short Hair, a very deep Dimple in his Chin, clumsey legs, and had a remarkable Cut in his left Knee, has a shambling Way of walking, and a slow soft Way of speaking.* George Dunn, *also belonging to Captain Delancey's Company, about* 5 *Feet* 9 *Inches high of a brown Complexion, thin Visage, long brown*

Hair, and a Shoemaker by Trade: He deserted in his Regimentals. William Washington, Corporal, in Capt. Forbes's Company, born in Old England, 5 Feet 10 Inches high, by Trade a Weaver, black Hair, of a dark Complexion, high nosed, with a Wart on it, of a down look, and was a Draft from the Old Buffs. James Kelsy, belonging to Captain Osborn's Company, born at Sheffield in Old England, 27 Years of Age, by Trade a Cutler, 5 Feet 8 Inches high, of a dark brown Complexion, slender made, frowning Appearance, and wants a Tooth. Whoever takes up and secures any of the above Deserters, shall have Twenty Shillings Reward paid by their respective Captains, or by Captain Mash, in New-York, besides what is allowed by Act of Parliament for apprehending Deserters.

The New-York Mercury, February 11, 1760; February 13, 1760.

RUN-away from John Vought on Tuesday last, a Servant Lad, named Hendrick Right, about 25 Years of Age, 5 Feet 2 Inches high, of a red Complexion, and his Nose crooked: Had on when he went away, a brown Jacket, greesy Leather Breeches, and white Stockings; took with him a large yellow Dog, with his fore feet white. Whoever takes up and secures the said Servant, shall have 20s. Reward, and all reasonable Charges
        paid, by   JOHN VOUGHT.
N. B. He formerly went by the name of Henry Miller.

The New-York Mercury, February 13, 1760; February 25, 1760.

DESERTED from his Majesty's Seventeenth Regiment of Foot, quartered at Ticonderoga, the following Persons, viz. John McIntosh, twenty three Years of Age, five Feet eight Inches high, well made, short necked, dark brown Hair, and a full smooth Complexion. born at Inverness, in Scotland, speaks both Earse and English equally well, by Trade a Silver-Smith.

    William Findley, twenty-four Years of Age, about five Feet seven Inches high, strait limbed, smooth Face, light brown Hair, and very talkative; born at Killebeg, in the County of Westmouth, in Ireland, by Trade a Weaver.

    For the better Encouragement of any Person or Persons to apprehend one or both of the said Deserters, shall receive Twenty Shillings for each, over and above what is allowed by Act of Parliament, which Money will be paid by Major John Campbell, of said Regiment, or Captain Howard, at Philadelphia; and at New-York, by Mr. Hugh Wallace, Merchant there.

    N. B. The abovementioned Persons deserted from a Serjeant's Party sent to Albany.

The New-York Mercury, March 3, 1760; March 10, 1760. See *The New-York Mercury*, November 10, 1760, for McIntosh.

RUN-away from Stephen Ward, of Eastchester, in Westchester County; an Indian Servant Boy, named Anthony Cockchick, about 15 Years of Age, and speaks good English: Had on when he went away, a Snuff coloured Broad-cloth Coat, blue everlasting Breeches, a Felt Hat, and strait Hair, about half grown. Whoever takes up and secures said Servant, so that his Master may have him again, shall receive Four Dollars Reward, and all reasonable Charges
       paid, by STEPHEN WARD.
The New-York Mercury, March 10, 1760; March 17, 1760; March 24, 1760.

RUN-away on Saturday the 8th of March, inst. from the Ship Two Friends, James Spellen, Master, a Servant Boy, named Bryant Carril, (but by most of his Acquaintance called Gilderoy) about 16 Years of Age: Had on when he went away, a Dutch Griggo, with a blue Jacket under it, a red Cap, a Pair of Trowsers with Drawers under them, and was seen going towards Jamaica, on Long-Island. Whoever takes up and secures said Servant, so that his Master may have him again, shall receive Twenty Shillings Reward, and all reasonable Charges paid,
      by JAMES SPELLEN.
The New-York Mercury, March 10, 1760.

           New-York, March 15, 1760.
SAturday Evening ran away from on board the Snow Sadler, a negro Boy, named Glasgow, aged about 18 Years, has got several Cuts on his Forehead, has a very clumsy Walk, and talks very broken English. Had on when he went away, a blue grey Coat, plain white Swan-skin Jacket, Pair of Trowsers, Pair of light blue Stockings, joined in the Middle, and new Shoes. Whoever takes up the said Boy, and brings him to his Master, shall have THREE POUNDS Reward, and all reasonable Charges
      paid by Capt. William Fitzherbert,
      now lying at the New Dock.
N. B. *All House-keepers, and Masters of Vessels are forbid to harbour the Boy, if they do, they may depend on being prosecuted according to Law.*
The New-York Gazette, March 17, 1760. See *The New-York Mercury,* March 31, 1760.

RUN-away on Saturday Evening, from on board the Snow Sadler, a Negro Boy, named Glasgow, aged about 18 Years, has several Cuts in his Forehead, a clumsy Walk, talks very broken English, and had on when he went away, a blue Great-Coat, plain white Swan-skin Jacket, a pair of Trowsers, light blue Stockings, joined in the Middle, and a pair of new Shoes: Whoever takes up and secures said Boy, and brings him to his

Master, shall have a Reward of Three Pounds, and all reasonable Charges paid by Capt. William Fitzherbert, now lying at the New Dock.

N. B. All House-keepers, and Masters of Vessels are forbid to harbour said Boy, if they do, they may depend on being prosecuted according to Law.

The New-York Mercury, March 31, 1760. See *The New-York Gazette*, March 17, 1760.

RUN-away, from Thomas Brown, of the City of New-York, a Servant Girl named Mary Rogerson: She is a portly Woman, has blue Eyes, and of a fair Complexion. Had on when she went away, a striped and cross-bar'd stuff gown, a homespun pettycoat, a round blue Satten Hat, went away the 30th of March, and was seen on Staten-Island. Whoever takes up and secures said Servant, so that her Master may have her again, shall receive THREE POUNDS Reward, from Joseph Mersereau on Staten-Island, or THOMAS BROWN.

N. B. 'Tis supposed she is gone to the Southward. All Persons whatsoever are forbid to harbour her.

The New-York Mercury, April 7, 1760; April 21, 1760; April 28, 1760; May 5, 1760.

Flushing, *on* Long-Island, *March* 30, 1760.
RUN *away from* Barnardus Ryder, *a negro man named* Caesar, *aged about 25 years, this country born, he is not a right black, but a little on the yellowish cast, a pretty lusty fellow, talks good English, but stutters a little in common, and if frightened, he stutters very much, and is remarkable for having lost one of his fore teeth: Had on when he went away, a light coloured* Devonshire *kersey coat, a soldiers red jacket and breeches, and a soldiers hat, a pair of old shoes. Whoever takes up the said negro man, and brings him to his said master, shall have* Forty Shillings *reward, and all reasonable charges, if taken on* Long-Island, *if taken off the said Island, shall have* Three Pounds *reward, and all reasonable charges,*
 paid by Barnardus Ryder,
 now living at Flushing.

N.B. *All house keepers, and masters of vessels, are forbid to harbour the said negro man; if they do, they may depend on being prosecuted according to law.*

The New-York Gazette, April 14, 1760; April 21, 1760; April 28, 1760; May 5, 1760; May 26, 1760. See *The New-York Mercury*, April 14, 1760.

Recruits which are deserted, belonging to the 4th Battalion or *Royal American* Regiment,

Joseph Monnet, born in Nottingham, in the County of Nottingham, by trade a blacksmith, of a dark complexion, aged 23 Years, 5 Feet 6 Inches high.

James Farning, born at Waterford, in the County of Waterford, by trade a Taylor, of a fair complexion, aged 23 years, 5 Feet 6 Inches high.

John Edward, born in Wales, in the county of Flintshire, by trade a Labourer, of a fair complexion, aged 28 years, 5 Feet 6 Inches high.

John Pike, born at Dover, in the same county, by trade a weaver, of a brown complexion, aged 23 years, 5 Feet 6 Inches high.

Whoever takes up and secures all or any of the said Deserters, so that the commanding Officer of the Battalion may have them again, shall have *Thirty Shillings* Reward for each, besides what the Law allows, and all charges paid.

The New-York Gazette, April 14, 1760.

RUN-away from Barnardus Ryder, on Long-Island, the 30th ultimo, a Negro Man named Caesar, aged about 25 Years, this Country born, and of a yellowish Cast, a pretty lusty Fellow, talks good English, but stutters a little, and if frightened, he stutters very much; is remarkable for losing one of his Fore Teeth: Had on when he went away, a light-coloured Devonshire Kersey Coat, and a Soldier's Jacket, Breeches and Hat, and a Pair of old Shoes. Whoever takes up the said Negro Man, and brings him to his Master, shall receive FORTY SHILLINGS Reward, and all reasonable charges paid, if taken up on Long-Island; and if off the said Island, Three Pounds, and all reasonable Charges paid.

by BARNARDUS RYDER,

N. B. All House-Keepers and Masters of Vessels are forbid to harbour the said Negro Man, at their Peril.

The New-York Mercury, April 14, 1760; April 21, 1760; May 5, 1760; May 26, 1760. See *The New-York Gazette*, April 14, 1760.

RUN-away from this City, about seventeen days since, a likely Negro fellow named Tom, about twenty seven years old, of a middle stature; had on when he went away, a blue cloth lapell'd coat, with brass buttons, a red cloth waistcoat, leather breeches, and a hat with a gold button and loop; he is supposed to be loitring in the country not far from town. Whoever takes up the said Negro, or will secure him, so that he may be had again, shall receive the sum of FIVE POUNDS Reward, by applying to the printer of this paper.

The New-York Mercury, April 14, 1760.

RUN-AWAY on the 27th of April last, a Negro Man, named Windsor, (Alias Jammy) aged about 20 Years, born in the West Indies, about 5 Feet 3 Inches high, a round full Visage, has several Pimples on his Face, especially on his Chin, a clumsy walk; had on when he went away, a full trim'd blue Livery Coat, with worsted Lace, and a Shoulder knot on the left Shoulder. a yellow cloth Waistcoat with the same Lace as the Coat, yellow plush Breeches, dark blue Stockings, and single channel'd Pumps, a beaver Hat with a Silk lining. Whoever takes up and secures the said Negro, shall have a Pistole Reward, and all reasonable Charges paid,
    by John Clopper in Stone-Street, New-York.
N. B. All House keepers and Masters of Vessels, are forbid to harbour or carry off the said Negro, if they do, they may depend on being prosecuted according to Law.
 The New-York Mercury, May 5, 1760; May 12, 1760; May 19, 1760; May 26, 1760; *The New-York Gazette*, May 5, 1760; May 12, 1760; May 26, 1760. The *Gazette* shows the runaway's alias as "Jemmy".
 See *The New-York Gazette*, June 23, 1760.

RAN away from *Erasmus Williams*, in *New-York*, on Thursday last the 8th Instant, a white Servant Wench, aged about 19 Year, has a pretty likely face, of a rudy complection, remarkably strong set, fat, and clumsy, wears a very dark blue and white striped Manchester cotton gown, striped homespun petticoat, a black sattin or straw hat, with two rows of flowncing round the Brim, besides what goes round the Crown; named *Easter Ashton*, born at *Ashton Underline*, in *Lancashire*.
Whoever apprehends and secures the said Servant, so that she may be had again, shall receive Forty Shillings Reward, and reasonable Charges paid,
    by said Williams.
N. B. It is imagined she went off with some of the Artillery Men.
 The New-York Gazette, May 12, 1760; May 26, 1760. See The *New-York Mercury*, May 12, 1760.

RUN AWAY from Josiah Pell, of the manor of Pellham near New Rochel, a negro wench, named Elcey, about 45 years old, has had the small pox, is not very black, but is pretty lusty. Whoever brings her home, or will send word where she may be found, so that her master may have her again, shall have FORTY SHILLINGS reward,
    From JOSIAH PELL.
 The New-York Gazette, May 12, 1760; May 19, 1760; June 9, 1760; June 23, 1760.

RUN AWAY from his Master, *Theodorus Van Wyck*, of *Dutchess* County, in the Province of *New-York*, a Negro Man named JAMES, aged about 22 Years, a short well made Fellow, goes stooping, with his Head forward, can talk nothing but English, and has a low Voice. Had on when he went away, a light blue Coat, a little grey under Waistcoat, laced; a check'd woollen Shirt, and Leather Breeches; is supposed to be gone to Albany to inlist into the Army, and has been taken up near Livingston's Manor, but escaped again.—Whoever shall take up said Negro, and send him to his said Master, or to *Theodorus Van Wyck*, Merchant, in New-York, shall have *Forty Shillings* Reward, and all reasonable Charges,
          paid by   THEODORUS VAN WYCK.   April 22, 1760.

In Case the said Negro should offer to inlist either in the Regular, or Provincial Forces, the enlisting Officer to whom he may offer himself, is desired to seize him, by Virtue of this Advertisement, and forward him to his said Master.

The New-York Gazette, May 12, 1760; June 23, 1760.

RUN-away from Erasmus Williams, of the City of New-York, on Thursday the 8th ultimo, a Servant Girl named Hester Ashton, born at Ashton under Line, in Lancashire; she is about 19 Years of Age, pretty likely Face, and of a ruddy Complexion, remarkable strong made, is fat and clumsy: Had on when she went away, a dark blue Manchester Cotton Gown, striped homespun Pettycoat, a Straw Hat, or a black Satten One, double flounced round the Brim, as well as round the Crown. Whoever apprehends and secures the said Servant, so that she may be had again, shall receive Forty Shillings Reward, and all reasonable Charges paid, by said Williams. It is imagined she went off with some of the Train of Artillery.

The New-York Mercury, May 12, 1760; May 19, 1760; May 26, 1760; June 2, 1760. See *The New-York Gazette*, May 12, 1760.

RUN-AWAY from John Thompson, at Jamaica, on Long-Island, a servant Woman named Rose McBride, born in Ireland, a lusty well looking young Woman of a fair Complexion, and light Hair, with Gold Earrings fixed in her Ears, having on a Dark coloured Callicoe Gown. Whoever takes her up, and secures her, so that her Master may have her again, shall receive forty Shillings Reward and all reasonable Charges paid.

    N. B. All Masters of Vessels, Boats, Shallops, and Ferry Men, are forbid to carry her off; and all manner of Persons are likewise forbid to Harbour, Conceal or Entertain the said Servant, as they will be prosecuted with the utmost Rigour of the Law
          by, JOHN THOMPSON.

The New-York Mercury, May 12, 1760; May 19, 1760.

Deserted, in his Regimentals, the 11th of April, from the 4th Battalion of the Royal American Regiment, at Fort Ontario, *Richard Coles,* of Captain *Willyamos*'s Company, 5 Feet 8 Inches high, 20 Years of Age, brown Complexion, round Visage, grey Eyes, brown Hair, born in England, in the County of Berkshire, Labourer, enlisted at Fort Ontario, out of the New-York Provincials, October 28, 1759.

The New-York Gazette, May 19, 1760; May 26, 1760.

RUN-AWAY, on Friday the 16th of May Inst. a Mulatto Wench named Sarah (Alias Jenny) born at New-Rochel, in the County of West-Chester; she is a well set likely Wench: Had on when she went away, a Green Penniston Petticoat, and brown Penniston Josey; also a very broad striped blue and white French Cotton Josey and Petticoat. Whoever takes up and secures said Wench, shall have Forty Shillings Reward, and all reasonable Charges paid,

By Hendrick Rutgers, Brewer.

N. B. All House-keepers, Masters of Vessels and others are hereby forbid to Harbour, Conceal or carry off said Wench, as they depend on being prosecuted according to Law. 'Tis supposed she is gone off with a white Man, towards the Southward.

The New-York Mercury, May 19, 1760; May 26, 1760; June 9, 1760; June 16, 1760; June 23, 1760.

Philipsburgh, in Westchester County, May 20, 1760.

THIS is to give Notice to all Persons whatever, that one *George Long,* an *Irishman,* aged 20 or 25 Years, about 5 Feet 9 Inches high, well set, and wore his own Hair, of a reddish brown, fled the 19th of this Inst. May, for committing a Rape on a Woman, whom he used very ill otherways, so that she is now in Danger of her Life: Had on when he went off, a blue Coat, much worn, a white Flannel Waistcoat, and little black speck check'd Trowsers: He is very much Pok-broken, blue Eyes, and a red Complexion. Whoever will apprehend the said Felon, and secures him in any of His Majesty's Goals, shall have *Three Pounds* Reward, and reasonable Charges, paid by *Wolvert Ecker,* of *Philipsburgh.*

N. B. He was inlisted under Capt. Gilchrist, of the New-York Forces, on the present Expedition; and it is supposed he will help himself to a Pass, as he has good Learning, for he has not got one from his Officer.

The New-York Gazette, May 26, 1760; June 16, 1760.

WHEREAS *Nelly Monro*, Wife of *James Mackinsey*, of the Royal Highlanders, stationed in New-York, discharged, left his Bed and Board on Friday Inst, and carried away Effects to considerable Value. She is of middle Size, of black Complexion, full Face, between 40 and 42 Years of Age, has a suitable Assortment of Cloaths, but in particular two Gowns of Tartan Plad, the one old, the other New. Any Person who will bring her to the Subscriber, living near the *Black-Horse*, shall have *Three Pounds* Reward, paid by *James Mackinsey*.

N. B. All Persons are forbid to harbour or conceal her at their Peril.

The New-York Gazette, May 26, 1760; June 16, 1760.

German Camp, May 11, 1760.

Run away from Major *Edmond Mathews*, a white Servant Boy, called *Patrick Corry*, about 14 Years old, stutters much in his Speech, had on two red Waistcoats, an old Pair of brown Breeches, and wears his own hair. Any Person that will take him up, so that his Master may have him again, shall have *Thirty Shillings* Reward, and all reasonable Charges paid, by EDMOND MATHEWS.

The New-York Gazette, May 26, 1760.

Run away from John Milligan, *in Beaver-street, a Negro Man named* TOM: *Had on when he went away, a pair of Trowsers, and a black cut Manchester Waistcoat, without Sleeves, and a check Shirt; he is stiff in the left Knee, and walks limping, can speak both* Dutch *and* English *and is a great Fiddler. Whoever takes up said Negro Man, and brings him to his Master, or secures him in any Goal, shall have* Twentyshillings *[sic] reward.*

All Masters of Vessels, and others, are hereby forbid to carry off said Slave, as they shall answer it at their peril.

The New-York Gazette, June 9, 1760.

RUN AWAY on the 2d Instant, from *James Barnard*, Inn-holder, at the *Kings-Bridge, Westchester* County, *Samuel Philipse*, an Apprentice of middle Stature, about 18 Years old, has dark brown Hair, with a Scar on his Forehead. Took with him a green cut Velvet Jacket, a pair of new Buckskin Breeches, a pair of brown Thread Stockings, wore a new Felt Hat, had two Flannel Jackets, one pair of Trowsers, and two check Shirts. It is very likely he may appear in a *New-York* Provincial Regimental Coat; and when he went off wore a pair of *Indian* Mockasins. Whoever takes up and secures the said Apprentice, so that his Master may have him again, shall have

FIVE DOLLARS Reward, and reasonable Charges
paid by   JAMES BARNARD.
N.B. Masters of Vessels, and others, are forbid to carry him off at their peril. It is supposed he is come down to *New-York*, in order to go to *Rhode-Island*, and was seen last Wednesday in this City, *New-York, June* 9, 1760.
The *New-York Gazette*, June 9, 1760; June 16, 1760; July 14, 1760; July 21, 1760; August 11, 1760; September 1, 1760.

Description of Deserters from the Hon.
Col. Montgomery*'s Regiment.*
Neil MacDonald, of Sir *Allan McLean*'s Company, 5 feet 7 inches high, 21 years of age, a Highlander, speaks little or no English, dark brown hair, light grey eyes, mark'd with the small-pox, swarthy complexion.

John Campbell, of said Company, size 5 feet 6 inches, aged 22 years, light brown hair, large white eyes, and thick lips, full fac'd, mark'd with the small-pox; both deserted from *Claverack*, and are supposed to be lurking thereabouts still.

Archibald Montgomery, of Capt. *Farquharson*'s Company, size 5 feet 6 inches, aged 45 years, complexion ruddy, large grey eyes, eye-brows, beard, and hair red, eyebrows remarkable large, snuffs and drinks to excess. wore a wig when he went off.

John Barnet, of said Company, size 5 feet 4 inches, aged 28 years, complexion black, grey eyes, a little mark'd with the small-pox, dark brown hair: The above two deserted from *Lunnenburgh*, and are supposed to have gone towards *York*.

Angus Stewart, of Capt. *Farquharson*'s Company, size 5 feet 4 inches high, born in *Scotland*, aged 30 years, jet black hair, black complexion, thin visage, blue eyes, deserted from *Albany*, and supposed to have gone towards *New-England*.

Robert Douglas, of Capt. *Robertson*'s Company, born in *North-Britain*, aged 19 or 20 years, 5 feet 5 inches high, pale hair cut short, redish complexion, blue eyes, round short visage, stoops forward much when he walks.

The *New-York Gazette*, June 9, 1760; June 16, 1760; July 14, 1760.

RUN-away from his Bail, one Dennis Delany: He is about 5 Feet 8 inches high, well set, of a sandy Complexion, speaks slow, and with the Brogue, and has a little Stopage in his Speech. Whoever takes up the said Delany, and secures him in any Goal in the Province, so they he may be brought to Justice, shall receive THREE GUINEAS Reward,
paid by   GERARD CHESNUT.

The New-York Mercury, June 9, 1760; June 16, 1760; June 23, 1760; July 7, 1760; July 21, 1760.

RUN AWAY, a Negro man, named *Andrase Peters,* middle size, smooth face, born at Corocoa, speaks bad English; had on a blue, and spotted swanskin waistcoat. Whoever takes up said Negro man, and brings him to THOMAS WATKINS, at New-York, shall receive Thirty Shillings reward, with all reasonable charges.
The New-York Gazette, June 16, 1760; June 23, 1760; July 7, 1760.

Staten-Island, June 9, 1760.
RAN-away, on Friday the 6th Day of *June,* from *Roger Barnes,* a Negro Boy, named *Tom,* 14 or 15 Years, born in *New-York,* pretty black. Had on when he went away.—a Felt Hat, an Oznabrig Shirt and Trowsers, a deep Blue Broad Cloth Jacket, the Fore Parts lined with two Colours of red and brown Cloth, with white Buttons. Whoever takes up the said Negro, so that his Master may have him again, shall receive Forty Shillings Reward and all reasonable Charges
        paid by,   Roger Barnes.
N. B. All persons are forbid to Harbour said Negro.
The New-York Gazette, June 16, 1760; June 23, 1760; July 14, 1760; *The New-York Mercury,* June 16, 1760; June 23, 1760; June 30, 1760; July 7, 1760; July 21, 1760. Minor differences between the papers. The *Mercury* shows the location and the date of June 6, 1760, at the bottom of the ad.

RUN-AWAY from the Subscriber, on Sunday the 15th instant, a Negro Fellow named Bromlow, aged about 24 Years, 5 Feet 7 Inches high, and has several Cutts in his Fore-head: Had on when he went away, an Ozenbrig Frock and Trowsers. Whoever takes up and secures the said Fellow, so that he may be had again, shall receive Forty Shillings Reward, and all reasonable Charges
        paid, by   HENRY RICHARDSON.
The New-York Mercury, June 23, 1760; June 30, 1760.

BROKE out of the Work-House, about a Fortnight ago, a negro man named *Windsor,* alias *Jemmy,* aged about 20 Years, born in the West-Indies, about 5 feet 3 inches high, a round full Visage, has several Pimple, on his Face, especially on his Chin, and has a clumsey Walk. Had on a brown colour'd cloth coat, Leather breeches, and oznabrigs shirt. Whoever takes up and secures the said Negro, so that he may be had again, or brings him to the Printer hereof, shall have a PISTOLE Reward, and all reasonable Charges paid by the Printer.

The New-York Gazette, June 23, 1760; June 30, 1760; July 14, 1760; *The New-York Mercury,* June 23, 1760; June 30, 1760; July 7, 1760; July 21, 1760. Minor differences between the papers. See *The New-York Mercury,* May 5, 1760.

Norwich, July 4, 1760.

BROKE jail last Saturday Night at Norwich one Christopher Squibb, an Indian Fellow belonging to Fitch's Regiment, about 20 Years old; had on when he broke Jail, a blue Coat lapelled with Scarlet, he deserted from Major Durkee at Albany.—Whoever shall apprehend said Fellow and bring him to the aforesaid Regiment, shall have four Pounds Reward, and all reasonable Charges
          paid, By   ELIHU HIDE, Ensign.
          per Major DURKEE's Order.

The New-London Summary, or, The Weekly Advertiser, July 11, 1760.

New-York, July 10, 1760

RUNAWAY from *Dennis Hicks,* of Philipsburgh, in Westchester County, and Province of New-York, a mulatto Slave, named Bill, aged about 20 Years, has a long sharp Nose, with a black Mole on the right Side of his Face, near his Nose: has very large Ears, speaks very good English, and pretends to be free, and can read and write well: Says he has a White Mother, and was born in New-England. He is of a middle size, and has a thin Visage, with his Hair cut off. All Persons are forbid to harbour him, and all Masters of Vessels are forbid to carry him off, as they will answer it at their Peril. TWENTY-FIVE POUNDS Reward for securing him in any Goal, or bringing him to me, so that I may have him again, and reasonable
          Charges paid by   DENNIS HICKS.

N. B. This Fellow was advertised in the New York Papers the 5th of June, and in New Haven the 11th of June 1759; was afterwards taken up in Waterbury, and was put into Litchfield Goal, from whence he was brought to Bedford, and there made his Escape from his Master again. Those who apprehend him, are desired to secure him in Irons. He was taken up by Moses Foot, of North Waterbury, in New-England. It is likely he will change his Cloaths, as he did before. The Mole abovementioned is something long.

N. B. By Information he was in Morris County, in the Jerseys all the Winter, and said he would enter into the Provincial Service.

The New-York Gazette, July 14, 1760; July 21, 1760; *The Pennsylvania Gazette,* July 24, 1760. Minor differences between the papers. See *The New-York Gazette,* June 11, 1759, *The New-York Gazette,* August 20, 1759, and *The New-York Gazette,* December 29, 1760.

L*Ast thursday night the wash-house of Timothy Wetmore, of Rye was broke open, and stole out of the wash-tub, three white linnen shirts, one marked F P on the breast, the other two T W on the tail gusset; one check shirt, with a patch on the breast, and on the back; 5 shifts, three of which were homspun, one pair of sheets, one marked I H on the corner, one diaper table cloth, a considerable number of linnen, cambrick and lawn handkerchiefs and caps, a parcel of child's cloths, and sundry other articles too tedious to mention. It is supposed they were taken by Moll Rogers, and that she has or will make towards New-York. Whoever will apprehend the thief, the person may be bro't to justice, shall have 8 dollars reward, paid by the subscriber. This wretch has been a great plunderer and disturber of the repose of the honest people of this province, particularly the country, for a long course of time, and has actually been in the hands of the authority time after time, and yet is as daring as ever in her villainy.*
                    TIMOTHY WETMORE.
The New-York Mercury, July 14, 1760; July 21, 1760; July 28, 1760.

RUN-away, from the Subscriber, a new Negro, named Castalio, has several Cuts in his Body, and his two fore Teeth filed; he has Holes in both his Ears. Had on when he went away, an Ozenbrigs Shirt and Trowsers, and a cross bard red Linnen Waistcoat. Whoever takes up and secures said Negro, so that he may be had again, shall receive 5 Dollars Reward,
        paid at Jamaica by   RICHARD BETTS.
The New-York Mercury, July 28, 1760; August 4, 1760; August 11, 1760.

RUN-away *from the Subscriber, on Saturday the 26th Inst. living in New-York, a Negro Fellow named Will, about 17 Years old, and very likely, born in the Island of Coracoa: Had on when he went away a round Hat, with white Binding, blue Jacket with white Linnen, Check shirt, and Ozenbrigs Trowsers. Whoever takes up and secures the said Fellow so that he may be had again shall have Forty Shillings Reward,*
        paid by   JOHN JOHNSON.
The New-York Mercury, July 28, 1760; August 4, 1760; August 11, 1760.

DESERTED from His Majesty's Royal Artillery, the two following Persons employed as Seamen on board the Sloop *True Briton, Charles Gyles,* Master, *Nathaniel Mayhew,* and *George Murfy,* both of Boston.

Whoever apprehends and secures in any of His Majesty's Goals in the Province of *New-York,* the *Massachusetts-Bay,* or County of *Albany,* either of the abovesaid Persons, or sends either or both of them to the Honorable Colonel *George Williamson,* with the Army under the Command of his Excellency Major-General AMHERST, shall immediately receive TEN DOLLARS Reward for each of them, and all other necessary Charges,
        by applying to me the Subscriber,
            or to Mr. *Alexander Boies* of *Boston* in *New-England.*

And all Masters of Vessels are hereby cautioned not to carry off or ship either of the abovementioned Persons, on any Pretence whatsoever.
      By Order of Colonel *George Williamson,* Commanding-Officer of Artillery in *America,*
          Wm. Saltonstall, Commissary Artillery.
Albany, June 21, 1760.
   The Boston News-Letter, July 31, 1760; August 7, 1760.

RUN away, on Tuesday the 29th ult. from Thomas Hill a negro wench named Princess; she is about 20 years of age, short of stature and speaks good english: Had on when she went away, a strip'd homespun josey and pettycoat, with silver earings; 'tis supposed she is harbour'd at some house in town, as she has been seen several times between the Old-Slip Market and the Exchange. Whoever takes up and secures said wench, or gives information where she is conceal'd, shall have Twenty Shillings reward, and all charges
         paid by   THOMAS HILL.
   The New-York Mercury, August 4, 1760; August 11, 1760.

               Cow-Neck, Long-Island, August 13. 1760.
RUN AWAY, *on Saturday Night last, from the Subscriber, a Negro Man named Primus, about* 20 *Years of Age, somewhat smaller than a middle Size, a likely well looking Fellow, speaks very good English and Low Dutch, plays on the Violin, can read and write, and has tended a Mill. He is supposed to have on, or taken with him, a good Castor Hat, a grey Ratteen Coat, lined with dark brown Camblet, with yellow mettal Buttons; a green Everlasting Jacket, faded yellowish, lined with Shalloon: a Pair of black Everlasting Breeches, a Pair of Check Trowsers, two Pair of Stockings, the one black, the other mix'd blue and white; a Pair of Pumps, three Shirts, one of fine Linnen, another of Homespun, and the other Oznabrigs. Any*

Person who takes up said Fellow and brings him to the Subscriber hereof, shall have Three Pounds *Reward, if taken on* Long-Island, *and* Six Pounds, *if taken off the Island.*
      Henderick Onderdonck.
N. B. It is likely he will forge a Pass.
 The New-York Gazette, August 18, 1760; August 25, 1760; September 1, 1760; September 15, 1760. See *The New-York Mercury*, August 18, 1760.

      Cow-Neck, (on Long-Island) August 13, 1760.
RUN-AWAY, on Saturday Night last from the Subscriber, a Negro Man named Primus, about 20 Years of Age, somewhat smaller than a middle Size, a likely well looking Fellow, speaks very good English and low Dutch, plays on the Violin, can read and write, and has attended a Grist Mill. He is supposed to have on, or taken with him, a good Castor Hat, a grey Ratteen Coat, lined with dark brown Camblet, with yellow mettal Buttons; a green Everlasting Jacket, faded yellowish, lined with Shalloon: a pair of black Everlasting Breeches, a pair of Check Trowsers, two pair of Stockings, the one black, the other mix'd blue and white; a pair of Pumps, three Shirts, one of fine Linnen, another of Homespun, and the other Oznabrigs. Any Person who takes up said Fellow and brings him to the Subscriber hereof, shall have three Pounds Reward, if taken on Long-Island, and Six Pounds, if taken off the Island, and all reasonable Charges paid, by HENDERICK ONDERDONK.
N. B. It is likely he will forge a Pass.
 The New-York Mercury, August 18, 1760; August 25, 1760; September 1, 1760; September 8, 1760; September 29, 1760. See *The New-York Gazette*, August 18, 1760.

RAN AWAY from Benjamin Tusten, of Goshen, in Orange County, on the 3d Day of August, a Negro Man, named Guy, aged about 30 Years, is very black, and has some small Scars on his Forehead: Had on when he went away, a mix'd colour homespun Coat, with horn Buttons, a blue Waistcoat, a new tow Shirt, short Trowsers, a Pair of white cotton Breeches, a pair of white worsted Stockings, a pair of good Shoes, and a new wool Hat. Whoever takes up said Negro Man, and brings him to his said Master, or secured him so that his Master may have him, shall have Forty Shillings Reward, and all reasonable Charges,
    paid by me *Benjamin Tusten.*
N. B. He is about 5 Feet 2 Inches high, talks broken English.
 The New-York Gazette, August 25, 1760; September 1, 1760; September 17, 1760; October 6, 1760.

TEN POUNDS Reward, and Reasonable Charges to any Person, securing or giving such Intelligence to the Subscriber, so as that he may get his Negro Man, named *Kinsale*, about 21 Years old, five Feet 6 to 8 Inches in Height, a thick well set strong Fellow, well known in this City. Had a large Head and Nose, very thick Lips. Speaks but indifferent *English* affecting the Negro Way; had a remarkable Scar near his left Temple, his Legs bowing outwards, and large flat Feet, subject to telling such as dont know him of his being a Freeman. This is therefore to give notice, that any Person harbouring, secreting or carrying off said Negro by Land or Water, and upon coming to my Knowledge, may depend upon being prossecuted in due course of Law,

by *JOHN LORD.* *September 8th*, 1760.

The New-York Gazette, September 8, 1760; September 15, 1760; *The New-York Mercury*, September 22, 1760; September 29, 1760. Minor differences between the papers. The *Mercury* shows his age as "about 22 Years of Age."

Albany, 9th September, 1760.
DESERTED His Majesty's 77th REgiment, or first Highland Battalion, commanded by the Hon. Col. *Archibald Montgomery*, and from the Hon. Capt. *John Gordon*'s Company of Grenadiers, *Duncan Cameron*, born in *Morganshire*, of *Argyle*, six Feet high, aged 24 Years, no Trade, hair Hair, full faced, fair Complexion, grey Eyes, went off in his Regimentals, and talks very bad *English*. Whoever apprhends and secures the said Deserter, or brings him to the commanding Officer in *New York*, shall have *Ten Guineas* Reward.

The New-York Gazette, September 15, 1760; September 22, 1760.

RUN-AWAY, on Sunday Night last, a Negro Man named Jack: Had on when he went away, a brown Jacket, without Sleeves, a pair of short Breeches, and no Hat, a Scar on his Left Cheek, speaks very good English and French. Any person that will take up the said Negro, and will bring him to the Printer hereof, shall have Thirty Shillings Reward, and all reasonable Charges.
N. B. All Masters of Vessels are forbid to Harbour the said Negro.
The New-York Mercury, September 15, 1760.

RAN-away on Saturday last, from Elizabeth Carpenter, a negro Fellow, named *Venture,* well known to attend the Stall at the Slip Market. Had on a green Jacket, short Trowsers, and a close trimed Hat, TWENTY

SHILLINGS, Reward, and Charges, for apprehending and securing him, paid by ELIZABETH CARPENTER.
The New-York Gazette, September 29, 1760. See *The New-York Gazette: or, the Weekly Post-Boy*, August 7, 1758, *Weyman's New-York Gazette*, April 30, 1759, *Weyman's New-York Gazette*, July 16, 1759. and *The New-York Gazette*, July 13, 1761.

RUN AWAY from the Subscriber, and taken with him sundry Things of Value, *John Lintner*, an indented Servant, of a fair Complexion, with long Hair, about 5 Feet 6 or 7 Inches high, a Native of Saxony, but speaks tollerable English. Had on when he went away, a Worsted Night Cap, two Jackets, the upper one red and white strip'd Flannel, with Sleeves, the under one a blue double breasted Ratteen, with Metal Buttons, a Pair of Oznabrigs Trowsers, new Shoes and Stockings, with Brass Buckles in his Shoes, but not paired. Whoever takes up and secures the above Fellow, shall have TWO PISTOLES Reward, by sending Notice to
  Mr. *Robert Wallace*, Carpenter, in *New-York.*
  George Black, Barrack-Master, in *Albany.*
The New-York Gazette, September 29, 1760.

RUN-AWAY from the Subscriber, the 12th of September last, a Negro Man, named Frank, speaks English pretty well, and a little French: Had on when he went away, a grey Watch Coat, a Pair of Trowsers, Stockings and Shoes, with carv'd Brass Buckles; is about 30 Years old, and 5 Feet and a half high. Whoever takes up and secures the said Fellow, so that he may be had again, shall have Fifty Shillings Reward, and all Charges paid, at the House of Mr. Evouts's
  by THOMAS MORLEY.
The New-York Gazette, October 13, 1760; October 27, 1760.

RUN-away from John Waddell, the 6th of October Instant, a Negro Man named Charles, aged about 24 Years, a likely middle-sized Fellow, talks good English, this Country born,, and formerly belonged to Col. Moore. He is well known in New-York, an at Harlem, and was seen as the latter the 11th Inst. Whoever takes up and secures the said Negro, so that his Master may have him again, shall receive FIVE POUNDS Reward,
  paid by JOHN WADDELL.
The New-York Mercury, October 13, 1760; October 20, 1760; October 27, 1760; November 4, 1760; November 17, 1760; November 24, 1760.

DESERTED *from Captain Oglivie's Independent Company, lying at Still-Water, the following Men, viz.* George Peters, *born in Philadelphia, a Serjeant; about* 5 Feet 9 *Inches high, well set and Square; of a fair Complexion, light brown Hair. Had on when he went away, his Regimentals; a Black-Smith by Trade.*

Barnaby Griffith, *about* 5 Feet 9 *Inches high, pretty thin, of a swarthy Complexion, straight long black Hair, long visage, grey Eyes. Had on, his Regimentals.*

James Greenland, *born in London, a Glazier by Trade, about* 5 Feet 7 *Inches high, well made, a round Vissage, brown Eyes, short black Hair. Had on, a pair of Buck Skin Breeches, with his Regimentals. Whoever taks up and secures the said Men, shall have the full Reward allowed by Act of Parliament for apprehending Deserters.*

The New-York Mercury, October 20, 1760; October 27, 1760; November 4. 1760.

RUN AWAY on Friday the 6th Day of *September,* from *Francis Silvester,* Cooper, on the City of *New-York,* A likely spry Negro Boy, named *CUDJO,* about 18 Years of Age: Had on when he went away, a dark brown Jacket, a white Shirt, and Trowsers. Any Person apprehending and securing the said Negro Boy, so that he may be had again, shall have *Twenty Shillings,* if taken in Town, and *Forty Shillings,* if out of Town, and reasonable Charges,
    paid by FRANCIS SILVESTER.

The New-York Gazette, October 27, 1760; October 30, 1760; November 3, 1760.

DESERTED the 7th of October Inst. from his Majesty's Inniskilling or 27th Regiment of Foot, commanded by the Right Honourable Lord Blakeney, and in Capt. Martin's Company, encamped at Crown-Point; John Wigg, 5 Feet 6 Inches high, without Shoes, straight black Hair, dark Complexion, aged about 21 Years, no Trade, born at Villverton in Norfolkshire. Had on when he went away, his Regimental Coat and Hat, and a brown Waistcoat; he formerly belonged to the Plymouth Division of Marines. Whoever apprehends him and lodges him in any of his Majesty's Goals, shall receive one Guinea Reward, over and above what is allowed by Act of Parliament, by applying to Mr. Hugh Wallace, Merchant in New-York, or Colonel Haviland, Commanding here. Likewise deserted at the same Time, James Marshall, of the same Regiment, and Major Skene's Company, 5 Feet 6 Inches and a half high, without shoes, aged 28 Years, a Printer by Trade, born in London, a Sallow Complexion. He went away in his Regimental Coat, and white Flannel Waistcoat. Whoever apprehends him, and lodges

him in any of his Majesty's Goals, shall receive what is allowed, by Act of Parliament for Apprehending any Deserters.
Camp at Crown-Point, October 9, 1760.
The New-York Mercury, October 27, 1760; November 10, 1760; November 24, 1760. See *The Boston Evening-Post*, November 3, 1760, for Wigg.

DESERTED the 7th Instant, *October*, from his Majesty's Inniskilling or XXVIIth Regiment of Foot, commanded by the Right Hon. Lord BLAKENEY, and in Capt Martin's Company encamped at *Crown-Point, John Wigg*, 6 Feet 6 Inches high without Shoes, streight black Hair, dark Complexion, aged about Twenty-one Years; no Trade, born at *Villverton* in *Norfolkshire*: Had on when he went away, his Regimental Coat and Hat, and a brown Waistcoat: He formerly belonged to the *Plymouth* Regiment of Marines.

Whoever apprehends him and lodges him in any of his Majesty's Goals, shall receive ONE GUINEA Reward, over and above what is allowed by Act of Parliament, by applying to Mr. *Anthony Brackett*, in School-Street, *Boston*; or to Colonel HAVILAND, Commanding Officer here.   Wm. MOORE. Adj't Inniskilling Regt.
Crown-Point, October 9th 1760.
The Boston Evening-Post, November 3, 1760; November 17, 1760; December 1, 1760; December 15, 1760; *Green & Russell's Boston Post-Boy & Advertiser*, November 3, 1760; November 17, 1760; *Boston News-Letter*, November 6, 1760; November 20, 1760. See *The New-York Mercury*, October 27, 1760.

Forty Dollars *Reward.*
AND *all reasonable Charges shall be paid to any Person that Secures and brings to William Kelly, of the City of New-York, Merchant A Negro Man, named NORTON MINORS, who Run away from his Masters, Mess. Bodkin and Ferrall of the Island of St. Croix, on the* 1st *Day of July last, is by Trade a Caulker and Ship Carpenter, has lived at Newbury in New-England, was the property of Mr. Mark Quane, who Sold him to Mr. Craddock of Nevis, from whom the above Gentlemen bought him about 3 Years ago, he is about 5 Feet 8 Inches high, aged about 37 Years, speaks good English, Reads and Writes, and is a very sensible Fellow, and his Masters suspected he came off in the Sloop Boscawen, Andrew Ford Master, who sailed from the above Island the very Day this Fellow eloped, bound for Louisbourg.*

The New-York Mercury, November 10, 1760; November 17, 1760; November 24, 1760; *Green & Russell's Boston Post-Boy &*

Advertiser, November 17, 1760; November 24, 1760; December 12, 1760; *The New-York Gazette*, December 1, 1760. Minor differences between the papers. The *Post-Boy* ends with: "*N. B.* If he is taken near *Boston,* and broughy to *Henry Lloyd.* Esq: the above Reward will be paid by him."

DESERTED from His Majesty's 17th Regiment of Foot, commanded by the honourable Brigadier General Robert Monckton, and in Capt. Paul Rycaut's Company of Grenadiers, on the 26th of October, 1760, from Fort Stanwix: Thomas Reed, aged 24 Years, 6 Feet 2 Inches high; he was born at Warfall, in the County of Stafford, in Old England, by Trade a Buckle maker, or a dark Complexion, remarkably slender and walks very upright. John M'Intosh, aged 25 Years, 5 Feet 8 Inches and an half high, he was born near Fort George, in Scotland, by Trade a Silver Smith, short neck'd, fresh Complexion, large Eyes, well set, has a small stoop in his Shoulders and speaks Irse and English equally well. John Guest, aged 28 Years, 5 Feet 8 Inches and an half high, he was born at Shifnall in the County of Salop, in Old England, by Calling a Labourer, of a swarthy Complexion, Squints with both Eyes, well set and a little Pock mark'd. Whoever apprehends and secures any one of the above Deserters, in any of his Majesty's Goals, shall receive Forty Shillings Sterling, over and above what is allowed by Act of Parliament, by applying to

Mr. Hugh Wallace, Merchant, in New-York.

The New-York Mercury, November 10, 1760; November 24, 1760. See *The New-York Mercury*, March 3, 1760, for McIntosh.

DESERTED from his majesty's 17th regiment of foot at Schenectady, October 20, 1760. John Murray, 32 years of age, 5 feet 7 inches and an 1-2 high, swarthy complexion, black hair, has a cast in his right eye, stoops in his shoulders, born in Ireland, a labourer, and professes dog-breaking. William Senior, 27 years of age, 5 feet 5 inches high, fresh complexion, well made, light brown hair, born in England, by trade a taylor. Paul Griffiths, 40 years of age, 5 feet 9 inches high, dark complexion, slender made, black hair, wounded through the mouth, and slobbers much in speaking, born in England, by trade a barber. William Allen, 27 years of age, 5 feet 5 inches high, fresh complexion, light brown hair, well limb'd, by trade a shoe maker. John Reece, 47 years of age, 5 feet 10 inches high, brown complexion, dark brown hair, knock knee'd, and turns out his toes in his walk and lame in his right arm, a labourer. Joseph Cavendish, 27 years of age, 5 feet 8 inches high, brown complexion, dark brown hair, full faced, broad shoulder'd, and thick legs, by trade a taylor. All persons whatsoever who employ or conceal any of the above deserters, will be prosecuted to the utmost severity of the law.

N. B. The above Joseph Cavendish is a notorious offender, and was try'd last spring at a general court martial at Crown-Point for desertion, and was pardon'd. Whoever secured the said Joseph Cavendish, so that he may be brought to justice, shall receive five guineas reward, to be paid by lieut. col. John Darby, or Mr. Hugh Wallace at New-York, over and above what the act of parliament allows, which sum of 20 shillings ster. will be paid for the apprehending and securing of each of the above-mentioned deserters, upon application to the commanding officer of the 17th regiment,
    or to Mr. Hugh Wallace at New-York.
The New-York Mercury, November 17, 1760; November 24, 1760

WHEREAS a Negro Man that went by the Name of Toby Hazard, runaway from his Master, from Charles Town, in the Province of Rhode-Island, in March 1760, and inlisted in Capt. Wright's Company, and passed for a free Man; and as the Campaign is now over, he has received his Pay, and absconded, in order as 'tis supposed to escape by Sea: He is between an Indian and a Negro, his Hair is not like a Negro's, but a little longer; about 5 Feet 6 Inches high, and plays on the Violin with his left Hand, is 25 Years old. Whoever takes up and secures the said Fellow, and brings him to the subscriber, at Charles-Town above mentioned, shall receive 20 Dollars, and reasonable Charges
    paid, by JOHN STANTON.
The New-York Mercury, November 24, 1760; December 1, 1760; December 8, 1760.

RUN-away from his Master Daniel Hubbard, of Poontoosuck, in the County of Hampshire, and Province of the Massachusetts Bay, on the 26th of this Instant, a Negro Man named Rob, (altho' he many Times calls himself Paul) and last year run-away from Mr. David Fowler of West-Chester in the Government of New-York; he is rather short of middling Stature, talks English well, is of the dark sort of Negros, has remarkable long Fingers, his Head has several Scars. Had on when he went off, an old Beaver Hat, two Jackets, one red, one blue, his Breeches old, made of Deer Skin, blue Stockings, and a pair of old Shoes. Whoever shall apprehend said Fellow, and bring him to his aforesaid Master, or secure him and give information where he may be had, shall have four Dollars Reward, and all necessary Charges   Poontoosuck, October 27, 1760.
    paid by me DANIEL HUBBARD.

The New-York Mercury, November 24, 1760; December 1, 1760. See *The New-York Mercury*, October 8, 1759, and *The New-York Mercury*, December 29, 1760.

RUN away from Capt. *Guysbert Mersalis*, a Negro Fellow named CHARLES, formerly belonging to *Thomas Willett*, aged about 19 Years, speaks good English; had on a black Jacket and Breeches, a brown Indian Coat, white Shirt, ribb'd Stockings, stripp'd Trowsers, coarse Hat: Whoever secures said Negro, and brings him to Mr. *John Livingston*, in *Wyncoop-Street*, shall have *Twenty Shillings* Reward, if taken in Town, and *Forty Shilings*, if in the Country, and all reasonable Charges paid: All Masters of Vessels are forewarn'd carrying him off.
The New-York Gazette, November 24, 1760; December 1, 1760.

RUN-*away from James Spellen, the* 19*th of September last, an Apprentice Boy, of about* 13 *Years of age, named Robert Bishup. Whoever takes up the said Boy, and brings him to his Master, shall receive three Pounds Reward.*
The New-York Mercury, November 24, 1760; December 1, 1760.

RUN-away, from his Majesty's Ship the Dover, Capt. Pursell, on the Night of the 20th Instant, the ten following Persons, viz. Samuel Barren, fresh Complexion. Having on him, a blue Coat and Waistcoat, with yellow Mettal Buttons, and a black Wigg. Matthew Limeburner, fair Complexion, wearing a white Wigg. William Smith, dark Complexion, and black Hair. John Clarke, brown Complexion, and bandy Knee'd. David Robertson, fresh Complexion, and light Hair. George Elliot, brown Complexion, and a brown Wig. Nicholas Crafton, brown Complexion, with long dark brown Hair, tied behind. David Thompson, brown Complexion, light brown Wig. Samuel Martin, black Complexion, short black Hair. Thomas Walsh, swarthy Complexion, short light brown Hair. Whoever takes up and secures any of the above Men, shall receive from Mr. Henry White, Agent Victualler, in New-York, Forty Shilling Sterling Reward, for each.
Nov. 24, 1760.
The New-York Mercury, December 1, 1760.

November 18, 1760.
RUN-away on Friday Night last about ten o'Clock, from the King's-Arms Tavern, in this City, a likely English Servant Girl, named Margaret Robinson, about 22 Years of Age, of a fair Complexion. Had on when she went away, a light brown gown; she was born in Cheshire, and has a little of that Country Accent; as she had conveyed her Cloaths out of the House

some Time before, there is Reason to believe she designs to go off in the Transports to Carolina. Any Person that will bring her to the King's-Arms, or secures her in any of his Majesty's Goals, so that she may be had again, shall have three Pounds Reward, and all reasonable Charges. And any Master of a Vessel or other Person that is mean enough to attempt to carry her off, may depend on being prosecuted to the utmost Rigour of the Law, is such Cases made and provided.
       THOMAS STEEL.
The New-York Mercury, December 8, 1760; December 22, 1760.

RUN-AWAY on Saturday morning last, from *Jacobus Louwin*, a Negro Man, named *Dick*, understands the Tanner's Business, is about 30 Years of Age; Had on a short rugged Sailors Jacket, of the *Grigo* kind, a Leather Pair of Breeches, and wore a large pair of Peticoat Trowsers over them; is well known among the Seafaring men, as having frequently been a Privateering, as a Sailor, &c. Whoever takes up and secures the said Negro, so that his master may have him again, or delivers him to Capt. *Balthazer Kip*, in *Broad-street, New-York*, shall have FORTY SHILLINGS Reward, and all reasonable Charges paid. Captains of Vessels, and others are forbid to carry him off, or harbour him, as they may be assured of a Prosecution for the same.
The New-York Gazette, December 8, 1760; December 15, 1760; December 29, 1760; January 5, 1761.

DESERTED the 10th Day of December Instant, from His Majesty's 17th Regiment of Foot, commanded by the Honourable Brigadier General Robert Monckton, JOHN ROBINSON, 23 Years of Age, 5 Feet 9 Inches high, by Trade a worsted Weaver, born in Manchester in Old England, fair smooth Complexion, stoops a little in his walking, and went off without his regimental Cloathing. Went off along with him, WILLIAM MENAGH, born in the North of Ireland, by Trade a Taylor, 22 Years of Age, 5 Feet 9 Inches high, slender made, black Complexion, black Eyes. Went off in a dark brown Coat, with Lappels at the Breast of it. Whoever takes up and secures any of the above Deserters, shall have Twenty Shillings Reward, besides what's allowed by Act of Parliament, paid by Col. Darby, at Philadelphia, or
    Mr. Hugh Wallace,   Merchant, in New-York.
The New-York Mercury, December 22, 1760; December 29, 1760.

      TWENTY-FIVE POUNDS Reward,
          New-York, December 29, 1760.

RUN AWAY from DENNIS HICKS, of Philipsburgh, in Westchester County, and Province of New-York, a mulatto man Slave, named BILL, aged about 20 Years, has a long sharp Nose, with a black Mole on the right side of his Face, near his Nose: has very large Ears, speaks very good English, and pretends to be free, and can read and write well: Says he has a white Mother, and was born in New-England. He is of a middle size, and has a thin Visage, with his Hair cut off. All Persons are forbid to harbour him, and all Masters of Vessels are forbid to carry him off, as they will answer it at their Peril.—TWENTY-FIVE POUNDS Reward for securing him in any Goal, or bringing him to me, so that I may have him again, and reasonable Charges
         paid by   DENNIS HICKS.

N. B. This Fellow was advertised in the New-York Papers the 5th of June, and in Newhaven the 11th of June 1759; was afterwards taken up in Waterbury, and was put into Litchfield Goal, from whence he was brought to Bedford, and there made his Escape from his Master again. Those who apprehend him, are desired to secure him in Irons. He was taken up by Moses Foot, of North Waterbury, in New-England. It is likely he will change his Cloaths, as he did before. The Mole abovementioned is something long.

N. B. By Information he was in Morris County, in the Jerseys all the Winter, and said he would enter into the Provincial Service, which he did; and was discharged after the Campaign, and is supposed to be either in this, the Jersies, or Connecticut Government.

The New-York Gazette, December 29, 1760; January 5, 1761. See *The New-York Gazette*, June 11, 1759, *The New-York Gazette*, August 20, 1759, and *The New-York Gazette*, July 14, 1760.

                        New-York, December 23, 1760.
RUN-away, about two Months ago, from the Subscriber, living at East-Chester, and Province of New-York, a Negro Man named Robin, aged 28 Years, Country born, and talks good English; about 5 Feet and an Inch high, stoops in his Walk, and has a pretended Pass. Whoever takes up and secures said Fellow so that he may be had again, shall receive Five Pounds Reward, and all reasonable Charges
         paid, by   DAVID FOWLER.

The New-York Mercury, December 29, 1760; January 12, 1761; February 9, 1761. See *The New-York Mercury*, October 8, 1759, and *The New-York Mercury*, November 24, 1760.

1761

RUN away from JOHN ANTHONY, Cordwainer, of the City of New-York, on Saturday the 27th of December, 1760, an Apprentice Boy, named Edward Lyal, between 18 and 19 Years of Age, about 5 Feet 5 Inches high, slender made, brown Hair, and smooth faced: Had on a blue Serge Coat, green Jacket, a light colour'd Hair Plush Breeches, blue ribb'd Stockings, and a white Shirt. Whoever takes up the said Apprentice, so that his Master may have him again, shall have THREE PISTOLES Reward, and all reasonable Charges paid. All Masters of Vessels are forewarn'd of carrying off the said Apprentice, as they shall answer it at their Peril.

The New-York Gazette, January 5, 1761; January 12, 1761.

RUN-away, on Friday the 26th of December last, from John Leake, of New-York, a Negro Man named Wall, aged about 40 Years: Had on, a new light colour'd Bearskin Jacket, lined with red Baize, black Jacket and Breeches, a check Shirt, an old Bearskin great Coat; was born at Oysterbay, on Long-Island, speaks good English, is about 5 Feet 6 Inches high, understands all sorts of Farming Work well. Whoever takes up and secures the said Negro, so that his Master may have him again, shall have Forty Shillings Reward,
          paid by   JOHN LEAKE.
N. B. He took sundry other Cloath besides those Advertised.

The New-York Mercury, January 12, 1761; January 19, 1761; January 26, 1761. See *The New-York Mercury*, May 4, 1761, and *The New-York Mercury*, April 12, 1762.

RUN-away, on Tuesday the 30th of December last, from William Bedlow, Sally Hutchenson, a white Girl, 13 Years old, born in the City of New-York, she is small of her age, a likely Face, with dark brown Eyes and Hair. Had on when she went away, a strip'd blue and white homespun Habit, strip'd homespun, blue Cloth, and white Flannel Petticoats; white Cap, check Handkerchief, leather Shoes, and blue worsted Stockings. Whoever takes up the said Girl and brings her home, shall have Twenty Shillings Reward.   WILLIAM BEDLOW.

The New-York Mercury, January 12, 1761.

ABSENTED himself a few days since, a Negro Man named PETER, about five and a half feet high, 25 years old, of a yellowish complexion; has very large wrist bones, and bandy legs. He took with him an old fustian coat, a flannel lapp'd jerkin, a pair of broad silver, and a pair of broad pinchbeck shoe-buckles, both square, but has been seen in a blue pea jerkin and trowsers about the wharfs and ship-yards. Whoever will take up the said Negro, so that his master may have him, shall have TEN DOLLARS reward, and all necessary charges paid. Enquire of the printer hereof.— Masters of vessels and others, are cautioned against concealing him, as they will answer it at their peril.

The New-York Gazette, January 19, 1761; January 26, 1761.

RUN-away from the subscriber, living in this City, on Monday night the 5th Inst. a likely Negro man, named TOM, about 22 years of age, and about 5 feet 8 or 9 inches high, has little or no appearance of the small pox, is very black: Had one when he went away, a blue broadcloth coat, a Jacket that had been turn'd, with mohair buttons of the same colour; and lined with white shalloon, and wore thickset breeches, a white shirt and cravat, with white or grey worsted stockings, and large silver buckles in his shoes. Whoever takes up the said Negro, or secures him in any goal, so that his master may get him again, shall have TWENTY DOLLARS reward, and all reasonable charges allowed by HENRY WHITE.

N. B. The above Negro was formerly the property of Robert R. Livingston, Esq; and has been seen several times since Rhe left his master in this city, and probably has not yet left it. All masters of vessels are cautioned not to carry him off, as they will be prosecuted with the utmost rigour of the law.

The New-York Gazette, January 19, 1761; January 26, 1761; *The New-York Mercury*, January 19, 1761. Minor differences between the papers.

DESERTED, belonging to His Majesty's Arm'd Ship the Lyon, Captain DAVID PRYCE, Commander,
HENRY TERRANT, Seaman, aged 28 Years, about 5 Feet 5 Inches high, brown Complexion, thin faced, hollow eyed, well made, wears a Wig or Cap.

WILLIAM WOOD, Captain's Clerk, pale Complexion, about 5 Feet 6 Inches high, aged 28 Years, wears his own Hair cued in a Tale of a dark brown Colour, pock marked.

Whoever apprehends the above Men, that they may be brought to Justice, shall have FORTY SHILLINGS Sterling Reward, for each Man.

Any Person entertaining either of them, after this advertisement, may depend on being prosecuted.

DAVID PRYCE.

The New-York Gazette, February 2, 1761; February 9, 1761; February 16, 1761.

New-York, February 5, 1761.

RUN-away, on Wednesday Night the 4th Instant, a German Servant Girl, named Catharine, and a Negro Wench, named Gin; The white Girl is remarkably short and thick, and pretty much Pock broken: Had on, a red and white Striped homespun Waistcoat and Pettycoat; the Negro Wench is about twenty Years of Age, very tall and strait; had on a Green Waistcoat and Pettycoat, but both had with them Sundry other Cloaths, as well of their own as of the Family's which they took with them on going off. Whoever takes up and secures the white Girl and Negro Wench, shall have Forty Shillings Reward, or Twenty Shillings for either,
   by JOHN TAYLOR.

N. B All Masters of Vessels and others are forbid to carry them off or harbour them.

The New-York Mercury, February 9, 1761.

RUN AWAY from the Subscriber, on the 20th of December last, a Negro or Mulatto Man Servant, aged about 28 Years, named Mark Edward, born near Byrams River, in the County of Westchester; a well set Fellow, near six Feet high, talks good English, goes commonly with his Head shaved, has two Crowns on the top of his head, small black specks or moles in his Eyes, with a scar near the middle of his Breast, and a mole on his left Breast. Had on when he went away, a good pair of Leather Breeches, a blue Broadcloth Jacket, a red Jacket under it, without sleeves, a good Beaver Hat. Whoever takes up and secures said Fellow, shall have FIVE POUNDS New-York Money Reward, and all reasonable Charges paid,
   by me ABNER SMITH, of New-Haven,
      in the Colony of Connecticut.

N. B. All House-keepers, and Masters of Vessels, are hereby forbid to harbour, conceal, or carry off said Fellow, as they may depend on being prosecuted according to Law. ABNER SMITH.

The New-York Gazette, February 16, 1761; February 23, 1761; March 2, 1761; March 16, 1761.

RUN-away, on Sunday Evening the 1st of February Inst. a Mullatto Wench named Suck, about 20 Years of Age, formerly belonging to the Buskirks. Had on when she went away, a homespun short Gown, with different colour'd Stripes, a blue and white Handkerchief, a quilted Petycoat, one Side light colour'd, and the other black, with a Pair of white Woollen Stockings. Whoever takes up and secures the said Wench, so that her Master may have her again, shall receive 30s. Reward, and all reasonable
   Charges paid, by ANTHONY HUNTER.

N. B. All masters of Vessels and others are forewarned to carry her off, or harbour her.
The New-York Mercury, February 23, 1761; March 9, 1761.

WHEREAS *John Jeffery*, Apprentice belonging to the General Wall Packet, left the said Ship last Friday. Whoever will bring Intelligence of him, so that he may be secured, shall have Forty Shillings Reward, upon applying to ALEXANDER COLDEN, Esq; The said Apprentice is about 19 Years of Age, middle Stature, broad shoulder'd, and of brown Complexion.
WALTER LUTWIDGE.
N. B. All Masters of Vessels are desired not to carry the said John Jeffery from hence.
The New-York Gazette, March 2, 1761; March 9, 1761.

RUN AWAY from George Burns, at the King's Head, New-York, February 29th, A bound Servant, named George Chrystie, about 26 Years old, born in Aberdeen, in Scotland, [tho' he is apt to say, he was born in Ireland] about five Feet eight Inches high, fair Hair, large grey Eyes, subject to breaking out in the Forehead and Chin: Had on when he went away, a short grey Coat, a Pair of Buckskin Breeches, and a light coloured Pair of ribb worsted Stockings. Whoever secures the said bound Servant, shall have FIVE POUNDS reward, New-York money, and all reasonable Charges
paid by me   GEORGE BURNS, Tavern-Keeper.
N. B. All House-keepers, and Masters of Vessels, are hereby forbid to harbour, conceal, or carry off the said Fellow, as they may depend on being prosecuted according to Law.   GEORGE BURNS.
The New-York Gazette, March 2, 1761; March 9, 1761; *The New-York Mercury*, March 9, 1761; March 23, 1761. Minor differences between the papers.

RAN-away on the 19th Day of *February* last from Captain *Ezibilon Ross* of *Dover*, in Dutches County in *New-York* Government, two Negro Fellows, one about 27 Years old, 5 Feet 6 Inches high; had on an all Wool Coat, lined with Flannel, and a red double Breasted Jacket, his left Leg is less than the right, and his Foot turns out:—The other about 17 Years old, and has lost one of his Fingers on his right Hand. Whoever shall take up said Fellows, and convey them to the Subscriber, in *Dover* aforesaid, or to *Jeremiah Ross* in *Windham* in *Connecticut*, shall have *Forty Shillings* York-Money Reward, and all necessary Charges
paid.   EZIBILON ROSS.

The Boston Gazette, and Country Journal, March 9, 1761; March 16, 1761; March 23, 1761.

40*S*. REWARD.

FOR taking up and securing Mary Brown, alias Edwards, a Pennsylvania born indented Servant, who ran away from the Service of the Subscriber, her Master, a few Days ago: She is a so-so-sort of a looking Woman, inclinable to Clumsiness, much Pock pitted, which gives her a hard Favour and a frosty Look, wants several of her Teeth, yet speaks good English and Dutch, about 26 or 28 Years old, perhaps 30. Had on and about her when she went off, a red quilted Pettycoat, a cross-barr'd brown and white Josey, a sorry red Cloak, and the making of a new stuff Wrapper, supposed to be gone towards Philadelphia, via New-York. The Subscriber hopes no body will harbour her, but on the contrary that every Body will be instrumental in causing her to be apprehended, so that her Master may have her again.

N. B. All reasonable Charges shall be paid,
   by JAMES CROFTON.

The New-York Mercury, March 9, 1761; March 16, 1761; March 23, 1761. A following ad shows that Crofton was living in Albany.

WHEREAS, Mary, the Wife of Bernhard Power, of the City of Albany, has eloped from her said Husband, gone off with George Gaub, and taken a Child of 8 Years old with her, a Girl, named Catherine. All Persons whatsoever are forbid to trust her on his Account, for he will pay no Debts of her contracting from the Date hereof. Should the Child be left with any Person, 'tis hoped they will acquaint him by a Letter.
   BERNHARD POWER.

The New-York Mercury, March 16, 1761; March 23, 1761.

TEN DOLLARS Reward,
If taken up off this Island, or Five Dollars if taken up on this Island.

RUN-away on Thursday Morning last, a Mulatto Fellow named Frank, formerly the Property of Mr. Flowers, of Philadelphia, but now belongs to Mr. Millena, Silversmith in this City: He is 5 Feet 6 Inches high, and well made. Had on when he went away, a green Jacket, much worn, and a brown striped one under it; a Pair of wide Trowsers, a pair of rib'd white Stockings and a pair of large Negro Shoes; likewise a round Hat, bound with black Tape, and pretends to be a free Man. Whoever takes up and secures the said Fellow, so that he may be had again, shall receive the above Reward,
   from John Farrell.

N. B. All Masters of Vessels are forbid to carry him off; and those that harbour him knowingly, may depend on being prosecuted.

The New-York Mercury, March 16, 1761; March 23, 1761; March 30, 1761; April 13, 1761.

RUN AWAY on Tuesday Night last, from *William Anderson*, of this City, Taylor, an Apprentice Lad named AMOS WHITE, about 17 Years old, small of his Age: Had on when he went away, a blue Cloth Coat, red Jacket and Breeches, a good Hat, Shoes and Stockings: He is suppos'd to be gone to *Middletown*, in the Jerseys. All Persons are forwarn'd carrying him off. *Twenty Shillings* Reward for apprehending and securing him, so that his Master may have him again.

The New-York Gazette, March 30, 1761.

RUN away last Wednesday, a Negro Boy about 15 Years old, named DICK, about 4 Feet 8 Inches high, very black, flat nosed, thick lipp'd: Had on a brown Breeches, ribb'd Stockings, and a blue Livery Coat, which he has since changed for a Jacket on board of a Snow lying opposite to the Earl of Loudoun Tavern, where he was for some Time employed. All Masters of Vessels, and others, are warned not to employ him, or take him off, at their Peril. He has attempted to pass on board the above Snow for a free Boy from Long-Island. Whoever brings him to the Printer hereof, shall have TWENTY SHILLINGS Reward, and all reasonable Charges paid.

The New-York Gazette, March 30, 1761; *The New-York Mercury*, May 11, 1761.

RUN-away, on Saturday the 28th of March last, a Servant Man, named John Willet, about 5 Feet 7 Inches high, aged 8 Years, [*sic*] a fair Complexion, with a cast in his Eye, has dark brown Hair, and speaks broken English and good French. Had on when he wen away, a blue Coat with white Lining and yellow Buttons, a striped Cotton Jacket of different Colours, and a pair of blue Breeches. Whoever takes up and secures said Servant shall have 20s. Reward, and all reasonable Charges paid by applying to the Printer hereof.

The New-York Mercury, April 6, 1761.

RUN-away, on Friday the 26th of December last, from John Leake, of New-York, a Negro Man named Wall, aged about 40 Years: Had on, a new light colour'd Bearskin Jacket, lined with red Baize, black Jacket and breeches, a check Shirt, an old Bearskin great Coat; was born at Oysterbay, on Long Island, speaks good English, is about 5 Feet 6 Inches high, understands all sorts of Farming Work well. Whoever takes up and secures

the said Negro, so that his Master may have him again, shall have Forty Shillings Reward,
paid by   JOHN LEAKE.
N. B. He took sundry other Cloaths besides those Advertised. Any Person that will send the said Negro, to Benjamin Waters, at Newtown, on Long-Island, will get the above Reward, or the said Negro will be sold to any Person, by said Waters, as he now is. If he will return to Benjamin Waters, all Faults will be forgiven.
The New-York Mercury, May 4, 1761; May 11, 1761. See *The New-York Mercury*, January 12, 1761, and *The New-York Mercury*, April 12, 1762.

Deserted from His Majesty's XXII Regiment of Foot, quartered at New-York, between the 30th March, and 27 April, 1761. *vizt.*
JOSEPH CRADDOCK, aged 23, 4 feet [sic] 10 inches, red complexion, born at Durham, Old England, by trade a weaver. DAVID WOOD, aged 24, 5 feet 9, dark brown complexion, born in Yorkshire, a labourer.—WILLIAM PRICE, aged 24, 5 feet 8½, brown complexion, born in Brecknochshire, a taylor. ROBERT STEWART, aged 22, 3 feet [sic] 9, sandy complexion, born at Donaghmore, a weaver.—JAMES CARSON, aged 25, 5 feet 8¼, light brown complexion, born in the county of Fermanagh, a labourer.—JAMES GALLAGHER, aged 22, 5 feet 9½, black complexion, born in the county of Tyrone, a weaver. JOHN GRIFFIN, aged 24, 5 feet 10½, dark brown complexion, born at Inniskilling, a labourer.—JOHN WRIGHT, aged 29, 6 feet 8, [sic] dark brown complexion, born at Carlow, a labourer. DAVID HERRON, aged 23, 5 feet 7¾, dark brown complexion, born in the county of Tyrone, a labourer.—PETER ROGERS, aged 27, 5 feet 9, ditto complexion, born in Flintshire, a labourer.—ROBERT SMITH, aged 23, 5 feet 10½, brown complexion, born in the county of Tyrone, a labourer.—CHARLES CIVILL, aged 24, 5 feet 8¾ dark brown complexion, born in Cheshire, a labourer.—WILLIAM SHELLY, aged 26, 5 feet 8½, red complexion, born at West Chester, a Shoemaker.— WILLIAM FAXON, aged 26, 5 feet 6½, brown complexion, born in Warwickshire, a Labourer. JAMES FRAZER, aged 22, 5 feet 5, fair complexion, born in Inverness, a labourer.—EDWARD RANDELLS, aged 26, 5 feet 8, dark brown complexion, born in the county of Caven, a shoemaker.—THOMAS CHANDLER, aged 29, 5 feet 10½, dark brown ditto, born in Warwickshire, a labourer.—MARK CARR, aged 23, 5 feet 10, brown complexion, born in Middlesex, a labourer.

N. B. *David Wood,* wanted the first joint of his little finger, on the left hand. *Robert Smith* and *William Shelly* were shot in the breast. Whoever apprehends and seizes any of the above deserters, and lodges them in any of

his majesty's goals in North-America, shall receive TEN DOLLARS reward for each of them, by applying to William Bayard in New-York.. The whole deserted in their Regimentals, or short blue jackets.
The New-York Gazette, May 11, 1761. See *The New-York Mercury,* May 11, 1761; May 18, 1761; June 8, 1761.

Deserted,

From his Majesty's XXIId Regiment of Foot, quartered at New-York, between the 30th March, and 27 April, 1761. viz.

JOSEPH CRADDOCK, aged 23, 5 Feet 10 Inches, red Complexion, born at Durham, in Old England, by Trade a Weaver. DAVID WOOD, aged 24, 5 Feet 9 Inches high, dark brown complexion, born in Yorkshire, a Labourer. WILLIAM PRICE, aged 24, 5 Feet 8 1-2, brown Complex. born in Brecknochshire, a Taylor. ROBERT STEWART, aged 22, 5 F. 9, sandy Complexion, born at Donaghmore, a Weaver. JAMES CARSON, aged 25, 5 Feet 8 3-4, light brown Complexion, born in the County of Fermanagh, a Labourer. JAMES GALLAGHER, aged 22, 5 Feet 9 1-2, black Complexion, born in the County of Tyrone, a Weaver. JOHN GRIFFIN, aged 24, 5 Feet 10 1-2, dark brown Complexion, born at Inniskilling, a Labourer. JOHN WRIGHT, aged 29, 5 Feet 8, dark brown Complexion, born at Carlow, a Labourer. DAVID HERRON, aged 23, 5 feet 7 3-4, dark brown complexion, born in the County of Down, a Labourer. PETER ROGERS, aged 27, 5 Feet 9, dark brown Complexion, born in Flintshire, a Labourer. ROBERT SMITH, aged 23, 5 Feet 10 1-2, brown Complexion, born in the County of Tyrone, a labourer. CHARLES CIVILL, aged 24, 5 feet 8 3-4. dark brown Complexion, born in Cheshire, a Labourer. WILLIAM SHELLY, aged 26, 5 Feet 8 1-2, red Complexion, born at West Chester, a Shoemaker. WILLIAM FAXON, aged 26, 5 Feet 6 1-2, brown Complexion, born in Warwickshire, a Labourer. JAMES FRAZER, aged 22, 5 Feet 5, fair Complexion, born at Inverness, a Labourer. EDWARD RANDELL, aged 26, 5 Feet 8, dark brown Complexion, born in the county of Caven, a Shoemaker. THOMAS CHANDLER, aged 29, 5 Feet 10 1-2, dark brown Complexion, born in Warwickshire, a Labourer. MARK CARR, aged 23, 5 Feet 10, brown Complexion, born in Middlesex, a Labourer.

N. B. David Wood, wanted the first joint of his little finger, on the Left Hand. Robert Smith and William Shelly were shot in the breast. Whoever apprehends and seizes any of the above Deserters, and lodges them in any of his Majesty's Goals in North-America, shall receive TEN DOLLARS reward for each of them, by applying to William Bayard in New-York. The whole deserted in their Regimentals, or short blue jackets.
The New-York Mercury, May 11, 1761; May 18, 1761; June 8, 1761.
See *The New-York Gazette,* May 11, 1761.

RUN away, a Dutch Servant Woman: Had on, a striped Gown, short red Cloak, black Bonnet, blue Shoes, and white Apron. Whoever takes her up, shall have Four Dollars Reward, and all reasonable Charges, so that they bring her to
     Mr. Leversage, Shipwright.
The New-York Gazette, May 18, 1761; May 26, 1761.

DESERTED the 10th of May, from Shenactady, from Capt. Barnaby Burns's Company, of the 1st New-York Regiment; the following Persons, viz
 EDWARD HAWKINS, 24 Years of Age, born in England; by Trade a Barber, 5 Feet 9 Inches, smooth Face Fair, Complexion, Light Hair and Brown Eyes.
 DAVID HERBERT, aged 46. born in Ireland, by Trade a Taylor; 5 Feet 8 Inches, Fair Complexion, Light Hair, Grey Eyes.
 EDWARD CHAMBERS, aged 38, born in Wales, a Marriner; 5 Feet 10 and half Inches high, Brown Complexion, Brown Hair, and Grey Eyes.
 Whoever secures the above Deserters, so that they may be delivered to the Regiment, or brings them to John Cruger, Esq; Mayor of this City, shall receive TEN POUNDS Reward.
The New-York Mercury, May 25, 1761; June 1, 1761; June 8, 1761.

DEserted from Captain Joseph Hait, of Stanford, on the 16th of May last, Ichabod Brooks, tall and slender, dark Complexion, with black curl'd Hair: Had on when he deserted a black broad cloth Coat, with a black velvet Collar, a brown cut velvet Jacket, a Pair of fustian Breeches, black Stockings, and Silver Shoe Buckles. Whoever takes up and secures said Deserter, and will bring him to Stanford, shall have Twenty Dollars Reward, and all necessary Charges paid,
    by JOSEPH HAIT. Captain.
The New-York Mercury, June 1, 1761; June 8, 1761.

         New-York, May the 30th, 1761.
LAST Night was broke open the Store of William Miliner, on the East Side of Coenties Dock, and sundry Sorts of Goods stolen, consisting as follows; one new red Watch-coat, one Dozen of worsted Stockings, three striped flannel Jackets, six check Shirts, one Piece of Silk Handkerchiefs, one Piece of Muslin, two Pair of Pumps, and five or six Pair of Trowsers, and some Money. This Robbery is supposed to be committed by one Ayers, a Man of about 30 Years of Age, of a sandy Complexion, and for some Time has been seen lurking in this City, and was at the Store the Day before the

Robbery was committed. This is therefore to desire, if the abovesaid Person, or any other should offer any of the said Goods to Sale, that they may be stopped; and if any Person can give Intelligence, who has committed this Robbery, and apprehends the Villain with the Goods, shall have Half the Value of the said Goods as a Reward,
    paid by me WILLIAM MILINER.
The New-York Gazette, June 8, 1761.

DESERTED *from his Majesty's 43d Regiment, John Savage, aged 25 Years, 5 Feet 9 Inches high, long dark brown Hair, fresh Complexion, round Shouldered, born at Great Markham, in Nottinghamshire, in England, went off in his Regimental Clothing, and a blue Waistcoat. Whoever shall secure in any of his Majesty's Goals the above mentioned Deserter, shall receive Twenty Shillings Sterling Reward, by applying to*
    Lieut. Shaw *of the said Regiment at New-York.*
The New-York Mercury, June 8, 1761.

DESERTED from his Majesty's Inniskilling Regiment of Foot, at Crown-Point, the 26th of May, 1761, Joseph Fish, 26 Years of Age, 5 Feet 7 Inches high, born in the Province of New-England, Town of Andover, in the County of Middlesex, brown Complexion, down Look, well made, smooth Face, by Trade a Carpenter, went off in a Blanket Coat, red Breeches, and green Waistcoat, has serv'd in the Rangers. George Roberts, 24 Years of Age, 5 Feet 6 Inches high, born in Ireland, County of Cork, Town of Glinward, brown Complexion, thin Face, strong made, by Trade a Cabinet maker, went off in his regimental Coat, blue Waistcoat and Breeches. Whoever apprehends and secures the above Deserters, shall receive 40s. for each besides what is allowed by Act of Parliament,
    by applying to Mr. Hugh Wallace.
The New-York Mercury, June 8, 1761; June 15, 1761; June 22, 1761.

DESERTED,

FROM the Inniskilling or 27th Regiment, Commanded by the Right Hon. Lord Blakeney, from Crown-Point, the 14th of May 1761, JOHN ROWE, 26 Year of Age, 5 Feet 6 Inches high, born in Shropshire, in England, professes himself a Porter, black Hair and Complexion, Pitted with the Small-Pox, well sett, and a down Look. ROBERT HOWEY, 22 Years of Age, 5 Feet 10 Inches high, born in Buckingham County, West-New-Jersey, in America, down Look, smooth Face, stoop in his Shoulders, brown Complexion, by Trade a Carpenter, tho' a very bad one. They both

had Blanket Coats when they Deserted. Whoever apprehends them, and lodges them in any of His Majesty's Goals, by applying to Mr. Hugh Wallace, Merchant, in New-York, or the Commanding Officer at Crown Point, shall receive Forty-Shillings Reward for each, over and above what is allowed by Act of Parliament.
The New-York Mercury, June 8, 1761; June 15, 1761; June 22, 1761.

RUN-away, on Tuesday the 9th Inst. from the Subscriber, living at Turtle-bay, a Mulatto Wench named Lena, 17 Years old, can speak good Dutch and English, and sings a good Song; is a handsome Wench, and may pass for a free Person, as she is very well featured all but her Nose and Lips, which are thick and flat: Had on when she went away, a homespun Josey and Pettycoat, but no Shoes nor Stockings. Whoever takes up and secures said Wench on the Island of New-York, so that she may be had again, shall have Forty Shillings Reward, and if in another Government Three Pounds,
              paid by   DAVID DEVORE.
N. B. All Persons were forbid to harbour or entertain said Wench at their Peril. Likewise, all Masters of Vessels are forbid to carry her off.
The New-York Mercury, June 15, 1761; June 22, 1761.

THAT on the Fifteenth Day of May last, a Person who called himself *Richard Benton*, left a Stone Horse in the Custody of *Baltus Van Kleeck*, Tavern-Keeper in Poghkeepsie, in Dutchess County, a chesnut brown, about 14 Hands high, a spotted Blaze in his Forehead, three white Feet, paces and trots, branded on the near Buttock with **B. S.** very plain. The said *Benton* was a man of about 5 Feet and Inches, [*sic*] well set, fair Complexion, had on a light coloured Fustian Coat, and was going from Albany to New-York. This is to notify said *Benton*, or any other Person who in the Owner of the said Horse, that the said Horse will be sold at publick Vendue at the House of said *Van Kleeck*, on the first Day of July next, to pay the Expences of his Keeping.
                                                        Dated June 16, 1761.
The New-York Gazette, June 22, 1761.

Deserted from the New-York Regiment,
1761,
JOHN MILLER, aged 37, 5 feet 1 inch, brown complexion. ISAAC BRIGGS, aged 21, 5 feet 7 inches, brown complexion. STEPHEN WARREN, aged 22, 5 feet 10 inches, sandy complexion. JOHN PRICE, aged 18, 5 feet 7, brown. JONATHAN DEAN, aged 18, 5 feet 7½ sandy complexion, JUSTUS GOLDING, aged 19, 5 feet 8, light complexion.

JOHN THOMPSON, aged 28, 5 feet 11, brown complexion. JOHN JONES, aged 43, 5 feet 3 inches, brown complexion. EDWARD DIVER, aged 25, 5 feet 10, brown complexion.
    All of Captain GILCHRIST's Company.
    DAVID CASH, aged 18, 5 feet 9½ brown complexion.
THOMAS WANSER, aged 22, 6 feet 1¼, fair complexion.
ALEXANDER McGRISOR, aged 24, 5 feet 6, brown complexion. Of Capt. HEIGHT's Company.
    JOSEPH MEANDERSON, aged 23, 5 feet 1, swarthy com.
GEORGE KEYS, aged 26, 5 feet 9, brown complexion. Of Captain WATER's Company.
    RIGING FARREN, aged 26, 5 feet 2, swarthy complexion.
NICHOLAS COLSKIN, aged 32, 5 feet 3, dark complexion. Of Captain THODEY's Company.
    OWEN SULLIVAN, aged 27, 5 feet 7, brown complexion. Of Captain WRIGHT's Company.
    CORNELIUS CLARK, aged 23, 5 feet 7, light complexion.
JOSEPH STORY, aged 25, 5 feet 8, light complexion.
JOHN DONEAN, aged 27, 5 feet 9, light complexion.
HUGH ROGERS, aged 30, 5 feet 10, light complexion.
JOHN SHEDMAN, aged 21, 5 feet 8, light complexion.
DENNIS HARRINGTON, aged 41, 5 feet 9, dark comp.
JAMES FORGUSON, aged 29, 5 feet 8, light complexion.
Of Captain PLATT's Company.
    Whoever takes up and secures any of the aforesaid deserters, so that the Officers may recover them, shall have THREE POUNDS Reward for each.
    The New-York Gazette, June 29, 1761; July 13, 1761; *The New-York Mercury,* June 29, 1761; July 6, 1761. Minor differences between the papers. The *Mercury* spells the last captain's name as Plat.

DESERTED from the Ship Mary, Capt. Deverson, now in this Harbour, David Carrick, and John Linn. In Case they return to the said Ship in three Days, they will be received
        by   WILLIAM DEVERSON.
    The New-York Mercury, July 13, 1761; July 20, 1761.

RUN away on Wednesday the 8th Instant, from *Elizabeth Carpender,* her Negro Man, named VENTURE, well known in this City, has a very aukard

Walk, in-knee'd, talks bad *English*: Had on when he went away, only a Shirt and Pair of Trowsers, suppos'd to be lurking in some Hay loft, or got on board some Vessel in the Harbour, in order to go off. All Masters of Vessels are hereby forwarned to carry him. Whoever will secure and bring him to his above Mistress, shall receive a Reward of THREE POUNDS.
Elizabeth Carpender.
The New York Gazette, July 13, 1761. See *The New-York Gazette: or, the Weekly Post-Boy,* August 7, 1758, *Weyman's New-York Gazette,* April 30, 1759, *Weyman's New-York Gazette,* July 16, 1759, and *The New-York Gazette,* September 29, 1760.

RUN away, about two Weeks since, from Sir *William Johnson,* of *Fort-Johnson,* a Negro Man named JO, 5 Feet 7 Inches high, of a yellow Cast, speaks good English, and is a very active Fellow: He was bought at publick Sale from Capt. *Thomas Seymour,* in May 1759, and it's suppos'd he is now in *New-York,* and will endeavour to make his Escape by Sea. Whoever takes up and secures the said Fellow, so that his Master may have him again, shall receive, *Three Pounds* Reward, and all reasonable Charges, in *New-York,* paid by WILLIAM KELLY.
The New-York Gazette, July 13, 1761; August 24, 1761. See *The New-York Mercury,* July 13, 1761.

RUN-away, about 2 Weeks since, from Sir *William Johnson,* of *Fort Johnson,* a Negro Man named *Joe,* 5 Feet 7 Inches high, of a yellow Cast, speaks good *English,* and is a very active Fellow: He was bought at public Sale from Capt. *Thomas Seymour,* in *May* 1759, and 'tis supposed he is now in *New-York,* and will endeavour to make his Escape by Sea. Whoever takes up and secures the said Fellow, so that his Master may have him again, shall receive *Three Pounds* Reward, and all reasonable Charges, in *New-York,* paid by WILLIAM KELLY.
The New-York Mercury, July 13, 1761; July 20, 1761; July 27, 1761; August 3, 1761; August 17, 1761. See *The New York Gazette,* July 13, 1761.

RUN-away on *Wednesday* the 8th Inst. a Negro Man called *Jack,* or *Selem*; he is about 20 Years old, born in *New-England,* speaks very good *English*; he is a short thick Fellow, and goes a little crooked on his right Foot: Had on when he went away, a blue Waistcoat, with Mettal Buttons, *French* make, and black Breeches. Whoever takes up the above Negro, and brings him to the Printer hereof, shall have Two Dollars Reward, if taken upon *New-York* Island, and all reasonable Charges; and Five Dollars if taken up

off the Island: He has been seen in the Mornings and Evenings about the outside of the City.
The New-York Mercury, July 13, 1761; July 20, 1761.

RUN-away from the Subscriber on Monday last, the 6th July, a Mullatto Boy, named Joe, about 5 Feet 4 Inches high, has black Hair, is broke out with Pimples on his Face, and has an Impediment in his Speech: Had on when he went away, a French Castor Hat, Nankeen Vest, lac'd behind, much worn, a Check Shirt and Trowsers, and Brass Buckles in his Shoes. Whoever takes up the said Negro, within the Limits of this City, shall have 20 and without 40 Shillings Reward, and all reasonable Charges allow'd on delivering him to me
JOHN GILL.
The New-York Mercury, July 13, 1761; July 27, 1761; *The New-York Gazette*, August 3, 1761.

DESERTED
From the *Inniskilling* Regiment of Foot, at *Crown-Point, May* 17, 1761;
JOHN DUNFORTH, Twenty-nine Years of Age, five Feet eight Inches high, born in *Bellacray*, in the Province of *New-England*; swarthy Complexion, brown Hair, smooth Face, well made, and professed himself a Shoemaker: Had on when he went off his Regimentals. Whoever takes up the above Deserter, so that he may be returned to the Regiment, by applying to Mr. Hugh Wallace, in New-York, shall have 40s. Reward, over and above what is allowed by Act of Parliament.
The New-York Mercury, July 13, 1761; July 20, 1761; July 27, 1761.

Westchester, July 20, 1761.
RUN away from the Subscriber, the 9th Inst. a lusty Mustee Wench, named Bet, about 40 Years old, and pretends to be free, speaks good English: Had on a striped Cotton Gown, a dark coloured short ditto, two Linsey Woolsey Petticoats, one black, and one striped, a Pair of old Leather heeled Shoes, and a Pair of wooden heeled ditto, and a sort of black silk Hat; both her Legs are sore, and she limps as she walks. Any Person apprehending, bringing, or securing her, so that her Master may get her again, shall have Forty Shillings Reward, and reasonable Charges for the same. I further forwarn any Person or Persons whatever, harbouring, entertaining, concealing, supporting or conveying her, under the Penalty of the Law, otherwise than to her Master, or common Goal.
JOHN FERRIS.

The New-York Gazette, July 20, 1761; July 27, 1761; August 31, 1761.

RUN-away on Monday the 6th of July Inst. from the Subscriber, living as Kocksackie, a Mulatto Man, named Anthony, aged 18 Years, speaks good Spanish, but very bad Dutch and English, has one Eye, and much Marked in the Face with the Small-pox; is about 5 Feet 8 Inches high: Had on when he went away, a Pair of Leather Breeches, a red Waistcoat, a felt Hat, and good Shoes and Stockings. Whoever takes up and secures the said Mulatto, so that he may be had again, shall have Three Pounds Reward,
    paid by me HENDRICK HOEGHTELEN.
 N. B. All Persons are forbid to harbour or entertain the said Mulatto Man at their Peril. Likewise all Masters of Vessels are forbid to carry him off.
The New-York Gazette, July 20, 1761; July 27, 1761; August 3, 1761.

RUN *away last Saturday Afternoon, from* John Leversage, *of this City, Ship-Wright, a Servant Woman, between* 40 *and* 50 *Years of Age. Had on a striped Cross-barr'd Gown, wore a Velvet Bonnet, blue Russel Shoes, has a Scar on her Forehead, and has lost the One Half of her Right Thumb.*
 Whoever apprehends and secures the said Servant, so that her Master may have her again, shall have THREE DOLLARS Reward, and reasonable Charges, *paid by* John Leversage.
The New-York Gazette, July 27, 1761; August 3, 1761.

                 31st July 1761.
DESERTED from his Majesty's First Battalion Royal Highland Regiment, John M'Invin, Soldier, in Col. Grant's Company, encamped on Staten-Island, aged 27 Years, size five Feet six Inches and an half, swarthy Complexion, Hair dark brown, black Eyes, round shoulder'd. thick and well made, went off in his Regimentals, born in Scotland, Shire of Argyle, and Parish of Morvin, speaks very bad English, Whoever secures the said Deserter, so that he may be brought to Justice, as a perjured Defrauder of the Publick, of his Colonel, and his Officers, and gives Notice of it to the Commanding Officer of said Regiment now encamped on Staten-Island, or to Mr. William Bayard, Merchant, at New-York, shall receive TWO GUINEAS Reward.
    FRANCIS GRANT, Colonel.
The New-York Gazette, August 3, 1761; August 10, 1761. See *The New-York Mercury*, August 3, 1761.

DESERTED the 31st ult. from the 1st Battalion of the Royal Highland Regiment encamped on Staten Island, and from Col. Grant's Company, John McInvin, of a swarthy Complexion, brown Hair, black Eyes, and round shouldred, about 27 Years old, 5 Feet 6 and half Inches high, and went off in his Regimentals. Whoever takes up said Deserter, and lodges him in any of his Majesty's Goals, shall have Two Guineas Reward,
   paid by Col. Grant,
     or William Bayard, Esq; Merchant, in New-York.
The New-York Mercury, August 3, 1761; August 10, 1761, August 17, 1761. See *The New-York Gazette*, August 3, 1761.

     FIVE POUNDS Reward,
RUN away from his Bail, at the City of *New York, ABRAHAM SLEATH*, Marriner.—A Man of a low Stature, square shouldered, flatish Faced, has a down Look, is of a brown Complexion, and wears his own Hair.
 Whoever apprehends him so that his Bail may have him again, shall have *Five Pounds* Reward, and all reasonable Charges
   paid, by *GEORGE BREWERTON.*
 All Masters of Vessels, and others, are hereby forewarn'd from either concealing or carrying off the said *Abraham Sleath* as they may expect to answer the same with the utmost Rigour of the Law.
 The Pennsylvania Journal, and Weekly Advertiser, August 6, 1761; August 20, 1761. See *The New-York Gazette,* August 10, 1761; August 17, 1761; August 24, 1761; August 31, 1761; September 14, 1761; September 21, 1761; October 13, 1761. Minor differences between the papers.

     New-York, 8th August, 1761.
DESERTED from under the Command of Captain David Pryce, borne on the Books of His Majesty's Arm'd Ship the Lyon, John Skelton, born at Scarborough, in England, walks erect, and wears his own Hair, of a dark brown. If he returns to his Duty, shall be forgiven; but if taken as a Deserter, he may expect to suffer as the Law directs; If inform'd of, the Reward paid agreeable to the Act for apprehending Deserters from His Majesty's Service.   DAVID PRYCE.
 The New-York Gazette, August 10, 1761; August 17, 1761; August 24, 1761; August 31, 1761.

     New-York, 24th August, 1761.
RUN-away from the Subscriber, living in the Bowery Lane, on Monday last, a yellow Fellow, named John, or Jack, (he gives his Name out for *John*

Smith) of about five Feet and an half high, broad shoulder'd, has an odd Walk, occasioned by his having no Toes on his Right Foot, has a slit in one of his Ears, has a very large black Beard, is a great Talker when he is a little in Liquor, and speaks good English and low Dutch, is a good Farmer, about 50 Years of Age. Had on when he went away, an old felt Hat, Homespun Jacket, striped black and white, an Oznabrigs Trousers, &c.

Whoever takes him up, and secures him so that he may be had again, shall have Forty Shillings Reward if taken on this Island, and Four Pounds if taken off the Island, and all reasonable Charges
    paid by CORNELIUS TEBOUT.

N. B.—All Masters of Vessels and others, are forbid to carry him off.

The New-York Gazette, August 24, 1761; *The New York Mercury*, August 24, 1761. Minor differences between the papers.

RUN-away from the Industry, Transport, Richard Killet, Master, lying in the North River, John Watson, an indented Servant, aged 29 Years middle stature, light Complexion, wears his own short light Hair: Had on, a strip'd sattee Waistcoat and Trowsers, a round Hat, bound with yellow, and carried away with him some goods of Value, belonging to his Master. If any Person can apprehend the said Apprentice, so that his Master may have him again, shall have ten Dollars Reward,
    paid by me JOHN ABEEL.

N. B. If any Masters of Vessels or others employ or harbour the said Apprentice, that will be prosecuted as the Law directs.

The New-York Mercury, August 24, 1761; September 7, 1761.

RUN away from Thomas Truxtun, on Jamaica on Long Island, the 19th Instant, while in the City of New-York, a very likely Negro Man, named Castalio, about 18 Years of Age, speaks good English, and is very likely; has been marked on the right Shoulder S. A. and had on when he went away a white Dimity Frock and Shirt, white Cotton Stockings, old Shoes, and dark colour'd Breeches, about 5 Feet 8 Inches high; a Mark over his left Eyebrow, occasioned by a Blow, and his Country mark about his Forehead and Temples, well known in York, the Ferry, (Jamaica, Hampstead, and in all Queen's County.) Whoever will apprehend him, and bring him to Mr. Joseph Greswold in the City of New-York, or to his Master at Jamaica aforesaid, or secures him in Goal, or otherwise, so that he may get him, shall over and above all reasonable Charges, receive a Pistole Reward.
    THOMAS TRUXTUN.   Aug. 24, 1761.

N. B. If he comes home he will not be punished. And all Persons are forbid to Harbour him on any Pretence whatsoever, and all Masters of Vessels, not to carry him off, as they will answer it to the Rigour of the Law.

The New-York Mercury, August 24, 1761.

RUN away on the 16th of August, from the Industry Transport, Richard Tillet, Master, lying in the North River, at New York, John Watson, an indented Servant, aged 19 Years, of a middle Stature, light Complexion, wears his own short light Hair, has used the Sea some time: Had on when he went away, a striped Sattee Waistcoat, Trowsers, and a round Hat, with yellow Binding, and took with him some Goods of Value belonging to his Master, supposed to be gone to Philadelphia. Whoever apprehends said Apprentice, and secures him, so as his Master may have him again, shall have Ten Dollars Reward,
          paid by   JOHN SIBBALD.
N. B. All Masters of Vessels and others are forbid to employ him, or they will be prosecuted as the Law directs.

The Pennsylvania Gazette, September 3, 1761.

RAN away last Sunday from Edward M'Ilroy, of this City Taylor, two Apprentice Lads, the one named *Alexander Wiley*, about 16 Years old, of a sandy Complexion, and wear his own Hair. Had on a Claret colour'd Coat lined with white, and has white Metal Buttons, a scarlet Jacket, and white Stockings.—The other named, *Gabriel Meeks*, about 14 Years old, of a dark Complexion, has his own dark Hair, and very much pock-mark'd. Had on a Bearskin Coat, striped Jacket, a black Everlasting Pair of Breeches, and white Stockings.

Whoever takes up and secures both or either of the said Apprentices, so that their Master may have them again, shall have Three Pounds Reward for each, and reasonable Charges
          paid by   *Edward M'Ilroy.*

The New-York Gazette, September 7, 1761; September 14, 1761; September 21, 1761; October 13, 1761.

RUN-AWAY from his Master George Townshend, of Norridge, in Oysterbay, a Negro Man named Will, a black Fellow, with a grey Beard and Hair; he talks loud and bold, and hard to be understood by some People who are not acquainted with him: He had on when he went away, a brown Jacket and Trowsers, and is remarkable for running his Shoes on one Side

and both one Way. Whoever takes up and secures the said Negro, so that his Master may have him again, shall receive Twenty Shillings Reward and reasonable Charges paid. And I do hereby forewarn all or any Persons not to entertain, harbour, or deal with the said Negro as they may expect to answer the contrary. The above-said Negro has told that he had been at New-York, and has been Traveling between New-York Ferry and Smith Town up and down most of the Time that he hath been run-away, which is about two Months; as I have heard that he has been seen and it is supposed that he has pillaged or stole in several Places, especially some Leather that Samuel Langdon, of Hampsted, hath taken from a Negro, and secured in his Hands, supposed to be the above said Negro, and the proper owner appearing who hath lost the said Leather, may have it again as Mr. Langdon told me after Days after he had it first, and that was some Time ago, I not having heard whether there is an Owner or not. And I do desire all Persons that they may take Care and Secure the above described Negro to prevent his doing any Mischief for the future, as must be supposed in sculking up and down that he can't subsist without.
    GEORGE TOWNSHEND.
      Norridge, in Oysterbay, August 22, 1761.
The New-York Mercury, September 7, 1761; September 14, 1761; September 28, 1761.

RUN AWAY on Friday last from Gotfreid Laeitabach, of this City, Baker, a Servant Lad, named PETER PITZ, 18 Years old, by Trade a Baker, of a tall Stature, brown Complexion, short Hair. Had on when he went away, a blue and white striped Homespun Jacket, a Pair of white Oznabrigs Trowsers, check Shirt, has old Shoes, and wears a round close trim'd Hat. Whoever takes up and secures the said Servant, so that his Master may have him again, shall have FIVE POUNDS Reward, and reasonable Charges
    paid by GOTFREID LAEITABACH.
The New-York Gazette, September 14, 1761; September 21, 1761; September 28, 1761; October 13, 1761.

RUN-away on Monday the 14th of September Inst. from Gale Yelverton, of Poughkeepsie, in Duchess County, a Negro Man named Prince, aged 30 Years, was brought up in New-England: Had on when he went away, a brown jacket, tore down a little in the back Part, and darn'd up again; a white Shirt, check Trowsers, light colour'd Stockings, and white Metal Buckles in his Shoes, is about 5 Feet 5 Inches high, and well Built. Whoever takes up and secures said Negro, so that his said Master may have him again, shall have Twenty Shillings Reward, and all other reasonable
    Charges paid by me *GALE YELVERTON*

The New-York Mercury, September 21, 1761; September 28, 1761; October 5, 1761; October 12, 1761; September 19, 1761. See *The New-London Summary, or, The Weekly Advertiser*, November 27, 1761.

Chester, September 22, 1761.
THIS Day was committed to Chester Goal, a Lad who calls himself by the Name of Thomas Brown, and on Examination says he belongs to John Johnston, Commander of a Sloop that sails out of New York. He appears to be 17 or 18 Years of Age, Irish Extraction. The Owner of said Servant is desired to come or send, defray the Charges, and taken him away.
    SAMUEL RAINE, Goaler.
The Pennsylvania Gazette, October 1, 1761.

New-York, September 15, 1761.
DESERTED, on Monday the 14th Instant, from New York, ROBERT BROWNE, of the Royal Artillery, and stole out of the Room of Lieutenant Parker, at Mrs. Gudgeon's, of the same Town, a Diamond Ring, the Stone large, a pair of Stone Shoe Buckles, and a Brace of Pistols. Whoever will apprehend the said Robert Browne, and secure him in any of his Majesty's Goals, shall receive a Guinea Reward, besides what is allowed for taking up Deserters. If the Ring should be offered for Sale, a Reward of Ten Pounds will be given to any Person that will stop it, by Mr. Rivington, Bookseller, in Market-street, Philadelphia. Robert Brown born at Williamsburg, in Virginia, aged 19 Years, about 5 Feet 8 Inches, thin visage, dark brown Hair, dark Complexion, black Eyes, with a very sober Countenance, andsoft Speech;—had on when he went away, a brown Coat.
The Pennsylvania Gazette, October 1, 1761.

RUN AWAY, the first day of October, from SAMUEL BOWNE, of New-York, Merchant, a Servant Lad, named THOMAS NOON, about 15 Years of Age, born in Ireland, came in the Ship Pitt, Capt. Montgomery: Had on when he went away, a plain Swanskin Jacket, Thicket Breeches, an old Castor Hat, check Shirt, blue worsted Stockens, a Pair of half worn Shoes, &c.—Whoever takes up and secures said Servant, so that his Master may have him, shall have TWENTY SHILLINGS Reward, and reasonable Charges paid, by SAMUEL BOWNE.
The New-York Gazette, October 13, 1761.

New York, October 8, 1761.
RUN away. on Sunday last, from the Snow Nottingham, Clement Cardiff, Master, now lying in the North River, in the Transport Service, an Irish

Lad, named Michael McGinnis, an indented Servant, about 17 Years of Age, thick set, and has a good Deal of the Irish Accent in his Speech: had on when he went away, a very good blue Cloth Jacket and Breeches, light Worsted Stockings, a SailorHat or Cap, and has a full Face, with dark brown Hair cut short. Whoever secures him, so that he may be had again, shall receive Eight Dollars Reward, by applying to Mr. John Franks, Merchant, in Philadelphia, or the above Capt. in New York.

N. B. He was seen on Staten Island on Sunday last, supposed on his Way to Philadelphia.

The Pennsylvania Gazette, October 15, 1761

And whereas on Friday last, one *Joseph Hallstock*, by Trade a Blacksmith, robbed my House, and has since absconded:—He is about 5 Feet 6 Inches, Pock-mark'd, wears a small curl'd Wig, is of a fair Complexion, and had on a blue Surtout Coat, with a Velvet Cape; wore a round carv'd Pair of Silver Buckles, and blue Broadcloth Pair of Breeches, with a black Manchester Velvet Jacket. Whoever apprehends the said *Joseph Hallstock,* so that he may be brought to Justice shall have *Three Pounds* Reward, if taken in this City, and *Five Pounds*, if taken out of it;
    paid by me JOHN JOHNS.
The New-York Gazette, October 19, 1761.

Stone-hook, (near Albany) October 5, 1761.

RUN-*away on the 20th day of August last, from the subscriber, James Griffith, servant to John Farrel, of Stone-hook, near Albany. The said Griffith is about 25 years of age, five feet three inches high, with long fair hair and has a great stopage in his speech; he was formerly a drummer in capt. Cruckshank's independent company. Any person who will bring the said Griffith to his master, shall have five pounds reward, or if lodged in any of his majesty's goals, so that his master can have him again, shall have 3 pounds currency on advice being sent to the said John Farrel. Any person who is found to harbour the said servant after this publick notice shall be punished with the utmost rigour of the law.*
    JOHN FARREL.
The New-York Mercury, October 19, 1761; October 26, 1761; November 2, 1761; November 9, 1761.

New-York, *October* 23, 1761.

RUN away Yesterday from the Ship Hanberry, Robert Necks, Master, from London, laying at Turtle-bay, loaded with Ordnance Stores, *Samuel Osbourn*, born in England, about 5 Feet 4 Inches high, an indented

Apprentice: Had on when he went away, a new double-breasted Jacket, a narrow brim'd Hat with a blue Edging to it; Wears a Wig, and dress'd in every Respect, pretty well as a Sailor: Therefore, as he is my Apprentice, I desire that no Master of a Ship or Vessel, will ship, or suffer him to be on board, as they may depend if ever known, who takes him from his Master, upon being prosecuted to the utmost Severity of the Law. And whoever will apprehend, and bring the said Apprentice, to his Master, shall receive a handsome Reward.

N. B. For Instance, a Master of a Ship now in this Port, was sued last Year in London, for shipping an Apprentice and carrying him the Voyage; was cast for One Hundred Pounds damages, besides paying him Twenty-five Pounds Wages.

The New-York Gazette, October 26, 1761; November 2, 1761; November 16, 1761; November 30, 1761.

WHEREAS *Rebaccah Johns,* the Wife of me the Subscriber, on Wednesday last, eloped from my Bed and Board, and it is apprehend will try to run me in Debt:—Notice by this Advertisement is given to all Persons, not to credit her on my Account, as they may rest assured I shall pay no Debts of her contracting after this Day. *Witness my Hand this* 18*th Day of October,* 1761.   JOHN JOHNS.

The New-York Gazette, October 26, 1761.

STOLEN out of the House of JACOB WANDEL, at the North-River, on Tuesday last, by one John Richmond, one green Plush Jacket, the Button Holes workt or turn'd inward with the same Stuff; one black Silk Jacket; and thee white Linen Shirts:—He is about 5 Feet & Inches, aged about 25 or 30 Years; having a Bruise on his Nose; is ready tongu'd, and has sore Eyes: He generally wears a blue grey Broadcloth Coat; but it is thought he will change his Apparel: Whoever apprehends the said John Richmond, so that he may be brought to Justice, shall have Five Dollars Reward, and Charges paid by   JACOB WANDELL.

N. B. The abovesaid Richmond, about 10 Days ago, brought to the House of Leonard Yates, at the Royal Hester, opposite to Old Slip, sundries of wearing Apparel, which he said he received as so much Wages that was due to him; some of which was bought in the said Yates's House, not knowing them to be stole; and which on Saturday last was delivered to the proper Owners.

The New-York Gazette, October 26, 1761; November 2, 1761; November 23, 1761; November 30, 1761.

Flushing, October 9, 1761.

RAN-away on Sunday Oct. 4, 1761, a Negro Man named Pollydore, about Twenty-four Years of Age; he had on when he ran-away, a new Sail Hat, snuff colour'd Thicksett Breeches, a slim Black Fellow, speaks pretty good English, and Shaves well, come from North Carolina, belongs to Mr. Mabion: Whoever takes up and secures the said Negro, shall have Twenty Shillings reward, and all reasonable Charges
                paid by,   SAMUEL CORNELL, at Flushing.
The New-York Mercury, October 26, 1761; November 2, 1761.

Twenty Shillings Reward,

RUN-away *on Sunday last, from Edward Price, a Negro Wench named Amelia, she is a likely young Wench, very Black and smooth Skin'd, a Creole born; had on when she went away, a green short Gown, homespun Petticoat, one red ditto, commonly Wares a Silk Handkerchief about her Head, with bunchy Hair about her Forehead, Gold Bobs in her Ears, and took with her likewise a red striped Holland Petticoat, one ditto of small check Linnen, with sundry other Cloaths. Whoever secures said Wench, so that her Master may have her again, shall have the above Reward, and all reasonable Charges*
                paid, by   EDWARD PRICE.

N. B. All Persons are forbid to harbour, conceal or carry off said Wench, at their Peril.

The New-York Mercury, November 2, 1761; November 9, 1761.

RUN away, on Tuesday the 10th Instant, an indented Servant Girl, named Nancy Welch, who had three Years of her Time to serve, was born in Ireland; she is red hair'd, pretty tall, and generally appears very slovenly in her Dress; which was (when she went away) a strip'd Josey, and strip'd home-spun Petticoat. Whoever apprehends the above Servant, so that her Mistress may have her again, shall have TWENTY SHILLINGS Reward, besides all Costs and Charges paid that may thereon accrue.—All Masters of Vessels, and others, are forewarned against carrying off or harbouring the above Delinquent, as they wou'd answer the same at their Peril.
        Apply to the Printer hereof, in Broad-Street.
The New-York Gazette, November 16, 1761; November 23, 1761; November 30, 1761.

RUN-away from the Subscriber the 5th Instant, living at Newtown, on Long-Island, a Negro Man, named LOO, about 30 Years old, 5 Feet 6

Inches, or rather less, high; pretty well made, and very Yellow for a Negro; his left Leg is very crooked, being broke about 12 Months ago: Had on a light-coloured Coat and Jacket, Buckskin Breeches, light-colour'd Stockings, and a Pair of new Shoes: He is supposed to be about Oysterbay, among the free Negroes there. Whoever takes up and secures the said Negro, so that he may be had again, shall have FIVE DOLLARS Reward, and all reasonable Charges,
     paid by JOHN GOSLINE.
The New-York Mercury, November 23, 1761; November 30, 1761; December 14, 1761.

RUN-away, this Day, from Edward Agar, in Beaver-Street; a Negro Lad, about five Feet five Inches high, about 30 Years of Age; well made, named Sylvester; had on when he went away, an old light mix'd colour'd cloath Coat, a Pair of red cloth Breeches: Whoever secures him, so that the said Edward Agar may have him again, shall be handsomly rewarded for their Trouble; all Masters of Vessels and others, are hereby warned not to harbour him, or carry him off, as they will be prosecuted for the same, to the utmost Severity of the Law.

 N. B. He is a French Negro, and speaks both French and English very well.   Nov. 21. 1760.
The New-York Mercury, November 23, 1761; November 30, 1761; December 14, 1761.

Deserted from his Majesty's First, or Royal Regiment of Foot, commanded by the Honourable Lieutenant General JAMES St. CLAIR, *Dennis Rouse*, 32 years of age, born in Limerick, 6 feet high, no trade, fair Complexion, and a mole on his right cheek. Edward Fennigen, 30 years of age, 5 feet 11 inches high, born in Cork, no trade, black hair, and a mole on his left cheek. *Thomas* and *Samuel Bowlers*, born in Barbados, 5 feet 10 inches high each, (brothers) by trade shoe-makers, black hair. *Thomas Hopeshaw*, 20 years of Age, 5 feet 9 inches high, born at Newton, in the Jersies, fair hair, by trade a cooper. John Acting, 27 years of age, 5 feet 7 inches high, born in Germany, by trade a cooper, dark brown hair, and halts a little in his walking, occasioned by a wound in his hip. *John Mullaly*, 25 years of age, 5 feet 5 inches high, born in Dublin, light brown hair, by trade a shoe-maker. *Joseph Munro*, 19 years of age, 5 feet 6 inches, born in Kingwood, in the Jersies, fair complexion, by trade a shoe-maker. *Peter Collons*, 26 years of age, 5 feet 7 inches, born in Cork, black complexion, speaks bad English. *Charles Martin*, 33 years of age, 5 feet 5 inches, born in Ireland, fair complexion, by trade a clothier. *Isaac Housley*, 22 years of age, 5 feet 5

inches, born in Pennsylvania, brown hair, by trade a carpenter. *William Hays*, 54 years of age, 5 feet 6 inches, born in England, brown hair, no trade. *Thomas Langley*, 27 years of age, 5 feet 8 inches, brown complexion, by trade a turner, born at Hopewell, and has a wife near justice Huff's, in the Jerseys. *John Mordent*, 31 years of age, 5 feet 8 inches, black complexion, has a wife in Philadelphia. *William Marsico*, 20 years of age, 5 feet 7 inches, yellow complexion, mark'd with the small-pox, a stoop in his shoulders, in-knee'd, and speaks thro' his nose. *James McGinnes*, 21 years of age, 5 feet 5 inches, born in the West-Jersies, by trade a shoe-maker, his left thigh crooked, and halts in his walking, occasioned by his thigh being broke. *Samuel Powell*, 24 years of age, 5 feet 8 inches, by trade a shoe-maker, born in America, dark brown hair. *William Hays*, jun. 29 years of age, 5 feet 8 inches, born in Ireland, and has a wife in New-England. *Thomas Sheppard*, 20 years of age, 5 feet 8 inches, born at Middletown, in the East-Jersies, by trade a carpenter, fair complexion. *James Marshall*, 22 years of age, 5 feet 8 inches, born in Ireland, by trade a weaver, fair complexion. *Thomas Holmes*, 22 years of age, 5 feet 8 inches, born in Old England, by trade a gardiner, fair hair, wants two of his foreteeth, and supposed to be along with *Marshall*. *John Sherock*, 20 years of age, 5 feet 6 inches, born in Philadelphia, by trade a rope-maker. *Thomas Thettson*, 23 years of age, 5 1/4 inches, born in Old England, no trade, squint ey'd and short sighted. *Robert Campbell*, 16 years of age, 5 feet 3 1/2 inches, no trade, fair complexion, born in the Jersies. *John Duffie*, 26 years of age, 5 feet 7 inches, born in Londonderry, by trade a baker, dark brown hair, pock mark'd, and full faced. *Joseph Oracks*, 30 years of age, 5 feet 6 1/2 inches, born in Old England, no trade, dark brown Complexion. *James McGrath*, 32 years of age, 5 feet 8 inches, born in Cork, no trade, dark brown complexion. *Henry Willson*, 29 years of age, 5 feet 7 inches, born in Newry, in Ireland, no trade, brown complexion.—Whoever apprehends any of the above Deserters, viz. *Holmes, Hays*, jun. *Rouse*, or *McGrath*, shall receive FIVE GUINEAS Reward for each of them, and for each of the rest FORTY SHILLINGS, over and above what is allowed by Act of Parliament, paid by Colonel FORSTER, commanding Officer of said Regiment, at Halifax,
      or by Lieut. RICHARD MARSHALL,
          of said Regiment, at New-York.

The New-York Gazette, November 24, 1760; December 8, 1760; *The Pennsylvania Gazette*, November 27, 1760. Minor differences between the papers. The *Pennsylvania Gazette* ends with "and if put into Philadelphia Goal, Mr. DAVID FRANKS, of that City, Merchant, will pay the Rewards there."

Ran-away on the 24th Day of *September last, from Gale Yelverton of Poghkeepse, in Dutchess County, a Negro Man, named PRINCE*, 30 Years

old, about 5 Feet 5 Inches high a well built Fellow; had on when he went away, a brown Jacket, tore a little down the back, but darned up again; a white Shirt, check'd Trowsers, Light colour'd Stockings, white Metal Buckles in his Shoes. Whoever shall take up said Negro and secure him so that his Master may have him again, shall have FIVE POUNDS Reward, and all reasonable Charges
    paid by me. GALE YELVERTON. October 31, 1761.
The New-London Summary, or, The Weekly Advertiser, November 27, 1761. See The New-York Mercury, September 21, 1761.

RUN-away, from the Masquerade Transport, Christopher Moon, commander, on Wednesday Night last, a Servant Lad, named Lawrence Davidson, (a Swede) about 17 or 18 Years of Age; 5 Feet high, a growing Lad, wears a Wig or Cap; had on when he run-away, a new blue double-breasted Waistcoat, and long Oznabrig Trowsers. Whoever secures the said Lad, or brings him on board the said Ship, lying off the Ship Yards, in the East-River, shall receive Three Dollars reward,
    by me CHRISTOPHER MOON.
 N. B. All Persons are forbid to harbour him, and Masters of Vessels carrying him off, as they will be prosecuted to the utmost Severity of the Law.
 The New-York Mercury, November 30, 1761; December 7, 1761; December 14, 1761.

RUN-away, the 3d Instant, from James M'Cartney, a Negro Man, named Peter, born in Jamaica. Had on when he went away, a blue jacket, a red inside Jacket without Sleves, and white Stockings; his right Leg seems as if it had been broke; he is Blind of one Eye. Whoever takes up and secures the said Negro, so that his Master may have him again, shall have, if taken up in Town, Twenty Shillings, and if in the Country, Forty Shillings Reward,
    paid by me JAMES M'CARTNEY.
 N. B. All Persons are hereby forbid to Harbour or Conceal him, and all Masters of Vessels are forbid to carry him off at their Peril.
 The New-York Mercury, December 7, 1761.

RUN-away the 3d Instant, a Negro Man named Jack or Selam; he is a short well-set Fellow, speaks good English, and limp in his right Foot: Had on when he wen away, a light green Coat, with white Mettal Buttons, a blue Waist-Coat, with brass Buttons, and Shag Breeches. Whoever brings the said Negro to the Printer hereof, shall have Two Dollars Reward, and all reasonable Charges paid.

N. B. All Masters of Vessels are desired not to carry off said Negro, or harbour him at their Peril.
The New-York Mercury, December 7, 1761.

RUN-away, on the 28th of November last, from Tunis Rapalye, a Negro Man named Harry; he understands a little of the Baking Business, about 32 Years old, 5 Feet 3 Inches high, and much Pitted with the Small-Pox: Had on when he went away, a blue Watchcoat, Buck-Skin Breeches, and wore a short dark brown Wig. Whoever takes up and secures said Negro, so that he may be had again, shall receive Twenty Shillings Reward, and all reasonable Charges,
    paid by TEUNIS RAPALYE.
The New-York Mercury, December 7, 1761; December 14, 1761; December 21, 1761; December 28, 1761; January 4, 1762.

RUN AWAY, at New-York, on the 8th Instant, December, from *Jacobus Van Kleeck*, of Poughkeepsie, a Negro Man, named ISAAC, about 30 Years of Age, 5 Feet 8 Inches high, has a clumsy Walk, speaks broken English: Had on a blue Broad-Cloth Coat, good Shoes, blue colour'd Stockings, brown Cloth Breeches, has two Woollen check Shirts, &c.—Whoever takes up the said Negro, so that he may be had again, shall have *Forty Shillings* Reward, and reasonable Charges
    paid, by JACOBUS VAN KLEECK.
The New-York Gazette, December 14, 1761; December 21, 1761; December 28, 1761; January 11, 1762; January 25, 1762.

RUN away Saturday Night last, from JOHN COOMBS, of Jamaica, on Long-Island, a Negro Fellow named *York*; 30 Years old, about 5 feet 7 Inches high, and very well made, and complaisant: Had on when he went away, a Great Coat of red Coating, a Pair of Leather Breeches, and Shoes and Stockings. Whoever takes up and secures the said Negro Fellow, so that his Master may have him again, shall have *Forty Shillings* Reward, and all
    Charges paid, by JOHN COOMBS.
N. B. All Masters of Vessels, and others, are forbid carrying him off.
The New-York Gazette, December 14, 1761; December 21, 1761; December 28, 1761; January 11, 1762; January 25, 1762; *The New York Mercury*, December 14, 1761; December 21, 1761. The *Mercury* spells the advertiser's last name as Comes. See *The New-York Mercury*, December 28, 1761, and *The Pennsylvania Gazette*, February 4, 1762.

THREE POUNDS REWARD.

RUN-away Saturday Night between the Twelfth and Thirteenth of December, from John Comes of Jamaica, on Long Island, a Negro Man named York, about 30 Years of Age, very likely, full Faced and Ey'd, well set, smooth Skin'd, his Knees a little bending in, a small Pit or two, on the left Side of his Nose, and one on his Forehead; had on when he went away, a Red Great Coat made of Coating, a red Waistcoat, and Leather Breeches. Whoever takes up said Negro Man and secures him, so that his Master may have him again, shall have the above Reward, and all Charges
               paid by   JOHN COMES.
N. B. All Masters of Vessels are forbid to carry him off.

The New-York Mercury, December 28, 1761; January 4, 1762; January 11, 1762; February 8, 1762; February 15, 1762. In the last two ads the reward is listed as "FIVE POUNDS." See *The New-York Gazette*, December 14, 1761, and *The Pennsylvania Gazette*, February 4, 1762.

FIVE POUNDS, Reward,

FOR *apprehending a certain man, who calls himself Thomas Partridge, and sometimes Wilson: He carried off the 28th of November, from New Brunswick Ferry, a saddle bags belonging to Eliphelat Plat, of Long-Island, containing 37 dollars and some linnen, &c. Whoever takes up and secures the said fellow so that he may be brought to justice, shall have the above reward paid by Francis Holeman, at Brunswick, or Eliphelet Plat, on Long-Island: He is about 5 feet 9 inches high, with black curled hair, is a little pitted with the small pox, and has a large scar on one of his cheeks.*

The New-York Mercury, December 14, 1761; December 21, 1761; December 28, 1761. See *The New-York Gazette*, April 5, 1762.

1762

RUN-away from the Ship King of Prussia, Thomas M'Glathery, Master, ROBERT BARKLEY, an Apprentice, 14 Years old, smooth ruddy Fac'd, fair Hair: Had on, an outside blue Jacket. Any Person giving Information to the Printer hereof where he may be found, will receive Thirty Shillings Reward. All Masters of Vessels and others are forbid to harbour him.

The New-York Mercury, January 11, 1762; January 18, 1762.

RUN-away, in the 5th of January Inst. from the Sloop Prince of Orange, of Bermuda, John Tod, Master, a Negro Man named Jacob, about 5 Feet 4 Inches high: Had on when he went away, a short blue Jacket, a grey Cap, two Pair of Oznabrig Trowsers, and white Stockings. Whoever takes up and

secures the said Negro, so that his Master may have his again, shall have Forty Shillings Reward,
    paid by Mr. Evouts.
The New-York Mercury, January 11, 1762; January 18, 1762.

RUN-away from Gabriel Leggett, a Negro Fellow named LONDON, about 30 Years old, 5 Feet 8 Inches high: Had on when he went away, a brown Bearskin Watch Coat, a Cap to the Cape, and large Mettal Buttons; a homespun Jacket; mixt colour'd, with Pewter Buttons, Leather Breeches, white Woollen Stockings, and thick Shoes, a Beaver Hat half worn; he has lost one of his Fore Teeth, and Talks broken English. Whoever takes up the said Negro, and secures him so that his Master may have him again, shall have Thirty Shillings Reward, and all reasonable Charges
    paid at Westchester, by GABRIEL LEGGETT.
The New-York Mercury, January 18, 1762.

RUN-*away on the 4th Instant from David Anderson, of North-Castle, in New-York Government, a Negro Man Servant named JAM, 28 Years of Age, 5 Feet 6 Inches high, or thereabouts, well built, and very square Shoulders, has a Scar on the right Side of his Nose, another under his left Eye, also one on the left side of his Head, plain to be seen, given to him by a Horse as he says, speaks good English and Low Dutch, is a very artful insinuating Fellow, and plays on the Fiddle:* Had on when he went away, an old Sail Hat, blue Jacket, red Great-Coat, blue Breeches with Trowsers over them, Tow Shirt, white Yarn Stockings, old Shoes, and large Brass Buckles. Whoever apprehends him and brings him to his aforesaid Master or secures him in any of his Majesty's Goals, to that his Master may have him again, shall have Twenty Shillings Reward, and all necessary Charges
    paid, by DAVID ANDERSON.
N. B. All Persons are forbid to harbour the above said Negro at their Peril.
The New-York Mercury, January 18, 1762.

RAN-away on the 19th Inst. *January, from* William Kar, *of this City, Taylor,—an Apprentice Lad, named* James Johnson, *but may want to pass by the Name of* James Kelly; *is about 16 Years old, very much Pock-markt. full faced, well-set, and wears long strait Hair.* Had on when he went away, a light brown colour'd Coat, a green colour'd Jacket, black Knit Breeches; a Pair of grey Woollen Stockings, square Brass Shoe Buckles, has an half worn Beaver Hat, and may wear a Callico Jacket.

Whoever takes up and secures the said Apprentice, so that his Master may have him again, shall have FORTY Shillings Reward, and reasonable Charges, paid by   William Kar.

N. B.—All Masters of Vessels are strictly forbid to carry him off; and all others are likewise forbid to harbour or conceal him, as they may depend on being prosecuted to the utmost Rigour of the Law.

The New-York Gazette, January 25, 1762; February 1, 1762.

RAN-away on the 14th Instant, *January,—A Negro Wench, named,* Nanny, *she has lost half the 2d Finger of one of her Hands; is a well-set Wench, and speaks good English. Had on a long blue Gown, of Baise, somewhat in Form to a Man's Banyan; and has a coarse Apron. Whoever takes up the said Wench, and secures her so that her Master may have her again, shall have TWENTY SHILLINGS, Reward, by applying*
     To   W. Weyman,   Printer, in Broad-street.

The New-York Gazette, January 25, 1762; February 1, 1762.

FIVE POUNDS Reward.

RUN away, Saturday Night the 12th Inst. from John Comes, of Jamaica, on Long Island, a Negroe Fellow, named York, 30 Years old, about 5 Feet 7 Inches high, very well made, and complaisant; has a forged Pass, and understands something of the SadlerBusiness: Had on when he went away, a Great Coat of red Coating, a Pair of Leather Breeches, Shoes and Stockings.—Whoever takes up and secures the said Negroe Fellow, so that his Master may have him again, shall have the above Reward, and all
          Charges, paid by   DAVID HALL, in Philadelphia,
     or JOHN COMES.   New York, December 22, 1761.
All Masters of Vessels are forbid to carry him off.

The Pennsylvania Gazette, February 4, 1762.See *The New-York Gazette,* December 14, 1761, and *The New-York Mercury,* December 28, 1761.

Philadelphia, February 18, 1762.
FIVE POUNDS REWARD.

MADE his escape on the 8th Instant, from Ellis Lewis of Philadelphia; an English Servant Man born in Yorkshire, named John Sims, about five Feet seven Inches high; of a swarthy Complexion, thin Visage, black Hair, and stoops much in the Shoulders: Had on when he went away, a light colour'd cloth Coat full trim'd, a crimson cut Velvet Vest, with short Skirts, Leather Breeches about half worn and dirty at the Knees; he formerly liv'd in Philadelphia, but has followed Peddling and Horse Jockying this twelve

Months past, about Trentown, New-York, and Connecticut Government; he is well known about Maroneck and the Purchase, and is very apt to talk about Horses: Has with him one Eleanor Debutcher, alias Catherine Cotton, an ordinary Woman, which he pick'd up at Trentown, and alledges to be marry'd to her, by shewing a Paper sign'd by one Fitz Patrick, but was sued in Burlington, by a Man that assum'd to be her lawful Husband. Whoever secures the said Servant in any Goal, so that his Master may have him again, shall receive the above Reward, paid by,
John Franklin of New-York,
or Ellis Lewis of Philadelphia.
N. B. They have been seen to pass in different Habits; the Woman says she was born in Boston, and is well known, in most Places along to Philadelphia.
The New-York Mercury, March 1, 1762; March 15, 1762.

RUN away about three Weeks ago, an indented Irish Servant Man, named JOHN McLAUCHLAN, aged about 30 Years, very low sized, and mean Appearance, and very indifferently cloathed: It's said he is gone to Rhode-Island, in his Way to Boston, to take Passage for Ireland or England. All Masters of Vessels or others whatever, are hereby forbid harbouring or entertaining the said John Mc Lauchlan: And any Person or Persons who take him up, and secure him in any of his Majesty's Goals, and give Information of the same to Mr. MALCOLM CAMPBELL, Merchant in New-York, shall have THIRTY SHILLINGS, as a Reward, and all reasonable Charges paid him.   *New-York, March 6*, 1762.
The New-York Gazette, March 8, 1762; March 15; 1762. See *The New-York Mercury*, March 8, 1762.

New-York, March 6, 1762.
RUN-away about 3 weeks ago, an indented Irish servant man, name John M'Laughlan, aged about 30 years, very low of stature, of a mean appearance, and very indifferently cloathed; 'tis said he is gone to Rhode-Island, in his way to Boston, to take passage for Ireland or England: All masters of vessels or others whatever, are hereby forbid harbouring or entertaining the said John M'Laughlan: And any person or persons who take him up, and secure him in any of his Majesty's goals, and give Information of the same to Mr. Malcolm Campbell, merchant in New-York, shall have thirty shillings, as a reward, and all reasonable charges paid him.
The New-York Mercury, March 8, 1762; March 15, 1762; March 22, 1762; March 29, 1762; April 5, 1762; April 12, 1762. See *The New-York Gazette*, March 8, 1762.

RUN-away from the Subscriber, a Negro Man named Sam, well known about Town: Had on, a brown Coat with yellow Buttons, a Waistcoat of the same; wears a Bob Wig, and is a very forward impudent Fellow. Whoever secures him so that his Master may have him again, shall receive Three Dollars Reward,
    paid by JAMES DE LANCEY.
 N. B. All Persons are desired not to harbour him, and all Masters of Vessels not to carry him off, on Pain of being prosecuted with the utmost Rigour of the Law.
The New-York Mercury, March 15, 1762.

            New-York, March 16, 1762.
     BROKE GOAL,
ON the Night of the 15th Instant Thomas Griffiths, alias, Tom Upon Occasion; He is about 25 Years of Age, 5 Feet 10 Inches high, of a brown Complexion, and was the only Evidence against Anderson and Van Arlam, at the last Supreme Court held here. Whoever takes up and secures the said Thomas Griffiths, so that he may be brought to Justice, shall have Five Pounds Reward,
    paid by John Roberts, Esq; High Sheriff,
      or his Deputy James Mills.
The New-York Mercury, March 22, 1762.

RUN-away, from Caleb Morgan, of East-Chester, on the 7th Instant, Negro Wench named Lucy, of a middle Stature, about 26 Years of Age, a likely looking Wench, talks good English and no other Language: Had on when she went away, a blue stuff Gown, a homespun Pettycoat, a black Hat or Bonnet, a lightish colour'd Broad-cloth Cloak, a Pair of Calf Skin Shoes, but possibly she may have changed them; she had on also a black quilted Pettycoat. Whoever takes up and secures the said Negro Wench in any of His Majesty's Goals, and sends me Word, so that I may have her gain, shall have Forty Shillings Reward, and all reasonable Charges,
    paid by me CALEB MORGAN.
 N. B. All Persons are forewarned not to harbour or conceal her on any Account whatsoever, as they may depend on being prosecuted with the utmost Rigour of the Law.
The New-York Mercury, March 29, 1762; April 5, 1762; April 12, 1762; April 19, 1762.

           New-York, March 24th, 1762.
RUN-away on Monday Morning last, from Eliphalet Plat, of Smith Town, Suffolk County, Long-Island;—An English Servant Man, named Thomas

Partridge, alias Wilson; about 25 Years of Age, 5 Feet 9 or 10 Inches high, dark Complection, grey Eyes, black curl'd Hair, and a little Pock-mark'd.— He has a remarkable Scar on the lower Part of one of his Cheeks. Had on when he went away,—a blue Coat, with red Lining;—green Jacket; a pair of Buckskin Breeches; Whoever takes up and secures the said Servant so that his Master may have him again, shall have THREE POUNDS Reward, if brought and confined in New-York Gaol; and all reasonable Charges
     paid by *ELIPHALET PLAT.*
The New-York Gazette, April 5, 1762. See *The New-York Mercury*, December 14, 1761.

RUN-away, Sunday the 4th Inst. from John Leake, in New-York, a Negro Man named WALL, aged about 40 Years, was born in Oysterbay, on Long-Island, speaks good English, is a sensible Fellow, about 5 Feet 6 Inches high, his Complexion between yellow and black, he understands all Sorts of Farming Work well: Had on when he went away, a short Bearskin Coat, lined with red Baize, Leather Breeches, and a Scotch Bonnet. Whoever takes up said Negro, and brings him to his Master, or secures him in any Goal, shall have Five Pounds Reward,
     paid by JOHN LEAKE.
N. B. All Masters of Vessels are forbid to carry him off.
The New-York Mercury, April 12, 1762; April 19, 1762; April 26, 1762; May 3, 1762. See *The New-York Mercury*, January 12, 1761, and *The New-York Mercury*, May 4, 1761.

RUN-*away, last Friday Night, from the Snow Cape-Breton, Robert Wilson, Master, the following Persons, Apprentices to the Owners of the said Snow, viz. John Wilson, 16 Years old, and of a ruddy Complexion; John Stewart, 18 years old, of a swarthy Complexion; and Robert Allan, about 16 Years old, and of a fair Complexion. Whoever takes up and secures the said Apprentices, and will deliver them to Greg, Cunningham, and Company, shall have* 20s. *as a Reward for each.*
The New-York Mercury, April 19, 1762; April 26, 1762; May 3, 1762; May 17, 1762.

New-York, Printing-Office, in Beaver-street, April 17, 1762.
RUN away, on Monday the 12th instant, from the Subscriber, a Mulatto Servant Man, named *Charles*, and known by the Name of *Charles Roberts*, or *German:* He is a likely, well-set Fellow, 28 or 30 Years of Age, about Five and a Half Feet high, and has had the Small-Pox. He has a Variety of Clothes, some of them very good, affects to dress very neat and genteelly, and generally wears a Wig. He took with him two or three Coats or Suits,

viz. A dark brown or Chocolate colour'd Cloth Coat, pretty much worn; a Dun or Dove colour'd Cloth, or fine Frize Coat, but little worn; and a light blue Grey Summer Coat of Grogram, Camblet, or some such Stuff; a Straw colour'd Waistcoat, edged with a Silver Cord, almost new; and several other Waistcoats, Breeches, and Pairs of Stockings; a blue Great Coat, and a Fiddle. His behaviour is excessively complaisant, obsequious and insinuating; he speaks good *English*, smoothly and plausibly, and generally with a Cringe and a Smile; he is extremely artful, and ready at inventing a specious Pretence to conceal a villainous Action or Design. He plays on the Fiddle, can read and write tolerably well, and understands a little of Arithmetic and Accounts. I have Reason to believe some evil-minded Persons in Town have encouraged and been Accomplices with him in his villanous Designs; and it is probable he will contrive the most specious Forgeries to give him the Appearance of being a Free Man: I have already been inform'd of a Writing he has shewn for that Purpose, by which he has imposed upon many People; who may all be easily satisfied that he has no legal Claim to Freedom, even from Slavery, nor any Pretence to it but by the very Law by which he is my Servant for 40 Years, as the Records of the Superior Court at *New-Haven* will Witness. At that Place where the former Owner of the said Slave lived, he was guilty of a Variety of Crimes and Felonies, for which he was several Times publicly whipped, and only escaped the Gallows by want of Prosecution. When he became my Servant, I intended to have shipped him to the *West-Indies*, and sold him there, and kept him in Prison till I should get an Opportunity; but on his earnest Request, solemn Promises of his good Behaviour, and seeming Penitence, I took him into my Family upon Trial, where for some Time he behaved well, and was very serviceable to me. Deceived by his Appearance of Reformation, I placed some Confidence in him, which he has villainously abused; having embezzled Money sent by him to pay for Goods, borrow'd Money, and taken up Goods in my Name unknown to me, and also on his Account, pretending to be a Freeman. By this villainous Proceeding I suppose he has collected a considerable Sum of Money, and am also apprehensive, that he has been an Accomplice in some of the late Robberies committed in and near this City.—Whoever will take up the said Servant, and bring him to me, or secure him in some of His MajestyGoals, so that I may get him again, if taken up in the City of *New-York*, shall have *FIVE POUNDS* Reward, and a greater, if taken up at a greater Distance, in Proportion to the Distance and Expence. Any Persons who take him up, are desired to be careful to carry him before the next Magistrate, and have him well search'd, leaving all the Money and Goods found upon him, except the necessary Clothes he has on, in the Hands of the said Magistrate; and to be very watchful against an Escape, or being deceived, for he is one of the most artful of Villains.

JOHN HOLT.
The Maryland Gazette, April 29, 1762; *The Pennsylvania Gazette,*
April 29, 1762; *The New-York Mercury,* May 3, 1762; May 10, 1762.
Minor differences between the papers.

New-York, April 27, 1762.
RUN-away, from the Transport Ship Three-Sisters, on Saturday Night last, the 24th Inst. a Servant Lad named James Jewell, West-Country born, 16 Years old, much marked with the Small Pox, and of a pale Complexion: Had on when he went away, a blue Jacket and Trowsers, has a sore Head, and wears a Cap. Whoever takes up and secures the said Servant shall have 20s. Reward, paid by Mr. Henry White, of New-York, or the Captain of said Ship JOHN MALTBY.
The New-York Mercury, May 3, 1762; May 17, 1762.

BROKE out of Gaol last Night, a Man named *Abraham Dewit,* near 6 Foot high. Had on when he went away, a blue Jacket, Leather Breeches, white Stockings, a Tow Shirt not whitened, with long curl'd Hair of a brown Colour, and brown Complexion, thin Visage, light grey Eyes. Whoever takes up, and brings him to me, or secures him in one of his Majesty's Gaols, so that he may be brought to Justice, shall have *Five Pounds* Reward, and all reasonable Charges, *May* 11, 1762.
  by me *William Holly,* Under Sheriff. *Goshen,*
The New-York Gazette, May 17, 1762; May 24, 1762; May 31, 1762;
The New-York Mercury, May 17, 1762; May 24, 1762; June 7, 1762.
Minor differences between the papers.

RUN away from his Master, being a Servant, on Sunday the 9th Instant, *James Simmerel,* by Trade a Taylor; Had on when he went away, a good Olive-coloured Thickset Frock and Breeches, and a fine blue Broadcloth Jacket, wears his own Hair, incling to a Flax Colour; he is near five Feet four Inches high, thick and chubby, full fac'd, and marked with the Small-pox, born at Carrickfergus, in Ireland, and is about 19 or 20 Years of Age, Whoever secures him, and brings him to the Subscriber, living at the Sign of the Hand and Sheers, near Beekman's Slip, and opposite Mrs. Keortricht's, in the Fly, shall have *Forty Shillings* Reward; and if taken out of New-York, all reasonable Expences borne. All Captains of Vessels and others, are forbid carrying him off, on Penalty of being prosecuted. *Dated* at New-York, 14*th Day* of May, 1762.
  James Grummel.
The New-York Mercury, May 17, 1762; June 14, 1762.

ON Tuesday Night last the 18*th of* May, Thomas Lovegrove's *House, at the Sign of the* Black Horse, *seven Miles from* New-York, *in the Road to* Kingsbridge, *was broke open and robb'd of a Silver Watch, and a small Leather Purse of about Fifty Shillings in small Silver, supposed to be done by* John Cambel, *formerly a Soldier: He entered the House by taking a square Pane of Glass out of the Window, and then putting his Hand through, unbutton'd it and got in, and came to the Head of the Bed, where said* Lovegrove *was asleep, and took his Breeches from under his Head, where the Money and Watch was. The aforesaid* Campbell *is a grand Villain. This is therefore to give Public NOTICE to take Care of him. He came from* Philadelphia, *as he said, and brought a sorrel Horse with him, which he sold to* Henry Schutz, *in* New-York, *near* Fresh-Water, *with Bridle and Saddle, for Four Pounds, for which he gave said* Schutz *a Receipt, in the Name of* Thomas Dawson. *After which he came to said* Lovegrove's *to lodge, and there staid three days, and passed by the Name of* Thomas Tawas: *And the last Place of his Lodging was at* Peter Waldron's *in* Harlem, *where he was obliged to go by his own Name first above mentioned, the People of the House knowing him when he waited upon an Officer of the* Royal Americans *at the same House. He will say sometimes that he is a Scotchman; and then that he was born on* Long-Island: *But he is an Irishman. He is a well-set Person, about five Feet five or six Inches high, with his own Hair, brown and not tied; is pretty much Pockmarked, dressed in a brown Camblet Coat, a striped Silk and Cotton Waistcoat, with the Stripes up and down; a Pair of Buff-coloured Buckskin Breeches, half dirty; a Pair of light brown mixed ribb'd Stocking, [sic] wears a Castor Hat, and carries with him a Tobacco-stopper with a Negro Head on it, in which there is a Magnet, and where-ever he goes, generally asks for a Bunch of Keys, in order to shew the Virtues of it by taking the Keys up with the said Magnet, which may be supposed is only done in order to take an Observation of them.*

Whoever apprehends the above mentioned Person so that the Owner of the said Watch and Money may receive his Own, and be brought to Justice, shall receive Fifty Shillings *Reward,*
    paid by   THOMAS LOVEGROVE.

N. B. *The Watch has a China Dial Plate, and the Outside and Inside Cases are both bruised pretty much by a fall. The Outside Case is lined with Crimson Sattin, with a white cut Paper over it; and has a green Silk String and Silver Seal, with a green Stone and a Bird thereon. The above Person hired a Horse at* East-Chester, *and is gone the Post-Road towards* Boston.

The New-York Gazette, May 24, 1762; May 31, 1762; June 14, 1762; July 5, 1762.

RUN-away a Negro Fellow, named Charles, is 30 Years old, Jamaica born, speaks English and French, pretends he is free: Had on a blue Plush Coat, is about 5 ½ Feet high; slender built; his Head, Nose, and Mouth, remarkably small for a Negro; his Teeth as white as Snow; and has several Cuts in his Face. Whoever secures him, and will give Notice to the Printer hereof, shall have Three Pounds as a Reward. He was seen in Town two Days age,—
May 31, 1762.
The New-York Gazette, May 31, 1762; June 7, 1762; June 21, 1762; *The New-York Mercury*, May 31, 1762; June 7, 1762; June 14, 1762.
Minor differences between the papers.

RUN-away the 14th Instant, from his Master, *Samuel Brookman*, a Servant Boy named *David Welch*. Had on when he went away, a brown Coat, a blue Pair of Breeches, black Stockings, an old Pair of Shoes, wore his own Hair, by Trade a Barber, and is about 16 Years of Age. Whoever takes up and secures the said Servant Boy, so that his Master may have him again, shall have Twenty Shillings Reward, and all reasonable Charges
        paid by   *Samuel Brookman.*
N. B. All Masters of Vessels and others are forbid to carry the said Boy off, as they will assuredly be prosecuted for the same.
N. York, May 22, 1762.
The New-York Gazette, May 31, 1762; June 7, 1762; June 14, 1762.

RUN-away, on Friday last, the 28th Instant, from the Subscriber, an Indian Servant Lad, named ———, about twelve Years old, and has a remarkable Scar on his Head: He went off without Shoes, Stockings, Wig, Hat, or Cap, having just come in from Jamaica, and had on only an Oznabrigs Frock and Trowsers: He is supposed to be gone to Long-Island. Whoever takes up and secures the said Lad so that he may be had again, shall have Forty Shillings Reward and all reasonable Charges,
        paid by   FRANCIS WELCH.
The New-York Mercury, May 31, 1762; June 7, 1762; June 14, 1762.

New-York, June 12, 1762.
RUN-away on Thursday Night last, from the Sloop *Sally, Joseph Carver*, Master, a Negro Fellow name *Quaco*, about 22 Years of Age; a stout lusty Fellow, about Five Feet Eight Inches high, with small Scars on his Cheeks, speaks bad English: Had on when he went away, a Felt Hat, a double-breasted dark-colour'd Bearskin Jacket half worn, lined with striped Flannel, Check Linnen Shirt, a Pair of Buckskin Breeches. Whoever takes up said Negro Fellow, and secures him in any Gaol, or delivers him to Mr.

John Byvanck, in *New-York*, opposite *Beekman's* Slip, shall have *Forty Shillings* Reward, and all reasonable Charges
     paid by John *Byvanck.*
 N. B. All Masters of Vessels and others, are forbid harbouring, concealing, or carrying off said Negro at their Peril.
The New-York Gazette, June 14, 1762.

Deserted from Nutten-Island, the 11th June, 1762, the following Soldiers, of the First New-York Regiment, and Capt. Thodey's *Company.*
 CHARLES BAKER, aged 31 Years, born in Old England, a Labourer, was inlisted by Lieut. Fitzpatrick in New-York, 5 Feet 9 Inches high, blue Eyes, light brown Hair, and swarthy Complexion.
 John Harden, aged 30 Years, born in Ireland, Baker by Trade, inlisted by Capt. Thodey, 5 Feet 6 Inches high, brown Eyes, black Hair, and ruddy Complexion.
 William Whitehead, aged 27 Years, born in Maryland, a Labourer, inlisted by Lieut. Fitzpatrick, 5 Feet 6 Inches high, blue Eyes, black Hair, and ruddy Complexion.
 Aaron Lambert, aged 20 Years, born in New-Jersey, Black-Smith, inlisted by Lieut. Fitzpatrick, 5 Feet 9 Inches high, grey Eyes, black Hair, and swarthy Complexion.
 Twenty Pounds will be paid for apprehending of the above Deserters, or *Five Pounds* or each to them that shall be secured in any of the Gaols of this Province, or delivered to the Regiment, either here or at Albany.
 The New-York Gazette, June 14, 1762; July 5, 1762.

LATELY Run-away from his Master, *Philip Solomon Flegelar*, of Dutchess County, a Negro Man Slave named *Primus*, aged about 20 Years, 5 and ½ Feet high, well set, very black Skin, when he talks he winks with his Eyes: He had on a light colour'd homespun Jacket, Buckskin Breeches, and Brass Buttons, thick Shoes, with Strings, blue Leggings, old Felt Hat, and Linen Shirt, talks good English, Low-Dutch, and High-Dutch. Whoever takes up and secures the said Negro Slave, so that his Master may have him again, shall have *Three Pounds* Reward, besides all reasonable Charges
     paid by *Philip Solomon Flegelar.*
 N. B. All Persons are forbid carrying him off, as they shall surely answer it at their Peril.   May 31*st*, 1761.
 The New-York Mercury, June 14, 1762; *The New-York Gazette*, July 5, 1762.

Marcus Hook, (in Pennsylvania) June 11th, 1762.
A Certain Alexander Crawford, having on or about the 24th of the Month of March last, absented himself from the usual Place of this Abode, with a Design, 'tis thought, to defraud his Creditors, to whom he owes divers large Sums: Notice is therefore given, that the said Crawford, who appears to be about 28 Years of Age, is much freckled, has a high Nose, is long visaged, and very slim: His wearing Apparel is not fully known, but is it certain he had on a brown Cloth Coat, with a light Velvet Cape to it, a black cut Wig, a black Velvet Jacket, Buckskin Breeches, and Thread Stockings: He was born in Ireland, and speaks a little on the Scotch Accent: He is a mighty Horse Jockey, and is always for swaping either Horses or indeed any other Article he may be possessed of when in Company: As he was seen some Days after he left the Place of his Residence on the Road that leads towards New-York, it is thought he has gone towards the Highlands in that Government, having Relations and Acquaintance there. Whoever takes up the said Crawford, and will secure him in any Goal, and gives Notice thereof in H. Gaine's Mercury, shall have a Reward of Ten Pounds, New-York Currency, and all other Charges they may be at paid besides,
        by   AARON HULTZ.
The New-York Mercury, June 14, 1762; June 21, 1762.

RUN-away, from the Care of the Constable in *Eastchester*, a Negro Man named Robin, belonging to Doctor *Thomas Wright*, of the same Place. The Negro is of a middling Size, square shoulder'd, and seems to stoop a little. He is somewhat thin visaged: He has a scar on his Left Arm, by Inocculation for the Small-Pox, and has several Corns on his Toes. He is about 28 Years of Age, born in *Westchester*, understands all Sorts of Country Business extremely well.

He had on when he went away, an old close bodied grey Rateen Coat, with Metal Buttons, a Check Shirt with a black Velvet Stock about his Neck, has a Pair of Leather Breeches, two new Pair of Trowsers with Horn Buttons, and an old Felt Hat. He also took with him, an old white Cloth Coat lined with Brown Holland with Silver Twist Buttons; and a blue Cloth Jacket without Sleeves, with Gold Vellum Button-Holes. It is supposed he took with him two white Shirts, one of which is ruffled: As also a long Pistol, remarkable for having a Sight on the Barrel, like a Gun. Tis supposed he is gone off with a likely young White Girl, by whom it is reported she is with Child; and Tis thought she will protect him under the Character of being her Servant. It is also supposed that he will try to get either to the Northern Parts of this Province or Connecticut, or for Maryland; all which Places he is well acquainted with.

If any Person will apprehend the said White Girl and Negro together, and secure them in any of his Majesty's Goals, and give Intelligence, to the said Master thereof, shall Forty Shillings Reward, and all reasonable Charges. And for the Negro alone TWENTY Shillings, if either brought home, or secured as above, to be paid by the Subscriber.
THOMAS WRIGHT.   Eastchester, the 25th of June, 1762.
The New-York Gazette, June 28, 1762; July 5, 1762; July 26, 1762.
See *The New-York Mercury*, July 12, 1762.

RUN-away, from the Subscriber, last Tuesday Night, a Servant Woman, named Margaret Smith, about 26 years old, of a fair Complexion, long visaged, pitted a little with the Small Pox, and has a large lump on her right Side: Had on when she went away, a striped Linnen Josey, and a homespun Pettycoat, wears a Cap that comes over her Face pretty much; speaks broad Scotch, and was born in Erwin, in Scotland. Whoever takes up and secures the said Servant, so that she may be had again, shall have Twenty Shillings Reward, if taken up in the City, and Thirty Shillings if in the Country,
paid by   GILBERT SHEARER.
The New-York Mercury, June 28, 1762.

RUN away from MICHAEL BUTLER, on Friday Night last the 2d Instant, a Servant Maid named Elizabeth Coteu, of a fair Complexion, blue Eyes, light Hair, and of middle Stature, about 21 Years old: Had on when she went away, a striped Linsy-wolsey Petticoat, and a striped Cotton short Gown, one Gold and one Tortishell Ring on her Fingers. Whoever takes up the said Servant, and brings her to her Master, living at Peck's Slip, shall have Twenty Shillings Reward, and all reasonable Charges
paid, by   MICHAEL BUTLER.
The New-York Gazette, July 5, 1762; July 12, 1762.

LATELY run away from his Masters *Andrius* and *Johannis A. Huycke*, of *Schadack*, a Negro Man named *Pomp*, 28 Years old; about six foot high, a pretty black Complexion, a little Pock-marked, well built, talks nothing but English, was born on Long-Island, and lately brought from there by Mr. Pemberton of Albany. Had on where he went away, a coarse homespun shirt, breeches and stockings; a coarse light-colour'd broad cloth Jacket, an old blue great coat, a Pair of black breeches, and an old blanket with him; His Shoes about half worn: His Hat cropped Jocky like. Whoever secures said Negro, so that his Masters may have him again, shall have Three Pounds Reward, and all reasonable Charges paid, if taken out of the county

of Albany; and if taken within the said county, Three Dollars, and all reasonable Charges,   *Schadack, 27th June,* 1762.
          paid by   Andries A. Huycke, *and* Johannis A. Huycke.
The New-York Mercury, July 5, 1762; July 12, 1762.

*R*UN *away from Mr. Bell's, Innholder in Roxbury, on the 9th Instant, Two Negro Men, lately imported from Martinico to New-York, and from thence to Boston, by the Way of Rhode-Island, about 23 Years of Age each, and speak no English. One of them had on a striped Flannel Waistcoat, and striped Linen Trowzers; the other a green Waistcoat and Breeches, and both bare-footed. Any Person who will apprehend the above Negroes, and send them to Melatiah Bourn, Esq; of Boston, or the said Bell, or secured them and give Notice to either of them, shall have FOUR DOLLARS Reward for each, and all Charges paid.*

All Masters of Vessels and others are cautioned against harbouring, concealing, or carrying off said Negroes, as they would avoid the Penalty of the Law.
      The Boston Evening-Post, July 12, 1762; July 19, 1762; July 26, 1762.

RUN-*away from the subscriber, an English Servant Man named* Benjamin Gansey, *aged about 23 or 24 Years, he says he was born in Stanford in Connecticut, is about 5 Feet 4 Inches high, a well-set Man, and has lost one or two of his Fore Teeth, has a down sheepish look, most of his Hair is cut off: Had on when he went away, a Tow Shirt and Trowsers, a blue Coat, a new felt Hat, old Shoes, but as he stole sundry Cloaths, and carried them away, he may change his Dress. Any Person that will bring him to the Subscriber, shall receive five Pounds Reward, and all reasonable Charges,*
          paid by   MICHAEL HOPKINS.
                                          Dutchess County, July 12, 1762.
The New-York Mercury, July 12, 1762; July 26, 1762.

RUN-away, from the Care of the Constable in East-Chester, a Negro Man named Robin, belonging to Doctor Thomas Wright, of the same Place: He is of middling Size, somewhat thin visaged, square shouldered, and seems to stoop a little; he has a scar on his Left Arm, by Innoculation, and has several Corns on his Toes; he is about 28 Years of Age, was born in West-Chester, understands all Sorts of Country Business extremely well, and pretends to be a good Brewer, and somewhat of a Shoemaker. He had on when he went away, an old close bodied grey Ratteen Coat, with White-Mettal figur'd Buttons, with Cat-gut Eyes; a Check Shirt, with a black

Velvet Stock, a Pair of Leather Breeches, two new Pair of coarse Tow Trowsers, with Horn Buttons, and an old Felt Hat. He also took with him, an old white Cloth Coat, lined with brown Holland, with Silver Twist Buttons, a blue Cloth Jacket without Sleeves, with Gold Vellum Button Holes, two white Shirts, one of which is ruffled, and also an old long Pistol, with a Sight on the Barrel, like a Gun. It is with the greatest probability imagined he has obtained a Pass from some ill disposed Person, and will try to get to the Northern Parts of this Province, and amongst the Five Nations of Indians, or at or near No. 4 in Boston Government, of else to the Northern Parts of Maryland or Virginia, all which Places he is well acquainted with by his elopement heretofore. If any Person will apprehend the said Negro, and safely return him in any of his Majesty's Goals, and will give Intelligence, or return him to his said Master, shall be rewarded for the same as follows, viz. If taken in West-Chester County, Twenty Shillings; if out of the County, and in any other Part of the Province, Three Pounds; and if among the Five Nations of Indians, or or in any other Province, the Sum of Five Pounds, and all reasonable Charges, to be paid by the Subscriber.   THOMAS WRIGHT.

   N. B. Whoever takes him are cautioned to secure him well, for he is an artful Fellow.

   The New-York Mercury, July 12, 1762; July 19, 1762; July 26, 1762. See *The New-York Gazette*, June 28, 1762.

WHEREAS, on Friday the 2nd Inst. a Man that went by the name of George Adams, hired a Pettyauger and a Boy from Edmond Pinfold, of White Stone, on Long-Island, with a Pretence to put a Surveying Instrument on board a Sloop that lay at Rye, for the Use of the College at Cambridge, in Massachusetts Government, but has neither returned the Petty auger nor the Boy since: He has been seen off Tinicunk, in the Sound, standing to the Eastward. 'Tis hoped all Persons will endeavour to intercept the said Fellow; he is a well-set Man, with a brown Silk Coat, and had a white Cap or a Wig; and if the Pettyaguer and Boy is returned to the Owner at White Stone, the Person that brings them shall be handsomly rewarded,
              by   ED. PINFOLD.
   The New-York Mercury, July 12, 1762.

                         Beaver-street, New-York, July 19th.
RUN-away Thursday Morning from the subscriber, between 7 and 8 o'Clock, an indented Servant Girl, named, Mary Godfrey, from Liverpool in Lancashire. She is about 17 Years old of a fair and ruddy Complexion, middling Stature, slim, but full breasted; her Hair light brow, her Nose short, with small blue Eyes, and a round Face. She is rather fawning than

complaisant, very liquorish, and has something lewd in her Behaviour, is much addicted to lying, and generally betrays herself by her Talkativeness. She ran away once before, and took the Name of Mary Everson. She had on when she went away, a purple and white coloured callico jersey with a small Bird in the Flowers, an English cotton Gown with black, blue, white, yellow, red, and greenish stripes; a linsey woolsey petticoat with yellowish, green, blue, and white narrow stripes; new leather Shoes, white cotton stockings, white metal buckles, and a plain new black satten round hat. Whoever takes up the above Servant, and secures her so that I may have her again, shall have Forty Shillings Reward, and all reasonable Charges
          paid by me   EVERT EVERSON.
The New-York Gazette, July 19, 1762.

RAN-away from the subscribers, on Sunday Morning the 11th Instant, supposed to be gone together, two Negro Men, one of them named Tom, a Brasier by Trade, and who also understands the Sugar-baking Business: He is 5 Feet 6 Inches high, 25 Years old, well-made, and has remarkable good Limbs: Had on when he went away, a blue double-breasted Jacket, and a Pair of light-coloured Serge Breeches. He took with him, a light-coloured Jacket, and a Buckskin Pair of Breeches; and can write and read.

The other named Pompey, 20 Years old, is straight and well-limb'd, has good Features, a Baker by Trade, and is about six Feet high: Had on when he went away, a blue Cloth Jacket and Breeches.

Whoever takes up and secures the above-mentioned Negroes, so that their Masters may have them again, shall have FIVE POUNDS Reward paid by each, if taken out of the Province THREE POUNDS for each if taken in any Part of the Province of New-York except the City and Suburbs; and FORTY Shillings for each if taken in City or Suburbs;
          paid by   Edward Man, jun.
                    James Bennett.

N. B. All Masters of Vessels are forwarned to carry them off, and all others are forbid to harbour him
The New-York Gazette, July 19, 1762; August 16, 1762.

New-York, July 9, 1762.
RUN away about two Months ago, a yellowish looking old Negro Fellow: He had on a brown Jacket without Sleeves, and has lost one of his Fingers: He has been seen wandering about *Greenwich* and the *Bowry-Lane*. Whoever takes him up, and carried him to the Work-House, shall there receive *Two Dollars*; and whoever will discover who it is that harbours him, shall be thankfully rewarded.
The New-York Gazette, July 19, 1762.

RUN-away, on the 21st Instant, from the snow George, Robert Crannel, Master, the 5 following Men, viz. Thomas Fitzgerall, Rowland Hillman, Francis Cook, John Doyl, and St. Baston Gonsalvo, the latter a Portuguese, and speaks very little English. Whoever will secure all or any of the above named Men, so that they may be brought to Justice, by applying to Christopher Heysham, in King-street, shall receive Five Dollars Reward for each man so secured.
The New-York Mercury, July 26, 1762; August 2, 1762.

ABsented himself of Tuesday last, from the Ship Mary, Capt. Deverson, a Sailor named Matthias Hureen, a Sweed, about 6 Feet high, stout, and well-made, and is much pitted with the Small-Pox. Whoever takes up and secures the said Hureen, and will bring him to the Ship lying at the New-Dock, shall receive as a Reward FIVE DOLLARS,
       by   WILLIAM DEVERSON.
The New-York Mercury, August 2, 1762.

RUN away, in New-York, on Wednesday the 4th. August Instant, from George Cornwall, of Hampsted, Long-Island, Boatman, an Apprentice Lad, named Charles M'Daniel; about 13 Years old, born in London, small Stature, of a light Complexion: had on a Pair of blue and white striped homespun Trowsers, and old light-brown Jacket, and wore a Scotch Bonnet; but 'tis probable he may change his Apparel, and cut off his Hair, which is of a light Colour. Whoever takes up and secures the said Apprentice, so that his Master may have him again, shall have *Twenty Shillings* Reward, and reasonable Charges
       paid by   GEORGE CORNWELL.
   N. B. All Commanders of Privateers, Masters of Vessels, and others, are hereby strictly forbid to carry him off, as they must expect to be prosecuted for the same.
The New-York Gazette, August 9, 1762; August 16, 1762.

RUN-*away, from the Subscriber, some Time ago, and is supposed to be on board the Privateer Brig Mars, Captain M'Gillycuddy, an Apprentice Boy named Samuel Juel: These are therefore to forewarn all Persons from purchasing any Prize Money, from the said Juel, or crediting him on any Account.*   JACOB BAKER,   Shoemaker.
The New-York Mercury, August 9, 1762; August 16, 1762.

RUN away on Monday the 9th August Instant, a Servant Lad, named John George Isling, German born, aged about 19, 5 Feet Stature, and fair Complexion. Carried away with him, a new Fustian Jacket and Breeches, Oznabrigs Trowsers, two new Check Shirts, an old Hat, and wears his Hair, a dark brown Colour. Whoever apprehends and secures said Servant, so that his Master may have him again, shall have *Forty Shillings* Reward, and all reasonable Charges
   paid by JOHN TALMAN.
 N. B. All Masters of Vessels and others, are forbid carrying off, concealing, or harbouring of him, as they will answer it at their Peril.
 The New-York Gazette, August 16, 1762; August 23, 1762.

RUN-away from the Subscriber, on Friday Night the 6th Inst. a Servant Girl named Sarah Hendrick, aged about 13 Years, has black Eyes, black Hair, and is of a swarthy Complexion; she was taken away by her Mother one Sarah Summers, about 5 Feet and an Half high, of the same Complexion, with one John Jones, a little Fellow, of a down Look, blue Eyes, and dark bushy Hair, born in England. Whoever will take them up and secure them, so that her Mistress may have them again, shall receive Three Pounds Reward, and all reasonable Charges,
   paid by *Elizabeth Dogworth.*
 The New-York Mercury, August 16, 1762; August 23, 1762; September 13, 1762.

          Kingston, July, 25, 1762.
TAKEN up here, and committed to Gaol, a Runaway Negro Fellow, suppos'd to be lately brought from his own Country; he can give no Account where he came from, nor who his Master is; he is a slim Fellow, about 5 Feet 6 Inches high; wears Snuff-colour'd Broadcloth Jacket, a blue Stroud Under-Jacket, a Pair of Leather Breeches, old Stockings and Shoes, and has with him a Gun, Powder-Horn, and Bullets. Whoever owns the said Negro, is desired to send for him speedily, to ABRAHAM LOW, Sheriff of Ulster County, or else he will discharge the said Negro from Goal.
 The New-York Mercury, August 23, 1762.

DESERTED from his Majesty's 35th Regiment of Foot, and Col. Oughton's Company, quartered at Fort-George, the 6th of July 1762; JOHN HARDIE, aged 22 Years, 5 Feet 5 Inches, and an half high, born at Philadelphia, by Trade a Shoemaker, hair Hair, rudy Complexion, a Cast in both Eyes, thick-sett and well made. DANIEL KIEFF, aged 21 Years, 5 Feet 6 Inches and an Half high, born at Casco-Bay in Boston Government, bred up to the sea, lank fair Hair, fresh Complexion, straight and well made. JOHN PATTER, aged 24 Years, 5 Feet 6 Inches high, born at Stoney Stratford, in Buckinghamshire, England, by Trade a Brazier, fair Hair, swarthy Complexion, very much pitted with the Small-Pox, a Scar under his left Eye, and slender made.

N. B. The above Deserters all went off in their Regimentals, and had their side Arms with them.

Deserted also from the above Regiment, and Captain Hargreave's Company, quartered at Albany; SOLOMON TAYLOR, aged 29 Years, 5 Feet 10 Inches and an Half high, born at Groton, in the County of New London, by Trade a Labourer, dark brown Hair, grey Eyes, brown Complexion, straight and well made, and had on when he went away, a green Jacket and Leather Breeches. WILLIAM PRICE, aged 24 Years, 5 Feet 5 Inches and an Half high, born at Newport Pagnell, in Buckinghamshire, by Trade a Butcher, light brown Hair, grey Eyes, greatly mark'd with the Small-Pox; had on when he went away, a white flannel Jacket, and a striped one under it. Whoever apprehends any of the above Deserters, and gives Notice thereof to the Commanding Officer at Albany, or to William Bayard, Esq; at New-York, shall receive a Reward of Forty Shillings Sterling for each of them, over and above what is allowed by Act of Parliament, for apprehending Deserters.

The New-York Mercury, August 23, 1762; August 30, 1762.

DESERTED,
OF Captain Cochran's Company,
of the first Battalion of the Royal American Regiment, from New-York, Andrew Fronheyser, a German, speaks tolerable good English, a good looking young mam, of an Olive Complexion, with black Hair, inclined to curl, 5 Feet 8 or 9 Inches high: Had on when he went off a Fustian colour'd Thick Set Coat with a red Waistcoat.

Christopher Brannan, 16 Years of Age, tall of his Years, good looking, with light brown Hair; born near York-Town in Pennsylvania: Had on when he went off a blue Coat with red button holes, and large red Cuffs.

Whoever apprehends One or both of them and secures them in any County Goal, or gives such information to the Printer hereof, that they may be apprehended, shall receive Five Pounds reward for each of them that is so secured, besides what is allow'd by act of Parliament. And whoever harbours or conceals them shall be prosecuted in the severest Manner.

> The New-York Mercury, August 23, 1762; August 30, 1762; September 6, 1762; The Pennsylvania Gazette, September 2, 1762. Minor differences between the papers. The *Gazette* states information of them is be given "to Mr. William Dunlap, Printer in Philadelphia...."

RUN away on Wednesday the first Inst. September, from JOHN ELLIOT, Taylor in New-York, an Apprentice Boy named JOHN HAUSE, about 19 Years of Age, about 5 Feet high, swarthy Complexion, long dark Hair. Had on when he went away, a blue Camblet Coat, and Nankeen Vest and Breeches. Whoever takes up said Apprentice, and secures him, so that his Master may have him again, shall have Forty Shillings Reward, and all reasonable Expences,
    paid by me *John Elliot.*
The New-York Gazette, September 6, 1762; September 13, 1762.

WHEREAS a few Weeks before Christmas last, John Causer, and Hester, his Wife, who lived near Brunswick, in New-Jersey, had committed to their Care on certain Conditions, a Boy about Ten Years of Age, named John Bryan, the Son of Archibald and Catherine Bryan, of the City of New-York; whom they were to return at the Expiration of Eleven Years:—And as the said John Causer has since gone into the Provincial Service, and as his Wife nor Boy to be heard of, it is apprehended they have disposed of him to some other Person or Persons, to the great Grief of the Parents.—If any Person or Persons can inform William Ouke, Esq; in New-Brunswick, or the Printer hereof, where the Boy is, so that he may be recover'd, it will be esteem'd a charitable Deed, and they thankfully rewarded.—The Lad is of a short thick Stature, Pock-markt, had a sore Head, brown Hair, and is very smart.— N. B. The Boy was clear'd at the Court held in August last at Brunswick.
The New-York Gazette, September 6, 1762.

RUN-away last Week, from the Subscriber, a Negro Man named Jack, has a Mole on his Chin, with Hair growing out of the same; is a thin magure Fellow, very active, and supposed to be gone on board some Vessel, or does intend it, therefore all Masters of Vessels are forbid to take him to Sea, as they will answer the same at their Peril. Whoever takes up and secures the said Fellow so that he may be had again, shall receive Five Dollars Reward, and all reasonable Charges,
    paid by THOMAS POOLE.
The New-York Mercury, September 13, 1762; September 27, 1762; October 4, 1762; October 11, 1762. See *The New-York Gazette*, October 4, 1762.

Deserted from his Majesty's 55th Regiment of
  Foot, and Colonel Oughton*'s Company, quartered at* Fort-George.
JOSEPH BRADBURN, aged about 29 Years, 5 Feet 7¼ Inches high, born at Lusford in Cheshire, England, by Trade a Garter Weaver; dark brown

Hair, grey Eyes, ruddy Complexion, greatly pitted with the Small-pox, stout and well made; he deserted off his Post when Centry, with his Arms and Accoutrements, and had on a new Sute of Cloathing.

WILLIAM BUCHAN, aged 24 Years, 5 Feet 5 Inches high, born in the Parish of St. Ninens, in the Shire of Stirling, North-Britain, by Trade a Carpenter, sandy Hair, blue Eyes, fresh Complexion, and went off in his new Regimentals.

Deserted also from the above Regiment, and Capt. Daly's Company, quartered at Fort-Edward.

DANIEL WATTS, aged about 30 Years, 5 Feet 7¼ Inches high, born in the Parish of Matlock, in Darbyshire, England, by Trade a Labourer, brown Hair, brown Eyes, fresh Complexion, a Mole under his left Eye.

WILLIAM WATSON, aged about 25 Years, 5 Feet 6 Inches high, born in Lambeth, in Surry, England, brought up to the Sea, dark brown Hair, grey Eyes, round full faced, ruddy Complexion.

Whoever apprehends any of the above Deserters, and gives Notice thereof to the Commanding Officer at Albany, or to William Bayard, Esq; at New-York, shall receive a Reward of Forty Shillings Sterling for each of them, over and above what is allowed by Act of Parliament for apprehending of Deserters, and four Dollars over and above will be given to any Person who apprehends the Deserter Joseph Bradburn.

The New-York Gazette, September 20, 1762; September 27, 1762.

Whereas a certain Gilbert Weakes, born in York Government, near the Borders of New-England, came to John Evelman's, with Pretence of having Orders to receive a Horse, left with said Evelman to be disposed of, and by his false Stories obtained said Horse. Said Weakes is of a middle Size, pretty fair Complexion, with blackish Hair and Eyes, has lost two of his fore Teeth; his Apparel not known, having several Changes of Clothes, and dresses very well, Whoever takes up and secures said Weakes, so as he be brought to Justice, shall have Five Pounds Reward,
   paid by John Evelman.
The Pennsylvania Gazette, September 23, 1762.

RUN-AWAY, a Negro Man named Philip, about 30 Years of Age, well made in Stature, speaks both English and French, having been brought up in Newrochel; is a good Farmer and Shoemaker: Had on when he went away, a Cloth Coat of a Brick Colour, lin'd with white, and Plate Buttons, Silk Waistcoat of near the same Colour, a Pair of Scarlet Worsted Breeches, with Silk Puffs and Garters Whoever apprehends him, and will deliver him

at the old City-Hall, in New-York, will receive Three Dollars Reward, and other reasonable Charges.
The New-York Gazette, September 27, 1762.

RUN away on Wednesday the 22d of September last, from THOMAS POOLE, of this City a Negro Man named Jack, about 5 ½ Feet high, has a Mole on one of his Cheeks, a Scar on his Forehead; is a thin meagre Fellow, very active and spry has lost his lower fore Teeth; his Cloathing uncertain; He formerly belonged to Mr. Allicock. Whoever takes up and secures the said Negro Fellow so that his Master may have him again, shall have FOUR POUNDS Reward, and reasonable Charges
    paid by *Thomas Pool.*
N. B. All Masters of Vessels, and others, are forbid carrying off, harbouring, or concealing said Negro, as they shall answer it at their Peril.
The New-York Gazette, October 4, 1762; October 11, 1762. See *The New-York Mercury*, September 13, 1762.

RUN away from the Subscriber on New-York, about three Weeks ago, a Negro Fellow, named Sam Black, about six Feet high, slim, is Bermuda born; talks good English; and is the Property of Mrs. CATHERINE HORTEN, of that Island. Had on when he went away, a blue colour'd Jacket, with a blue and white striped one under it; an Oznabrigs Trowsers, and Check Shirt. Whoever takes up and secures the said Fellow, so that he may be had again, shall have Twenty Shillings Reward, and reasonable
    Charges paid by JOHN TUDOR.
N. B. It is thought he is still in New-York; all Masters of Vessels are forbid to carry him off; and others forbid either to harbour or employ him, 'til further Orders from me J. T.
The New-York Gazette, October 4, 1762; October 11, 1762; October 25, 1762.

RUN away from *Korl Toll*, of Schenectady, on the 18th of July last, a Negro Man, named Jack, about 26 Years of Age: Had on when he went away, a white French Coat, Leather Jacket, a Pair of blue Camblet Breeches, and a Pair of Homespun Trowsers over them, has likewise taken with him a Gun: He is about 6 Feet high.—Also a Negro Wench, his Wife, named GIN, about 5½ Feet high, aged about 35 Years, has taken with them a Boy of 3 Years old: She had on a striped Holland short Gown, a striped Homespun Petticoat, and a striped stuff one. Whoever apprehends the said Negroes, or either of them, and secures them in any Gaol, so that their Master may have them again, shall have a Reward of FIVE POUNDS,
    paid by me Koral Toll, or by Richard Waldron,
    in New-York, with the Charges attending.

The New-York Gazette, October 4, 1762; October 11, 1762; October 25, 1762; December 13, 1762; December 20, 1762; January 3, 1763.

          Tappan, Orange County, Sept. 26, 1762.
RUN away from his Master, Johannis Blauveldt, Blacksmith a Negro Fellow named, as he says Adonis, but by us Doon; he is of yellow Complexion, being a mixed Breed, speaks and reads Low Dutch pretty well, and speaks little English; he is a very good Blacksmith, and understands a little of the Cordwainers and Carpenter's Business is about 5½ Feet high, full fac'd, short black Hair, is about 20 or 21 Years old: Had on when he went away, a Homespun Shirt and Trowsers, grey Waistcoat, Felt Hat: Took with him a Check Shirt and Trowsers, and one white Shirt, a blue cloth Breeches, and a homespun Waistcoat: He had been whipt the Day before he went off, which may be seen pretty much on his Right-side; he pretends to be free, and perhaps by that Means may procure a Pass. Whoever takes up and secures said Fellow, so that his Master may have him again, shall have *Three Pounds* Reward, and all reasonable Charges
      paid by *Johannis Blauveldt.*
N. B. All Masters of Vessels and others, are forbid carrying him away.
The New-York Gazette, October 4, 1762; October 25, 1762.

THERE is now in the Goal, of Jamaica, on Long-Island, a Negro Fellow about 5 Feet 9 Inches high, pretty slender, and speaks French or Spanish, and will speak no English. He was taken up in the Woods near Jamaica, on Wednesday Evening last, by William Watts. Whoever owns the said Fellow may have him again, proving their Property and paying Charges, by
      applying to said   WILLIAM WATTS.
The New-York Mercury, October 11, 1762.

RUN-*away, 12 days ago, from Long Island; a negro man named Harry, about 26 years old, near six feet high: had on when he went away, a round sailors hat, red striped woollen cap, new check'd trowsers, wears sometimes white, sometimes check trowsers, and sometimes and oznabrigs frock; speaks English, Dutch and Spanish, flat fac'd, tho' a tolerable good countenance; and may pretend to be free. Whoever apprehends and brings him to William Cobbam, at the Gold Hand, in Hanover-Square, shall have ten dollars reward, and all reasonable charges. All masters of vessels are forewarned to employ him, or carry him off at their Peril.*
  The New-York Mercury, October 11, 1762; October 18, 1762.

RUN away from his Master, a Negro Man, named Jack: Had on when he went away, an old Beaver Hat, clouded Coat, spotted Jacket, white Linen Shirt, and brown Cloth Breeches: Aged about 23; has a surly Look, and a Scar on his Chin: He is middling well set, about 5 Feet 4 Inches high: He formerly belonged to Mr. *Jacob Remsen*, near the Exchange, New-York. Whoever takes up and secures said Negro, so that his Master may have him again, shall have *Forty Shillings* Reward, paid by Jacob Remsen, or his Master, near the Court-House, at Freehold, East New-Jersey. All Masters of Vessels, and others, are forewarn'd carrying him off, harbouring, or concealing him, as they shall answer it at their Peril.
The New-York Gazette, October 18, 1762.

RUN-away the 12th Instant, a Negro Man named JACK, alias Salem, a short sett Fellow, a little lame in his right Foot, speaks good English: Had on when he went away, a brown Broad-cloth Coat, (which it's probably he may change for some other) and a Check Shirt. Whoever brings the said Negro to Christopher Heysham, in King-street, shall have Three Dollars Reward, if taken within the City, and Ten Dollars if taken without, and all necessary Charges, paid by the said Heysham. All Persons are forbid harbouring or carrying off said Negro at their Peril.
The New-York Mercury, October 18, 1762; November 15, 1762; November 22, 1762; December 27, 1762. Last ad shows he ran away "the 12th of September last."

RUN-*from the subscriber, living in Ulster County, near Coldenham, the beginning of October inst. a servant lad named Francis Quin: He is about 20 years old, pretty pock mark'd about the nose, short, and well-set, with black hair, pretty short on the crown: Had with him when he went away, a white cloth jacket, lined with red, with a turned up cuff, and a cape of the same cloth and colour; also a brown cloth jacket, a new felt hat, with a black ribband for a band, a pair of old leather breeches, and short trowsers; and is supposed to be gone to the Southward. Whoever takes up and secures the said servant, so that he may be had again, shall receive three Dollars Reward, and all reasonable charges,*
           paid by   DENNIS M'PEAK.
The New-York Mercury, October 18, 1762.

RUN-away, from Joseph Forman, of New-York, the 29th of October last, a Negro man named Joe, well set, about 5 feet 7 inches high, yellow complexion, much pock-mark'd, and speaks good English: Had on, a brown coat, striped jacket, leather Breeches, and a felt hat, sharp cock'd. Whoever secures the said Negro, shall have three pounds reward, and all reasonable charges, paid by said Forman.

The New-York Mercury, October 18, 1762. See *The New-York Gazette*, February 14, 1763, and *The Pennsylvania Gazette*, July 21, 1763.

RUN-*away, the 16th ultimo, from John Griffiths, in Albany, a servant man, named, Thomas Jones; dark complexion, about five feet ten inches high, and well set: Had on when he went away, a red great coat, blue jacket without sleeves, and a check shirt, his other clothes not known; it is supposed he was taken on board of a sloop (by a certain person,) 6 miles below Albany, and is gone to New-York. Whoever secures said servant man, and returns him to his said master in Albany, or to Messieurs Griffiths and M'Combs, Merchants, in New-York, shall receive* Five Dollars *Reward, and reasonable Charges.*

The New-York Mercury, November 1, 1762.

FIVE DOLLARS REWARD.

RUN away from the Subscriber, on Monday Evening 25th of October last, a Negro Man, named Somerset, but often goes by the Name of Joe, formerly the Property of Mr. Theodorus Van Wyck: about 30 Years of Age, and near 5 Feet and a Half high, speaks tolerable good English, but often affects to speak like a new Negro, and pretends to be free: Had on when he went off a Jacket and Trowsers, which is probable he has changed for some other Apparel: It is imagined he keeps somewhere nigh the City. Whoever apprehends said Negro, and brings him, or gives Notice of it to his Master, living in Smith-street, nigh the old Dutch Church, shall have the above Reward, and all reasonable Charges paid; and if taken up at any Distance from the City, shall be handsomely rewarded, over and above the Sum aforesaid. All Persons are forewarned to harboar [sic] him, and Masters of Vessel to employ him, or carry him off at their Peril.

Manuel Josephson.

The New-York Gazette, November 8, 1762; November 15, 1762; *The New-York Mercury*, November 8, 1762; November 15, 1762.

WHEREAS Edward Price, and John Robinson, has absented themselves from the Brotherly Love Transport:—This is to give Notice, that the Ship is under Sailing Orders; and if they do not immediately repair on board, they will lose their Wages,

WILLIAM ARMSTRONG.

The New-York Gazette, November 15, 1762.

WHEREAS I the Subscriber gave my Negro Fellow Jabez, Liberty to go Huntington, on Long-Island, the 25th of October last, to return in 15 Days; he not returning according to Order, is supposed to be absconded. He is a well built slim nimble Fellow, about 5 Feet, 9 Inches high; active, of a yellowish Complexion. Had on when he went away, a brown Camblet Coat, and Duffles Great-Coat faded; red Breeches. Whoever takes up said Fellow, and secures him in any of his Majesty's Gaols, or otherwise, that his Master may have him again, shall have Forty Shillings Reward, and all Charges occuring, paid by   *Theodorus Van Wyck.*
Fishkills, 11th Nov. 1762.

P. S. It is probably said Fellow will endeavour for Rhode Island to go to Sea. All Masters of Vessels are forbid carrying off, or any other Person whatsoever to harbour said Fellow.

The New-York Gazette, November 15, 1762; November 22, 1762.

Fifteen Pounds, Reward.

RUN-away from the subscriber, on Sunday evening the 31st of October, 3 apprentice lads, viz, James Anderson, aged 19 years, a tanner by trade, about 5 feet 7 inches high: Had on when he went away, a snuff colour'd coat, blue broad cloth breeches, striped jacket, a white shirt and two check ditto. Uzal Woodruff, aged 18 years, about 5 feet 6 inches high: Had on when he went away, a blue broad cloth coat, jacket, and breeches. Also, Epenetus Beech, about 5 feet 5 inches high: Had on when he went away, a blue broad cloth coat, a green jacket, a pair of thick-sett breeches; both [sic] cordwainers, or shoe-makers. Whoever will secure the said apprentices, so that their master may have them again, shall have the the above reward, or FIVE POUNDS, New-York currency, reward, for each,
paid by   MOSES OGDEN.

N. B. All persons are forbid harbouring or carrying of [sic] said apprentices at their peril.

The New-York Mercury, November 16, 1762; November 22, 1762; January 3, 1762.

RUN away from his Master the 24th Instant, a Servant Man, named Bartholomew Joy. Had on when he went away a blue stroud Jacket with a Leather Patch on the left shoulder, a woollen check shirt, a pair of bucskin [sic] breeches, a pair of green Indian stockings, and an old felt hat. He is of middling stature, somewhat pitted with the small-pox, and has very large hands and feet. Whoever apprehends the said servant, so that his Master may have him again, shall have Twenty shillings reward, and all reasonable charges paid by the subscriber, or by Mr. Martin, in Albany.
JAMES JONES.

Willoge, Albany County, Oct. 8, 1762.
The New-York Gazette, November 22, 1762; November 29, 1762.

RUN away from the Subscriber the 3d Inst. Nov. a likely Negro Fellow, named WITLOW, aged 28 or 29 Years, of a yellowish Complexion, about five Feet 10 inches high, lusty and well built, a Blacksmith by Trade, speaks tolerable good English, with a coarse Voice. Whoever takes up the said Negro, or secures him in any of his Majesty's Gaols, so that his Master may have him again, shall receive FIVE DOLLARS, and all reasonable
                     Charges paid by   ADAM DOBBS, PETER WESSELS,
                            or W. WEYMAN, Printer, in Broad-street.
N. B. All Masters of Vessels, and others, are forbid harbouring, concealing, or carrying off the said Negro, as they shall answer it at their Peril.
The New-York Gazette, November 22, 1762; November 29, 1762.

RUN-away, from the Subscriber, Master of the Hercules Transport, David Ross, an Apprentice, about 18 Years of Age, short Stature, fair Complexion, with dark brown Hair, was born at Edinburgh, but has quite left the Scotch Accent: he has taken something with him belonging to the Ship, and is thought to be concealed about this City. Whoever will secure the said David Ross, and bring him on board the said Ship lying at Degrushe's Wharf, shall receive Two Guineas Reward; and if any Person or Persons shall harbour or conceal the said Apprentice, they may depend on being prosecuted at the Law directs,
                    by   JOHN JUMP.
The New-York Gazette, November 29, 1762; December 6, 1762.

Staten-Island, 26th November, 1762.
RUN away the 22d Inst. Nov. from ANTHONY WATERS, a Negro Man named SIRO, about 5 Feet 2 Inches high, yellow Complexion, black curl'd Hair, and bow Legs: Had on when he went away, a green Jacket, with a white Swanskin one under it, Leather Breeches, Blue Stockings, and strings in his Shoes. Whoever takes up said Servant, and brings him to his Master, or secures him in any of his Majesty's Gaols, so that his Master may have him again, shall receive Forty Shillings Reward, and all reasonable Charges
                     paid by   Anthony Waters, jun. or Edward Waters.
The New-York Gazette, November 29, 1762; December 6, 1762; December 20, 1762.

ABSENTED every since the 29th of October last, a Negro named CAESAR, formerly belonging to Mr. Lattouch, now to William Smith, jun. about 5 Feet 10 Inches high, well set, aged 20 or 22 Years, can read and write; is supposed to be lurking about the City of New-York, and seeking an Opportunity to get off in some Vessel: Has for Dress a Leather Breeches, and green Jacket, or a Suit of blue Cloth. Whoever will secure and return him, shall have FIVE POUNDS Reward.
The New-York Gazette, November 29, 1762; December 6, 1762; December 13, 1762; December 20, 1762.

RAN away from the Subscriber, the 14th inst. a lusty well built Negro Fellow, named Pompey, aged 24 Years, his left Legg is a wooden one. Whoever takes up said Negro, or secures him in any of his Majesty's Gaols, so that his Master may have him again, shall receive FIVE DOLLARS, and all reasonable Charges
        paid by *J. Sebastian Stephany.*
        Chemist near the New Dutch Church.
N. B. All Masters of Vessels, and others, are forbid harbouring, concealing, or carrying off the said Negro, as they shall answer it at their Peril.
The New-York Gazette, November 29, 1762; December 6, 1762.

RUN away from Mr. ADRIAN VAN BRENTS, of Eutricht, a Wench about 14 Years old, between the Indian and Negro Breed; was bought last October from Mr. Jaques De Nise, of Eutricht; her name is Nanny. Whoever brings her to Mr. Van Brents, shall be well rewarded for their Trouble: Or if any one can give Information of any Person that harbours her, on Proof thereof, shall have Five Pounds Reward.
The New-York Gazette, December 13, 1762; December 20, 1762; January 3, 1763; January 10, 1763. See *The New-York Mercury*, December 20, 1762, *The New York Gazette*, January 17, 1763, and *The New-York Mercury*, January 17, 1763.

RUN away the 12th Instant December, from the House of Daniel Toton, a Man named Samuel Greenfields, and took with him a small black Mare, has been bit by a Horse on the Breast, and a Tit appears in the same Place. Said Greenfields owes said Toton Seven Pounds Ten Shillings. Had on when he went away, a light colour'd Great-Coat with a Velvet Cape, and a dark brown Body Coat. He is about 5 Foot 7 Inches high, has a large Head, and very talkative, and much given to Drink, aged 40 or 50 Years. Any Person that apprehends and secures him, so that Daniel Toton may have him again,

shall have Forty Shillings Reward, and all reasonable Charges paid by me Daniel Toton, at Philipsbourg, near the Upper-Mills.
The New-York Gazette, December 20, 1762; January 3, 1763; January 10, 1763.

RUN-away from Adrian Van Brents, of Eutricht, a Wench about 15 Years old, between the Indian and Negro Breed; Was bought last October from Mr. Jaques De Nise, of Eutricht; her name is Fanny. Had on, a striped Gingham Josey, and homespun Pettycoat. Whoever brings her to Mr. Van Brents, shall be well rewarded for their Trouble: Or if any one can give Information of any Person that harbours her, on Proof thereof, shall have Five Pounds Reward.
The New-York Mercury, December 20, 1762; December 27, 1762; January 3, 1763. See *The New-York Gazette*, December 13, 1762, *The New-York Gazette*, January 17, 1763, and *The New-York Mercury*, January 17, 1763.

FIVE POUNDS REWARD.

RUN away, on the 14th Instant, a Servant Man, named Emanuel Lightin, about 19 or 20 Years of age, 5 Feet 7 or 8 Inches high, fair Complexion, smooth fac'd, long Visage, and has long light brown Hair, plaited and tied up: Had on a blue thin Coat, a white double-breasted Flannel Jacket, with red Spots and Buttons, good Leather Breeches, Yarn Stockings, strong Shoes and half-worn Fur Hat, &c. He has stolen a middle-sized brown or Mouse-coloured Horse, about 12 Years old, in good Order, shod before, trimmed under the Bridle, a small Star and Snip, has a Lump on the off Side of his Belly near the Flank, paces and trots, and had on an old hunting Saddle, with Leather Housins, and snaffle Bridle: He has likewise stolen a light coloured Great-Coat a Snuff coloured close bodied Ditto, two or three fine Shirts, a half-worn Fur Hat, a large Pair of Silver Buckles, with some other Things, and probably will change his Cloaths. Whoever secures said Servant, so that his Master may have him again, shall have the above Reward of Five Pounds, and reasonable Charges, or Forty Shillings for the Horse &c. paid by JOHN ROBERTS, Miller.
N. B. It is supposed he will go towards New-York or Albany.
The New-York Mercury, December 20, 1762; December 27, 1762; January 3, 1763; January 10, 1763; January 24, 1763.

RUN-away, the 19th instant, at night, from the subscriber, living at Esopus, in Ulster County, a negro fellow named Prince, about 28 years old, about 6 feet high, and slender, has been used to the sea, and followed boating many

years; he is much of the Madagascar colour, and smooth skined: Had on when he went away a kersey great coat, leather breeches, and a white linnen shirt. Whoever takes up the said negro, and secures him, so that his master may have him again, shall receive ten dollars Reward, and all reasonable charges paid by MICHAEL DEVOE.
All Masters of Vessels are forbid to carry him off.
The New-York Mercury, December 27, 1762; January 3, 1763; January 10, 1763; January 24, 1763.

1763

MIssing since Christmas day, and supposed to be inveigled by some bad person, a Negro woman, about 40 years of age, very short, but well made, is marked much by scars in the face, neck, breast and arms, when she was a child; she was very well dress'd in a purple and white callicoe gown. Whoever give information where she is, so that she may be had again, shall have ten pounds reward, paid by Oliver De Lancey. She was seen on Christmas afternoon a little beyond the college, in her way home to Greenwich, and has not been heard of since.
The New-York Mercury, January 3, 1763.

DEserted from his Majesty's 35*th regiment of foot, the* 25*th of December, at New-York; John Smith, aged* 23 *years,* 5 *feet* 7 *inches high; dark brown hair, pale faced, wants the first joint of his left hand thumb: Had on when he deserted, a black coat, and plaid waistcoat. Any person who apprehends and confines him in any of his majesty's goals, so that he may be returned to his said regiment, shall have Twenty Shillings sterling, by applying to any justice of the peace,*
       or to Major Hamilton, at New-York.
The New-York Mercury, January 3, 1763.

THREE POUNDS REWARD,
RUn-away, from Albany, the 18th day of November 1762, from the subscriber, living in Pennington, West New-Jersey; an indented servant man, named John White, about 21 years of age, 5 feet 6 inches high; a shoemaker by trade, of a pale countenance, well set, wears his own hair, of a light colour, much given to card playing: Had on when he went away, a Jersey regimental coat, red waistcoat, buckskin breeches, yarn stockings, old shoes with steel buckels, and a narrow brim'd hat; he is supposed to have gone to some part of New-England, where he has some acquaintance. Whoever takes up said servant, and brings him to the subscriber, or secures him in any of his Majesty's goals, so as his master may have him again, shall receive the above reward, and all reasonable charges

paid, by   JIERARD SAXTON.
The New-York Mercury, January 3, 1763; January 10, 1763.

RUN away in November last, from the Subscriber, a Negro Woman, named VILET, of a yellow Complexion, with her Hair shaved back on her Forehead; squints with one Eye: It is thought she has dress'd herself in Man's Clothes, as she has taken with her a Pair of Boots and a blue Coat. Whoever takes up said Wench, so that her Master may have her again, shall have THREE POUNDS Reward, and all reasonable Charges
    paid by   ELBERT HERRING.
The New-York Gazette, January 10, 1763; January 17, 1763.

New-York, January 15, 1763.
RUN away from the House of Mr. *Adrian Van Brent*, of *New Utricht*, in *December* last, a Girl about 14 Years of Age; between the Negro and Indian Breed, bought of Mr. *Jaques Denise*, of *Utricht*, with whom her Mother and Sister now lives; known by the Name of Nanney, has not had the Small Pox, with remarkable white broad Teeth, talks little English, mostly Dutch. Had on when she went away, a striped Gingham Josie, and a Linsey-woolsey Petticoat. Whoever delivers her to Captain *David Pryce*, at *New-York*, shall have Three Pounds Reward, and all reasonable Charges paid them; Or any one that gives Information of any White Person that harbours her, on good Proof thereof, shall have Six Pounds,
    paid by,   DAVID PRYCE.
The New York Gazette, January 17, 1763. See *The New-York Gazette*, December 13, 1762, *The New-York Mercury*, December 20, 1762, and *The New-York Mercury*, January 17, 1763.

RUN-away, on Saturday Night, the 15th Inst. from her Mistress Margaret Long, and supposed to be gone with a Soldier, Catharine Carty, an indented Servant, aged about 18 years, of a brown Complexion, black Hair and Eye-Brows, a thick-set Girl, born in Ireland. Whoever secures said Girl, so that her Mistress may have her again, shall have Five Dollars Reward, and all reasonable Charges,
    paid by   Margaret Long, on Cruger's Wharf.
The New-York Mercury, January 17, 1763; January 24, 1763.

RUN away from Adrian Van Brent, of Eutricht, in December last, a Girl about 14 Years old, between the Indian and Negro Breed; was bought of

Mr. Jaques De Nise, of New Eutricht, with whom her Mother and Sister now lives; known by the Name of Nanney, has not had the Small-Pox, with remarkable white broad Teeth: Had on when she went away, a striped Gingham Josey, and Linsey-woolsey Pettycoat. Whoever delivers her to Captain David Pryce, at New-York, shall have Three Pounds Reward, and all reasonable Charges paid them: Or any one that gives Information of any White Person that harbours her, on Proof thereof, shall have Six Pounds paid by. DAVID PRYCE.

The New-York Mercury, January 17, 1763; February 7, 1763. See *The New-York Gazette*, December 13, 1762, *The New-York Mercury*, December 20, 1762, and *The New York Gazette*, January 17, 1763.

DESERTED,
From His Majesty's 44th Regiment, now lying at Montreal, the under-named Men, viz.

EDward Brown, aged 26 years, 5 feet 4 1-2 inches high, ruddy complexion, round visage, black eyes, red hair, his dress not known, born in the county of Cavan, in Ireland, a labourer, deserted the 14th of September, 1762. Matthew Collins, aged, 26 years, 5 feet 1-2 inches high, brown complexion, round visage, grey eyes, brown hair; had on, his regimentals, born in the country of Cork, in Ireland, a labourer, deserted the 14th of September, 1762. Thomas Williams, aged 23 years, 5 feet 5 1-2 inches high, fair complexion, long visage, grey eyes, brown hair; had on his regimentals, born in the county of Maidenhead, in East Jersey, a weaver, deserted the 14th of September, 1762. John Rice, aged 30 years, 5 feet 8 inches high, ruddy complexion, round visage, grey eyes, brown hair, his dress not known, born in Germany, a labourer, deserted the 25th of November, 1762: The above four deserters belonging to Lt. Col. Eyre's company.

Joshua Frost, alias Kettenger, aged 25 years, 5 feet 10 3-4ths high, swarthy complexion, long visage, grey eyes, dark hair, had on, his regimentals, born in Boston, in New-England, a sailor, deserted the 11th of October, 1762. Joseph Ralston, aged 28 years, 5 feet 2 inches high, fair complexion, long visage, brown eyes, brown hair; had on a blanket coat, born at Newcastle, in Pennsylvania, a labourer, deserted thee 11th of October 1762. Thomas Farrel, aged 23 years, 5 feet 10 inches high, fair complexion, long visage, grey eyes, fair hair; had on a blanket coat, born in Georgetown, Maryland, a labourer, deserted the 11th of October, 1762: The above three belonged to Capt. Dunbar's company.

William Vickers, of Capt. Ault's company, aged 31 years, 4 feet 10 inches high, ruddy complexion, round visage, grey eyes, light brown hair; had on, his regimentals, born at Talbot, in Maryland, a labourer, deserted the 11th of October, 1762.

Joseph Thomas, of Capt. Treby's company, aged 27 years, 5 feet 6 1-2 inches high, fair complexion, long visage, grey eyes, light brown hair; had on, his regimentals, born in Philadelphia, a hatter, deserted the 9th of November, 1762. Whoever take up any of the above-mentioned deserters, and secures them in any goal, or brings them to Lt. Col. Eyre, in New-York, shall have twenty shillings sterling reward.
The New-York Mercury, January 31, 1763; February 7, 1763.

RUN away on Friday the 4th inst. February, from David Kelly, a Servant Girl, named Rose Flanagin, about 28 Years of Age, born near Newry, in Ireland, talks that Dialect broad. She is stout and lusty, mark'd a little with the Small-pox, and black hair'd. Had on when she went away, a Callico Gown, a homespun Petticoat, with a coarse black one under it. Whoever takes up, and secures said Girl, so that her Master may have her again, shall have Five Dollars Reward, and all reasonable Charges paid by me, David Kelly, living on Cowfoot-Hill.—N. B. All Masters of Vessels, and others, are forbid harbouring or carrying her off, as they shall answer it at their Peril.
The New-York Gazette, February 7, 1763.

RAN away Yesterday Morning, from Francis Panton, of this City, Peruke-maker, living in Broad-street,—A Servant Man, named John Boyer, about 18 Years old, brought up to the Peruke-Business; he is of middle Stature, a very swarthy Complexion, has a Scar close under one of his Cheeks, He took with him several Suits of Clothes, and undoubtedly will change his Dress. It is thought he waits an Opportunity to go to Sea: Masters of Vessels are therefore strictly forbid to carry him off. Whoever takes up the said Servant, and secures him so that he may be had again, shall have THREE POUNDS Reward, and reasonable Charges
        paid by   F. Panton.
The New-York Gazette, February 7, 1763; February 14, 1763.

Twelve Dollars Reward.
RAN away from *Epenetus Smith* of Smith-Town Long-Island, a Mustee Slave named Cesar, thin Visage, tall and slim, Indian hair, discovers guilt in his Look, has lost all his Toes on one Foot; I think the right. Whoever takes up said Slave and brings him to his said Master or *Benjamin Giles* of Groton, Connecticut, shall have the aforesaid Reward and all necessary Charges.
The New-London Summary, or, The Weekly Advertiser, February 18, 1763.

RUN away from Joseph Forman, of New-York, the 21st of December last, a Negro Man named JOE, about 5 Feet 7 Inches high, aged 24 Years, of a yellow Complexion, much Pock-mark'd, has something of a down Look, Country born, speaks good English and Dutch. Had on when he went away, a brown Coat with red Lining, a red double-breasted Jacket, a Pair of Thickset Breeches, Yarn Stockings, Felt Hat, is a pretty good Sailor. Whoever takes up said Negro, so that his Master may have him again, shall have FOUR POUNDS Reward, and all reasonable Charges paid.

The New-York Gazette, February 14, 1763; February 21, 1763; March 14, 1763. See *The New-York Mercury*, October 18, 1762, and *The Pennsylvania Gazette*, July 21, 1763.

Middletown-Point, Jan. 31, 1763.
RUN-away from the subscriber, a Negro man named Joe, about 6 feet high, long visaged, speaks good English, and is this country born: Had on when he went away, a felt hat, a worsted cap, an oznabrig shirt a blue duffle great Coat, a brown kersey vest, lined with strip'd homespun, a green vest without sleeves, a pair of sheepskin breeches, a pair of blue rib stockings, and an old pair of pumps. It is supposed he will endeavor to get on board some vessel. Whoever takes up the said Negro, and secures him, so that his master may have him again, shall have five dollars reward, and all reasonable charges,
         paid by me   WILLIAM HENDRICKS.
The New-York Mercury, February 14, 1763; February 21, 1763; February 28, 1763.

BROKE out of Dutchess County Gaol, DAVID SMITH, about 5 Feet 6 Inches, and 27 Years of Age, thin visag'd, slender built, brown Hair, was committed for stealing; he, some Time ago, lived at Goshen. Whoever shall apprehend the said Prisoner, and deliver him to me at Poughkeepsie, shall be rewarded for his Trouble.
        JAMES G. LIVINGSTON, Sheriff.
The New-York Gazette, February 21, 1763; March 14, 1763; March 28, 1763.

RUN away, a Dutch Servant Man about 25 Years of Age, a Joiner by Trade, named Frederick Myers. Had on when he went away, a brown Watch-Coat, Leather Breeches, and blue Jacket; it is suppos'd he is gone towards Philadelphia. He run away last August, was taken up and put into Philadelphia Gaol. Whoever takes up said Servant, and secures him in any County Gaol, so that his said Masters can have him again, shall have a Reward of Five Pounds,
        paid by   *William Brown*,   and *Nicholas Bayard*.

The New-York Gazette, February 21, 1763.

New York, March 1, 1763.
Twenty Dollars Reward.
RUN away on Monday, the 21st of February last, from Jacob Arden, of this City Butcher, an Apprentice Lad, named Peter Wilt, about 18 Years of Age; had on, when he went away, a red duffle Watchcoat, a light coloured jacket, a brown Jacket, and a striped homespun One under them; also, either a light coloured Pair of cloth or buckskin Breeches; had likewise on a Check Shirt, a Pair of blue knit Stockings, with a Pair of new Shoes, and a half worn Castor Hat. Whoever takes up and secures said Apprentice, so that his Master may have him again, shall be intitled to the above Reward,
    paid by me JACOB ARDEN.
 N. B. All Masters of Vessels and others, are forbid carrying him off, as they shall surely answer it at their Peril.
The Pennsylvania Gazette, March 10, 1763.

WHEREAS, the house of Josiah Disborow, tavern-keeper, at Marrowneck, was broken open on Saturday Night, the 26th inst. and the following things were stolen, viz. A coat and jacket, almost new, of a reddish snuff colour; one blue taffaty gown; a dark cotton chintz negligee; a black bombazeen gown, one homespun gown, worked in sprigs with a needle; one velvet cloak; one black peeling cardinal, with gimp round it; one short red broad cloth cloak; one peeling hat scolop'd, with double gimp round it; one red callimancoe pettycoat; one white linen quilted ditto; some shirts, shoes, buckles, linen, and sundry other articles. The person who is suspected to have stolen the above goods, is a likely young Irishman, of about 25 or 30 years of age, middling size, is an agreeable, merry fellow, was lately advertised for robbing one Mrs. Hodge, in Smith street, in New-York, and was taken up by Benjamin Brown, of Rye; from whom he made his escape. All persons are hereby desired to stop the above goods if offered for sale, for which an adequate reward will be allowed, as follows, viz. If the thief is taken, and safety confined in any of his Majesty's goals, with the goods stolen, so that he may be brought to justice, the sum of six pounds, and all reasonable charges; and for the goods along, if the whole, the sum of three pounds; and less in proportion, and all necessary charges,
    paid by me, JOSIAH DISBOROW.
The New-York Mercury, April 4, 1763; *The New-York Gazette*, April 11, 1763; April 18, 1763. Minor differences between the papers. The *Gazette* calls the woman Mrs. Hodges.

STOLEN out of the House of James Wetmore, at Rye, on the 16th of this Month, in the Night, by Mary Barrington, an Irish Woman, three Silver Watches, and sundry other small Articles: one of the Watches is of French made, and winds up on the Dial-Plate; the second is an old fashion'd frosted Dial-Plate; the other is a common China Dial Plate. This Woman is about 5 Feet 6 Inches high, about 33 Years old, broad face, has a leering Look, is very soft spoken, redish Hair, her fore Finger on her Left Hand is crooked, commonly wears a purple Callicoe Gown, short light coloured Allopeen Josey; and says she is married in Boston. Whoever apprehends the above Woman, and secures her, or the said Watches, shall be entitled to receive five Dollars Reward, or delivering her to Goal,
or the above Goods to said Wetmore,
N. B. All reasonable Charges will be paid in the Bargain.
The New-York Mercury, April 4, 1763.

RUN away on the 4th Instant, from Garrat Cosine, of Bloomingdale, a Molato Man Slave, named Jack, of a dark Complexion, and long Visage, with a surly Countenance; has long black curl'd Hair, and pitted with the Small-pox. Had on when he went away, a half-worn Beaver Hat, pale red Watchcoat, a blue Camblet Jacket and Breeches, and pale blue Worsted Stockings; he plays on the Fiddle, and has often been strolling in and about this City. Whoever takes up the said Slave, and delivers him to his Master, or secures him in the Work-House, so that his Master may have him again, shall have *Forty-Shillings* Reward, and all reasonable Charges
         paid by me,   GARRAT COSINE.
All Masters of Vessels, and others, are forbid concealing or carrying him off, as they shall answer it at their Peril.
The New-York Gazette, April 18, 1763; April 25, 1763; May 2, 1763.

RUN away from John Green, of North-Castle, on Sunday the 24th of April, a Negro Man named JIM, about 30 Years of Age, speaks Dutch and English plain: Is about 5 Feet 3 Inches high: Had on when he went away a brown homespun Coat, and white Swanskin Jacket, a Pair of Buckskin Breeches, and blue Stockings: Has a remarkable Scar on his Nose. Whoever takes up said Negro, and secures him, so that his Master may have him again, shall have Forty Shillings Reward, and all reasonable Charges
         paid by   JOHN GREEN.
N. B. All Masters of Vessels, and others, are forbid carrying him off, as they shall answer it at their Peril.
The New-York Gazette, May 2, 1763; May 9, 1763; May 16, 1763.

RUN away from Edward Agar, in Broad-street, on Sunday the 24th of April 1763, a Negro Fellow named George, lately came from the Havannah, then belonging to Lieutenant Pierce, of the Royal Artillery: Was born in Antigua, in the West-Indies: He is about 5 Feet 10 Inches high, rather of swarthy black Colour, and pretty thin; talks quick, tho' plain to be understood. Had on when he went away a blue Coat; was seen on Monday, by several People, at the Horse Race at Jamaica, on Long-Island, and is not suppos'd to be sculking somewhere about the Country. Whoever secures him, so that his Master may have him again, shall receive Forty Shillings Reward for their Trouble, and all reasonable Charges
    paid by me, EDWARD AGAR.
 The New-York Gazette, May 2, 1763; May 9, 1763. See *The New-York Mercury,* May 16, 1763.

RUN-away from the Subscriber the 18th of April a Negro Wench, named Amelia, middle sized, about 22 Years of Age, West-India born, and talks a little like the Creoles: Had on when she went away, two homespun Pettycoats, a homespun Josey, and has a Handkerchief about her Head. Whoever apprehends the said Wench, and brings her to the Subscriber, shall have 20 Shillings Reward, and reasonable Charges,
    paid by me PHILIP KISSICK.
 N. B. All Persons are hereby forbid harbouring the said Wench, and all Masters of Vessels from carrying her off at their Peril, as she has a Fancy to go to the West-Indies.
 The New-York Mercury, May 2, 1763; May 9, 1763. See *The New-York Mercury*, December 5, 1763.

     TWENTY FIVE POUNDS Reward.
ON Monday, the 2d of May instant, between the Hours of 12 and 1 o'Clock at Night, was assaulted in New-York, and robbed of a considerable Sum of Money, to the Amount of Four Hundred and Sixty Pounds, New-York Currency (the greatest Part of said Money was in Jersey Bills) also a Silver Watch, with a Brass Chain, the Key hanging a little lower than the Seal. The Persons who are suspected to have committed said Robbery are, Lawrence Poor, William Farril, and John Donwith, all three Taylors. Said Poor is about five Feet ten Inches high, of a brown Complexion, sandy coloured Hair, with a long Nose, and a Rocking in his Walk, about 35 Years of Age, wearing a blue Coat, Vest and Breeches, when he left New-York, but may have changed them. Farril is a short well built Person, wears a Crimson Coat, blue Vest, and light grey Breeches, about 31 Years of Age. Donwith is a short well-built Person, wears a dark grey Coat, about 25 Years of Age.—They were seen in Philadelphia (by Information) the 6th or 7th Instant. Whoever takes up said Persons, especially Lawrence Poor, and

commits him to any of his Majesty's Goals, so that he or they may be brought to Justice, giving Notice to the Subscriber, living in Elizabeth-Town, East Jersey, shall have Twenty-five Pounds Reward, if taken with the Money, or Ten Pounds if otherwise.
Given under my Hand, this Ninth Day of May, 1763.
      JAMES CARTER.
N. B. All Masters of Vessels are forbid to carry them off.
The Pennsylvania Gazette, May 12, 1763.

RUN *away from JOSEPH MOTT, living in Poughkeepsie, Dutchess County, in the Province of New-York, a Negro Fellow named Cuff, about 5 Feet 10 Inches high, can talk High and Low Dutch very well, also English. Had on when he went away a litish colour'd Jacket, and a double-breasted blue Broadcloth Jacket, and a Pair of black Everlasting Breeches, grey Yarn Stockings, Indian made Shoes, a chequer'd woolen Shirt, and Beaver Hat about half worn: The said Negro is about 35 or 36 Years of Age. Whoever takes up said Negro, and confines him, or conveys him to his Master, or to* John Cannon, *Shipwright in New-York, shall have* Forty Shillings *Reward, and all reasonable Charges*
    paid by   JOSEPH MOTT, *or said* CANNON.
The New-York Gazette, May 16, 1763; May 30, 1763.

WHEREAS *Joseph Concklin,* hath escaped out of my Custody, on Process for Debt; he is supposed to be somewhere about the Drowned Land. Whoever shall take the said Joseph, and deliver him to the Gaoler at Poughkeepsie, in Dutchess County, shall receive Three Pounds Reward, or in any Part of Dutchess County, to me, or Bernard Filkin, Isaac Burton, Azeriah Newcomb, or Henry Ludenton, my Under Sheriffs, or either of them, shall receive Forty Shillings Reward, and all Charges
    paid by   James G. Livingston, Sheriff.
The New-York Gazette, May 16, 1763.

RUN-*away from Edward Agar, in Broad-street, on Sunday the* 8*th of May inst. a Negro fellow, named George, about 5 feet 10 inches high, of a swarthy black colour, and very thin, talks very quick, tho' plain: Had on when he went away, a brown striped homespun jacket, and leather breeches. Whoever secures him, so that his master may have him again, shall be handsomely rewarded for their Trouble, and all reasonable charges paid. All Persons are hereby forbid to harbour him, and all masters of vessels to carry him off, as they shall be prosecuted for so doing to the utmost rigour of the law.*

The New-York Mercury, May 16, 1763; May 23, 1763. See *The New-York Gazette,* May 2, 1763.

New-York, May 8, 1763.
DEserted, from his Majesty's 17th Regiment of Foot, commanded by the Hon. Major General Robert Monckton, and from Col. John Darby's Company, Serjeant Alvery Hodgson, born at Woolverhampton, Staffordshire, England; by Trade a Wig maker, about five Feet ten Inches high, light brown Hair, gray Eyes, thin, well made; had on a blue Surtout Coat, a Pair of stript Linnen Trowsers, supposed to be gone to Boston. Whoever apprehends the above Deserter, and secures him in any of his Majesty's Goals, and gives Notice to the Regiment thereof, shall have five Guineas Reward, over and above his Majesty's Bounty, paid by the commanding Officer of the 17th Regiment,
 or Mr. Hugh Wallace, Merchant, in New-York.
The New-York Mercury, May 16, 1763; May 23, 1763.

RUN-away, the first Day of May, from James Thompson, a Negro Man named Cato; he is likely and well made, has a Sore on one of his Legs; had on when he went away, a white Shirt, a brown Rateen Coat, a black Cloth Waistcoat, with brown buttons, and Buckskin Breeches, an old Pair of gray Yarn rib'd Stockings, a Pair of Shoes, with odd Brass Buckels, a Beaver Hat. Whoever takes up and secures said Negro, so that his Master may have him again, shall have twenty Shillings Reward, if in Town, and if out of Town, forty Shillings, and all reasonable Charges paid; all Captains of Vessels and others, are forwarned to harbour or carry off said Negro at their Peril.
The New-York Mercury, May 16, 1763.

RUN away on the 14th of May last, from GEORGE BURNS, of this City, a Negro Man named *Sam,* formerly belonging to Capt. De Lancey; and noted as a Cook. It is thought he will changed his Clothes; but had on when he went off, a grey short Coat, dark Wig, &. Whoever takes up said Negro, and secures him, so that his Master may have him again, shall have Twenty Shillings, if taken in Town, and Forty Shillings, if taken out of it; and reasonable Charges
 paid by GEORGE BURNS.
The New-York Gazette, June 6, 1763.

RUN away from his Bail, on Saturday the 4th June, Instant, a Man named JOHN CROSS, by Trade a Cabinet maker: He is about 5 Feet 8 Inches high, of a pale Complexion, has black Hair, a long Nose, much given to

Liquor, and is very quarrelsome. Whoever takes up and secures said Fellow in New-York Gaol, shall have TEN POUNDS Reward, and all reasonable Charges paid by THOMAS BROOKMAN.
N. B. All Master of Vessels are forbid to take him away.
The New-York Gazette, June 13, 1763; June 20, 1763; *The New-York Mercury*, June 20, 1763. Minor differences between the papers.

RUN-away, a Negro Wench named Priscilla, about 16 Years old, late the Property of Samuel Hodge. Any Person that take up said Wench, and brings her to the Subscribers, shall have Twenty Shillings Reward, and all reasonable Charges paid, by her present Owners.
RENSSELAER and SHIPBOY.
The New-York Gazette, June 20, 1763; June 27, 1763.

RUN-away, on Friday the 17th Inst. from their Master, Mr. Theodore Godet, two Negro Men, one called John, the other Champaign; the former a black well-set Fellow, supposed to be about 30 Years old; is a good Cook; left handed; plays tolerably well on the Violin; and was dressed in Sailors Clothes. The other a tall likely black Fellow, about 21 or 22 Years of Age; understands shaving and dressing of Hair: Had on when he went away, a black waistcoat, without Sleeves; a Pair of knit Breeches, and a Straw Hat. Whoever takes up and secures said Negroes, so that their Master may have them again, shall have Forty Shillings Reward for either of them, and all reasonable Charges,
paid by THOMAS DURHAM.
N. B. All Masters of Vessels and others, are forbid carrying said Negroes off, or employing them.
The New-York Mercury, June 20, 1763; June 27, 1763.

FIVE GUINEAS Reward.
RUN away at the Havannah, from the Snow Hibernia, John Troy, Master, a Negroe Man, who called himself Jack Jones, was formerly a Slave to Colonel Jones, of the Vineyard, near Philadelphia, who sold him to Mr. Byrns, at the King's Arms Tavern, in New York, from whom said Troy bought him. Said Negroe Man is about 45 Years of Age, stout built, of a tawney Colour, is fond of Liquor, and talks a little French: it is supposed he will endeavour to pass for a Free Negroe. Whoever takes up said Negroe, and delivers him to Mr. Hugh Wallace, Merchant in New York, or to Mr. John Flanagan, in Philadelphia, or the Keeper of any Prisons, so that they

may have him again, shall receive from either of them the above Reward, and reasonable Charges.
The Pennsylvania Gazette, June 23, 1763.

RUN away on Saturday the 18th of June Inst. from PHILIP HESS, of this City, an Apprentice Lad, named John Coomes, about 17 Years old, a tall slender Person, thin Visage, and has short black Hair: Had on when he went away, a short Double-breasted Flannel Jacket without Sleeves, a long striped Pair of Trowsers, Check Shirt, a Pair of old Shoes, and a large thick Pair of Pewter Buckles: Whoever takes up and secures the said Apprentice, so that his Master may have him again, shall have Forty Shillings Reward, and reasonable Charges
           paid by   PHILIP HESS.
The New-York Gazette, June 27, 1763; July 4, 1763.

RUN-AWAY,
From on board the Snow CHARMING NANCY, Francis Haines, Master; a Molatto Negro, about 18 Years of Age, his Hair curls much, speaks good English. Had on when he went away, a striped Waist-Coat. Whoever takes up said Negro, and will bring him to Lawrence Kortright, shall have Forty Shillings, and all reasonable Charges, paid.
N. B. All Masters of Vessels are forwarned not to carry said Negro off.
The New-York Mercury, June 27, 1763; July 4, 1763.

RUN away on Monday Night the 27th of June last, from KILLEYAEN MULLER, of Clavarack, in the County of Albany, a likely tall Negro Fellow, named JIM, about 19 Years old, speaks good English and Dutch. Had on when he went away, a Woolen Shirt, striped Woolen Jacket, red Duffles Great Coat, Linen Drawers, and blue mill'd Stockings; he had also with him another Woolen Shirt, and a Pair of Leather Breeches. Whoever takes up said Negro Fellow, and secures him, so that his Master may have him again, shall have *Five Dollars* Reward, and reasonable Charges
           paid by me   KILLEYAEN MULLER.
N. B. It is suppos'd he is gone towards New-York, in order to go off in some Vessel; therefore all Master of Vessels, and others, are forewarn'd from carrying him off, as they shall answer it at their Peril.
The New-York Mercury, July 4, 1763; July 11, 1763; July 25, 1763.
See *The Providence Gazette; And Country Journal*, July 30, 1763, *The Massachusetts Gazette, and Boston News-Letter*, September 15, 1763, and *The New-London Gazette*, December 9, 1763.

RUN-away, last Thursday Morning from the Snow Lamb, Captain Moore, an indented Servant Man named John Maddin, aged about 22Years, 5 Feet 9 Inches high, long streight light colour'd Hair, much freckled, and pretends to be a School-Master: Had on when he went away, an old blue Coat, with a black Cape, blue Jacket, and a Pair of old black Leather breeches. Whoever takes up and secures said Servant, so that his Master may have him again, shall receive Forty Shillings Reward,
By WILLIAM MOORE.
The New-York Mercury, July 4, 1763; July 11, 1763.

RUN-away, on Monday the 27th of June, a Negro Man called Jacob, belonging to George Wray, of Albany, about 23 Years old, 5 Feet 6 Inches high, without Shoes, has a Scar on the right Side of his Forehead, another on his left Temple, both just at the Edge of his Hair, two large Pock Marks on the upper Part of his left Cheek, high Cheek Bones, had a Hair Mole under his Chin, but has lately cut the Hair off it; the Calves of his Legs remarkably high, stoops forward in walking, speaks English very well, some French, and a little Spanish, of an insinuating Address, very apt to feign plausible Stories, has a stammering in his Speech, when in Liquor, and may call himself free. Whoever takes up the said Negro, and secures him, so that he may be had again, shall have TWO DOLLARS Reward, and all reasonable Charges paid,
by George Wray, at Albany, or the Printer hereof.
The New-York Mercury, July 4, 1763; July 11, 1763. See *The New-York Mercury*, February 27, 1764, *The Boston Gazette, and Country Journal*, March 5, 1764; and *The Boston Gazette, and Country Journal*, July 23, 1764.

DESERTED from His Majesty's 55th Regiment of Foot, commanded by Colonel GANSEL, and Capt. Daly's Company of Grenadiers, quarters at Crown-Point, 22d May, 1763,
JOSEPH BLACKHAM, aged 26 Years, 5 Feet 9½ Inches high, born in the Town of Berwick upon Tweed, and was brought up to the Sea; dark Complexion, dark brown Hair, round visag'd; can speak good French, Italian, Spanish, and German. Also.
DANIEL ALLY, aged 25 Years, 5 Feet 10 Inches high, born at Dover, in the County of Kent, South-Britain, by Trade a Labourer; brown Complexion, round visag'd, well built, speaks slow; and went off in his Regimentals.
Deserted likewise from the above Regiment, and Capt. Hargreave's Company, quartered at Albany,

Corporal WILLIAM PELL, aged about 30 Years, 5 Feet½ Inches high, born at Sheffield, in Yorkshire, by Trade a Cutler, dark brown Hair, blue Eyes, swarthy Complexion, a little in-knee'd, and went off in his Regimentals.

Whoever secures the above Deserters in any of His Majesty's Gaols, and gives Notice to Capt. Winepress, of the 55th Regiment, commanding at Albany, or to William Bayard, Esq; at New-York, shall receive FIVE DOLLARS Reward for each of them, over and above what is allowed by Act of Parliament for apprehending of Deserters.

The New-York Gazette, July 11, 1763; July 18, 1763.

RUN-away, from the Subscriber, last Tuesday Morning, Master of the Ship Brotherly Love, an Apprentice Lad named Joseph Cox, about 14 Years old, thin visaged: Had on when he went away, a Check Shirt, and Canvas Trowsers. Whoever takes up and secures the said Lad, so that his Master may have him again, shall have Twenty Shillings Reward,
    paid by Elisha Bell.
The New-York Mercury, July 11, 1763.

The commanding Officer of his Majesty's 17th Regiment, has obtained Pardon from his Excellency, the Commander in Chief, for Serjeant Hudson, who some time ago deserted; he is therefore desired to join his Corps as soon as possible.
    JOHN CAMPBELL, Lieut. Col.
    New-York, June 13th, 1763.
The Boston Gazette, and Country Journal, July 13, 1763.

RUN away from Thomas Tredwell, of the City of New York, an Irish Servant Girl, about 22 Years of Age, named Elizabeth Lee, a short well-set Girl, fair Complexion, light Eyes, and light colour'd curl'd Hair: Had on when she went away, a short strip'd Gown and Pettycoat, blue Stockings, and Men's Shoes. Whoever takes up said Girl, and brings her to her said Master, shall have two Dollars Reward, and all reasonable Charges,
    paid by said Tredwell.
The New-York Mercury, July 18, 1763; July 25, 1763.

RUN away from Stephen Forman, of the City of New York, a Negroe Man, named Joe, about 5 Feet 7 Inches high, a good deal Pock marked, has a plain Scar under one of his Eyes, speaks very proper English, and, if he pleases, can speak Dutch; he is about 25 Years of Age. Whoever takes up

and secures said Negroe, so that his Master may have him again, shall have Five Pounds Reward, and all reasonable Charges,
    paid by me STEPHEN FORMAN.
The Pennsylvania Gazette, July 21, 1763. See *The New-York Mercury*, October 18, 1762. See *The New-York Gazette*, February 14, 1763.

RUN away from his Bail, on Thursday the 14th Instant, a Man called William Bowen, a Taylor by Trade, and is supposed to be gone to some part of Connecticut: He is about 5 Feet 9 Inches high, 28 Years old, and can speak Dutch, French, and Irish. Whoever will bring him to the Subscriber, shall have three Dollars Reward.
    WILLIAM THORNE.
The New-York Mercury, July 18, 1763; August 1, 1763.

RUN away from the Subscriber on Thursday Night last the 21st Instant, three new Negroes, two Men and one Woman; talks a little English, is scarrified on her Face, and had on when she went away an Oznabrigs Josey and Petticoat with Beads round her Arms and Neck, but it's suppos'd she may alter her Dress, as she took away with her several Things mark'd E T H and others belonging to a Negro Wench in the House; the Men had Oznabrigs Frocks and Trowsers, one of them a brown Cloth Waistcot without Sleeves. As they must be unacquainted with the Country, it's suppos'd they can't be gone far. Whoever discovers and secures said Negroes, so that the Owner may have have them again, shall receive Ten Shillings Reward for each if taken in the City, or Twenty Shillings each, if taken out of Town, and all reasonable Charges, by applying to the Printer, or the Subscriber, in Stone-Street,
  PETER HILL.   New-York, July 23, 1763.
The New-York Gazette, July 25, 1763; August 1, 1763; August 22, 1763. See *The New-York Gazette*, August 1, 1763.

July 9, 1763.
TAKEN *up by Stephen Sly, Esq; of Smithfield, and now in the Possession of the Subscriber, a Negro Man, supposed to be a Run-away; And as he says, his Name is James, and is a Slave belonging to one Muller, in the Town of Claaverack, within 35 Miles of Albany, in New-York Government.—Any Person claiming said Negro, after proving their Property, and paying the Cost of securing, advertising, &c. may have him of*
    DANIEL MOWRY, jun. *of Smithfield.*

The Providence Gazette; And Country Journal, July 30, 1763. See *The New-York Mercury*, July 4, 1763, *The Massachusetts Gazette, and Boston News-Letter*, September 15, 1763, and *The New-London Gazette*, December 9, 1763.

RUN-away from their Master, last Thursday Night, the 21st ult. three New Negroes, viz. Two Men and a Woman; they cannot speak English: They are each about 25 Years old, and has several of their Country Marks in their Foreheads: The two Men had on an Ozenbrigs Shirt and Trowsers, and the Woman had on an Ozenbrigs Pettycoat, and Josey. Whoever will take up and bring the said Negroes to Thomas Hill, if taken in Town, shall have ten Shillings Reward for each, and all reasonable Charges paid; and if taken out of Town, twenty Shillings for each.

The New-York Gazette, August 1, 1763. See *The New-York Gazette*, July 25, 1763, and *The New York Mercury*, September 5, 1763.

RUN away, on Thursday last, from EDWARD AGAR, at Newfoundland, commonly called the Glass-House, A (French) Negro Boy about 16 Years of Age, speaks very little English, very black Colour: Had on when he went off, a brown strip'd home-spun Jacket, and a Pair of long white Trowsers. Whoever secures him, so that his Master may have him again, shall be handsomely rewarded for their Trouble, and all reasonable Charges paid.

The New-York Gazette, August 8, 1763.

STOLEN on Saturday the 6th Instant, from SUSANNAH HILSON, of this City,—One Silver Watch, having *William Kerson* engraved on the upper Part of the Plate; she had fixe to her a very rusty Steel Chain, having a French Silver Seal to it. Also One Gold Spanish Ring, having a Heart and Hand Cypher on the Top.—The Man that committed to Robbery, is one Philip Jacobs, an High-Dutchman, formerly belonging to the 40th Regiment. 'Tis thought he is in Town still.—He is of a very fair Complexion, with very fair long Hair, is about 5 Feet 7 Inches high, very well made, and talks good English. He generally wears a red Fly Coat, or a white Frock; a red, a white or a striped Jacket; Has also a Pair of white Petticoat Trowsers, a long Check ditto, and a Pair of Scarlet Breeches, with white Drawers. Whoever takes up and secures the said Thief, so that he may be brought to Justice, shall have a Reward of Five Dollars,
   paid by me SUSANNAH HILSON, at Mr. Jones's,
    at the Sign of the Ship, near the Fresh Water Pump.
The New-York Gazette, August 15, 1763; August 22, 1763.

RUN away on Saturday last, the 13th August, from the Subscriber, a well-set Negro Fellow, named Pompey, about 20 Years of Age, has well made Legs, Scars on his Shins, a thick flat Foot, thick Neck, little Eyes, no Beard, short Fingers, and a Cast in his Hand which is also thick: He is about five Feet 8 Inches high, was bought out of Capt. Richards, and his Name on board was Apollo. Had on a fine Check Shirt, having a white Patch on the Back of it; a Linsey Woolsey double-breasted Jacket without Buttons on the Sleeves; a red Cap, long striped Trowsers that has a Patch on one Thigh, and a Check one on the other; has no Shoes or Stockings, but a coarse bit of Linen for a Neckcloth: He has a Hole in each Ear, and a Resemblance of the Small-pox. All Masters of Vessels and others, are strictly forbid carrying him off, to harbour or conceal him, as they must assuredly answer it in Law. Whoever secures him in any of his Majesty's Gaols, so that he may be had again, shall have FIVE POUNDS Reward, with reasonable Charges,
    paid by, ARTHUR M'NEIL.
The New-York Gazette, August 15, 1763.

RUN away from the Subscriber, living in the Bowry Lane, in New-York, a Negro Man, named *Cuff*, aged about 20 Years, this Country born has woolly Head of Hair, pretty low on his Forehead, has Marks of the Small-Pox on his Face. Had on when he went away, an old brown Jacket, an Oznabrigs Shirt and Trowsers, bare-headed and legged. Whoever takes up and secures said Negro, and brings him to his Master, shall have *Five Dollars* Reward, and reasonable Charges
    paid by ELBERT HERRING.
The New-York Gazette, August 22, 1763; August 29, 1763; September 5, 1763; September 19, 1763; September 26, 1763. See *The New York Gazette*, October 3, 1763.

RUN away Yesterday Morning, very early, from JUDAH HAYS of New-York, a Negro Man, named Aron, lately the property of Capt. William Murray; he is about 5 Feet 4 Inches high, well set Fellow about 25 or 26 Years old: Had on when he went away, a Thickset Coat with scarlet Cuffs and Cape, and scarlet Button-holes, and Brass Buttons, and Waistcoat and Breeches of the same, also with scarlet Button-holes and Brass Buttons, blue Yarn Hose, a Pair of old Pumps, and Brass Buckles; he has taken with him two Pair Oznabrigs Breeches, and one Waistcoat with Whitemetal Buttons, one white Linen, and two Ozenbrigs, and one Check Shirts. Whoever takes up, and secures the said Negro, so that his Master may have him, shall have a Reward of Twenty Shillings, if taken in this City, and Forty Shillings if taken out of it, and reasonable Charges,
    paid by JUDAH HAYS.

New-York, August 22d, 1763.
The New-York Gazette, August 22, 1763; August 29, 1763; September 5, 1763. See *The New-York Gazette,* October 24, 1763.

Last Monday Ran away from John Van Cortlandt's Sugar House,—A Negro, Fellow, Named Boatswain, About thirty-five years of age, five foot Nine Inches high; had on when he went away, an Oznabrigs Shirt, and Tow Cloth Trowsers, Shoes, and Stockings, and a felt hat. As he has formerly been to Sea, therefore all persons are Desired Not to Carry him off; A Reasonable Reward will be paid to the Person that will apprehend him, and bring him to his Master.
The New-York Gazette, August 22, 1763; August 29, 1763.

RUN away on Monday the 15th Instant, from on board the Brig Sally, WILLIAM BEATHELL, Master, a strong well-set Negro fellow, about 6 feet high, known well in this Town by the name of GOLIA; remarkable for having a very large Mouth, and the Loss of his Left Eye: He formerly belong'd to Mr. Cornelius Tebout, in the Bowery Lane; has taken in Capt. James Oman last Cruize, and condemn'd at Fort Dauphin as a Slave, and there sold at Vendue as such, bought by a Dutchman of St. Eustatia, and afterwards there sold to one Capt. Leacraft, who transfer'd his Property to the Owners of the Brig Sally. Any Person delivering the said Negro to me, or to the Keeper of the Work-House in this City, will be well rewarded. All Persons are hereby forewarned to harbour, conceal, entertain, or give any Encouragement to him, as they must expect to answer it to the Severity of the Law of this Province that is made and provided for in such Cases.
    WILLIAM BEATHELL, for the Owners.
The New-York Gazette, August 22, 1763; August 29, 1763; September 5, 1763.

RUN-away from the Subscriber, the 20th Instant, a Negro Fellow named York, about 19 Years old, 5 Feet three Inches high, and stutters when he speaks: Had on when he went away, a green short Jacket without Sleeves, and a Pair of Trowsers; and is a very active Fellow. Whoever brings the said Fellow to his Master, shall have FIVE DOLLARS Reward and all reasonable Charges,
          paid by me,   SAMUEL BRIDGE.
The New-York Mercury, August 22, 1763.

TWENTY DOLLARS Reward.

RUN-*away from John Leake, a Negro Man named Wall*, about 40 *Years of Age, five Feet* 6 *Inches high, yellow Complexion, one Leg a little thicker than the other, his Head bald; born at Oyster-bay, speaks good English: Had on when he went away, a red Coat, a Manchester Velvet Jacket, white Thread Stockings, and new shoes. Whoever brings him to his said Master at New-York, shall have the above Reward, and all reasonable Charges.*
The *New-York Mercury*, August 29, 1763; September 5, 1763.

WHEREAS one *James Matthews*, of *Plainfield* in *Connecticut*, hired a Horse of the Subscriber at *Providence*, to go to *Plainfield*, instead of which he proceeded to *Boston*, where he sold the Horse: Whoever will give Information to the Subscriber, or to *Richard* and *Samuel Draper*, Printers, so that the said *Matthews* be secured and brought to Justice, shall have TEN DOLLARS Reward.   KNIGHT DEXTER.

Aug. 24. 1763.

N. B. The said *Matthews* is about 25 Years of Age, about 5 Feet high, a thick well-set Fellow, of a freckled and brown Complection, sandy Hair, sometimes with a black Bag or Pig-tail, a very genteel talkative Fellow: He had on a Claret-colour'd Broadcloth Coat, metal Buttons, white Jacket, black knit Breeches; he had one Ruffle-Shirt: It is said he kept a Tavern in *Albany* some Time since, and buried his Wife in that City.

The *Massachusetts Gazette, and Boston News-Letter*, August 25, 1763; *The Boston Gazette, and Country Journal*, August 29, 1763; September 5, 1763; *The Boston Post-Boy & Advertiser*, August 29, 1763.

Fishkill, August 26, 1763.

RUN away from his Master, the Rev. Mr. Chauncy Graham, of the Fishkill, in the County of Dutchess, and Province of New-York, a Negro man named *Trace*, aged 25 Years; a spry well-built Fellow; bred in New-England; looks very brazen, prompt and likely; talks flippant; has a flat Forehead, and the lower Part of his Face something prominent; his Hair cut on the Top, with a Tupee Foretop; plays on the Violin: Had with him an old blue Great-Coat, a Pair Leather Breeches, ditto Trowsers, a white Shirt, ditto Check, ditto Ozenbrigs, a red under Jacket, a new Castor Hat, a Pair blue and white Stockings. Whoever takes up and secures said Negro, so that his said Master may have him again, shall have Forty Shillings Reward, and all reasonable Charges

paid by   *CHAUNCY GRAHAM.*

N. B. All Persons are hereby forbid to conceal, harbour, or carry off said Negro, as they shall answer it at their Peril.

The New-York Gazette, September 5, 1763; September 12, 1763; September 26, 1763.

                  Ten Shillings Reward for each,
RUN-away, from their Master, last Thursday Night, the 21st of July last, three New NEGROES, viz. Two Men and a Woman; they cannot speak English: They are each about 25 Years old, and has several of their Country Marks in their Foreheads: The two Men had on an Ozenbrigs Shirt and Trowsers, and the Woman had on an Ozenbrigs Pettycoat, and Josey. Whoever will take up and bring the said Negroes to Thomas Hill, if taken in Town, shall have ten Shillings Reward for each, and all reasonable Charges paid; and if taken out of Town, twenty Shillings for each.
The New York Mercury, September 5, 1763. See *The New-York Gazette*, July 25, 1763, and *The New-York Gazette*, August 1, 1763.

RUN-away, the 22d Inst. a Negro Man, named Baptist, belonging to the Estate of Mr. Robert Kennedy; he is a French Negro, about Forty Years old, five Feet eight or ten Inches high, a little pitted with the Small-Pox: He had good Cloaths, a good Hat, and generally wears a green Jacket, with a stripped Holland Shirt, and speaks but bad English. Whoever secures said Fellow, and brings him to Mrs. Fararo's, shall be well rewarded, and all Charges paid them,
                  by   GEORGE TRAILE.
The New York Mercury, September 5, 1763.

RUN-away the 12th of August, ult. from Peter Benedict, of Salem, in Westchester County, a Negro Man, named Tom; aged about 30 Years, 5 Feet 7 Inches high; speaks tolerable good English, only is apt to use the Words, is and to, instead of, it and to. He had on when he went away, a Frock and Trowsers, and Felt Hat; and took with him a blue Coat, with white Mettle Buttons, and a Callico Vest, a Holland Shirt, a Pair of Leather Breeches, and two Pair of blue Woolen Stockings: He was born at St. John's, in Antigua; has followed the Seas, but of late Years has been employed at Husbandry, but always seems to have an Inclination to go to Sea; therefore all Masters of Vessels, and Seafaring Men, are hereby forbid to Harbour said Negro, on the Peril of the Law; and whosoever will take up, or secure said Negro, so that his Master can have him again, shall be rewarded Forty Shillings, and all reasonable Charges
                 paid by me   PETER BENEDICT.
The New York Mercury, September 5, 1763.

RUN-away, the first inst. from Leonard Yeats, an Irish servant boy, named Francis Buglis, aged 14 years. Had on when he went away, an old blue jacket, with red lining, a pair of red breeches, no shoes, nor stockings, and an old check shirt; he was bought from Mr. Kennedy, merchant: he speaks very thick; has streight hair; he rob'd his master. All masters of vessels are forbid to harbour him. Any person that secures the said boy, shall have FORTY SHILLINGS reward,
                paid by me   Leonard Yeats,
                              living at the sign of the Royal Hester.
The New York Mercury, September 5, 1763; September 12, 1763; September 19, 1763.

RUN-away, the 8th Instant, a Negro Wench, born in the County of Westchester, named Kate, about 5 Feet 6 Inches high; she took a Child with her, a Boy about 15 Months old, and is supposed to be harboured in New-York. Whoever brings her to the Printer hereof, so that her Master may have her again, shall be handsomly rewarded.
The New York Mercury, September 12, 1763; September 19, 1763.

RUN-away from the Subscriber, of *Claverack*, in the County of *Albany*, a Negro Man about 19 Years old, speaks good English and low Dutch, he is about 6 Feet high; had on when he went away a red Great coat, a woolen Shirt, blue mill'd Stockings, old leather Breeches, and had with him another pair of blue mill'd Stockings, and a woolen check'd Shirt. Whoever takes him up and will bring him to his Master, shall have FIVE DOLLARS Reward, and all charges paid by me
            Killiaen Muller, of *Claverack.*
The Massachusetts Gazette, and Boston News-Letter, September 15, 1763; September 22, 1763. See *The New-York Mercury*, July 4, 1763, *The Providence Gazette; And Country Journal*, July 30, 1763, and *The New-London Gazette*, December 9, 1763.

STOLEN the 6th of August last, from the Subscriber, a black Mare, 14 Hands high; six Years old this Spring; Trots well, but when she Trots she throws her Fore Feet very much out: The Person who took her goes by the Name of David Hanley, and was a Serjeant in Capt. Wright's Company from Long-Island; aged 30 Years; 5 Feet 9 Inches high, and has red Hair. Any Person that secures either Mare or Thief, shall have Five Pounds Reward, paid by Joseph Hagerman, at the Ferry on Long-Island.
    N. B. She is branded on the near Thigh **P**.

The New York Mercury, September 19, 1763; September 26, 1763.

RUN away on Thursday last, the 15th Inst. Sept. from on board the Schooner Little Taff, lying at the Whitehall, an Irish Servant Lad, about 19 Years old, a stout well made Person, fair Complexion, and went off in Sailor's Clothes. All Masters of Vessels are strictly forbid carrying him off. Whoever takes up the said Servant and secures him so that he may be had again, shall have *Thirty Shillings* Reward, and Reasonable Charges,
    paid by *William Anderson*, or Captain *John Dalton.*
The New York Mercury, September 19, 1763; *The New-York Gazette*, September 26, 1763.

RUN away from JAMES BARNARD, Inn-holder, at the King's-Bridge, a Negro named Windsor, about 23 Years of Age, a stout bluff looking Fellow, walks bow-legg'd: Had on when he went away, a green Jacket, with a white Flannel one under it, a striped Cotton Shirt, old Trowsers, and a black Leather Jockey-Cap. Whoever takes up and secures the said Negro, so that his Master may have him again, shall have *Twenty Shillings* Reward, and reasonable Charges
    paid by JAMES BARNARD.
N. B. Masters of Vessels are strictly forbid to carry him off.
The New-York Gazette, September 26, 1763; October 3, 1763; November 7, 1763.

RUNAWAY,
On the 5th Instant, September, from the Subscriber, at the Province Arms, in New-York,

A Negro Man named Sam, well limb'd, round faced, about 30 years of age, but looks younger; French born, but speaks pretty good English; is a good Cook, and was lately bought of Capt. James Delaney. He had on when he went away a narrow brimmed black Hat, somewhat worn, cock'd on one Side, which he commonly wore behind; a light brown Coat, Short Skirts; a Scarlet pair of Breeches, Pewter Buckles, and black Worsted Stockings.— But he may probably change his Dress. He is well known in this City, and it is supposed in now lurking and concealed therein. Whoever will take up and secure the said Negro, so that I may get him again, shall have Forty Shillings Reward,
    paid by GEORGE BURNS.
N. B. Masters of Vessels, and all other persons, are desired not to carry off, conceal or harbour the said negro, as they will answer the Penalty of the Law, in such Cases made and provided.
The New-York Mercury, September 26, 1763; October 3, 1763.

New-York, October 3, 1763.

RUN away in August last from the Subscriber, living in the Bowery Lane, in New-York, a Negro Man, named CUFF, aged about 20 Years, this Country born, has woolly Head of Hair, pretty low on his Forehead, has Marks of the Small-Pox on his Face. Had on when he went away, an old brown Jacket, an Oznabrigs Shirt and Trowsers, bare-headed and legged. Whoever takes up and secures said Negro, and brings him to his Master, shall have *Five Dollars* Reward, and reasonable Charges

paid by   ELBERT HERRING.

N. B. He has since been apprehended, and brought back; but immediately ran away, a second Time: It is certain he changes his Clothes; so that cannot be depended on. All Masters of Vessels are strictly forbid to carry him off, or others to Harbour him, as they must expect to be prosecuted for the same.

The New York Gazette, October 3, 1763; October 10, 1763; October 24, 1763. See *The New-York Gazette*, August 22, 1763.

RUN-*away, the* 10*th of August,* 1763, *from John Farrell, a Mulatto Wench, named Sarah Bradey, born in Albany, aged* 25 *Years. Whoever secures the said Wench in the City of New-York, shall have* TWENTY SHILLINGS *Reward, paid by the Subscriber; but if in Albany, or elsewhere,* FIVE DOLLARS, *by applying to*

Mr. Benjamin Williams, in Albany.

The New-York Mercury, October 10, 1763; October 17, 1763; October 24, 1763.

RAN away Wednesday Evening last, from Judah Hayes, of New-York, a Negro Man, named Aaron, or Hiram, late the Property of Capt. William Murray, deceased. He is a well-set lusty Fellow, about 5 Feet 4 Inches high, and 26 or 28 Years old, speaks broken English, and pretends to be something of a Sailor. Had on when he went away, a brown Thickset Jacket, with red Button Holes and Brass Buttons; and a red Half-thick Soldier's Jacket over that, with white Metal Buttons; a Pair of brown Thickset Breeches of the same as the Jacket; black Worsted Stockings, a Pair of old Pumps, an Oznabrigs Shirt, and a striped Worsted Cap; he may have taken some Oznabrigs Shirts with him. Whoever takes up and secures the said Negro Man, so that his Master may have him again, shall receive a Reward of *Twenty Shillings*, if taken in the City, and *Forty Shillings*, if taken any Distance without the City, and all reasonable Charges

paid by   JUDAH HAYS.

All Persons whatsoever are hereby forewarn'd not to detain, conceal, or carry off the said Negro, as they may depend on being prosecuted to the utmost Severity of the Law. *New-York, 20th. October,* 1763.
The New-York Gazette, October 24, 1763; October 31, 1763. See *The New-York Gazette,* August 22, 1763.

ABSCONDED from the Snow Lamb, William Moore, Commander, from Belfast, lying at New-York, a Redemptioner, named Philip Traner, about five Feet seven Inches high, with dark Eyebrows. Also an indented Servant Woman, about 19 Years of Age, named Honor Kelly, middling thick set, and fresh coloured. Whoever apprehends and brings them to John Moore, Merchant, in Chestnut-street, or to the Workhouse in Philadelphia, or the Subscriber, in New-York, shall have Forty Shillings Reward for each, and reasonable Charges,
    paid by WILLIAM MOORE.
The Pennsylvania Gazette, October 27, 1763.

Deserted from his Majesty's 44th Regiment of Foot, and Lieut. Col. *William Eyres* Company, the undermentioned Persons, viz.
 David Farrington, aged 21 Years, five Feet eight Inches high, without Shoes, round Face, fair Hair and Complection, born in *Flushing, Long-Island,* Long Island, by calling a Labourer.
 Thomas Mills, aged 28 Years, five Feet five and 3-qr Inches high without Shoes, full Face, fair Hair, ruddy Complection and well made, born in Old-England, by Callings a Labourer. They both went off in their Regimentals.
 WHOEVER apprehends the above Deserters, and gives them up to any Officer commanding a Post, Garrison or Cantonment, shall receive TWENTY SHILLINGS Sterling Reward.
       Crown-Point, September 26, 1763.
The Boston Post-Boy, & Advertiser, October 31, 1763; November 7, 1763; November 14, 1763.

RUN-away, on Thursday last the 27th of October, from the Subscriber, an Apprentice, about 19 Years of Age, much marked with the Small-Pox, has dark strait Hair, and a down Look. Had on when he went away, a dark coloured claret Coat and Breeches, the Coat lined with green, having yellow gilt buttons; has a red Jacket; a Pair of new Pumps, carv'd silver Buckles; and an half-worn Beaver Hat. He took with him a blue Surtoit Coat with yellow gilt Buttons to it; and stole, at least, Ten Half Johannes. Whoever takes up and secures the said Apprentice, so that his Master may have him

again, shall have FIVE DOLLARS Reward, and reasonable Charges paid by William Carr.
N. B. The Boy is a Taylor by Trade.
The New-York Gazette, October 31, 1763.

To the PUBLICK,

WHEREAS there is a certain Woman called Ann Gilliland, now in Town, who has been some Years past a Resident in Albany; and. as I am informed, reports she was married to me. Now, least any Person should be imposed upon by her, I affirm I never was married to her, nor do I allow any Person to credit her on my Account, as I never intend paying what she or any such person shall contract. Witness my Hand at the City of New-York, October 21st, 1763.
        his
    William X Gilliland, Butcher,
       Mark
The New-York Gazette, October 31, 1763.

RUN-away from the Subscriber, living in Gold-Street, New-York, an Apprentice Boy, named Andrew Mitchell, a Cordwainer by Trade, 16 Years old, black Hair, and marked with the Small-Pox: Had on when he went away, a light coloured Cloth Jacket, and a white Flannel one under it; a Pair of black Cloth Breeches, Ozenbrig Trowsers, new Shoes and Brass Buckles, and 'tis supposed is gone to Sea. Therefore all Masters of Vessels are forbid to carry him off. Whoever takes up and secures the said Boy, and will bring him to his Master, shall have Twenty Shillings Reward, and all reasonable Charges,
     paid by HENDRICK BARR.

The New-York Mercury, October 31, 1763; November 7, 1763; December 5, 1763; December 12, 1763.

RUN away from JOHN RAFF, of Albany, on Friday the 5th Inst. Nov, a Negro Man named *Jack*, aged about 33, speaks but little English, about 5 ½ Feet high: Had on a green Jacket, Buckskin Breeches, brown knit stockings; took with him a French Blanket; has an outward Bend in his right Foot, which obliges him to brace the hind Part of his Shoe round his Ancle to keep it up, both his Great Toes are nearly frozen off. Whoever takes up and secures said Negro so that his Master may have him again, or brings him to Waldron Blau, on the Great Dock, in New-York will receive a Reward of *Five Dollars*, from either of them, and lawful Charges.

The New-York Gazette, November 7, 1763; November 14, 1763; December 5, 1763. See *The New-York Gazette*, December 3, 1764.

TAKEN up as a Runaway at Cecaicos in the County of Bergen, at the House of Renier Vangesen, Esq; on Sunday Morning the 6th Inst, November, an Indian Servant Lad, aged about 16 or 17 Years, is 5½ Feet high: Had on when taken up, a Pair of old Tow Trowsers, a white Flannel Under Jacket, and an old homespun Jacket, middling good Shoes, and a Pair of old Leggings, and, as he says, his Name is Ben Jathro, and belongs to William Nicoll, Esq; a Lawyer upon Long-Island. Whoever proves his Property to the aforesaid Indian Servant, at the Gaol of Hackinsack, may have him again, paying all Charges to the High Sheriff of said County.
    ISAAC KINSLAND, Sheriff of said County.
 The New-York Gazette, November 14, 1763; November 21, 1763; *The New-York Journal,* November 21, 1763.

RUN-away on Friday the 3d of November, a Servant Boy, named *James M'Gee,* about 5 Feet 5 Inches high, and about 19 or 20 Years of Age; small round visag'd; is strong and heavy made; and inclined to a fair, but freckled, Complexion; is the Property of *James Williams,* and came Passenger from Ireland on board the Dunluce, John Munfoort. Whoever apprehends the said Man-Servant, and puts him in the first convenient Gaol, or sends him to this City to Mr. *Benjamin Payne,* on Cromelin's Wharf, shall have *Forty Shillings* Reward.
 The New-York Gazette, November 28, 1763; December 4, 1763. See *The New-York Mercury,* December 5, 1763.

RUN away the 21st Day of November last, from Philip Kissick, a black Negro Wench named Amelia, about 23 Years of Age; she is a middle Size Wench: Had on when she went away, a green Short Gown, and a striped Homespun Petticoat blue and white, and a whitish Cloth one underneath, and a Pair of thick Woollen Stockings, and a Pair of Mens Slippers. Whoever takes up and secures the said Wench, so that her Master may have her again, shall have Twenty Shillings Reward, and all reasonable Charges paid. She is a Barbados Wench, and she is very desirous to go to her own Country; all Persons and Masters of Vessels, are forbid to harbour her or to carry her off; if they do, they may depend on being prosecuted according to Law.
 The New-York Mercury, December 5, 1763. See *The New-York Mercury,* May 2, 1763.

Five Pounds Reward,
RUN-away from the London Coffee-House, on Thursday Night last, a white Man Servant, named *James Stevenson,* about 5 Feet 5 Inches high, of a fair Complexion, smooth Face, his Teeth very irregular, and wears his

own short curling Hair, says he was born in Yorkshire: Had on when he went away, a red Frize Coat, a brown Cloth Waistcoat and Breeches; carried with him five new white Shirts, one Pair of turn'd Pumps, and a Pair of Shoes. It's thought he went towards Albany. Whoever secures said Servant, and brings him to the London Coffee-House, shall receive the above Reward, and all reasonable Charges,
                paid by   THOMAS OUGSTON.

The New-York Gazette, December 5, 1763; December 12, 1763; December 26, 1763; *The New-York Mercury*, December 5, 1763; December 12, 1764. Minor differences in the papers. The *Mercury* shows "his Feet very iregular."

RUN-away on Friday the third of November, Inst. from James Williams, living in New-York, an Irish Servant Boy, named James Magee, 19 or 20 Years of Age, five Feet five Inches high, strong and well made, small round visaged, and freckled: Had on when he went away, a drab coloured Cloth Coat and Jacket, Sheep-skin Breeches, a Hat and Wig, a Pair of Stockings, and a Pair of Shoes with Brass Buckles in them. Whoever takes up and secures said Servant, so that his Master may have him again, shall have Forty Shillings Reward, paid by his said Master,
                or Benjamin Payne, on Crommelin's Wharf.

The New-York Mercury, December 5, 1763; December 16, 1763. See *The New-York Gazette*, November 28, 1763.

RAN away from his Master (*Killien Miller,* of *Claverick*, in the County of *Albany*, and Province of *New-York*), on the 27th of *June* last; A Negro Man Servant named *JAM*, about 20 Years of Age, about Six Feet high, slender built, speaks good English and Low Dutch, this Country born. Had on a red duffil great Coat, a strip'd homespun Jacket, woolen check Shirt, a pair of old leather Breeches, blue mild Stockings, coarse felt Hat. Whoever will take up said Servant and give Notice thereof to his Master, by advertising him in the New-York Papers, or otherwise, so that his Master may have him again, shall receive Twelve DOLLARS reward, and all necessary Charges
                paid by   *KILLIEN MILLER.*
                New-London, December 3d, 1763.

The New-London Gazette, December 9, 1763. See *The New-York Mercury*, July 4, 1763, *The Providence Gazette; And Country Journal*, July 30, 1763, *The Massachusetts Gazette*, and *The Boston News-Letter*, September 15, 1763.

RUN away for these six Weeks past, a Negro Man named James, a Taylor by Trade, speaks broken English, and pretends to be a free Man from

Jamaica, in the West Indies; is now supposed to work in private Families, to mend Cloaths. Whoever secures said Negro, and brings him to the Printer hereof, shall be well rewarded for their Trouble; and whoever harbours him, may depend on being prodecured according to Law.

The New-York Mercury, December 12, 1763; December 19, 1763.

RUN away from the Subscriber, living in Gold-Street, New-York, an Apprentice Boy named Andrew Mitchell, a Cordwainer by Trade, 16 Years old, black Hair, and marked with the Small-Pox: Had on when he went away, a light coloured Cloth Jacket, and a white Flannel one under it; a Pair of black Cloth Breeches, Ozenbrig Trowsers, new Shoes and Brass Buckles, and 'tis supposed is gone or will go to Sea. Therefore all Masters of Vessels, are forbid to carry him off. Whoever takes up and secures the said Boy, and will bring him to his Master, shall have Forty Shillings Reward, and all reasonable Charges
            paid by   HENDRICK BARR.

N. B. He went away with a Portugueze Boy named John, and has been seen in Connecticut, and is supposed to be gone to Rhode Island.

The New-York Mercury, December 12, 1763.

Albany, 28th November, 1763.

DESERTED from his Majesty's 55th Regiment of Foot, and Capt. Daly's Company of Grenadiers;

Andrew Krigeur, Sergeant, 5 Feet 8 Inches high, Age 26 Years, straight body'd. well limb'd, swarthy Complexion, round Visage by Trade a Malster: Had on when he went off his Regimental Coat, plain Beaver Hat, Buff Breeches, and strip'd Waistcoat, born in Scotland.

Andrew M'Kechne, Grenadier, foresaid Regiment, Age 22 Years, thick made, well limb'd, round shoulder'd, brown Complexion, round Vissage, with a Cut across his Nose, 5 Feet 9 Inches high, by Trade a Weaver, born in Scotland.

Henry Mereband, Lieut. Col. Elliot's Company, said Regiment, Age 23 Years, 5 Feet 5 Inches high, grey Eyes, black Hair, mark'd with the Small-pox, long Visage, brown Complexion, wants a Finger on the Right Hand, has on the Inside, mark'd thus, M: M: He went off in a shirt red plain Coat, and plain Hat; born in London, by Trade a Brick-maker, And

Isaac Norris, of the aforesaid Regiment, Capt. Gardner's Company, about 26 Years of Age, 5 Feet 7 Inches high, well made, thick limb'd, brown Complexion, black Complexion, [*sic*] black Hair, long Visage, born in Old England, by Trade a Chandler. Had on when he went off, a plain red Coat fac'd with green, a Gold lac'd Hat.—Whoever apprehends the above said Deserters, or any of them, by applying to William Bayard, Esq; at

New-York, or to Lieut. Colonel Elliot, commanding at Albany, shall receive One Guineas Reward for each, over and above what is allow'd by Act of Parliament for apprehending Deserters.
R. ELLIOT.
The New-York Gazette, December 19, 1763.

RUN-away, from the Snow LORD DUNLUCE, John Monford, Master, on Friday the 16th Instant, two Apprentice Lads, one named John Mc. Vicker, with black curled Hair, and about 5 Feet 6 Inches high. The other named Hugh Mc. Killip, wore his own black Hair also, a little freckled, and about 5 Feet 4 Inches high. Whoever takes up and secures the said Lads, so that they may be had again, shall have 40s. Reward for each, and reasonable Charges, by applying to
Mr. Waddell Cunningham, Merchant, in New-York.
The New-York Mercury, December 19, 1763; December 26, 1763.

DEserted from his Majesty's second Battalion of the Royal Regiment of Artillery, whereof George Williamson, Esq; is Col. Commander. Edmund Layn, born in New-England, by Trade a Carpenter, 24 Years of Age, 5 Feet 8 Inches high, rudy Complexion; inlisted in 1761, at Nova Scotia, by Capt. Ferguson, and deserted from his Guard at New-York, the 11th of December 1763. Whoever apprehends the said Edmund Layn, and secured him in any of his Majesty's Goals, to that he may be brought to Justice, shall, by applying to John Godwin, Esq; Lieutenant Colonel, and commanding Officer of Artillery in North-America, at New-York; or to Thomas Hancock, Esq; at Boston, or Capt. Thomas Ferguson, at Halifax, receive Twenty Shillings Sterling, over and above what is allowed by Act of Parliament
The New-York Mercury, December 19, 1763.

RUN-AWAY,

FROM *on board the Ship Manchester, James Chambers, Master, on Monday the 28th of November last, a young English Lad, aged about Nineteen, brought up to the Shoemaking Branch, about five Feet five Inches high, fair Complexion, pitted with the Small-Pox, and wore his own light streight Hair, rather inclining to be lusty: Had on when he went away, a light colour'd Thickset Coat, &c. Any Person securing the above Lad, and bringing him to said Chambers, or Mr. Theophilact Bache, shall receive a handsome Reward, with all Charges. N. B. If the said Lad will return, he shall be kindly receive and the Offence forgiven; and any Person harbouring the said Lad, will be prosecuted to the utmost Severity of the Law.*

The New-York Mercury, December 19, 1763.

RUN-*away from Hugh Campbel, at Fort Anne, near Fort Edward, on the 20th ult. Three Spanish Negro Men, the Property of Major Philip Skene; one named M'Gile; had on when he went away, a blue Jacket and Breeches. The other named Havannah, had on a white Oznabrig Frock, with red Cuffs. And the other named Jacco; had on, a blanket Coat: They took with them two Guns. Whoever apprehends them, or either of them, and brings them to the said Hugh Campbell, or Mr. Hugh Wallace, in New-York, or to John M'Comb, in Albany, or lodges them in any of his Majesty's Goals, and gives Notice thereof, shall be by either of the above Persons well rewarded.*

The New-York Mercury, December 19, 1763; December 26, 1763.

DEserted from his Majesty's second Battalion of the Royal Regiment of Artillery, whereof George Williamson, Esq; is Col. Commander. Edmund Layn, born in New England, by Trade a Carpenter, 24 Years of Age, 5 Feet 8 Inches high, rudy Complexion, inlisted in 1761, in Nova Scotia, by Capt. Ferguson, and deserted from his Guard at New-York, the 11th of December 1763. Whoever apprehends the said Edmund Layn, and secures him in any of his Majesty's Goals, so that he may be brought to Justice, shall, by applying to John Godwin, Esq: Lieutenant Colonel, and commanding Officer of Artillery in North-America, at New-York; or to Thomas Hancock, Esq; at Boston, or Capt. Thomas Ferguson, at Halifax, receive Twenty Shillings Sterling, over and above what is allowed by Act of Parliament.

The New-York Mercury, December 26, 1763.

1764

DEserted from the second Battalion of his Majesty's 60th, or Royal American Regiment, and Capt. Holland's Company, James Bryan, 34 Years of Age, 5 Feet 7 Inches high, ruddy Complexion, born in London, went off in a Soldiers Coat of the 47th Regiment, and was a Draught from said Regiment. Whoever secures the above deserter shall receive two Guineas Reward, over and above what is allowed by Act of Parliament, from the commanding Officer of the second Battalion of the Royal American Regiment.   JAMES MURRAY.

The New-York Mercury, January 2, 1764; January 9, 1764.

DESERTED from His Majesty's Ship Coventry, *Archibald Kennedy*, Esq; Commander: *Robert May*, of the seventh Company of Marines, born at Canterbury, Kent, 23 Years of Age, 5 Feet 5 Inches high, brown Complexion, black Hair, and round shouldered, deserted from the Hospital in New-York the 10th of November, 1763.

Evan Jones, of the 19th Company of Marines, born in Cowbridge, Glamorganshire, 19 Years of Age, 5 Feet 5½ Inches high, fair Complexion, light brown Hair, full faced, deserted from the same Ship the 21st of December, 1763.

Samuel Rugg, of the 10th Company of Marines, born at Crookhorn, Somersetshire, 26 Years of Age, 5 Feet 6 Inches high, brown Complexion, brown Hair, well set, deserted from the same Ship the 21st of December 1763.

Thomas Gray, of the 40th Company of Marines, born at Norwich, Norfolk, 28 Years of Age, 5 Feet, 5½ Inches high, fair Complexion, sandy Hair, deserted from the same Ship the 30th of December, 1763.

Henry Johnson, of the 4th Company of Marines, born at Peterborough, Northamptonshire, 25 Years of Age, 5 Feet 6½ Inches high, brown Complexion, dark brown Hair, well set, deserted from the same Ship the 30th December, 1763.

Whoever apprehends any of the above Marines, and secures them in any of His Majesty's Gaols, so that they may be brought to justice, shall, by applying to Lieut. *Edward Owen*, Commanding Officer of the Marines on board the same Ship, receive Forty Shillings Reward.

The New-York Gazette, January 16, 1764; January 23, 1764; February 13, 1764.

WHEREAS *a Negro Man, named Cyrus, but calls himself Harry, had a Pass from the Subscriber, to go to Elizabeth Town, and return on Saturday the 7th inst. and is still absent: Whoever takes up said Negro, and brings him to his Master, shall have Forty Shillings Reward, and all reasonable Charges*

paid by JEREMIAH STANTON.

N. B. *The said Negro is 28 Years of Age, but looks much older; is about 5 Feet 2 Inches high, a good deal mark'd with the small Pox, speaks Dutch, and very bad English. Had on when he went away, a blue Watch Coat, with Brass Buttons, Leather Breeches, and a white Shirt.*

Staten-Island, Jan. 18, 1764.

The New-York Gazette, January 23, 1764; January 30, 1764; February 20, 1764; *The New-York Mercury*, January 20, 1764. Minor differences between the papers.

DESERTED, on Wednesday January 25th 1764, from the Snow Bristol Merchant, Robert Keir, Master; JAMES WELCH, a Boy about fourteen years of Age, of a fair Complexion, wearing a Capor Wigg. Had. Had on when he deserted a blue Jacket, check Shirt, blue Breeches, light grey Stockings, a new Pair turn'd Pumps, is of a thin Stature, and of a pale Face, is a little Pock-mark'd,—Whosoever brings the aforesaid Boy to the above Robert Keir, shall Receive two Dollars Reward.—
The New-York Gazette, January 30, 1764; February 6, 1764.

The Names of the Men deserted from Capt. John Brant's Company, 10th January, 1764, after the Receival of their Bounty and Cloathing.
SILL CAVANAUGH, inlisted 29th Dec. 1763, of Ireland: Had on when deserted, a Claret colour'd Coat, Buckskin Breeches, a Pair of Silver Buckles in his Shoes, fair fac'd, grey Eyes, brown Hair, about 5 Feet 7 ½ Inches high, formerly a Waiter at the White-Hall Coffee-House, and at the Province Arms.
   JOHN WILLIAMS, 2d Jan. 1763, of Wales, Old England: When deserted had on his Regimentals, being about 5 Feet 8 Inches high, broad fac'd and fair, brown curl'd Hair, and round shoulder'd.
   HENRY STUTES, Corporal, 4th Jan, 1763, of Germany: When deserted, had on his Regimentals, and since have changed them, and left behind in this City at the House of Mr. Rudolph, be he being about 5 Feet 4 ½ Inches high, brown Complexion, and black curl'd Hair, and broad shoulder'd, formerly in the Province Service, and in the Company commanded by Capt. Gillchrist.
   Whoever apprehends the above Deserters, or either of them, and secures them in any of his Majesty's Gaols, shall have Forty Shillings Reward for each, by applying to the Printer hereof.
   The New-York Gazette, January 30, 1764; February 6, 1764.

WHereas on Wednesday last between two and three o'clock in the Afternoon, a Chest belonging to James Gelston, was broke open in his Lodging, at the House of Mrs. Barbait, in Chappel-Street, and 22 Dollars taken therefrom; and 'tis supposed was done by a Lodger in the said Hose that went by the Name of Thomas North, he having absconded that Day, without taken Leave of his Landlady: He has been seen on Long-Island: He is about 5 Feet 6 Inches high, well-set, and of a fair Complexion; wore a Linen Cap, and said he was a Stone Cutter and Mason by Trade, and born in Ireland: Had on a light coloured Watch-Coat, a Thickset under Coat, a Linen Jacket, and a Pair of dirty Leather Breeches. Whosoever takes up and

secures said Fellow, so that he may be brought to Justice, shall have 40s. Reward,
    paid by JAMES GELSTON.
The New-York Gazette, January 30, 1764.

RUN-away last Monday Morning, from the Subscriber, living in New York, an Apprentice Lad, named John Young, a Cordwainer by Trade, about 18 Years old, has short dark brown Hair, a smooth full fac'd Lad, but swarthy; his right Foot has been broke and is crooked: Had on a blue Coat, and a red Plush Jacket, with Buckskin Breeches. Whoever takes up and secures the said Lad, so that his Master may have him again, shall have three Pounds Reward,
    paid by WILLIAM MARINER.
The New-York Mercury, February 6, 1764; February 13, 1764.

RUN-away, the 13th Instant February from Thomas Hamersly, of this City, Goldsmith, a Negro Man, named Duke, aged 33 Years, about 5 Feet 8 Inches high, of a yellow Complexion, and thick lipp'd: Had on when he went away, a red Frize Coat somewhat dirty, a light coloured Cloth Waistcoat, black Cloth Breeches, and brown Worsted Stockings. Whoever takes up and secures the said Negro, so that his Master may have him again, shall have Forty Shillings Reward, if taken out of the City, and Twenty if taken within it.
 N. B. He has been seen sundry Times since he went away, at and near the Ship-Yards in this City.
 The New-York Gazette, February 20, 1764; *The New-York Mercury*, February 20, 1764; February 27, 1764. Minor differences between the papers. The *Mercury* shows his age as 35. See *The New-York Mercury*, August 30, 1756.

On Wednesday Night last,
EDWARD AGNEW, an indented Servant, run away from the Subscriber, and took with him two Pair of Buckskin Breeches, one Beaver Hat, and one white Shirt; he is a likely Lad about 20 Years old, smooth fac'd, fresh colour'd, wears slink brown Hair generally tied, speaks fluently, is apt to get drunk, and about 5 Feet 6 Inches high: Had on when he went away, a light coloured coarse Cloth Frock, a white Flannel Jacket, a Pair of the above mentioned Buckskin Breeches, a coarse Felt Hat, a tucker'd white Shirt, old grey Yarn Stockings, turn'd Pumps with carv'd Steel Buckles in them. Whoever secures the said Servant, and brings him to the Subscriber, shall have Forty Shillings Reward, if taken in this Province, or Three Pounds, if taken in any other Province,

paid by   WILLIAM GILLILAND.
New-York, Feb. 18, 1764.
The New-York Gazette, February 20, 1764; February 27, 1764; *The New-York Mercury*, February 20, 1764; February 27, 1764. See *The Boston Evening Post*, April 2, 1764.

RUN away on Saturday the 24th of February, a Negro Fellow named Jack: He is about 5 Feet 8 Inches high, of a very black Complexion, and pretty much pitted with the Small-pox, his Hair pretty long, and stares very much; was born at Hackensack; when he talks he speaks very quick: He had on when he went away, a short scarlet Duffil Waistcoat made without Flaps, (but buttoning close to the Waistband of his Breeches) and a red Watchcoat, a Pair of long Trowsers. Whoever secures the said Negro, so that his Master may have him again, shall have Five Dollars Reward, and all reasonable Charges,
paid by me   EDWARD AGAR.
N. B. All Masters of Vessels are hereby forewarn'd not to carry him off; and all Persons are forbid to harbour him, as they shall answer it at their Peril.

The New-York Gazette, February 27, 1764; March 5, 1764; March 12, 1764. See *The New-York Mercury*, March 12, 1764, and *The New-York Mercury*, May 14, 1764.

Albany, February 12, 1764.
RUN-away on Friday Afternon the 10th Instant, a likely Negro Man, named Jacob, belonging to George Wray, at Albany; the said Negro is about 24 Years old, 5 Feet 6 3-4 inches high without Shoes, has a Scar on the right Side of his Forehead, one on his left Temple, (both just on the Edge of his Hair) and another on the Crown of his Head; two large Pock-marks on the upper Part of his left Cheek; high Cheek-bones, crooked Legs, the Calves of his Legs remarkably high, a lump on each shoulder by being flogg'd some Time past, stoops forward in walking, and hangs down his Head; speaks good English, some French, and a little Spanish, but little or no Dutch; of an insinuating Address, very apt to feign plausible Stories, and may perhaps call himself a free Negro. Whoever apprehends the said Negro, and brings him to his Master above-mentioned, or secures him in any Goal, giving his Master Notice of it, shall receive Five Dollars Reward, and all reasonable Charges. He had on when he went away, a Blanket Coat, Green Leggings and Moccasins, Buckskin Breeches and a red Worsted Cap. It is supposed he had with him, a black and white spotted Dog, answering to the Name of Venture.

The New-York Mercury, February 27, 1764; March 5, 1764; March 12, 1764. See *The Boston Gazette, and Country Journal*, March 5, 1764,

The New-York Mercury, July 4, 1763, and *The Boston Gazette, and Country Journal*, July 23, 1764.

RAN-away on Saturday Morning the 11th of February, a Negro Man nam'd Jacob, belonging to George Wray at Albany. He had on when he went off, a Blanket Coat with red Stripes, Buckskin Breeches, green Leggins, a pair of Moccasins and red Worsted Cap; and tis suppos'd he had a black & white spotted Dog with him, answering to the name of Venture. Said Negro is 24 Years old, 5 Feet 6 3-4 Inches high without Shoes, has a scar on the right Side of his Forehead, another on the left Temple, both just in the Edge of his Hair, and another on the Crown of his Head, two large Pock-marks under his left Eye, high Cheek-bones, crooked Legs, the Calves of his Legs remarkably high, a Lump on each Shoulder by being flogg'd some Time past, hands down his Head, and stoops forward in walking speaks good English, some French, a little Spanish but little or no Dutch; had a stammering in his Speech when in Liquor, to which he is much addicted; is very artful and apt to feign plausible Stories, and may perhaps call himself a free Negro. Whoever apprehends the said Negro, and secures him in any Goal, or brings him to his Master in Albany, shall receive FIVE DOLLARS Reward, and all reasonable Charges
    paid by me GEORGE WRAY.

The above Negro was bought of Isaac Kibbe the 3d of Enfield in the County of Hartford, and has been seen going that Road.

The Boston Gazette, and Country Journal, March 5, 1764. See *The New-York Mercury*, July 4, 1763, *The New-York Mercury*, February 27, 1764, and *The Boston Gazette, and Country Journal*, July 23, 1764.

STOLEN from the House of James Hyon, in Byram, a dark brown Horse between 5 and 6 Years old, pace, trots, and gallops, and goes very wide and stiff behind, had a Saddle on with red Housing and red fringe, supposed to be taken away by one John Roberts, a Stranger, about 26 Years of Age, much mark'd with the Small-pox, by Trade a Carpenter, and sings very well: Had on a light-colour'd Coat, red Jacket, brown Great Coat, and a Tail Wig. Whoever takes up the said Horse and Thief, so that the Horse may be recovered, and the Thief brought to Justice, shall be handsomely rewarded, and have all necessary Charges paid by the Subscriber, near Byram.
  BENJAMIN HAYS.   Feb. 15. 1764.

The New-York Gazette, March 5, 1764. See *The New-York Gazette*, October 8, 1764.

RUN *away on Saturday the 24th of February, a Negro Fellow named Jack: He is about 5 Feet 8 Inches high, of a very black Complexion, and pretty much pitted with the Small-pox, his Hair pretty long, and stares very much; was born at Hackensack; when he talks he speaks very quick: He had on when he went away, a short scarlet Duffil Waistcoat made without Flaps, (but buttoning close to the Waistband of his Breeches) and a red Watchcoat, a Pair of long Trowsers. Whoever secures the said Negro, so that his Master may have him again, shall have Five Dollars Reward, and all reasonable Charges,*

    paid by me EDWARD AGAR.

N. B. Since he went first away, he came privately into the House at Night, and has taken away the rest of his Cloths, viz. A Blue Camblet Coat, and a Pair of Leather Breeches, Shoes and Stockings, so that he may possibly change his Dress and appear in them. All Masters of Vessels are hereby forewarn'd not to carry him off; and all Persons are forbid to harbour him, as they shall answer it at their Peril.

  The *New-York Mercury*, March 12, 1764. See *The New-York Gazette*, February 27, 1764, and *The New-York Mercury*, May 14, 1764.

       BURNET'S-FIELD, February 12, 1764.
DEserted from the New-York Service, and Capt. John De Garimo's Company, John Camoran, born in the Highlands of Scotland, speaks bad English, aged 32 Years, short dark-brown Hair, smooth Face, gray Eyes, stout made, about 5 Feet 5 Inches high: Had on when he went away, his regimental Coat, a Pair of Buckskin Breeches, and a white Flannel Waistcoat. Whoever will apprehend the above Deserter, and secure him in any of his Majesty's Goals, and give Notice to the commanding Officers of the York Troops, shall receive Forty Shillings Reward.

    JOHN DE GARMO, Captain.

The New-York Mercury, March 19, 1764.

RUN-away, last Tuesday, from John Cornell, of Long-Island, Butcher, an Irish Servant Man, named John Smith, 20 Years old, 5 Feet 6 Inches high, short black Hair, and stutters: Had on when he went away, a red Great Coat, and a Pair of old Velvet Breeches. Whoever takes up and secures the said Run-away, so that he may be had again, shall have 20s. Reward, and all reasonable Charges,

    paid by the said JOHN CORNELL. March 26.

The New-York Mercury, March 26, 1764.

    On WEDNESDAY Night, the 22d *February*,
EDWARD AGNEW, an indented Servant, run away from the Subscriber, and took with him two Pair of Buckskin Breeches, one Bever Hat, and one

white Shirt; he is a likely Lad about 20 Years old, smooth fac'd, fresh colour'd, wears slink brown Hair generally tied, speaks fluently, is apt to get drunk, and about 5 Feet 6 Inches high: Had on when he went away, a light coloured coarse Cloth Frock, a white Flannel Jacket, a Pair of the above mentioned Buckskin Breeches, a coarse Felt Hat, a tucker'd white Shirt, old grey Yarn Stockings, turn'd Pumps with carv'd Steel Buckles in them.

Whoever secures the said Servant, and brings him to the Subscriber in *New-York*, Mr. S*amuel Blodget* at *Medford*, near *Boston*, Mr. *Thomas Mumford*, in *New-London*, or to *John Ledyard*, Esq; in *Hartford*, or lodges him in any of his Majesty's Goals, so that his Master may have him again, shall have TEN DOLLARS Reward, and all reasonable Charges
           paid by   WILLIAM GILLILAND.

☞ Said Runaway was met on the Road to *Boston* (where he said he was going) and had on then a blue Surtout and light colour'd Breeches.

The Boston Evening Post, April 2, 1764; April 9, 1764; April 16, 1764; April 30, 1764; May 7, 1764. See *The New-York Gazette*, February 20, 1764.

New-York, March 30, 1764.

RUN-away from the Subscriber, on Thursday last, a Servant Man, named John Black, 5 Feet 6 Inches high, pale Complexion, a little Pox-mark'd, speaks several Languages, and pretends to know the World well; says he is an Irishman, but talks more like a High-Dutcher: Had on when he went away, a black Thickset Coat, a black Plush Jacket pretty much worn, black Stocking Breeches, and black Stockings, a Pair of new turn'd Pumps, and a Pair of small square japan'd Steel Buckles, and a black cut Wig, with lofty Hair under it, to which he may tie a Cue: a Beaver Hat half worn; an impertinent, talkative, boasting Fellow. Whoever secures the said Fellow, so that I may have him again, (if taken in Town) shall have 40s. Reward, and if in the Country, 5l.
           paid by me,   DAVID GRAHAM.
The New-York Mercury, April 2, 1764; April 9, 1764.

TEN POUNDS REWARD.

King's College, New-York, April 7th, 1764.

R*AN away from his Master, an Irish indented Servant, Name* Patrick Field, *about* 23 *or* 24 *Years of Age,* 5 *Feet* 6 *or* 7 *Inches high, of a ruddy Complexion, his Eyes somewhat prominent, the White a little larger than common, one Fore-Tooth in his Under-Jaw wanting; well made, and active. Had on when he went away, a light brown Cloth Livery faced with green, a dark colour'd Wig with one Curle; is very soon intoxicated, and stares remarkably when he is so: Broke open, and took out of a Desk about* 50

Dollars, some smaller Spanish Silver, two Guineas, one of his present Majesty, some English Silver, two Mourning Rings, one for Mr. Joseph Haynes, the other for Archibald Kennedy, Esq; his Indenture, made over to the Subscriber by Mr. Deane; and is supposed to have counterfeited his Master's Name, that he might pass for a Freeman: Took out of the same Desk likewise, several Shirts, Handkerchiefs, Cravats, Stockings, marked M. C. and a Pair of large oval Silver Buckles; and bought, the Evening he went away, a thin Jacket, and a Pair of Musqueto Trowsers. Whoever apprehends the said Patrick Field, so that he may be brought to Justice, shall have the aforesaid Reward from
     MYLES COOPER.
The New-York Gazette, April 9, 1764; April 16, 1764; *The New-York Mercury,* April 16, 1764; April 23, 1764; April 30, 1764. Minor differences between the papers. The *Mercury* shows the date at the top as April 9.

RUN-away from the Subscriber, living in New-York, a Servant Boy, named Francis Bugles, aged 13 Years; had on when he went away, a red Pea Jacket, a round Hat, light brown Plush Breeches. Whoever takes up and secures the said Boy, so that he may be had again, shall have 20s. Reward, and all reasonable Charges
   paid, by WILLIAM ALBERSPE.
The New-York Mercury, April 9, 1764; April 16, 1764; April 23, 1764.

         Fort-Stanwix, March 28, 1764.
DESERTED *from his Majesty's* 17*th regiment of foot, and Lieut. Col. John Darby's company, Ebenezer Hodgkins, aged* 32 *years,* 5 *feet* 6 *inches high, born at Grotton, New England, by trade a shoemaker, dark brown hair, brown eyes, swarthy complexion, full faced and well made. Also deserted from said company, Peleg Stevens, private soldier, aged* 30 *years,* 5 *feet* 7 *inches high, born in Newport, Rhode-Island, in New England, by trade a wig-maker, dark brown hair, black eyes, swarthy complexion, and stoops much.*

  Also deserted the same time from Capt. Richard Montgomery's company, Joseph Sheron, a private solder, aged 27 *years,* 5 *feet* 9 *inches high, born in Lancashire, Old England, by trade a silk troller, dark brown hair, grey eyes, swarthy complexion, straight, well set. Also deserted from said company, Nicholas Kennisen, aged* 22 *years,* 6 *feet high, born in Hampshire, New-England, by trade a shoemaker, light brown hair, brown eyes, swarthy complexion, straight well made. The above men deserted in their regimentals. Whoever apprehends any of said deserters, and secures them in any of his Majesty's goals, giving notice thereof to the regiment*

shall have 40*s. sterling reward for each.*
JOHN CAMPBELL, *Lt. Col* 17*th Regt.*
The New-York Mercury, April 9, 1764; April 16, 1764; April 23, 1764.

DESERTED from his Majesty's 44th Regiment of Foot, and Lieutenant-Colonel WILLIAM EYRE'S Company.

John Blear, Drummer. He is about 20 Years of Age, 5 Feet 7 Inches high without Shoes, fair Complection, round faced, grey Eyes, dark brown Hair, born in *Germany,* by Trade a Caulker.

N. B. Received a large cut on the Bridge of his Nose, since he went on Furlough; has with him his Discharge from the late Col. *Murray*'s Regiment at *Quebec,* as Drum Major, went off in the 44th's Regimentals.

Deserted also from Capt. FALCONER's Company in the abovesaid Regiment the following Persons, *viz.*

Samuel Nichols, 26 Years of Age, 5 Feet 7 Inches high, swarthy Complection, long Visage, black Eyes, black Hair, born in the County of *Chester* in *Old-England,* by Trade a Cordwainer, is a thin made Fellow, and went off in his Regimentals the 26th of *November* last.

John Gildow, 25 Years of Age, 5 Feet 6 Inches high, fair Complection, round faced, grey Eyes, born in *Germany,* by Trade a Cordwainer, is a well-made Fellow, and went off in his Regimentals the 26th of *November* last.

Daniel Loveall, Labourer, 24 Years of Age, 5 Feet 6 Inches high, brown Complection, round faced, grey Eyes, light brown Hair, born in *Germany,* thin made, and went off in his Regimentals the 26th of *November* last.

WHOEVER secures the said Deserters and delivers them up to any Officer, Civil or Military, so as they may be brought to the Regiment shall receive FORTY SHILLINGS Sterling Reward for each or either of them.

Crown-Point, April 5, 1764.
The Boston Post-Boy & Advertiser, April 30, 1764; May 7, 1764; May 14, 1764; May 21, 1764.

Six Pounds Reward.
Deserted from Capt. Alexander White's Company, of New-York Troops, in Albany, the 20th of March, 1764;

WIlliam Annelly, about 5 Feet 6 Inches high, dark brown streight Hair, uncommon long Nose, born in Ireland, and by Trade a Taylor; used formerly to lodge at one Welsh's, next Door to Mr. Plantin's, in the Fields of New-York. Thomas Singleton, 5 Feet 7 Inches high, brown streight Hair, supposed to be born on Long-Island; naturally very dirty, and by Trade a Shoe-maker, and for some Years past, worked at Newtown and Flushing,

on Long-Island, and used to work likewise at Peeks-Kill and Philipse's Manor. Whoever takes up the said Deserters, or either of them, shall have £. 3 for each, besides what the Law allows for apprehending Deserters, and to lodge them in any Goal; to be paid by me the Subscriber.
            ALEXANDER WHITE, Capt.
            German Flats, March 20, 1764.
The New-York Mercury, April 9, 1764; April 16, 1764; April 23, 1764.

RUN-away, from his Bail in the City of New-York, Saturday last, John Williams, 6 Feet high, a well-looking Man, black Complexion, and Beard; about 40 Years old, a Carpenter to Trade, and lately worked with Samuel Nevill, Esq; at Amboy, in New-Jersey: Had on when he went away, a blue Broadcloth Coat, with a Velvet Colar: a black Velvet Jacket trim'd with Silver Twist, and wore his own black Hair. Whoever takes up the said John Williams, and will secure him so that he may be had again, shall have 10 Dollars if taken in this City; 20 Dollars if in the Jersies; and £. 15, if in the Province of Pennsylvania, and all reasonable Charges
            paid by   Mr. Shipboy in New-York,
                      or at Albany, by Benjamin Williamson.
The New-York Mercury, April 30, 1764.

RUN-away from the Subscriber, an Apprentice Boy, named John Thompson, born in Ireland, aged about 17 Years, about 5 Feet 7 Inches high, round faced and bulky, fair Complexion, his Hair cut short before, and not long enough to tie: Had on when he went away, a blue Cloth Coat, a striped Cotton Waistcoat, a brown Pair of Breeches, a narrow brim'd Hat, bound with Tape. Whoever secures him in any of his Majesty's Goals, so that he may be had again by the Subscriber, shall have 40s. Reward, and all reasonable Charges,
            paid by   RICHARD DEANE.
All Masters of Vessels are forbid at their Peril not to take him off.
The New-York Mercury, May 7, 1764; May 14, 1764.

RUN-away the 13th of April ultimo, from Simon Fleet, of Huntington, of Long Island, an indented Indian Apprentice, named Charles; he is Long-Island born, and 18 Years old: Had on a Pair of Tow Trowsers, and a homespun Great Coat, and is supposed to be gone towards New-York. Any Person apprehending and securing said Apprentice, if on Long-Island, shall have 30s. Reward, or if taken in New-York, 40s. and all reasonable
            Charges, paid by   SIMON FLEET.
All Masters of Vessels are hereby forbid to carry him off.
The New-York Mercury, May 7, 1764.

New-York, May 14, 1764.

RUN-away from the Subscriber, about 10 Days ago, a Negro Fellow named Jack, born at Hackinsack, late the Property of Mr. Hailet, at Hell Gate; is of a very black Complexion, and pretty much marked with the Small-pox, talks quick, speaks both Dutch and English: Had on when he went off, an old scarlet double-breasted Waistcoat, and a Pair of black Worsted Breeches. Whoever secures the said Negro, so that his Master may have him again, shall receive 20s. Reward, if taken any where upon the Island; and 40s. if taken up any where else, and all reasonable Charges,
paid by   EDWARD AGAR.

All Masters of Vessels and others, are hereby forbid to harbour or secret him, as they shall, on being detected, be prosecuted to the utmost Severity of the Law.

The New-York Mercury, May 14, 1764; May 21, 1764. See *The New-York Gazette*, February 27, 1764, and *The New-York Mercury*, March 12, 1764.

RUn away from the Subscriber, living in New-Providence Township, Philadelphia County, on the 6th of this instant May, A Servant Man, named Ebenezer Mirrit, this Country born, about 25 Years of Age, 5 Feet 10 Inches high, of a swarthy Complexion, down looking, black Hair, inclined to buckle, thin Visage: Had on when he went away, a new Coat, of Country Cloth, Lead coloured, with broad White metal Buttons, lined with half-worn Linsey, broad Stripes, blue and green half worn Linsey Jacket, wanting Sleeves, of a light blue, without Lining, half-worn Sheepskin Breeches, half-worn cotton Stockings, mixed blue and white, but most Part blue, new Pumps, with large square Brass Buckles, Check Shirt, Felt Hat, and a new Flag Handkerchief about his Neck. Whoever takes up and secures said Servant in any County Goal so as his Master may have him again, shall have Three Pounds Reward, and reasonable Charges,
paid by   WILLIAM SHEPHERD.

N. B. Perhaps he may change his Name, and call himself John Miller. It is thought he will make to New York, as he says he was born away above New York, and his Friends live there, so that he will make that Way.

The Pennsylvania Gazette, May 17, 1764.

DESERTED from the New-York Troops, commanded by Major WILLIAM W. HOGAN, Esq: at Schenectady.

ABRAHAM SUTHARD, aged 30 Years, 5 Feet 10 Inches high, born in New-Jersey, dark short Hair, of Capt. Richard Ray's Company.

PETER THORN, born in Dutchess County, 5 Feet 10 Inches high, dark Complexion, dark brown Hair, blue Eyes, of Capt. Grant's Company.

JOHN FALKNER, born in Ireland, 5 Feet 7 Inches high, brown Complexion, dark brown Hair, aged 25 Years, of Capt. Dawson's Company.

JOHN WELSH, born in New-York, 25 Years old, 5 Feet 6 Inches high, brown Complexion, blue Eyes, brown Hair, a Scarr upon his Forehead.

JOHN PALMER, born in Old England, aged 30 Years, 5 Feet 8 Inches high, dark colour'd Hair, blue Eyes.

JOHN TAYLOR, born in Ireland, 42 Years of Age, 5 Feet 7 Inches high, dark colour'd Hair, blue Eyes.

ROGER GIDDONS, born in New-Jersey, 5 Feet 8 Inches high, light Hair, blue Eyes, of Capt. White's Company.

GEORGE VARDEE, 5 Feet 8 Inches high, 37 Years of Age, dark Complexion, a curl'd Wig, or short Hair, born in Ireland, by Trade a Ropemaker.

ADAM M'CAIN, born in New-York, 5 Feet 9 Incehs high, fair Complexion, short brown Hair.

Of Capt. DEGARMO'S Company.

JOHN GRIXIN, aged 26 Years, born in Old England, 5 Feet 6 Inches high, brown Complexion, grey Eyes, light Hair.

JAMES ANNEN, aged 19 Years, born New-York, by Trade a Cooper, 5 Feet 6 Inches high, fair Complexion, black Hair, black Eyes.

PETER M'ENTIRE, aged 20 Years, born in Scotland, Labourer, 5 Feet 7 Inches high, black Hair, dark Complexion, grey Eyes.

HENRY HAZARD, born in Ireland, Mariner, 5 Feet 5 Inches high, dark brown Hair, fair Complexion, black Eyes.

JOHN CHANDLER, born in England, black Hair, dark Complexion, black Eyes.

All the above Deserters had on when they went away their Regimentals. Any Person taking up any of them, and secures them in any of his Majesty's Goals, shall receive from the Commanding Officer of New-York Troops, *Forty Shillings*, Reward.

WILLIAM HASLIP, born in Old England, 5 Feet 8 Inches high, light colour'd Hair, blue Eyes, round Visage, fair Complexion, of Ray's Company.

JOHN STEUART, born in Ireland, 5 Feet 8 Inches high, black Hair, sore Eyes, dark Complexion, thin Visage.

FELIX QUIN, born in New-England, 5 Feet 9 Inches high, sandy Complexion, blue Eyes.

JOSEPH WHITE, born in Old France, 5 Feet 10 Inches high, dark Complexion, black Hair, black Eyes, speaks much upon the French Accent, of Capt. White's Company.

NICHOLAS CURTEE, born in Old France, 5 Feet 5 Inches high, dark Complexion, black Hair, black Eyes, speaks much upon the French Accent.

PETER DENNISTON, born in Ireland, by Trade a Labourer, 5 Feet 8 Inches high, fair ruddy Complexion, short dark brown Hair, blue Eyes, round Visage.

OLIVER WESTOVER, by Trade a Blacksmith, born in New-Jersey, 5 Feet 9 Inches high, fair Complexion, short black Hair, Round Visage, brown Eyes.

JAMES THOMPSON, born in Old England, 5 Feet 10 Inches high, fair Complexion, black Hair, black Eyes, thin Visage, a Blemish in one of his Eyes.

THOMAS NORTON, by Trade a Mariner, 5 Feet 9 Inches high, born in Old England, brown Hair, brown Eyes, round Visage, of Capt. Grant's Company.

The New-York Gazette, May 21, 1764; May 28, 1764. See *The New-York Mercury*, May 21, 1764.

DESERTED from the New-York Troops, commanded by Major WILLIAM W. HOGAN, Esq: at Schenectady. Of Capt. Richard Rea's Company, Abraham Suthard, aged 30 Years, 5 Feet 10 Inches high, born in New-Jersey, dark short Hair. William Haislip, born in Old England, 5 Feet 8 Inches high, light coloured Hair, blue Eyes, round Visage, fair Complexion. John Stewart, born in Ireland, 5 Feet 8 Inches high, black Hair, sore Eyes, dark Complexion, thin Visage. Felix Quin, born in New-England, 5 Feet 9 Inches high, sandy Hair, fair Complexion, blue Eyes. Of Capt. Grant's Company, Peter Thorn, born in Dutchess County, 5 Feet 10 Inches high, dark Complexion, dark brown Hair, blue Eyes. Thomas Norton, by Trade a Mariner, 5 Feet 9 Inches high, born in Old England, brown Hair, brown Eyes, round Visage. Of Capt. Dawson's Company, John Falkner, born in Ireland, 5 Feet 7 Inches high, brown Complexion, dark brown Hair, aged 25 Years. John Welsh, born in New-York, 23 Years old, 5 Feet 6 Inches high, brown Complexion, blue Eyes, brown Hair, a Scar upon his Forehead. John Palmer, born in Old England, 42 Years of Age, 5 Feet 7 Inches high, dark coloured Hair, blue Eyes. Roger Giddons, born in New-Jersey, 5 Feet 8 Inches high, light coloured Hair, blue Eyes. Of Capt. White's Company, George Vardee, 5 Feet 8 Inches high, born in Old England, 25 Years of Age, fair Complexion, short dark brown curled Hair. Thomas Jorden, 5 Feet 10 Inches high, 37 Years of Age, dark Complexion, a curled Wig, or short Hair, born in Ireland, by Trade a Rope Maker. Adam Mc. Cain, born in New-York, 5 Feet 9 Inches high, fair Complexion, blue Eyes, short brown Hair. Joseph White, born in Old France, 5 Feet 10 Inches high, dark Complexion, black Hair, black Eyes, speaks much upon the French Accent. Nicholas Curle, born in Old France, 5 Feet 5 Inches high, dark Complexion, black Hair, black Eyes, speaks much upon the French Accent. Peter Dennison, born in Ireland, by Trade a Labourer, 5 Feet 8 Inches high, fair, rudy Complexion, short dark brown Hair, blue Eyes, round Visage. Oliver Westover, by Trade a Blacksmith, born in New-Jersey, 5 Feet 9 Inches high, fair Complexion, short black Hair, Round Visage, brown Eyes. James Thompson, born in Old England, 5 Feet 10 Inches high, fair Complexion, black Hair, black Eyes, thin Visage, a Blemish in one of his Eyes. Of Capt. Degarmo's Company. John Grizin, aged 26 Years, born in Old England, 5 Feet 6 Inches high, brown Complexion, grey Eyes, light coloured Hair. James Annen, aged 19 Years, born in New-York, by Trade a Cooper, 5 Feet 6 Inches high, fair Complexion, black Hair, black Eyes. Peter Mc.Entire, aged 20 Years, born in Scotland, a Labourer, 5 Feet 7 Inches high, black Hair, dark Complexion, grey Eyes. Henry Hazard, born in Ireland, a Mariner, 5 Feet 5 Inches high, dark brown Hair, fair Complexion, black Eyes. John Chandler, born in England, black Hair, dark Complexion, black Eyes. All the above Deserters had on when they went away their Regimentals. Any Person taking up any of them, and secures them in any of his Majesty's Goals, shall receive from the Commanding Officer of New-York Troops, Forty Shillings, Reward.

The New-York Mercury, May 21, 1764. See *The New-York Gazette*, May 21, 1764.

RAN-away from the Subscriber, a Negro Man, named Sharp, is about 5 Feet 7 Inches high, well-set, and a good Countenance: He was dressed in a red Jacket, blue Breeches, and white+ Stockings when he went off. Whoever secures the above Negro, and gives Notice thereof, shall have a Reward of Four Pounds,
          paid by JOHN REID.
                        Beaver street, New-York, May 21, 1764.
The New-York Mercury, May 21, 1764; May 28, 1764.

RAN away, *on Monday the 28th of May last, from the Subscriber, in New-York, an Irish Servant Man, named John Read; aged about 20; 5 Feet 8 or 9 Inches high; wears his own dark brown Hair; is of a fair Complexion, and walks limping, owing to Rheumatick Pains in the great Toe of his Right Foot. Had on when he went away, a light colour'd napt Jacket, a white Cloth Breeches grease on the Knees, which has a brown colour'd Piece of Cloth as a Patch on the Seat of it; an old Felt Hat; has Yarn Stockings; Brass Buckles, and a good Pair of Shoes. He is full of Talk, and has much of the Brogue, and seemingly has been well educated. Whoever secures him so that his Master may have him again, shall have FIVE POUNDS Reward, and reasonable Charges*

     paid by DANIEL WIGGINS.
  The New-York Gazette, June 4, 1764; June 11, 1764; June 25, 1764.

RUN-away from the Subscriber, on the 24th Instant May, a Negro Man, named Emanuel; Speaks broken English, is a lusty likely Negro Fellow, very black, about 22 Years of Age. Had on when he went away, a brown colour'd Cloth Coat double breasted, short brown Vest, light grey Breeches, old Stockings and Shoes with large brass Buckles, small brim'd Hat, Check Shirt. Whoever takes up, and secures said Negro Man, so that his Master may have him again, shall receive Three Dollars Reward, if taken on this Island, and Six if taken out of the Province, and all reasonable Charges,
     paid by THOMAS IVERS.
N. B. All Masters of Vessels and others, are forbid to harbour or carry off said Negro Man, as they may depend on being prosecuted according to Law.
 The New-York Gazette, June 4, 1764.

RUN away on the 22d of January last from the Subscriber, living in the County of Burlington, a Dutch Servant Man, named Joseph Bayard, about 21 Years of Age, and about 5 Feet 5 or 6 Inches high: Had on when he went away, an old Beaver Hat, an old brown Broadcloth Coat, new Swanskin Jacket, good Leather Breeches, a white Shirt, blue Worsted Stockings, and old Shoes or new Pumps; but it is very likely he has chang'd all or most of his Dress: He has served a Time with Joseph Taylor, near Monmouth Court-House, and if he has not chang'd his Name, may shew his old Indenture for a Pass; and its believ'd he has worked near a Month with George Garrison, on Staten-Island, by the Name of David McConney, and went from there to New-York. He is a well set down-looking Fellow, and remarkable for looking red about the Eyes, and has a Scar which causes something of a Bunch on the out-side of one of his Legs. Whoever takes up and secures said Servant in any of his Majesty's Gaols, so that his Master may have him again, shall have Five Pounds Reward, and reasonable
    Charges paid by JOB LIPPINCOTT. June 2, 1764.
 The New-York Gazette, June 11, 1764; June 18, 1764; July 2, 1764.

DESERTED from his Majesty's 44th Regiment of Foot, George Brewin, a private Soldier in Capt. Thomas Falconer's Company, 5 Feet 8 1-2 Inches high without Shoes, about 32 Years of Age, dark Complexion, long Visage, dark brown Eyes, black Hair, born in the County of Roscommon, by Trade a Sawyer.

As Likewise John Farrel, a private Soldier, in Capt. Charles Davers's Company, 5 Feet 7 Inches high, without Shoes, about 31 Years of Age, dark Complexion, long Visage, grey Eyes, black Hair, born in the County of Derry, by Calling a Labourer.

The above Men deserted at Albany, the 8th of May, 1764, when on Command with Ensign Harper, of said Regiment. Whoever apprehends the above Deserters, and delivers him or them to any Officer, Civil or Military, shall receive 20s. Sterl. Reward,

THOMAS EYRE, Lt. 44th Regt.

Crown-Point, May 20, 1764.

The New-York Mercury, June 11, 1764; June 18, 1764; July 2, 1764.

RUN away from WILLIAM Douglass, of Staten-Island, a Negro Man named GEORGE, aged about 21 Years, near 5 Feet 10 Inches high, slinder built, talks a good deal upon the New-England Accent; large Eyes with a good deal of White in them: Had on when he went away, a speckled Flannel Shirt, a Pair of twill'd Bagging Trowsers piec'd, a Pair of black Stockings, new Pumps with carved Silver Buckles, a homespun brown upper Jacket, and a red Waistcoat without Sleeves under, lin'd with buff-colour'd Flannel, a Felt Hat not half worn. Any Person taking up, and securing the above Negro in any Gaol, so that his Master can have him again, shall receive the Sum of Forty Shillings, and all reasonable Charges,
    paid by me WILLIAM DOUGLASS,
           living on Staten-Island.

The New-York Gazette, June 11, 1764.

Philadelphia, June 11, 1764.

RUN away last Night from the Snow Pitt, two Servant men; the one named Patrick Thompson, remarkable for a Hair Lip, and a great Stoppage in his Speech, bred a Tallow-chandler, about 24 Years of Age, fair complexion, 5 Feet 10 Inches high; had on a light coloured Coat, and a short brown Wig. The other named William Donnavan, of a dark complexion, wears his own Hair tied behind; had on a blue Cloth Coat and white Shirt; about 5 Feet 6 Inches high, 28 Years of Age. It is probable they may take the Road to New-York, as Thompson said he had some Relations there. Whoever takes up and secures both or either of said Servants, shall have forty shillings Reward for each, with reasonable Charges, paid by Captain Baily, on board the Snow off Market-street Wharff, or by

CONYNGHAM and NESBITT.

The Pennsylvania Gazette, June 14, 1764; June 21, 1764. See *The Pennsylvania Journal; and Weekly Advertiser*, June 14, 1764, for both. See *The Pennsylvania Gazette,* July 10, 1766, and *The New-York Mercury,* July 28, 1766, for Thompson.

June 14.

RUN away, on Sunday Night last, from the Snow Pitt, two servant men; the one named Patrick Thompson, remarkable for a hairlip and a great stoppage in his speech, bred a Tallow chandler, about twemty four years of age, fair complexion, 5 feet 10 inches high; had on a light coloured coat and a short brown wig. The other named William Donnavan, of a dark complexion, wears his own hair tied behind, had on a blue cloth coat and white shirt; about 5 feet 6 inches high, aged twenty eight years: Its probable they may take the road to New-York, as Thompson said he had some Relations there. Whoever takes up and secures both or either of said Servants, shall have FORTY SHILLINGS Reward for each, with reasonable charges paid by Capt. Baily, on board the Snow off Market-street wharf,
    or by CONYNGHAM and NESBITT.

The Pennsylvania Journal; and Weekly Advertiser, June 14, 1764; June 21, 1764; June 28, 1764; July 12, 1764; July 26, 1764. See *The Pennsylvania Gazette,* June 14, 1764, for both. See *The Pennsylvania Gazette,* July 10, 1766, and *The New-York Mercury,* July 28, 1766, for Thompson.

RAN-*away on Tuesday Morning last, the* 12*th* JUNE, *from* JOHN LASHER, *of this City, a Negro Lad about 15 Years of Age, but has something of the yellow Cast; he is well set for his Age, tho' short; and has at the back Part of his Head, a Sore something like a Scald, where there is no Hair, and he wears a Cap on Account thereof. Had on when he went away, a green Jacket, a brown Pair of Breeches, had Stockings with him but their Colour is uncertain, has middling Shoes, and an half-worn Beaver Hat. He speaks both English and Dutch.*

Whoever takes up and secures the said Lad, so that his Master may have him again, shall have Twenty Shillings *Reward if taken in Town, and* Forty Shillings *if out of it,*
   paid by JOHN LASHER.

Commanders of Vessels, and others, are forbid to employ or carry him off the Island.

The New-York Gazette, June 18, 1764.

RAN away on Sunday the 12th June, from Johannes Van Waganen, on Staten-Island, a lusty Negro Man, about 5 Feet high, named JACK; Coromante born, has the usual Negro Cuts on his Cheeks, being full faced, and has a sore Finger. Took with him a bluish grey colour'd Coat, a blue Jacket, a red Pair of Breeches, and a Pair of Trowsers. Whoever apprehends

said Negro, so that his Master may have him again, shall have Forty Shillings Reward, and reasonable Charges,
> paid by   Johannes Van Waganen.

N. B. He formerly belonged to Abraham Bush, of Rye. He has been used to the Sea, therefore all Masters of Vessels are forbid carrying him off at their Peril.

The New-York Gazette, June 18, 1764; July 9, 1764.

RUN-away, Yesterday, from on board the Snow Prince of Wales, Robert Wilson, Master, a Redemptioner, named Ronald Donnaldson, of a fair Complexion, 23 Years old, about 5 Feet 6 Inches high: Had on when he went away, a dark grey Coat, Nankeen Waistcoat, and was pitted with the Small-Pox. Run-away at the same Time, a Servant Man named Hugh Daniel, has a down Look, and of a dark Complexion: Had on when he went away, a brown Jacket, and a flowered one under it; had short black Hair: They are both Sailors, and are supposed to be gone towards Philadelphia. Whoever takes up and secures the said Run aways, so that they may be had again, shall have 40s. Reward for each, and all reasonable Charges,
> paid by   Greg, Cunningham, and Co.   June 18.

The New-York Mercury June 25, 1764; July 2, 1764.

RUN *away from Daniel Campbell, of Schenectady, and County of Albany, an indented Servant Man, named Daniel Baily: He is 19 Years and 6 Months old, about 5 Feet 7 Inches high, well set, whitish colour'd Hair, which he wears hanging down about his Shoulders: He is very pale in the Face, vastly full of Freckles, and was born on Long-Island: When he went off he had with him a green Coat and Waist Coat, with yellow Buttons, lined with green Shaloon, black breeches, turn'd Pumps, a Pair of mixed Silk and Worsted Stockings, square Brass Shoe Buckles; one white Shirt, and one check ditto, an old Beaver Hat, which he generally wears uncock'd: He has likewise with him, a Gun, and a Pair of old Saddle-Bags. He left this Place the King's Birth-Night, in Company with one John Grannis, a Carpenter, who also ran away from his Employ. It's thought they took the Road towards New-Haven, in Connecticut, where the said Grannis inform'd he lived at. Whoever takes up and secures the said Baily, so that he may be had again, shall receive £. 3 New-York Currency, Reward, and all reasonable Charges,*
> paid by   H. Gaine, or   DANIEL CAMPBELL.

Schenectady, June 11.

The New-York Mercury June 25, 1764; July 2, 1764; July 9, 1764.

DESERTED

FROM His Majesty's 44th Regiment of Foot, and in Lieut. Colonel William Eyrs's Company, JOHN SMITH, private Soldier & Muscianer, aged 24 Years, 5 Feet 8 Inches high, without Shoes, brown Complection, long Visage, grey Eyes, brown Hair, very much mark'd with the Small Pox, thin Made, straight Body and Limbs, walks with a genteel Air, Plays extraordinary well on the Bassoon, and likewise on the Violen; had on when he went off, a green Frock, trim'd with plate Buttons, scarlet Waistcoat and Breeches, and a new beaver Hatt, with a very narrow Brim. Whoever apprehends the said Deserter and delivers him to any Officer, Civil or Military, so as he may be brought to the Regiment shall receive Twenty Shillings Sterling Reward, over and above the Act of Parliament.

   THO's EYRS, Lt. 44th Regt. Commanding at Crown-Point,
               Crown-Point, 1st June 1764.

The New-London Gazette, June 29, 1764.

DESERTED from the PENNSYLVANIA REGIMENT, since the First of July Instant, the following Soldiers, viz.

  From Capt. JOHN WEBB'S Company... Reuben Halbert, born in York Government, 16 Years of Age, five Feet six Inches, brown Complexion, a Farmer....

  Whoever takes up and secures the said Deserters, or either of them, in any of the Goals of this Province, or brings them to the Regiment, shall have THREE POUNDS Reward for each of them,
     paid by JAMES YOUNG,
       Commissary of the Musters, P. F.

The Pennsylvania Gazette, July 19, 1764.

Broke Bridewell last Night, a Negro Man, named Jacob, belonging to Mr. George Wray of Albany. He is about 24 Years of Age, has lately had the Small-Pox, and is very much Pock-broken, 5 Feet 6 Inches 3-4 high without Shoes, speaks good English, some French, a little Spanish, but little or no Dutch: he has a Scar on the right Side of his Forehead, another on the left Temple, both just on the Edge of his Hair, and another on the Crown or his Head, his Cheek Bones, crooked Legs, hangs down his Head, and stoops forward in walking; had on a green Pea Jacket, and large Silver Buckles in his Shoes. Whoever takes him up, and will convey him to his Master in Albany or to Edes and Gill in Boston, shall have TWO DOLLARS Reward, and all reasonable Charges paid. All Masters of Vessels and others are hereby cautioned against harbouring concealing or carrying off said Negro on Penalty of the Law.

The Boston Gazette, and Country Journal, July 23, 1764. See *The New-York Mercury*, July 4, 1763, *The New-York Mercury*, February 27, 1764, and *The Boston Gazette, and Country Journal*, March 5, 1764.

RAN-away on Wednesday the 18th Instant, from JOSEPH ANTHONY, of Courtlandt's Manor, a Negro Man, named JACK, is very black, has no front upper Teeth, and talks good English. Had on when he went away, a Soldier's old red Jacket, check Shirt, an old Pair of Buckskin Breeches, with Ozenbrig Petticoat Trowsers over them. He is supposed to be gone to the House of Mr. John Coomb's, at Jamaica, on Long-Island; or otherwise to Mr. Palmer's, at Whiteplains, Westchester County, from each of whom he has been sold. Captains of Vessels are desired to be careful in not carrying him away; and Feryman forbid to carry him across Ferries; as they must answer the Damages. Whoever takes up and secure the said Negro, so that his Master may have him again, shall have FORTY SHILLINGS Reward, and reasonable Charges
          paid by   JOSEPH ANTHONY.
The New-York Gazette, July 23, 1764.

RUN-Away *from the Subscriber, on Sunday the 15th inst. July, an indented Servant, named* JOHN HARDIC, *a Joiner and Carpenter by Trade, who serv'd his Time with his Father, in Great Poultney-street, London; he is about 5 Feet, 8 or 9 Inches high, a thin pale-faced down-looking Fellow, about 22 or 23 Years of Age, with short Hair; had on when he went away, a dark olive colour'd corded Fustian Coat and Breeches, a Nankeen Waistcoat, white ribb'd cotton Stockings, a pair of Steel Shoe-Buckles, plated with Silver, and a light colour'd Surtout Coat. Whoever takes up and secures the said Servant, in any Goal, or delivers him to his Master, shall have* FIVE POUNDS *Reward,*
          paid by   CHRISTOPHER BLUNDELL, *in New-York.*
All Commanders of Vessels, and others are forbid harbouring, employing, or carrying him off at their Peril.   New-York, July 23, 1764.
The New-York Gazette, July 23, 1764; July 30, 1764.

DESERTED from his Majesty's 44th Regiment of Foot, William Goodchild, of General Abercromby's Company, about 33 Years of Age, 5 Feet 8 Inches and three-fourths high, without Shoes, fair Complexion, long Visage, blue Eyes, black Hair, born in Hereford, in Old England, by Trade a Taylor. Whoever takes up and secures the above Deserter, in any of his Majesty's Goals, shall have Twenty Shillings Reward, over and above what is allowed by Act of Parliament.

The New-York Mercury, July 23, 1764.

Livingston's Manor, July 12, 1764.
Five Pounds Reward.

RAN-away from his Master, Jacob Platneer, in the County of Albany, on the 3d Instant, a NEGRO MAN, named JACK, about 35 Years of Age, of a middling stature, has a Scar of a Bullet on his left Leg: He had on when he went away, a stript home-spun Jacket, a Shirt of home-spun Linen, and short Breeches of the same. Whoever will take up said Negro, and secure him, so that his Master may have him again, shall receive the above Reward, and all necessary Charges
paid by me   JACOB PLATNEER.

The New-York Gazette, July 30, 1764; August 6, 1764; August 13, 1764; August 20, 1764.

RUN-away, on Sunday the 15th of July, from Andrew Myer, of New-York, a Negro Man, named Charles, about 5 Feet 9 Inches high, of a black Complexion, and a little pitted with the Small-Pox; he is very remarkable for his white Teeth, and on his Breast he is marked in character Letters, P. Lecount: Had on when he went away, a brown Thickset Coat, a black Silk Vest, a Pair of black Manchester Velvet Breeches, and a good Felt Hat, with a Brass Button in it. Whoever secures the said Negro, so that his Master may have him again, shall receive a Reward of Five Dollars, if taken in this Province; and Six if in any other Province, and all reasonable
Charges, paid by   ANDREW MYER.

The New-York Mercury, July 30, 1764. See *The New-York Mercury*, June 30, 1766, and *The New-York Gazette, and Weekly Post-Boy*, October 16, 1766.

RUN-away from the Brigantine Neptune, William Cockran, Commander, the 26th at Night, an indented Servant, named James Dunavan, about 18 or 19 Years of Age, about 5 Feet 6 or 7 Inches high, wears his own Hair, born in Ireland: Had on when he went away, a blue pea Jacket, and waistcoat of the same. Whoever takes up said Servant, and brings him to Mr. David Van Horne, of the City, Merchant, shall have Four Dollars Reward, and all reasonable Charges.   July 30.

The New-York Mercury, July 30, 1764; August 13, 1764; August 20, 1764.

New-York, August 13, 1764.

RUN-away, on Saturday Night the 4th Inst, from on board the Brigantine Fanny, Thomas Stevenson, Master, a Negro named Robbin, of a yellow Complexion; he has a Wen on the middle Joint of his Right Fore-Finger,

and a Scar across his Throat, where he attempted to cut it; has lost one of his Fore-Teeth, and is pitted a little with the Small-Pox: Had on when he want away, a Sailor's old Frock and Trowsers, a dirty Handkerchief about his Head, and is bare footed. Whoever secures the said Negro, and brings him on board the said Brigantine, now lying in Rotton-Row, shall receive a Reward of Thirty Shillings, and all reasonable Charges
   paid by THOMAS STEVENSON.
  N. B. All Persons are forewarned not to harbour, carry off or employ said Negro; if they do, that will be prosecuted according to Law.
The New-York Mercury, August 13, 1764.

          East-Hampton, August 10, 1764.
RUN-away from the Subscriber, living at East-Hampton, at the East End of Long-Island, a Mullatto Fellow named Sharp or Sharper; a short, thick, well-set Fellow, and is very much pitted with the Small-Pox: Had on, a short blue Jacket, double breasted; Check Trowsers, and blue Plush Breeches under them, and a Sailor's Hat. Whoever takes up and secures said Fellow, so that his Master may have him again, shall have Five Dollars Reward, and all reasonable Charges,
   paid by THOMAS TILLINGHAST.
The New-York Mercury, August 20, 1764; August 27, 1764.

RUN-away, from the Subscriber, on Tuesday last the 21st Instant, a High Dutch Servant Man, named John Seymour, 36 Years old, and about 5 Feet 3 or 4 Inches high, red short Hair, wore a Cap, and was od a ruddy Complexion: Had on when he went away, a light coloured Camblet Jacket, and an Ozenbrigs Frock under it, long Trowsers of Ozenbrigs. Who ever takes up and secures said Servant, so that he may be had again, shall receive Five Dollars Reward, and all reasonable Charges,
   paid by Capt. Joseph French,
     at Henry Carmer's, or, JOHN M'CLEAN.
The New-York Mercury, August 27, 1764; September 3, 1764; September 10, 1764.

STOLEN out of the House of Abraham Sarzadas, in Oswego street, Saturday morning last the First Instant, the following Wearing Apparel, supposed to be stolen by one Mary Dennis, by which Name she hired herself a Servant to Mr. Sarzedas about a Week past, but is known to some by the Name of Mary Hughes, and others Mary M'Griggor; she is a pretty bulky Woman of low Stature, much freckled in the Face, and very black Eyes: Had on when she went away, a short Calico Gown, and a blue stript homespun Petticoat. The things she has taken are, 1 Chintz Gown, 1 blue

and white Calico ditto, 2 Holland Shifts, 1 Holland Apron, 1 Minionet and 1 Gauze Apron, 1 black and 1 white silk Hat, 1 black sattin Cardinal trimm'd with Ermin, 1 new black Barcelona Handkerchief, 1 Yard new cambrick, 2 pair thread hose, 1 pair new pockets, 1 pair womens black shamoy shoes, and one pair large open work'd buttons, and sundry other things. Whoever takes up and secures the said Mary Dennis, so that the goods, or any part of them maybe recovered, shall has 40s. Reward, and all reasonable Charges   N. York, Sept. 3d, 1764.
       paid by   MOSES M. HAYS.

The New-York Gazette, September 3, 1764; September 10, 1764; September 17, 1764.

Three Pounds Reward,
RAN-away from the Subscriber, on Monday Afternoon, the 27th of August, an indented Servant Man named EDWARD MARTIN, about 32 Years of Age, born in Greenwich near London, a Black-smith and Farrier by Trade, about 5 Feet 7 Inches high, a square Set Fellow, Pale faced, and pitted with the Small-pox, has a Mark on his left Cheek near his Nose, very apt to get in Liquor, forward and talkative; had on when he went away, a Check Shirt, a pair of dirty Buck-skin Breeches, ribb'd mottled worsted Stockings, had a Pair of close work'd Silver Buckles in his Shoes, and wore a good dark brown Cut Wig. It's not well known what upper Clothes he may have on, as he went off and left his Coat, Waistcoat and Hat, where he was at Work; he is well known in and about the City, at most Gentlemen and Innkeeper's Stables, as Horse Doctor. He was spoke with on Thursday last, about 30 Miles from New-York, on the New-England Road; had then on, an old green Jacket, was in Company with a Man in Sailor's dress, and is supposed to be gone towards Boston.—Whoever takes him up and delivers him to his Master at New-York, or Secures him in any Goal, giving Notice as above, or to Hugh Gaine, shall receive Three Pounds Reward, and all reasonable Charges.   New-York, 3d September, 1764.
       WILLIAM WOOD.

The New-York Gazette, September 3, 1764; September 10, 1764; September 17, 1764; *The New York Mercury,* September 3, 1764. Minor differences between the papers. See *The Boston Gazette, and Country Journal,* September 17, 1764, *The Newport Mercury,* October 8, 1764, and *The New-York Mercury,* December 3, 1764.

RUN-away from her Master, JOHN FARRELL, at Stone-hook, in the County of Albany, about four Weeks ago, a tall likely Negro Wench named JEAN, round visag'd, her Hands a little crooked, on each Temple a square Mark. Whoever takes up and secures the said Negro Wench, so that her

Master may have her again, shall have Forty Shillings Reward, and all necessary Charges   Stone-hook, August 14, 1764.
        paid by me   JOHN FARRELL.
The New-York Gazette, September 3, 1764; September 10, 1764; September 17, 1764; October 22, 1764. See *The New-York Mercury*, September 3, 1764.

RAN-away from her Master, John Farrel, at Stone-Hook, in the County of Albany, about four Weeks ago, a tall Negro Wench, named Jane, round Visage, her Hands a little crooked, on each Temple a square Mark: Whoever takes up and secures the said Negro, so that her Master may have her again, shall have Forty Shillings Reward, and all necessary Charges
        paid by me   John Farrell, or
        Joseph Greswold, Distiller, in Pearl-street, New-York.
The New-York Mercury, September 3, 1764; September 10, 1764. See *The New-York Gazette*, September 3, 1764,

RAN AWAY on Friday Night, the 24th of August last, from Johannes Veeder, of Coknawaga on the Mohawk's River: A Negro Man, named CAESAR, about 32 Years of Age, spoke broken English, Low and High Dutch, is remarkable for being prick'd with Gun-Powder, like Diamonds on his fore-Head, and down each Cheek: Had on when he went away, an old Homespun Coat, white Linen Drawers, two speckled Shirts, a coarse Hat, Shoes and Stockings. Whoever takes up and secures the above Negro Man, and gives Notice, shall receive Forty Shillings, and reasonable Charges,
        to be paid either by me or
        Simon J. Veeder, at Albany.
The New-York Mercury, September 10, 1764; September 17, 1764; September 24, 1764.

RUN-away from Stephen Forman, a Negro Man named JOE; he is of middle Stature, pretty well set, pock mark'd, yellowish Complexion, speaks good English and Dutch; he ran away some time ago, and it is said was seen in Town last Week; when seen last he had on, a blue Jacket and Sailors Hat; it is supposed he has a Pass, and says he is a free Negro: His Ears are very small, and imagine they have been pared, as it's said he was once cropt for Roguery. Whoever secures him, shall have Forty Shillings Reward, and all reasonable Charges,   September 3.
        paid by   STEPHEN FORMAN.
The New-York Mercury, September 10, 1764.

£.3 New-York Currency Reward.

RAN away from the Subscriber in New-York, on Monday the 27th of August, an indented Servant Man named Edward Martin, about 32 Years of Age, born in Greenwich near London, a Blacksmith & Farrier by Trade, about 5 Feet 7 Inches high, a square well-set Fellow, pale faced, and pitted with the Small-Pox, has a Mark on his left Cheek near his Nose, and several Cuts on his Head: very apt to get in Liquor, forward & talkative, particularly about doctoring Horses: Had on when he went away a Check Shirt, a pair of dirty Buck-skin Breeches, ribb'd mottled worsted Stockings, had a Pair of close work'd Silver Buckles in his Shoes, and wore a good dark brown Cut Wig; it is not well known what upper Cloaths he may have on, as he went off and left his Coat, Waistcoat and Hat where he was at Work. He was spoke with on the Thursday following, about 30 Miles from New-York, on the New-England Road; had then on, an old green Jacket, was in Company with a Man in Sailor's dress, and is supposed to be gone towards Boston, or New-London. As he is a good Horse Doctor it's suppos'd he'll made Application to some Smith for Work, and to Innkeepers in want of a Farrier, and will perhaps change his Name. All Blacksmiths, Innkeepers, and others, are forwarn'd from harbouring or employing said Servant. And whoever apprehends and delivers him to Messiers Eales and Gill, at Boston, or secures him in any Goal, giving Notice to the Subscriber, or to Hugh Gaine, Printer in New-York, shall receive the above Reward, and all reasonable Charges.   New-York, 3d Sept. 1764.
WILLIAM WOOD.

The Boston Gazette, and Country Journal, September 17, 1764; September 24, 1764; October 1, 1764; October 8, 1764; October 22, 1764. See *The New-York Gazette*, September 3, 1764, *The Newport Mercury*, September 24, 1764, and *The New-York Mercury*, December 3, 1764.

RAN-AWAY on Monday the 27th of August last, from Casparis Coughlin of Orange-Town, in the County of Orange, a Guinea Negro Man, named Tom Well; about 5 Feet 6 or 7 Inches high, speaks broken English, and has a down Look; is Pock broken, full faced, and had on when he went away a black Cloth under Jacket, and a gray home-spun Jacket over it, a tow Shirt, striped Linsey Woolsey Trowsers, an old Felt Hat, no Stockings or Shoes. Whoever takes up said Negro Man and secures him, so that his Master may have him again, shall have Thirty Shillings Reward, and all reasonable Charges paid by. CASPARIS COUGHLIN.
Orange-Town, September 11, 1764
The New-York Gazette, September 17, 1764.

RUN away on the 21st of August last, from the Subscriber, living in New-York, an Apprentice Lad, named William Seaman, about 18 Years of Age, about 5 Feet 6 Inches high, smooth fac'd, strait brown Hair, slender built; was seen on board a Schooner the 22d of August, lying at Beekman's Slip, bound to Seabrook, in Connecticut, New-England. Had on when on board said Schooner, a new Check Shirt, a Silk Handkerchief round his Head, a blue Jacket and old Leather Breeches or Trowsers, but it is likely he has changed all or most of his Dress: He was in Connecticut in September 1762, and is supposed to be gone there again; is by Trade a Gunsmith. And as he has run me in Debt for Goods, and attempted to borrow Money in my Named, whoever takes up said Apprentice, and Secures him in any of his Majesty's Gaol, so that his Master may have him again, shall have Three Pounds Reward, if taken out of this Province, if in it, Forty Shillings, and reasonable Charges,

   paid by EDWARD ANNELY.

The New-York Mercury, September 17, 1764; September 24, 1764; *The New-York Gazette*, October 8, 1764; October 22, 1764; October 29, 1764.

Three Pounds N. York Currency Reward.

R*AN away from the Subscriber in New-York, on Monday the* 27*th of August, an indented Servant Man, named Edward Martin, about* 32 *Years of Age, born in Greenwich near London, a Blacksmith and Farrier by Trade, about* 5 *Feet* 7 *Inches high, a square well-set Fellow, pale faced, and pitted with the Small-Pox; has a Mark on his left Cheek near his Nose, and several Cuts on his Head; very apt to get in Liquor, forward & talkative, particularly about doctoring Horses: Had on when he went away a Check Shirt, a pair of dirty Buckskin Breeches, ribb'd mottled worsted Stockings, had a Pair of close work'd Silver Buckles in his Shoes, and a good dark brown cut Wig; it is not known what upper Cloaths he may have on, as he went off and left his Coat, Waistcoat and Hat where he was at Work. He was spoke with on the Thursday the* 30*th of August following, two Miles beyond New-Rochell, on the New-England Road; had then on a green Jacket and a pair of short Trowsers;, was in Company with a Man in a Sailor's dress; and is supposed to come to some Seaport in New England, where he may apply to Persons in Want of a Farrier, or endeavour to get on board some Vessel bound outwards, and will perhaps change his Name. All Masters of Vessels and others, are forewarned from employing or carrying off the said Servant. And whoever takes him up, and delivers him to the Printer hereof, or to his Master, or to Hugh Gaine, in New-York, or secures him in any Gaol, giving Notice thereof, shall receive Three Pounds New-York Currency Reward, and all reasonable Charges,*

paid by WILLIAM WOOD.
The Newport Mercury, September 24, 1764; October 1, 1764; October 8, 1764; October 15, 1764. See *The New-York Gazette*, September 3, 1764; *The Boston Gazette, and Country Journal*, September 17, 1764, and *The New-York Mercury*, December 3, 1764.

TAKEN up on Staten-Island, and now in Gaol at Richmond-Town, a Negro Fellow that appears to be about 30 Years of Age, is slim bodied, and has the usual Negro Cuts in his Face; says his name is MINGO; has been about two Years in the Country, speaks bad English;—has on a French Soldier's Coat turned up with Blue; says his Master's Name is William Bennet, and that his House was burned and he was put in Goal, and one John Abraham's took him out, with whom he lived about four Months, and then Run-away from him. The Owner can have him by applying to the Sheriff of Statten-Island, and paying the Charges.
New-York, September 17, 1764.
The New-York Gazette, September 24, 1764; October 1, 1764.

RUN-away, an Indian Wench a Slave, calls herself Mary she has been about Eight Weeks from Montreal, speaks and reads broken English, 26 Years of Age, short and thick Set; had on when she went away, a Cap with a black Ribbon tied under her Chin, wears her Hair platted, a Calico short Gound, with the colours washed out, a black Pettycoat, bare-footed, with a Rag bound round her Heel, having been hurted. Whoever secures him in any of His Majesty's Goals, or brings her to the Work-House of this City, and delivers her to Mr. Forbes, shall receive Four Dollars Reward, and all reasonable Charges paid.—N. B. All Masters of Vessels are forbid at their Peril to take her off. [October 1.]
The New-York Gazette, October 1, 1764.

RAN-away, Sunday the 23d of Sept. last, from William Goforth, of this City, Cordwainer, an Apprentice Boy named William Pelton, born in Connecticut: He is short and thick-set, and wears his Hair commonly tied, and sometimes cued. Had on when he went away, a blue Coat, a green double-breasted Jacket, a Pair of Buckskin Breeches, a Pair of white ribb'd Stockings, white Shirt, and a Castor Hat. It is supposed he took his working Cloaths with him, a Pair of wide Trowsers, and a Check Shirt. Whoever takes up the said Apprentice, and delivers him to his Master, in New-York, shall receive, if taken in this City, Forty Shillings; if taken in this Province,

out of the City, Three Pounds; and if taken out of this Province, Five Pounds, and reasonable Charges,
        paid by   WILLIAM GOFORTH.

N. B. All persons are forbid to employ the said Apprentice, or to conceal him, or to contract with him; and all Masters of Vessels are forbid carrying him off at their Peril.

The New-York Mercury, October 1, 1764; October 15, 1764.

LATELY made his Escape out of Suffolk County Gaol, on Long-Island, in the Province of New-York, a Man something less than Middle Stature, pale, and thin Vissage, pretty much poc-pitted, by Trade a Carpenter and Painter; committed by the Name of John Roberts, for Horse-stealing; at other Times went by the Name of John Jones. Whoever will take and secure the said John Roberts in any of his Majesty's Gaols, giving me Notice thereof, shall have *Five Pounds* Reward, and all reasonable Charges
        paid by me,   BENAJAH EDWARDS,
                      Keeper of Suffolk County Gaol.

The New-York Gazette, October 8, 1764; October 22, 1764; October 29, 1764. *The New-York Gazette*, March 5, 1764.

RUN-away from the Subscriber, a Negro Lad named Jack, he is about 5 Feet 7 Inches high, is of a yellowish, tawny colour, long black Hair, is marked in the Face with the Small-pox, speaks both English and Dutch very well, and plays well on the Violin, and always pretends to be a Free Man; had on when he went away, a white Swan-skin Jacket, check Shirt, a pair of long Oznabrigs Trowsers, a Beaver Hat pretty much worn. If taken on York Island 20 Shillings Reward, if out of the Island 40 Shillings for bringing him to any of his Majesty's Goals, or to his Master at Bloomendale, shall have the above Sum mentioned, and all reasonable Charges
        paid by me   GARIT COSSINE.
                    New-York, September 30, 1764.

N. B. All Masters of Vessels and others are forbid to carry him off.— He took with him Clothes which he may change.—

The New-York Gazette, October 8, 1764; October 22, 1764.

RUn-away on the 7th Inst. a Scotch Boy, named Daniel McDaniel, of about 5 Feet 4 Inches high, well set: Had on when he went away, a brown Broadcloth Coat, Leather Breeches, and a felt Hat, run-away once before, from Philadelphia, and was taken up in this City, last Spring. Whoever takes up said Lad, and secures him, so that he may be had, shall have Five

Dollars, besides all other reasonable Charges
paid by Franklin and Underhill,
living on Cannon's Dock, N. York.
The New-York Mercury, October 15, 1764.

Goshen Precinct, County of Orange, July 25, 1764.
TAKEN up, supposed to be a Run-away, a Mulatto Fellow, who calls himself Ben, talks good English, is about 18 Years of Age, and about 5 Feet 6 Inches high; has large Lips, frizzled Hair, is very broad over the Shoulders, and his Toes has been frozen: He says he is a free Man, was taken up endeavouring to cross the North River, and said he was going to the Little Nine Partners, or to Albany. The Owner of the above-described Fellow may have him again, paying Charges,
by applying to PHINEAS RUMSEY.
The New-York Mercury, October 29, 1764; November 5, 1764. See *The New-York Mercury,* November 28, 1764.

TEN POUNDS REWARD,
FOR apprehending a certain Person, called HENRY STEVENS, having carried away 52 Spanish milled Dollars, the Property of a Person who intrusted him with the Care of his Money: He came from Philadelphia last Thursday, in the Stage Boat, and absconded the same Morning, and 'tis imagined he is gone to Albany, having lately been, as he said, a Sergeant in the Army: He is about 5 Feet 7 Inches high, black hair, pretty long, tied up with a Ribbon, and had a blemish on one of his Eyes: Had on when he went away, a blue Surtout Coat, a blue undercoat, and a red Jacket. Whoever takes up and secures the said Fellow, so that the Cash may be had again, shall have the above Reward,
paid by W. Weyman. November 5.
The New-York Gazette, November 5, 1764; November 12, 1764, See *The New-York Mercury,* November 5, 1764.

Ten Pounds Reward,
FOR *apprehending a certain person, called Henry Stevens, having carried away 52 Spanish milled dollars, the property of a person who intrusted him with the care of his money: He came from Philadelphia last Thursday, in the state boat, and absconded the same morning, and 'tis imagined he is gone to Albany, having lately been, as he said, a serjeant in the army: He is about 5 feet 7 inches high, black hair, pretty long, tied up with a ribband, and had a blemish on one of his eyes: Had on when he went away, a blue surtout coat, a blue under coat, and a red jacket. Whoever takes up and*

secures the said fellow, so that the cash may be had again, shall have the above Reward,
          paid by   HUGH GAINE.
The New-York Mercury, November 5, 1764; November 12, 1764. See *The New-York Gazette*, November 5, 1764.

DESERTED the 23d Inst. from His Majesty's 55th Regiment, and Lieut. Col. Elliot's Company, lying at Albany, Edward Campbell, a private Soldier, says he was born in Scotland; but by his talking the Irish Language, is supposed to be born in Ireland; by Trade a Sadler, aged 21 Years, 5 Feet 7 Inches high, straight bodied, well limb'd, black Hair, grey Eyes, fair Complexion, full faced, has a large Scar upon the Shin of his left Leg; has been in the marine Service, and is supposed to have deserted from the Juno Frigate. He went off in a brown Great Coat, regimental Waistcoat and Buckskin Breeches. He stole from one Archibald Mc. Donald (a discharged Soldier of the said Regiment) his Discharge, and many other Things, and whose Name it it supposed he may go by. Whoever apprehends the said Deserter, and delivers him to Major Moncreiffe, at New-York, or to Ensign Bell at Albany, shall receive one Guinea Reward, over and above what is allowed by Act of Parliament.
      THOMAS BELL, Ensign to the 55th Regiment.
                                          New York, October 28.
The New-York Mercury, November 5, 1764.

RUN-away from Christopher Duyckinck, of this City, Sail-maker, in Monday the 26th of October last, a Negro Man, named Boston, is very black, and speaks good English: Had on when he went away, a brown double-breasted Jacket, white Shirt and Stockings, wide tarry Trowsers, and red Plush Breeches. Whoever takes up and secures the said Negro, so that his Master may have him again, shall have Forty Shillings Reward, and all reasonable Charges,
          paid by   CHRISTOPHER DUYCKINCK.
The New-York Mercury, November 12, 1764.

                                      New-York, November 12, 1764.
RUN-away together last Tuesday Night, from the Subscriber, two Negro Men, one named Tom, about 5 Feet 6 Inches high, well-made, and a surly looking Fellow, much pitted with the Small-Pox, and spoke very bad English: Hand on, [*sic*] or took with him, a blue Watchcoat, brown Jacket, a Pair of Buckskin Breeches, and brown Stockings. The other named Fortune, smooth-faced, very talkative, has a very large Mouth, and spoke bad English: Had on, a grey Watchcoat, brown Jacket, and brown Stockings, 17

Years old, not more than 5 Feet 4 Inches high, and well-made. Whoever takes up the said Negroes, and secures them, so that they may be had again, shall have Three Dollars for each, or Six Dollars for both, and all reasonable Charges,
    paid by WILLIAM BATES.

N. B. All Persons are hereby cautioned not to harbour or entertain the said Fellows, or either of them, on pain of incuring the Penalty of the Law, in such cases provided; and all Masters of Vessels are forbid to carry them, or either of them off, at their Peril.

The New-York Mercury, November 12, 1764.

             Roxbury, November 23, 1764.

RUN away from the Subscriber, in Roxbury, early this Morning, an Irish Servant Man, named THOMAS BLAIR, a tall thick Fellow, judg'd to be about 6 Feet high; had on when he went away, a light Bearskin Pea Jacket, a strip'd Swanskin Waistcoat, much wore, a Pair of yellow Buckskin Breeches, and Yarn Stockings, and wears his own Hair. He stole and carried off sundry Articles of English Goods, and a Pair of Boots.—He was brought from New-York to Providence, about 6 Weeks ago, and 'tis imagined he has gone that Way.—Whoever takes up said Fellow, and delivers him to me, or secures him in His Majesty's Goal in Providence, and gives me Information thereof, shall receive FIVE DOLLARS Reward, and have all reasonable Charges
    paid, by JOSHUA LORING.

The Providence Gazette; And Country Journal, November 24, 1764; December 1, 1764; January 8, 1764.

        Goshen Precinct, County of Orange, July 23, 1764.

RUN away, from the Subscriber, a Mulatto Fellow, who calls himself Ben, talks good English, is about 18 Years of Age, and about 5 Feet 6 Inches high; has large Lips, frizzled Hair, is very broad over the Shoulders, and his Toes has been frozen: He says he is a free Man, was seen as he was endeavouring to cross the North River, and said he was going to the Little Nine Partners, or to Albany. Whoever takes up, and secures the said Fellow, so that he may be had again, shall receive Five Dollars Reward,
    paid by PHINAS RUMSEY.

The New-York Mercury, November 28, 1764. See *The New-York Mercury*, October 29, 1764.

RUN away some Time in August last, from Jury Weaver, at the German Flatts, Mohawk River, a Negro Man named JACK, about 30 Years old, and near 6 Feet high: He has both his great Toes froze off;—had on when he went away, an old red Stroud Waistcoat, a pair of Buckskin Breeches,

Shoes tied with Strings, and an old Woolen Hat. Whoever takes up and secures the said Negro, so that his Master may have him again, shall receive FIVE POUNDS Reward, and all reasonable Charges
    paid by JURY WEAVER, and JOHN RAFF, at Albany,
    or WALDRON BLAU in New-York.—
N. B. All Masters of Vessels are forbid to carry him off, as they shall assuredly be prosecuted for the same.   December 3.
The New-York Gazette, December 3, 1764; December 10, 1764; January 28, 1765. See *The New-York Gazette,* November 7, 1763.

RUN away from William Holly, of Goshen, an Irish Servant Boy, named Thomas Noon, about 18 Years of Age: Had on when he went away, an old Wooll Hat with a Hole in the Crown, a light-coloured Jacket, a Pair of old Leather Breeches, and black Worsted Stockings: He is full-faced, Pock marked, red Complexion, with short yellowish Hair. Whoever takes up said Boy, so that his Master may have him again, shall have 20s. Reward, and all reasonable Charges paid, by the Printer hereof
    or WILLIAM HOLLY.
The New-York Gazette, December 3, 1764.

RAN-away, the 27th of August last, from the Subscriber in New-York, and indented Servant Man, named Edward Martin, about 32 Years of Age, from in Greenwich near London; a Blacksmith and Farrier by Trade, about 5 Feet 7 Inches high, a Square set Fellow; pale faced and pitted with the Small-Pox; has a Mark on his left Cheek, near his Nose, and several Cuts on his Head; very apt to get in Liquor, forward and talkative, particularly about doctoring of Horses: He has been seen since he Ranaway, up the Country, and then wore a green Jacket, with a white or strip'd one under it: Had on a Pair of dirty Buckskin Breeches, and short Trowsers over them, had a Pair of close worked silver Buckles in his Shoes, wore and old Hat, and a good dark cut Wig; and has been several Times since he ran-away seen in Company with a Man in a Sailor's Dress, with a green Jacket, and a Pair of long Trowsers. As he had Money with him, when he went away, its likely he has changed his Cloaths and Name, and is supposed to be some where imployed, in the Country. All Persons are forwarned from harbouring or employing the said Servant and Masters of Vessels from carrying him off. And whoever apprehends and secures him, in any Goal, and gives Notice thereof, to the Subscriber, or H. Gaine in New-York, shall receive three Pounds Reward, and all reasonable Charges,
    paid by WILLIAM WOOD.

The New-York Mercury, December 3, 1764. See *The New-York Gazette*, September 3, 1764, *The Boston Gazette, and Country Journal*, September 17, 1764, and *The Newport Mercury*, September 24, 1764.

RUN-away, on Wednesday last, the 5th instant, from on board the ship Newry, Capt. Russel, an Irish servant Man, named Patrick White, about 21 years old, supposed to be 5 feet 8 inches high, of a fair and clear complexion, has dark strait coloured hair; and a very great impediment in his speech. He went off with cloaths which he artfully afterwards changed for others; as, a blue sailors jacket, an under black waistcoat, a pair of long narrow striped trowsers, with a pair of white ribb'd stockings, and broad round pewter buckles Whoever takes up (in this City) and secures the said servant, so that his master may have him again, shall have four Dollars Reward; and if taken out of the town, and secured on like conditions, shall have five Dollars Reward, and reasonable charges
           paid by   JOSEPH WHITE, on board said ship,
           or Mr. ACHESON THOMPSON; Merchant in New-York.
The New-York Gazette, December 10, 1764; December 17, 1764.

WHEREAS on Tuesday Night the 4th of December Inst. was stolen out of the Pasture of Thomas Wright, of Westchester, and Province of New-York, a large brown Mare, about 15 Hands high, with a curled Mane and Tail, can pace and trot, and has a large Lump on here near Fore Foot, was 6 Years old last Spring. The same Night was stolen out of the Pasture of John Crane, of Westchester aforesaid, a brown Mare also, 6 Years old, 14 hands high, has a Star in her forehead, her Mane trim'd pretty far back from her Ears, a Comb-Cut on her Mane, square dock'd, a natural Pacer, and paces pretty fast. The Person who who 'tis supposed stole the above mentioned Mares, borrowed the same Day from Charles Haight, of Westchester, a small Russet Saddle, with green Plush Housing, whose name is John Rogers, taught School at Westchester, and absconded the same Night: He was seen the same Night also with one of the Mares, and 'tis supposed is gone to some of the Iron Works in New-Jersey, or this Government: The said Rogers is about 5 Feet 7 Inches high, black Hair, had very thick Legs, and said he was an Englishman: Whoever takes up the Thief with the Mares, shall have Ten Pounds Reward, or Five Pounds for any of the Mares, with the Thief, and all reasonable Charges,
           paid by   Thomas Wright, or John Crane.
The New-York Mercury, December 31, 1764.

1765

RUN-away from their Bail, in this City, last Week, a Portugueze Man, named John, and spoke pretty good English: He is a slim Fellow, and about 5 Feet 4 Inches high. The other was named Nicholas Duvell, a Frenchman, and can speak but little English; had on a Purser's Jacket and Breeches, and marbled Stockings. Whoever will take up the said Fellows, shall have two Dollars for each, or four for both,
          paid by   JAMES FORBES.
The New-York Gazette, January 7, 1765; January 14, 1765; January 21, 1765.

RUN away, from the Subscriber, at Maroneck, in Westchester County, the first Day of this Inst. January, a Negro Wench named JIN, about 20 Years old, very black, and flat-faced, was very well dressed, having on when she went away, a striped Josey, a brown homespun Gown, and a red and black Petticoat; and formerly belonged to Mr. Thomas Franklin, of this City, and supposed to be in or about the same. Whoever takes up and secures the said Wench, so that she may be had again, shall receive Forty Shillings Reward,
          from   Joseph Grigs, or JAMES HORTON, Jun.
The New-York Mercury, January 14, 1765; January 21, 1765; January 28, 1765.

RUN-*away, from his Lodgings, on Sunday the 31st Instant, a Servant Man named Henry McDonagh, a Shoemaker by Trade,* 30 *Years old, of a fair Complexion, wore his own brown Hair, was a little pitted with the Small-pox; and has on when he made his Exit, a white Fustian Coat, a striped Flannell Waistcoat, a Pair of blue Cloth Breeches, and it is supposed gone to Philadelphia.* Whoever takes up and secures said Fellow, so that he may be had again, shall receive Forty Shillings Reward, and all reasonable
          Charges paid   , by GREG, CUNNINGHAM, and Co.
The New-York Mercury, January 14, 1765; January 21, 1765; February 11, 1765.

LEFT his Master's Service the 24th of December last, an Apprentice Lad named William Morrell, 19 Years of Age, born at Newtown, on Long-Island, 5 Feet 6 Inches high, his Hair and Complexion, fair, smooth-faced, and look'd boyish; by Trade a Shoemaker; does Men's Work well and ready, speaks and laughs loud, has a lazey, clumsey walk, and a little stooping: Took nothing with him but his working Dress, consisting of a half-worn Castor Hat, light brown Wig, half-worn white Cloth Coat without Buttons, and was too short for him, a brown Sagothee double-breasted Jacket, Leather Breeches, a new Check Shirt, black Worsted Stockings, and

a Pair of Half-boots, speaks English fluent and a little Low Dutch, is obliging and good-natured, and was lately seen on Staten-Island. All Masters of Vessels are forbid to carry him off; and whoever takes up and secures the said Lad so that he may be had again, shall have THREE DOLLARS Reward, and reasonable Charges
                paid, by   JOHN CREE.
The New-York Mercury, January 21, 1765.

WHEREAS a certain John Patton, that came to these parts of the Country some Time last June from New York, and as we are informed ran away from thence considerably in Debt, and did pretend to follow the Fuller's Business at a Fulling mill belonging to Mr. George Lawson, in Cecil County, Maryland, where he run greatly in Debt, and absconded from the said Place without discharging the same; those that will take up and secure the said Patton in any Goal on the Continent, shall be rewarded with Fifteen Pounds, on giving Notice to the Subscribers. Said Patton is a Scotch man, and has been on board a Man of War, is about 5 Feet 10 Inches high, a well looking Man, wears black Hair; had on, when he went away, a half worn Fur Hat, blue Coat, light coloured Velvet Jacket, black Leather Breeches, blue Stockings, good Shoes, and rode a bay Horse, about 9 Years old, with good Saddle and Bridle; he is pretty talkative, and given to extol himself by the Way of Lying, and pretends to be a Seaman; it is supposed, he will endeavour to get on board some Vessel. Whoever secures the said John Patton, shall be entitled to the above Reward,
              paid by   THOMAS COOK, JOHN STRAWBRIDGE,
              JOHN LOCHRIDGE, and ROBERT CORRY.
N. B. All Masters of Vessels are forbid to carry him off at their Peril.
The Pennsylvania Gazette, February 28, 1765.

RUN-away, from the Subscriber, an Irish Servant Man, named John Miller, of a fair Complection, about 24 Years of Age, middle Stature, sandy Hair, has a light grey Irish Frize Coat, black satten Jacket, black Everlasting Breeches. Whoever secures the said Servant, shall have 5 Dollars Reward, so that his Master may have him again. He attended the Barr at the Ferry. All Masters of Vessels are forbid to carry him of.
              FRANCIS KOFFLER.
The New-York Mercury, March 11, 1765; March 18, 1765. See *The New-York Mercury,* November 2, 1767, and *The New-York Journal; or, the General Advertiser*, November 5, 1767.

RUN-away from the Subscriber, on Saturday the 2d inst. an Irish Servant named Robert English, indented for 7 Years: He is about 15 Years old, full-

faced, and of a good Complexion: Had on when he went away, a light coloured Coat with darn'd Buttons on the breast and Sleeves; check Shirt, and black Stockings; it is supposed that he has applied or may apply to some Master of a Vessel to carry him off, this is to caution all such from taking him on board. And any Person that secures the abovenamed English, and brings him to the Subscriber, shall have three Dollars Reward.
      ROBERT PILSON.
The New-York Mercury, March 11, 1765; March 18, 1765.

RAN *away on Saturday the 9th Instant, from the Place of her Hire in this City, an Indian Slave Wench named,* Mary, *but will probably say her Name is* Frances, *as she was formerly called; is about* 26 *Years of Age, has long black Hair, and a remarkable Scar on one of her Breasts, uncertain which, was born in* Canada, *can read English and French, tho' little of the former. Had on a black Petticoat, a short Homespun Gown. Whoever takes up the said Wench, and secures her so that she may be had again, shall have* THREE DOLLARS *Reward, and reasonable Charges. ALL Persons are forbid to harbour of conceal her; and all Masters of Vessels are strictly forbid to carry her off. Give Notice to the Printer hereof when she is apprehended and secur'd.*
The New-York Mercury, March 18, 1765; May 6, 1765.

Forty Shillings Reward.
RUN-away, on Friday the 29th ult. from the Subscriber, an indented Irish Servant Lad, named Alexander Bradburn, by Trade a Barber, about 17 or 18 Years of Age, about 5 Feet high, smooth Face, large Mouth, chews Tobacco, and generally puts a deal in his Mouth at once: Had on when he went away, a Thickset Coat, blue Cloth Jacket, black Stocking Breeches, dark blue Stockings, a Pair of turn'd Pumps, plain Pinchbeck Buckles, and an old Hat. Whoever takes up and secures said Servant, so that his Master may have him again, shall have the above Reward, and all reasonable Charges,   paid by ROBERT ORR, Peruke Maker,
    in King-Street, or H. GAINE.
  N. B. All Masters of Vessels and others are forbid to harbour him, or carry him off at their Peril.
The New-York Mercury, April 1, 1765; April 8, 1765; April 15, 1765; May 6, 1765.

              New-York, April 19, 1765.
RUN-*AWAY from the Subscriber, on Saturday Evening last; together, Three indented Servants, Natives of Ireland, who have been about five*

Months in this Colony, and will nearly answer the following Description, VIZ. TIMOTHY SULLIVAN, aged about thirty Years, fair Complexion, short brown Hair, much marked with the Small-Pox, has not so much of the Brogue as usual, about five Feet nine Inches high, slender made, walks sprightly and upright, he will probably endeavour to pass for a Sailor, but is a Calenderer by Trade.

TIMOTHY M'CARTY, aged about Twenty-two Years, fresh Complexion, smooth Face, dark brown Eyes, short black Hair, has a large Scar in his Forehead; about five Feet six Inches high, a square well made Fellow, by Trade a Woolen-Weaver.

PHILIP M'CARDELL, aged about Twenty-four Years, a short thick made Fellow, round shoulder'd, stoops when he walks, very aukward in his Gait, has more of the Brogue than either of the above Persons, has short curled brown Hair, and a fair Complexion, by Trade a Brewer and Distiller.

They had on when they went away, short brown Frize Coats all of one Piece, green Baize Lining, white Metal Buttons, Waistcoats, white Flanel Linings, and plain white Metal Buttons, good Buckskin Breeches, Homespun Stockings, and good Shoes. Whoever takes up and secures the said Servants, or either of them, so that their Master may have them again, shall receive THREE POUNDS Reward for each of them, if taken within this Colony, and FIVE POUNDS if taken in any of the neighbouring Colonies and all reasonable Charges
    paid by LEONARD LISPENARD.
The New-York Gazette, April 22, 1765; April 29, 1765. See *The New-York Mercury*, April 22, 1765.

DESERTED from his Majesty's 44th regiment of foot, and in Capt. Daniel Desney's company.— FRANCIS PIERCEL, Musician, about 24 years of Age, 5 feet 7 inches high, without Shoes, fair complexion, long visage, grey Eyes, light brown Hair, born in Ireland, Dublin; by calling a Labourer, Went off in his Regimentals, viz.—A red Coat faced with yellow, a yellow Cape, and yellow Button-holes, the Cape and Cuffs has Drummers lace of the regiment round them, his Regimental Waistcoat yellow, with red Button-holes. Whosoever apprehends the above deserter, and delivers him up to any Officer, Civil, or Military, shall receive TWENTY SHILLINGS Sterling Reward, according to Act of Parliament.

N. B. The above Deserter plays on the Hautboy, and took his Instrument along with him. *Crown-Point, April* 5, 1765.
The New-York Gazette, April 22, 1765; April 29, 1765.

RUN-AWAY from the Subscriber, on Saturday Evening the 19th Inst. April, together, Three indented Servants, Natives of Ireland, who have been about five Months in this Colony, and will nearly answer the following Description, viz. Timothy Sullivan, aged about 30 Years, fair Complexion, short brown Hair, much mark'd with the Small-pox, has not so much of the Brogue as usual, about 5 Feet 9 Inches high, slender made, walks sprightly and upright; he will probably endeavour to pass for a Sailor, but is a Callenderer by Trade. Timothy M'Carty, aged about 22 Years, fresh Complexion, smooth Face, dark brown Eyes, short black Hair, has a large Scar in his Forehead; about 5 Feet 6 Inches high, a square well made Fellow, by Trade a Woolen-Weaver. Philip M'Cardell, aged about 24 Years, a short thick made Fellow, round shoulder'd, stoops when he walks, very awkward in his Gate; has more of the Brogue than either of the above Persons, has short curled brown Hair, and a fair Complexion, by Trade a Brewer and Distiller They had on when they went away, short brown Frize Coats all of one Piece, green Baise Lining, White-metal Buttons, red Waistcoats, with white Flannel Linings, and plain White-metal Buttons, good Buckskin Breeches, homespun Stockings, and good Shoes. Whoever takes up and secures the said Servants, or either of them, so that their Master may have them again, shall receive Three Pounds Reward for each of them, if taken within this Colony, and Five Pounds, if taken in any of the neighbouring Colonies, and all reasonable Charges,
        paid by   LEONARD LISPENARD.
The New-York Mercury, April 22, 1765; April 29, 1765. See *The New-York Gazette,* April 22, 1765.

RUN away from Jost Bush, of Fish-Kill, in Dutchess County, on Monday the 14th of March, an Indian Servant, about 19 Years old, about five feet and an half high, midling slim, full faced, strait black Hair, has a Scar on his Left Arm, and several Marks on his Left Leg and Thigh: Took with him, a Wool Hat, an Homespun Jacket, a red Great Coat and a Leather Britches.— Whoever secures him so that his Master may have him again, shall have the above Reward and Charges
        paid by   JOST BUSH.   Ap. 15. 1765.
The New-York Gazette, April 29, 1765; May 13, 1765; May 20, 1765; May 27, 1765.

        Eastchester, May 6, 1765.
RAN away from Stephen Ward, on Eastchester, and County of Westchester, on Monday the 20 Day of April, a Negro Man named Daniel, a likely spry Fellow, of a middle Size, speaks good English, about 20 Years of Age. Had on a blue camblet Coat an old double-breasted Jacket with flat metal Buttons, old Felt Hat, a pair of thickset Britches, and a check Woolen

Shirt. Whoever takes up and secures the said Negro, so that his Master may have again, shall have FORTY SHILLINGS Reward, and all reasonable Charges paid by STEPHEN WARD.
All Masters of Vessels and others are forbid to carry him off, or harbour him, at their Peril.
The New-York Gazette, May 6, 1765; May 13, 1765.

RUN away from the Subscriber, Wig-Maker on the New-Dock, on Monday Night the 29th of April, an indented Irish Servant, named Mary Clancy. She was inticed away, and went off with one Thomas Brown, (who has been for two Months past in the Work-House, and is a Servant to Messrs. Greg, Cunningham, and Co.) She is about 24 Years of Age, middle Size, a dark brown Complexion, and much freckled in the Face; she has much of the Brogue in her Speech, and had on a brown Camblet Gown, and a long Cloak of the same, a black Calimancoe Petticoat not quilted, and without Lining, a broad check'd Apron, bad Shoes and Stockings, and no Hat. Whoever takes up and secures the said Servant, so that her Master may get her again, shall receive Forty Shillings Reward, and all reasonable Charges paid by JAMES MORRISON.
N. B. All Persons are desired at their Peril, not to harbour them; and Masters of Vessels not to carry them away, as they will be prosecuted with the utmost Rigour of the Law,
The New-York Mercury, May 6, 1765; May 13, 1765; June 3, 1765.
See *The Pennsylvania Journal, and Weekly Advertiser*, May 30, 1765.

FIVE POUNDS REWARD.
RUN-*away from his Bail, on Friday the 26th Day of April ult. a young Man about* 24 *Years of Age, named Joseph Pye, of a middle Stature about five Feet* 7 *Inches high, by Trade a Saddletree-Riveter; he is very much given to Drinking, and when in Liquor is very much giving to talking, and of a loud Speech: he some Time ago worked Jorney work with one Robert Boyd of the City of New-York, and from thence went to Elizabeth-Town, and worked opposite the Sign of the Roe-Buck, near Capt. Ephraim Terrill's, within two Miles and a Half of the Town: Had on when he went away, a light claret coloured Coat, a blue double brested Jacket and a Pair of blue broad cloth Breeches; he wares his Hair, of a dark brown Colour, he has had one of his little Fingers broke, which makes it less than the other: He is supposed to be kept concealed near the King's Stores at the North River, in New-York, it is likewise supposed that he intends for North-Carolina, as soon as possible, therefore all Captains of Vessels and others, are forbid to harbour, conceal or carry him off, on their Peril. He was born at Bermingham in Old England. Any Person taking up said Run-away, and*

securing him, so that his Bail may have him again, shall have Five Pounds Reward, and all reasonable Charges
        paid by   JOHN CRAIG.   Elizabeth-Town, May 2.
The New-York Mercury, May 6, 1765; May 13, 1765.

Three Pounds Reward.

RUN-away the 19th of March, and indented Servant, named Edward McEllroy, by Trade a Joiner; about 20 Years of Age, middle sized, short dark Hair, brown Complexion, and pitted with the Small-Pox; has also lost a Piece of one of his Fore Teeth: Had on a brown Thickset Coat, light coloured Cloth Waistcoat and Breeches, but has got other Cloths along with him. Whoever takes up and secures the said Servant, so that his Master may have him again, shall receive the above Reward, and all reasonable Charges
        paid by   JOHN KEATING.

N. B. All Masters of Vessels are forbid to carry him off, as they will answer it at their Peril.

The New-York Mercury, May 6, 1765; May 13, 1765; June 3, 1765.

WHEREAS Samuel Buffinton, on the 2d Day of November, 1764, chartered the Sloop Ranger, Joseph Earle, Master, belonging to me the Subscriber, for Hartford, in Connecticut; which Sloop sailed from Egg Harbour on or about the 6th Day of the same Month, but has not yet returned; and on Enquiry, I have Intelligence, that on the 6th Day of November last, the said Buffinton sold the above Sloop to Mr. Zephaniah Anthony, of Dartmouth, in the Province of Massachusetts-Bay, and assuming my Name, forged a Bill of Sale agreeable thereto, and afterwards absconded:—I hereby promise a Reward of FIFTEEN DOLLARS to any Person or Persons who shall apprehend and secure the said Samuel Buffinton, so that he may be bro't to Justice, and all necessary Charges
        paid.   ISAAC BELLAMY.

N. B. Said Buffinton is a tall, slim Man, about 36 Years of Age, thin favoured, walks fast, and wears a Cap or Wig, and belongs to a Place called the Nine Partners, in the Province of New-York. He has worked at the Joiner's Business in Newport.

The Newport Mercury, May 13, 1765; May 20, 1765; May 27, 1765.

FIVE POUNDS Reward.

RUN away, on Wednesday the 24th Day of April, from the Subscriber, living in the Mannor of Cortlandt, in the County of West-Chester, a Negro Wench, named Gin, aged 25 Years, she may change her Name; she is Slim and Straight bodied, of a middle Size, of a pale black, has long narrow Feet, she has a large bump like a Scar on her Stomach, one of her upper fore-

Teeth is out, she has a black Mold 'twixt her Eyebrows, and Speaks English and Dutch, she is handy at all sorts of Work, she had several sorts of Cloaths homspun and others, with some Mens Cloaths to appear like a Negro Man; it is said she went off in a Boat from Peeks-Kill, with two Men one a German named Roouger, the other is called Hoogeboom; its thought she has a forged Pass and bill of Sale by which they may offer her for Sale. Whoever takes up and Secures the said Negro Wench so that her Master may have her again shall have the above Reward, paid by all reasonable
     Charges by PHILIP VERPLANCK,
The New-York Gazette, May 13, 1765; May 20, 1765; May 27, 1765.

RUN-away, from Benjamin Westervelt, of Poughkeepsie, the 28th of October last, a Negro Man named Cato, about 28 Years old, 5 Feet and half high, full-faced, was very black, and is supposed to be at Work in some Part of Connecticut. Whoever takes up and secures the said Fellow, so that he may be had again, shall receive Five Pounds Reward, paid by the said
    BENJAMIN WESTERVELT.
The New-York Mercury, May 13, 1765.

RUN-AWAY from the Subscriber, living in New-York, the 11th of this Instant, May, an Apprentice Lad, named, John Clark, 19 Years old, of Scotch Parents, and can talk Earse, [*sic*] black Hair, and of a dark Complexion: Had on when he went away, a brown Jacket lined with green Baise, a Pair of Buckskin Breeches, and blue Yarn Stockings. All Masters of Vessels are forbid to carry him off; and whoever will bring home said Lad, shall have Two Pounds Reward,
    paid by JONATHAN COWDERY.
The New-York Mercury, May 20, 1765; May 27, 1765.

STOLEN from the subscriber of Goshen, on the West side North river, in New-York Government, on Thursday the 16th of May instant, a dark bay horse, four years old, branded thus **AD** on the left thigh, small blaze in his face, natural pacer, about 14 hands high. The person that stole him, is an Irishman, about 6 feet high, and slim, pitted with the small-pox, hallow ey'd, wears his own hair, had on a blue coat, and a jacket figur'd in imitation of seal-skin; he is something talkative, a great story-teller, card-player and song-singer; he says his name is Henry Gote. Whoever shall take up said thief and horse, and bring them to the subscriber, or secure the thief in any of his Majesty's goals, so that he may be brought to justice, and inform where the horse is, so that the owner may have him again, shall

receive a reward of FIVE DOLLARS, and all necessary charges,
> paid by me   JONAS DUBOIS.

N. B. He was in Hartford last Monday, and the next day set off as is supposed, for Boston.

The Connecticut Courant, May 27, 1763; June 3, 1765.

RUN away from the Subscriber, living in Albany, an Indented Irish Servant, named Matthew Shees, but it is likely he will change his name, by Trade a Taylor, about Nineteen years of Age, 5 Feet 6 Inches high, short brown Hair, full smooth Faced, brown Eyes remarkably blue under: Had on when he went away, a brown Coat turn'd, with Button-holes on each breast, round topt, yellow Buttons, blue Sagathee Waistcoat, lined with white Flannel, a Check Shirt, black Barcelona Handkerchief, a good Beaver Hat, a Pair of blue Cloth Breeches, blue Worsted Stockings, new Shoes, Pinchbeck Buckles; very apt when Angry to Swear in Irish. Whoever takes up and Secures said Servant, so that his Master may have him again, shall have FIVE DOLLARS Reward, and reasonable Charges
> paid by   MATHEW WATSON,

N. B. All Masters of Vessels, are forbid to carry him off, as they shall answer the same at their Peril.   Albany, May 21, 1765.

The New-York Gazette, May 27, 1765; June 3, 1765. See *The New-York Mercury*, May 27, 1765.

RUN away on Tuesday Night last, from Jacob Dyckman at Kingsbridge, a Negro Fellow named Will, or Wilthier, about 40 Years old, 5 Feet 8 Inches high, very Crooked Leggs: had on when he went away, a blue Broad Cloth Coat very short, Homspun Trowsers, a Beaver Hat, half worn, with a hole through the Rim; he formerly belonged to Mr. Alsop, and likewise Mr. Kateltass; he was seen at Whitehall Yesterday, Whoever takes up the said Negro, and sends him to the Work-House, shall have 3 Dollars Reward,
> paid by JACOB DYCKMAN.   New-York, May 23, 1765.

The New-York Gazette, May 27, 1765.

RUN-away the 20th inst. from the subscriber, living in Albany, an indented Irish servant, named Matthew Shees, but it is likely he will change his name, by trade a taylor; about 19 years of age, five feet 6 inches high, short brown hair, full smooth face, brown eyes, remarkably blue under: had on when he went away, a brown coat turned, with button holes on each breast, round-topt, yellow buttons, blue sagathee waistcoat, with yellow buttons to the bottom of the skirt; a short double breasted red waistcoat lined with white flannel; check shirt, black Barcelona handkerchief, good beaver hat, a blue cloth breeches, blue worsted stockings, new shoes, pinch-beck buckles,

very apt when angry to swear in Irish. Whoever takes up and secures the said servant, so that his master may have him again, shall have Five Dollars reward, and reasonable charges
          paid me   MATTHEW WATSON,
The New-York Mercury, May 27, 1765; June 3, 1765. See *The New-York Gazette*, May 27, 1765.

                  FIFTEEN POUNDS Reward.

RUN away from Carlisle Iron works, in Cumberland County, Pennsylvania, two indented Servants, the one named James Bishop, but it is likely will change his Name; he is an Englishman, about 5 Feet 8 Inches high, thick and well set, about 28 Years of age, pale Complexion, and has a sour down Look, a Scar on his Forehead, made, he says, by a Musket Ball, he is apt get drunk, and when so, is a very talkative, searing, rude, quarrelsome Fellow; he has been used to work in the Forge, and can work pretty well in a Finery Fire; had on, when he went away, an old Beaver Hat, Ozenbrigs or Country made Linen Shirt, a light coloured Nap Coat, made short, about half worn, a Pair of brown Thickset Breeches, patched with light coloured Cloth, spotted Yarn Stockings, half worn Shoes and Pewter Buckles; he has worked at most of the Iron-works in the Jersey and York Governments, has been on board Men of War, and in the Army. The other is named John Johnson, an Irishman, about 26 Years of age, 5 Feet 7 or 8 Inches high, pretty well set, fair Complexion, smooth Face, and a likely innocent Look; had on, and took with him, a light coloured Cloth Coat, Jacket and Breeches, pretty much worn, an old brown Fustian Coat, with Horn Buttons, a striped Tickin Jacket, and a spotted Flannel one, old brown Yarn Stockings, half worn Shoes, and Steel Buckles. They went away in Company with one Jacob Wolfe, a Dutchman, but speaks good English, is a short well set Fellow, pitted with the Small-Pox, and has a Gun with him; Wolfe has also worked at Iron-works in the Jersies. Whoever takes up said Servants, and secures them, so that their Masters may have them again, shall have the above Reward, or Ten Pounds for Bishop, and Five Pounds for Johnson, and reasonable Charges, if brought to said Works,
          paid by   ROBERT THORNBRUGH.
The Pennsylvania Gazette, May 30, 1765; June 6, 1765; June 13, 1765; June 20, 1765; October 24, 1765; October 31, 1765.

                                                                       May 10.
RUN away from the Subscriber, wig-maker, on the New-Dock, New-York, on Monday night the 29th of April, an indented Irish servant, named Mary Clacy. She was inticed away, and went off with one Thomas Brown, (who has been for two months past in the work-house, and is a servant to Messrs. Greg, Cunningham, and Co.) She is about 24 years of age, middle size, a

dark brown complexion, and much freckled in the face; she has much of the brogue in her speech, and had on a brown camblet gown, and a long cloak of the same, a black calimancoe petticoat not quilted, and without lining, a broad check'd apron, bad shoes and stockings, and no hat. Whoever takes up and secures either of the above servant, so that their masters may have them again, shall receive FORTY SHILLINGS Reward, and all reasonable Charges paid by applying to James Morrison aforesaid in New-York, or John James, wig maker and hair dresser in Market street, Philadelphia.
JAMES MORRISON.
N. B. All Persons are desired at their Peril, not to harbour them; and Masters of Vessels not to carry them away, as they will be prosecuted with the utmost Rigour of the Law,
The Pennsylvania Journal, and Weekly Advertiser, May 30, 1765. See *The New-York Mercury*, May 6, 1765.

RUN-away on Monday Afternoon, the 27th of May last, from John McKinney, of this City, Taylor, an Irish Servant Man, named Michael Haley; of middle Size, not very thick, Pock-mark'd, black Beard, has strait black Hair cued. Had on when he went away, a redish brown Coat, Jacket of the same, black Stocking Breeches, a Pair of white Thread ribb'd Stockings, and another ribb'd Pair of mixed grey Worsted: an old Hat, and good new Shoes. Whoever takes up, and secures the said Servant, so that he may be had again, shall have THREE POUNDS Reward, and all reasonable
Charges, paid by   JOHN McKINNEY.
The New-York Mercury, June 3, 1765; June 10, 1765; July 1, 1765; August 5, 1765; September 2, 1765.

RUN away from the Subscriber, living at the North Side of Hempstead, on Long-Island, an Irish Servant Man, named Henry Bokels, aged about 18 Years, he is somewhat thick, short and clumzey, wears his own black curl'd Hair, and is sometimes subject to Fits. Whoever takes up said Servant, and secures him, so that his Master may have him again, shall have Forty Shillings Reward
by me   JOSEPH VALENTINE.
N. B. He has wrote himself a Pass, by which he may endeavour to plead his Freedom.
The New-York Mercury, June 3, 1765; June 10, 1765; July 17, 1765.

FIVE POUNDS *Reward.*
New-York, May 29, 1765.
RUN-away from John Leversage, shipwright, an apprentice lad, about 17 years of age, five feet 8 inches high, of fair complexion, with light hair, blue eyes, and white eyebrows. Had on when he went away, a long stone-grey

cloth coat, with a tape of the same cloth, the sleeves in the fashion; a claret colour'd jacket of Irish knap, without sleeves, a pair of Buckskin britches, new hemp stockings, new shoes, a new English castor hat; and metal buckles; talks something on the cant [sic] order; was born at Cow-Neck, Long-Island, where it is supposed he is gone. Whoever takes up the said run-away, and brings him to his masters or secures him in any of his majesty's goals, shall have the above reward, and all necessary charges paid by me,   JOHN LEVERSAGE.

N. B. All masters of vessels are forewarned of carrying him off, upon their Peril of suffering the Law.

The New-York Gazette, June 3, 1765. See The New York Mercury, June 3, 1765.

FIVE Pounds Reward.

Run away from John Leversage, Ship-Wright, an Apprentice Lad, about 17 Years of Age, 5 Feet 8 Inches high, fair Complexion, with light Hair, blue Eyes, and white Eye Brows: Had on when he went away, a long stone grey cloth Coat, with a Jacket of the same Cloth, the Sleeves in the Fashion; and a Claret colour'd Jacket, of Irish nap, without Sleeves, a Pair of Buckskin Breeches, new Hemp Stockings, new shoes, a new English Castor Hat; and Metal Buckles; talks something on the Cant [sic] Order, was born at Cow-Neck, Long-Island, and is supposed to be gone that Way. Whoever takes up the said Run-away, and brings him to his Master, or secures him, in any of his Majesty's Goals, shall have the above Reward, and all necessary
        Charges paid by   JOHN LEVERSAGE.

N. B. All Masters of Vessels are forewarned not to carry him off, upon their Peril of suffering the Law.

The New-York Mercury, June 3, 1765; June 10, 1765. See The New-York Gazette, June 3, 1765.

DESERTED on the 25th of May last, from a Recruiting Party of the First Battalion of Royal Americans, one Hugh O'Dannel, born in the County pf Donnegale, in Ireland, is of a dark Complexion, and about 5 Feet 6 Inches high, aged about 35 or 26 Years. Whoever shall secret him in any of his Majesty's Goals, at New-York or Philadelphia, so that he may be delivered to the Regiment, shall receive Ten Pounds Currency Reward, to be paid by
        I. M. PREVOOST, Capt. 1st. Bat. Royal Americans.

The New-York Mercury, June 3, 1765; June 10, 1765.

RUN away from the Subscriber, on Wednesday the 5th Inst. June, an Irish Servant Man, named Edward Joice, thin Visage, light brown Hair, about 23 Years old, speaks broken English. Had on when he went away, a dark

brown Coat lin'd with white Flannel, Buckskin Breeches, a double-breasted blue Jacket with Horn Buttons, grey ribb'd Worsted Stockings. Whoever takes up said Servant, and secures him in any Goal, or brings him to his Master, shall have Forty Shillings Reward, and all reasonable Charges
                    paid by   DANIEL AMONS, living near Greenwich.
The New-York Mercury, June 17, 1765.

RUN-away, from Hendrick Hoghtaling, of Coxsahkie, in [the] County of Albany, a Negro Man named Tone: he [is a] Spaniard and talkes crooked: he is blind of one of his Eyes, and has long Hair, and yellow Complexion. Whoever takes up said Negro Man, and secures him so that his Master may have him again, shall be handsomely rewarded for their Trouble.
It is suspected that he is gone to New-York.
                  HENDRICK HOGHTLAING.
The New-York Mercury, June 17, 1765.

TAKEN-up, and is now in the Goal, at Jamaica, on Long-Island, Negro Man between 19 and 20 Years of Age, that will give no Account of himself: He is a tall slim Fellow, very black, and speaks bad English: he has on a red Broad-Cloth Coat and Jacket, blue Cloth Breeches, good shoes and Stockings, and a Felt Hat: He is much mark'd on the Cheeks and had about him when taken up, a Silver Tea Spoon marked G. B. The owner may have him again, by applying to Benjamin Hageman, paying Charges.
The New-York Mercury, June 17, 1765; June 24, 1765.

RUN-away the 12th of June, inst. from William Gilliland of this city, an Irish servant woman named Catharine Welch, of a low size, but thick and strong made; a homely face, with a disagreeable cast in her eyes. Had on when she went away, a green camblet gown, black calimanco petticoat, check apron, and handkerchief; leather shoes with high heels, and a pair of blue worsted stockings, &c. Whoever takes up and secures the said servant, so that the subscriber may have her again, shall have Five Dollars reward, and reasonable charges
                paid, by WILLIAM GILLAND.
The New-York Mercury, June 24, 1765; July 1, 1765.

RUN-away, the 7th of June Instant, from Charles Miller, of this City, Baker, an indented Servant Boy named Philip Sparling, about 15 Years old, much pitted with the Small Pox, light Hair, was born in Ireland, speaks High Dutch and English, and discovers a melancholly and suspicious Countenance when threatened: Had on when he went away, a whitish brown Ratteen Jacket, double-breasted, a Pair of long Oznabrigs Trowsers much worn, a small Beaver Hat, white Stockings, new Shoes and old Check

Shirt. Whoever apprehends and secures said Servant, so that his Master may have him again, shall receive 20 Shillings Reward, besides all reasonable Charges, paid by   *Charles Miller.*

All Masters of Vessels and others, are forbid to conceal or harbour said Servant, as they shall answer it at their Peril.

The New-York Mercury, June 24, 1765; July 1, 1765. See *The New-York Journal; or, General Advertiser*, March 2, 1769, and *The New-York Gazette; and the Weekly Mercury*, April 10, 1769.

RUN-away from the subscriber, on Tuesday the 18th instant, an apprentice lad named John Foster, by trade a blacksmith, about 17 years of age, born in Newark, in New-Jersey, about 5 feet 8 inches high, a good deal pitted with the smallpox, having had it this last winter; he had on when he went away, a blue frize coat bound with tape, a jacket of the same colour, and a pair of buck-skin breeches. Whoever takes up and secures the said apprentice, so that his master may have him again, shall have Forty Shillings reward, and all reasonable charges
paid by   Robert Andrews.

New-York, June the 26th, 1765.

N. B. All masters of vessels and others are forewarn'd not to conceal, or carry him off, as they may depend they will answer for it, as the law directs.

The New-York Gazette or Weekly Post Boy, June 27, 1765. See *The New-York Gazette; and the Weekly Mercury*, September 5, 1768.

RUN-away, about the 27th of June ult. from the Subscriber, living in New-York, an indented Servant Girl, named Catharine Luter, about 14 Years of Age, was somewhat pitted with the Small-Pox, and had white curled Hair: Had on when she went away, a striped Pettycoat, homespun short Gown, and speckled Apron. Whoever takes up and secures the said Girl, so that she may be had again, shall receive Twenty Shillings Reward, and all
reasonable Charges paid, by   GEORGE HORNER.

The New-York Mercury, July 1, 1765; July 8, 1765.

RUN-away the 28th of June last, a Negro Boy, named Prince, about 18 Years of Age, middle sized, very black: Had on when he went away, a Check Shirt, black Breeches, and blue Stockings. Whoever will take up said Negro, and bring him to his Master *Isaac Gomez*, in New-York, shall be well rewarded for their Trouble; and those that harbours or entertains him, may depend on being prosecuted.

All Masters of Vessels or others, are forewarned not to carry him off one their Peril.
The New-York Mercury, July 15, 1765. See *The New-York Mercury*, December 1, 1766.

RUN-away from the Subscriber, at Rye, the 8th of June last, a Negro Wench named Peg, belonging to the Estate of Mrs. Elizabeth Straing, deceased: All Persons are forbid to harbour or conceal her at their Peril. Whoever takes up said Wench, and will send her to me at New-York, shall have Forty Shillings Reward,
   paid by RICHARD VAN DYCK, Administrator.
The New-York Mercury, July 22, 1759; July 29, 1765.

RUN-away from the Subscriber, on Tuesday the 9th Instant, July, a Negro Man, named Toby, this Country born, yellow Complexion; about 5 Feet 7 Inches high, or thereabouts, and about 22 Years of Age: Had on when he went away, a brown Fustian Jacket, Oznabrigs Shirt and Trowsers, and an old Beaver Hat; but 'tis very likely he may change his Dress, and endeavour to pass for a free Negro. Whoever takes up, and secures the said Negro, so that his Master may have him again, shall receive Three Pounds Reward, and all Charges
   paid by AUGUSTUS VANHORNE.
All Masters of Vessels, and others, are forewarned not to conceal or carry him off, as they may depend they will answer for it as the Law directs.
The New-York Mercury, July 22, 1759; July 29, 1765; August 5, 1765; September 2, 1765. The last ad shows he ran away "9th of July last" and omits the line beginning with "All Masters".

RUN-*away, the* 22d *Instant, from the Subscriber, living at Tappan in Orange County, and Province of New-York, a Negro Man named Hector, about* 30 *Years old, a well-made, full-faced spry Fellow, a little pitted with the Small-pox, and about* 5 *Feet* 8 *Inches high. Had on when he went away, a blue Camblet Coat, black Silk Jacket, Cloth Breeches, white Thread Stockings, a Castor Hat, a Pair of good Pumps, and can talk both Dutch and English. Whoever takes up and secures the said Fellow, so that his Master may have him again, shall receive Five Dollars Reward, and all reasonable Charges,*
   paid by JOHN PELL, *Miller.*
The New-York Mercury, July 29, 1765.

RUN-away from the Subscriber, living in this City, on the 26th Inst. July, a Negro Man named WILL, about 5 Feet 5 Inches high: Had on when he went away, a blue Coat with yellow Lining, and White-metal Buttons; a double breasted Swanskin Waistcoat much worn; a Pair of Ozenbrigs Trowsers, and a half-worn Castor Hat. He is very apt to get in Liquor, and is somewhat stupid when so. Whoever takes up said Fellow, and secures him, so that his Master may have him again, shall have Forty Shillings Reward, and reasonable Charges,
    paid by AARON BUCK.
The New-York Mercury, July 29, 1765.

RUN-away from Philip Livingston's Distillery, on Long-Island, Edward Laverty, an indented Servant, aged about 28 Years; he is an Irishman, and has the broad Way of speaking common to the lower Sort of People of that Country; he is about 5 Feet 5 Inches high, full Face, dark Complexion, short Hair; a thick well-set, strong-limb'd Fellow, he has a down Look, and a surly Countenance: He had on when he went away, a blue Jacket, checked Shirt, striped Wilton Coat bound with Tape, not lined, on the said Coat are 14 Silver Buttons, with a Lawrel engraved on each Button; he professes himself to be a Maltster; it is supposed he is gone to some Part of Connecticut, New-London, Middletown, or Hartford, are the most likely Places, from some Hints he dropped before he went off. Five Pounds Reward will be given by Philip Livingston, besides all reasonable Charges, to any Person who will be so kind to secure the said Servant, in any Goal in this or any of the Neighbouring Colonies.
The New-York Mercury, July 29, 1765; August 5, 1765.

FIVE POUNDS REWARD.

MADE his Escape out of Philadelphia Prison, a certain Cornelius Clark, on or about the Month of September, in the Year of 1762. It is thought that he is near Elizabeth-Town, in East New-Jersey, as he has a Brother and other Relations living at, or near, a certain Place called Ash Swamp; he is a thin space Man, long sharp Nose, thin visaged, and about 5 Feet 10 Inches high; his Age about 35 or 36 Years; when he went away he wore long Hair, of a darkish brown Colour, and used to live in a Swamp, and followed the Weaving Business with a Brother he had there, but in New-York followed the Ship Carpenter's Business. Whoever apprehends the said Runaway, and secures him in any of His Majesty's Goals, till Information be given to James Alexander, Turnkey, shall be entitled to the above Reward, and if returned to Philadelphia Prison, shall receive said Reward, and all reasonable Charges, from
    WILLIAM PARR, Sheriff,
      or JAMES ALEXANDER, Turnkey.

The Pennsylvania Gazette, August 1, 1765; August 15, 1765.

TEN DOLLARS REWARD.

RAN away from the subscriber, a Negro man named Peter, aged about 26 years. Took with him a blue coat, and a blue camblet vest, a blue cut Manchester pair of breeches, and some other cloathing. The said Negro was bred at Rhode Island, is of a clear black, speaks good English, and is about 5 feet 6 inches high. Also a white apprentice boy, aged 15 named Henry Wiltse, had on when he went away a light colour'd homespun jacket, a striped linen under jacket, blue ever-lasting breeches, two trowsers, a small brim'd felt hat, bound with ferret, light colour'd hair tyed in his neck, black eyes. Whoever shall take up said Negro and boy, and secure them so that their master can have them, shall be entitled to the above reward, and all necessary charges
paid, By   JAMES WILTSE.   Fish Kills, July 21st, 1765.
The Connecticut Courant, August 5, 1765; August 19, 1765.

Eight Pounds Reward.

WHEREAS *Robert Erwin, by some called William Erwin, battoeman, who calls himself a carpenter by trade, about the age of 30 years or upwards, has been seen last night at Mr. Shaw's in this city, and has stolen from me the subscriber, my servant maid, a girl of about 26 years of age; being a fat jolly girl, of a red complexion, having light hair, grey eyes, and had a cut over her left eye; she had on a white bed gown, and a strip'd linsey woolsey petticoat, black callimanco shoes, and light grey stockings; and her companion had on a buckskin short coat with lapells, a light colour'd jacket turned, a buckskin pair of breeches, and a castor hat; was of a down look having a long peaked nose, red beard, and sandy hair. Whoever secures and takes up said runaways, and places them within any goal within this province, shall have the above reward of eight pounds, or four pounds for securing any one of them, and all reasonable charges,*
   paid by me   William M'Cew.
   N. B. That she my said servant named Catherine M'Gra, is a tayloris by trade, and has stole several things from me.   Albany, July 30, 1765.
The New-York Mercury, August 12, 1765.

BROKE-out of Flatbush Goal, on Long-Island, last Friday Night, a certain Jacob Sherman, confined for Debt; he is a tall Man, goes stooping, raw-bon'd, and of a brown Complexion: Had on when he went away, a brown Cloth Coat, and a Nankeen Jacket. Whoever takes up and secures the said Jacob Sherman, so that he may be committed to said Goal again, shall receive Five Pounds Reward,

from JEREMIAH VANDERBELT, jun. Sheriff.
The New-York Mercury, August 19, 1765. See *The New-York Mercury*, September 23, 1765, and *The New-York Mercury*, October 7, 1765.

RUN-away the 3d Inst. Sept. from the Subscriber, living in Scotch-street, an indented Irish Servant Girl, named Mary Delaney, has three years of her Time to serve, about 18 or 19 Years of Age, of a ruddy Complexion, smooth-featur'd, short Stature, and thick set: Had on a Callico Gown, with a white ground and purple Sprig Flower, and a Pair of red Calimanco Shoes. Whoever will bring the said Servant to the Subscriber, or give Information where she is harbour'd, shall receive Forty Shillings Reward; and whoever harbours or conceals her, may expect to be punished as the Law directs.
RICHARD HARRIS.
The New-York Mercury, September 9, 1765; September 16, 1765.

BROKE the Goal of the City of New-York, in the Night of the 13th of September Instant, and made his Escape, a Negro Fellow taken up some Time since among the Enemy Indians, and was formerly advertised for Sale: He is a sturdy well-made Fellow, and about 40 Years old, Whoever takes up and secures said Fellow, so that he may be had again, shall receive TEN POUNDS Reward,
paid by JAMES MILLS, D. Sheriff.
The New-York Mercury, September 16, 1765; September 23, 1765; September 30, 1765.

RUN-away on the Night of the 2d instant, Sept. from John Duncan, of Schenectady, Esq; a Negro Man named Charles, about 38 Years of Age, and about 5 Feet 7 Inches high, a clean well-made Fellow, speaks good English, French, and a little Dutch, has a small Spot on the Crown of his Head without any Hair on it, about the Breadth of a Dollar, and a white Speck on the lower Side of one of his Eyes. Had on when he went away, a blue Coat with a red Collar, brown Jacket, and Scarlet Breeches: He plays little on the Violin. Whoever takes him up, and secures him to his Master, shall have Three Pounds Reward, and reasonable Expences, if taken up in this Province; if taken out of it, Five Pounds, and all reasonable Expence
paid by JOHN DUNCAN.
N. B. Said Negro was taken from Doctor Blair, of the Artillery, the Day of General Braddock's Defeat, carried to Canada, when he was in the Possession of Mons. De VaDriel, until the taking of Montreal, then delivered up to his former Master, and soon after sold to Walter Rutherford, Esq; in New-York.

The New-York Mercury, September 16, 1765; September 23, 1765; September 30, 1765. See *The New-York Mercury*, August 18, 1766.

RUN-away, from John Macomb, of the City of Albany, on Wednesday the 4th Inst. Sept. an indented Servant Man, named Ricket Donivan, born in Ireland, about 20 Years of Age, 5 Feet 10 Inches high, clean and well-made, a little pitted with the Small-pox, wears his own Hair, of a blackish Colour, speaks fast, and with the Irish Accent. Had on when he went away, a mottled coloured Ratteen Coat with Brass Buttons, Scarlet Jacket without Sleeves, and Raven Duck Trowsers. He went off in Company with one John Curtin, an indented Servant belonging to Cortlandt Schuyler, Esq: of this City, a stout-made Fellow, about 5 Feet 8 Inches high, a little round-shouldered, and stoops. Whoever takes up the said Ricket Donivan, and secures him in any of his Majesty's Goals, and gives Notice thereof, or brings him to the said John Macomb, or Mr. Hugh Wallace Merchant, in New York, shall receive THREE POUNDS Reward, and all reasonable Charges.

The New-York Mercury, September 16, 1765; September 23, 1765; September 30, 1765.

BROKE out of King's County Goal, on Friday Night the 20th Instant, September, one Jacob Shearman: A tall Man, brown Complexion, a Scar on his upper Lip, walks a little stooping: Had on when he went away, a Brownish Boat, [sic] Nankeen Waistcoat and Breeches, wears a brown Wig or a Worsted Cap: The said Jacob Shearman, broke out of said Goal some Time ago, and was apprehended by the Sheriff of the said County. Whoever apprehends the said Jacob Shearman, and brings him to me, shall have Five Pounds Reward, and all reasonable Charges

          paid by me,   JEREMIAH VANDER BILT, jun. Sheriff.

The New-York Mercury, September 23, 1765. See *The New-York Mercury*, August 19, 1765, and *The New-York Mercury*, October 7, 1765.

RAN-AWAY from *Stephen Hopkins* of the *Nine-Partners*, a Negro Man named *Simon*, about 24 Years of Age, near 6 feet high, well proportioned, had on when he went away, a blue Coat, brass Buttons with round Tops, a light-colour'd, double-breasted Waistcoat, a white Tow Shirt, short Tow Trowsers, black and white Stocking, [sic] two Threads twisted together, an old felt Hat with a small Brim. Whoever shall take up said Negro, and secure him in any of his Majesty's Goals, so that his Master may have him again, shall have *Five Dollars* Reward, and all necessary Charges

          paid by   STEPHEN HOPKINS.

The Connecticut Courant, September 30, 1765; October 7, 1765.

Forty Shillings Reward.
Albany, September 19, 1765.

RUN away from the Subscriber yesterday, a Mulatto Negro Man, a Spaniard named Joseph; about 25 Years old, short well-made Fellow, speaks broken English; (he went off with a big Spanish Negro belonging to Mr. Bayard, of New-York, sent here to sell.) He had on when he went away, a blue Jacket, an old light-colour'd ratten ditto, without Sleeves, an Ozenbrigs Shirt, old Leather Breeches, a Pair of black ribb'd Stockings, a Hat bound with Worsted Binding, and a Pair of new Shoes with Brass Buckles. Whoever takes him up, and secures him in any of his Majesty's Goals, so that his Master may have him again, shall have the above Reward, and all reasonable Charges paid by Mr. John Ernest, Merchant, in New-York, or the Subscriber, in Albany.
    BARENT TEN EYCK.

The New-York Mercury, September 30, 1765; October 7, 1765; *The Newport Mercury,* November 4, 1765; November 11, 1765; November 18, 1765; December 9, 1765. The latter paper ends with: "All Masters of Vessels and others, are forbid to conceal, harbour, entertain, or carry off the said Servant, as they will answer it at their Peril."

RUN-away, from the subscriber, in New-York, last friday, an apprentice boy named Alexander Oyl, about 14 years old, a taylor by trade: had on when he went away, a light coloured serge-jacket and velvet breeches. Masers of vessels and others are forbid to carry him off, or entertain him. Whoever will take up and secure the said lad, so that his master may have him again, shall have twenty shillings reward,
    paid by   WILLIAM THORNE.
The New-York Mercury, October 7, 1765.

These are to certify, that Jacob Shearman, who formerly broke King's County Goal, and made his Escape, is now at Liberty to follow his Business as usual, and the Reward offered for apprehending him is void from this Day, As Witness my Hand,
    Jeremiah Vanderbilt, Sheriff.   Oct. 5, 1765.
The New-York Mercury, October 7, 1765. See *The New-York Mercury,* August 19, 1765, and *The New-York Mercury,* September 23, 1765.

RAN *away, yesterday, from the subscriber living on Rotton-Row, a new Negro man, named Dublin, he is about 21 years old, and speaks but little*

English: had on an ozenbrigs frock and a red jacket, with blue breeches. Whoever takes up said Negro, and returns him to his master, shall have 20s. reward paid by   WILLIAM GRAHAM.
The New-York Mercury, October 14, 1765; October 21, 1765.

RUNaway from the subscriber, living in New-York, last Monday, and was seen near King's-Bridge the same day, an Irish servant man named Philip Mc Manus, about 17 or 18 years old, 5 feet 5 inches high; is much freckled, and stoops much as he walks: He had on when he went away, a grey Irish rateen coat, striped flannell jacket, a check shirt, & black stocking breeches. Whoever takes up and secures the said servant, so that his master may have him again, shall receive FORTY SHILLINGS reward, and all reasonable charges, paid by   SMITH RAMADGE.
The New-York Mercury, October 14, 1765; October 21, 1765. See *The New-York Mercury,* June 16, 1766, and *The New-York Mercury,* February 9, 1767.

RUN-*away, the 10th Instant, a Negro Man named Robbin, and a Wench named Rose, both this Country born, short and well-set, the Man about 27, and the Woman about 30 Years of Age, far gone with Child, and the Man is round-shouldered; he was some Years ago on an Expedition on the Frontiers, and it is supposed they are both gone that Way. Whoever apprehends the abovementioned two Slaves, so that their Master may have them again, shall have Forty Shillings Reward,*
   paid by Doctor Thomas Wright, of Eastchester, or
      David Wright, lately moved to Peck's-Slip, in New-York.
The New-York Mercury, October 21, 1765.

Philadelphia, November 4, 1765.
EIGHT DOLLARS Reward.
RUN away last night from the Subscriber, in Strawberry Alley, an Irish servant man, named John Harford, by trade a taylor, about 5 feet 7 inches high, well set, of a dark complexion, wears his own hair, which is black, and is very much inclined to curl: Speaks middling good English:—Had on, when he went away, grey coat, with white metal buttons, grey waistcoat, with yellow buttons, blue breeches, light-blue stockings, a pair of half-worn shoes, with yellow buckles, white shirt, half worn-hat, sharp cocked. The said servant has a flesh mark on one of his shoulders (which he calls a strawberry.) Whoever apprehends said servant, and secures him, so that his master may have him again, shall receive the above reward, and reasonable charges,
      paid by   THOMAS HARRISON.

N. B. All masters of vessels, and others are forbid harbouring or carrying him off, as they will answer it at their peril.

The Pennsylvania Gazette, November 28, 1765; December 5, 1765; December 12, 1765. See *The New-York Gazette; and the Weekly Mercury*, October 10, 1768.

ABSENTED himself from the Ship Minerva, Capt. Tillet, lying at the New-Dock, the 19th ult. a certain Benjamin Jones, shipped for Chief Mate in the Port of London, and signed Articles to compleat the Voyage, tho' when he went away the Ship was but little better than half unloaded. Whoever employs, or harbours the said Jones, shall be prosecuted as the Law directs in such Cases.

Absented themselves also, from the said Ship, last Monday Night, two Men, one of which was named Thomas Billsbury, a Mariner and Cooper; the other named John Bowden, a Glazier and Mariner. Whoever takes up and secures the two last mentioned Persons, so that they may be had again, shall receive Twenty Shillings Reward for each,
     paid by THOMAS TILLET.

The New-York Mercury, December 2, 1765; December 9, 1765; January 20, 1766.

RUN-away from ROBERT ANDREWS, on Thursday the 2d Day of December, an Irish Servant Girl named KATY COLEBY, about 20 years of Age, has red Hair, and pretty much freckled in her Face; had on when she went away, a check'd short Gown, and black quilted Petticoat. Whoever takes her up, &c. shall have TWENTY SHILLINGS Reward, and all reasonable Charges.—All Masters of Vessels and others, are cautioned against carrying her off, harbouring or concealing her, as they will answer it at their Peril.

The New-York Gazette, December 9, 1765; December 16, 1765; December 23, 1765; December 30, 1765.

WHEREAS on Saturday the 21st day of December, at seven o'clock at night, as the Goalers was up in the goal, locking up the prisoners in their several wards, the said prisoners rose upon them, knocked them down, and forced the keys from them, opened the doors and made their escape. Underneath is a list of the prisoners, with their several discriptions.— Whoever takes up and secures any of the aforesaid prisoners, in any of his majesty's goals in this province, shall receive a reward of FIVE POUNDS current money of the province; and as a greater reward, whoever brings back, or secures Thomas Allen, Robert John Livingston, Charles Gerome, and Samuel Still, or any one of them, shall receive TWENTY POUNDS for

each and every one they shall so secure, that they may be had again,
paid by   J. ROBERTS, Sheriff.

THOMAS ALLEN, of New-London, about 5 feet 9 inches high, thin vissage, and streight grey hair.

ROBERT JOHN LIVINGSTON, about 5 feet 10 inches high, thin visage, with long light-coloured hair, and his face full of carabuncles.

SAMUEL STITT, about 5 feet 5 inches high, well sett, light hair, which ties behind, and almost bald upon the top of the head.

CHARLES GEROME, about 5 feet 10 inches high, a lusty well set man, with long black hair which ties behind, and is remarkable for speaking broken English, and is generally known by the name of the FRENCH MILLINER.

PATRICK HACKET, about 5 feet 6 inches, a taylor by trade, has a crooked nose, and long black Hair.

ALEXANDER M'LEAN, about 5 feet 7 inches high, well sett, fair complexion, and long black hair curled behind.

JOHN ROBERTSON, about 5 feet 10 inches high, a slender man, round shoulder'd, pitted with the small-pox, and wore a dark cut wig.

JUDAH JACOBS, about 5 feet 8 inches high, well sett, and long long black hair which ties behind.

SAMUEL MUNROW, about 5 feet 10 inches high, an elderly man, grey bushy hair, and well sett.

TUNIS DE KLERKE, upwards of 6 feet high, an old man, with one eye, and wore an old piss-burnt wig.

The New-York Gazette, December 23, 1765; December 30, 1765; January 6, 1766.

RUN-away from the Subscriber, on Sunday the 15th Instant, a Mulatto Slave, named NICK, about 22 Years of Age, and about 5 Feet 10 Inches high; a well-made Fellow, remarkably active and sprightly, and speaks very good English. Had on when he went away, a Beaver Hat, half worn, a brown cut Periwig, but generally goes in his own Hair, a brown Devonshire Kersey Jacket, or Waistcoat, with a green Cloth one under it, which somewhat exceeded the other in Length, black knit Breeches, and grey ribb'd Worsted Stockings. Whoever shall take up and secure said Runaway, so that his Master may have him, shall have Forty Shillings Reward, if taken in the City of New-York, and Three Pounds, if taken elsewhere, and all reasonable Charges
paid by me,   LEWIS MORRIS.

All Masters of Vessels, and others, are hereby forbid to harbour, conceal, or carry off said Run-away, as they will answer it at their Peril.

The New-York Mercury, December 23, 1765; December 30, 1765; January 6, 1766; January 20, 1766; January 27, 1766.

1766

Five Pounds Reward.
RAN-away on Friday the 22d Day of November last, a Negro Man Named Pomp, but may go by the Name of Jemmy: by Trade a Blacksmith. He is about 5 Feet 5 Inches and an Half high: Talks very good English, Low-Dutch, and something of the High-Dutch. Had on when he went away, a thick Jacket, a round Castor Hat, bound round the Edge; an old Pair of Trowsers, Check Shirt, Shoes with very large Brass Buckles; it is supposed he is harbouring in the Woods, upon Long Island. Whoever takes up the said Negro, and brings him to his Master, in the City of New-York, shall receive Five Pounds Reward, and all reasonable Charges
    paid by me, ANTHONY SHAKERLY.
N. B. All Masters of Vessels, are forbid carrying away said Negro, as the will be prosecuted as the Law directs. *New-York, January* 20, 1766.
The New-York Gazette, January 20, 1766; January 27, 1766; February 3, 1766; February 10, 1766.

R*AN-away from her Master,* Alexander McNeill, *of* New-London, *in the Evening of the 21st Instant, an Indented Indian Woman, about 26 Years old, is a very tall, likely, strait Limb'd, active Wench, both speaks good English and reads well: She was brought up by one* Greene *of* Narraganset, *and is called* Hannah Greene, *but 'tis probable she will change her Name: She had on and carried with her, a dark striped flannel Gown, and a striped linnen Ditto, two Quilts, and sundry other Cloathing; 'tis probable she may have gone towards Albany & Crown-Point, having as she says, been in a Campaign.*
 Whoever will return said Servant, or give Information of her to her said Master, so that he may have her again, shall have all necessary Charges paid them, if to the amount of TEN POUNDS lawful Money, besides a handsome Reward, in proportion to their Trouble,
    paid by ALEXANDER McNeill,
        New London, Jan. 23*d*, 1766,
 The New-London Gazette, January 31, 1766.

RUN-AWAY the 29th of January, from JOHN POLHEMUS, at Jamaica, on Long-Island, a Negro man named MINK, about 5 Feet 10 Inches high, a well set Fellow of a lightish Complexion, and had on when he went away, a light colour'd Homespun Great Coat, with Horn Buttons; a Forrest Cloth Jacket, with Horn Buttons; a Pair of blue Everlasting Breeches: And took with him, a Pair of Buckskin Breeches with Silver Buttons, a Pair of white Stockings, and a Pair of blue and white ditto, a Pair of double soaled half

worn Shoes.—Whoever takes up said Runaway, and secures him in any Goal, so that he may be had again, shall have FIVE DOLLARS Reward,
        paid by WILLIAM PUNTINE, at the Fly-Market,
          or his said Master, JOHN POLHEMUS.—
    N. B. All Masters of Vessels are forbid carrying him off, as they shall assuredly answer it at their Peril.
    The New-York Gazette, February 3, 1766; February 17, 1766.

RUN away, from the Subscriber, at the New Lots, on Long-Island, a Negro Man named Toney, about 40 Years old: Had on when he went away, a homespun Coat and Jacket, and a Linen Jacket under the whole, coarse Stockings, and a new Hat. Whoever takes up said Fellow, and lodges him in the Work-House or Goal, shall have Forty Shillings Reward,
        paid by   JOCOB SNEDIKER.
    The New-York Mercury, February 17, 1766; February 24, 1766; March 24, 1766.

                        New-York, March 7th, 1766.
WHEREAS NICHOLAS MEZIERES, a French Servant belonging to his Excellency the Governor, has absented himself privately from his Service: This is therefore to caution all Masters of Ships from taking him on board their Vessels, or any other Persons from harbouring him.
    The New-York Gazette, March 17, 1766; March 24, 1766; March 31, 1766; April 7, 1766; April 14, 1766; April 21, 1766.

        Run-away from Johnson-Hall, *in the County
      of Albany, about four Weeks ago, an Irish Servant Man,*
              Named CONNOR O''ROURK,
ABOUT 26 Years of Age, is round faced, and is much freckled: He is a well Set short Fellow, wore a blackish Bob Wig, and wore a Blanket Coat when he ran off.—Whoever takes up and secures the said Servant in any Goal, or Work-House, so that he may be had again, and gives Notice to WILLIAM DARLINGTON, in Beaver-Street, New-York, shall have THREE POUNDS Reward, and all reasonable Charges
        paid by   WILLIAM DARLINGTON.
    N. B. It is thought he has changed both his Name and Clothes. All Masters of Vessels are strictly forbid to carry him off, or any other to harbour him.
    The New-York Gazette, March 24, 1766; March 31, 1766; April 7, 1766; April 14, 1766; April 21, 1766.

FIVE DOLLARS REWARD.
New Haven, March 27, 1766.

RUN-away, from Doris Van Wyck, of Oyster Bay, on Long-Island, a Negro Man, named Dick, but now calls himself John Dickerson; he is of a middle Stature, has a wildish whitish Look with his Eyes, especially when frightened, a likely Fellow, about Forty Years of Age. He talks as if he has a Cold, and had on when he went away grey yarn Stockings, Pumps, large Silver Buckles, blue Broad Cloth Breeches, a blackish thickset Jacket, a whitish Broad Cloth Coat, and a grey Homspun great Coat, a Cap and a large Beaver Hat, cock'd. About a fortnight ago he went over Milford Ferry, with a false dirty Pass all written by one Hand, with the Names of 6 or 7 Long-Island Justices of the Peace, at the Bottom. He enquired the Road to Boston and 'tis supposed he is gone that Way, to see an Acquaintance. Whoever secures the said Negro so that his Master may have him again, shall have Five Dollars Reward, and all reasonable Charges. And 'tis desired he may be delivered to Michael Peck, of Milford, living at the Ferry, who will pay the Reward and Charges,
for the said   DORIS VAN WYCK.
The Boston Gazette, April 7, 1766; April 14, 1766; April 28, 1766.

RUN-away from the Subscriber, living near Clark's-Town, Orange County, and Province of New-York, the first Inst. a Negro Man named Harry, a well-set Fellow, about 5 Feet 8 Inches high, and is very black: Had on when he went away, a Pair of dirty Buckskin Breeches, a Tow Shirt, brown Yarn Stockings, and 'tis imagined he has changed his Cloths. All Masters of Vessels are forbid to carry him off, and other Persons from harbouring him. Whoever takes up and secures the said Fellow, so that he may be had again, shall receive Forty Shillings Reward, and all reasonable Charges
paid by   JOHN RIDER.
The New-York Mercury, April 7, 1766; April 14, 1766.

Three Pounds Reward.
RUN away from the Subscriber, about four Weeks ago, an indented Man-Servant, named John Miller, about 40 Years of Age, says he was born in Swisserland, speaks broken English, German tolerably well, but the French Language is most natural to him; he is about 5 Feet 9 Inches, thick set, dark long brown Hair, generally queu'd; walks a little stiff: Had on when he went away, a Broadcloth brown colour'd Coat and Waistcoat, blue Breeches with Silver Knee-garters. Whoever secures him in New-York Goal, and gives Notice of it to the Subscriber, shall receive Three Pounds
Currency Reward, from   J. M. PREVOST.
The New-York Mercury, April 7, 1766; April 14, 1766.

RUN-away from the subscriber on the 12th instant, a German servant girl, named Eve Hukel, aged about twelve years, well-set, pail [sic] complexion, large eyes, and brown hair: Had on when she went away, a striped linsey petticoat and joseph, check linen handkerchief, and leather shoes with low heels. Whoever takes up said girl, and brings her to her said master, shall have 20s. reward. All people are forwarned harbouring her.
      L. GARRISON.
 The New-York Mercury, April 14, 1766.

      Five Pounds Reward.
DESERTED *from his Majesty's Ship Coventry, William Colvin, late Midshipman on board the said Ship: He is about 5 Feet 7 Inches high, stout made, swarthy Complexion, wears his own long black Hair, and supposed to be about 30 Years of Age: He was lately Mate of the Merchant Ship Aletto, which he left in Distress, and enter'd voluntarily into his Majesty's Service. Whoever shall secure the said William Colvin, and deliver him on board his Majesty's Ship Coventry, or into the Goal of this City, shall receive the above Reward, to be paid by the commanding Officer of his Majesty's said Ships.—*

 Merchants, and Owners of Ships, or other Vessels, are desired to be cautious how they employ the said William Colvin, circular Letters being wrote to Europe, and to the Commanders of his Majesty's Ships on the Coast of America, and in the West-Indies, to apprehend the said William Colvin, wherever he shall be found.
            Coventry April 26, 1766.
 The New-York Mercury, April 21, 1766; May 5, 1766; May 12, 1766.

RUN-away from Mr. Moses Clements, on Sunday the 13th of April, two indented Servants, Christian Fry, and Margareta Fry, his Wife, both Germans, of a brown Complexion, speaks no English, they are short and pretty thick set: he had on a brown Coat and blue Waistcoat, with small white Buttons, red Soldier's Breeches, and coarse white stockings, a pretty good Castor hat, cock'd in the French Form. She had on a blue German Vest, a striped homespun Petticoat, a black quilted Petticoat, and a brown Petticoat; the first of which she has sold. All Persons are forewarn'd of harbouring, or carrying said Servants away on their Peril, as they will be prosecuted as the Law directs; And any Person that discovers said Servants, and will bring them to said Clements, in the Broad-Way, opposite the New Church, shall have Four Pounds Reward.

 N. B. She had on a black German quilted Cap with Wire in the Border. They may have changed their dresses, as they have sold several Things.

The New-York Mercury, April 28, 1766; May 5, 1766. See *The New-York Mercury*, July 28, 1766, and *The New-York Mercury*, September 15, 1766.

WHEREAS my late Wife, Sarah Burch, otherwise Sarah Wheeler, did, on Sunday Night the 23d Day of March, elope from me without any manner of Occasion, and by the Assistance of one who calls himself John Spencer, and says he was born in North-Caroline, did rob the House of me her lawful Husband, to the amount of Forty Pounds and upwards in Cash, wearing Apparel, and Household Furniture, and stole a large Canoe with them from Scodack. Said Spencer is about 5 Feet 6 or 7 Inches high, wears his own Hair, cut short, of a dark brown Colour, has a down Look, speaks English, but no Dutch: Sarah was born on Long-Island. Whoever secures the said Runaways in any of his Majesty's Goals, shall have Five Pounds Reward, by me the Subscriber, at Sodack, in Albany County.
        DAVID BURCH.

N. B. Sarah reported she was born at Flushing, on Long-Island. She is corporate, [sic] and fresh colour'd.

The New-York Mercury, April 28, 1766.

Ten Pounds Reward.

WHEREAS a Person that goes by the Name of WILLIAM SHEEHAN, came some Weeks since to the House of Richard Sands, at Cow-Neck, in Queen's-County, and on Friday the 9th of May, Instant, hired of Ezekel Cooper, a sorrel Mare, with a Pretence of going to a Place, called the Oyster-Ponds, in Suffolk County; but after he left the said Neck, it was found that he had forged a Note of Hand on one James Burlen, of New-Town, and other Circumstances concurring, he is suspected to be gone off:—He is a well Set, likely Man, wears his own Hair, a light-colour'd Suit of Clothes, Buckskin Breeches; also has a blue Suit trim'd with Twist; the Horse is a natural Pacer, and has a large Star in his Forehead.—The same Evening a Woman who passed for his Wife, absconded from her Lodging at said Sands's, and took with her 15 Yards of Irish Huccaback, a long blue Cloth Cloak, one Poplin Gown, one black Calamanco Quilt, two under Petticoats, several Pair of Sheets, several Yards of Linen, and two Cloth [sic] one Cambrick Apron; two double Cambrick Handkerchiefs, and sundry other Things: She goes by the Name of NELLY, is pretty tall, long visage, Pock-broken, and has N. K. marked on her Hand. Whoever apprehends either of said Persons, so that they may be brought to Justice, shall have FIVE POUNDS Reward for each, and all reasonable Charges
        paid by   RICHARD SANDS.

N. B. If any of said stolen Goods are offered to Sale, pray stop them and give Notice.

The New-York Gazette, May 12, 1766; May 26, 1766; June 9, 1766.
See *The New-York Mercury*, May 12, 1766.

TEN POUNDS, Reward.
WHEREAS a Person that goes by the Name of William Sheehan, came some Weeks since to the House of Richard Sands, of Cow-Neck, in Queen's-County, and on Friday the 9th of May Instant, hired of Ezekel Cooper, a sorrel Mare, with a Pretence of going to a Place, called the Oyster-Ponds, in Suffolk County; but after he left the Neck, it was found that he had forged a Note of Hand on one James Burling, of Newtown, and other Circumstances concurring, he is suspected to be gone off; he is a well-set likely Man, wears his own Hair, a light-coloured Suit of Cloths, Buckskin Breeches, and has a Suit of Blue trimmed with Twist; the Horse is a natural Pacer, and has a large Star in his Forehead.—The same Evening, a Woman who passed for his Wife, absconded from her Lodging at said Sands's, and took with her 15 Yards of Irish Huckaback, a long blue Cloth Cloak, one Poplin Gown, one black Calamincoe Quilt, two under Pettycoats, several Pair of Sheets, many Yards of Linnen and tow Cloth, one Cambrick Apron, two double Cambrick Handkerchiefs, and many other Things. She goes by the Name of Nelly, is pretty tall, long visaged, Pock broken, and has N K marked on her Hand. Whoever apprehends either of said Persons, so that they may be brought to Justice, shall have Five Pounds Reward for each, and all reasonable Charges,
      paid by   RICHARD SANDS.
If any of the above Goods are offered for Sale pray stop them.
The New-York Mercury, May 12, 1766. See *The New-York Gazette*, May 12, 1766.

RUN-away from Charles Doughty, a negro man named cato, [*sic*] aged about thirty four years, about 5 feet 7 inches high, of a tawny colour, and has lost his upper teeth before: Had on when he went away, a brown homespun coat, a reddish waistcoat, a pair of buckskin breeches, and speaks good English and Dutch. Whoever takes up and secures the said negro, shall have forty shillings reward, and all reasonable charges,
      paid by   Charles Doughty.
                              Westchester, April 29, 1766.
The New-York Mercury, May 12, 1766.

RUN away from the subscriber in New-York, indented Irish servant, named Martin Doxey, by trade a dyer; he is about 5 feet 6 inches high, had on when he went away, a black coat, jacket and breeches, but is supposed to have changed his cloaths, as he carried off different cloths, silks, and other things intrusted to his care. He is much stooped in his shoulders, down

looking, badly limbed, wore his own black hair, is very deaf, and is very much addicted to swearing; he is supposed to be gone either to the Jersies or Philadelphia. Whoever will apprehend the said Martin Doxey, and lodge him in any of his Majesty's goals, shall receive three pounds,
    by applying to Henry Pillson.
          New-York, May 9, 1766.
The New-York Mercury, May 12, 1766; May 19, 1766; May 26, 1766.

      South-Hold, on Long-Island, May 12, 1766.
RAN-AWAY from their Masters (Michael Moore, and Abraham Corey) on Saturday Night last, two Negro Men, one named Prince, about 30 Years of Age, of a middling Stature, well set, one of his upper for Teeth gone, of an Olive Complexion; had on when he went away, a light-blue homespun Broad-Cloth Coat; he some Time since belonged to the Rev. Mr. Barber of Groton. The other is 25 Years of Age, 5 Feet 9 Inches high, well set, has lost half of one of his upper fore Teeth, is very black, named Crank; had on when he went away, a homespun Broad-Cloth Coat, of a light blue, trimmed with black, and double-breasted, black Everlasting Waistcoat, black Leather Breeches, blue ribb'd Yarn Stockings, thin Shoes, with plain Silver Buckles, and a new Castor Hat; speaks good English.—Whoever shall take up the said Negroes, or either of them, and secure them, so that their Masters may have them again, shall have a Reward of FIVE DOLLARS for each, and all necessary Charges,
    paid by me, ABRAHAM COREY.
The Newport Mercury, From May 12, to May 19, 1766; From May 19, to May 26, 1766; From May 26, to June 2, 1766; From June 2, to June 9, 1766; From June 9, to June 16, 1766.

          New-York, May 12, 1766.
THE Public is hereby informed, *and cautioned to beware* of an IMPOSTER, who has lately been detected in this City, but too late to be secur'd.
  He offered to enlist as a Recruit, but having a scurbutick Sore on the out Side of his Right Leg, and several suspicious Scars on his Limbs, he was therefore rejected: Nevertheless, by a plausible Tale he artfully related of his Misfortunes and Situation, he impos'd so far as to excite Compassion, and obtain charitable Assistance in curing his Leg.
  He called himself JAMES CUMING, born in Carlisle in Cumberland, Old England; gave out that he had been formerly in his Majesty's Service as a Soldier, but that he had an authentic Discharge; which, with some other Papers and Effects, he had left *as he said*, with one Mr. Richardson, a Justice of Peace, in some remote Part of New-Jersey, at whose house, he gave out, he had kept a School for some Time past; but had been obliged to

Abscond from thence on Account of a small Debt he had contracted. As his Hand writing is fair and distinct, he was employed to Copy some Papers, and on receiving Money as a Reward, he became profligate and careless, and at last eloped on the 25th of last Month, since which he has not been seen or heard of.—He is now discovered to have deserted from the 31st Regiment of Foot in England, in 1763; and to have been guilty and detected in several Forgeries, in drawing Bills, and otherwise: His real Name to be JOSEPH COOK, a Native of Ireland.

He appears to be between 30 and 40 Years of Age, is about 5 Feet 8 Inches high, round shouldered, lean, and somewhat emaciated in his Body, Limbs, and Face; has grey Eyes, a hollow Voice, is much pitted with the Small-Pox, his Hair cut short, and almost entirely grown Grey; his Complexion sallow and swarthy; he wore an old Snuff-colour'd Cloth Coat, with yellow plated Buttons, and grey Stuff Vest, brown Breeches, and grey Stockings, and an old Hat generally slouch'd.

He is a specious insinuating Fellow, and seems to be a thorough bred Villain: In order therefore, if possible, to prevent his doing any farther Mischief, (and that he may, if found out, be apprehended) this Account and Description of him is published.

The New-York Gazette, May 26, 1766.

RUN away from the Subscriber, on the 20th Day of May, a Servant Man, named Alexander McCormack, an Irishman, about 40 Years old, and about 5 Feet 9 Inches high, of a darkish Complexion, short black curl'd Hair, chews Tobacco, and is apt to get drunk, much given to talking and singing, and passes for a Ditcher, has a Wife in New-York, named Mary, with a Son about 18 Months old: Had on a lightish colour'd Coat, his other Clothes uncertain. Whoever takes up said Servant, so that his Master (living in Morris-Town, New-Jersey) may have his again, shall have Three Dollars Reward, and all reasonable Charges
    paid by me, TIMOTHY DAY.
The New-York Mercury, May 26, 1766; June 2, 1766.

WHEREAS John Raft, my Apprentice, hath absented himself for some Time from my Service; this is therefore to forewarn all Joiners, Carpenters, and others from harbouring or employing him; and all Masters of Vessels are forbid concealing or carryying him off: And if any Person shall harbour, employ, or carry off said Appretice, they shall be prosecuted to the utmost
    Extent of the Law. ANDREW BURN.
The New-York Mercury, May 26, 1766.

SIX POUNDS, Reward.

RUN-away from the Subscribers, living in the Counties of Essex and Morris, and Province of New-Jersey, the 24th of May Instant, three Mulatto Fellows, viz, Robin, Ben and Dick; they are all about 5 Feet 10 Inches high, and pretty yellow; two of them have Indian-like Hair, and the other's is cut off, and 'tis imagined they intend for the back Country, as one of them has been in Albany in the King's Service: Ben can read and write. Dick took with them a suit of blue Camblet; the other two have each Camblet Coats, one brown and the other green. Whoever takes up and secures the aforesaid Fellows, so that they may be had again, shall receive six Pounds for the Three, or forty shillings for each of them,
     paid by DANIEL WICKS, Doctor Wm. BUDD,
       or Captain BENJAMIN WILLIAMS.
The New-York Mercury, June 2, 1766.

DESERTED,

FROM the second Battalion of his Majesty's 60th, or Royal American Regiment, and Major Bayard's Company, quartered at New-York; John Caventish, otherwise John Miller, which last Name he enlisted by, as Drummer and Fifer; David Cochran and William Cochran; John Caventish is about 19 Years of Age, 5 Feet 6 Inches high, pale Complexion, grey Eyes, brown Hair. born in Dublin, Ireland, by Trade a Weaver, which Trade he work'd at on Long-Island, before he enlisted; David Cochran is about 20 Years of Age, 5 Feet six Inches high, red Complexion, red Hair, born in the North of Ireland, by Trade a Labourer; William Cochran he is about 21 Years of Age, 5 Feet 10 Inches high, reddish Complexion, brown Hair, born in the North of Ireland: Whoever secures the said Deserters, or any one of them, so that he, or they, may be brought to Conviction, shall receive a Guinea Reward for each, over and above what is allowed by Act of Parliament, by applying to Major Bayard, at Fort George, New-York.
The New-York Mercury, June 2, 1766; June 9, 1766.

RUN away from the subscriber, living in Oyster-Bay, Long-Island, an Apprentice, named Joseph Youngs, by trade a house-carpenter: He is about 5 feet 10 inches high, of a brown complexion: Had on when he went away, a purple cloth coat much faded, a cut velvet jacket, and brown serge breeches, and carried with him sundry other Cloaths; he is sturdy and well-built, and wore his own Hair. Whoever employs or conceals the said Apprentice, may expect to be prosecuted according to Law,
    by me JAMES WHIPPO.
The New-York Mercury, June 9, 1766; June 16, 1766.

Three Pounds Reward.

RUN-away from the subscriber, on Monday the 21st of April last, a yellowish Negro fellow named Bill, formerly belonging to Mr. Cornelius Clopper, at Rariton Landing, in New-Jersey; appears to be about 20 or 22 years of age, about 5 feet 6 inches high, speaks good English, and low Dutch fluently; has a Scar across the Bridge of his Nose. He is a Baker by trade, and understands his Business very well. Had on when he went away, an old red Cloth Jacket, a Pair of old Homespun Trowsers, and an Iron Collar; which last it is supposed he had found Assistance to get taken off. Whoever takes up and returns, or secures him so that I may get him again, shall have THREE POUNDS reward for their Trouble, if taken in this City, and FOUR POUNDS if taken out of it, besides all necessary expences. All Masters of Vessels and other Persons, are warned not to carry off, conceal, or harbour the said Run-away, as they would avoid a Prosecution in the law.
    JOHN KLEIN.   New-York, May 1, 1766.
N. B. No higher Reward will be given.
The New-York Gazette, June 9, 1766; June 16, 1766; June 23, 1766; June 30, 1766 *The New-York Mercury*, June 9, 1766. Minor differences between the papers.

Twenty DOLLARS *Reward.*

MADE *his Escape from the Goal of Somerset County, a certain Doctor Anennias Randell, aged about 25 Years, born upon Long-Island, about 5 Feet 6 Inches high, dark brown Hair, commonly wears it queued, fair Skin, black Eyes; took with him a blue stuff Coat, Buckskin Breeches, generally wears ruffels. Whoever takes up the aforesaid Person, shall receive the above Reward, and all reasonable Charges*
    paid by   Cornelius Lott, *Sub Sheriff.*
                Millstone, June 11.
The New-York Mercury, June 16, 1766. See *The Pennsylvania Gazette*, June 19, 1766, and *The New-York Mercury*, July 28, 1766.

RUN *away on Sunday the 26th Day of May, Philip Mac Manus, an Irish Servant Man, 19 Years old, about 5 Feet five Inches high, has a remarkable Stoop, is much freckled, and has short strait Hair, of a sooty Colour:* Had on when he went away, a grey Ratteen Coat, and Waistcoat, lapelled, a Pair of Leather Breeches, and check'd Shirt.—He is supposed to be gone to Rockaway, or towards Philadelphia; he went off in Company with a white Chimney-Sweeper, who goes by the Name of Tom Vanderill, and 'tis probable he may follow that Business. Whoever secures the said Runaway in any of his Majesty's Goals, so that the Subscriber may have him again, shall be paid Two Pounds Reward, with all reasonable Charges.

JOHN KEATING.   New-York, June 4, 1766.
The New-York Mercury, June 16, 1766; July 7, 1766; July 14, 1766. See *The New-York Mercury*, October 14, 1765, and *The New-York Mercury*, February 9, 1767.

TWENTY DOLLARS Reward.
Millstone, June 11, 1766.

MADE his Escape from the Goal of the County of Somerset, and Province of New-Jersey, a certain Doctor Ananias Randall, aged about Twenty-five Years, born upon Long-Island, about Five Feet 6 Inches high, dark brown Hair, commonly wears it cued, fair Skin, black Eyes; took with him a Stuff Coat, Buckskin Breeches, generally wears Ruffles. Whoever takes up the aforesaid Person, and brings him to the Subscriber at Millstone, shall receive the above Reward, and all reasonable Charges,
   paid by JOB STOCKTON, High Sheriff, or
       CORNELIUS LOTT, Sub Sheriff.

Likewise made his Escape from the Goal of Somerset County, aforesaid, one Robert Mouston, a Taylor, by Trade, born in Scotland, about Five Feet Six Inches high, black Hair, fair Skin, wore a blue Broadcloth Coat and Breeches, and a red Vest. Whoever takes up the aforesaid Person, and brings him to the Subscriber, at Millstone, shall receive TEN DOLLARS Reward, and all reasonable Charges,
   paid by SAMUEL BREWER, Goaler.
The Pennsylvania Gazette, June 19, 1766; July 3, 1766; July 24, 1766. See *The New-York Mercury*, June 16, 1766, and *The New-York Mercury*, July 28, 1766, for Randell.

RUN-away, from the Subscriber, living at New-York, the Beginning of June 1766; a Negro Fellow named Charles, about 5 Feet 10 Inches high, very black, Pock-pitted, and remarkable for his white Teeth; speaks both French and English, Jamaica born, and mark'd under his left Breast P. Le Count: Had on when he went away, a brown Jacket, and a blue short Waistcoat under it, a pair of Trowsers, and a Sailor's round Hat. Whoever takes up the said Negro, and secures him, so that he may be had again, shall have Forty Shillings Reward, and all reasonable Charges,
   paid by ANDREW MYER, in Dock-Street.

N. B. All Masters of Vessels, and others, are hereby warn'd not to harbour of carry off said Servant, at their Peril, as they will answer it as the law Directs.

The New-York Mercury, June 30, 1766. See *The New-York Mercury*, July 30, 1764, and *The New-York Gazette, and Weekly Post-Boy*, October 16, 1766.

RUN-AWAY from his Master, in New-York, the 2d Instant, an Apprentice Boy named Thomas Turner, about 18 Years old; very tall, marked with the small-Pox, can work very well at the Cooper's Trade, and took with him two different Dresses, viz. A new Chocolate-coloured Broad-cloth Coat, with Mettal Buttons, and Breeches of the same; a blue Alopeen Waistcoat without Sleeves, half-worn; the other his common working Dress. All Persons are hereby forbid from securing or employing said Apprentice. Whoever takes him up and secures him, so that his Master may have him again, shall have Twenty Shillings Reward,
paid by James Neavin, Cooper,
in French-Church-Street.

The New-York Mercury, June 30, 1766; July 7, 1766.

Skenesborough, July 11, 1766.
RUN-away from Major Philip Skene at Skenesborough, on Monday morning the 7th Instant; a Negro Man named Cesar, about 5 Feet 6 Inches High, very well set; his fore Teeth are remarkably Wide and Sharp-pointed: He had on when he went away, a brown colour'd coarse Cloth Coat, Soldiers Jacket, Sailors Trowsers, blue Legings, and a Pair of Mokasins adorn'd with Porcupine Quills; the Hair has been lately cut off his Head, except just over the Forehead and Temples, which was left in the Form of a Toupe. Whoever takes up the said Negro and delivers him to his Master at Skenesborough, or to Doctor Samuel Stringer at Albany, shall receive a Reward of one Half-Joe, from either of them.

The New-York Gazette, July 21, 1766; August 11, 1766; August 18, 1766; August 25, 1766. The second and third ads do not have the location and date at the top. See *The New-York Mercury*, July 21, 1766.

RUN-away from Major Philip Skene, at Skenesborough, on Monday Morning the 7th Instant; a Negro Man, named Caesar, about 5 Feet 6 Inches High, very well set. His Fore Teeth are remarkably wide and sharp-pointed. He had on when he went away a brown coloured coarse Cloth Coat, a Soldier's Jacket, Sailor's Trowsers, blue Leggings, and a Pair of Mokasins. adorn'd with Porcupine Quills. The Hair has been lately cut off his Head, except just over the Forehead and Temples, which was left in the Form of a Toupee. Whoever takes up the said Negro, and delivers him to his Master at Skensborough, or to Doctor Samuel Stringer, at Albany, shall receive a Reward of one Half-Joe, from either of them.

The New-York Mercury, July 21, 1766; July 28, 1766; August 11, 1766. See *The New-York Gazette*, July 21, 1766.

Goshen, Orange-County, July 14, 1766.

RUN-away, from the Subscriber, on the 14th Instant, and Apprentice Lad named Barnabas Munro, a likely fresh coloured well set Lad, with dark brown hair, about 19 Years of Age, & about 5 Feet 8 Inches high: Had on when he went away, a new pail-blue [sic] homespun Coat trim'd with white mettal Buttons, with Catgut Eyes, and lin'd with dark blue Shalloon, a strip'd double breasted Linsey-Woolsey Jacket, a Pair of Leather Breeches, butened up before, a Pair of Pumps, and a half worn Castor Hat; took with him also, a dark coloured Soldier's Coat, with Philadelphia Buttons, and a Pair if Linen and a Pair of Woollen Stockings. Whoever takes up said Apprentice Lad, and secures him, so that his Master may have him again, shall receive three Pounds Reward, and all reasonable Charges,
   paid by SAMUEL WICKHAM.

The New-York Mercury, July 21, 1766; July 28, 1766; August 4, 1766; August 11, 1766.

Twenty DOLLARS *Reward.*

MADE *his Escape from the Goal of Somerset County, a certain Doctor Anennias Randell, aged about 25 Years, born upon Long-Island, about 5 Feet 6 Inches high, dark brown Hair, commonly wears it queued, fair Skin, black Eyes; took with him a blue stuff Coat, Buckskin Breeches, generally wears ruffels. Whoever takes up the aforesaid Person, shall receive the above Reward, and all reasonable Charges*
   paid by *Cornelius Lott, Sub Sheriff.*
             Millstone, June 11.

The New-York Mercury, July 28, 1766; August 18, 1766. See *The New-York Mercury*, June 16, 1766, and *The Pennsylvania Gazette*, June 19, 1766.

Queensburgh, in Orange–County, July 10, 1766.
Ten Dollars Reward.

RUN-away, from Moses Clement, two High-Dutch indented Servants, named Christian Fry, and Margaret Fry, his Wife; they are both short, the Man about 5 feet 4 or 5 Inches, hair Complexion, round Face, short black Hair: Had on when he went away, slop't Hat, which has been cut round the Brim; a blue Jacket without Sleeves, with small white Buttons, long Oznaburg Trowsers, shirt of the same, white Worsted Stockings and black Buckles in his Shoes. The Woman shorter than the Man, brownish Complexion, long Vissage, black Eyes and black Hair: Had on when she went away, a white Cap, a straw Hat bound with black, a black quilted Coat and a homespun Check Apron, a blue and white Handkerchief, a red and white do. They carried away large bundles with them, which contains a Soldier's new Coat faced with Green, white Buttons, two large Feather Bed

Pillows, a Pewter Bason, some new Oznaburgs Shirts and Trowsers: The Woman a coarse blue Jacket and a Linnen do, with blue faded Flowers; two Oznaburg Jackets without Sleeves, some white Stockings, and several other Things. All Persons are forewarned from harbouring, imploying, or carrying them away, as they shall answer it at their Peril. Whoever takes up and secures them, in any of his Majesty's Goals, so that their Master may have them again, shall have the above Reward, and all reasonable Charges,
paid by   MOSES CLEMENT.

N. B. They are the same advertised the 13th of April last. They have been seen at Quequiate-Friday, the 11th Inst. where they have sold some of their Cloathing, but could not learn which Way they went: Queensburgh lies bout 4 Miles above Haverstraw, 3 Miles West of Col. Matthew's Furnace.

The New-York Mercury, July 28, 1766; August 4, 1766; August 11, 1766. Only the first ad has the location at the top. See *The New-York Mercury*, April 28, 1766, and *The New-York Mercury*, September 15, 1766.

DESERTED from his Majesty's Royal Regiment of Artillery, MARMADUKE BERWICK, Matross, in Capt. Joseph Walton's Company, at New-York; 5 Feet 7 inches high, smooth fac'd, fresh Complexion, light brown Hair, has a large deep Hole in the upper Part of his right Wrist: Had on when he went away his Regimentals. Whoever apprehends or secures the said Deserter in any of the Goals, and gives Information to Capt. Lieut. Thomas Davies, commanding the said Company at New-York, shall receive the Sum of Twenty Shillings, over and above the Reward offered by Act of Parliament for apprehending Deserters.

The New-York Mercury, July 28, 1766; August 4, 1766; August 11, 1766; August 18, 1766.

RUN-away, on Monday Morning, the 7th Inst. an Irish Servant Man, named Patrick Thompson, 5 Feet 8 Inches high, thin Visage, pale Complexion, has an Impediment in his Speech, occasioned by a Hair Lip, which renders him difficult to understand, magnifying Matters, can read, write a tolerable good Hand, and understands Figures: Had on when he went away an old Beaver Hat, a black cut Wig, new Olive-coloured Thickset Coat, lined with blue Shalloon, with Mohair Buttons the Colour of the Coat, uncertain whether he took a Waistcoat, Shirts, new Buckskin Breeches, much sullied, white Cotton Stockings, and old Shoes, with Brass Buckles, professes the Business of Tallow-Chandler. Whoever secures said Servant, so that his Master may have him again, shall have 30 Shillings Reward, and reasonable Charges,
paid by Smith Ramadge, in New-York,

or ARCHIBALD GARDNER, of Philadelphia.
Queensburgh, in Orange-County, July 10, 1766.
The New-York Mercury, August 4, 1766.

RUN-away from JACOBUS MONTANY, and Company, on Friday the 18th of July, a German Servant Man, named PETER CLOSSEN, a Baker by Trade; about 5 Feet 6 Inches high, thin and swarthy Complection, black Hair and black Eyes, speaks good English and French, about 25 Years old: He is supposed to be gone towards Goshen; has lately been seen at Haverstraw.—Whoever takes up the said Servant, and delivers him to said JACOBUS MONTANYE and Company, at Burling-Slip, shall receive FIVE POUNDS, and all reasonable Charges.   August 11, 1766.

The New-York Gazette, August 11, 1766; August 18, 1766; August 25, 1766; September 1, 1766. See *The New-York Mercury*, August 11, 1766.

RUN-away from *Jacobus Montanye*, and Company, on Friday the 18th of July, a German Servant Man, named Peter Clossen, a Baker by Trade, about 5 Feet 6 Inches high, thin, and swarthy Complection, black Hair, and black Eyes, speaks good English and French, about 25 Years old: Supposed to be gone towards Goshen; has lately been seen at Haverstraw. Whoever takes up the said Servant, and delivers him to said Jacobus Montanye and Company, at Burling's-Slip, shall receive a Reward of *Five Pounds*, and all reasonable Charges.

The New-York Mercury, August 11, 1766; August 18, 1766. See *The New-York Gazette*, August 11, 1766.

RUN-away on Sunday the 10th of this Instant, from JOHN MICHAEL WILL, of this City, Cordwainer, an Apprentice Lad, named JACOB PITT's, about 16 Years of Age, is about four Feet ten Inches high, has a stoop in his Walk, round shoulder'd, wears his own long brown-colour'd Hair: He was seen to cross King's Bridge on Wednesday last;—had on when he went away, an old patch'd Jacket, a Pair of old Leather Breeches, Check Shirt, old Stockings and Shoes, with a Felt Hat. Whoever takes up and secures the said Apprencice, [*sic*] so that his Master may have him again, shall have Two DOLLARS Reward, and reasonable Charges
paid by   JOHN MICHAEL WILL.

Note, Whoever harbours or conceals him, will be prosecured as the Law directs.

The New-York Gazette, August 18, 1766; August 25, 1766; September 1, 1766; September 15, 1766.

RUN-away from John Duncan's Farm, near Schenectady, on Tuesday the 5th of August, a Negro Man, named Charles, well known in the neighbouring Country, and is supposed to be lurking about Norman's Kill, or between Albany and Schenectady. Any Person that will apprehend said Negro, and secures him, so that his Master may have him again, shall receive Two Dollars Reward,
     from JOHN DUNCAN.
 N. B. Said Negro is acquainted in New-York, as he lived some time with Walter Rutherford, Esq; He speaks French, Dutch and English, has a Pearl on one of his Eyes: If he is apprehended out of the County of Albany, Twenty Shillings Reward will be paid, and all reasonable Expences.
 The New-York Mercury, August 18, 1766; August 25, 1766; September 1, 1766. See *The New-York Mercury*, September 16, 1765.

RUN away from the subscriber, of Staten-Island, on Sunday the 17th day of August last, a Negro man, named Toney: Had on when he went away a tow shirt and trowsers, and an old beaver hat; he is about 5 feet 8 inches high, a well set fellow, has a small blemish in his right eye; and 'tis suppos'd is gone towards New England, as he formerly lived there. Whoever takes up the said Negro, and secures him, so that his master may have him again, shall have Forty shillings reward, and all reasonable charges
    paid by ANTHONY WATERS.
 N. B. All Masters of Vessels, and others, are forbid to harbour, conceal, or carry off said fellow, as they will answer it at their Peril.
 The New-York Mercury, September 1, 1766; September 15, 1766; September 22, 1766; September 29, 1766.

RUN-away on Thursday last, a Negro Man, named Tom, has lost two of his Fingers off his Left Hand, is about 5 feet 6 inches high, speaks English and French, and is about 23 Years old. Had on when he went off, a Thickset Jacket ,ad grey Cloth Breeches, a black Handkerchief, a small cock'd Hat, and took with him a Bundle containing a Thickset Coat, a Cotton Knit Jacket, two Pair of black worsted Stockings, a Pair of Shoes half worn, and a Pair of plain Pinchbeck Buckles. Whoever takes up and secures the said Negro, so that I may have him again, shall have *Twenty Shillings* Reward, and all reasonable Charges
    paid by *ALEXANDER STEUART.*
 N. B. None must dare carry him off, employ him, or conceal him, or they must answer the Consequence.

The New-York Gazette, September 15, 1766; September 22, 1766; September 30, 1766.

RAN-away on Friday Night the 5th September, Instant, from Daniel Wiggins of the City of New-York, a Negro Man (Slave) named Peter, about 5 Feet 9 Inches high, has his long thick Wool on his Head, and the Fore-Finger of his Left Hand is remarkably short, the upper Joint inclining on the Back of the Hand about 3 quarters of an Inch, contrary to its usual Situation, and is somewhat stiff in its Use: He speaks both English and French proper, Had on when he went away an old Swanskin Jacket, double breasted, and slash sleev'd, lined with brown Linnen, a check Shirt, long Ozenbrigs Trowsers, no Stockings, but old Shoes, with one Steel and one Pewter Buckle; and had neither Hat or Cap. Whoever takes up said Negro, and brings him to his Master, or secures him so that he may be had again, shall have Twenty Shillings Reward, and all reasonable Charges
          paid by   DANIEL WIGGINS.

N.B. All Persons are strictly forbid to employ, harbour, conceal, or carry him off, as they will be dealt with severely: He understands the Tallow-Chandler's Business.

The New-York Gazette, September 15, 1766. See *The New-York Journal, or General Advertiser,* November 13, 1766.

RUN-away the 3d instant, from the subscriber in New-York, a negro boy, named Tom, about 16 years old, part Indian; he has had the small-pox, and has a scal'd head, part of the top of the head bald: Had on when he went away, a white shirt, two trowsers, an old double breasted swanskin jacket, and a sailor's hat. Whoever takes up said run-away, and brings him to the subscriber, shall have Forty Shillings reward, and all reasonable charges,
          paid by   ROBERT HALLETT.

N. B. All masters of vessels are forewarned from carrying him off, at their peril.

The New-York Mercury, September 15, 1766.

Ten Dollars Reward.

RUN-away, from MOSES CLEMENT, of Orange County, in the Province of New-York, the 10th of July last, two High Dutch indented Servants, named Christian Fry, and Margaret Fry, his Wife; they are both short; the Man about 5 feet 4 or 5 Inches, hair Complexion, round fac'd, short black Hair: Had on when he went away, a flapt Hat cut round the Brim; a blue Jacket without Sleeves, with small white Buttons, long Ozenbrigs Trowsers, Shirts of the same, white Worsted Stockings and black Buckles in his Shoes. The Woman is shorter than the Man, brownish Complexion, long Vissage, black Eyes and black Hair: Had on when she went away, a white

Cap, a straw Hat bound with black, a black quilted Petticoat, and a homespun one, with broad white stripes, Check Apron, a blue and white Handkerchief, and a red and white do. They carried with them large Bundles, which contain'd a Soldier's new Coat fac'd with green, and white Buttons, two large Feather-bed Pillows, a Pewter Basons, some new Ozenbrigs Shirts and Trowsers, a Woman's coarse blue Cloth Jacket, and a Linen one with blue faded flowers, Tow Ozenbrigs Jackets without sleeves, some white stockings, and several other Things. They are gone to the Southward, and have been pursued along the Road towards East-Town, on Delaware: They tell plausible stories as they go, that they are going to see a Brother of his, who has sent for them to work on a Farm upon Shares, and many such like stories to deceive People: They never go together to ask for the Road, he enquires for one Place and she for another; she often complains of being oblig'd to travel in shoes; they have often try'd to buy her shoes, but could not; they have sold several of their Things along the Road, and has offer'd the Soldier's Coat for Twenty Shillings; he pretends to be a good Farmer and Gardener, and she a good Spinster: They both speaks but little English, as they have been in this Country but since last March; it is suppos'd they will soon change their Names and Cloathing; but as they are so remarkable in their sizes, it is hoped some good Persons will secure them before they can effect it. All Persons are forewarned from harbouring, employing, or carrying them away, as they shall answer it at their Peril: Whoever takes up and secures said Servants in any of his Majesty's Goals, so that their Master may have them again, shall have the above Reward, and all reasonable Charges,
         paid by   MOSES CLEMENT.

N. B. Direct for me opposite the New Dutch-Church, in the Broadway, New-York.

The New-York Mercury, September 15, 1766; September 22, 1766.
See *The New-York Mercury*, April 28, 1766, and *The New-York Mercury*, July 28, 1766.

DESERTED from his Majesty's Royal Regiment of Artillery, and Captain Farrington's Company, WILLIAM FORDER, Mattross; he is 25 Years of Age, 5 Feet 9 Inches high, fair Complexion, dark brown Hair, by Trade a Bricklayer; born at Newport in the Isle of Wight; Whoever shall secure the said William Forder in any Goal, or so as he may be brought to Justice, and give Notice thereof to the Commanding Officer of the Regiment at New-York, shall receive TWENTY SHILLINGS, over and above his Majesty's Bounty allowed by Act of Parliament.

The New-York Gazette, September 22, 1766.

RUN-away from the Subscriber, a Negro Man named Caesar, about 5 Feet 5 Inches High: Had on and took with him when he went away, a black and white Kersey Jacket, a brown Duroy Jacket, with blue Lining, Tow Trowsers, Buckskin Breeches and rib'd Linen Stockings; he has bandy Legs, and walks lame, speaks very bad English. Whoever takes him up, and brings him to the Subscriber, shall have 20*s*. Reward and all reasonable Charges, paid by   JOHN SLOSS HOBART.
Manor of Eatton, Suffolk County, Sept. 26, 1766.
The New-York Mercury, September 29, 1766; October 6, 1766. See *The New-York Journal, or General Advertiser*, October 23, 1766, and *The New-York Journal, or General Advertiser*, January 1, 1767.

RUN away on Friday last, from John Milligan, in Beaver-street, a Negro Wench named Phillis, Speaks bad English, is remarkable for her Hobling Gates, [*sic*] and has lost some of the Joints of her Fingers.—Whoever Secures said Wench, so that her Master may have her again, shall have TWO DOLLARS Reward.
    N. B. All masters of Vessels and others, are forbid to Harbour or carry off said Wench, as they shall Answer it at their Peril.
New-York, Oct, 10, 1766.
The New-York Gazette, October 13, 1766.

RUN-away from Henry Holland's Place, on the North Side of Staten-Island, on Wednesday the 1st instant, a negro Man named Cyrus, about 30 Years of Age, about five Feet seven Inches high, he is pretty much wrinkled, with a Monkey Face; he can read and write, and has learned some Latin and knows the Greek Characters: He took with him a new Canoe with an iron Chain, and is painted with Spanish Brown and Tar. Whoever apprehends him, so that his Master may have him again, shall have Forty Shillings reward, and all Charges paid.
The New-York Mercury, October 13, 1766; October 20, 1766; October 27, 1766. See *The New-York Gazette*, From Monday January 5, to Monday January 12, 1767, and *The Massachusetts Gazette, and Boston News-Letter*, February 5, 1767.

RAN away from the Subscriber, in New-York, an Irish Servant Man named Thomas Holmes, 19 Years of Age, about 5 Feet 8 Inches high, pitted with the Small-Pox, light Hair and Eyes, speaks English and Dutch fluently, had on or took with him, a blue great Coat, a Sailors blue Waistcoat with tin Buttons, a Blue Sagathy Coat, a grey Ratteen double breasted Waistcoat, and a Pair of black Breeches. Whoever takes up the said Servant, and

returns him to me or secures him in Gaol, shall have FORTY SHILLINGS Reward, and all reasonable Charges
        paid by   HENRY MARSELIS.
    N. B. All Masters of Vessels and others, are forbid to harbour or carry him off, as they will answer it at their Peril.
    The New-York Gazette, and Weekly Post-Boy, October 16, 1766.

    RAN-AWAY from the Subscriber, living in New-York, the Beginning of Junes Inst. a Negro Fellow named Charles, about five Feet ten Inches high, very black, Pock-pitted, and remarkable for his white Teeth; speaks both French and English, Jamaica born, and mark'd under his left Breast P. le Count; had on when he went away, a brown Jacket, and a blue short Waistcoat under it, a Pair of Trowsers, and a Sailor's round Hat.—Whoever takes up said Negro, and secures him so that he may be had again, shall have FORTY SHILLINGS Reward, and all reasonable Charges
        paid, by   ANDREW MYER, in Dock-Street.
    N. B. All Masters of Vessels and others, are hereby warn'd not to carry off said Servant, at their Peril, as they will answer as the Law directs.—.
    The New-York Gazette, and Weekly Post-Boy, October 16, 1766; *The New-York Journal; or General Advertiser*, October 23, 1766; October 30, 1766; November 13, 1766. See *The New-York Mercury*, July 30, 1764, and *The New-York Mercury*, June 30, 1766.

                FORTY SHILLINGS REWARD.
    RUN-AWAY from the Manor of Eaton, in Suffolk County—A Negro Man, named Caesar, about five Feet five Inches high—he is bandy legged, walks lame, has thick Lips, and speaks very broken English—took away with him a black and white Kersey Jacket, a brown Duroy Jacket without Sleeves, lined with blue, Leather Breeches, and Tow Cloth Trowsers.—He has been seen in this City, in the Fields, near where Major James formerly lived.— Whoever takes him up and brings him to the Printer, at the Exchange, or gives Information so that he may be secured, shall have the above Reward. All Persons are forbid to harbour of conceal the said Runaway, at their Peril.
    The New-York Journal, or General Advertiser, October 23, 1766; October 30, 1766. See *The New-York Mercury*, September 29, 1766, and *The New-York Journal, or General Advertiser*, January 1, 1767.

    RUN-AWAY, a few Days since, from the Subscriber, living in New-York, an Irish Servant Lad named JAMES RONEY, about 5 Feet 10 Inches high;

he is a Lad about 19 Years of Age, much pitted with the Small-pox, has straight light-coloured hair, with a surly kind of Vissage, commonly wears a brown Cloth Jacket, with Brass Buttons without Sleeves, Breeches of the same, and Trowsers over them, and a speckled Shirt with a large single Check: He also took with him, a Cloth Coat, with Brass Buttons, and a second-hand Beaver Hat. All Masters of Vessels and others are hereby warned not to carry off said Servant, at their Peril. Whoever apprehends and secures said Run-away, so that his Master may have him again, shall receive Three Pounds Reward, and all reasonable Charges paid, by JOHN PROVOOST.
The New-York Mercury, October 27, 1766; November 3, 1766.

RUN away from Robert Andrews, who lodges at Mr. John Peasly's, in Maiden-Lane, next door to the coppersmiths shop, an indented servant named Charels Berry; had on when he went away, a suit of blue cloaths, white metal buttons, wears his own hair generally tied, dark complexion, a waver [sic] to trade, about 5 feet 5 inches high, well built, smoth fac'd. Any person that apprehends said Berry, and brings him to his said master, or lodges him in one of his Majesty's goals, so that his master may have him again, shall receive 40 shillings reward, and all reasonable charges paid.
The New-York Mercury, November 3, 1766; November 10, 1766; November 17, 1766.

RUN-away from the Snow James and Mary, John Moor, Master, William Cook, about 20 Years old, wears his own hair, of a fair complexion, about 5 feet 6 inches high: Had on when he went away, a Sailor's white Jacket and trowsers, smooth fac'd, good like, [sic] and wears a sailor's hat.

Likewise John Cook, about 19 years of age, wears his own hair, fair complexion, about 5 feet 6 Inches high, was when he went away, in Sailor's dress, with jacket and trowsers, smooth, thin-faced and good-like.

Likewise James Coulter, about 18 years old, wears a wig, brown complexion, about 5 feet 7 inches high, served part of his time to a Barber: Had on when he went away, an old blue coat, a pair of thickset breeches, good-like, smooth-fac'd: Whoever apprehends all or any of said servants, shall have Forty Shillings for each, by applying to said Master, and all reasonable expences paid; likewise all Masters of vessels on their peril, are discharged from countenancing or carrying them off the Continent.
The New-York Mercury, November 10, 1766; November 24, 1766; December 1, 1766; December 8, 1766; December 15, 1766; December 22, 1766; December 29, 1766.

RAN-away on Sunday the 2d Inst. from Daniel Wiggins of the City of New-York a Negro Man (Slave) named Peter, about 5 Feet 9 Inches high, has long thick Wool on his Head, and the Fore-Finger of his Left Hand remarkably short, the upper Joint inclining on the Back of the Hand about 3 quarters of an Inch, contrary to its usual Situation: He speaks both English and French properly. Had on when he went away an old light colour'd Frize Jacket, double breasted, and slash-sleev'd, with light colour'd Horn Buttons, a blue and white strip'd Linsey Waistcoat, an old Felt Hat, an old Worsted Cap, a check Shirt, long Oznaburgs Trowsers, mill'd Stockings, old Shoes, and Pinchbeck Buckles. Whoever takes up said Negro, and brings him to his Master, or secures him so that he may be had again, shall have a Dollars Reward, and all reasonable Charges

   paid by   DANIEL WIGGINS.

 N. B. All Persons are strictly forbid to employ, harbour, conceal, or carry him off, as they will be dealt with severely: He understands the Tallow-Chandler's Business.

The New-York Journal, or General Advertiser, November 13, 1766.
See *The New-York Gazette*, September 15, 1766.

STOLEN from Doctor Joseph Munsell, of Smith's Clove, in Orange County, and Province of New-York, by one James Brimingham, and one James Colters; two large Horses, two Saddles, and two Briddles, both of them Irishmen, and are apt to drink; Brimingham is a well-set Fellow, wears a brown Coat, and a yellow Wig, can sing very well; the other is a slim Fellow, wears his own Hair of a light Colour: About four Weeks after this Theft was committed, both these Villains robbed a New-England Gentleman between Kinderhook and Albany, and the next Day were taken, but made their Escape from the Officer. Whoever will apprehend both or either of them, shall have Five Pounds Reward for each, if committed to any of his Majesty's Goals,

   paid by me   JOSEPH MUNSELL.

The New-York Mercury, November 17, 1766.

RUN away on Friday Night, the Fourteenth Instant, from Samuel Waldron, at the Ferry, Long-Island; An Irish Servant, named John Boyle, about five Feet nine Inches high, has short brown curled Hair, fresh coloured, and fair Complexion; had on when he went away, a blue Pea Jacket, and a green one under it, blue Breeches, and blue Stockings.

 Whoever takes up the said Servant, and returns or secures him, shall have Forty Shillings Reward, and all reasonable Charges,

   paid by   SAMUEL WALDRON.

N. B. All Masters of Vessels and others, are warned not to harbour, conceal, or carry him away, as they will answer it at their Peril.
The New-York Journal, or General Advertiser, November 20, 1766; December 4, 1766. See *The New-York Gazette*, From January 16, to February 2, 1767.

RUN-away from the subscriber, on the 16th of November instant, an Irish servant girl, named Margaret M'Donald, about 18 years of age, black hair.—Had on when she went away, a green camblet gown, a red short cloak and a round black hat. Any person or persons that takes up the said servant girl and will bring her to her said master at Beekman's slip, shall have TWO SHILLINGS reward; and I hereby forewarn all or any person or persons, from harbouring or entertaining the said servant girl, at their peril, he or they shall be prosecuted according to law for so doing.
          THOMAS POOLE.   *New-York, November* 17, 1766.
The New-York Journal, or General Advertiser, November 20, 1766; December 4, 1766; December 11, 1766.

RUN-away from his Master, Isaac Gomez, a Negro Lad named Prince, about 20 Years old, very black, pretty slim, talks good English, and has been often seen in this City in different Dresses, tells a plausible story, has taken all his Cloths with him, and 'tis imagined will go the sea if possible; therefore this is to forewarn all Masters of Vessels and others, not to carry him off or harbour him, as they must answer it at their Peril. Whoever takes up said Negro, and brings him to his said Master, shall be well rewarded for their Trouble.
The New-York Mercury, December 1, 1766. See *The New-York Mercury*, July 15, 1765.

WHEREAS a certain *Joshua Gowing*, who came to *America*, with Major James, (as a Servant) last Spring, absented himself from his Master's Service some Days since, and 'tis supposed to be concealed in some House in this City.—He is about 26 Years of age, fair Complexion, wears his Hair, is genteely made, about 5 Feet 7 Inches high, with a tetter'd [*sic*] Face, hazle eyed, but a forbidden Leer under his Brow, and a smooth spoken Tongue. The Cause of his absconding was owing to the many Convictions of recent Frauds: He has borrowed Monies to a considerable amount, from different People in this Place, without the Approbation or Knowledge of his Master or Mistress: He has received Monies to pay different Tradesmen, and not perform'd his Trust: He has even had the Impudence to borrow Money, and given Orders upon the Major: He has drank his Wine; and being convicted of tapping a Pipe and Quarter Cask, he had the Assurance to tell the Major and his Lady, "*he did it to taste!*" He is a most abominable

Liar, and a Person that can be by no Means trusted; I therefore publish this Advertisement to all Mankind, to warn the Gentlemen in North-America, from taking so base a Scoundrel into their Service; who had all the Encouragement a good Servant could have expected.

The Major sends his Servants to Market with Money; He never gives a Servant, or any other Person whatever, an Order or Authority to borrow Money in his Name; as William Foreman, Esq; is his Agent; and to whom he shall always wait on himself.

A. JAMES.

The New-York Mercury, December 1, 1766; December 15, 1766.

December 1, 1766.

RUN-away from his Master, Isaac Mann of Still Water, near Albany, about the 18th of November last, a Negro Man named HAM, middling Size, about 30 Years old, had on a furr'd Cap, red cloth Leggins, check'd Shirt, strip'd flannel Vest, Dutch Blanket—took with him a Musket—has a counterfeit Pass, sign'd with Capt. Murry's Name. Whoever takes up said Run-away, and secures him so that his Master may have him, shall receive three Dollars Reward, and all necessary Charges

paid by   ISAAC MANN.

N. B. He formerly liv'd with, and was owned by J. Chandler, Esq; of N. Haven.

The Connecticut Courant; and the Weekly Advertiser, December 8, 1766; December 15, 1766.

TEN DOLLARS Reward.

RUN-away, the first of December Instant, from the Subscriber, living opposite the Coffee-House, in New-York, an Irish Servant Man named Michael M'Mullen, a Skinner and Breeches-maker by Trade, about 5 Feet 6 or 7 Inches high, well set, 28 Years of Age, of a surly Look, and very hollow from the Crown of his Head to his Temples, has just lost one of his fore Teeth, chews Tobacco, and is much addicted to swearing and drinking: Had on, and took with him, a white Wilton Coat, lappelled, brown Holland Lining, one Cotton and Silk cross-bar'd Waistcoat, and another of Irish striped Woollen, Leather Breeches, and wears a light-coloured Wig, but his own Hair is black. Whoever takes up and secures the said Servant, so that his Master may have him again, shall receive the above Reward, and all reasonable Charges

paid, by   CORNELIUS RYAN.

N. B. All Masters of Vessels and others, are hereby forewarn'd to harbour or carry him off at their Peril.

The New-York Mercury, December 8, 1766.

Philadelphia, December 9, 1766.

WHEREAS Susannah McGlocklin hath been confined in the Workhouse of this City for six Weeks past, and her Master, John Hanlin, in New York, hath had Notice of it; these may serve to let said Hanlin know, that if he does not come or send for said Servant, in two Weeks from the above Date, and pay the Charges, she will be sold out for the same, by

JAMES WHITEHEAD, Keeper of said Workhouse.

The Pennsylvania Gazette, December 11, 1766; December 18, 1766.

Fifteen Dollars Reward.

RUN away from their Master in New-York, two indented Servants, one an English Man, named Joseph M'Nabb, aged about thirty-five Years, write a good Hand, is a tolerable Scholar; he is about five Feet ten Inches high, of a tawny Complexion, speaks good English; had on when he went away, a brown Wig, a Wool Hat, a dark colour'd Coat and Breeches, striped Waistcoat, grey Stockings and a white Shirt.—The other a Scotch Man, named William Rankin, a Shoe-maker by Trade, about twenty-three Years of Age, a little pitted with the Small-Pox, wears his own Hair; he is about five Feet six Inches high; had on when he went away, a brown coloured Coat and Breeches, striped Drugget Waistcoat, and grey Stockings.— Whoever secures them, so that their Master may have them again, shall have Ten Dollars for M'Nabb, and Five for Rankin, as a Reward, and reasonable Charges

paid by ALEXANDER M'CULLUGH,
at Mr. Elkanah Deane's, Broad-Street, New-York,

N. B. It has been remarked by several, that none elopes but Irish People, but it is evident from the above, that there are other People of as bad a Species as the Hibernians.

The New-York Journal, or General Advertiser, December 20, 1766; January 1, 1767; January 15, 1767; January 22, 1767; January 29, 1767.

WHEREAS a young Woman named Anne Simmons, left her Parents at Charlestown, in South-Carolina, about five Years ago, and came to this Place; if she be now living, and will apply to Capt. John Schermerhorn, in New-York, she will hear of something much to her Advantage. 'Tis supposed since her Departure, she is married to a Person of the Name of Manning.

The New-York Mercury, December 29, 1766.

1767

FORTY SHILLINGS REWARD.

RUN-AWAY in October last, from the Manor of Eaton, in Suffolk County—A Negro Man, named Caesar, about five Feet five Inches high—he is bandy legged, walks lame, has thick Lips, and speaks very broken English—took away with him a black and white Kersey Jacket, a brown Duroy Jacket without Sleeves, lined with blue, Leather Breeches, and Tow Cloth Trowsers.—He has been seen in this City, in the Fields, near where Major James formerly lived.—Whoever takes him up and brings him to the Printer, at the Exchange, or gives Information so that he may be secured, shall have the above Reward.

All Persons are forbid to harbour of conceal the said Runaway, at their Peril.

The New-York Journal, or General Advertiser, January 1, 1767; January 8, 1767; January 15, 1767; January 22, 1767; January 29, 1767. See *The New-York Mercury*, September 29, 1766, and *The New-York Journal, or General Advertiser*, October 23, 1766,

FIVE DOLLARS Reward,

RAN away from the Subscriber, an Indented Servant named Alexander Johnston; about twenty-one Years of Age, five feet, six or seven inches high; a strong well built fellow, of a dull sullen countenance: had on when he went away a brown Coat, claret coloured waistcoat, a blue under ditto, a check shirt, Wool Hat, black worsted shagg breeches, grey worsted stockings, new shoes, with a pair of open wrought steel buckles, has dark brown hair generally tied. Whoever secures said Servant, and brings him to his Master, in Smith Street, New-York, at the Corner of the float, shall have the above Reward, and all reasonable Charges paid by me   RICHARD SAUSE, Cutler.

The New-York Gazette, From Monday January 5, to Monday January 12, 1767; From Monday January 12, to Monday January 19, 1767; From Monday February 2, to Monday February 9, 1767.

RUN away from HENRY HOLLAND's Place on the North Side of Staten Island, in the Colony of New-York, on the first Day of October last, a Negro named Cyrus, between 25 and 30 Years of Age, about 5 Feet 8 Inches high, he has a mean look with a Monkey Face, he can read and write, has learn'd some Latin and knows the Greek Characters: It is supposed he is gone towards Boston where he was born, in the Rev. Samuel

Auchmuty's Fathers Family, whoever apprehends him, so that his Master may have him again shall have FIFTEEN Spanish DOLLARS Reward.

The New-York Gazette, From Monday January 5, to Monday January 12, 1767; From Monday January 12, to Monday January 19, 1767; From Monday January 26, to Monday February 2, 1767; From Monday March 2, to Monday March 9, 1767. See *The New-York Mercury*, October 13, 1766, and *The Massachusetts Gazette, and Boston News-Letter*, February 5, 1767.

RUN-away the 2d of this Month, from Capt. John Schermerhorne, a Negro Boy named ORONOCO, generally called NOK, about 16 or 16 Years old, a likely black Boy; had on when he went away, a blue Pea Jacket, lined with red Baize, Leather Breeches, Yarn Stockings and white mill'd Cap.— Whoever will take up the said Boy and bring him to his Master at New-York, shall have Forty Shillings Reward and all reasonable Charges paid.

The New-York Journal, or General Advertiser, January 15, 1767; January 22, 1767; January 29, 1767; February 5, 1767.

WHEREAS a certain John Connor, an indented servant of mine, hath absented himself from my service, and taken sundry articles from different people in my name. This is to forewarn any person from crediting him, as I will pay no debts that he has, or may contract. A reward of twenty shillings will be given to any person who apprehends the said run-away, and brings
        him to   THOMAS WHITE.

The New-York Mercury, January 19, 1767.

RUN-away, from the Subscriber, the 1st Inst. living at Clavarack, a Negro Man, named Crispus Cross 6 Feet high, of a yellow Cast, and raw-boned: Had on when he went away, a half-worn Felt Hat, a dark brown Frize Coat, white Shirt, Mettal Buttons, and an old Thickset Coat, Buckskin Breeches, blue homspun Stockings, and red Indian Stockings over them. Whoever takes up and secures the said Negro, so that his Master may have him again, shall receive Five Pounds Reward, and all reasonable Charges,
        paid by me   JOHN FREDERICK RIES.

The New-York Mercury, January 19, 1767; January 26, 1767; February 9, 1767; March 2, 1767. See *The Connecticut Courant; and the Weekly Advertiser*, February 9, 1767.

                      New-York, January 22.
RUN-away, on Friday the 26 of last month, from his master, the subscriber, an indented Irish servant boy, called Isaac Beatie, about 14 years of age, likely, and of a fair complexion, with dark coloured hair, about 4 feet 11 or

5 feet high: had on when he left his master a superfine blue cloth coat, much wore, a red flannel waistcoat, blue plush breeches, and a large beaver hat. He was seen at Newark in the province of New-Jersey about a fortnight ago, and is supposed on his way to Philadelphia. Whoever takes up the above described servant and brings him to his master at New-York, shall have THREE POUNDS reward, or if secured in any of his Majesty's goals in the provinces of New-York, Jersey, or Pennsylvania, notice being sent to his master, FORTY SHILLINGS reward and all reasonable charges
              paid by   PHILIP J. LIVINGSTON.

The Pennsylvania Journal, and the WeeklyAdvertiser, January 22, 1767; January 29, 1767; February 12, 1767; February 26, 1767.

              Run-away, from his Bail,

IN this City, last Monday Night, a certain Michael Thomas, of Ulster County, and Province of New-York; he went off with his Wife; Thomas is about 5 Feet 10 Inches high, has black Hair and Eyes, very brown Complexion, is a German, but talks pretty good English, about 40 Years old, and 'tis supposed is concealed in New-York, by some of this Countrymen; his Wife is a very brown Woman: Had on when he went away, a blue Great-Coat, but had several Cloths with him, and among them a Claret-coloured Coat. Whoever takes up or secures him in any Goal, so that he may be brought to Justice, shall have Five Pounds Reward, paid by the Subscriber, living in Ulster-County.
            JOHN WHARRY.

The New-York Mercury, January 26, 1767; February 2, 1767; March 2, 1767.

              New-York, February 1, 1767.

RUN away on Monday last the 27th of January from Samuel Waldron at the Ferry, Long-Island, an Irish Servant, named John Boyle, about 5 Feet 9 Inches high, has short brown curl'd Hair, is fresh colour'd, and of a fair Complexion. Had on when he went away, a striped Blanket Coat, with flat Pewter Buttons to it, a blue Pea Jacket, and a green one under it, and a brown colour'd Pair of Broad Cloth Breeches, blue Yarn Stockings; had a good Hat, and generally wears it uncock'd; and has a particular kind on grinning Smile when he talks, with a quick Motion of his Eye-Lids at the Time.—Whoever takes up the said Servant, and returns him to his Master, or secures him so that he may be had again, shall have FORTY SHILLINGS Reward, and all reasonable Charges
            paid by   SAMUEL WALDRON.

    N. B. All Masters of Vessels and others, are forewarned not to harbour, conceal, or carry him off, as they will answer it at their Peril.

The New-York Gazette, From Monday January 26, to Monday February 2, 1767; From Monday February 2, to Monday February 9, 1767; From Monday February 23, to Monday March 2, 1767; From Monday March 9, to Monday March 16, 1767; From Monday March 16, to Monday March 23, 1767; From Monday March 23, to Monday March 30, 1767; From Monday April 6, to Monday April 13, 1767. See *The New-York Journal, or General Advertiser,* November 20, 1766.

RUN-away from *Henry Holland's* Place on the North Side of *Staten-Island,* in the Colony of *New-York,* on the First of *October* last, a Negro named *Cyrus,* between 25 and 30 Years of Age, about 5 Feet 8 Inches high, he has a mean look with a Monkey Face, he can read and write, has learn'd some Latin, and knows the Greek Characters: It is supposed he is gone towards *Boston* where he was born, in the Rev. *Samuel Auchmuty's* Fathers Family, whoever apprehends him, so that his Master may have him again shall have *Fifteen Spanish Dollars* Reward.

If the Negro should be taken up near *Boston,* it is desired he may be secur'd, and Notice give to *R. & B. Draper,* Printers

The Massachusetts Gazette, and Boston News-Letter, February 5, 1767; February 12, 1767; February 19, 1767. See *The New-York Mercury,* October 13, 1766, and *The New-York Gazette,* From Monday January 5, to Monday January 12, 1767.

RUN-away, from the Rev. John-Frederick Rees of Clovarack, on the First of January last, a Molatto Negro Man, named Crispus Cros, about Six Feet high, and raw-bon'd, had on when he went away, a dark brown long friz'd Coat, half worn felt Hat, red Indian Stockings, knock-kneed, speaks good English, writes and reads well, he pretends to understand the Fulling Business; he was bought of one Harris near Rhode-Island. Whoever shall take up said Slave, and bring him to the Printer herof, shall receive Five Pounds New-York Currency reward, and all reasonable Charges.

Feb. 2, 1767.

The Connecticut Courant; and the Weekly Advertiser, February 9, 1767; February 16, 1767. See *The New-York Mercury,* January 19, 1767.

THREE DOLLARS, Reward.

RUN-away, in the Night of the 3d instant, from his Lodgeings in the Meadows, Thomas Higgins, otherwise John Higgins, otherwise John Ornals, and stole 4 large Gammons, a new Pair of blue Breeches, follows the Sea, commonly wears a blue Jacket, a brown Wig, a brown Pair of

Breeches, blue Stockings, has very small Eyes, and much pock-mark'd; he is about 5 Feet 4 or 6 Inches high: Whoever will takes up the said Thief, and secures him in one of his Majesty's Goals, shall receive the above Reward from me   JACOB NICE.

N. B. All Masters of Vessels are desired to secure him, if he should offer to ship himself, as he gave Notice he was going to Sea.

The New-York Mercury, February 9, 1767; February 16, 1767; March 2, 1767.

RUN-away from the subscriber, on saturday evening last, an indented servant man named Philip McManus, about 19 years old, five feet 6 inches high, born in Ireland, of a swarthy complexion, sooty colour'd hair, has a remarkable stoop, and is very round shoulder'd. Likewise Dublin, a Negro lad about 18 years old, about the same size as McManus, has remarkable thick lips and big mouth, and when accused of a crime, or in a passion, stammers much in his speech: They are both chimney sweepers, and have took no clothes with them but their working dress. Whoever apprehends and secures the said run-aways, so that their master may have them again, shall have, if taken in the city, Ten shillings for each; if any distance from the city a reward accordingly,

paid by   John Keating.

N. B. All masters of vessels are hereby forewarn'd of carrying off either of said run-aways.

The New-York Mercury, February 9, 1767. See *The New-Mercury*, October 14, 1765, and *The New-York Mercury*, June 16, 1766, for McManus.

RUN *away, on Tuesday night the 10th inst. a negro man called Peter, about 5 feet 7 inches high, marked with the small-pox, about 22 years of age: Had on when he went away, a brown cloth coat, red cuffs and cape, buttons and holes of the same, the waistcoat trimmed the same way; also the lining red, a pair of black worsted breeches, grey worsted stockings, and a pair of shoes half worn. Said negro talks good French and Spanish. Any person bringing him to the subscriber, shall have twenty shillings, and all reasonable charges*

paid by me, RICHARD MERCER, *living in King-street.*

The New-York Mercury, February 23, 1767; March 2, 1767; March 9, 1767.

RUN away the first instant, from the subscriber, a servant man, named Lodwick Abel, a German, about 24 years of age, black straight hair, about 4 feet [sic] 4 inches in height, has a large nose, speaks no English, had on when he went away and took with him, a light bluecoat and waistcoat, with red lining, sheep-skin breeches, round brass buckles, a wool hat, two coarse white shirts, and mill'd stockings: whoever takes up said servant, and brings him to Mr. Robert Murray, merchant in New-York, shall have two dollars reward and reasonable charges paid,

JACOB SPEIRA, Gardiner.

The New-York Journal, or General Advertiser, March 5, 1767; March 12, 1767; April 2, 1767; *The New-York Mercury*, March 30, 1767; April 6, 1767; April 13, 1767; April 27, 1767. Minor differences between the papers.

RUN away from the House of *Jeremy Hoogboom*, at Claverack, in the County of Albany, an indented Servant Man, named *Jacob Rooss*, and from the House of *Jasper Cole*, near Claverack, an Indented Servant Man, named *Jacob Thom*, the said Servants are both Germans, and Millers by Trade: *Jacob Rooss*, is about 24 Years of Age, about 5 Feet 7 Inches high, is a strong well built Fellow, wears his Hair which is of a light colour and generally wears a Comb in it, is full Fac'd and hard Featur'd.—*Jacob Thom*, is about 20 Years of Age, 5 Feet 9 Inches high, light Hair and is well looking Young Man: They both commonly wore Soldiers red Coats faced with blue, but 'tis not unlikely they may change them.—Any Person who discovers and secures the said Servants, and gives Notice thereof to Mr. *Dudley Davis*, at Katts-Kill, or to Mr. *John Deas*, Peruke-maker, in New-York, shall have a Reward of FIVE DOLLARS for each; and the same Reward shall be given, and all reasonable Charges paid by any Person who shall deliver the said Servants to the said

Dudley Davis, at Katts-Kill.

The New-York Gazette, From Monday March 30, to Monday April 6, 1767; From Monday April 6, to Monday April 13, 1767; From Monday April 20, to Monday April 27, 1767.

A GERMAN Man, his wife, with two small children, one at the breast, have absented themselves from their master, since Thursday last, and are supposed to be lurking in some house among their countrymen in this city; all such people are forewarn'd by this Advertisement, from entertaining them at their peril: And any person informing the Printer hereof where they are, so that they may be had again, shall receive Five Dollars reward. The man is a short fellow, has a remarkable hump on one of his shoulders, and a broad flat face, thick bushy hair, and wears a Soldier's short red coat: The woman of a middling stature, small features, and fair complexion.

The New-York Mercury, April 13, 1767; April 20, 1767; April 27, 1767.

RUN-away on Tuesday the 21st ult. a Negro Wench, named Daphne; she is tall and likely, not very black, has a Scar on one Hand, that looks as if it has been scalded: Her Cloathing, when she left Home, consisted of a brown Tow-cloth Shift, and green Stuff Waistcoat and Pettycoat, with a blue and white Homespun under Pettycoat. Whoever brings said Wench to her Master, or secures her, that he may get her, shall have Twenty Shillings Reward, and reasonable Charges,
          paid by   MYER MYERS.
    N. B. All Persons are herby forbid harbouring said Wench, or Masters of Vessels carrying her off.
The New-York Mercury, May 4, 1767; May 11, 1767.

RUN-away, a few Days ago, from JOHN COMBES, of Jamaica, on LONG-ISLAND, a Negro Man named PRIMUS, about 25 Years old, about 5 Feet 6 Inches high, well set, is a little deformed in the Wrist of his Left Arm, by its being bent, and a little bigger than the other: Had on when he went away, a blue Frize Coat and Leather Breeches, with blue Stockings, and 'tis likely has taken a great Coat with him. Whoever takes up and secures the said Negro, so that his Master may have him again, shall if taken on the Island, have TWENTY SHILLINGS Reward; and if any other Place, FORTY SHILLINGS, and all reasonable Charges
          paid, by   JOHN COMBES.
N. B. All Masters of Vessels are forbid to carry him off.
The New-York Mercury, May 11, 1767; May 18, 1767; June 8, 1767; June 14, 1767.

RUN-AWAY, from the subscriber, living in King-street, New-York, on Thursday the 17th instant, a Negro wench, named SYLVIA, formerly the Property of Mr. Ralph Furman, about 28 Years old, stoops much when she walks, and has a small scar on her right cheek: Had on when she went away, a pettycoat, one side blue, and the other yellow, a green quilt about her shoulders, and 'tis imagined is harbour'd in this city. Whoever takes up and secures said Wench, so that she may be had again, shall receive FOUR DOLLARS reward, and all reasonable charges,
          paid by   WILLIAM STEWART.
The New-York Mercury, May 25, 1767; June 1, 1767.

WHEREAS the subscriber, MATTHEW BRETT, of the Fishkills, in Dutchess county, purchased a Negro Boy of OBADIAH ROBINSON, in the 6th day of this instant May, for £. 40 New-York currency, of which he paid him in hand £. 22-1, and gave him a note of hand for 17-19, to be paid next May ensuing; but finding the said Robinson to be an arrant rogue, and that the sale was an horrid cheat, as the said boy he sold was free-born, tho' he sold him as a slave for life. These are therefor to forbid any person after this date, to accept or receive the said note, or an order upon it, in any payment whatsoever, as I am determined never to pay its contents. The said Robinson is a well-built man, near 6 feet high, brown hair, having a dark brown coat on, a black lappell'd jacket bound with black, buckskin breeches, and a hat bound with black ferriting, &c. Whoever takes up the said fellow, and continues him in any of his Majesty's goals, and sends notice to the subscriber, shall have THREE POUNDS New-York currency,
reward, paid by MATTHEW BRETT.
The New-York Mercury, May 25, 1767; June 1, 1767.

New-York, June 13, 1767.
RAN-away, the 8th Inst. June, from the Subscriber, at Romapough, a Negro Man named Hack, about 30 Years of Age, 5 Feet 4 Inches high, well set, had on a white Broadcloth Coat, a black Calimanco Waistcoat, yellow Breeches and black Stockings:—Whoever takes up the said Negro, and returns or secures him, so that his Master may get him again, shall have Forty Shillings New-York Money Reward; and all Persons are hereby warned not to entertain, conceal, or remove him away, as they will answer it at their Peril:—Note, he is suspected to be now in New-York. He speaks Dutch and English well.
LAWRENCE JACOBUS VAN BUSHKIRCK.
The New-York Journal; or The General Advertiser, June 18, 1767; June 25, 1767; July 2, 1767.

TAKEN up in the County of Orange, and Province of New-York, and now in Confinement in the Court-House of Orange-Town, a Negro Man, about 5 Feet 4 Inches, aged, as he says 26 Years, has on a blue Coat and a pair of strip'd Ticking Trowsers, and likewise says he belongs to CHARLES BURNFIELD, Merchant, in Eden town, North-Carolina, and his Name is Sheford, and run-away from the Schooner Lydia, John Miller, Commander, when he was at Staten-Island, near N. York, when they were taking in Water: The said Negro was put into Confinement the 11th of June, Ins. and is now under the Care of
EBENEZER WOOD, Dep. Sheriff.
The New-York Gazette, From Monday June 15, to Monday June 22, 1767; From Monday June 29, to Monday July 6, 1767.

SIX POUNDS, Reward.

DESERTED from his special Bail, a few Days again, near the Pond, in the Precinct of Haverstraw, County of Orange, and Province of New-York, a certain NATHANIEL BAREMORE; he is middle-sized, of a dark Complexion, very fair and insinuating in Conversation: He took with him a Stallion and a Mare, which he before had made over by Bill of Sale to his said Bail: The Mare is 11 Years old, 13 Hands high, a Sorrel, with a drooping Star in her Face, and was in Foal by BRITAIN. The Stallion is about 14 Hands high, a dark Bay, with a drooping Star in his Face, rising three Years, got by BRITAIN, and could often have been sold for £60. Whoever apprehends the said Baremore with the Stallion and Mare, and will brig him to the Subscriber, living at the Place above mentioned, shall receive 40s. for the Man or either of the Horses, and reasonable Charges,
    paid by WILLIAM FELTER.   June 22, 1767.

The New-York Mercury, June 22, 1767; June 29, 1767; July 20, 1767; August 17, 1767.

New-York, June 25, 1767.

WHEREAS on Tuesday Evening last, a young Man about 5 Feet and a half high, well set, fresh coloured, freckled Face, sandy coloured Hair, had on a red Waistcoat without Sleeves, a Check Shirt and black Breeches, came to my Shop, near the Oswego-Market, told me he was the Son of Mr. John Riker of this City, that he was lately come from Sea with Captain Prince (who frequents my Shop) on his Account, to take of me such Clothes as were necessary for his outfit.—Not doubting the Truth of a Story, told with so many probable Circumstances, I delivered him such Goods as he chose, viz. Three Yards of blue and Pink mixt seven Quarter broad Cloth, yellow double gilt Metal Buttons, with all other Trimmings suitable for a Coat and Breeches, amounting in the whole to £. 7-11, which he carried away. But next Morning I discover'd that he had no Orders from Captain Prince, was neither the Son of Mr. Riker, nor known to either of them; nor have I yet been able to discover who he is.—These are therefore to desire, that if any of the said Articles are offer'd to sale, carried to any Taylor to be made up, or can otherwise be discovered, that they may be stopped, the Man secured, and Notice given to me; for which, if the Goods are recovered a handsome Reward will be given in Proportion to the Service done, besides all reasonable Charges
    paid, by THOMAS FISHER.

The New-York Journal; or The General Advertiser, June 25, 1767; July 2, 1767; July 9, 1767; July 16, 1767.

RUN away on the 17th of *June*, from *Tanton* Forge, in the County of *Burlington*, in *New-Jersey*, three Servant Men; one named PHILIP HALL, by Birth a *German*, about 35 Years old, round Visage, and fresh Complection, black Hair and dark Eyes, square set and fleshy, and it is thought has a small hair Mole on one Cheek; He pretends to have a Wife at *New-York*, and was taken up there a few Months ago, and upon fair Promises, bought by the Subscriber out of the Workhouse at *Philadelphia*.

One other named DANIEL DAYLEY, an *Irishman*, about 24 Years old, five Feet two Inches high, black Hair, dark Eyes, thick lipp'd. well set, and corpulent; has a Brogue on his Tongue, is smooth spoken, and apt to beg.

One other named JOHN COURTNEY, born in *Ireland*, aged about 24 Years, light brown Hair, with Curls; thick Lipp'd, good Teeth, and they stand distinct or apart from each other, fair Countenance, and a good Look, about 5 Feet, 5 Inches high.

About four Months ago, Run away from the same Forge, a Servant Man named JOHN SHIRLOCK; he understands the Taylor's Trade, and any Sort of Country Work: He is about 28 Years old, 5 Feet, 5 Inches high, black Hair, Pock-marked, thick Negro-lipp'd, his Eyes a little sunk in, loves Liquor, and is abusive and foul mouthed: He had Buck-skin Breeches, a good blue Coat short skirted; the Cloaths of the others unknown. It is expected they are gone towards *New-York*. Whoever takes up any of them, and delivers them into the Gaol of *New-York*, or any of the Goals of *New-Jersey*, so that the Owner may have them again, shall receive *FORTY SHILLINGS* Reward for each,

        paid by me,   *CHARLES READ.*

The New-York Gazette or The Weekly Post-Boy, June 25, 1767; July 2, 1767; July 9, 1767; July 16, 1767; July 30, 1767; August 6, 1767.

RUN-away the 6th instant, July, from Joseph Wicks, of Huntington, on Long-Island, cooper, an apprentice, named David Kelly, a lusty young man, of about 19 years of age, light complexion, and sandy coloured hair; had on when he went away, a blue broad cloth waistcoat, white shirt, whitish strip'd or tow trowsers, a felt hat, worsted stockings, and old shoes— Whoever takes up said apprentice, and secures him in any goal, and sends me word, shall have Two Dollars reward, and all reasonable charges,

        paid by   JOSEPH WICKS.

The New-York Journal; or The General Advertiser, July 9, 1767. See *The New-York Journal; or The General Advertiser*, July 30, 1767.

        Newburgh (in Ulster County) July 13, 1767.

Run away from James Stickney in Ulster County, in New-York, 7th Inst. a White Servant Man, named Asahel Nickson—he is about twenty-five Years

of Age, of a dark Complexion, short, black Hair, black Eyes, his fore Teeth very much broke out—he is about five Feet nine Inches high, speaks good English. He had on, when he went away, a felt Hat, dark flannel Shirt, dark check'd linentt long Trowsers, and old Shoes. Whoever will take up said Servants, and give Notice or bring him to his said Master, shall have three Pounds, Lawful Money Reward, and all necessary Charges
      paid by me,   JAMES STICKNEY.
  The Connecticut Courant, July 20, 1767; July 27, 1767. See *The New-York Mercury,* August 3, 1767.

RUN-away the 29th of June, an Irish servant man, named Florence Crawley, had on when he went away a waistcoat without sleeves, with red fore parts, and blue back parts; a light coat, yarn stockings, is much pock-mark'd, has much of the brogue is knock-kne'd, has clumsy legs and a heavy gait, and pretends to be a surgeon. ALSO RUN-away the 20th instant, another servant, named Joseph Jessop, had on when he went away an old brown cloth coat, and dark brown waistcoat and breeches, grey ribb'd stockings, check shirt, Sailor's round hat, and brown wig, is much pitted with the small-pox, is disabled in both arms, so as he cannot straighten them, has two spots on his head where no hair grows, and pretends to be a taylor and weaver, Whoever takes up and secures said servants or either of them, and brings them to the printer hereof shall receive 20 shillings reward, for each, and all reasonable charges,
            New-York, July 22, 1767,
  The New-York Journal; or The General Advertiser, July 23, 1760; July 30, 1767; August 13, 1767.

BROKE goal, last thursday night, the 24th inst. out of Morris county goal, Alexander M'Cormick, an Irish man, about 40 years of age, 5 feet 10 inches high, with short black curled hair, has much of the Brogue, on his tongue: had on when he went away an old blue cloath coat, a green jacket, blue everlasting breeches, grey yarn stockings, pumps, and pretends to play on the bag-pipes; and it is supposed to be gone towards New-York, as his wife is there.—Whoever shall take up the said M'Cormick, a Prisoner for debt, and him secure, in any of his Majesty's goals, shall have 10 Dollars reward,
     paid by   *Daniel Cooper,* sheriff.
  The New-York Mercury, July 27, 1767; August 3, 1767; August 17, 1767.

TAKEN up, and is now in the Goal in Orange-Town, in the County of Orange, a Negro Man who calls himself Abraham Smith, and says he belonged to Benjamin Smith, of Rhode-Island, but that his Master was dead, and he left free: He says he is about 30 Years: He is 6 Feet high, well-

set, thick lips, long Vissage, his Back well marked by Stripes, has a Scar across the main Sinnew of the right Leg; and has on a black jacket, Check Shirt, and an Ozenbrigs Trowsers. The Owner is desired to send for said Negro, and pay Charges,
to   EBENEZER WOOD, Under-Sheriff.
The New-York Mercury, July 27, 1767; August 3, 1767; August 10, 1767; August 17, 1767.

RUN-away from the Subscriber living in New-York, an Apprentice, named Edward Sparger, A Shoemaker by Trade, about 6 Feet 8 Inches high, [sic] swarthy Complexion, a down Look, and probably cannot straighten the little Finger of his Hand, as it was lately bruised, and is much addicted to chewing Tobacco. He had on when he went away, or took with him, an old Check Shirt, two Pair of coarse Oznaburgs Trowsers, one Pair of old Shoes, one Pair of large square Silver Shoe Buckles, and a green half worn Cloth Waistcoat. He is supposed to be gone towards New-Haven. Whoever brings home the said Apprentice, or secures him so that his Master gets him again, shall have FOUR DOLLARS Reward and all reasonable Charges,
paid by   EDWARD SELOOVER.
All Masters of Vessels and others, are desired not to harbour, conceal, or take him away, as they will answer it at their Peril.
New-York, July 28, 1767.
The New-York Journal; or The General Advertiser, July 30, 1767; August 6, 1767; August 13, 1767; August 20, 1767; August 27, 1767.

RUN-away from the Subscriber in Long-Island, a stout well made Negro Man, named James, about five Feet two Inches high, seems to be about twenty-four Years of Age, and speaks very much after the New-England Manner. He had on when he went away, a homespun Shirt and Trowsers, a blue Jacket and a Scots Bonnet. Any Person that takes up and returns the said Negro, or secures him in any Gaol, giving Notice so that I may get him again, shall have Ten Dollars Reward, and all reasonable Charges
paid,   ROBERT PICKEMAM.
N. B. He has made several Attempts to go off by Sea, therefore all Masters of Vessels, and others are warn'd not to harbour, conceal, or carry him away, as they will answer it at their Peril.
The New-York Journal; or The General Advertiser, July 30, 1767.

FIVE POUNDS REWARD.
RUN-away the 6th instant, July, from Joseph Wicks, of Huntington, on Long-Island, cooper, an apprentice, named David Kelly, a lusty young man,

of about 19 years of age, light complexion, and sandy coloured hair; had on when he went away, a blue broad cloth waistcoat, white shirt, whitish strip'd or tow trowsers, a felt hat, worsted stockings, and old shoes—Whoever will bring the said apprentice to me shall have Five Pounds reward, or if secured in any gaol, giving me notice, so that I get him again, shall have Three Pounds reward, and all reasonable charges,
    paid by me JOSEPH WICKS.
  ☞ All masters of vessels and others are desired not to harbour, conceal, or carry him away, as they will answer it at their peril.

The New-York Journal; or The General Advertiser, July 30, 1767; August 7, 1767; August 13, 1767; August 20, 1767; August 27, 1767; September 3, 1767. See *The New-York Journal; or The General Advertiser*, July 9, 1767.

RUN away, from the Subscriber living in New-York, a Negro Man named Tom about 24 Years of age by trade a Baker, about 5 Feet 10 Inches high, of yellow Complexion, a little marked with the Small pox, and has a scar down his forehead, had on when he went away a new Tow cloth Jacket, with Sleeves, and a pair of long tow cloth trowsers; whoever takes up the said Negro man and Secures him that the Master can have him again shall have FORTY SHILLINGS reward and all Charges
    paid by MATTHEW HYER.

The New-York Gazette, From Monday July 27, to Monday August 3, 1767; From Monday August 3, to Monday August 10, 1767; *The New-York Mercury*, August 3, 1767; August 10, 1767; August 17, 1767. Minor differences between the ads. The *Mercury* shows he ran away "the 29th ult."

RUN away on Sunday the 12th of July past, from JOHN HURSEN, of Bloemendale, near the City of New-York, a Mulatto Fellow named *Squire*, aged about 26 Years, is of a middle Size, well set, tho' thin Visag'd; has a remarkable Scar on the side of one of his Legs, and his Hair of the Mallagasco kind, long and frizzel'd.—Had on when he went away, an Oznabrigs Shirt and Trowsers, an Allapeen jacket without Sleeves, which is thought he would exchange, and a Pair of old Shoes. He went off with a Squaw named *Charity*, she is well set, and has an extraordinary Scar or Mark under each Ear, just below the Jaw-Bone.—Her Cloathing uncertain. They have been seen together on Long-Island, and afterwards to cross White-Stone Ferry. Whoever takes and secures the said Mulatto Fellow, so that his Master may have him again shall have THREE POUNDS Reward, and all reasonable Charges
    paid by JOHN HURSEN.

The New-York Gazette, From Monday July 27, to Monday August 3, 1767; From Monday August 3, to Monday August 10, 1767; From Monday August 10, to Monday August 17, 1767; From Monday August 17, to Monday August 24, 1767; From Monday August 24, to Monday September 1, 1767; From Monday September 14, to Monday September 21, 1767; From Monday September 21, to Monday September 28, 1767; From Monday September 28, to Monday October 5, 1767.

Newburgh, Ulster County, July 7, 1767.

RUN-away, from *James Stickney*, the 7th of *July*, a white servant Man, named, *Abel Nickson*, about 25 Years of Age, dark Complexion, short black Hair, black Eyes, his Fore Teeth very much broke out, about 5 Feet 9 Inches high, speaks good English: Had on when he went away, a Felt Hat, dark check Flannel Shirt, dark check Linen long Trowsers, and old Shoes. Whoever takes up said Servant, and gives notice of, or brings him to his said Master, shall have *Forty Shillings* Reward, and all necessary Charges paid, by me, JAMES STICKNEY.

The New-York Mercury, August 3, 1767; August 10, 1767; August 17, 1767. See *The Connecticut Courant*, July 20, 1767.

RUN-AWAY, from JACOB ARDEN, of Kakiat, in Orange County, a Negro Man of a yellow Complexion, called CATO: He is about 40 Years of Age, and about 5 Feet 2 Inches high: Had on when he went away, a brown homespun Coat, a white Jacket, an Ozenbrigs Shirt and Trowsers, a Pair of light blue Worsted Stockings, a Pair of Pumps, and an old Beaver Hat newly clean'd: Whoever takes up the said Negro, and secures him, so that his Master may have him again, shall have Three Pounds Reward, and all reasonable Charges,
paid JACOB ARDEN.

The New-York Mercury, August 3, 1767; August 10, 1767; August 17, 1767.

DESERTS his Master's Service from Time to Time, and quits his Master's House almost every Night, Benjamin M'Vaugh, an Apprentice Lad, near 21 Years old:—He is a PRINTER by trade; is prodigiously forward with his Tongue, and apt to use scurrilous Language; wears his Hat Soldier like, across Ship: is broad featur'd, square stern'd, broad shoulder'd, and has a most lazy, idle, lounging, clumsy Way of Walking, with a hang-down look.—A DOLLAR Reward to inform who it is that harbours him, and good Reason there is to think it is in the Street that leads from BURNS's

Corner to the North-River;—and Two DOLLARS to put him in Confinement, in any Place erected by Authority,
                  paid by,—the Printer hereof.
The New-York Gazette, From Monday August 3, to Monday August 10, 1767; From Monday August 10, to Monday August 17, 1767.

RUN away from the Subscriber, on Saturday Night last, a likely Negro Man named *Prime*, about 25 Years of Age, and about Five Feet Four inches high; he took with him when he went away, two striped Linsey Woolsey Jackets, a red Cloth one, and a blue Camblet one: He was seen coming out of the Mouth of the Kills in a Canoe on Sunday Morning last, with an Intention of coming to *New-York*, in Order to get on Board some Vessel: Whoever takes up and secures said Negro, so that his Master may have him again, shall have a Reward of FIVE DOLLARS, and all reasonable Charges
                paid by   JOHN MERCEREAU.
N. B. All Masters of Vessels and others are forbid to carry him off or harbour him at their Peril.—It is very likely he is gone to Mr. *David Provost's* Farm, about Six Miles from *New-York*, as he formerly lived there.
                        Staten-Island, August 11, 1767.
The New-York Gazette or the Weekly Post-Boy, August 13, 1767; August 20, 1767; August 27, 1767; September 10, 1767.

WHEREAS on the Second Day of June last, came to the House of *Prudence Irwin*, of the Precinct of Shawngunck, in the County of Ulster, Widow, a Man who called himself *Hanas Vandebergs*, and left with her a light bay Horse, about 14 Hands (or More) high, is branded on the near Buttock with the Letters **WH**, to be kept in her Pasture, and promised he would come for him in a Month after, and pay her for keeping said Horse; but hearing a few Days after, that he was committed to Goal at Kingston, in said County, and was there arraigned by the Name of *Hanas Pick, &c. &c.* and burnt in the Hand for a Felony he had committed, and having come by the said Horse, it is generally suspected he has stole him, and the said Widow being advised by one of the Magistrates of the said County, to advertise the said Horse in one of the Publick Papers of this Province: There are therefore to give Publick NOTICE, to whom it may Concern, that the said Horse is at present in here Pasture, where she intends to keep him 6 Weeks from the Date hereof, unless the said Person who left him with her will bring sufficient Proof before that Time, that he came lawfully by the said Horse.
The New-York Gazette, From Monday August 10, to Monday August 17, 1767.

RUN-away the 18th Instant, from the Subscriber, living in New-York, an indented Servant, named Erasmus Ferrer; he is about 18 Years old, 5 Feet 6 Inches high, or thereabout, smooth faced, and has light curled Hair: Had on when he went away, a napt Jacket of a dark Colour, Tow Trowsers, black grained Shoes, has pretty much of the Brogue; he is a Shoemaker, and understands both Men and Womens Work well; His fore Finger of his right Hand is remarkably clumsy at the End; he is supposed to be lurking at the back Part of this Town. Whoever takes up and secures the said Servant, so that he may be had again, shall, if taken in or about Town receive Two Dollars, and if at any distance Three Dollars Reward, and all reasonable Charges paid, by   JOHN CREE.

The New-York Mercury, August 24, 1767; August 31, 1767; September 7, 1767; September 28, 1767.

RUN-away from the Subscriber, living at Poughkeepsie Precinct, the latter End of August last, a Negro Man named SAM, 22 Years old, 6 Feet high, smooth-faced, goes stooping, and has large Feet: Had on when he went away, a Tow shirt and Trowsers. Whoever takes up and secures the said Fellow, so that his Master may have him again, shall be handsomely rewarded, and have all reasonable Charges paid,
by   JOHANNIS HOGHTALING.

The New-York Mercury, September 7, 1767; September 14, 1767; September 28, 1767.

RUN-away from his Lodgings, on Golden Hill, in this City, on Friday Night last, a certain *William Trench*, Mariner, and carried with him a Pair of Nankeen Breeches, and a double-breasted Jacket of the same Sort, and several other Things: He is about 24 Years old, much pitted with the Small-pox, and of a swarthy Complexion: Had on when he went away, a green Jacket, and long Canvas Trowsers. Whoever takes up and secures the said *William Trench*, and will bring him to the Subscriber, shall receive Forty Shillings Reward,
paid by   DANIEL BANE.

The New-York Mercury, September 7, 1767; September 14, 1767; September 21, 1767; September 28, 1767.

TAKEN up on Tuesday last, by the subscriber, living in New-York, and is now in the Work-House, a Run-away servant, who calls himself John Price, but is supposed to be Robert Randall, and it is thought he belongs to Charles Hollis, who lives in some of the southern Governments, as a written Advertisement was taken out of his pocket when taken up, signed Charles Hollis, and the cloths and other marks, answering, in every particular, to what he had on when taken: He says he came from Philadelphia, but tells

many lies. Whoever this may concern, are desired to make speedy application to   JOHN JONES.
The New-York Mercury, September 14, 1767; September 21, 1767.

Ten Pounds Reward,
BROKE Joal, at Kingston, Ulster County, in the Province of New-York, on Wednesday the [ ] of August, ult. one George Burne, late of the Wall-Kill in [ ] County, who was confined in Joal for Debt: The said Burne [is a] likely young Man, about 28 or 30 Years old, and about 5 Feet [ ] Inches high, brown Eyes, long brown Hair, either clubb'd or [   ]d, fair Complexion, and read Cheeks. [*sic*] It is suppos'd that [he] had on a Blue Cloath Coat, with Brown under Cloths, but not [   ]in, as he wore a Shirt and Trowsers in Joal only. Any Person [who] will apprehend said Burne, and deliver him to the Subscriber, [at] Kingston, shall have the above Reward, of Ten Pounds, for apprehending him and securing him, in any Joal in the Province [of] New-York, or elsewhere, so that the Subscriber may have him again, shall have Five Pounds Reward,
          paid by   DANIEL GRAHAM, Sheriff.
The New-York Mercury, September 28, 1767.

RUN away from his Master, James Raymond, living in Bedford, in New-York Province, a Molatto Negro Servant, named DOVER, about 18 years of Age, about 5 Feet 9 Inches high—Had on when he went away, a Beaver-Hat, red Jacket, light colour'd Breeches, long Trowsers, bare Foot—All Masters of Vessels are forbid carrying him away; also Ferrymen are desired to take Notice of the same.
   Whoever takes up said Servant, and brings him to his said Master at Bedford, or secures him, giving Notice of the same, shall have FIVE DOLLARS, reward, and all reasonable Charges,
          paid by me   JAMES RAYMOND.
The New-York Journal; or The General Advertiser, October 1, 1767; October 8, 1767; October 15, 1767; October 22, 1767.

                    Huntington, September 20th, 1767.
RUN away from Joseph Lewis of Huntingdon, in Suffolk County, 1 Negro Man, named Daniel, about 21 Years of Age; and 1 Negro Boy, named Ben about 13 Years old:—Daniel, had on when he went away a light brown coat, brown jacket, leather breeches and check linen shirt; wears his hat with a peak cock, and white button; is about 5 feet 7 or 8 inches high, a very likely strait limb'd fellow, the boy had on when he went off a light blue camblet coat, check shirt and tow trowsers, is remarkable for having one sore eye, and lost one joint of his little fingers: Whoever takes up and secures both, or either of said negroes, so that their master may have them

again, or give notice to Thomas Tucker in New-York, shall be reasonably rewarded, and all charges paid.
                    JOSEPH LEWIS.
The New-York Journal; or The General Advertiser, October 1, 1767; October 8, 1767; October 15, 1767.

                    Three Pounds Reward.
RUN-AWAY, on Wednesday the 6th Instant, an indented Irish Servant Man, named Robert Byrne; he sometimes calls himself Robert Stratford Byrne; Had on when he went away, a light grey Coat and Waistcoat, and black Stocking Breeches; he also took with him a blue Sagothie Coat, with yellow Buttons, and an entire suit of Pompadour Clothes: He has dark short Hair, is about 5 Feet 8 Inches high, a genteel looking young Fellow, and his Face broke out in Pimples, writes and understands Accounting extremely well, remarkable talkative, very plausible and greatly addicted to Lying: It is supposed he has the Counterpart of his Indentures with him, and by that Means may endeavour to pass for a Free Man. Whoever secures the said Servant, and delivers him to the Subscriber, shall receive the above Reward, with all reasonable Charges paid by the Printer hereof,
      or   CHARLES RAMADGE.   New-York, October 9, 1767.
N. B. All Masters of Vessels are hereby forbid to carry off the said Byrne at their Peril.
The New-York Mercury, October 12, 1767; October 19, 1767; October 26, 1767.

ON the 11th Day of May last, a Negro Man named TOM, about five Feet and five Inches high, run away from the Subscriber living on the Mohawke River; he had on when he went away, a red Cloth Jacket without Sleeves, a dark Woollen Check Shirt, Leather Breeches, and a Cap made of a Piece of a Blanket; without Shoes, Stockings or Hat: He can talk but very little English, having lately come into this Country from Guinea; had a Scar under his right Eye, Holes through his Ears, and is without his two foremost under Teeth; walks with his Knees wide apart, and has the Figure of a Deer pricked on his Belly after the Fashion of the Guinea Negroes:
    Whoever takes up and secures him in any of his Majesty's Gaols in this Province, and gives Notice to his Master thereof, or brings him to his said Master, shall receive a Reward of THREE POUNDS, and charges
            paid by   SAMUEL A. BRATT.
                    Schenectady, September 30, 1767.
The New-York Journal; or The General Advertiser, October 15, 1767; October 22, 1767; October 29, 1767.

RUN away on Monday the 21st Instant, from JOHN THOMAS, Esq; of Westchester County, in the Province of New-York, an Indian Slave, named ABRAHAM, he may have changed his Name, about 23 Years of Age, about 5 Feet 5 Inches high, yellow Complexion, long black Hair something curl'd; a thick set Fellow, one of his four Teeth [sic] in the lower Jaw broke off;—had on when he went away, a white double breasted Vest, made with full'd Homespun cloth with white Metal Buttons, the over Vest made with yellow brown Homespun Cloth, and Breeches of the same, blue Stockings Shoes made with the Grain outward, a new Felt Hat:—Whoever takes up said Fellow, and secures him in any of his Majesty's Gaols, or brings him to his said Master, shall have FIVE POUNDS Reward and all reasonable Charges paid,
     by me JOHN THOMAS. *Rye, September* 21, 1767.

The New-York Journal; or The General Advertiser, October 22, 1767; October 29, 1767; November 12, 1767; November 19, 1767; *The New-York Gazette*, From Monday October 19, to Monday October 26, 1767; From Monday November 12, to Monday November 19, 1767; From Monday November 23, to Monday November 30, 1767; From Monday November 30, to Monday December 6, 1767; From Monday December 7, to Monday December 14, 1767; *The New-York Mercury*, October 26, 1767; November 2, 1767; November 9, 1767; November 16, 1767. Minor differences between the papers. See *The New-York Journal; or, The General Advertiser*, September 28, 1769.

New-York, October 19, 1767.

BROKE out of the Work-House last Night, a Negro Man, belonging to Mr. BARD, named SAM, who formerly lived with Mr. BURNS of this City:— Whoever will bring the said Negro to the Printer of this Paper, shall receive TEN DOLLARS Reward.

 N. B. All Masters of Vessels and others; are cautioned not to harbour or conceal the said Negro.

The New-York Journal; or The General Advertiser, October 22, 1767; October 29, 1767; November 12, 1767; November 19, 1767.

RUN away from the Subscriber, on the 17th Inst. an English Servant Girl, named CATHARINE BURCHALL, of a low Stature, pitted with the Small-Pox; and is supposed to be concealed from her said Master, by some ill disposed Person: This is therefore to forewarn all Persons whatsoever, from harbouring or concealing the said Servant, or carrying her away, as they will answer at their Peril.—Whoever takes up the said Servant Girl, and brings her to her said Master, or secures her in any of his Majesty's Goals,

so that he may have her again, shall have Forty Shillings Reward, and all reasonable Charges
    paid by ROBERT ANDREWS.
The New-York Journal; or, the General Advertiser, October 29, 1767; November 5, 1767.

RUN-away from FRANCIS KOFFLER of Brooklyn-Ferry, the 1st of this Instant November, an Irish indented Servant, named John Miller, which kept the Bar, and made Punch at his House; is about 26 Years of Age, is of a fair Complexion, sandy streight Hair: Had on him when he went away, a new blue Wast Coat, with blue Lining and Buttons, a new blue Wast Coat, and blue Buttons and white Lining, Deer Skin Breeches, speckled Yarn Stockings, double-soaled Shoes and Brass Buckles, and a Beaver Hat. Any Person that secures the said Run-away, so that his Master may have him again, shall have FIVE DOLLARS Reward, and all reasonable Charges,
    By FRANCIS KOFFLER.
The New-York Mercury, November 2, 1767; November 9, 1767; November 16, 1767; November 23, 1767; November 30, 1767. See *The New-York Mercury*, March 11, 1765. and *The New-York Journal; or, the General Advertiser*, November 5, 1767.

TAKEN up, on Saturday Night, the 24th of October last, at Corlear's Hook, near New-York, by the Subscriber, a Negro Fellow, who says his name is *SAM*; he is a lusty well-looking Fellow, 6 Feet high, and can give by a bad Account of himself, as appears to be but a short Time from his own Country; he has large Feet, and has on a Tow Shirt and Trowsers. He is now in the Work-House, and his Master may have him again, paying a Reward and Charges, by applying at Corlear's Hook,
    to JASPER MILLER.
The New-York Mercury, November 2, 1767; November 9, 1767.

RUNAWAY from Francis Koffler of Brookland-Ferry, the 1st of November 1767, an Irish indented Servant, named John Miller, which kept the Bar and made Punch at his House; is about 26 Years of Age, is of a fair Complexion, sandy streight Hair:—Had on him when he went away, a new blue Coat, Lining and Buttons blue, Waistcoat and Buttons white Linen, Dearskin Breeches, Yarn speckled Stockings, double soled Shoes, Brass Buckles, Beaver Hat.—Any Person securing the said Runaway, shall have 5 Dollars Reward and all reasonable Charges,
    paid by FRANCIS KOFFLER.
The New-York Journal; or, the General Advertiser, November 5, 1767; November 12, 1767; November 19, 1767; November 26, 1767.

See *The New-York Mercury*, March 11, 1765, and *The New-York Mercury*, November 2, 1767.

RUN-away, from Alexander Leslie, of New-York, the 31st Day of October, 1767, an indented Irish servant Boy, named Daniel M'Namar, was learning to be a Peruke-maker and Hair-cutter, is about 16 Years old, of a fresh Complexion, round faced, Chesnut brown hair, cut short and inclining to curl, a down Look, and speaks when he is in a good Humour, very much like a Girl; carried off with him, a new Green livery plush Coat, with red Lining, red Button holes and large Brass Buttons: Had on him when he ran away, an old blue Coat, a brown Cloth Waistcoat, with a few large white Buttons on, an old powdery Hat, a pair of greasy Buckskin Breeches, a Check Shirt and some other Shirts, a black Neckcloth about his Neck, a strong Pair of Shoes pieced at the Heels and soaled, the Coat broke under the Arms and tore on the right Hip, and took with him two new Razors, one marked G. Smith, the other no name on it; was formerly a Servant of Capt. Wilson, of the 59th Regiment and will endeavour to change his Cloaths: Any Person securing the said Run-away, on this Island or in Town, shall have Twenty Shillings Reward, or if off of the Island, Five Dollars, and all reasonable Charges on bringing him to me. This is therefore to forewarn all Persons to harbour or conceal the said Run-away, and all Masters of Vessels or others from carrying him off, as they will answer the same to the Subscribers. ALEXANDER LESLIE.

The New-York Mercury, November 9, 1767; November 16, 1767; December 28, 1767; January 4, 1768; January 11, 1768.

RAN-away, on Monday Night the 23d of November, from John Michael Will, of the City of New-York, Cordwainer, an Apprentice Lad named, David Littleye Simpson, about 17 Years old, of a proper Lad Size, has middle colour'd round trim'd brown Hair, is something Pock-marked, has a limping Walk, and very free with his Tongue in either old or young Company: Had on when he went away, and old Felt Hat, a double breasted nap Jacket lin'd with flannel, a check Shirt, a Pair of Sheepskin Britches, long Trowsers, blue Stockings, a Pair of good thick soal'd Shoes, with Pinchbeck Buckles, and has a bold Look.—Whoever takes up and secures the said Apprentice, so that his Master may have him again, shall have TWO DOLLARS Reward, and reasonable Charges
paid by, John Michael Will.

N. B. Masters of Vessels, and Boatmen, are forbid to carry him off; and a reward will be given to inform who harbours or employs him in or out of the City of New-York.

The New-York Gazette, From Monday November 23, to Monday November 30, 1767, From Monday November 30, to Monday December 7, 1767; From Monday December 7, to Monday December 14, 1767.

RUN-away on Friday last, from the Subscriber, an Apprentice named John Shopman, he is a likely Lad, about 5 Feet 6 Inches high, of a fair Complexion, wears his own dark Hair, tied behind, has lost the first Joint of his right Thumb, and speaks very broad Yorkshire, being lately come over.—He had on when he went away, a dark brown Coat, black Waistcoat, Buckskin Breeches, and coarse worsted Stockings: He pretends to know a little of the Dying Business, and it is thought, is now in Philadelphia. Whoever will bring the said Apprentice to Stephen Brown at Thomas Ivers's, Rope-Maker in New-York, shall receive Six Dollars Reward, and all reasonable Expences
        paid by   STEPHEN BROWN.
The New-York Journal; or, the General Advertiser, December 3, 1767; December 10, 1767; December 17, 1767; December 31, 1767.

RUN-AWAY from the Subscriber, the 10th of November last, a Servant Boy, named *John Babtist Disseau,* of French Parents, born in Canada: He is about 14 Years old, of a fair Complexion, and speaks good English and French: Had on, when he went away, a blue Coat and Breeches, and a brown Waistcoat; commonly known by the name of JACK. He went off in Company with one Joseph Fletcher, about 17 Years old, Son of Joseph Fletcher of this Place: He is of a dark Complexion: Whoever will secure the said JACK, so that his Master may have him again, shall receive Forty Shillings Reward, and all reasonable Charges
        paid, by   JOHN LILBURN.
The New-York Mercury, December 14, 1767; December 21, 1767.

RUN-away, from the Ship Three-Brothers, the 12th Inst, lying in the Harbour of New-York, an Indented Servant named Dennis Reilley, 30 Years old, of a fair Complexion, wears his own Hair of a light Colour, & very straight, one of his upper Teeth broken, likes Company, plays very well on the Violin, and is supposed to be gone to Philadelphia: Had on when he went away, a black Coat, Jacket, and Breeches, and a Sailor's Hat. Whoever takes up and secures the said Run-away, and will bring him to Messrs. Thompson and Alexander, in New-York, or Messrs. Carson, Barclay, and Mitchell, in Philadelphia, shall receive Three Pounds Reward, and all reasonable Charges, [   ] the Captain.

JOHN GWINN.
The New-York Mercury, December 28, 1767; January 4, 1768.

1768

New-York, Jannary [sic] 11. 1768.
RUN away about 2 Months ago, a French Negro Man, named *John Baptist*, speaks French and broken English, pitted with the Small-Pox, flat Nose, square built, about 5 Feet 6 Inches high, his little Finger of his Left Hand, stiff and straight, his Age about 45 or 50 Years: He has Holes in each Ear for Earings. Whoever takes up said Negro, and sends Word to the Subscribr, shall have *FORTY SHILLINGS* Reward, and all Charges
    paid by WILLIAM DARLINGTON.
The New-York Gazette or the Weekly Post-Boy, January 11, 1768; January 18, 1768; January 25, 1768; February 4, 1768; February 15, 1768; January 22, 1768; March 7, 1768; March 14, 1768; *The New-York Journal; or, the General Advertiser*, January 14, 1768; January 21, 1768; January 28, 1768; February 4, 1768; February 18, 1768. Minor differences in the papers.

*R**UN**-away from the Subscriber at West-Chester, a Negro Man, named Mingo, formerly known by the Name of Jim: He is about five Feet eight or nine Inches high, not very black, has a large Scar, partly upon his Nose, and another near the middle of his Forehead.—He has very often changed his Master; but has lived last with one Jones, a Black-smith, at, or near Haverstraw, towards which place he is supposed to have directed his Course.—He plays tolerably well upon the Fiddle, and has taken one with him;—he is an insinuating Fellow, and can tell a plausible Story.—As he has taken all the Clothes he had, with him; it is not known in what Dress he chuses to appear.—He took his Departure during the Christmas Holidays; and whoever shall take him and bring him to his Master, shall have Forty Shillings Reward, and all reasonable Charges,*
    paid by *ISAAC WILKINS.*
The New-York Journal; or, the General Advertiser, January 14, 1768; January 21, 1768; January 28, 1768; February 4, 1768.

WHEREAS Alexander Philips, weaver, did, on Monday, the 18th instant, abscond from the House of Peter Read, at Cakeat, in Orange county, and 'tis supposed took with him, a new beaver hat, a brass-mounted hanger, with a leather scabbard, made by a saddler: He is about 5 feet 8 inches high, fat and lusty, and talks with the Irish accent; had black hair tied behind, about 20 years old, is a stranger in the country: Had on a blue surtout coat,

brown broad cloth breeches, and a jacket much of the same colour. Whoever takes up the said Alexander Philips, so that he may be brought to justice, and found guilty of the above crime, shall have three pounds reward, paid by   PETER READE.
The New-York Mercury, January 25, 1768; *The New-York Gazette; and the Weekly Mercury*, February 1, 1768; February 8, 1768.

NOTICE is hereby given, that there is now in the Gaol of Goshen in Orange County, committed as a Runaway, a well set Negro Man, who calls himself James Gale, says he came from Judge Horsmanden, is about 5 Feet 5 Inches high, and is supposed to be about 23 Years of Age: He has a large Scar across his Nose, several on his right Temple and Head, a large Bump on his Forehead resembling a Bile, and has scabby Shins: He had on an oldish Shirt, ruffled at the Bosom, an old blue Broadcloth Coat, on which are several Sorts of Buttons, a green lapell'd Waistcoat with white Backs, a Pair of Oil dressed Sheep-Skin Leather Breeches, pretty good Stockings and Shoes, and a middling good Castor Hat.—The Owner may have him on Application to the Subscriber, and paying Charges.
     JOHN HUDSON, S. Sheriff.
The New-York Journal; or, the General Advertiser, January 28, 1768.

                              Philadelphia, February 1, 1768.
WHEREAS....ISAAC BEATE, servant to Philip Levingston, in New York...being confined in the public goal of this county, as runaway servants, public notice is hereby given to the masters of the said servants, that I intend to apply to the court of quarter sessions, to be held in the city of Philadelphia, for the county of Philadelphia, on Monday, the 7th day of March next, for an order to sell the said servants for their fees, unless their masters redeem them before that time.
     JEHU JONES, goaler.
The Pennsylvania Gazette, February 4, 1768; February 11, 1768; February 25, 1768.

              FOUR DOLLARS REWARD.
Run away from the subscriber in September last, a Negro man named Stephen, born in Lebanon, in the colony of Connecticut, is a stout fellow, frouzled hair, is part Indian, hath remarkable scars made by the king's evil breaking under his ears and chin, had with him an old fine black broad cloth coat. Any person that will bring him to me, or confine him in any of his majesty's goals, shall have the above reward, and al reasonable charges   paid by   ROSWELL HOPKINS, of the Nine Partners.
N. B. All Persons are forbid to harbour, conceal or carry him off.

The Connecticut Courant, February 15, 1768; February 22, 1768.

New-York, March 14, 1768.
RUN away from the City of New-York, on Saturday Night last, being the 12th of March, 1768, three indented German Servants, viz. One belonging to John Slidell, Soap-boiler and Tallow-chandler, in the Broad-Way, named Johannes Finckensor, a tall Man, about Six Feet three or 4 Inches high, a well limb'd person, has a Scar from his Mouth almost half Way his left Cheek: Had on when eloped, a short brown Napt Coat, without Lining, a blue Vest, and old Buckskin Breeches, new Castor Hat, old Shoes, with a Piece cut out upon the left Foot, occasioned by a Cut with an Axe; short brown Hair, speaks broken English, is pitted somewhat with the Small-Pox: Forty Shillings Reward, if taken and returned. The other Servants, one belonging to Mr. Peter Hassenclever, named Burgert, had on a green Livery Suit, and a white Cloth great Coat, round Face, aged about 24 Years, is about five Feet; the other belonging to Mr. Philip Lidack, Baker, named John George Tiebolt, aged about 24 Years, had on new Buckskin Breeches, a blue Coat, and a white Cloth Coat; has his Hair tied up, and walks stooping a little, has a smooth looking Face; about five Feet high. Whoever apprehends those Servants, shall have Forty Shillings for each, if returned to New-York, or Six Pounds for the three, with reasonable Charges.
    JOHN SLIDELL, PHILIP LIDACK,
      PETER HASSENCLEVER.
 N. B. Two of them are Bakers by Trade: No Person to carry them off at their Peril, or harbour them, as they will answer it at Law.
The New-York Journal; or, the General Advertiser, March 17, 1768; *The New-York Gazette or the Weekly Post-Boy*, March 21, 1768; March 28, 1768; April 4, 1768. Minor differences between the papers. See *The New-York Gazette; and Weekly Mercury*, March 21, 1768; and *The New-York Journal; or, the General Advertiser*, March 24, 1768.

RUN-away, from John Slidell, of this City, Soap Boiler, and Tallow-Chandler, an indented German Servant Man, named Johannis Frokinger; he went off in Company with two others of his Countrymen, one of which belonged to Peter Hassenclever, Esq; and the other to Philip Lidack, of this Place, Baker: Frokinger is about 6 Feet 4 Inches high, streight, and well made; had on a short brown Coat of knapt Cloth, a new blue Jacket, Leather Breeches, new Castor Hat, and old Shoes with Steel Buckles, and there is about the Bigness of a Dollar cut out of the upper Leather of his left Foot. Mr. Lidack's Servant is about 5 Feet 4 Inches high, his Dress uncertain, but may have on a blue and grey Coat. Mr. Hassenclever's Servant is supposed to have on short green Cloathing, and is about 5 Feet high. Six Pounds

Reward will be given for apprehending the above mentioned Run-away's, or 40s, for each, by their Masters in New-York.

The New-York Gazette; and Weekly Mercury, March 21, 1768; March 28, 1768; April 4, 1768; April 11, 1768. See *The New-York Journal; or, the General Advertiser*, March 17, 1768, and *The New-York Journal; or, the General Advertiser*, March 24, 1768.

New-York, March 14, 1768.

RUN away on the 12th Inst. from the City of New-York, three indented German Servants, viz. one belonging to John Slidell, Soap-Boiler and Tallow-Chandler, in the Broad-Way, named Johannes Finckensor, a tall well made Man, about Six Feet three or four Inches high, short brown Hair, has a Scar from his Mouth almost half Way his left Cheek, is somewhat pitted woth the Small-Pox, and speaks broken English: He had on when went away, a short brown napp'd Coat without Lining, a blue Waistcoat, old Buckskin Breeches, a new Castor Hat, old Shoes, with a Piece cut out of one of them by the Stroke of an Ax.

Another of the Servants, belonging to Mr. Peter Hassenclever, is named Alexander Burgert, about Five Feet high, has a round Face, is aged about 24 Years, had on a green Livery Suit, and a white Cloth Great Coat. The other, belonging to Mr. Philip Lidack, Baker, named John George Tiebolt, aged about 24 Years, Five Feet high, has a smooth well looking Face, walks a little stooping and wears his Hair tied up. He had on a blue, and a white Cloth Coats, and Buckskin Breeches. Two of the said Servants are Bakers by Trade.—Whoever takes up and returns the said Servants, or any of them to Few-York, [*sic*] shall have Forty Shillings New-York for each so returned, and all reasonable Charges paid.

N. B. All Persons on their Peril, are warned not to harbour, conceal or carry away the said Servants, or either of them.

        JOHN SLIDELL,   PHILIP LIDACK,
        PETER HASSENCLEVER.

The New-York Journal; or, the General Advertiser, March 24, 1768; April 9, 1768; April 28, 1768. See *The New-York Journal; or, the General Advertiser*, March 17, 1768, and *The New-York Gazette; and Weekly Mercury*, March 21, 1768.

RUN-away, a Negro man named Harre, about 30 or 35 years of age, is short, has broad shoulders, large staring eyes, remarkable small legs, large feet, and walks something lame, having had his toes frozen; he speaks English and low Dutch, has lived formerly in the counties of Orange, Dutches, and Albany, with Mr. Dingman of Kinderhook. Whoever brings home the said Negro, or secures him in any gaol, giving notice to Mr. James

Abeel, merchant in New-York, or to the subscriber in Albany, shall receive three pounds reward, and reasonable charges.

    PHILIP SCHUYLER.   Albany, 12th April 1768.

The New-York Journal; or, the General Advertiser, May 5, 1768; May 12, 1768; May 19, 1768; May 26, 1768; *The New-York Gazette; and Weekly Mercury*, May 16, 1768; May 23, 1768; May 30, 1768; June 6, 1768. The *Mercury* does not have the location and date at the bottom.

RUN away May the 14th 1768, from the subscriber in Middletown, a Negro Man named York, about five feet nine inches high, 18 years of age, well set, has one of his fore teeth broke near the gum; had on when he went away, a suit of homespun mixt grey clothes, shoes and stockings, brass buckles, and a cock'd felt hat, with a large metal button.—Whoever takes up said Negro and secures him, so that his master can have him again, shall have twenty shillings reward, and all charges,

   paid by me CYRENIUS VAN MATER.

The New-York Journal; or, the General Advertiser, May 19, 1768; May 26, 1768; June 2, 1768; June 4, 1768.

             New-York, May 30, 1768.
WHEREAS one Elizabeth Harrison, (an indented servant to Mr. John Ramsay, of this city merchant) on Sunday last, came to me (wife of Thomas Clay, a soldier in his Majesty's 16th regiment) told me she had disobliged her master, and desired me to intercede with him on her behalf, and gave me the counter part of her indentures, which she desired me to keep for her:—As I was just going to church, (my husband and son being from home) I left the room in her care till my return from church,—when I found she had lock'd the door, and was gone off with the key, and had robbed to room of the following goods and money, viz.

One red and white, and 1 purple and white chintz gowns, 1 striped linen, and 1 dark ground callico short gowns; 4 new check aprons, 2 plain, 1 cross barred lawn aprons: 5 mens, 4 boys shirts, of new Irish linen at 3s. 6d. a yard; 5 shifts of new Irish linen at 2s. 2d. a yard, 7 pair of womens fine linen sleves; 16 womens caps of fine linen, with thin borders, one of them has a large iron mould on one side, near the bottom; 1 black small figured silk cloak, had been torn on the left shoulder, and mended with blue thread, the head border'd with silk lace and lined with silk, the rest lined with black tammy; 1 white Barcelona silk handkerchief, with pale and deep red borders; 1 crossed barred purple flowered gauze handkerchief, 2 check linen handkerchiefs; 1 pair mens plain gray, 2 pair cotton stockings; 4 pair womens blue worsted do. 3 pair boys cotton hose mark'd T. C. all quite new; 2 pair mens new shoes, 1 pair womens callimanco do. 1 pair leather pumps a little worn; 2 large silver table spoons, mark'd M. C. 1 silver milk or cream pot, mark'd M. C. within the hoop of the handle; 1 large silver salt cellar on 3 feet, a human face on each, and mark'd M. C. on the bottom, near one of them; 4 silver tea spoons, not mark'd, the ends of the handles rather broader than common; 1 large plain gold ring, mark'd B. M. coast [sic] a guinea; 1 pair large square wrought silver shoe buckles, mark'd T. C. cost 40s. in this city; sundry ribbons, child's clothes and other small things. Also, sundry paper money bills, among which was a New-Jersey- 30s. bill, the whole amounting to 11 dollars; small silver and coppers amounting to 1 dollar, and 20 Spanish dollars, most of them milled. Whoever secures the said Elizabeth Harrison, so that she may be brought to justice, shall receive Three Dollars reward, and all reasonable charges; and whoever will stop and secure the said goods or any of them, or give intelligence of them so that the owner may get them again, shall be thankfully rewarded for their trouble.

Elizabeth Harrison is a tall lusty woman, seems to be between 20 and 30 years of age, pale sallow complexion, dark hair, parted on the forehead; came from Liverpool, has been brought up to the farming business, and has been but little used to the needle; she had on a yellow petticoat and white short gown. It is hoped that no person will be so unjust as to carry off, harbour or conceal her, or any of the goods she has stolen.—Inquire at the house of Mr. Oyster, next door to the house Major James lived in, back of the college. MARGARET CLAY.

The New-York Journal; or, the General Advertiser, June 2, 1768; June 9, 1768.

RUN-away from Bartholomew Hadden, of Westchester, on the 23d day of April last, a negro man named Hannable, a short well-set fellow, of a yellow complexion, and has remarkable large lips: Had on when he went away, a red duffils coat, and red colour'd vest, with wide trowsers.—As his master is a poor old blind man, it is requested of all good people to use their endeavours in apprehending said fellow, and securing him, so that his master may have him again, for which he offers a reward of five dollars, with reasonable charges.

The New-York Gazette; and Weekly Mercury, June 6, 1768; June 13, 1768; June 27, 1768. See *The New-York Gazette; and Weekly Mercury*, September 12, 1768.

RUN-away from the subscriber, living at Jamaica, on Long-Island, being the 26th instant, an Irish servant lad, named George Adams, about 18 years old, 5 feet 5 inches high, with streight light hair: Had on when he went away, (which he stole) a blue broad cloth coat, with brass buttons, a green velvet jacket, and buckskin breeches. He also stole a 30. Jersey Bill, and a

plain gold ring. Whoever takes up and secures the said run-away, so that he may be brought to Justice, shall receive five dollars reward,
    paid by DANIEL REMSEN.
The New-York Gazette; and Weekly Mercury, June 6, 1768; June 13, 1768.

              Long-Island, June 13, 1768.
RUN away on Saturday Morning last, from me the Subscriber, living at Success, in *Hampstead* Township, on *Long-Island*, an indented Servant Man, named William Scott, about 5 Feet, 9 Inches high, well set, straight black Hair, intermixed with some grey Hairs, aged about 25 Years; had on, when he went away, a dark brown Cloth Coat, a white Linen Jacket, a Pair of Leather Breeches, black Stockings, and a Pair of new Pumps: Whoever takes up said Servant, and secures him, so that his Master may had him again, shall have FORTY SHILLINGS Reward,
    paid by me WILLIAM FORBUSH.
 N. B. All Masters of Vessels, and others, are forbid to harbour or carry off said Servant at their Peril.
The New-York Gazette or the Weekly Post-Boy, June 13, 1768; June 27, 1768; July 4, 1768; July 11, 1768.

RUN-away the first inst. from the subscriber, living in Rye, Westchester county, a negro man called Peter, about thirty five years of age, well made, of a middle size, and can work at the shoemakers or bakers trade, and probably may follow one of these employments; and he is very self-conceited: Had on or carried with him, a blue duffle watch coat, with large plate buttons on it, 2 light colour'd jackets without sleeves, leather breeches, and two pair of sailors trowsers, a pair of blue yarn hose, half worn shoes, and an old beaver hat; he is supposed to be in this city, as he formerly lived with Leonard Lispenard, Esq; Whoever takes up the said run-away, shall receive twenty shillings reward, and all reasonable charges,
    paid by ADAM SIMMONS.
The New-York Gazette; and Weekly Mercury, June 20, 1768; June 27, 1768; July 4, 1768.

RUN-away from the subscriber, living in this city, on the 29th day of February last, two apprentice lads, aged about 18 years each; Squire Davis, by trade a shoemaker, about 5 feet 6 inches high, dark complexion, a down look, and black hair: Had on when he went away, a new nap'd coat (of a mouse colour) with brass buttons, a blue waistcoat double breasted, with pewter buttons, and a new English castor hat. Nathaniel Street, about 5 feet 5 inches high, has a surly look, and light colour'd hair: Had on when he went away, a brown forrest cloth double breasted waistcoat, and an old hat.

All persons are forewarn'd to harbour or entertain said run-aways, as they will be prosecuted according to law; and whoever shall take up and secures them, so that their masters may have them again, shall receive *Three Pounds* for each, and all reasonable charges,
    paid by John Jones, and *Phineas Lockwood.*
The New-York Gazette; and Weekly Mercury, June 20, 1768; June 27, 1768; July 4, 1768.

RUN-away from his Master, Caleb Cornwell, living in Hempstead, Queen's County, on Long-Island, a Negro Man named SHIER, about 40 Years of Age, five Feet four Inches high, or thereabout; slightly mark'd with the Small-Pox, and is by Trade a Caulker: Had on when he went away a Castor Hat, homespun Cloth colour'd Jacket, Trowsers, blue rib'd Stockings, and Brass Buckles in his Shoes. All Masters of Vessels are forbid carrying him off; and whoever takes up said Negro, and brings him to his said Master, at Hempstead, shall have Twenty Shillings Reward, if taken on the Island; and if off the Island, Thirty Shillings, and all reasonable Charges,
    paid by CALEB CORNWELL.
The New-York Gazette; and Weekly Mercury, June 20, 1768; June 27, 1768; July 4, 1768.

            Baltimore Town, June 20, 1768.
TAKEN up, and committed to Baltimore Town Goal, on suspicion of being runaways, viz.

Timothy Mahony, an Irishman, about 5 feet 10 inches high, dark brown hair, tied behind, his nose somewhat bent more towards one side than the other, he writes a very good hand, and is well acquainted with the inhabitants at North-River, quite up to Albany, and from whence, he says, he came last March; he had on, when taken up, a ruffled shirt, with the mark cut out from the side gushet, and he is remarkably fond of liquor; a letter has been found, wrote by him, which he dates from Quebec, and therein mentions, that he left Sugar Loaf in March last, this letter was directed to Edmund Keho, on Cow-foot Hill, near the tanyard, New-York.

If not claimed, and fetched away, in one month from the date hereof, they will be sold out for their fees,
    By DANIEL CHAMIER, Sheriff.
The Pennsylvania Gazette, June 30, 1768.

RUN-away from the subscriber, at Hosack, near Albany, an indented Irish Servant man, named James M'Kinzie, about 25 Years old, and about 5 Feet 9 Inches high, a strong clumsy made Fellow, black Hair, his Countenance not the most pleasing, is, not sensible, yet much oppinionated, and speaks much with the Irish Accent; his Hands rather remarkably large, and has a

fresh Scar on the upper Part of his Head: Had on when he went away a dark purple nap Coat, lapelled, with white Mettel Buttons, black Calimanco Jacket, and Buckskin Breeches. Whoever secures him so that his Master may have him again, shall receive Five Dollars, and all reasonable Charges, paid by   JOHN MACOMB.
N. B. He lived about 18 Months with Mr. Peter Martin, at Cherry-Valley.

The New-York Gazette; and Weekly Mercury, July 4, 1768; July 11, 1768.

DESERTED from Capt. *David Hay's* Company, of the Royal Regiment of Artillery, viz. *THOMAS SEAL*, Matross, aged Twenty-seven Years, Five Feet Nine Inches high, born in the West of England, and pretends to be a Coachman; he has a fresh Complexion, dark brown Hair, wore a false Tail, when he went away; his Clothes cannot be described, as he left his Regimentals.—N. B. He has his Wife along with him: She is a thick short Woman, sandy Hair, fair Complexion, aged about Thirty-two Years, born in Ireland; she has served some time in *Philadelphia* as a Nurse. Whoever secures the above Deserter, shall have Two Guineas Reward,
          from   Capt. *David Hay*, of the above Regiment.

The Pennsylvania Chronicle, and Universal Advertiser, From Monday, June 27, to Monday, July 4, 1768; From Monday, July 11, to Monday, July 18, 1768; *The New-York Gazette; and the Weekly Mercury*, July 18, 1768; July 25, 1768; August 1, 1768. Minor differences between the papers. The *Weekly Mercury* ends with "His Wife may call herself McClone, as she was married before."

THIS Day was taken up by *Benjamin Blagge*, Esq; and committed to Bridewell, in this city, on suspicion of being a Run-away; a young man, who calls himself James Lawler, born in Ireland, about 23 or 24 years of age, about 5 feet 5 inches high, well set, round visag'd, short brown hair; has on a blue coat, with red lining, and brass buttons; a red striped flannel waistcoat, with the stripes across, a pair of leather breeches, brown yarn stockings, a pair of old shoes with brass buckles, and an half-worn felt hat: He says he belongs to Cornelius Ten Brock, Esq; of Albany, and pretends to be a great buffer. Whoever owns the said servant, by applying to said *Benjamin Blagge*, Esq; or the keeper of the Bridewell; proving their property, and paying charges, may have him again.

The New-York Gazette; and Weekly Mercury, July 11, 1768; July 18, 1768.

STOLE from the Widow STOCKER, in Front-street, next door to Capt. HAY's. a new BLUE CLOTH COAT, lined with deep blue shalloon, is has

a cloth cape, slash cuffs, and blue buttons; a SILK and COTTON DOUBLE BREASTED JACKET, with red and white stripes, and is not quite finished, the size holes not being sewed down, but has been wore, and the fore parts are sullied; also a NEW TWENTY-FIVE SHILLING HAT, made by Joseph Baker, in Market-street.—A young fellow, who goes by the name of THOMAS RIVINGTON, is supposed to have taken them; he is about eighteen years old, square built, five feet two or three inches high, has light brown hair, and a smooth and innocent countenance, which deceives strangers. He pretends to be a printer, as well as a seaman. Some time since he lived in New-York, whither it is thought he is now gone. Whoever secures the clothes and thief, so that he be brought to justice, shall have FOUR DOLLARS reward, and all reasonable charges.
     REBECCA STOCKER.

The Pennsylvania Chronicle, and Universal Advertiser, From Monday, July 11, to Monday, July 18, 1768; From Monday, July 18, to Monday, July 25, 1768.

     TWO POUNDS REWARD.
RUN-AWAY on the 14th of July inst. from the Subscriber, living in Charlotee Precinct, Dutchess County, an Irish Servant Man named Francis Kidd, by Trade a Weaver, six Feet high, broad Face, flat Nose, thick Lips, fair Complexion, black Hair, and has much of the Brogue on his Tongue: Had on when he went away a claret coloured Coat, a jacket with red fore Parts, and check Trowsers; 'tis supposed he took with him a Pair of Buckskin Breeches, and an old Felt Hat bound with green Ferriting; he is much given to Drink. Whoever secures him so that his Master may have him again, shall have the above Reward,
   paid by SAMUEL ROWLAND.

The New-York Gazette; and Weekly Mercury, July 25, 1768; August 1, 1768; August 8, 1768; August 15, 1768; August 22, 1768.

             New-York, July 21, 1768.
     TWENTY POUNDS Reward.
RUN away from his special Bail, *Alexander Whyte*, late Clerk of the Markets in this City, born in *Ireland*, a well-built Man, about 5 Feet 8 Inches high, mark'd with the Small-pox; has a large Nose, grey Eyes, is apt to swear much, pretends to know a good deal about Lands, and is very positive in his Arguments, on any Subject; so that he may be known by speaking to him: His Legs are almost from Top to Bottom of a Thickness; and is well acquainted in this City; has been a Captain in the *New-York* Provincials, and was with Col. *Broadstreet*, in the Year 1763 and 1764. Whoever takes up and secures the said *Alexander Whyte*, in any Place, and acquaints me the Subscriber, so that I can come at him, shall have the above

Reward.—All Masters of Vessels, Boats, Ferry Boats, or any other small Crafts, are hereby warned not to carry the said *Whyte* out of this City, as they, or any of them that does, will be prosecuted with the utmost Rigour of the Law: Or any Person whatever, that shall be found to harbour or conceal, or in any Ways to assist him the said *Whyte*, in getting away from his special Bail, will be obliged to answer the Consequences of it unto
                    MICHAEL THODY.
    N. B. If taken within the Limits of the City, a farther Consideration will be allowed.
    The New-York Gazette or the Weekly Post-Boy, July 25, 1768; August 1, 1768; August 8, 1768; August 22, 1768; *The New-York Gazette; and Weekly Mercury*, July 25, 1768; August 1, 1768. The *Mercury* does not have the date and location at the top. See *The New-York Gazette; and Weekly Mercury*, July 25, 1768, for Whyte's rebuttal. See *The New-York Gazette; and Weekly Mercury*, August 1, 1768.

WHEREAS Michael Thody has put up a most scandalous and malicious Advertisement, entirely with a Design to injure my Character in the Eyes of the Publick, and not our of Fear of my absconding from my Bail, which can be proved by my Letter in May last; wherein I told him, I would be back in two or three Months and settle; which Promise in coming back, I have performed in two Months from Pensacola; and since my Arrival have corresponded together by Letter from Time to Time, with an Intention to get my Affairs settled; and if Mr. Thody's Letter of the 19th, he acknowledges I have performed by Promise, and that the look'd on me as a Man of *Honour* and *Honesty*. I hope the Public will not be unfavourable in their Opinion of me, as it is evident, I need not have come back, if I have an Intention to deceive him, now would I have corresponded with him here. It is true, I did not want to deliver myself to Goal, until I had made up my Accounts, and convinced the Corporation of my Loss, which was great. If he should have been arrested, I would have delivered myself up, as my Letter to him shews.
                    ALEXANDER WHYTE.
    The New-York Gazette; and Weekly Mercury, July 25, 1768; August 1, 1768. See *The New-York Gazette or the Weekly Post-Boy*, July 25, 1768, and *The New-York Gazette; and Weekly Mercury*, August 1, 1768.

WHEREAS Alexander Whyte, has, since my being obliged to advertise him, spread a Report that his Departure from hence in May last, was with my Advice and Consent.—I am obliged to convince the Public to the contrary by the following Affidavit, viz.

New-York, *ff*. PERSONALLY appeared before me, Michael Thodey, of this City, and maketh Oath, that, he never knew of Mr. Whyte's leaving this Place, 'till after he was sail'd; nor did he ever consent to his going, That in about three or four Days after his Departure, he receive a Letter from said Whyte, which informed him of it; which Letter he seems to refer to for his Honesty. And he farther deposeth, That since his Return, he has, as far as a Man of Honour can, promised Mr. Whyte, by Letter (as he would not let me see him, and kept close) if he would let me see him, or call on me privately, that I would do all in my Power, to extricate him from the difficulties he laboured under with the Corporation of this City; and did, in said Letters, promise I would not confine him in Goal; this he did not comply with; and therefore the Advertisement were put up; tho' not before I was informed that Preparations were making for a second Departure; and that he had conveyed every Thing away, in his Power, for me, before he left this in May last.   MICHAEL THODEY.
Sworn before me this 23*d of* July, 1768.
DIRCK BRINKERHOFF.
The New-York Gazette; and Weekly Mercury, August 1, 1768. See two ads in *The New-York Gazette or the Weekly Post-Boy*, July 25, 1768.

RUN-away on friday evening last, a negroe man named Norway, about 33 years of age, but has an older look, near 5 foot high, marked with the small-pox, talks slowly and very indifferent English; he some time since liv'd with Mr. William Ralston, innkeeper, in Philadelphia, but about a year past with Mr. William Provoost, in the city of New-York: Had on when he went away, a blue coat with silver thread buttons, a reddish mixed coloured cloth waistcoat and white plush breeches. Whoever brings the above negroe to Mr. Provoost in New-York, shall receive five dollars reward with all reasonable charges.
The New-York Gazette; and Weekly Mercury, August 1, 1768; August 8, 1768; August 15, 1768; August 22, 1768; August 29, 1768.

TWO POUNDS REWARD,
RUN-away from the subscriber, living in New-York, a Welch servant man named William Walters, by trade a mason, six feet high, thin face, red nose, fair complexion, ball'd [*sic*] on his head, long eyebrows, came in the ship New-Hope, from Bristol: Had on when he went away, a blue jacket, new hat, new shoes; he has a wife with him, a Welch woman, both aged about 48 years, and are much given to drink: She had on a brown silk gown, black hat and petticoat; very remarkable in her talk, and is supposed to be gone towards Mr. Griffith's iron works. Whoever secures him so that his Master

may have him again, shall have the above reward, and all reasonable charges, paid by   JOHN GIFFORD.

The New-York Gazette; and Weekly Mercury, August 1, 1768; August 8, 1768; August 15, 1768; August 22, 1768; August 29, 1768. *The New-York Journal; or, the General Advertiser*, August 4, 1768; August 11, 1768; August 18, 1768; August 25, 1768. See *The Pennsylvania Chronicle, and Universal Advertiser*, From Monday, August 1, to Monday, August 8, 1768, and *The New-York Gazette or the Weekly Post-Boy*, August 8, 1768.

TWO POUNDS REWARD,

RUN away from the Subscriber, living in *New-York*, a *Welch* servant man named WILLIAM WALTERS, by Trade a Mason, 6 Feet high, thin Face, red Nose, fair Complexion, bald on his Head, long Eye Brows, came in the Ship *New Hope* from *Bristol*; had on when he went away, a blue Jacket, new Hat, and new Shoes: He has a Wife with him, a *Welch* Woman, both aged about 48 Years, and are much given toDrink. She had on a brown Silk Gown, black Hat, black Petticoat, very remarkable in her Talk; supposed to be gone towards Mr. *Griffith's* Iron Works. Whoever secures him, so that his Master may have him again, shall have the above Reward, and all reasonable Charges,
          paid by   JOHN GIFFORD.

The New-York Gazette or the Weekly Post-Boy, August 8, 1768; August 15, 1768; August 22, 1768; August 29, 1768; September 5, 1768. See *The New-York Gazette; and Weekly Mercury*, August 1, 1768, and *The Pennsylvania Chronicle, and Universal Advertiser*, From Monday, August 1, to Monday, August 8, 1768.

Forty Shillings Reward.

RUN away from the subscriber, living in New-York, a Welch servant man, named William Waters, by trade a mason, six feet high, has a thin face, red nose, fair complexion, bald head, large eye-brows, came from Bristol in the ship Hope; had on when he went away, a blue jacket, new hat, new shoes; took his wife with him, a Welch woman; she is much given to strong drink, both aged about 48 years. She had on a brown silk gown and petticoat, is very remarkable in her speech, and has a red nose.—Whoever takes up and secures the said servants, so that their master may have them again, shall have the above reward, and all reasonable charges,
          paid by John Gifford, of New-York,
          or John Jervis, jun. in Philadelphia.

N. B. All masters of vessels and others are hereby forbid to carry them off. New-York,—1768.

The Pennsylvania Chronicle, and Universal Advertiser, From Monday, August 1, to Monday, August 8, 1768; From Monday, August 8, to Monday, August 15, 1768. See *The New-York Gazette; and Weekly Mercury*, August 1, 1768, and *The New-York Gazette or the Weekly Post-Boy*, August 8, 1768.

RUN away from the Subscriber living in New-York, an Apprentice Lad, named Jacob Horsen, by Trade a Blacksmith, being between 18 and 19 Years of Age, and near 6 Feet high, very slim built, with black Hair, which he used to wear tied: Had on when he went away, a blue Broadcloth Coat with gilt Buttons, a brown Stocking pattern'd Jacket with gilt Buttons, also, a Pair of half worn Leather Breeches, white rib'd worsted Stockings, a white Shirt, a Pair of Silver Buckles in his Shoes, and a Castor Hat: It is something likely he may be gone towards Blooming-Dale, where he was brought up.—Whoever secures the said Apprentice so that his said Master may have him again, shall receive Twenty Shillings if taken in this City, and Forty Shillings if taken within this Province, out of the Boundaries of the City, and Four Pounds and all reasonable Charges if taken out of the Province.—All Masters of Vessels are desired to be careful not to carry off the said Apprentice: And all Persons whatever are hereby warn'd not to harbour said Apprentice, as they may depend on answering it at their Peril.
    EDWARD MEEKS. *New-York, August* 10, 1768.
The New-York Journal; or, the General Advertiser, August 11, 1768; August 18, 1768; August 25, 1768.

WENT away from the House of Christopher Heysham, in Flushing, (supposed to be persuaded by some evil minded Persons) on the 26th of July last, a hired Servant Man, named John Brown, born in Switzerland, speaks French and broken English, of a middle Stature, dark Complexion, has short black Hair, and walks irregular hobbling on his Heels: Had on when he went away, an old Hat with a Brass Button on it, a striped homespun Jacket lined with coarse Toe [*sic*] Cloth, a new check Shirt, old Buckskin Breeches, and grey yarn Stockings with the Feet cut of, and Pieces of old Hat tied round the Tops of his Shoes; he is much addicted to Liquor, and as he was intoxicated when he went away, may be asham'd to return; but as he has committed no Fault, if he returns he shall have all his Cloaths which he left behind him, and be kindly received. And it is requested of all Persons that may see said Brown, to persuade him to his Interest, and return to his Master.
 The New-York Gazette; and Weekly Mercury, August 15, 1768; August 22, 1768.

RUN-away from the subscribers, last Saturday night, the 20th of August, two negro boys, one 20 years of age, a likely tall fellow, has a little scar on his forehead, has lost one nail off his great toes, branded on both breasts HF, born in St. Kitts, his name is GARRICK. The other about 18 years of age, a likely black fellow, about five feet in heighth, and is a little deaf; born in the island of Jamaica, and has been in this country two years, speaks good English; his name is QUASH. Whoever takes up said negroes, and secures them so that the subscribers may have them, shall receive a reward of TEN DOLLARS, for both; or five for either of them, and all reasonable charges, paid by either of the subscribers.
    HENRY A. FRANKIN, PETER REMSEN.

 N. B. All person or person are hereby forewarned either to conceal or carry off either of the above said negroes, as they will be prosecuted to the utmost rigour of the law.

The New-York Gazette; and the Weekly Mercury, August 29, 1768; September 5, 1768.

RUN-away from *William Mott,* of *Great-Neck,* on Long-Island, on Monday the 15th Instant, a young Indian Servant Fellow, named Stephen, but sometimes Pompey, about 5 Feet 6 Inches high: Had on when he went away, a Tow homespun Shirt and Trowsers, a grey homespun Jacket, a Pair of old Shoes, and an old Felt Hat; is well-set, and has streight black Hair. Whoever takes up and secures the said Fellow, so that his Master may have him again, shall, if found on Long-Island, receive Twenty Shillings Reward; and if taken up off the Island, 40s. and all reasonable Charges,
    paid by WILLIAM MOTT.

N. B. It is supposed he may have a Pass.

The New-York Gazette; and the Weekly Mercury, August 29, 1768; September 5, 1768; September 12, 1768; September 19, 1768; October 3, 1768.

RUN-away from the subscriber, an apprentice lad named JOHN FOSTER, born in the Jersies, about 5 feet 8 inches high, of a dark complexion, and pitted with the small-pox, wears his own hair with a false que to it; is supposed to be gone towards Amboy. He took with him a blue coat and jacket, the coat bound with blue takes, and has metal buttons studded with steel. Whoever takes up said apprentice and brings him to his master, shall have FORTY SHILLINGS reward, and all reasonable charges,
    paid by me, ROBERT ANDREWS.

The New-York Gazette; and the Weekly Mercury, September 5, 1768; September 12, 1768; September 19, 1768; October 3, 1768; October 10, 1768. See *The New-York Gazette or Weekly Post Boy,* June 27, 1765.

City of *New-Brunswick, August* 25.
NOTICE is hereby given that on Monday the 22d Inst. were taken up and committed to Goal, two likely young Negroe Fellow; one calls himself LONDON, about 5 Feet 6 Inches high; the other ROBERT, about 5 Feet 3 Inches: They pretend to be free; say that they did belong to a Gentleman a Merchant from *St. Christophers*; that they came with their Master to *New-York*, who lodged them with the Widow *Richardson*, on *Rotten Row*; that their Master died there last Spring, and before his Death gave them free.— The chief Cloathing about them, was contain'd in a good Ozenbrigs Bay, mark'd P. R. No. 19, viz, a White Fustian Coat, lined with Shalloon, a pair of Leather Breeches, one White Linnen Jacket, 5 White Shirts, one pretty shoe, mark'd W. I. 2 pair of Cloth Breeches, 2 pair of Trowsers, one pair of Yarn, and a pair of Worsted ribb'd Stockings, and one White Handkerchief, one Duffields Great Coat; had on each a Beaver Hat, one about half worn; Jackets, coarse Shirts and Trousers, Calf Skin Shoes, pretty good, and in Appearance had belonged to a Gentlemen.—Whoever claims said Negroes, are desired to be speedy in taking them out.—Or if Mrs. *Richardson*, or any other Person knows them to be free, are desired to give Notice thereof, that upon paying Charges, they may be set at Liberty.

The New-York Gazette or the Weekly Post-Boy, September 5, 1768.

Six DOLLARS Reward.
RUN away from MOSS KENT, of Dutches-County, on Monday the 15th of July last, a Negro Man, named TOM, he speaks English pretty well, is about 30 Years of Age, of a pretty black Complexion, is near six Feet High, slim built, his Cheeks something fallen in: Had on when he went away, a striped Linsey Woolsey lapel'd Jacket, an old Linen Shirt, an old Beaver Hat, with the Brims in Part sewed on the Crown, and a Pair of Tow-Cloth Trowsers. Whoever apprehends the about Run away Negro Man, and secures him, so that his said Master may have him again, shall be paid the above Reward, and all reasonable Charges,
by the said   MOSS KENT.

The New-York Journal; or, the General Advertiser, September 8, 1768; September 15, 1768; September 22, 1768; September 29, 1768.

RUN-away, last Night, being Sunday, the 4th of September Instant, from the Subscriber, living at Flushing, on Long-Island, an Irish Servant Lad, named James Lawson, about 21 Years old, his Nose is pretty long, a little pitted with the Small-Pox, short black Hair, and of a dark Complexion, pretty slender, and about 5 Feet 10 Inches high: Had on and took with him when he went away, a brown Homespun Coat, Jacket and Breeches, 2 short Coats, and a Pair of Trowsers, an old Hat, and a Pair of old Shoes. Whoever

takes up and secures the said Run-away, so that he may be had again, shall receive Forty Shillings Reward, and all reasonable Charges,
   paid by ABRAHAM LAWRENCE.
The New-York Gazette; and the Weekly Mercury, September 12, 1768; September 19, 1768; September 26, 1768; October 3, 1768; October 10, 1768. See *The New-York Journal; or, the General Advertiser*, February 2, 1769.

Five Pounds Reward.

RUN-away from the Subscriber, living in the Borough of Westchester on the 23d of April last, a Negro Man named Hannibal: He is a short well-set Fellow, of a yellow Complexion, has a high Forehead, very large lips, with a remarkable Scar under his right Jaw, occasioned by a Gathering;—he is a remarkable Fellow on a Farm, for Ploughing, Cradleing, and Mowing, and is very talkative: Had on when he went away, a red Duffils Coat, Lead Colour'd Waistcoat, and wide Trowsers, but perhaps has changed his Apparel. Whoever takes up and secures the said Fellow, so that his Master (who is *a poor blind Man*) may have him again, shall receive the above Reward, and all reasonable Charges,
   paid by BARTHOLOMEW HADDEN.
The New-York Gazette; and Weekly Mercury, September 12, 1768; September 19, 1768; September 26, 1768; October 3, 1768. See *The New-York Gazette; and Weekly Mercury*, June 6, 1768.

RUN-away from the subscriber, on monday the first of august last, and Irish servant man named Christopher Grumbley: He is about 22 years of age, 5 feet 6 inches high, pitted with the smallpox, short red hair, and is of a sandy complexion, he speaks the Latin and English tongue well: Had on when he went away, a red coat and jacket, oznaburg Shirt and Trowsers; he has been seen at Batten-Kill and White Creek in the county of Albany. Whoever takes up said servant, and brings him to his master at Fort Edward, or secures him in any of his Majesty's goals, shall have ten dollars
   reward, from PATRICK SMYTH.
N. B. The subscriber will pay upon conviction, a reward of five pounds, to any person who who will inform him who it was that shew'd the said servant the way from Fort Edward to White Creek.
The New-York Gazette; and Weekly Mercury, September 19, 1768; September 26, 1768; October 10, 1768.

RUN-away from the SUBSCRIBER, living at Foster's Meadow, Hempstead, the 18th instant, an indented Irish servant man, named Thomas Mullin;—he is about 26 years of age, and 5 feet 5 inches high, of a fair complexion, a little marked with the small-pox, and short black hair: Had on when he went away, a light coloured short coat, with small cuffs; old leather breeches, grey stockings, a new felt hat, and half worn shoes. Whoever takes up and secures the said servant, so that his master may have him again, shall receive Twenty Shillings reward, and all reasonable charges, paid by   GEORGE REIRSON.

The New-York Gazette; and the Weekly Mercury, October 3, 1768; October 10, 1768; October 24, 1768.

RUN-AWAY last Thursday Morning, an Apprentice Lad, named Thomas M'Cowen, a Tanner and Currier by Trade; he is about 19 Years old, about 5 Feet high, thick and well-set. Had on when he went away, a light-colour'd Jacket and Breeches, and took with him a full Suit of grey Cloth, wore a Wig and a Wool Hat. Whoever takes up and secures the said Run-away, and will bring him to JAMES M'CARTNEY, in Bayard-street, New York, shall have Forty Shillings Reward, and all reasonable Charges paid.

The New-York Gazette; and the Weekly Mercury, October 3, 1768; October 10, 1768; October 17, 1768; October 24, 1768.

ABSCONDED *from the House of the Subscriber, (Dyer and Scourer, on Golden-Hill, opposite the Harp and Crown, New-York) one Fargie Flin, an Irish Man, a dark looking Fellow, about* 30 *Years of Age, black Hair, smooth tongued, by Trade a Blacksmith; and had on a mixt greyish Coat, and a lapped Beaver Hat. He took with him a Chest from the House of the said Subscriber, in his Absence and in a clandestine Manner.—Whoever will take up and bring the said Fargie Flin, to the Subscriber, shall have Two Dollars Reward and all reasonable Charges,*
          HENRY BRABAZON.

The New-York Journal; or, the General Advertiser, October 6, 1768; October 13, 1768.

Philadelphia, October 3, 1768.
FOUR DOLLARS Reward.

ABSCONDED from his bail, living in Strawberry Ally, an Irishman named John Harford, by trade a taylor, about 5 feet 7 inches high, well-set, of a dark complexion, wears his own hair, which is black, and very much inclined to curl, speaks middling good English. Had on when he went away, a grey coat with buttons of the colour, grey waistcoat, black stockings, blue breeches, halfworn shoes, with yellow metal buckles, white shirt, halfworn hat sharp cock'd, walks very upright. Said runaway has a flesh-mark on one of his shoulders, which he calls a Strawberry. Whoever apprehends said runaway, so that he maybe had again, shall have the above reward and reasonable charges,
          paid by   THOMAS HARRISON.

N. B. 'Tis suppos'd he is gone to New-York, as he has a wife whom he married at the time he was advertised as a runaway servant about two years ago. By virtue of which advertisement he was taken in New-York. All masters of vessels and others, are forbid harbouring or carrying him off, as they will answer the same at their peril. P. S. The place of his wife's residence probably may be heard of at Mrs. Ann Able's, in New-street, near the Old English Church, or at Mr. Ennis Graham's, Taylor, near the Coffee-House, where said runaway formerly worked.

The New-York Gazette; and the Weekly Mercury, October 10, 1768; October 17, 1768; October 24, 1768; October 31, 1768; November 7, 1768. See *The Pennsylvania Gazette*, November 28, 1765.

MADE his Escape from the Subscriber, Under-Sheriff for the County of Orange, on the North Side of the Highlands, one JOHN MOORE, Waggon and Chairmaker; he is about 6 Feet high, something pock-mark'd, walks very nimble, born in Ireland. Had on when he went away, a blue Coat, a green Calimanco Vest, with the Fore-skirts patch'd, a black knit Breeches. Said Moore formerly work'd at the Fishkills. Whoever takes up said John Moore, and brings him to the Subscriber, shall have Forty Shillings Reward, and all reasonable Charges,

paid by me   JEREMIAH COLMON, Under-Sheriff.

The New-York Gazette; and the Weekly Mercury, October 10, 1768; October 17, 1768; October 24, 1768.

NORWICH, October 17th, 1768.

Last Friday Evening the Shop of Mr. John M'Carthy of Norwich was opened, and two pair of new buck-skin breeches were taken from thence; several shirts, &c. were taken from people's bedges, the same night—and on Sunday, two transient fellow were taken up at Pomfret, and the following articles were found in their packs, viz. 18 keys of different sizes and constructions, 5 files sorted, a very large iron spike hardened and sharp at the end, one hammer, one tinder box, tinder, steel, matches, flints and brimstone, a phial, supposed to contain aquasortice, so that it appears they were furnished with a variety of useful instruments for executing their business. One of then is an Englishman, about 50 years of age, red face and hair, short stature, crooked shape, and lame, wears a blue jacket and trowsers, and says his name is John Wood. The other is a German about 30 years old, calls himself Jacob Hendrick, had on a blue coat and trowsers, wears his own hair, and is lame in one of his knees. they both say, that they come from Albany. The articles that were stolen from Norwich being found in their packs, they were this day whipt, and committed to goal.

come from Albany. *The articles that were stolen from Norwich being found in their packs, they were this day whipt, and committed to goal.*
The Connecticut Journal, and New-Haven Post-Boy, October 21, 1768.

TAKEN-up a few Days ago, and committed to the Goal of the Borough of Elizabeth, in New-Jersey, by order of John Stites, Esq; Mayor, a Negro Man about 24 Years old, very thick Lips, talks both Dutch and English, says he is a free Man, and that he lived some Time at Bloomindale, near New-York: When taken up he had on a blue Coat, old Shoes, without Stockings. The Owner may have him again, paying Charges, and proving his Property, by applying to the said John Stites, Esq;
   or the Goaler, Benjamin Miller.
The New-York Gazette; and the Weekly Mercury, October 24, 1768.

RUN-AWAY from Henry Grigg, Inn-keeper, in the city of New-York, last saturday night, an Irish servant boy named William Brown, 17 years old, of a fair complexion, had a down look, was much freckled, has streight brown hair, about 5 Feet 2 Inches high, taper shouldered, a lazy walk, and his right ankle bends in: Had on when he went away, a brown cloth waistcoat and breeches patched on both knees, and two under-waistcoats, the one blue, and the other white flannel, a check shirt, with a silver broach at his breast, a pair of white shoes with stiffening in the quarters, a small round hat bound on the edges, and a pair of blue stockings. Whoever takes up and secures the said Run-away, so that he may be had again, shall receive *Three Dollars* reward, and reasonable charges,
    from HENRY GRIGG.
The New-York Gazette; and the Weekly Mercury, October 31, 1768; November 7, 1768.

RUN-away, belonging to the Estate of John Schermerhorne, deceased, about the first of October, a Negro Boy about sixteen years of Age, named NOKE: Whoever brings said Boy to Luke Van Ranst, Isaac Sears, Jeremiah Brower, or Lawrence Kortright, Executors to said Estate; or can give any Account of him, so that he may be had again, shall receive a Reward of Forty Shillings, and all reasonable Charges paid them.
The New-York Gazette; and the Weekly Mercury, November 21, 1768; November 28, 1768; December 5, 1768; December 19, 1768; December 26, 1768.

RUN-away from the subscriber, living in the city of New-York, a negro man named CUFF, about 5 feet 9 inches high, aged about 25 years, and as the marks of the small-pox in his face very plain: Had on, when he went away, (which was about 5 weeks ago) a brown jacket, a pair of new shoes, and trowsers. Whoever takes up said negro, so that his master may have him again, if taken in the city, shall have 20s. if in the country 40s. and all reasonable charges,
     paid by ELBERT HERRING.

The New-York Gazette; and the Weekly Mercury, December 19, 1768; January 2, 1769; January 16, 1769; January 30, 1769.

INDEX

The index contains all the names found. If a person is listed only by a title and last name the title is given, otherwise titles are omitted. If no name is associated with a person, the person is listed such as "Men, unknown." Negroes and Indians are listed by race, and if they have a first and last name, they are also listed with last name, then first name. Mustees, persons of mixed but unspecified races, are also listed separately.

Abeel, James, 381
Abeel, John, 205
Abel, Lodwick, 360
Abercrombie, James, 114
Abercromby, General, 294
Able, Ann, 396
Abraham, John, 301
Acting, John, 212
Adams, George, 230, 383
Afey, john, 42
Agar, Edward, 212, 252, 253, 260, 278, 280, 285
Agnew, Edward, 277, 280
Akerly, Benjamin, 130, 131
Alagon, Richard, 113
Alberspe/Albrespy, William, 282, 125
Alexander, James, 4, 42, 323
Alexander, John, 106
Alexander, Mr., 377
Alexander, Robert, 116
Algee, David, 70
Allan, Robert, 221
Allen, Henry, 94
Allen, Mary, 55
Allen, Mr., 55
Allen, Thomas, 330
Allen, William, 184
Allicock, Mr., 237

Ally, Daniel, 257
Alsop, Mr., 316
Amherst, Major General, 178
Amons, Daniel, 320
Anderson, Capt., 71
Anderson, David, 217
Anderson, James, 241
Anderson, Mr., 220
Anderson, William, 194
Andrew, John, 6
Andrews, Robert, 321, 329, 351, 375, 392
Annelly, William, 283
Annely, Edward, 300
Annen, James, 286, 288
Annow, John, 109
Anthony, John, 189
Anthony, Joseph, 294
Anthony, Zephaniah, 314
Arden, Jacob, 250, 369
Arding, Charles, 26
Armstrong, William, 240
Arnold, Benedict, 147, 148
Arnold, Valentine, 75
Arrowsmith, Michael, 80
Ash, Gilbert, 1
Ashfield, Richard, 4, 5
Ashton, Easter, 170
Ashton, Hester, 171

Ashton, William, 106
Auchmuty, Samuel, 356, 359
Ault, Capt., 247
Ayers, Mr., 197
Ayres, Charles, 115
Ayscough, John, 60, 76
Bache, Theophilact, 273
Backus, Lieut., 139
Baddeley, John, 111
Bagnel, Benjamin, 24
Baily, Captain, 290, 291
Baily, Daniel, 292
Baker, Charles, 226
Baker, Jacob, 232
Baker, Joseph, 67, 387
Bane, Daniel, 371
Banker, Jores, 41
Banks, James, 60
Baptist, John, 378
Barbait, Mrs., 276
Barber, Mr., 337
Barbutt, William, 1
Barclay, Mr., 377
Bard, Mr., 374
Baremore, Nathaniel, 364
Barkley, Robert, 216
Barnard, James, 173, 266
Barnes, Richard, 161
Barnes, Roger, 175
Barnet, John, 174
Barns, Capt., 123
Barr, Hendrick, 269, 272
Barren, Samuel, 186
Barrington, Mary, 251
Barton, James, 103
Bates, William, 305
Bavard, Sam., 27

Bayard, Joseph, 289
Bayard, Major, 339
Bayard, Mr., 327
Bayard, Nicholas, 43, 44, 54, 63, 89, 249
Bayard, Samuel, 133
Bayard, Stephen, 35, 40
Bayard, William, 74, 196, 203, 204, 234, 236, 258, 272
Bayly, Richard, 90
Bear, John, 115
Beate, Isaac, 379
Beathell, William, 262
Beatie, Isaac, 357
Bedlow, William, 189
Beech, Epenetus, 241
Beekman, Gerard G., 122
Beekman, Henery, 21
Beezley, Capt., 48
Bekers, Frederick, 61
Belcher, John, 121, 129
Bell, Elisha, 258
Bell, John, 7, 15, 54, 95
Bell, Mr., 229
Bell, Thomas, 304
Bell, Tom, 56
Bellamy, Isaac, 314
Bellamy, John, 156
Bellew, Captain, 98, 103, 113
Bellross, Pierre Joseph, 78
Benedict, Peter, 264
Bennet, William, 301
Bennett, James, 231
Benton, Richard, 199
Berry, Charels, 351
Berwick, Marmaduke, 344
Beslee, Robert, 130

Bethel/Bethell, Benjamin, 39, 105
Bethune, Henry, 79
Betts, John, 57
Betts, Richard, 177
Betts, Thomas, 26
Bevan, Robert, 8
Bicker, Lieut., 139, 140
Bill, James, 68
Billing, Moses, 44
Billsbury, Thomas, 329
Bird, James, 98
Bishop, James, 317
Bishop, Richard, 7
Bishup, Robert, 186
Black, George, 181
Black, John, 281
Blackham, Joseph, 257
Blackmore, William, 60
Blackwood, Hamilton, 130
Blackwood, John, 147, 148
Blage/Blagge, Benjamin, 91, 386
Blair, Doctor, 325
Blair, Thomas, 305
Blakeney, Lord, 182, 183, 198
Blau, Waldron, 269, 306
Blauveldt, Johannis, 238
Blear, John, 283
Blodget, Samuel, 281
Bloodgood, Francis, 54
Blundell, Christopher, 294
Bodkin, Mr., 183
Boies, Alexander, 178
Bokels, Henry, 318
Bollard, Robert, 24
Bond, John, 19

Borhite, Barnet, 110
Boskirk, Susanna, 142
Bosomworth, Captain, 120
Bostick, William, 2
Bouls, Mary, 40
Bourineau, Stephen, 23
Bourk, John, 110
Bourn, Melatiah, 229
Bowden, John, 329
Bowen, William, 259
Bowlers, Samuel, 212
Bowlers, Thomas, 212
Bowne, Samuel, 140, 208
Bownes, Mrs., 65
Boyd, Robert, 313
Boyde, James, 98
Boyer, John, 248
Boyer, Samuel, 29
Boyle, John, 352, 358
Boyle, Robert, 116
Brabazon, Henry, 395
Brackett, Anthony, 183
Bradburn, Alexander, 310
Bradburn, Joseph, 235
Bradford, Andrew, 4
Bradford, James, 68
Bradford, William, 10, 15, 23, 39
Bradly, Francis, 102
Bradt, Arent, 17
Brannan, Christopher, 234
Brant, John, 276
Bratt, Johannes, 29
Bratt, Samuel A., 373
Breasted, Andrew, 107
Breese, John, 27
Breese, Mrs., 70
Breese, Sidney, 146

Brereton, Ensign, 118
Brett, Francis, 48
Brett, Matthew, 363
Brewer, Edward, 99
Brewer, Samuel, 341
Brewerton, George, 204
Brewin, George, 289
Brewster, Daniel, 84
Brian, Dennis, 29
Bridge, Samuel, 93, 262
Briggs, Isaac, 199
Brimingham, James, 352
Brinkerhoff, 389
Broadstreet, Col., 387
Brock, William, 130
Brook, Joseph, 16
Brookman, Samuel, 225
Brookman, Thomas, 255
Brooks, Ichabod, 197
Brower, Jeremiah, 397
Brown Thomas, 168
Brown, Benjamin, 250
Brown, Capt., 80
Brown, Edward, 247
Brown, James, 99
Brown, John, 125, 391
Brown, Jonathan, 32, 99
Brown, Margery, 8
Brown, Mary, 193
Brown, Stephen, 377
Brown, Thomas, 78, 208, 313, 317
Brown, William, 249, 397
Browne/Brown, Robert, 208
Brownejohn, William, 142
Brush, Abner, 36, 37
Brush, Isaac, 112

Bryan, Archibald, 235
Bryan, Catherine, 235
Bryan, George, 151
Bryan, James, 274
Bryan, John, 235
Buchan, William, 236
Buck, Aaron, 323
Buckelew, Francis, 42
Budd, Mrs., 144
Budd, Undrell, 61
Budd, Wm., 339
Buffinton, Samuel, 314
Bugles, Francis, 282
Buglis, Francis, 265
Burch, David, 335
Burch, Sarah, 335
Burch, Thomas, 39
Burchall, Catherine, 374
Burgert, Alexander, 381
Burgert, Mr., 380
Burlen/Burling, James, 335, 336
Burling, Benjamin, 40
Burn, Andrew, 338
Burn, John, 117
Burne, George, 372
Burnfield, Charles, 363
Burnham, Samuel, 41
Burns, Barnaby, 197
Burns, George, 76, 192, 254, 266
Burns, Mr., 374
Burton, Colonel, 144
Burton, Isaac, 253
Bush, Abraham, 292
Bush, Amaziah, 35
Bush, Jost, 312
Butler, John, 15
Butler, Michael, 228

Butterfield, William, 20
Buxton, Ruben, 41
Byrn, Arthur, 32
Byrne, Robert, 373
Byrns, Mr., 255
Byvanck, Anthoney, 37
Byvanck, Ever/Evert, 86, 100
Byvanck, John, 226
Byvank, John, 18
Caldwell, Capt., 100
Cambel/Campbell, John, 224
Cameron, Duncan, 180
Camoran, John, 280
Campbell, Archibald, 29
Campbell, Daniel, 88, 292
Campbell, Edward, 304
Campbell, James, 140
Campbell, John, 2, 90, 121, 166, 174, 258, 283
Campbell, Malcolm, 219
Campbell, Robert, 108, 213
Campbell, William, 156
Campbell/Campbel, Hugh, 274
Campble, Mr., 24, 25
Can, Matthew, 149
Cannon, John, 9, 253
Cannon, William, 52
Cardiff, Clement, 208
Carmer, Henry, 296
Carney, Mary, 49
Carpenter/Cardender/Carpder, Elizabeth, 133, 146, 151, 180, 200
Carr, Mark, 195, 196
Carr, William, 269
Carrall, James, 164
Carre, Pierre Joseph, 78

Carrick, David, 200
Carril, Bryant, 167
Carrol/Carroll, James, 114, 119
Carson, James, 195, 196
Carson, Mr., 377
Carter, David, 119
Carter, James, 253
Carty, Catharine, 246
Carver, Joseph, 225
Caselicth/Caselick, James, 63
Cash, David, 200
Castle, Robert, 96
Causer, Hester, 235
Causer, John, 235
Cavanaugh, Sill, 276
Cavenaugh, Thomas, 32
Cavendish, Joseph, 184, 185
Caventish, John, 339
Chadwicke, John, 132
Chambers, Edward, 197
Chambers, James, 5, 273
Chamier, Daniel, 385
Chandler, J., 354
Chandler, John, 286, 288
Chandler, Thomas, 195, 196
Chapman, Daniel, 149
Chapman, William, 102
Charles, Andrew, 142
Chelwell, Thomas, 150
Chesnut, Gerard, 174
Chew, Richard, 30
Chombrier, Capt., 102
Christell, John, 100
Christian, John, 132
Christopher, John, 36
Chrystie, George, 192
Cicere, Dorothy, 106

Civil/Civill, Charles, 195, 196
Clancy/Clacy, Mary, 313, 317
Clark, Cornelius, 200, 323
Clark, John, 1
Clarke, George, 24, 25
Clarke, John, 186
Clarkson, David, 94
Clarkson, Mathew, 17
Clay, Margaret, 383
Clay, Thomas, 382
Clemens, Charles, 60
Clement/Clements, Moses, 73, 104, 334, 343, 347
Clopper, Cornelius, 340
Clopper, John, 170
Clossen, Peter, 345
Clymer, Christopher, 34
Cobbam, William, 238
Cochran, Captain, 234
Cochran, David, 339
Cochran, William, 339
Cockchick, Anthony, 167
Cockran, William, 295
Colam, Ephraim, 30
Colden, Alexander, 192
Cole, Jacob, 94
Cole, Jasper, 361
Coleby, Katy, 329
Coles, Richard, 172
Colford, Patrick, 95
Collens, Luke, 42
Collin, John, 129
Collins, Matthew, 247
Collins, Thomas, 115
Collons, Peter, 212
Colman, Mr., 42
Colmon, Jeremiah, 396

Colquhoon, Hugh, 113
Colskin, Nicholas, 200
Colters, James, 352
Colvin, William, 334
Combes, John, 362
Combs. James, 149
Comes, John, 218
Comes, Solomon, 60
Comfort, Baily, 51
Concklin, Joseph, 96, 253
Conkling, Deliverance, 130
Connar, Daniel, 78
Connel/Connell, William, 134
Connely, Roger, 121
Conner, John, 130
Connor, John, 357
Conway, John, 129
Conyngham, Mr., 290, 291
Cook, Francis, 232
Cook, John, 351
Cook, Joseph, 338
Cook, Richard Clark, 62
Cook, Thomas, 309
Cook, William, 351
Cooly, Henry, 131
Coomb, John, 294
Coombs/Comes, John, 215, 216
Coomes, John, 256
Coomes, Robert, 36, 37
Cooper, Daniel, 366
Cooper, Ezekel, 335, 336
Cooper, James, 78
Cooper, Myles, 282
Cooper, Samuel, 132
Coppner, Gabriel, 112
Corey, Abraham, 337
Cornelison, Mr., 144

Cornell, John, 280
Cornell, Mary, 59
Cornell, Samuel, 211
Cornie, Zepheria, 129
Cornwall/Cornwell, George, 232
Cornwell, Caleb, 385
Corry, Patrick, 173
Corry, Robert, 309
Cosby, William, 27
Cosine, Garrat, 251
Cossine, Garit, 302
Coteu, Elizabeth, 228
Cotton, Catherine, 219
Couglin, Casparis, 299
Coulter, James, 351
Courter, Capt., 7
Courtney, John, 365
Cowdery, Jonathan, 315
Cox, Capt., 112
Cox, John, 36, 69
Cox, Joseph, 258
Coxetter, Bartholomew, 154
Craddock, Joseph, 195, 196
Craddock, Mr., 183
Crafton, Nicholas, 186
Crane, John, 307
Crannel, Robert, 232
Crawford, Alexander, 227
Crawley, Florence, 366
Cree, John, 309, 371
Cregier, Simon, 62
Crew, Captain, 134
Crofton, James, 193
Crofts, Dudley, 41
Croker, Thomas, 38
Crooke, Gabriel, 22
Crookshank, Capt., 107

Crookshanks, Thomas, 157
Cross, James, 147
Cross, John, 254
Cross/Cros, Crispus, 357, 359
Cruckshank, Capt., 209
Cruger, John, 47, 197
Cuming, James, 337
Cummings, Donald, 127
Cunningham, John, 145
Cunningham, Mr., 132, 221, 292, 308, 313, 317
Cunningham, Samuel, 145
Cunningham, Waddel/Waddell, 116, 125, 273
Curle, Nicholas, 287
Curry, Margery, 122
Curtee, Nicholas, 287
Curtin, John, 326
Daily, Sam, 17
Dally, Cornelius, 93
Dalton, John, 266
Daly, Capt., 236, 257, 272
Damsel, Andrew, 101
Daniel, Hugh, 292
Danolson, Archibald, 156
Darby, Col., 187
Darby, John, 38, 185, 254, 282
Darlington, William, 76, 332, 378
Dart, Joseph, 47
Daugherty, Michael, 61
Davers, Charles, 290
Davidson, Lawrence, 214
Davies, Thomas, 344
Davis, Dudley, 361
Davis, John, 42
Davis, Squire, 384

Davis, Thomas, 30, 158
Dawson, Capt., 286, 287
Dawson, Thomas, 224
Day, Thomas, 338
Dayley/Dayly, Daniel/Danial, 365
De Boutemant, Glove, 81
De Garmo/De Garimo, John, 280
De Klerk, Theunis, 41
De Klerke, Tunis, 330
De Lancey, Capt., 254
De Lancey, James, 220
De Lancey, Justice, 35
De Lancey, Oliver, 245
De Lancey, Peter, 57
De Peyster, Cornelius, 5
De Peyster, Gerardus, 17
Dean, Jonathan, 199
Deane, Elkanah, 355
Deane, Le Chevalier, 86, 87
Deane, Mr., 282
Deane, Richard, 284
Deare, John, 42
Deas, John, 361
Deaver/Deavers, Patrick, 89
Debutcher, Eleanor, 219
Decker, Charles, 21
Decker, Joseph, 130
DeForest, Mrs., 96
Degarmo, Capt., 286, 288
Degrushe, Elias, 74
Delancey, Captain, 165
DeLancey, Col., 120
Delaney, James, 266
Delaney, Mary, 325
Delany, Dennis, 174
Delaplaine, Joshua, 23

Demere, Paul, 92
Denise/DeNise, Jaques, 243, 244, 246
Dennis, Mary, 296
Dennison/Denniston, Peter, 287, 288
Denton, Daniel, 3
Derota, Maria, 91
Derry, Cornelius, 93
Desney, Daniel, 311
DeVaDriel, Mr,, 325
Devenport, Samuel, 135
Devereux, James, 142
Deverson, William, 200, 232
Devoe, Michael, 245
Devore, David, 199
Dewit, Abraham, 223
Dicker, Gabriel, 129
Dickerson, John, 333
Dingman, Mr., 381
Disborow, Josiah, 250
Disseau, John Babtist, 377
Disseaux, Colonel, 102
Diver, Edward, 200
Dixon, Captain, 107, 134
Doadel, Owen, 3
Dobbs, Adam, 242
Dobson, Thomas, 92
Dogworth, Elizabeth, 233
Donaldson, William, 72
Donean, John, 200
Dongan, Richard, 157
Dongan, Walter, 3
Donivan, Ricket, 326
Donnaldson, Ronald, 292
Donnavan, William, 290, 291
Donum, Samuel, 35

Donwith, John, 252
Dooly, Michael, 145
Dougherty, Jno., 110
Doughty, Charles, 336
Douglas, Robert, 174
Douglas, Thomas, 90
Douglass, John, 116
Douglass, William, 290
Dow, Folkert Hendrick, 45
Dowhanty, William, 42
Down, John, 101
Downs, Mr., 130
Doxey, Martin, 336
Doyl, John, 232
Draper, Messrs., 359
Draper, Richard, 263
Draper, Samuel, 263
Dubois, Jonas, 316
Ducard, Jean Jacob, 77
Ducart, George, 77
Duddon, Joseph, 130
Dudley, Francus, 66
Dudley, John, 147
Duffie, John, 213
Duggan, John, 60
Dulany, William, 3
Duley, Philip, 38
Dumont, Henry, 103
Dunahoe, Thomas, 42
Dunavan, James, 295
Dunbar, Capt., 247
Duncan, John, 325, 346
Dunforth, John, 202
Dunkin, John, 36
Dunlap, John, 14
Dunlap, William, 234
Dunn, George, 165

Dunn, Hezekiah, 118
Dunscomb, Daniel, 74
Dunsten, Doctor, 68
Durham, John, 139
Durham, Thomas, 255
Durkee, Major, 152, 176
Durrem, William, 27
Duryee, John, 146
Duvell, Nicholas, 308
Duyckinck, Christopher, 304
Dwight, Edmund, 42
Dyckman, Jacob, 316
Dyer, John, 22
Dyer, Mr., 83
Eage, Jacob, 163
Eagon, John, 26
Eales, Mr., 299
Earle, Edward, 101
Earle, Joseph, 314
Ecker, Wolvert, 172
Ederenton, John, 38
Edward, John, 169
Edward, Mark, 191
Edward, William, 162
Edwards, Benajah, 302
Edwards, Mary, 193
Eiles, Robert, 42
Elbert, Margaret, 138
Eliot/Elliott, John, 130, 235
Elliot, George, 186
Elliot, Lt. Col. R., 272, 304
Elsworth, George, 31
Engelbert, Anthony, 23
English, Robert, 309
Ennis, Frederick, 38
Erein, Elenor, 56
Ernest, John, 327

Erwin, Robert, 324
Erwin, William, 324
Erwine, John, 79
Evans, John, 129
Evelman, John, 236
Everit, Clear, 95
Everit, John, 3
Everson, Evert, 231
Everson, Mary, 231
Evouts, Mr., 181, 217
Evouts, Peter, 141
Exelby, John, 153
Eyre, Lt. Col., 247
Eyre, Thomas, 290
Eyre, William, 283
Eyres, William, 268
Eyrs, Tho's, 293
Eyrs, William, 293
Fairfield, William, 160
Falconer, Captain, 141, 283
Falconer, Thomas, 289
Falkner, John, 286, 287
Fanueil, Andrew, 1
Fararo, Mrs., 264
Farmar, Samuel, 86
Farning, James, 169
Farquharson, Capt., 174
Farrant, John, 7
Farrel, John, 209, 290
Farrel, Thomas, 247
Farrel/Farrell, John, 110, 193, 267, 297, 298
Farren, Riging, 200
Farril, William, 252
Farrington, Captain, 348
Farrington, David, 268
Faxon, William, 195, 196

Felter, William, 364
Fennigen, Edward, 212
Ferguson, Capt., 273
Ferguson, Thomas, 273, 274
Ferrall, Mr., 183
Ferrari, Mary, 89
Ferrel, John, 56
Ferrer, Erasmus, 371
Ferris, Caleb, 113
Ferris, John, 202
Field, Patrick, 281
Filkin, Bernard, 253
Fincher, Henry, 6
Finckensor/Frokinger, Johannes/Johannis, 380, 381
Findley, William, 166
Finn, William, 16
Fish, Joseph, 198
Fisher, Jacob, 136, 137
Fisher, John, 144
Fisher, John Sighmont, 108
Fisher, Thomas, 364
Fitch, Col., 152, 176
Fitch, James, 58
Fitz Morris, Richard, 80
Fitzgerald, John, 121, 129, 131
Fitzgerall, Thomas, 232
Fitzherbert, William, 167, 168
Fitzpatrick, Lieut., 226
FitzPatrick, Mr., 219
Fitzpatrick, Stephen, 135
Flanagan, John, 255
Flanagin, Rose, 248
Flanley, Patrick, 86
Fleet, Simon, 284
Fleglar, Philip Solomon, 226
Fletcher, Capt., 113

Fletcher, Henry, 114
Fletcher, Joseph, 377
Fletcher, Major, 102
Fletcher, William, 2
Flin, Fargie, 395
Flowers, Mr., 193
Foine, Thomas, 115
Folliot, George, 103, 151
Fonda, Abraham, 109
Foot, Moses, 155, 176, 188
Forbes, Capt., 166
Forbes, James, 308
Forbes, John, 119
Forbes, Mr., 301
Forbush, William, 384
Ford, Andrew, 183
Forder, William, 348
Foreman, Col., 90
Foreman, William, 354
Forguson, James, 200
Forman, Aaron, Jr., 124
Forman, Joseph, 239, 249
Forman, Stephen, 258, 298
Forsey, Benjamin, 126, 127
Forsey, Thomas, 126, 127
Forster, Colonel, 213
Foster, John, 321, 392
Foster, Jonas, 20
Foster, Ralph, 136
Fowler, David, 158, 185, 188
Fowler, Jeremiah, 5
Franklin, Henry A., 392
Franklin, John, 219
Franklin, Mr., 303
Franklin, Thomas, 308
Franks, David, 213
Franks, John, 209

Franks, Mathias, 41
Frazer, James, 195, 196
Freidure, John Baptist, 92
Freits, John Milcus, 140
French, Capt., 116
French, Joseph, 296
Frey, Margaret, 347
Frokinger/Finckensor, Johannes/Johannis, 380
Fronheyser, Andrew, 234
Frost, Joshua, 247
Fry, Christian, 334, 343, 347
Fry, Margaret/Margareta, 334, 343
Fuller, General, 40
Furman, Ralph, 362
Furnance, Anthony, 41
Gaffe, Thomas, 120
Gage, Thomas, 94
Gaine, Hugh, 297, 300, 304, 306, 310
Gale, James, 379
Gallagher, James, 195, 196
Galusha, Daniel, 95
Gansel, Colonel, 257
Gansey, Benjamin, 229
Gardner, Archibald, 345
Gardner, Jeremiah, 19
Gardner, Thomas, 132
Garrison, A., 5
Garrison, George, 289
Garrison, L., 334
Gatefield, William, 102
Gaub, George, 193
Gelston, James, 276
Gerbus, John, 129
Gerome, Charles, 330

Giddons, Roger, 286, 287
Gifford, John, 390
Gilchrist, Adam, 164
Gilchrist, Captain, 172, 200
Gilderoy, Bryant, 167
Gildow, John, 283
Giles, Benjamin, 248
Gill, John, 202
Gill, Mr., 299
Gill, Samuel, 163
Gillchrist, Capt., 276
Gillet, John, 157
Gilliam, William, 4, 5
Gilliland, Ann, 269
Gilliland, David, 132
Gilliland/Gilland, William, 269, 278, 281, 320
Gland, Thomas, 117
Glen, George, 103
Goad, John, 63, 64
Goald, David, 36, 37
Goddard, Nicholas, 165
Godet, Theodore, 255
Godfrey, Benj., 1
Godfrey, Mary, 230
Godwin, Capt., 115
Godwin, John, 273, 274
Goforth, William, 301
Golding, Justus, 199
Gombauld, Moses, 22, 23
Gomez, Isaac, 321, 353
Gonsalvo, St. Baston, 232
Goodchild, William, 294
Goodwin, Capt., 80
Gordon, John, 148, 180
Gosline, John, 212
Gote, Henry, 315

Gover, John, 60
Gowing, Joshua, 353
Graham, Chauncey/Chauncy, 84, 263
Graham, Daniel, 372
Graham, David, 281
Graham, Dr., 156
Graham, Edward, 29, 86, 109
Graham, Ennis, 396
Graham, Gardon, 129
Graham, William, 328
Grangent, Hugh, 65
Grannis, John, 292
Grant, Capt., 287
Grant, Col., 204
Grant, Francis, 203
Grasset, John, 36, 37
Gray, Adam, 13
Gray, Joseph, 54
Gray, Thomas, 275
Greem, Capt., 101
Green, James, 60
Green, John, 251
Greene, Hannah, 331
Greene, Mr., 331
Greenfields, Samuel, 243
Greenland, James, 182
Greg, Mr., 132, 221, 292, 308, 313, 317
Greswold, Joseph, 205
Griffin, John, 81, 195, 196
Griffith, Barnaby, 182
Griffith, James, 209
Griffith, Mr., 389, 390
Griffiths, John, 240
Griffiths, Mr., 240
Griffiths, Paul, 184

Griffiths, Thomas/Tom, 220
Grigg, Henry, 397
Grimes, Cornelius, 42
Grinnell, Capt., 83
Griswold, Joseph, 135
Grizin/Grixin, John, 286, 288
Groesbeek, John, 57
Grumbley, Christopher, 394
Grummel, James, 223
Gudgeon, Mrs., 208
Guerard, Mr., 1
Guest, John, 184
Guion, Isaac, 81
Gwinn, John, 378
Gyles, Charles, 178
Haber, Christian, 8
Haber, Frederick, 8
Hacket, Patrick, 330
Hadden, Bartholomew, 383, 394
Haddon, Richard, 79
Hagerman, Benjamin, 320
Hagerman, Joseph, 265
Haigt, Charles, 307
Hailet, Mr., 285
Haily, Jacob, 114
Haines, Francis, 256
Haislip, William, 287
Hait, Joseph, 197
Halbert, Reuben, 293
Haley, Michael, 318
Halkett, Peter, 90
Hall, David, 218
Hall, Philip, 365
Hall, Thomas, 11
Hallock, Jesse, 108
Hallstock, Joseph, 209
Hambleton, Charles, 164
Hamersley/Hamersly, Thomas, 97, 277
Hames, George, 89
Hamilton, Alexander, 116
Hamilton, Col., 65, 66
Hamilton, Major, 245
Hammond, Joseph, 4
Hamsen, James, 149, 150
Hana, William, 71
Hancock, Thomas, 273, 274
Handlin, John, 139
Hanley, David, 265
Hanlin, John, 355
Hanna, Archibald, 40
Hannawell, Enoch, 84
Hardcastle, Henry, 91
Harden, John, 226
Hardic, John, 294
Hardie, John, 233
Harding, James, 15
Harford, John, 328, 395
Hargreave, Captain, 234, 257
Harper, David, 38
Harper, Ensign, 290
Harring, Elbert, 267
Harrington, Dennis, 200
Harris, Mr., 359
Harris, Richard, 142, 145, 325
Harris, William, 38
Harrison, Elizabeth, 382
Harrison, John, 395
Harrison, Thomas, 328
Hart, Mordecai, 110
Hartley, Henry, 16
Harvey, Arthur, 60
Haskell, John, 8
Haslip, William, 286

Hassenclever, Peter, 380, 381
Hassert, Arent, 17
Hastier, John, 122
Hatfield/Hetfield, Joshua, 161
Hause, John, 235
Haviland, Colonel, 182, 183
Hawkins, Edward, 197
Hawkins, John, 161
Hawxhurst, Benjamin, 55
Hawxhurst, William, 55
Hay, Capt., 386
Hay, David, 386
Hay, Mr., 19
Haydock, John, 91
Hayes/Hays, Judah, 106, 267
Haynes, Joseph, 52, 282
Haynes, Samuel, 115
Hays, Benjamin, 279
Hays, Francis, 116
Hays, Judah, 65, 66, 123, 125, 128, 261
Hays, Moses M., 297
Hays, William, 213
Hays, William, Jr., 213
Hayt/Hait, Captain, 163
Hazard, Henry, 286, 288
Hazard, Nathaniel, 9
Hazard, Toby, 185
Heath, William, 138
Hedy, Arabella, 159
Height, Capt., 200
Heisterberg, Christinus Fredericus, 81
Hendrick, Jacob, 396
Hendrick, Sarah, 233
Hendricks, William, 249
Henery/Hendry, Margaret, 49

Hepburn, Patrick, 28
Herbert, David, 197
Herring, Elbert, 246, 261, 398
Herring, Lieutenant, 121
Herron, David, 195, 196
Hess, Philip, 256
Hetfield, Abraham, 156
Hetfield, Joshua, 155
Heurtin, William, 14
Heysham, Christopher, 120, 232, 239, 391
Hickenbottom, Samuel, 36
Hickey, John, 22
Hicks, Dennis, 148, 155, 176, 188
Hiddiels, John, 36, 37
Hide, Elihu, 152, 176
Higgins, John, 26, 359
Higgins, Thomas, 359
Higgins, William, 20
Highland, Michael, 6
Hildreth, Mr., 162
Hill, Peter, 259
Hill, Robert, 9
Hill, Thomas, 178, 260, 264
Hillman, Rowland, 232
Hilson, Susannah, 260
Hinds, Abraham, 161
Hobert, John Sloss, 349
Hobson, Samuel, 94
Hodge, Samuel, 49, 50, 52
Hodge, Thomas, 126
Hodge, Vincent, 149
Hodge/Hodges, Mrs., 250
Hodgkins, Ebenezer, 282
Hodgson, Alvery, 254
Hoeghtelen, Hendrick, 203

Hoff, Leonard, 44
Hogan, William W., 285, 287
Hogg, Robert, 28
Hoghtaling, Johannis, 371
Hoghtaling/Hoghtlaing, Hendrick, 320
Hold, Mr., 6
Holeman, Francis, 216
Holland, Capt., 274
Holland, Henry, 349, 356, 359
Holland, Thomas, 11
Hollet, Jacob, 56
Hollis, Charles, 371
Holly, William, 223
Holmes, James, 147, 148
Holmes, Samuel, 24
Holmes, Thomas, 213, 349
Holms, Isaac, 34
Holt, John, 223
Honeyman, John, 41
Honeywell, Israel, Jr., 90
Hood, Zachariah, 101
Hoogboom, Jeremy, 361
Hoogeboom, Mr., 315
Hopeshaw, Thomas, 212
Hopkins, Mathew, 145
Hopkins, Michael, 229
Hopkins, Roswell, 379
Hopkins, Stephen, 326
Hopson, Samuel, 19
Horn, George, 142
Hornbeck, Matthew, 71
Horner, George, 321
Horsemanden, Mr., 154
Horsen, Jacob, 391
Horsmanden, Judge, 379
Horten, Catherine, 237
Horton, James, 44
Horton, James, Jr., 308
Housley, Isaac, 212
Houtvat, Mrs., 99
Howard, Captain, 166
Howard, James, 23
Howard, Joseph, 108
Howath, James, 40
Howey, John, 13
Howey, Robert, 198
Hubbard, Daniel, 185
Hubbel, Ichabod, 95
Hudson, John, 379
Hudson, Serjeant, 258
Huff, Justice, 213
Hughes, Mary, 296
Hughes, Patrick, 150
Hughes, Timothy, 90
Hukel, Eve, 334
Hulet, Capt., 149, 150
Hultz, Aaron, 227
Hunt, John, 90, 159
Hunter, Anthony, 191
Hunter, Robert, 36, 37
Hunter, Samuel, 14
Huntt, Obadiah, 55
Hureen, Matthias, 232
Hurry, Thomas, 123
Hursen, John, 368
Hurst, John, 132
Hutchenson, Sally, 189
Hutchinson, James, 132
Hutchinson, Thomas, 47, 55
Huttur, Michael, 102
Huycke, Andrius/Andries A., 228
Huycke, Johannis A., 228

Hyatt, Gilbert, 67
Hyer, Matthew, 368
Hyer, Victore, 46
Hylton, Ralph, 47
Hyon, James, 279
Indians, Abraham, 374; Charity, 368; Indians, Charles, 284; Cockchick, Anthony, 167; Cooly, Henry, 129; Emery, Joseph, 1; Galloway, 27; Grace, 1; Greene, Hannah, 331; Hezekiah, 12; Jack, 53; Jacob, 70, 109; James, 54; Job, 12; Kate, 124; Mahane, James, 25; Mary, 301, 310; Nanny/Nanney/Fanny, 243, 244, 246, 247; Pero, 22, 23; Pompey, 392; Shadrack, 96; Squibb, Christopher, 176; Stephen, 379, 392; Store, Gersham, 42; Teer, 11; Tierce, 39; Tom, 347; unnamed, 42, 225, 270, 312
Ingoldey, Coll., 4
Innes, John, 59
Insull, Thomas, 41
Irwin, Prudence, 370
Isling, John George, 233
Ivers, Thomas, 289, 377
Ivey, John, 8
Jackson, Benjamin, 98
Jackson, James, 11, 139
Jacobs, James, 33
Jacobs, Judah, 330
Jacobs, Philip, 260
Jamain, Nicholas, 1
James, A., 353

James, John, 318
James, Major, 350, 356, 383
James, Thomas, 142
James, Thomas Bubount, 76
Jaquet, Joseph, 122
Jathro, Ben, 270
Jefferies, Capt., 123
Jefferies, Mr., 129
Jeffery, John, 192
Jenkins, Thomas, 74
Jervis, John, Jr., 390
Jessop, Joseph, 366
Jewell, James, 223
Johns, John, 209, 210
Johns, Rebaccah, 210
Johnson, Henry, 275
Johnson, James, 217
Johnson, John, 177, 317
Johnson, Marthinus, 35
Johnson, Mr., 110
Johnson, William, 130, 132, 201
Johnston, Alexander, 356
Johnston, Christopher, 132
Johnston, John, 208
Joice, Edward, 319
Jones, Benjamin, 329
Jones, Colonel, 255
Jones, Evan, 275
Jones, Francis, 28
Jones, Jack, 255
Jones, James, 18, 241
Jones, Jehu, 379
Jones, John, 108, 150, 200, 233, 302, 372, 385
Jones, Mr., 260, 378
Jones, Owen, 75
Jones, Samuel, 95

Jones, Thomas, 149, 240
Jones, William, 132
Jorden, Thomas, 287
Josephson, Manuel, 240
Joy, Bartholomew, 241
Juel, Samuel, 232
Jump, John, 242
Kar, William, 217
Kateltass, Mr., 316
Katiens, Robert, 149
Keating, John, 314, 341, 360
Keef, Philip, 102
Keese, William, 123
Keho, Edmund, 385
Keir, Robert, 276
Keller, Ebenezer, 152
Kelly, David, 248, 365, 367
Kelly, George, 32
Kelly, Honor, 268
Kelly, Hugh, 52
Kelly, James, 217
Kelly, Margaret, 49, 50
Kelly, Patrick, 132
Kelly, William, 82, 100, 183, 201
Kelsall, Johanna, 12
Kelsy, James, 166
Kennedy, Archibald, 275, 282
Kennedy, Bartholomew, 132
Kennedy, Mr., 265
Kennedy, Robert, 264
Kennisen, Nicholas, 282
Kent, Moss, 393
Keortricht, Mrs., 223
Keriger, George Henry, 23
Kernon, Thomas, 129
Kerson, William, 260

Keteltas, Peter, 141
Kettenger, Joshua, 247
Keys, George, 200
Keys, James, 26
Kibbe, Isaac, 279
Kidd, Francis, 387
Kieff, Daniel, 233
Killet, Richard, 205
King, Richard, 45
Kinsland, Isaac, 270
Kip, Abraham, 39, 42
Kip, Balthazar, 187
Kip, Henry, 105
Kip, Jacobus, 104
Kip, Richard, 119
Kissick, Philip, 252, 270
Klein, John, 340
Knapshneider, John, 156
Knite, John, 141
Knowland, James, 79
Koffler/Kofeler, Francis, 309, 375
Kortright, Lawrence, 256, 397
Kout, Elizabeth, 93
Kremer, Philip Barnet, 89
Krigeur, Andrew, 272
Lacy, Daniel, 42
Laeitabach, Gotfreid, 207
Laforey, John, 122
Laight, Edward, 92
Lake, John, 58
Lakerman, Isaac, 21
Lambert, Aaron, 226
Landram, William, 29
Lane, John, 18
Langden, Capt., 19
Langdon, Amos, 20

Langdon, Richard, 35
Langdon, Samuel, 207
Langley, Thomas, 213
Langston, Peter, 121
Larzelere, Nicholas, 53
Lasher, John, 112, 291
Latouch/Lattouch, Mr., 19, 243
Lauder, Robert, 162
Lavenue, John, 153
Laverty, Edward, 323
Lavolet, Anthony, 81
Lawler, James, 386
Lawrance, Lawrence, 130
Lawrence, Abraham, 394
Lawrence, John, 92
Lawrence/Lawrenc, Joseph, 31
Lawson, George, 309
Lawson, James, 393
Layn, Edmund, 273, 274
Leach, Stephen, 87
Leacraft, Capt., 262
Leake, John, 144, 189, 194, 221, 263
Ledyard, John, 281
Lee, Edward, 75
Lee, Elizabeth, 258
Lee, Thomas, 140
Leech, James, 60
Leech/Leach, Stephen, 126, 128, 131
Legget, William, 12
Leggett, Gabriel, 54, 217
Leslie, Alexander, 376
Lester, John, 15
Leteler, William, 121
Leversage, John, 126, 203, 318, 319
Leversage, Mr., 197
Levingston, Philip, 379
Levy, Joshua, 154
Lewis, Benjamin, 149
Lewis, Charles, 162, 164
Lewis, Ellis, 218
Lewis, Joseph, 372
Lidack, Philip, 380, 381
Ligget, Gabriel, 152
Lightin, Emanuel, 244
Lilburn, John, 377
Limeburner, Matthew, 186
Link, Jacob, 120
Linn, John, 200
Lintner, John, 181
Lippincott, Job, 289
Lispenard, Leonard, 311, 312, 384
Livesly, Richard, 114
Livingston, James G., 249, 253
Livingston, John, 52, 186
Livingston, Mr., 125, 152
Livingston, Philip, 6, 78, 163, 323, 358
Livingston, Robert James, 59
Livingston, Robert John, 330
Livingston, Robert R., 190
Lloyd, Henry, 184
Lochridge, John, 309
Lockwood, Phineas, 385
Long, George, 165, 172
Long, Margaret, 246
Long, Michael, 102
Lookwhite, Mary, 73
Lord, John, 180
Loring, Joshua, 305
Lott, Cornelius, 340, 341, 343

Lottridge, Robert, 89
Loudon, Earl of, 96
Loughton, Joseph, 47
Lounsberry, John, 41
Louwin, Jacobus, 187
Loveall, Daniel, 283
Lovegrove, Thomas, 224
Low, Abraham, 233
Low, Peter, 30, 105
Low, Rachael, 105
Ludenton, Henry, 253
Ludlow, Henry, 94
Luter, Catharine, 321
Lutwidge, Walter, 192
Lutz, Simon, 157
Lyal, Edward, 189
Lyneall, Richard, 77
Mabion, Mr., 211
MacAulay, Lieut., 109
MacDonald, Neil, 174
Machree, Patrick, 116
Mackadee, James, 42
Mackeffee, Daniel, 24
Mackett, Lawrence, 102
Mackinsey, James, 173
Mackintosh, Charles, 34, 35
MacLanghlin, James, 18
MacManus, Daniel, 145
MacManus/McManus, Philip, 340, 360
Macomb, John, 326, 386
Macoy, William, 15
Maddin, John, 257
Magee, John, 118
Magee, Patrick, 93
Magee/McGee, James, 271
Magrah, Roger, 80

Mahony, Timothy, 385
Makist, John, 24
Malcolm, George, 39
Malley, Cornelius, 50
Maltby, John, 223
Man, Edward, Jr., 231
Mann, Isaac, 354
Manning, Anne, 355
Marceloe, Isaac, 14
Margison, James, 114
Mariner, William, 277
Marisco, William, 213
Markeshin/Markessixhe, John, 146
Markham, John, 22
Marselis, Henry, 350
Marshall, James, 182, 213
Marshall, Richard, 213
Martin, Captain, 161, 182, 183
Martin, Charles, 212
Martin, Colonel, 141
Martin, Edward, 297, 299, 300, 306
Martin, Josiah, 70
Martin, Mr., 241
Martin, Peter, 386
Martin, Samuel, 186
Mash, Captain, 166
Masterman, George, 146
Mathews/Matthews, Edmond, 119, 173
Matthews, Edward, 160
Matthews, James, 263
Matthews/Mathews, Edmund/Edmond, 159
Matthis, Edmond, 160
Matthison, Nicholas, 6

Maulkin, Ralph, 13
Maxwell, George, 116
May, Robert, 275
Mayhew, Nathaniel, 178
McAlster, John, 129
McBriage, James, 42
McBride, Rose, 171
McCain, Adam, 286, 287
McCall, John, 28
McCamly, David, 6
McCammel, Charles, 19
McCan, Hugh, 32
McCaniel, James, 42
McCardell, Philip, 311, 312
McCarthy, John, 396
McCartney, James, 214, 395
McCarty, Alexander, 42
McCarty, James, 42
McCarty, Timothy, 311, 312
McCew, William, 324
McChelhow, Margaret, 154
McClaren, James, 85
McClean, John, 296
McClean, Mary, 163
McCleur, Ensign, 120
McClone, Mrs., 386
McCollister, Alexander, 39
McCombs, Mr., 240
McConney, David, 289
McCormack, Alexander, 338
McCormack, Mary, 338
McCormick, Alexander, 366
McCowen, Thomas, 395
McCoy, Daniel, 152
McCullom, Andrew, 42
McCullough, David, 132
McCullugh, Alexander, 355

McDaniel, Charles, 232
McDaniel, Daniel, 302
McDaniel, Nicholas, 71
McDonagh, Henry, 308
McDonald, Archibald, 304
McDonald, Margaret, 353
McDonald, Peter, 35
McDonald, William, 72
McDonalson, Roger, 65
McEllroy, Edward, 314
McEntire, Peter, 288
McEvey, John, 117
McFarrel, Richard, 36, 37
McGee, Patrick, 94
McGee/Magee, James, 270
McGill, Michael, 122
McGillycuddy, Captain, 232
McGinnes, James, 213
McGinnis, Michael, 209
McGirr, John, 132
McGlathery, Thomas, 216
McGlocklin, Susannah, 355
McGra, Catherine, 324
McGrath, James, 213
McGriggor, Mary, 296
McGrisor, Alexander, 200
McGuire, Capt., 90
McHugh, James, 61, 85, 163
McIlroy, Edward, 206
McIntaylor, John, 25
McIntire, Matthew, 70
McIntire, Peter, 286
McIntosh, John, 166, 184
McInvin, John, 203, 204
McKeane, Lieut., 107
McKechne, Andrew, 272
McKenzie, Thomas, 129

McKillip, Hugh, 273
McKinney, John, 318
McKinzie, James, 385
McKoy, William, 38
McLauchlan/McLaughlan, John, 219
McLean, Alexander, 330
McLean, Allan, 174
McMahon, John, 29
McManus/MacManus, Philip, 328
McMeck, Henry, 35
McMullen, Michael, 354
McMullin, John, 71
McNabb, Joseph, 355
McNamar, Daniel, 376
McNeel, Arthur, 143
McNeelage, Donald, 148
McNeil, Arhur, 261
McNeill, Alexander, 331
McPeak, Dennis, 239
McQueede, Henry, 48
McQuoid, Hugh, 132, 133, 162
McVaugh, Benjamin, 369
McVicar, Hugh, 63, 64
McVicker, John, 273
Meanderson, Joseph, 200
Medway, Isaac, 65
Meeks, Edward, 391
Meeks, Gabriel, 206
Men, unnamed, 16, 147, 250, 266, 268, 272, 273, 308, 318, 319, 361
Menagh, William, 187
Mercer, Richard, 360
Mercereau, John, 370
Mereband, Henry, 272

Mereditch, Reese, 140
Merrils, Mr., 24
Mersalis, Guysbert, 186
Mersereau, Jacob, 106
Mezgan, Abraham, 130
Mezieres, Nicholas, 332
Milegan, John, 151
Miliner, William, 197
Millena, Mr., 193
Miller, Benjamin, 397
Miller, Charles, 320, 321
Miller, Grissel, 16
Miller, Henry, 130, 166
Miller, Jasper, 375
Miller, John, 129, 199, 285, 309, 333, 339, 363, 375
Miller, John Christophel, 160
Miller, Killien, 271
Milligan, John, 173
Milligar, John, 349
Milliner, French, 330
Mills, Daniel, 130
Mills, James, 49, 56, 136, 220, 325
Mills, Thomas, 268
Mirrit, Ebenezer, 285
Mitchell, Andrew, 269, 272
Mitchell, James, 81
Mitchell, Mr., 377
Monckton, Robert, 184, 187, 254
Moncreiffe, Major, 304
Monnet, Joseph, 169
Monro, Nelly, 173
Montany/Montanye, Jacobus, 345
Montford, John, 273

Montgomery, Archibald, 148, 174, 180
Montgomery, Capt., 208
Montgomery, Col., 174
Montgomery, Richard, 282
Moon, Christopher, 214
Mooney, John, 91
Moor, John, 3, 351
Moore, Captain, 121
Moore, Col., 103, 181
Moore, Francis, 120
Moore, James, 92
Moore, John, 4, 396
Moore, Michael, 337
Moore, Wm./William, 183, 257, 268
Mordent, John, 213
Morgan, Caleb, 220
Morley, Thomas, 181
Morrell, William, 308
Morris, Lewis, 330
Morris, Nicholas, 156
Morris, Richard Fitz, 80
Morrison, James, 128, 131, 313, 318
Morrow, Martin, 12
Morsby, John, 14
Moss, Capt., 149
Moss, Patrick, 83
Mott, Joseph, 253, 255
Mott, Patrick, 83
Mott, William, 97, 392
Mount, Mathias, 147
Mous, Joshua, 36, 37
Mouston, Robert, 341
Mowry, Daniel, Jr., 259
Muirhead, John, 32
Mulhall, Henry, 72
Mullaly, John, 212
Mullar, Anthony, 109
Muller, Killeyaen/Killiaen, 256, 265
Muller, Mr., 259
Mullin, Thomas, 394
Mumford, Thomas, 281
Munfoort, John, 270
Munro, Barnabas, 343
Munro, Joseph, 212
Munrow, Samuel, 330
Munsell, Joseph, 352
Murfey, William, 42
Murfy, George, 178
Murphey, Edmund, 121
Murphy, David, 150
Murphy, John, 84
Murphy, Richard, 4, 5
Murphy, Robert, 132
Murray, Col., 283
Murray, James, 274
Murray, John, 184
Murray, Robert, 361
Murray, Thomas, 165
Murray, William, 261, 267
Murry, Capt., 354
Mustees, Bet, 202; Cesar, 248
Myer, Andrew, 295, 341, 350
Myer, Ide, 131, 132
Myer, Margreta, 91
Myers, Frederick, 249
Myers, Myer, 362
Nealan, Bridget, 143
Neavin, James, 342
Necks, Robert, 209

Negroes, Aaron, 267; Adonis, 238; Amelia, 211, 252, 270; Andrew, 43; Anthony, 153, 154, 203; Apollo, 261; Aron, 261; Baptist, 264; Baptist, John, 378; Bell, 52; Ben, 65, 303, 305, 339, 372; Bet/Bett, 144, Bett, 59; Bill, 155, 176, 188, 340; Black Peter, 98; Black, Sam, 237; Boatswain, 262; Bohenah, 159; Bolton, 56; Booth, Mingo, 108; Boston, 304; Bradey, Sarah, 267; Bristol, 136; Bromlow, 175; Caesar, 3, 72, 88, 97, 168, 169, 243, 298, 349, 350, 356; Caesar/Cesar, 342, Cambridge, 109; Castalio, 177, 205; Cato, 45, 254, 315, 336, 369; Cesar/Caesar, 342; Champaign, 255; Charles, 88, 105, 181, 225, 295, 325, 341, 346, 350; Claus, 107; Coffey, 26; Crank, 337; Cromwell, Isaac, 31; Crook, 74; Cross/Cros, Crispus, 357, 359; Cuba, 125; Cudjo, 182; Cuff, 84, 106, 253, 261, 267, 398; Cuffey, 108; Cyrus, 275, 349, 356, 359; Daniel, 312, 372; Daphne, 362; Dick, 71, 153, 187, 194, 333, 339; Dick/Richard, 99; Dickerson, John, 333; Dinah, 52; Domingo, 48; Don Pedro, 107; Dover, 372; Dublin, 327, 360; Duke, 97, 277; Elcey, 170; Emanuel, 289; Fanny, 127, 158; Fortune, 304; Franck, 100; Frank, 46, 61, 105, 181, 193; Frank/Francois, 135; Gale, James, 379; Garrick, 392; George, 104, 252, 253, 290; German, 221; Gin, 191, 237, 314; Glasgow, 167; Golia, 262; Grace, 114; Green, Jack, 157; Guy, 179; Hack, 363; Ham, 354; Hamstead, 47; Handrick, 37; Hank, 37; Hannable/Hannibal, 383, 394; Hannah, 131, 132; Hannibal/Hanibal, 51, 117, 118; Harre, 381; Harry, 21, 46, 57, 142, 162, 164, 215, 238, 275, 333; Harry/Harrie, 69; Havannah, 274; Hazard, Toby, 185; Hector, 32, 58, 64, 76, 97, 99, 322; Henricus, John, 3; Henry, 135; Hiram, 267; Holliday, 70; Isaac, 57, 215; Issabel, 52; Jabez, 241; Jacco, 274; Jack, 21, 49, 52, 94, 106, 142, 165, 180, 201, 204, 214, 235, 237, 239, 251, 269, 278, 280, 285, 291, 294, 295, 302, 305; Jack/John, 86, 87; Jacob, 152, 216, 257, 278, 279, 293; Jam, 217, 271; James, 26, 171, 259, 271, 367; Jammy/Jemmy, 170; Janneau, 52; Jasper, 122; Jean/Jane, 297, 298; Jemmy, 331; Jemmy/Jammy, 175;

172; Jerrey, 159; Jerry, 85; Jim, 251, 256, 378; Jin, 308; Jo/Joe, 201; Joe, 97, 113, 202, 239, 240, 249, 258, 298; Joe/Joseph, 83; John, 65, 134, 204, 255; Jack, 255; Joseph, 327; Jupiter, 22; Kate, 265; Kinsale, 180; Lamdon, 152; Lena, 199; Lewis, 52; Licum, 94; London, 217, 393; Loo, 211; Lucy, 220; McGile, 274; Methias, 90; Mingo, 301, 378; Mink, 331; Minors, Norton, 183; Nanny, 218; Nanny/Nanney/Fanny, 243, 244, 246, 247; Ned, 103, 112; Nell, 59; Nick, 330; Nok/Noke, 357, 397; Noke, 397; Norway, 389; Ohnech, 131, 132; Oronoco, 357; Paul, 185; Peg, 322; Peggy, 125; Peter, 31, 48, 161, 189, 214, 324, 347, 352, 360, 384; Phaebe, 62; Philip, 236; Phillis, 349; Phoenix/Phenix, 126, 127; Pollydore, 211; Pomp, 228, 331; Pompee, 33; Pompey, 231, 243, 261; Prime, 370; Primus, 154, 178, 179, 226, 362; Prince, 29, 31, 134, 154, 207, 213, 244, 321, 337, 353; Princess, 178; Priscilla, 255; Quaco, 225; Quash, 5, 392; Ralph, 116, 140; Rick/Rieck, 103, 104; Rob, 158, 185; Robbin, 295, 328; Robert, 393; Roberts,

Charles, 221; Robin, 132, 188, 227, 229, 339; Rose, 114, 152, 328; Salem, 239; Sam, 45, 57, 220, 254, 266, 371, 374, 375; Sandy, 117, 118; Sarah, 9, 65, 66, 172; Scipio, 110, 111; Selam, 214; Selem, 201; Sharp, 288; Sharp/Sharper, 296; Sheford, 363; Shier, 385; Simon, 52, 143, 326; Sippeo, 41; Siro, 242; Smith William, 17; Smith, Abraham, 366; Smith, John, 204; Somerset, 240; Squire, 368; Stephen, 379; Storde, 43; Street, Sarah, 149, 150; Suck, 191; Sylvester, 212; Sylvia, 362; Tamer, 52; Toby, 322; Tom, 54, 55, 83, 104, 141, 142, 145, 157, 160, 169, 173, 175, 190, 231, 264, 304, 346, 347, 368, 373, 393; Tone, 320; Tone/Toon, 153, 154; Toney/Tony, 53, 332, 346; Trace, 263; Negroes, unnamed, 7, 9, 18, 60, 72, 78, 119, 141, 158, 159, 160, 192, 229, 231, 233, 238, 245, 256, 259, 260, 264, 265, 291, 320, 325, 363, 397; Venture, 146, 151, 180, 200; Vilet, 246; Wall, 189, 194, 221, 263, Wan, 48, 51; Weldon, James, 32; Well, Tom, 299; Whithaven, 93; Will, 37, 155, 162, 177, 206, 323; Will/Wilthier, 316; William,

148; Windsor, 170, 175, 266;
Witlow, 242; Wright,
Hezekiah, 152; Yaff, 4; York,
44, 123, 130, 215, 216, 218,
262, 382;
Neill, Arthur, 132
Neilson, Samuel, 73
Nelson, Thomas, 42
Nesbitt, Mr., 290, 291
Nevil, Samuel, 284
Nevins, David, 59
Newcom, Mr., 64
Newcomb, Azeriah, 253
Newkerk, Cornelius, 107
Nice, Jacob, 360
Nicholas, John, 82
Nicholls, Thomas, 58
Nichols, Samuel, 283
Nicholson, William, 81
Nickson, Abel, 369
Nickson, Asahel, 365
Nicoll, William, 270
Nixon, Mr., 134
Noon, Thomas, 208, 306
Norman, Edward, 145
Norris, Daniel, 36, 37
Norris, Isaac, 272
Norris, Mathew, 3
North, Thomas, 276
Norton, George, 143
Norton, Thomas, 287
Nutlees, Edward, 42
Nuttle, Francis, 77
O'Brien, John, 113
O'Connor, John, 43
O'Dannel, Hugh, 319
O'Dowley, Daniel, 42

O'Konnor, John, 44
O'Rourk, Connor, 332
Obrian, John, 24
Ogden, Moses, 241
Oger, Jacob, 56
Oglivie, Captain, 182
Oliver, Andrew, 67
Oman, James, 262
Onderdonck/Onderdonk,
  Henderick, 179
Oracks, Joseph, 213
Ormsby, Capt., 124
Ornals, John, 359
Orr, John, 132
Orr, Robert, 310
Orvis, David, 5
Osborn, Captain, 166
Osborne, Ambrose, 132
Osbourn, Samuel, 209
Otlay, Anthony, 146
Otterson, William, 143
Otway, Charles, 102
Otway, General, 98
Oughton, Colonel, 233, 235
Ougston, Thomas, 271
Ouke, William, 235
Owen, Edward, 275
Owens, John, 76
Oyl, Alexander, 327
Oyster, Mr., 383
Pacqueran, Mr., 1
Page, Thomas, 133
Pallester, Catherine, 164
Palmer, John, 286, 287
Palmer, Mr., 294
Palmer, Nehemiah, 61
Palmer, Samuel, 149

Palmer, Stephen, 119
Panton, Francis, 248
Pardy, John, 145
Parker, James, 10, 42
Parker, Lieutenant, 208
Parr, William, 323
Parsco, Simon, 134
Partridge, Thomas, 216, 221
Paterson, Henry, 78
Patter, John, 234
Patterson, John, 98
Patterson, William, 43, 44
Pattison, John, 99
Patton, John, 309
Paul, John, 123
Pay, Thomas, 129
Payne, Benjamin, 270, 271
Payton, Samuel, 19
Pearson, William, 98
Peasly, John, 351
Peck, Michael, 333
Pell, John, 52, 322
Pell, Josiah, 170
Pell, William, 258
Pelton, William, 301
Penny, James, 113
Pepperrell, William, 42
Perry, Mr., 75
Pert/Pertt, Aelxander, 85
Peters, Andrase, 175
Peters, George, 182
Peters, William, 48
Petty, John, 53
Pheffer, Michael, 112
Philips, Alexander, 378
Philips, John, 98
Philipse, Coll., 27
Philipse, Samuel, 173
Phillips, William, 132
Pick, Hanas, 370
Pickman, Robert, 367
Pierce, Lieutenant, 252
Piercel, Francis, 311
Piercy, John, 30
Pike, John, 169
Pillson, Henry, 337
Pilson, Robert, 310
Pinfold, Edmond, 230
Pinkney, William, 90
Pitt, Jacob, 345
Pitz, Peter, 207
Plantin, Mr., 283
Plat, Eliphalet, 216, 220
Platneer, Jacob, 295
Platt/Plat, Captain, 200
Plymun, Margrietta, 86
Polhemus, John, 331
Polly, Samuel, 123
Poluck, Johannes, 17
Poole, Richard, 74
Poole/Pool, Thomas, 235, 237, 353
Poor, Lawrence, 252
Potter, Capt., 150
Pougher, Daniel, 2
Powell, Samuel, 213
Power, Bernhard, 193
Power, Catherine, 193
Power, Mary, 193
Powers, Charles, 150
Prevoost, I. M., 319
Prevost, J. M., 333
Price, Edward, 211, 240
Price, George, 55

Price, John, 163, 199, 371
Price, Thomas, 55
Price, William, 116, 195, 196, 234
Prichard, Richard, 114
Prince, Captain, 364
Proctor, Carden, 82
Provoost, David, 89
Provoost, John, 351
Provoost, William, 389
Provost, David, 370
Pryce, David, 190, 204, 246, 247
Puglsey, John, 159
Puntine, William, 332
Puntiner, William, 165
Purcel, Michael, 122
Pursell, Capt., 186
Pye, Joseph, 313
Pyra, Mary, 87
Quackenbusch, Cornelius, 18
Quane, Mark, 183
Quin, Felix, 286, 287
Quin, Francis, 239
Radman, Philip, 38
Raff, John, 269, 306
Raffele, Thomas, 132
Raft, John, 338
Ragen, John Danel, 73
Raine, Samuel, 208
Ralston, Joseph, 247
Ralston, William, 389
Ramadge, Charles, 373
Ramadge, Smith, 328, 344
Ramsay, John, 382
Rand, William, 77
Randall, Robert, 371

Randall/Randell, Ananias/Anennias, 340, 341, 343
Randell, Edward, 196
Randells, Edward, 195
Randle, Patrick, 120
Rankin, William, 355
Rapalye, Tunis/Teunis, 215
Ray, Francis, 28
Ray, Richard, 285, 286
Raymond, James, 372
Rea, Richard, 287
Read, Charles, 365
Read, John, 288
Read/Reade, Peter, 378
Reade, Joseph, 9, 154
Reader, Jacob, 161
Reece, John, 184
Reed, Benjamin, 53
Reed, Leonard, 63, 64
Reed, Thomas, 184
Reese, Robert, 157
Reffly, Francis, 120
Reid, John, 288
Reilley, Dennis, 377
Reirson, George, 395
Remer, George, 134
Remsen, Daniel, 384
Remsen, Jacob, 239
Remsen, Peter, 392
Renold, Richard, 32
Rensselaer, Mr., 255
Reynolds, George, 20
Rice, Abraham, 130
Rice, Andrew, 130
Rice, Daniel, 42
Rice, John, 247

Richard, John, 38
Richard, Stephen, 82
Richard, Warner, 38
Richards, Capt., 261
Richards, Nathaniel/Nathanial, 35, 36, 37
Richards, Paul, 27
Richards, Robert, 144
Richardson, Francis, 14
Richardson, Henry, 175
Richardson, Mr., 13, 337
Richardson, Mrs., 393
Richmond, John, 210
Ridden, Rufford, 130
Riddle, John, 136
Rider, John, 333
Ries/Rees, John Frederick, 357, 359
Rigby, Thomas, 13
Right, Hendrick, 166
Riker, John, 364
Rikor/Rickor, John, 149
Rivington, Mr., 208
Rivington, Thomas, 387
Roberts, Anthony, 19
Roberts, George, 198
Roberts, J., 330
Roberts, John, 65, 220, 244, 279, 302
Robertson, Capt., 174
Robertson, David, 186
Robertson, John, 330
Robertson, Robert, 129
Robeson, Nathaniel, 46
Robinson, Beverly, 38, 40
Robinson, Charles, 7
Robinson, James, 85

Robinson, John, 187, 240
Robinson, Margaret, 186
Robinson, Obadiah, 363
Robinson, Thomas, 42, 103
Rodman, James, 16
Rodman, Thomas, 10
Roe, Benjamin, 52
Roe, John, 51
Rogers, Hugh, 200
Rogers, John, 307
Rogers, Moll, 177
Rogers, Peter, 195, 196
Rogers, Samuel, 61
Rogers, William, 48
Rogerson, Mary, 168
Rollar, Capt., 102
Roney, James, 350
Roorbach, Johannis/Johannes, 153, 154
Rooss, Jacob, 361
Roouger, Mr., 315
Rose, Johannis, 36
Rose, William, 45
Roseman, James, 124
Ross, Charles, 96
Ross, David, 242
Ross, Ezbilon, 192
Ross, James I., 153
Ross, James Isaiah, 72
Ross, Jeremiah, 192
Ross, Johaunis, 37
Rouse, Thomas, 212
Row, James, 40
Rowe, John, 198
Rowland, Samuel, 387
Rowley, Edward, 17
Rubie, Edward, 62, 111

Rudolph, Mr., 276
Rugg, Samuel, 275
Rumsey, Phineas/Phinas, 303, 305
Russel, Capt., 307
Rutgers, Cornelia, 64
Rutgers, Hendrick, 172
Rutherford, Captain, 120
Rutherford, John, 121
Rutherford, Walter, 325, 346
Ryan, Cornelius, 354
Ryan, John, 156
Rycaut, Paul, 184
Ryckman, Isaac, 107
Ryder, Barnadus, 169
Ryder, Barnardus, 168
Ryder, Hugh, 98
Ryder, Joseph, 67
Ryersz, Adrian, 58, 76
Ryker, John, 150
Sacket, Joseph, 96
Salm, Martin, 38
Saltonstall, Wm., 178
Sample, John, 150
Sands, Richard, 335, 336
Sappen, Sarah, 83
Sarefield/Sarefeald, William, 158, 159
Sarly, Anthony, 99
Sarzadas, Abraham, 296
Saunders, John, 29
Saunders, Philemon, 42
Saunders, Thomas, 46
Sause, Richard, 356
Savage, John, 198
Saxton, Andrew, 11
Saxton, Jierard, 246

Sayers, Eavan, 101
Sayre, John, 28
Schermerhorn/Schermerhorne, John, 111, 355, 357, 397
Schinkle, Hendrick, 93
Schlosser, Capt., 121
Schultz, Henry, 224
Schuyler, Cortlandt, 326
Schuyler, Peter, 1
Schuyler, Philip, 382
Scot, George, 103
Scot, Thomas, 98
Scot, William, 384
Scott, Hugh, 40
Scott, John, 22, 35
Scramshire/Scramshair, Thomas, 127
Scurlock, Thomas, 3
Seal, Mrs., 386
Seal, Thomas, 386
Seaman, William, 300
Searisbrook, James, 132
Sears, Isaac, 397
Sebring, Abraham, 138
Seloover, Edward, 367
Senior, William, 184
Sennet, Peter, 83
Senthus, Matthew, 45
Sergeant, Jonathan, 60
Seymour, Captain, 32
Seymour, John, 296
Seymour, Thomas, 201
Shakerly, Anthony, 331
Shano, Isaac, 62
Shaw, Hezekiah, 42
Shaw, James, 38
Shaw, Lieut., 198

Shaw, Mr., 324
Shearer, Gilbert, 228
Shedman, John, 200
Sheehan, Nelly, 336
Sheehan, Richard, 335
Sheehan, William, 335, 336
Sheels, Timothy, 128, 131
Sheerer, James, 67
Shees, Matthew, 316
Sheldon, Isaac, 163
Shelly, William, 195, 196
Shepherd, William, 285
Sheppard, Thomas, 213
Sherer, Robert, 46
Sheringham, James, 114
Sherman/Shearman, Jacob, 324, 326, 327
Sherock, John, 213
Sheron, Joseph, 282
Shilling, Barnet, 89
Shipboy, Mr., 255, 284
Shirley, John, 114
Shirlock, John, 365
Shoemaker, Philip, 93
Shopman, John, 377
Sibbald, John, 206
Sickles, Hendrick, 38
Sifirey, Dorothy, 123, 125, 128
Silea, John, 138
Silvester, Francis, 182
Simkin, Daniel, 41
Simmerel, James, 223
Simmons, Adam, 384
Simmons, Anne, 355
Simpson, David Littleye, 376
Sims, John, 218
Sims, William, 25
Simson, Joseph, 136
Sinclair, John, 7
Singleton, Thomas, 283
Sinnet, Ellinor, 47
Siveck, Jois, 20
Skelton, John, 204
Skene, Major, 182
Skene, Philip, 274, 342
Skey, Boughey, 133
Skey, Captain, 138
Sleath, Abraham, 204
Slideborn, Henry, 24
Slidell, John, 380, 381
Sly, Stephen, 259
Smith, Abijah, 95
Smith, Abner, 191
Smith, Abraham, 366
Smith, Benjamin, 366
Smith, Cornelius, 151
Smith, David, 249
Smith, Epenetus, 248
Smith, James, 107
Smith, John, 8, 77, 98, 141, 142, 245, 280, 293
Smith, Margaret, 228
Smith, Marmaduke, 114
Smith, Morgan, 36
Smith, Mr., 154
Smith, Obadiah, 25
Smith, Philip, 69
Smith, Robert, 195, 196
Smith, Thomas, 114
Smith, William, 96, 147, 162, 186
Smith, William P., 87
Smith, William Peartree, 134
Smith, William, Jr., 243

Smyth, Patrick, 394
Snediker, Jocob, 332
Sniffen, Henry, 108
Solly, Nathan, 58
Sparger, Edward, 367
Sparhawk, Mr., 42
Sparling, Philip, 320
Speira, Jacob, 361
Spellen, James, 167, 186
Spencer, John, 335
Springer, James, 126
Squibb, Christopher, 176
St. Clair, James, 212
St. Clair, John, 120
Stager, Frederick, 101
Stagner, Andrew, 141
Stagner, Daniel, 101
Standard, Thomas, 47
Stanton, Jeremiah, 275
Stanton, John, 185
Steel, Thomas, 187
Steel, William, 130
Stephany, J. Sebastian, 243
Stephens, Francis, 161
Sterling, Alexander, 82
Steuart, Alexander, 346
Steuart, John, 286
Stevenar, Christenar, 121
Stevens, Henry, 130, 303
Stevens, John, 74
Stevens, Peley, 282
Stevenson, James, 270
Stevenson, Thomas, 295
Steward, John, 42
Steward, Patrick, 29
Stewart, Angus, 174
Stewart, Captain, 141

Stewart, James, 135
Stewart, John, 221, 287
Stewart, Lewis, 134
Stewart, Robert, 195, 196
Stewart, William, 35, 362
Stickney, James, 365, 369
Stike, Nicholas, 154
Stiles, Daniel, 43
Stilwill, John, 38
Stinson, James, 122
Stites, John, 397
Stitt, Samuel, 330
Stocker, Rebecca, 386
Stockton, Job, 341
Stoop, John, 50
Story, Enoch, 101
Story, Joseph, 200
Story, William, 19
Stouten, Timothy, 36
Stow, Jonathan, 12
Straing, Elizabeth, 322
Strawbridge, John, 309
Street, Nathaniel, 384
Stringer, Robert, 146
Stringer, Samuel, 342
Strong, William, 38
Stutes, Henry, 276
Stuyvesant, Mr., 6
Sulivan, John, 11
Sullivan, Mary, 66
Sullivan, Owen, 200
Sullivan, Timothy, 311, 312
Summers, Sarah, 233
Suter, John, 148
Suthard, Abraham, 285, 287
Sutphen, Barnet, 42
Sutton, John, 129

Swan, James, 50, 130
Swanson, Samuel, 34
Sweeny, Lawrence, 156
Swetanham, Ensign, 119
Swetnam, Henry, 60
Symonson, Rem, 106
Talman, John, 233
Tawas, Thomas, 224
Taylor, Daniel, 24
Taylor, Isaac, 33
Taylor, John, 165, 191, 286
Taylor, Joseph, 289
Taylor, Solomon, 234
Taylor, William, 35
Tebout, Cornelius, 205, 262
Teebout, Albartus, 36, 37
Teebout, Cornelia, 36, 37
Ten Brock, Cornelius, 386
Ten Eyck, Anthony, 107
Ten Eyck, Barent, 327
Tenbrook, Wessel, 33
Terrant, Henry, 190
Terrel, Abraham, 80
Terrill, Ephraim, 313
Thettson, Thomas, 213
Thodey, Captain, 200, 226
Thody/Thodey, Michael, 388, 389
Thom, Jacob, 361
Thomas, John, 374
Thomas, Joseph, 248
Thomas, Michael, 358
Thomas, Mrs., 358
Thompson, Acheson, 307
Thompson, David, 186
Thompson, James, 70, 100, 254, 287, 288
Thompson, John, 171, 200, 284
Thompson, Mr., 377
Thompson, Patrick, 290, 291, 344
Thompson, William, 42
Thorn, James, 127
Thorn, John, 31
Thorn, Peter, 285, 287
Thornbrugh, Robert, 317
Thorne, William, 259, 327
Tiebolt, John George, 380
Tiebout, Cornelius, 117, 118
Tillet, Richard, 206
Tillet, Thomas, 329
Tillinghast, Thomas, 296
Tingley, Samuel, 43
Tod, John, 216
Todd, Robert, 12
Toll, Korl/Koral, 237
Toms, Simeon, 95
Toton, Daniel, 243
Townshend, George, 206
Traile, George, 264
Traner, Philip, 268
Treby, Capt., 248
Tredwell, Thomas, 258
Trench, William, 371
Trent, William, 34
Troy, John, 255
Truxtun, Thomas, 205
Tucker, Henry, 141
Tucker, Henry, Jr., 141
Tucker, Thomas, 373
Tudor, John, 237
Tully, Hugh, 38
Turner, Thomas, 342
Tusten, Benjamin, 179

Tuthill, Capt, 150
Tuthill, Daniel, 88
Tuthill, John, 53
Underdown, Morris, 69
Underhill, Mr., 303
Uresher, John Mattuse, 2
Valentine, Joseph, 318
Van Allen, Adam, 51
Van Arlam, Mr., 220
Van Brent/Van Brents, Adrian, 243, 244, 246
Van Bushkirck, Lawrence Jacobus, 363
Van Buskirk, Jacob, 106
Van Cleef, Laurence, 38
Van Cortlandt, John, 262
Van Cortlandt/Van Courtlandt, Jacobus, 11
Van Dervoort, Michill, 38
Van Devemter, Barent, 37
Van Dyck, Francis, 109
Van Dyck, Richard, 322
Van Gelder, Mrs., 46
Van Horne, Cornelius, 19
Van Horne, David, 295
Van Horne, Jacob, 106
Van Kleeck, Baltus, 199
Van Kleeck, Jacobus, 215
Van Mater, Cyrenius, 382
Van Rans, Cornelius, 29
Van Ranst, Cornelius, 134
Van Ranst, Luke, 397
Van Ranst, Mrs., 134
Van Schaick, Jacob, Jr., 103, 104
Van Waganen, Johannes, 291
Van Wagenan, Jacob, 160
Van Wagenen, Jacob, 115

Van Wyck, Cornelius, 62
Van Wyck, Doris, 333
Van Wyck, Theodorus, 171, 240, 241
Van Wyck, Thomas, 72
Van Zandt, John, 89
Vandebergs, Hanas, 370
Vander Heyden, David, 62
Vander Heyden, Dirk, 62
Vanderbelt/Vander Bilt, Jeremiah, 326, 327
Vanderbelt/Vander Bilt, Jeremiah, Jr., 325
Vanderill, Tom, 340
Vandorn, Abraham, 84
Vangesen, Renier, 270
Vanhorne, Augustus, 322
Vanhorne, Cornelius, 59
Vantile, Othis, 106
Vardee, George, 286, 287
Vaughan, Jason, 7
Veeder, Simon J., 298
Veeder, Johannes, 298
Veile, Petrus, 73
Verplanck, Philip, 315
Vickers, William, 247
Vought, John, 166
Vredenburgh, William, 41
Waddell, Hugh, 13
Waddell, John, 181
Waldron Peter, 224
Waldron, John, 43
Waldron, Resolved, 48, 51
Waldron, Richard, 237
Waldron, Samuel, 352, 358
Walker, John, 73

Wallace, Hugh, 98, 103, 148, 166, 182, 184, 185, 187, 198, 199, 202, 254, 255, 274, 326
Wallace, James, 6, 8
Wallace, John, 16
Wallace, Robert, 181
Walsh, Peter, 62
Walsh, Thomas, 186
Walsh, Walter, 103
Walton, Henry, 129
Walton, Joseph, 344
Wandel/Wandell, Jacob, 210
Wanser, Thomas, 200
Ward, Mrs., 144
Ward, Nathaniel, 60
Ward, Stephen, 167, 313
Ward, Thomas, 16
Ware, Charles, 83, 86
Waring, Mr., 5
Warren, Stephen, 199
Wary, George, 278
Washington, William, 166
Watens, William, 121
Waters, Anthony, 242, 346
Waters, Anthony, Jr., 242
Waters, Benjamin, 81, 195
Waters, Captain, 200
Waters, Edward, 242
Waters/Walters, Mrs., 389, 390
Waters/Walters, William, 389, 390
Watkins, Thomas, 175
Watson, John, 143, 205, 206
Watson, Mathew, 316
Watson, Matthew, 317
Watson, William, 236
Watts, Daniel, 236
Watts, William, 238
Weakes, Gilbert, 236
Weatherly, Benjamin, 157
Weaver, Jury, 306
Weaver, William, 134
Webb, John, 293
Weissenburg, Catherine, 19
Welch, Catharine, 320
Welch, Francis, 225
Welch, James, 276
Welch, John, 149, 150
Welch, Nancy, 211
Welch, Nicholas, 88
Welch, Richard, 116
Welchman, David, 225
Well, Tom, 299
Wells, David, 42
Wells, Obadiah, 53, 54, 88
Welsh, John, 286, 287
Welsh, Mr., 283
Wessels, Gilbert, 45
Wessels, Peter, 242
West, John, 143
Westervelt, Benjamin, 315
Westover, Oliver, 287, 288
Wetmore, James, 251
Wetmore, Timothy, 177
Wettersroom, G. C., 96
Weyman, W., 156, 218, 242, 303
Wharry, John, 358
Whealton, Caleb, 127
Wherton, John, 42
Whilen, John, 6
Whippo, James, 339
White, Alexander, 283
White, Amos, 194
White, Capt., 286, 287

White, Henry, 190, 223
White, John, 245
White, Joseph, 286, 287, 307
White, Mr., 123
White, Patrick, 307
White, Thomas, 26, 357
White, Townsend, 30
Whitehead, James, 355
Whitehead, William, 226
Whiting, Major, 147
Whitle, Henry, 186
Whitmore, Edward, 116
Whyte, Alexander, 387, 388
Wickham, Samuel, 49, 343
Wicks, Daniel, 339
Wicks, Joseph, 365, 367
Wiel, Thomas, 121
Wigg, John, 182, 183
Wiggins, Charles, 42
Wiggins, Daniel, 289, 347, 352
Wilde, Thomas, 109
Wiley, Alexander, 206
Wiley, James, 32
Wilhelmen, Christina, 78
Wiliams, William, 41
Wilkins, Isaac, 378
Wilkinson, Nathaniel, 67
Wilkot, Amos, 129
Will, John, 93
Will, John Michael, 345, 376
Willcox, Capt., 110
Willet, Gilbert, 5
Willet, John, 72, 194
Willet, Thomas, 147, 148
Willett, John, 65, 70
Willett, Thomas, 186
Willey, James, 22

Williams, Benjamin, 136, 267, 339
Williams, Betsy, 144
Williams, Cadwalider, 15
Williams, Charles, 147, 148
Williams, Erasmus, 170, 171
Williams, James, 43, 44, 270, 271
Williams, John, 130, 131, 139, 140, 276, 284
Williams, Lydia Mary Anne, 87
Williams, Mark, 144
Williams, Mr., 13
Williams, Rice, 30
Williams, Richard, 34
Williams, Thomas, 247
Williamson, Benjamin, 284
Williamson, George, 178, 273, 274
Willson, Henry, 213
Willson, Joseph, 17
Willyamos, Captain, 172
Wilson, Capt., 376
Wilson, Francis, 79
Wilson, James, 85
Wilson, John, 221
Wilson, Robert, 221, 292
Wilson, Thomas, 216, 221
Wilt, Peter, 250
Wiltse, Henry, 324
Wiltse, James, 324
Winepress, Capt., 258
Winn, Peter, 30
Wisely, James, 59
Wiswal, Thomas, 35
Withers, John, 133
Wolfe, Jacob, 317
Women, Catharine, 191

Women, unnamed, 10, 158, 159, 160, 197, 203, 227
Wood, David, 195, 196
Wood, Ebenezer, 363, 367
Wood, John, 396
Wood, Stephen, 21
Wood, William, 190, 297, 299, 301, 306
Woodhouse, Robert, 67
Woodman, Jonathan, 68
Woodruff, Uzal, 241
Woodstock, Capt., 79
Woodward, Joseph, 15
Wooly, John, 18
Wooters, John, 119
Wray, George, 257, 279, 293
Wright, Captain, 149, 200, 265
Wright, David, 328
Wright, Hezekiah, 152
Wright, John, 195, 196
Wright, Mary, 82, 87
Wright, Mr., 27
Wright, Thomas, 227, 229, 307, 328
Wright, William, 103
Wyngaard, Luykas, Joh,, 52
Yates, John, 130
Yates, Leonard, 210
Yeats, Leonard, 265
Yelverton, Gale, 207, 213
Young, James, 293
Young, John, 4, 142, 277
Youngs, Joseph, 339
Zaensker, Johann Ernst Frederick, 85
Zenger, John Peter, 21, 30
Zepperly, Frederick, 21
Zobel, Capt., 116

www.ingramcontent.com/pod-product-compliance
Lightning Source LLC
Chambersburg PA
CBHW052112010526
44111CB00036B/1680